Enterprise Cybersecurity Study Guide

How to Build a Successful Cyberdefense Program Against Advanced Threats

Scott E. Donaldson
Stanley G. Siegel
Chris K. Williams
Abdul Aslam

Apress®

Enterprise Cybersecurity Study Guide: How to Build a Successful Cyberdefense Program Against Advanced Threats

Scott E. Donaldson
Falls Church, Virginia, USA

Chris K. Williams
San Diego, California, USA

Stanley G. Siegel
Potomac, Maryland, USA

Abdul Aslam
San Diego, California, USA

ISBN-13 (pbk): 978-1-4842-3257-6
ISBN-13 (electronic): 978-1-4842-3258-3
https://doi.org/10.1007/978-1-4842-3258-3

Library of Congress Control Number: 2018935923

Managing Director, Apress Media LLC: Welmoed Spahr
Acquisitions Editor: Todd Green
Development Editor: Laura Berendson
Coordinating Editor: Rita Fernando

Cover designed by eStudioCalamar

Cover image designed by Freepik (www.freepik.com)

Distributed to the book trade worldwide by Springer Science+Business Media New York, 233 Spring Street, 6th Floor, New York, NY 10013. Phone 1-800-SPRINGER, fax (201) 348-4505, e-mail orders-ny@springer-sbm.com, or visit www.springeronline.com. Apress Media, LLC is a California LLC and the sole member (owner) is Springer Science + Business Media Finance Inc (SSBM Finance Inc). SSBM Finance Inc is a **Delaware** corporation.

For information on translations, please e-mail rights@apress.com, or visit http://www.apress.com/rights-permissions.

Apress titles may be purchased in bulk for academic, corporate, or promotional use. eBook versions and licenses are also available for most titles. For more information, reference our Print and eBook Bulk Sales web page at http://www.apress.com/bulk-sales.

Any source code or other supplementary material referenced by the author in this book is available to readers on GitHub via the book's product page, located at www.apress.com/9781484232576. For more detailed information, please visit http://www.apress.com/source-code.

Printed on acid-free paper

To my growing family: Shelly, Ashleigh, Melanie, Manoli, Nick, Stephanie, David, Jackson, Mason, Julia, Laura, and Justin

—Scott Donaldson

To Bena, my wife, and our grandchildren: Eva, Ezra, Avi, Raffi, Tal, Eli, Zoe, Sarah, Emma, and Simcha

—Stan Siegel

To my father, Dennis, who taught me to protect those whom you love, and love those whom you protect

—Chris Williams

To my parents: Zahida, Maqbool, Shamim, and Imam. And to my loves: Sharu, Ishaq, Farhan, and Zayd

—Abdul Aslam

Contents at a Glance

Contents

About the Authors

Scott E. Donaldson's professional experience includes working in federal, commercial, and university marketplaces as well as in the defense industry. His expertise includes multimillion-dollar program management, systems development, information technology, business operations, business development, and technology cultural change. He has served in a wide variety of leadership roles including Chief Technology Officer (CTO), IT Director, Chief Systems Engineer (CSE), Program Manager, Line Manager, and Business Development Capture Manager. He has developed new technologies, techniques, and practices to bring in new business by solving real-world problems.

Donaldson teaches software engineering, software process improvement, and information management courses at the Johns Hopkins University's Whiting School of Engineering. Johns Hopkins honored him in 2009 with an Excellence in Teaching Award. He has a BS in Operations Research from the United States Naval Academy and a MS in Systems Management from the University of Southern California.

Donaldson has co-authored three software engineering books: *Successful Software Development: Making It Happen, 2nd Edition* (Prentice Hall PTR, 2001); *Successful Software Development: Study Guide* (Prentice Hall PTR, 2001); and *Cultivating Successful Software Development: A Practitioner's View* (Prentice Hall PTR, 1997).

Donaldson has contributed to other software engineering books, including the *Encyclopedia of Software Engineering: Project Management—Success Factors* (CRC Press, 2010) and the *Handbook of Software Quality Assurance: Software Configuration Management—A Practical Look, 3rd Edition* (Prentice Hall, 1999).

Donaldson also co-authored *CTOs at Work* (Apress, 2012) and *Enterprise Cybersecurity: How to Build a Successful Cyberdefense Program Against Advanced Threats* (Apress, 2015).

Dr. Stanley Siegel has progressive professional experience as a systems engineer, mathematician, and computer specialist. He holds a nuclear physics doctorate from Rutgers University. He started his career with the US government in the Department of Commerce and then the Department of Defense. After his government service, he worked with Grumman for 15 years and Science Applications International Corporation (SAIC) for over 20 years. He helped SAIC grow to an 11-billion-dollar leader in scientific, engineering, and technical solutions with hundreds of millions of dollars in new business.

While at SAIC, he served as a senior technical advisor and director on a wide spectrum of projects in areas such as software engineering methodology assessment, software requirements analysis, software testing and quality assurance, and technology assessment.

In the 1990s, Siegel and Donaldson developed the Object Measurement Methodology, which appears in *Enterprise Cybersecurity*. This methodology can be used to quantify an enterprise's cybersecurity effectiveness in warding off cyberattacks. As the book explains, the enterprise can improve its cyberdefenses by taking corrective actions by using this methodology.

Siegel and Donaldson have jointly taught graduate courses since the mid-1990s. They teach both in-class and online software systems engineering courses at Johns Hopkins University's Whiting School of Engineering. Johns Hopkins honored them both in 2009 with an Excellence in Teaching Award.

Siegel has co-authored four software engineering books including the seminal software engineering textbook *Software Configuration Management: An Investment in Product Integrity* (Prentice Hall, 1980). He has contributed to a number of books, including the *Encyclopedia of Software Engineering: Project Management—Success Factors* (CRC Press, 2010) and the *Handbook of Software Quality Assurance: Software Configuration Management—A Practical Look, 3rd Edition* (Prentice Hall, 1999).

Chris Williams has been involved in the cybersecurity field since 1994. He has held both US military and commercial positions. He has been with Leidos (formerly SAIC) since 2003, focusing on enterprise cybersecurity and compliance. Previously, he worked with EDS (now HP) and Booz Allen Hamilton. He is a veteran of the US Army, having served five years with the 82nd Airborne Division and 35th Signal Brigade. He has worked on cybersecurity projects with the US Army, Defense Information Systems Agency, Department of State, Defense Intelligence Agency, and numerous other commercial and government organizations, designing integrated solutions to protect against modern threats. Williams holds a BSE in Computer Science Engineering from Princeton University and a MS in Information Assurance from George Washington University.

Williams co-authored *Enterprise Cybersecurity: How to Build a Successful Cyberdefense Program Against Advanced Threats* (Apress, 2015). He holds a patent for e-commerce technology and has published technical papers with the Institute of Electrical and Electronics Engineers (IEEE). He has presented on cybersecurity at RSA, Milcom, the International Information Systems Security Certification Consortium (ISC), the Information Systems Security Association (ISSA), and other forums.

Abdul Aslam has over 20 years of experience in devising risk acceptance and compliance frameworks, application security, security operations, and information protection. He is the Director of Cyber Security Audit for Leidos tasked to evolve and maintain the corporate Cyber Security assessment and audit program. He was the Director of Cyber Security Governance, Risk, and Compliance for Leidos where he was in charge of delivering secure and scalable security solutions, policy governance, and strategic technology support. He has worked on numerous IT projects with a proven record of pioneering innovative systems analysis processes and secure application designs that improve availability, integrity, confidentiality, reliability, effectiveness, and efficiency of technology services.

Aslam has a MS in Systems Engineering Management and Information Assurance from the George Washington University and a BS in Engineering in Electronics and Telecommunications from Osmania University (India). He also has CISSP certification.

Aslam co-authored *Enterprise Cybersecurity: How to Build a Successful Cyberdefense Program Against Advanced Threats* (Apress, 2015) and has presented on cybersecurity at International Information Systems Security Certification Consortium (ISC)^2 and the Information Systems Security Association (ISSA).

About this Study Guide

Preface

This study guide is an instructional companion to the book *Enterprise Cybersecurity: How to Build a Successful Cyberdefense Program Against Advanced Threats*. This study guide increases students' understanding of the book's ideas, whether they are using it in the classroom or for self-study. The study guide is structured to be self-explanatory and is intended to augment the book's content. For additional information and detail on the topics covered in this study guide, please reference *Enterprise Security: How to Build a Successful Cyberdefense Program Against Advanced Threats* by Scott E. Donaldson, Stanley G. Siegel, Chris Williams, and Abdul Aslam (Apress, 2015) (`www.apress.com/9781430260820`).

Implementing a successful cyberdefense program against real-world attacks is what *Enterprise Cybersecurity* is about. Often in cybersecurity, everyone knows *what should be done*, but resources *to do it* are not sufficient. Organizations must prioritize their efforts to deploy an incomplete solution that they "hope" is sufficient. The challenge lies in how to prioritize resources so security can be as successful as possible. As shown in Figure P-1, the Cybersecurity Conundrum often gets in the way of what needs to be done, leaving gaps in enterprise cyberdefenses that are exploited by clever attackers.

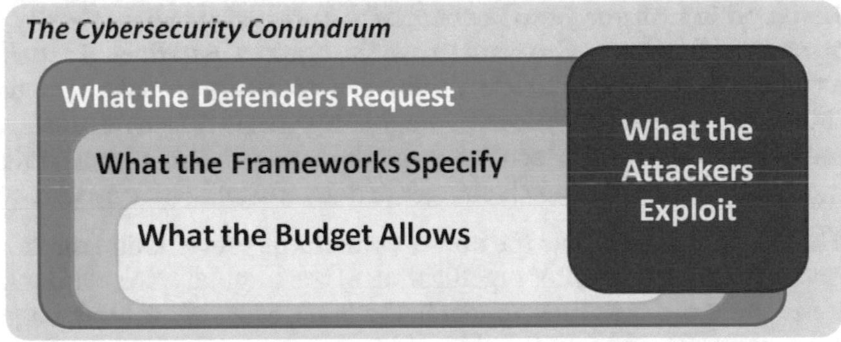

Figure P-1. *Even though the cybersecurity conundrum presents significant challenges, implementing a successful cyberdefense program that works against real-world attacks is achievable.*

One Cybersecurity Conundrum challenge is that cybersecurity professionals want to implement more than what control frameworks specify and much more than what the budget allows. Ironically, another challenge occurs even when defenders get everything that they want; clever attackers are extremely effective at finding and exploiting the gaps in defenses, regardless of their comprehensiveness. The overall challenge, then, is to spend the available budget on the right protections so that real-world attacks can be thwarted without breaking the bank and that they also comply with mandated regulatory requirements.

Intended Audiences

As shown in Figure P-2, people involved in or interested in successful enterprise cybersecurity can use this study guide to gain insight into an effective architecture for coordinating an entire cyberdefense program.

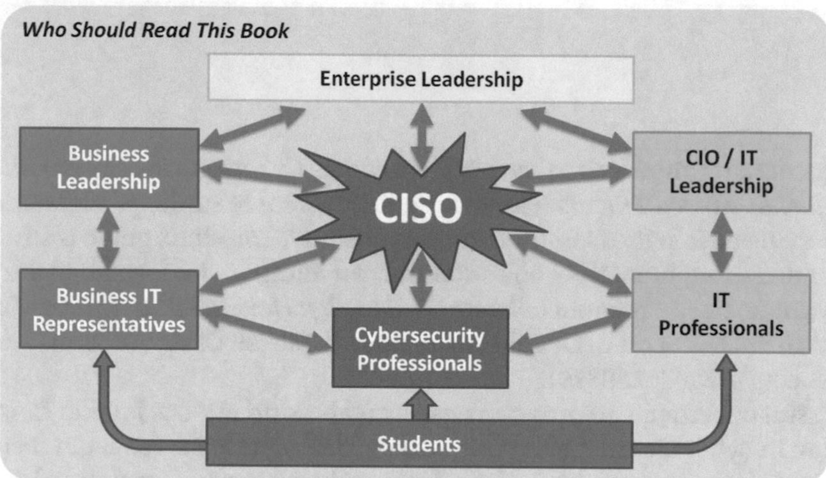

Figure P-2. *Successful enterprise cybersecurity is a team sport.*

This study guide is intended for the following audiences:

- **Everyone involved in or interested in successful enterprise cybersecurity**. This study guide offers material for those who want to use the book to help them do their work. Such individuals can use this material to learn about cybersecurity and its challenges, cybersecurity implementation, effective cyberdefenses, pragmatic cyberincident response, cybersecurity program assessments, and cybersecurity program management. In short, this study guide helps those who need to understand the challenges of delivering effective cybersecurity solutions.
- **Students**. This study guide recasts the book's contents as presentation material. This material is organized according to the chapter organization of the original book, with major points appearing generally in the same order as they appear in the book. Most of the book's figures, or adaptations of these figures, appear in this study guide. Students can use this material in a number of ways in conjunction with the text to include the following examples:
    - Before reading a chapter or part of a chapter from the book, students can go to the corresponding study guide pages to get a quick look at the chapter or chapter part and understand its major points and themes.
    - While reading a chapter or chapter part, students can, in parallel, look at the corresponding study guide pages. Sometimes a different look at the same material can facilitate learning.
    - After reading a chapter or chapter part, students can go to the corresponding study guide pages to quickly review key points, concepts, and descriptive figures.

- **Instructors**. This study guide offers material that instructors can use to develop classroom presentations based on the book's contents. Instructors can also use these pages to incorporate material from the book into other courses. For example, an instructor may be teaching a course (or part of a course) on the topic of cybersecurity assessments. If such a course is presenting different approaches to cybersecurity assessments, "Chapter 11: Assessing Enterprise Cybersecurity" and/or "Appendix D: Cybersecurity Sample Assessment" in this study guide may offer the instructor ready-made material for demonstrating one example of a comprehensive assessment methodology.

Using Study Guide Material

This study guide material can be used in a number of ways that include the following:

- **Corporate Education**. This material can be used to teach a short course to employees within an organization or to teach a more detailed course targeted at cybersecurity professionals. The course can address all the book's material or selected material for special topics.
- **University Education**. This material is suitable for a course at the undergraduate and graduate levels. The material can be covered quickly in a single overview course, or it can be covered in more detail as part of a larger cybersecurity instruction program. When considered in depth, the material of this study guide may be too extensive to be thoroughly covered in a one-semester, three-credit course.

  This guide can be used to structure short presentations on selected topics from the book. In the university environment, this approach can be used to structure a graduate-level special topics seminar spanning multiple weeks, and perhaps meeting for a couple of hours each week to discuss detailed topics drawn from the book and other industry literature. Such a seminar might be used to help students conduct their own research and assess other information sources from books, literature, and the Internet.
- **Professional Conferences and Meetings.** The authors offer the following suggestions to those involved with establishing cybersecurity training programs:
  - This material can be used to give presentations at professional conferences and other meetings pertaining to cybersecurity (such as the Information Systems Security Association [ISSA]).
  - This material can be used to structure short presentations (say, one hour) to introduce employees to key cybersecurity-related topics such as common cybersecurity attacks, cybersecurity frameworks, cybersecurity policy, and cybersecurity operational processes.
  - This material can be used to structure half-day or longer presentations dealing with the how-tos of such topics as cybersecurity assessments audits and measuring a cybersecurity program.

- The material can be used to augment existing training activities:
    - The material found in "Appendix C: Object Measurement" can be added to an existing presentation on measurement. One purpose of such an addition would be to illustrate alternative ways of addressing the challenging problem of meaningful cybersecurity measurement.
    - This material can be added to a new module as a self-contained presentation. For example, a company may have one or more training modules dealing with different aspects of the business case for cybersecurity improvement. This material could be included in a module that focuses on return on investment, while another module might focus on cybersecurity effectiveness.

How This Study Guide Is Organized

- ***Introduction***
  The introduction lays the groundwork for subsequent discussions on how to start, continue, and improve an enterprise's cybersecurity. This section provides an introductory understanding of cybersecurity and explains how cybersecurity is with us to stay.
- ***Part I: The Cybersecurity Challenge***
  Part I is about the cybersecurity challenge and how cybersecurity has changed over the past decade. Due to this evolution, the cyberdefense methods that worked well in the past are doomed to fail in the future.
    - *Chapter 1: Defining the Cybersecurity Challenge*
      This chapter defines the cybersecurity challenge facing the modern enterprise and discusses the threats against its defenses and why those threats are succeeding at an alarming rate.
    - *Chapter 2: Meeting the Cybersecurity Challenge*
      This chapter describes how the cybersecurity challenge can be met and how cybersecurity controls and capabilities can be organized to prevent, detect, document, or audit malicious behavior.
- ***Part II: A New Enterprise Cybersecurity Architecture***
  Part II introduces a new enterprise cybersecurity architecture that is designed to organize and manage every aspect of an enterprise cybersecurity program, including policy, programmatics, IT life cycle, and assessment.
    - *Chapter 3: Enterprise Cybersecurity Architecture*
      This chapter describes the new enterprise cybersecurity architecture and explores 17 functional areas in terms of their goals and objectives, threat vectors, and underlying capabilities.
    - *Chapter 4: Implementing Enterprise Cybersecurity*
      This chapter discusses how to implement the new enterprise cybersecurity architecture by identifying security scopes, defining security policies, and selecting security controls to counter anticipated threats.

- *Chapter 5: Operating Enterprise Cybersecurity*
  This chapter explains how to operate enterprise cybersecurity capabilities and processes, including 17 operational processes and 14 supporting information systems essential to effective enterprise cybersecurity.
- *Chapter 6: Enterprise Cybersecurity and the Cloud*
  This chapter discusses how cloud computing is different from the conventional data center and explains how the new architecture needs to be tailored for cloud computing environments.
- *Chapter 7: Enterprise Cybersecurity for Mobile and BYOD*
  This chapter describes the trends of mobile computing and Bring Your Own Devices (BYODs) and how these two trends solve problems and introduce challenges for the new architecture.

- ***Part III: The Art of Cyberdefense***
  Part III discusses the art of cyberdefense and how the new architecture is deployed and used to provide effective risk mitigation and incident response for cybersecurity crises.
  - *Chapter 8: Building an Effective Defense*
    This chapter examines why attackers have great success against legacy cyberdefenses, how the steps of the attack are sequenced and how to disrupt them, and how to layer cyberdefenses so they effectively thwart targeted attacks.
  - *Chapter 9: Responding to Incidents*
    This chapter describes the incident response process in detail by considering what the enterprise needs to do on an ongoing basis to investigate, contain, and remediate cybersecurity incidents when they occur.
  - *Chapter 10: Managing a Cybersecurity Crisis*
    This chapter discusses how severe cybersecurity incidents become crises and how the enterprise must behave differently in a crisis situation while it struggles to restore normal operations.
- ***Part IV: Enterprise Cyberdefense Assessment***
  Part IV establishes a methodology for quantitatively and objectively assessing cybersecurity using the enterprise cybersecurity architecture and then mapping those assessments against major frameworks for reporting purposes.
  - *Chapter 11: Assessing Enterprise Cybersecurity*
    This chapter explains the cybersecurity assessment and auditing process, and provides four worked-out examples using the new architecture to assess cybersecurity posture and effectiveness.
  - *Chapter 12: Measuring a Cybersecurity Program*
    This chapter provides a comprehensive method for objectively measuring an enterprise's cybersecurity by looking at risk mitigations, cybersecurity functional areas, and security operations.
  - *Chapter 13: Mapping Against Cybersecurity Frameworks*
    This chapter explains how to take the results of an enterprise cybersecurity assessment and map them against other cybersecurity frameworks for the purpose of evaluation, audit, or compliance reporting.

- ***Part V: Enterprise Cybersecurity Program***
  Part V brings together the concepts of the rest of the book into a comprehensive enterprise cybersecurity program that combines assessment, planning, prioritization, implementation, and operations.
  - *Chapter 14: Managing an Enterprise Cybersecurity Program*
    This chapter explains the cybersecurity program management process and shows how the enterprise can use it to manage cybersecurity decision-making and prioritize improvements to get the best possible value for the investment.
  - *Chapter 15: Looking to the Future*
    This chapter concludes the study guide by discussing the evolution of generations of cyberattacks and cyberdefenses, and how enterprise cybersecurity architecture will evolve over time to support the enterprise's needs now and in the future.
- ***Part VI: Appendices***
  The appendices provide greater detail than the chapters and provide important details and examples for cybersecurity practitioners who want to use the enterprise cybersecurity architecture described in this study guide.
  - *Appendix A: Sample Cybersecurity Policy*
    This appendix provides a sample enterprise information security policy document, organized into the 11 functional areas of the new architecture described in this study guide.
  - *Appendix B: Cybersecurity Operational Processes*
    This appendix contains detailed flowcharts for the 17 operational processes of enterprise cybersecurity, and it also introduces the 14 supporting information systems.
  - *Appendix C: Object Measurement*
    This appendix introduces the Object Measurement Methodology for objective assessment and explains how to use it to measure and report enterprise cybersecurity architecture effectiveness.
  - *Appendix D: Cybersecurity Sample Assessment*
    This appendix provides an example enterprise cybersecurity assessment using the methodology contained in this study guide, providing multiple levels of details showing how different types of assessment can be performed.
  - *Appendix E: Cybersecurity Capability Value Scales*
    This appendix contains detailed, example Object Measurement value scales for measuring the performance of each of the 113 enterprise cybersecurity architecture capabilities, grouped by the 11 functional areas.

Summary

- This study guide is an instructional companion to the book *Enterprise Cybersecurity: How to Build a Successful Cyberdefense Program Against Advanced Threats.*
- This study guide contains landscape-formatted pages that recast the book's content and new content as presentation material.
- This material is organized according to the chapter structure of the original book and is laid out in the order that it appears in each chapter.
- This study guide is intended for everyone involved in or interested in successful enterprise cybersecurity (business professionals, IT professionals, cybersecurity professionals, students, and so on).
- Students, cybersecurity professionals, and IT professionals can use this study guide in a self-study manner. Students can also use this study guide to facilitate note-taking in the classroom.
- Instructors can use this study guide to develop classroom presentations based on the book's contents.
- This study guide, in conjunction with the book, can be used by anyone who wants to learn and apply what it takes to build a successful cyberdefense program against advanced threats.

Introduction

Enterprise Cybersecurity Study Guide:
How to Build a Successful Cyberdefense Program Against Advanced Threats

Today's Discussion

- Overview
- Intended Audience
- What is an ***enterprise***?
- What is ***cybersecurity***?
- Cybersecurity Conundrum
- Axioms of a "Next-Generation" Cyberdefense
- The Cyberattacks of Today
- Successful Cybersecurity Program
- Cybersecurity Program Cycle
- Future Discussion Topics

Overview

- Provide an introductory understanding of cybersecurity
- Explain why cybersecurity is with us to stay
- Explain why everyone needs to understand cybersecurity
- Lay the groundwork for subsequent discussions that detail ***how to*** start, continue, and improve an enterprise's cybersecurity

Intended Audience

- ***Enterprise Leadership***
  - Oversight responsibility for information technology and cybersecurity concerns within an enterprise (for example, organization, business, or government agency)
- ***Business or Organizational Leadership***
  - Responsible for achieving enterprise objectives while using information technology systems and protecting sensitive and valuable information
- ***Business or Organization IT Representative***
  - Responsible for delivering business capabilities using information technology and complying with cybersecurity requirements
- ***Chief Information Security Officer (CISO)***
  - Responsible for overseeing a comprehensive enterprise cybersecurity program
- ***Cybersecurity Professional***
  - Responsible for managing, deploying, and operating effective cyberdefenses within the enterprise
- ***Chief Information Officer (CIO) or Information Technology (IT) Leadership***
  - Responsible for deploying information technology solutions to deliver business value while complying with regulatory and security requirements

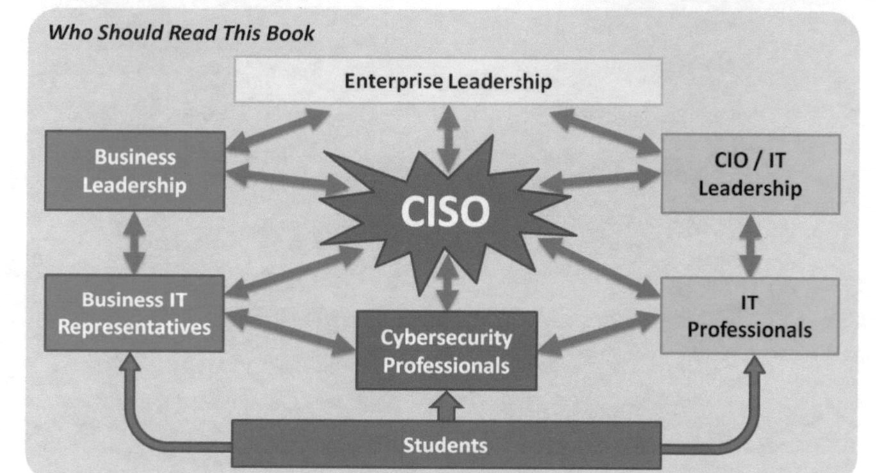

- ***IT Professionals***
  - Responsible for ensuring information technology solutions have adequate cybersecurity while also delivering value to the enterprise
- ***Students***
  - Learning about business, information technology, or cybersecurity, and need to understand the challenges of delivering effective cybersecurity solutions

What is an *enterprise*?

- An ***enterprise*** is an organization that uses computers and computer networks for personal, business, nation-state, or other purposes, and has authority over those computers and computer networks.

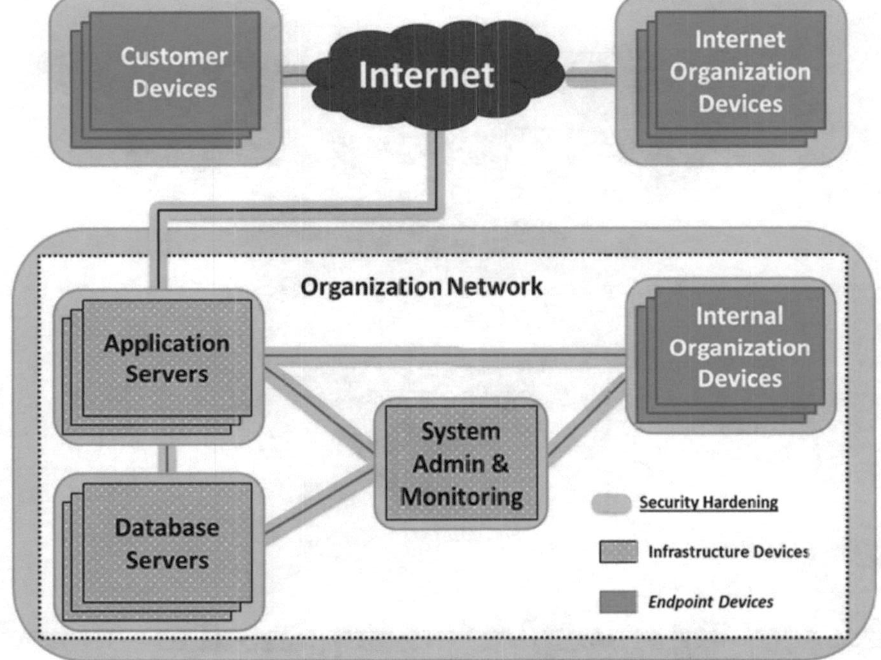

- An ***enterprise*** may range from an individual's personal computer and network to a corporate or governmental entity with thousands or hundreds of thousands of computers connected to networks spanning the globe.

What is *cybersecurity*?

- ***Cybersecurity*** is the practice of protecting the *confidentiality, integrity*, and *availability* of enterprise IT assets.

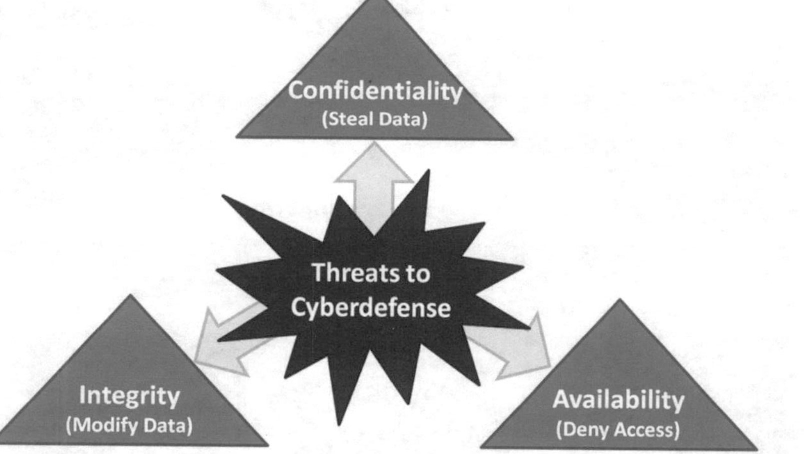

- ***Cyber***- is a prefix that identifies properties related to IT systems including computers and computer networks

Cybersecurity Conundrum

- The reality is cyberthreats are just one of many threats against the enterprise and, from a budget perspective, are relatively small threats.
- Therefore, the enterprise has to prioritize limited resources to get the best possible security for the available budget.
- Cybersecurity will *never* be funded to do everything that is desired, or even mandated, by available *best practice* cybersecurity frameworks.

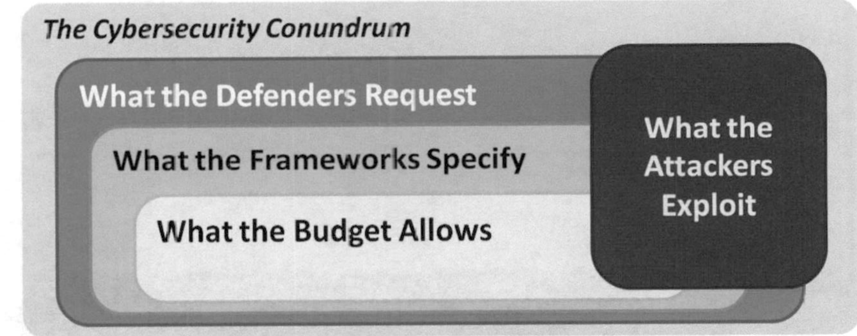

- **Enterprise CEO to IT Manager**

  I want the truth!
- **IT Manager**

  You can't handle the truth!

Axioms of a "Next-Generation" Cyberdefense

- Cybersecurity needs to be planned around the idea of achieving only partial security, rather than being resourced to do everything perfectly all the time.
- Major cybersecurity frameworks
  - Lay out what the *ideal* practice should be; and
  - Have little, if any, guidance on how to deploy a *partial* solution for available funding.
- Cybersecurity professionals must learn how to work with the business to find a balance between defenses that are only partially successfully, but effective in the eyes of the business.

Assume an intelligent attacker will eventually defeat all defensive measures.

Design defenses to detect and delay attacks so defenders have time to respond.

Next-Generation Cyberdefense Axioms

Layer defenses to contain attacks and provide redundancy in protection.

Use an active defense to catch and repel attacks after they start, but before they can succeed.

The Cyberattacks of Today *(1 of 2)*

- Compared to today, cybersecurity used to be relatively simple.
  - Major cyberthreats were viruses, worms, and Trojan horses.
- Transformation started to take place.
  - Cyberattackers started getting inside enterprise networks.
  - Once inside, cyberattackers operated surreptitiously.
- *We are using outdated, conventional defenses to guard against cutting-edge innovative malware. We are no more prepared to do this than a 19th-century army trying to defend itself against today's weaponry.*[1]

- Common Cyberattacks
  - Phishing / Spear Phishing
  - Drive-By / Watering Hole / Malvertising
  - Code Injection / Webshell
  - Keylogging / Session Hacking
  - Pass-the-Hash and Pass-the-Ticket
  - Credential Harvesting
  - Gate-Crashing
  - Malware / Botnet
  - Distributed Denial-of-Service (DDoS)
  - Identity Theft
  - Industrial Espionage
  - Pickpocket
  - Bank Heist
  - Ransomware
  - Webnapping
  - Hijacking
  - Decapitation
  - Sabotage
  - Sniper / Laser / Smart Bomb
  - Smokeout / Lockout
  - Infestation / Whack-a-Mole
  - Burndown
  - Meltdown
  - Defamation
  - Graffiti
  - Smokescreen / Diversion
  - Fizzle

[1]FireEye, "Advanced Malware Exposed," fireeye.com/wp_advmalware_exposed.html, 2011.

The Cyberattacks of Today *(2 of 2)*

- There is a rise of a new type of adversary—the Advanced Persistent Threat (APT).
- An APT attacker is skilled in the art of cyberattack and leverages IT technologies effectively to breach enterprises and systematically bypasses all their protections, one at a time.
- What makes APT different from earlier cyberattack types is the persistence of the attack.

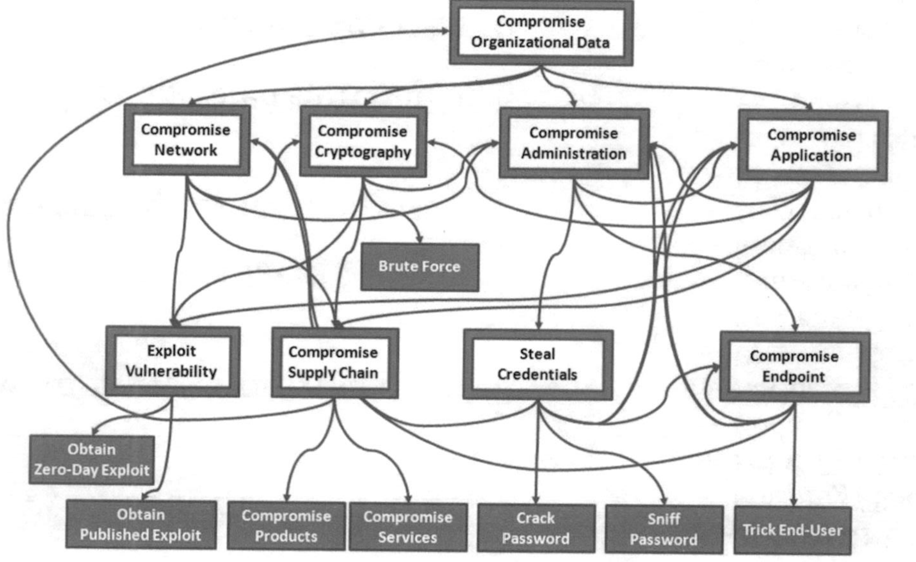

- APT makes cyberattacks much more focused and effective because now they are under the control of an intelligent actor who has an objective to achieve.
- An APT attacker constantly adjusts the attack to get past the latest round of defenses.

Successful Cybersecurity Program *(1 of 2)*

Characteristics

- A cybersecurity program is about much more than buying cybersecurity technologies and deploying them.
- A successful cybersecurity program facilitates the coordination of policy, programmatics, IT life cycle, and cybersecurity assessments.
- These major components work together to *guide, build,* and *operate* an enterprise cybersecurity program.

Challenges

- ***Policy frameworks*** do not align well with how people are typically organized or with how cybersecurity is usually assessed.
- ***Programmatic frameworks*** focus on business considerations and deal with cybersecurity at a high level of abstraction such that their guidance is not actionable, except in the most general terms.
- ***IT life cycle frameworks*** deal with cybersecurity in broad terms and generally do not consider how cybersecurity needs to be decomposed for management and reporting purposes.
- ***Assessment frameworks*** tend to group cybersecurity controls and capabilities in ways that are not aligned with how people or budgets are typically organized.

Successful Cybersecurity Program *(2 of 2)*

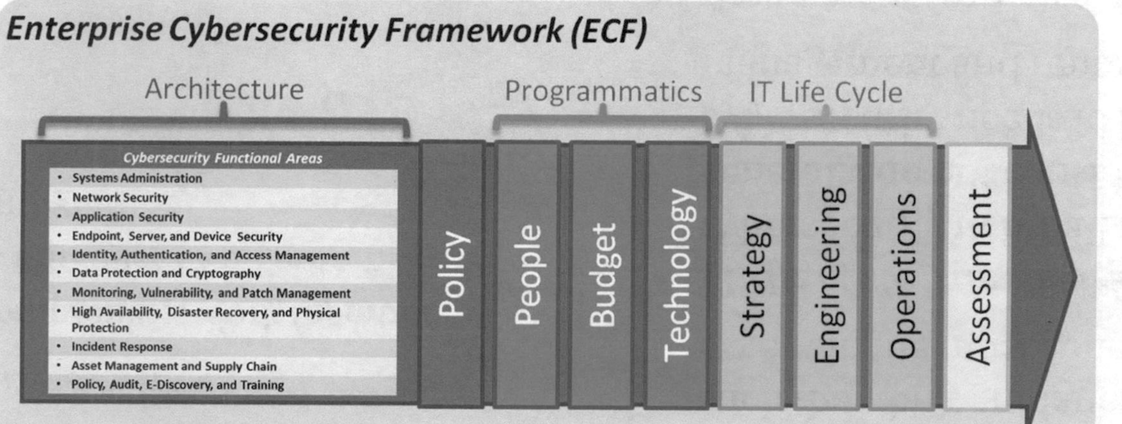

- Cybersecurity Program requirements include the following:
  - Tie together **architecture**, **policy**, **programmatics**, **IT life cycle**, and **assessments** using a single ***Enterprise Cybersecurity Framework (ECF)*** for delegation and coordination.
  - Break down enterprise cybersecurity into a number of sub-areas to communicate that there is more to effective cybersecurity than just firewalls and anti-virus software.
  - Align sub-areas relatively well with real-world skills of cybersecurity professionals, budgets supporting those professionals, and technologies purchased and maintained with the budgets.
  - Enable sub-areas quick and efficient reporting of cybersecurity status so executives can understand the big picture of what is and is not working well.
  - Support the business decision-making process via the sub-areas and help leaders define strategy and prioritization.

Cybersecurity Program Cycle

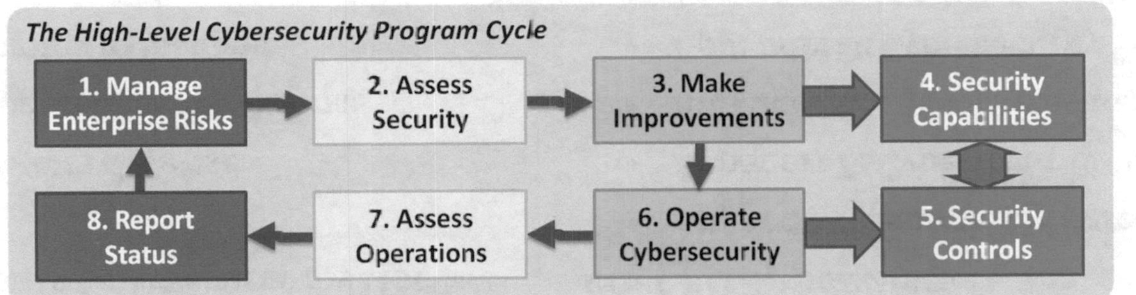

1. ***Manage Enterprise Risks*** involves assessing risks to the enterprise and scoping enterprise IT systems to contain those risks and deploy mitigating controls and capabilities.
2. ***Assess Security*** involves evaluating the security that is currently deployed to assess its *effectiveness* and *comprehensiveness* compared to the negotiated business need.
3. ***Make Improvements*** involves planning improvements to enterprise cybersecurity by deploying or improving technologies and processes.
4. ***Security Capabilities*** are what are delivered by cybersecurity technologies and processes and what enable the enterprise to accomplish its cybersecurity objectives.
5. ***Security Controls*** apply those capabilities to address specific concerns, providing prevention, detection, forensics, or audit of the behavior that is of interest.
6. ***Operate Cybersecurity*** involves operating cybersecurity technologies, processes, capabilities, and controls to deliver cybersecurity to the enterprise.
7. ***Assess Operations*** involves measuring cybersecurity performance to understand what cybersecurity threats are occurring and how well defenses are serving to counter those threats.
8. ***Report Status*** involves reporting cybersecurity status both internally according to internally negotiated frameworks and standards, and externally to regulators, insurers, and other interested parties.

Future Discussion Topics

Part I: The Cybersecurity Challenge

- Chapter 1: Defining the Cybersecurity Challenge
- Chapter 2: Meeting the Cybersecurity Challenge

Part II: A New Enterprise Cybersecurity Architecture

- Chapter 3: Enterprise Cybersecurity Architecture
- Chapter 4: Implementing Enterprise Cybersecurity
- Chapter 5:Operating Enterprise Cybersecurity
- Chapter 6: Enterprise Cybersecurity and the Cloud
- Chapter 7: Enterprise Cybersecurity for Mobile and BYOD

Part III: The Art of Cyberdefense

- Chapter 8: Building an Effective Defense
- Chapter 9: Responding to Incidents
- Chapter 10: Managing a Cybersecurity Crisis

Part IV: Enterprise Cyberdefense Assessment

- Chapter 11: Assessing Enterprise Cybersecurity
- Chapter 12: Measuring a Cybersecurity Program
- Chapter 13: Mapping Against Cybersecurity Frameworks

Part V: Enterprise Cybersecurity Program

- Chapter 14: Managing an Enterprise Cybersecurity Program
- Chapter 15: Looking to the Future

Part VI: Appendices

- Appendix A: Sample Cybersecurity Policy
- Appendix B: Cybersecurity Operational Processes
- Appendix C: Object Measurement
- Appendix D: Cybersecurity Sample Assessment
- Appendix E: Cybersecurity Capability Value Scales

Part I: The Cybersecurity Challenge

- Chapter 1: Defining the Cybersecurity Challenge
- Chapter 2: Meeting the Cybersecurity Challenge

CHAPTER 1

Defining the Cybersecurity Challenge

S. E. Donaldson et al., *Enterprise Cybersecurity Study Guide*, https://doi.org/10.1007/978-1-4842-3258-3_1

Overview *(1 of 2)*

- This study guide describes ***effective cybersecurity*** that
  - works against advanced cyberthreats;
  - evolves over time to handle increasingly sophisticated adversaries in an increasingly interconnected world;
  - is involved as a partner, coach, and scorekeeper for IT, rather than just as a naysayer standing in the way of progress; and
  - works when you are faced with an adversary who is well-funded, intelligent, sophisticated, and persistent.
- Cybersecurity challenges and technologies continue to evolve quickly—attackers and defenders are not standing still.

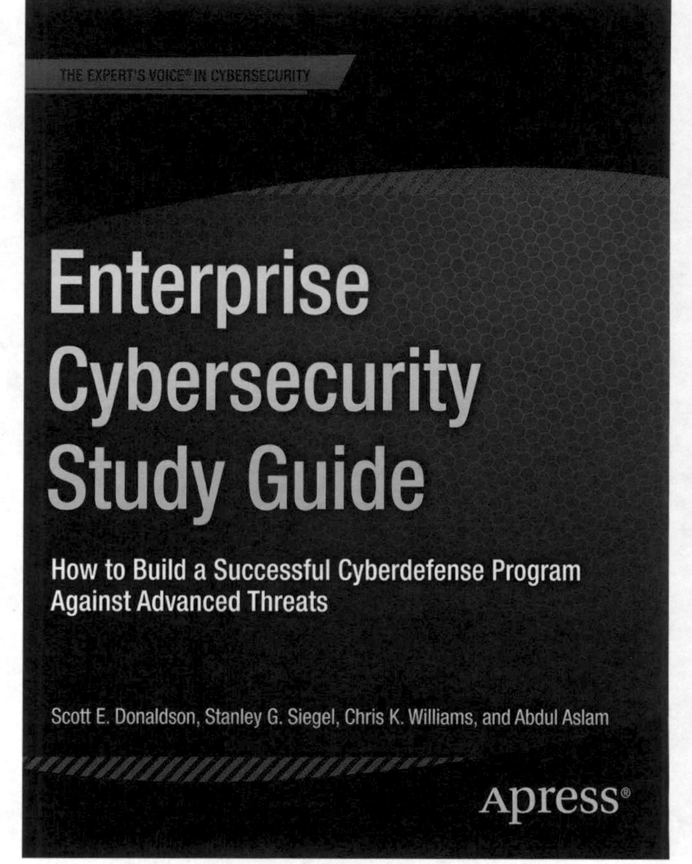

Overview *(2 of 2)*

- This study guide describes a ***cohesive*** *Enterprise Cybersecurity Framework* that integrates
  - ***architecture*** consisting of cybersecurity capabilities organized into functional areas that make capabilities easier to track, manage, and delegate;
  - ***cybersecurity policy*** designed to balance security needs against business priorities;
  - ***programmatics*** involving people, budget, and technology that are allocated to day-to-day operations and projects;
  - an ***IT life cycle*** aligned with IT departments responsible for strategy and architecture, engineering, and operations; and
  - ***cybersecurity assessments*** that are conducted periodically to help prevent cybersecurity program obsolescence.

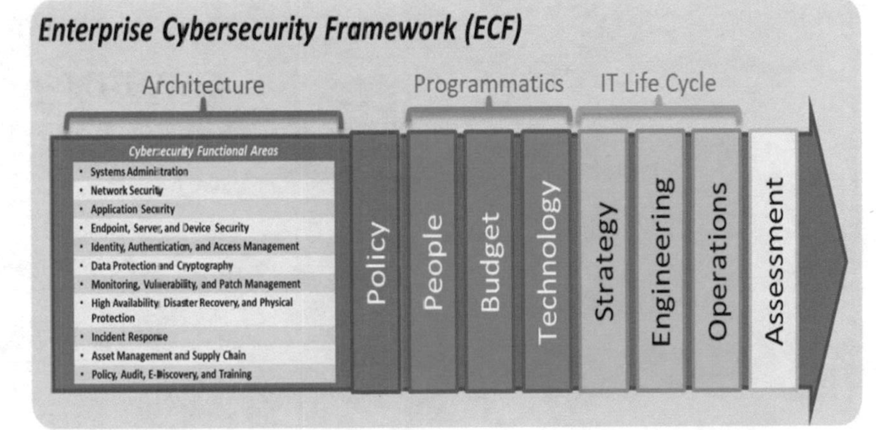

- The *Enterprise Cybersecurity Framework* is pragmatic, realistic, and designed for battling today's cyberthreats as well as tomorrow's next-generation cyberthreats.

Topics

- The Cyberattacks of Today
- Types of Cyberattackers
- Types of Cyberattacks
- The Steps of a Cyberintrusion
- Why Cyberintrusions Succeed
- A New Cybersecurity Mindset
- An Effective Enterprise Cybersecurity Program

The Cyberattacks of Today *(1 of 5)*

Context

- Compared to today, cybersecurity used to be relatively simple.
  - Major cyberthreats were viruses, worms, and Trojan horses.
- Transformation started to take place.
  - Cyberattackers started getting inside enterprise networks.
  - Once inside, cyberattackers operated surreptitiously:
    - They took control of infected machines.
    - They connected infected machines to remote command-and-control systems.
    - They escalated their privileges to systems administration. ...
- *"We are using outdated conventional defenses to guard against cutting-edge innovative malware. We are no more prepared to do this than a 19th century army trying to defend itself against today's weaponry."*[1]

- Breaches in the News
  - In 2011, RSA's enterprise was breached, and the security keys for many of its customers were believed to have been stolen.
  - In 2013, Target's point of sale network was compromised, resulting in the loss of personal information and credit card numbers for over 40 million customers.
  - In 2014, a German steel mill was affected by a hacking incident that caused one of its blast furnaces to malfunction, resulting in significant physical damage to the plant and its facilities.
  - In 2015, Anthem reported its IT systems had been breached and personal information on over 80 million current and former health care network members was compromised.
- These examples are but a handful of cybersecurity breaches that are indicative of trends.

[1]FireEye, "Advanced Malware Exposed," fireeye.com/wp_advmalware_exposed.html, 2011.

The Cyberattacks of Today *(2 of 5)*

The Sony Pictures Entertainment Breach of 2014

- In November 2014, an attacker took over the employees' computers.
  - The nonfunctional computers displayed a message from the Guardian of Peace.
  - By the end of the day, most computers had been completely disabled, which impacted the company's business—or lack thereof.
  - The cyberattacker published proprietary data to include salaries and personal e-mails of Sony's senior executives.
- Key Lessons Learned
  - Attackers did what cyberattackers have been able to do all along, but have chosen not to—they put the reality of the Sony hack in full view of the press and public.
  - It is reasonable to assume Sony's cyberdefenses were consistent with industry norms, but reflected ***what is*** and ***what is not*** being done at companies around the world.
  - Effectiveness of the Sony hack was likely amplified by the consolidation of IT systems administration that has occurred over the past 20 years.
    - A single systems administrator used to manage a handful of servers.
    - Today, this same administrator may have privileged access to hundreds of systems or even thousands.
  - Professional attackers, who understand how modern IT works and how it is managed, can effectively turn an enterprise's IT infrastructure against the enterprise.
  - IT infrastructures are largely designed for functionality—not security—and often lack compartmentalization to contain an attack.
  - Attack underscores the *fear factor* that devastating cyberattacks can have on an industry or nation.
- ***Megatrend***—As further described, such attacks are moving *"down market"* over time and becoming more common.

The Cyberattacks of Today *(3 of 5)*
Advanced Persistent Threats

- ***Advanced Persistent Threat (APT)*** is rising as a new type of adversary.
- An APT attacker is skilled in the art of cyberattacks and leverages IT technologies effectively to breach enterprises and systematically bypass all their protections, one at a time.
- What makes APT different from earlier cyberattack types is the persistence of the attack.
- APT cyberattacks are much more focused and effective because they are under the control of an intelligent actor who has an objective to achieve.
  - If their objective is to break into a company and steal corporate secrets, attackers persist until they succeed.
  - If their objective is to break into a government and steal national security information, they persist to find a weakness to exploit.
- Conventional Cyberattacks
  - Defenses only need to block the malware and the attacker will move on to other targets.
  - Simply having defenses is no longer effective when an opportunistic attacker can exploit a ***single*** mistake.
- An APT attacker constantly adjusts the attack to get past the latest round of defenses.
  - ***Given enough time, an APT attacker eventually gets through.***
  - To stop an APT attacker, the defenses have to ***work perfectly*** and ***be maintained perfectly.***
  - An APT attacker will exploit any mistake.
- APT requires a new type of defense method—one that adapts to the attack as quickly as the attack adapts to the defense.

The Cyberattacks of Today *(4 of 5)*

Waves of Malware (1 of 2)

- Over the past 20 years, there have been a number of generations, or *waves*, of malware technologies.

1. *Static Viruses*
- a) Propagated from computer to computer via floppy disks and boot sectors of hard drives
- b) Had little impact on system operations

2. *Network-Based Viruses*
- a) Propagated across the open Internet from computer to computer, exploiting weaknesses in operating systems or configurations
- b) Were effective because computers were often directly connected to each other without firewalls or protection

3. *Trojan Horse*
- a) Propagated across the Internet via e-mail and from compromised or malicious web sites
- b) Can infect large number of victims, but does so relatively arbitrarily since it is undirected

4. *Command and Control (C^2)*
- a) Allows attacker to remotely control its operation within the target enterprise
- b) Enables compromised machines to become footholds within the enterprise

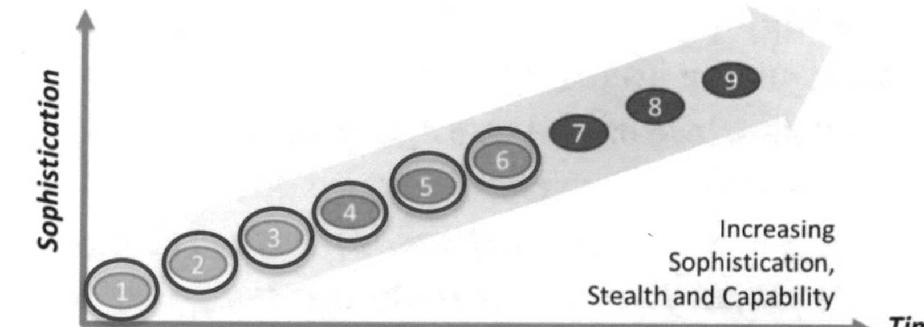

- c) Allows footholds to be manipulated by the attacker

5. *Customized*
- a) Developed for a particular target
- b) Sent directly to specific targets via phishing e-mails, drive-by web sites, or downloadable applications such as mobile apps
- c) Is not not recognized by signature-based defenses since this malware is customized for each victim

6. *Polymorphic*
- a) Designed not only to take administrative control of victim networks, but also to dynamically modify itself so it can continuously evade detection and stay ahead of attempts to remediate it

The Cyberattacks of Today *(5 of 5)*

Waves of Malware *(2 of 2)*

7. ***Intelligent***
    a) Analyzes a victim network, moves laterally within it, escalates privileges to take administrative control, and then extracts, modifies, or destroys its target data or information systems
    b) Does all its actions autonomously, without requiring human intervention or external command and control
8. ***Fully Automated, Polymorphic***
    a) Combines the features of polymorphic and intelligent malware
    b) Takes control autonomously and dynamically evades detection and remediation to stay one step ahead of defenders at all times
9. ***Firmware and Supply Chain***
    a) Takes fully automated, polymorphic malware to its logical conclusion by delivering malware capabilities through the supply chain, either embedded in product firmware or software products before they are shipped
    b) Is virtually undetectable
    c) Is difficult to differentiate the supply chain malware from the other features ***coming from the factory***

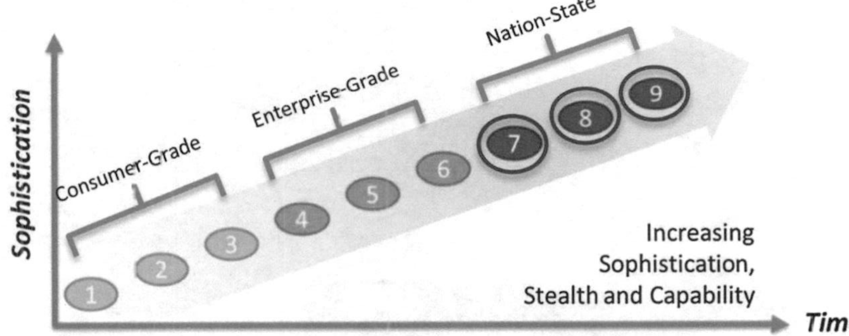

- Many people are familiar with malware waves 1, 2, and 3 because they represent the majority of consumer-grade cyberthreats, and many of the attacks are covered by the mainstream press.
- Enterprises are experiencing malware waves 4, 5, and 6 on a regular and increasing basis, but few outside of specialized cybersecurity fields understand the malware.
- Nation-state attackers use malware waves 7, 8, and 9, which require significant resources and expertise.

Types of Cyberattackers *(1 of 7)*

Context

- *Who are these mysterious cyberattackers hacking into systems and causing media headlines?*
- Cyberattackers are people who choose to create, distribute, and use malware or other tools and techniques to do things on computers they shouldn't be doing.
- The graphic shows five groups of cyberattackers grouped by their intent and objectives:
  - Commodity Threats
  - Hacktivists
  - Organized Crime
  - Espionage
  - Cyberwar

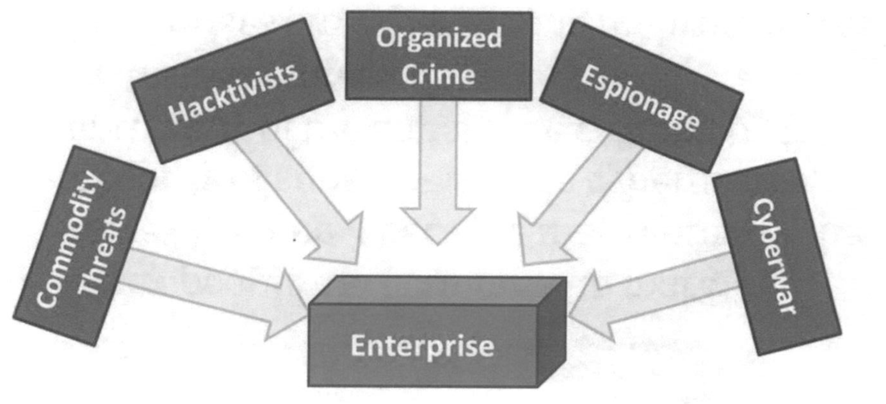

Note: There can be significant overlap in the tools and technologies used by these groups.

Types of Cyberattackers *(2 of 7)*

Commodity Threats

- Commodity threats include random malware, viruses, Trojans, worms, botnets, and ransomware.
- Commodity threats are propagating on the Internet all the time. Commodity threats
  - are undirected and opportunistic;
  - may exploit cyberdefense vulnerabilities;
  - do not adjust or adapt in order to work their way around protections that are in place;
  - can be destructive, but limited;
  - can be a starting point for more dangerous, ***targeted*** threats; and
  - be stopped if defenders block the commodity threat's attack vector, making the defenders safe.
  - For other cyberattack threat categories, simply blocking the initial attack vector is only a start.

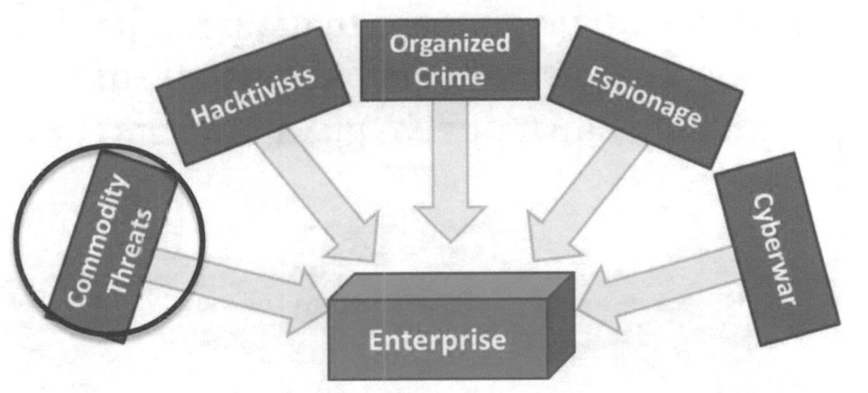

- Targeted cyberattackers
  - These cyberattackers may start their efforts by going to botnet operators and purchasing access to computers and servers that are already compromised inside the target environment.
  - Purchasing access can make the attackers' initial entry into the enterprise easier and save them valuable time and money.

Types of Cyberattackers *(3 of 7)*

Hacktivists

- Activist hacking, or *hacktivism*, consists of targeted attacks that
  - make public or political statements;
  - are used against individuals, enterprises, or governments;
  - seldom set out to hurt anyone or do significant physical damage;
  - are simply looking to get a message out and draw attention to a cause;
  - tend to use mostly commodity tools and techniques that are widely available on the Internet; and
  - take advantage of vulnerabilities that are unpatched or open.
- Defenses to protect against these tools and techniques are also usually widely available.

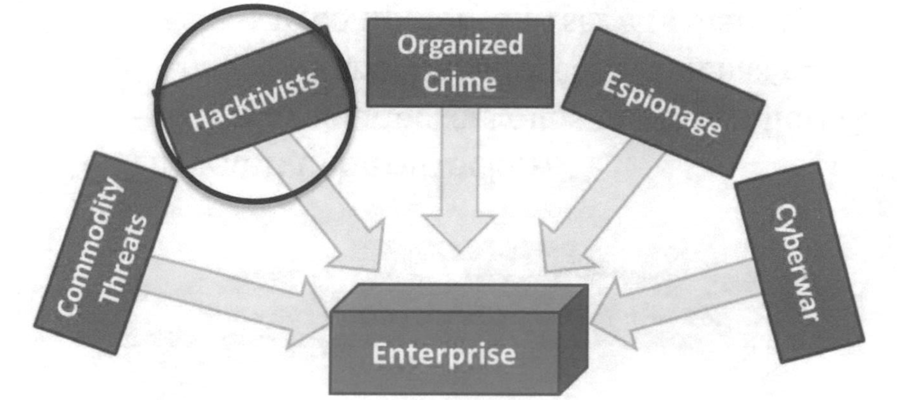

- Hacktivists will try and try again until the defenders make a mistake that allows them to accomplish their goal of bolstering their cause or embarrassing their adversaries.

Types of Cyberattackers *(4 of 7)*

Organized Crime *(1 of 2)*

- Organized crime attacks are targeted attacks.
- Criminals and criminal organizations have found there is serious money to be made on the Internet.
  - ***Easy Access***
    - On a global, interconnected network, the so-called ***good*** and ***bad*** neighborhoods are just a click apart.
    - Criminals can reach most anyone in the world without leaving their easy chairs.
  - ***Lack of Attribution***
    - It can be difficult to track down attackers, especially when they cover their tracks.
    - With criminals in one country and victims in another country, national boundaries make attribution even more difficult.
  - ***Wholesale Data***
    - Why steal money from one person at a time when you can rob the bank instead?
    - With the consolidation of data into huge corporate databases, wholesale data theft can be relatively easy to carry out.

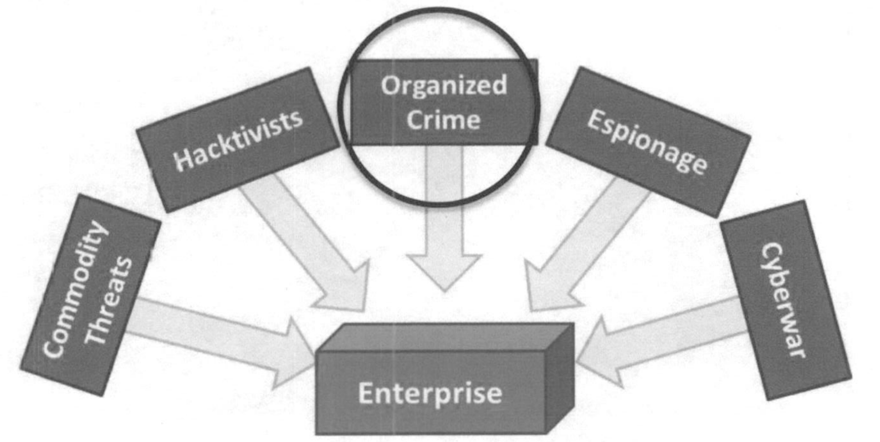

- Data theft is big business.
  - Stolen credit cards or social security numbers typically sell for $1 each.
  - Medical records can sell for $10 or more.
  - Stealing one million records can make real money, which can be used to support an entire shadow industry willing to lend their services for a piece of the action.

Types of Cyberattackers *(5 of 7)*

Organized Crime *(2 of 2)*

- There are many ways to make money through cyberattacks:
  - Business banking accounts
  - Ransomware
  - Payroll accounts can be relatively easy to carry out
  - Direct deposits

Types of Cyberattackers *(6 of 7)*

Espionage

- What organized crimes start, espionage agents take to the next level.
- Cyberespionage is more complex than organized crime.
  - It may be financially driven, but other drivers are much less forward.
  - It centers on stealing trade secrets for commercial advantage or national secrets for political or military advantage.
- In the cases of international business, trade secrets and national secrets can be closely aligned.
- Secrets can include the following:
  - Blueprints, formulas, or software code that is considered critical for success
  - Plenty of other information such as organization charts, budgets, project schedules, and meeting minutes that are vitally useful to the competition

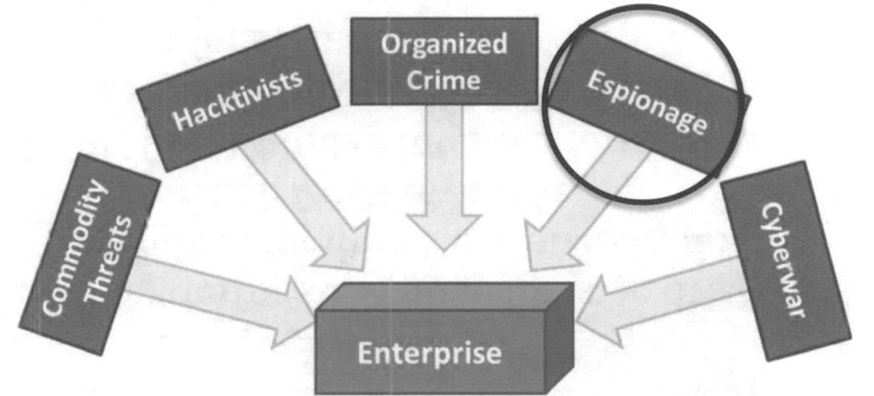

- Cyberespionage practitioners frequently use APT-style methods because they tend to be effective against enterprises with legacy-style cyberdefenses.
  - Why hack the CEO's laptop when, for the same amount of effort, you can get control of every laptop in the enterprise?
- Cyberespionage campaigns can be
  - conducted at the nation-state level; and
  - can be made up of multiple parts or phases (stepping stones).

Types of Cyberattackers *(7 of 7)*

Cyberwar

- Whereas espionage is generally focused on ***stealing*** information, the focus of cyberwar is on ***damaging*** the ability of enterprises or governments to operate in cyberspace.
- Damage can done by the following:
  - Overwhelming, overloading, disabling, or destroying IT systems used by victims
  - Using victim IT systems to cause physical systems to malfunction and damage themselves or their operators
- Everything is increasingly computerized and networked—the damage from cyberspace continues to increase.
- Cyberwar's cousin is cyberterrorism. Unaffiliated individuals or terrorist organizaions use the same techniques:
  - Denial of service
  - Data destruction
  - Control system manipulation
- Cyberwar supports national interests.

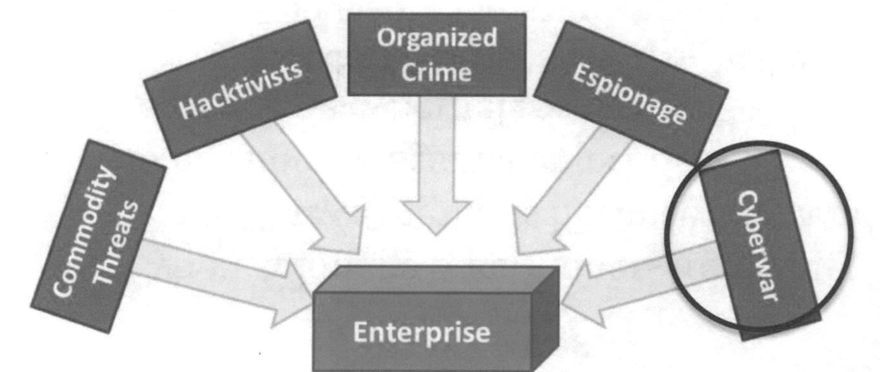

- Cyberterrorism is done for an activist agenda or for the sake of anarchy and destruction for its own sake.
- In 2007, Estonia's Internet infrastructure (telephone, financial, and government operations) was targeted.
- The Stuxnet worm infiltrated the Iranian nuclear program and ruined nuclear centrifuges.
- The 2012 cyberattack of Saudi Aramco resulted in damaging tens of thousands of computers.

Types of Cyberattacks *(1 of 5)*

Context *(1 of 2)*

- Regardless of their objective or techniques, cyberattacks generally can do three things to an enterprise or its data.
- Cyberattacks compromise
  - ***confidentiality*** by stealing data;
  - ***integrity*** by modifying data; and
  - ***availability*** by denying access to data, services, or systems.
- Some attacks combine two or more of the three types, but the three cyberattack types are the building blocks for most malicious cyberactivities.
- Cyberdefenses must focus on protecting confidentiality, integrity, and availability of data and the IT systems that process data.

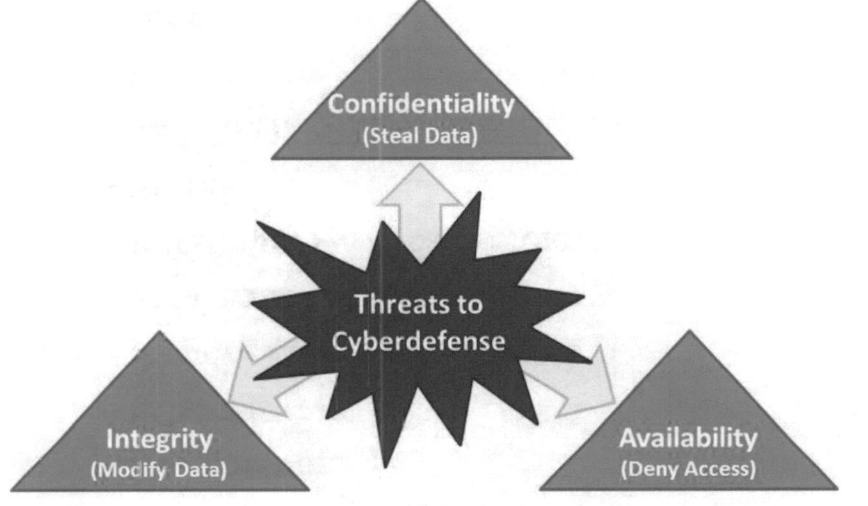

Types of Cyberattacks *(2 of 5)*

Context *(2 of 2)*

- Following are common cyberattacks:
  - Phishing / Spearsphishing
  - Drive-By / Watering Hole / Malvertising
  - Code Injection / Webshell
  - Keylogging / Session Hijacking
  - Pass-the-Hash and Pass-the-Ticket
  - Credential Harvesting
  - Gate-Crashing
  - Malware / Botnet
  - Distributed Denial-of-Service (DDoS)
  - Identity Theft
  - Industrial Espionage
  - Pickpocket
  - Bank Heist
  - Ransomware
  - Webnapping
  - Hijacking
  - Decapitation
  - Sabotage
  - Sniper / Laser / Smart Bomb
  - Smokeout / Lockout
  - Infestation / Whack-a-Mole
  - Burndown
  - Meltdown
  - Defamation
  - Graffiti
  - Smokescreen / Diversion
  - Fizzle

Types of Cyberattacks *(3 of 5)*

Confidentiality—Steal Data

- Confidentiality breaches steal data, sell data to the highest bidder, and often make headlines:
  - Social security numbers
  - Credit card numbers
  - Bank account information
  - Electronic health records
  - Confidential corporate secrets and executive correspondence
- Breaches focus on getting access to data at-rest or in-transit locations.
  - ***Databases***
    - Large pools of data
    - Relatively well-protected deep inside enterprise architecture
  - ***Backups***
    - Contain critical business information and customer data
    - Frequently do not get much security consideration
    - May be unencrypted

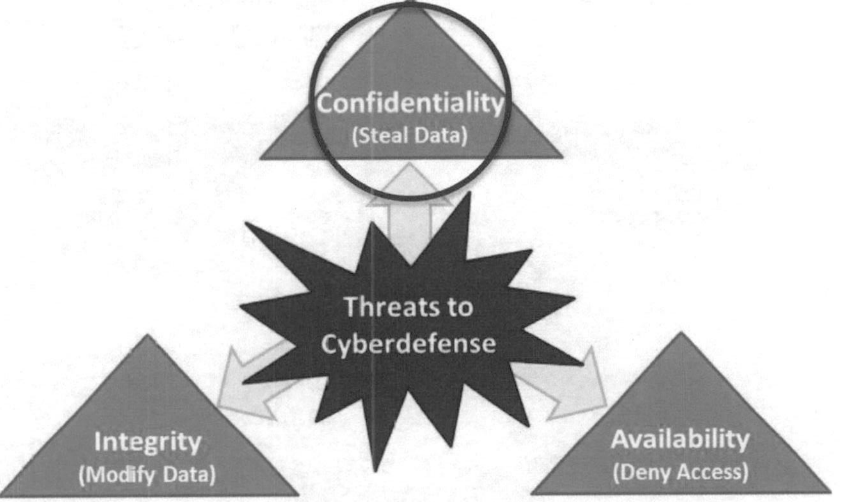

  - ***Application Servers***
    - Front-end application servers with access to data are frequently directly connected to the Internet.
    - Breaching such servers can provide access to data through applications, bypassing encryption, and other protection.
  - ***Systems Administrators***
    - They are the Achilles' heel of most enterprises.
    - Access to these credentials enable attackers to bypass data protection with little or no audit trail.

Types of Cyberattacks *(4 of 5)*

Integrity—Modify Data

- Integrity attacks involve modifying data that can result in various impacts:
  - Reputational impacts if the data is public-facing such as web sites
  - Financial reporting impacts, particularly for publicly traded corporations
  - Losses of actual money if data is bank-routing numbers or financial command to banks handling corporate accounts
- Integrity attacks include the following:
  - ***Hijacking***
    - Hijackers alter infrastructure data about Internet property (domain names, social medial identities, or registered network locations).
    - Much of the Internet's real estate is secured only by an e-mail address.
  - ***Sarbanes-Oxley***
    - Unauthorized changes to financial data can have serious audit and regulatory outcomes.
  - ***Online Banking***
    - Bank accounts including payroll, investments, and stock funds worth thousands or millions of dollars.

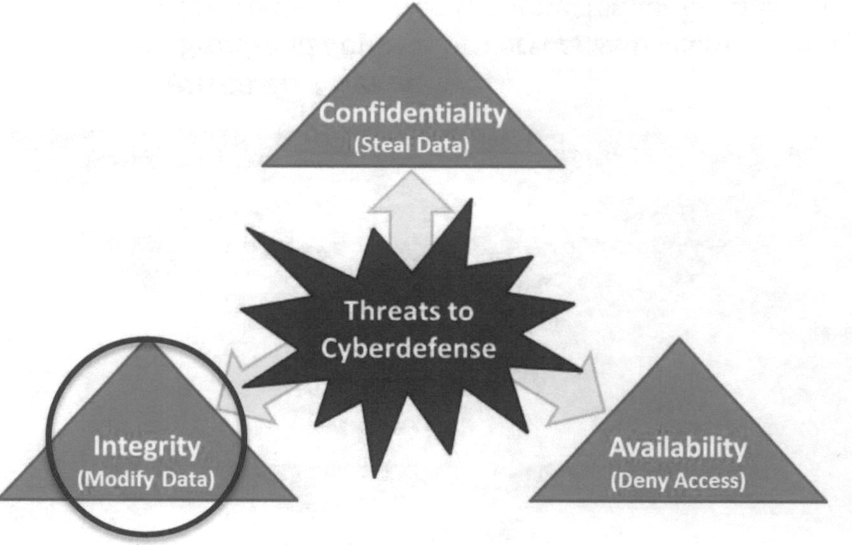

  - ***Direct Deposits***
    - Vulnerable to thefts where paychecks are re-routed to attacker accounts.
  - ***Vandalism***
    - Malicious actors deface web sites or other public materials with the intent of embarrassing the victim.
    - Internet-facing systems can be hard to protect perfectly as a single vulnerability or configuration mistake is all an attacker needs to strike.

Types of Cyberattacks *(5 of 5)*

Availability—Deny Access to Data, Services, or Systems

- Availability attacks affect the availability of systems and deny access to the systems.
  - Can be difficult to diagnose, especially if systems are impaired but not disabled
  - Can cause failures by overwhelming systems and infrastructure
- Deliberate availability attacks can be grouped into three categories:
  - ***Distributed Denial of Service (DDoS)***
    - Used to effectively disable services in the victim enterprise or country
    - Can take significant portions of victim's Internet capabilities offline for some time until they are mitigated
  - ***Targeted Denial of Service***
    - Involves hacking into the victim's enterprise and then disabling systems so they have to be rebuilt or recovered
    - Can be time-consuming for IT personnel to recover systems and restore service, particularly if backups are affected

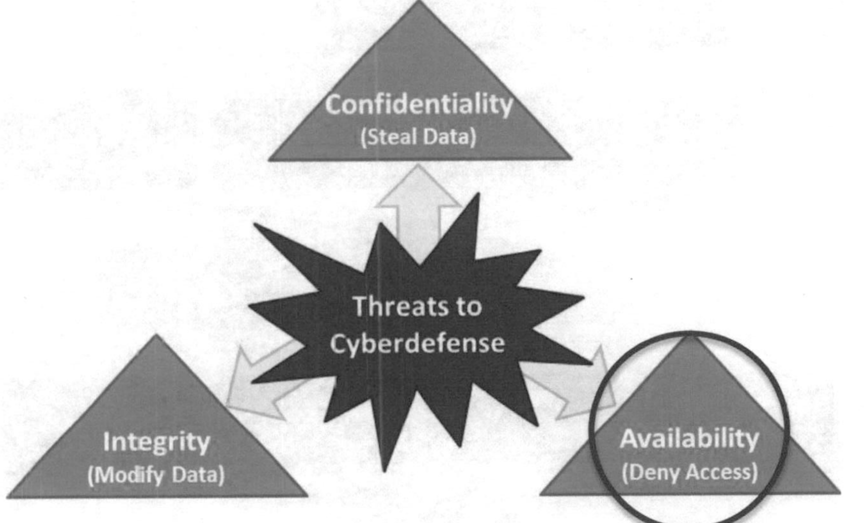

  - ***Physical Destruction***
    - This type of availability attack Involves using cyberattacks to cause physical destruction.
    - Stuxnet is a computer worm that sabotaged centrifuges used by the Iranian nuclear program.
    - As more and more critical systems are computer-controlled, these types of attacks will become potentially more dangerous and destructive over time.

The Steps of a Cyberintrusion *(1 of 11)*

Attack Trees and Attack Graphs (1 of 2)

- *How do cyberattacks occur?*
  - Hackers actually take control of computers and accounts inside of victim enterprise.
  - It is helpful to work out steps required for intrusion to succeed.
- Attack Trees and Attack Graphs
  - In 1999, Bruch Schneider published an article introducing a methodology for analyzing attacks, called ***Attack Trees***.
  - An attack tree begins with the objective of the cyberattack (such as stealing enterprise data).
  - Then the attack tree works backward to consider the various ways the objective could be achieved and the steps involved to accomplish the objective.

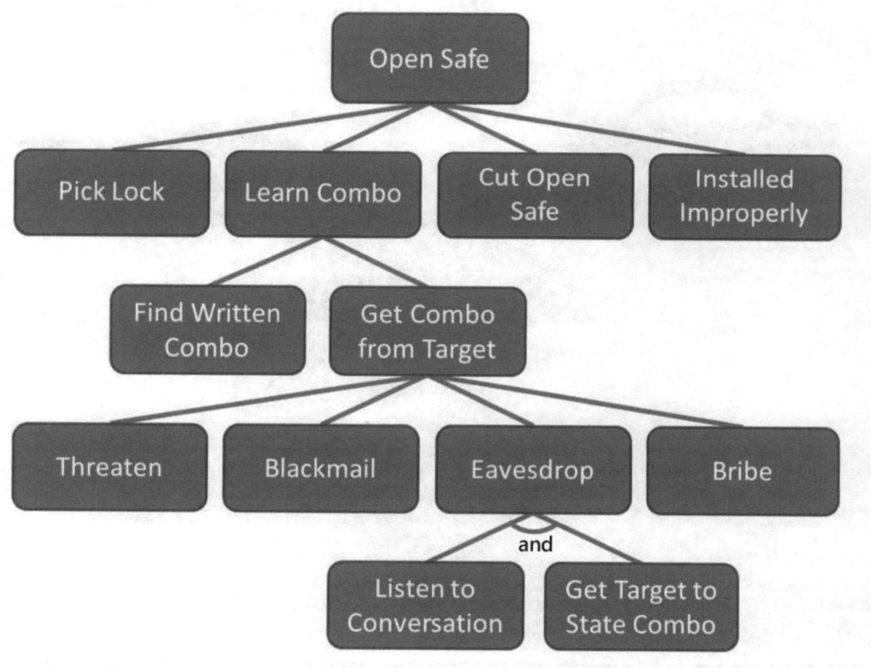

- The graphic depicts a notional attack tree Mr. Schneider analyzed for the case of trying to break into a safe.

The Steps of a Cyberintrusion *(2 of 11)*

Attack Trees and Attack Graphs (2 of 2)

- Each attack tree step is an opportunity to apply defenses and make the overall attack harder.
  - Attack steps can trigger an alarm and cause the entire attack to be detected.
  - Defenses can also add steps the attack must take before it can succeed.
    - Putting money in a safe means the attackers have to figure out how to get into the safe before they can get to the money.
    - Putting data into "virtual safes" can have the same effect.
  - Defensive steps don't make stealing the data impossible, as no defense is perfect, but they can make the attack significantly more difficult, time-consuming, and expensive.
- Significant academic research is ongoing using attack trees and a generalized version of attack trees called ***Attack Graphs***.
  - A graph is just like a tree, except the dependencies can loop back on themselves.
- Attack graphs have been computed for massive networks.
  - Research shows how vulnerabilities interconnect and how attackers can step from one compromised computer to another until they reach their target.
  - This research is of limited use.
    - Attack graphs of more than a handful of machines considering more than a handful of potential vulnerabilities become incredibly complex.
    - It is difficult to turn results into actionable intelligence.

The Steps of a Cyberintrusion *(3 of 11)*

Lockheed Martin Kill Chain (1 of 3)

- *What kind of graph is* useful?
  - Attack-tree and attack-graph methodologies provide a generalized model of the sequence of cyberintrusion activities.
    - Defenders can analyze multiple options of attacker activities.
    - Defenders can then focus their defenses on disrupting such options.
    - The attack tree can be generalized into a model that is simpler to analyze, but powerful in terms of providing specific, actionable results.
- When simplified, the attack tree gets reduced down to a sequence.
- The sequence has many labels, including ***Kill Chain***, ***Attack Life Cycle***, and ***Attack Sequence***.
- In 2011, several researchers from Lockheed Martin published a paper[2] that analyzed Advanced Persistent Threat (APT) attack campaigns.
- Attackers followed a sequence of seven steps; defenders could apply defenses at each step to attempt to thwart the attack.

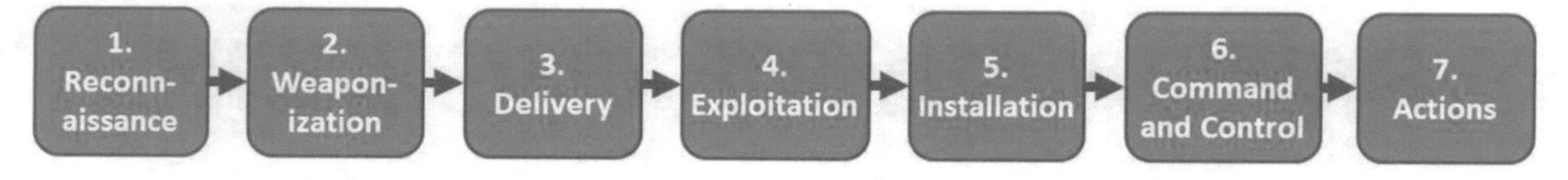

[2]Eric M. Hugchins, Michael J. Cloppert, and Rohan M. Amin, Ph.D., "Intelligence-Driven Computer Network Defense Informed by Analysis of Adversary Campaigns and Intrusion Kill Chains," `www.lockheedmartin.com/content/dam/lockheed/data/corporate/documents/LM-White-Paper-Intel-Driven-Defense.pdf`, 2011

The Steps of a Cyberintrusion *(4 of 11)*

Lockheed Martin Kill Chain *(2 of 3)*

1. ***Reconnaissance***
   a) Research, identify, and select targets.
   b) Crawl Internet web sites such as conference proceedings, mailing lists for e-mail addresses, social media sites, and so on.
2. ***Weaponization***
   a) Attackers couple a remote access Trojan with an exploit into a deliverable payload, typically by means of an automated tool (weaponizer).
   b) Adobe Portable Document Format (PDF) and Microsoft Office documents often serve as the weaponized vehicle.
3. ***Delivery***
   a) Delivery denotes the transmission of the weapon to the targeted environment.
   b) Lockheed Martin Computer Incident Response Team reported for the years 2004–2010, the three most prevalent delivery vectors for APT weaponized payloads were e-mail attachments, web sites, and USB removable media.
4. ***Exploitation***
   a) After the weapon is delivered to the victim host, exploitation triggers the intruder's code.
   b) Exploitation often targets an application or operating system vulnerability, but it can also target the users or leverage an operating system feature that auto-executes code.

The Steps of a Cyberintrusion *(5 of 11)*

Lockheed Martin Kill Chain (3 of 3)

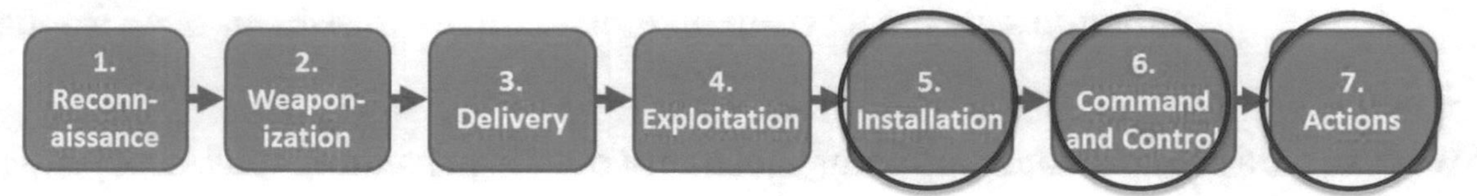

5. ***Installation***
   a) Installation of a remote access Trojan or back door on the victim system allows the adversary to maintain persistence inside the environment.

6. ***Command and Control (C^2)***
   a) Typically, compromised hosts must beacon outbound to an Internet controller server to establish a C^2 channel.
   b) APT malware typically requires manual interaction rather than activity conducted automatically. Once the C^2 channel is established, intruders have "hands-on-the-keyboard" access inside the target environment.

7. ***Actions on Objectives***
   a) After progressing through the first six steps, intruders take actions to achieve the objectives.
   b) The typical objective is data exfiltration—collecting, encrypting, and extracting information from the target environment; violations of data integrity or data availability are also potential objectives.
   c) Alternatively, intruders may use the initial victim box as a "hop point" to compromise additional systems and move laterally inside the network.

The Steps of a Cyberintrusion *(6 of 11)*

Mandiant Attack Life Cycle (1 of 3)

- Mandiant published a Lockheed Martin-like kill chain methodology called the *Attack Life Cycle.*[3]

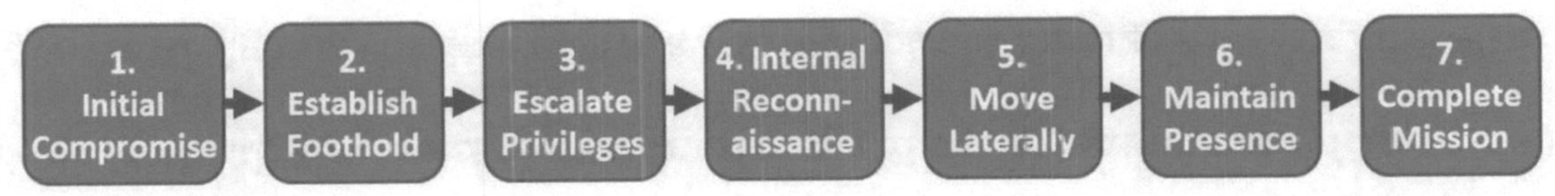

- The Mandiant Attack Life Cycle contains seven steps that start at the initial compromise.
- The process breaks out the steps of accomplishing the mission in greater detail than the Lockheed Martin Kill Chain.
- Mandiant believes China used such techniques to spy on governments and corporations in the United States and elsewhere.

[3]Mandiant, "APT: Exposing One of China's Cyber Espionage Units," http://intelreport.mandiant.com/Mandiant_APT1_Report.pdf, 2013

The Steps of a Cyberintrusion *(7 of 11)*

Mandiant Attack Life Cycle *(2 of 3)*

1. ***Initial Compromise***
   a) This step represents the methods intruders use to penetrate a target organization.
   b) APT intruders frequently target individual users or look for technical vulnerabilities in public-facing infrastructure.
2. ***Establish Foothold***
   a) By establishing a foothold, APT threat groups can access and control one or more victim computers from outside the network via back doors.
   b) Back doors give the APT groups basic access to a system, typically through a command shell or graphical user interface.
3. ***Escalate Privileges***
   a) This step involves acquiring administrative access to resources within the victim environment.
   b) Administrative access can be obtained through usernames and passwords, Public Key Infrastructure (PKI) certificates, Virtual Private Networking (VPN) connectivity, or control of systems administration computers.
4. ***Internal Reconnaissance***
   a) Attackers collect information about the victim environment.
   b) Data of interest may take different forms, most commonly consists of documents, the contents of user e-mail accounts, or databases.
   c) Attackers may use custom scripts to automate the process of reconnaissance and identification of data of interest.

The Steps of a Cyberintrusion *(8 of 11)*

Mandiant Attack Life Cycle *(3 of 3)*

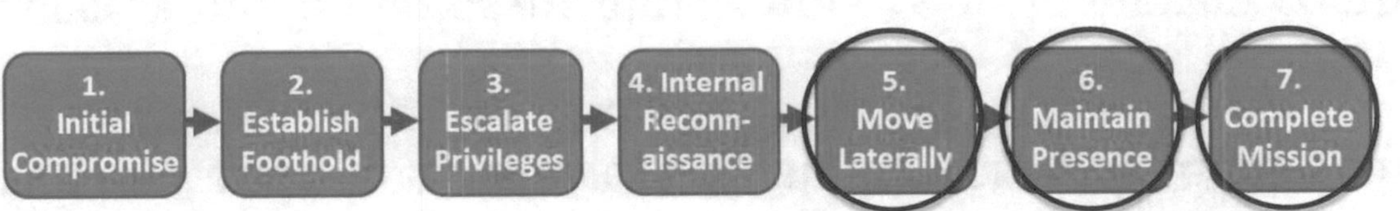

5. ***Move Laterally***
   a) In most cases, the systems intruders initially compromise do not contain the data they want.
   b) Moving laterally within a network to other computers is necessary for mission success.
   c) APT groups leverage compromised user credentials or pass-the-hash tools (that steal user credentials) to gain access to additional victim computers and devices.

6. ***Maintain Presence***
   a) Intruders take actions to ensure continued control over key systems in the network environment from outside the network.
   b) They may install different families of malware on multiple computers and use a variety of command and control addresses.
   c) Different malware families provide redundancy and make it difficult to identify and remove all intruder access points.

7. ***Complete Mission***
   a) The APT intrusion goal typically is to steal data (for example, intellectual property, business contracts or negotiations, policy papers, and internal memoranda).
   b) Once APT groups find files of interest on compromised systems, they often pack them into archive files before exfiltrating them.
   c) A variety of methods are used to transfer files out of the victim network, including file transfer protocol (FTP), file sharing tools, and web upload sites.

The Steps of a Cyberintrusion *(9 of 11)*

Enterprise Cybersecurity Attack Sequence *(1 of 3)*

- Based on the authors' experience building and operating defenses against real-world APT actors, they adopted a simplified version of the attack sequence process they call the ***Enterprise Cybersecurity Attack Sequence.***

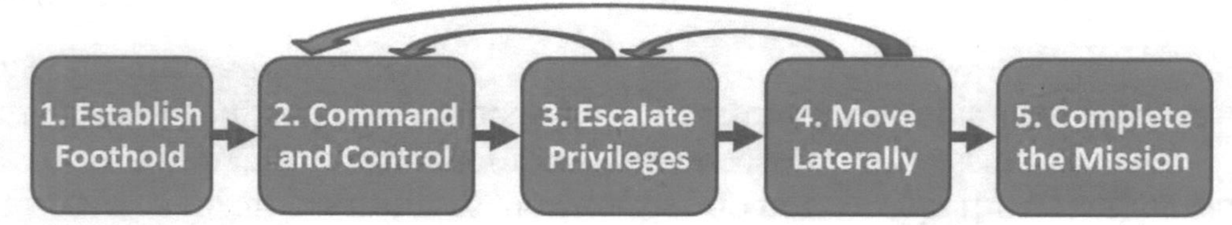

- This attack sequence is derived from the preceding work and simplifies it somewhat to align more closely with how and where defensive capabilities are often deployed in enterprise defenses.
- Initial attacker access and footholds are almost impossible to prevent completely.
- The attack sequence includes ***iterative cycles*** among steps 2, 3, and 4, as attackers move around the target enterprise in search of their objective.
- During steps 2, 3, and 4, attackers often generate considerable telemetry activity that can be used to detect their presence and repel their attacks before those attacks can succeed.

The Steps of a Cyberintrusion *(10 of 11)*

Enterprise Cybersecurity Attack Sequence *(2 of 3)*

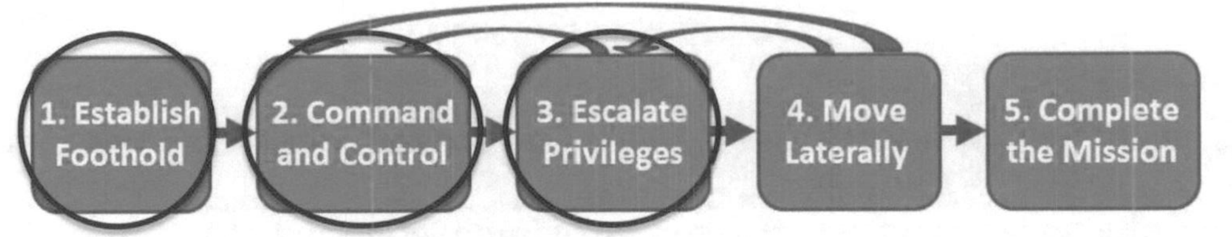

1. ***Establish Foothold***
   a) Attackers can accomplish this activity by exploiting vulnerabilities in servers and applications, compromising end-user workstations, or buying access through criminally operated botnet networks.
   b) Footholds can consist of a compromised server, endpoint computer, mobile device, or simply a user account with access into the victim enterprise network.
2. ***Command and Control***
   a) Attackers establish remote command and control capabilities so they can manually run commands in the target environment.
   b) These connections can be made via inbound connections to Internet-facing servers, outbound connections from internal endpoints, or various forms of protocol tunneling, including encrypted connections.
3. ***Escalate Privileges***
   a) Attackers gain control of user accounts with the privileges needed to accomplish the attack objective.
   b) In environments with username and password authentication for systems administrators, this activity can be trivially easy to accomplish.
   c) In more complex environments, this activity may take more time as attackers must identify and circumvent multiple layers of protections around the privileges the attackers want.

The Steps of a Cyberintrusion *(11 of 11)*

Enterprise Cybersecurity Attack Sequence (3 of 3)

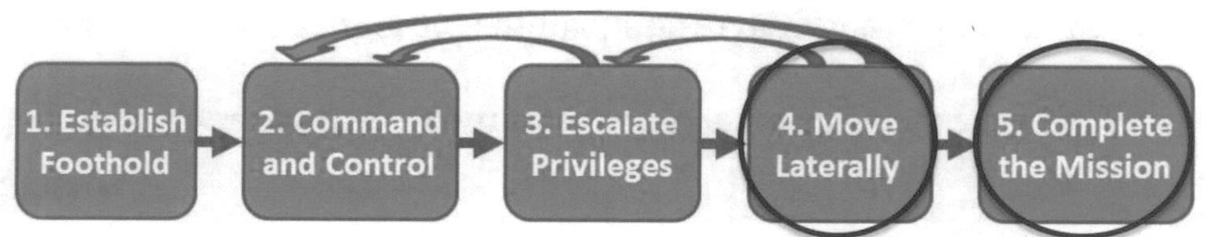

4. ***Move Laterally***

    a) While escalating privileges, attackers may also move laterally from computer to computer.
    b) This movement can involve transiting network zones, bypassing firewalls, compromising machines, and stealing credentials.
    c) Lateral movement may then feed back into multiple rounds of privilege escalation and command-and-control establishment.
    d) In complex environments, this cyclical process may take weeks or months to get from the starting point to the ultimate objective.

5. ***Complete the Mission***

    a) Once the objective has been accessed, the attackers can complete their mission.
    b) If the objective is to ***steal data***, attackers will bundle the data up and exfiltrate it.
    c) If the objective is to ***modify data***, attackers will make the desired changes or initiate the desired transactions.
    d) If the objective is to ***damage availability***, attackers will disable the targeted systems.
    e) At the end of this step, attackers may cover their tracks.

Why Cyberintrusions Succeed *(1 of 8)*

Context

- Successful attacker cyberintrusions require the following:
  - Successfully performing multiple steps
  - Defeating potential defenses and defensive technologies
- *Why are cyberintrusions successful?*
  - No single or simple answer exists.
  - A number of factors, when taken together, is making it harder for cybersecurity defenses to succeed.
- Factors impacting enterprises' abilities to protect themselves include the following:
  - The Explosion in Connectivity
  - Consolidation of Enterprise IT
  - Defeat of Preventive Controls
  - Failure of Detective Controls
  - Compliance over Capability
  - The Gap in Cybersecurity Effectiveness

Why Cyberintrusions Succeed *(2 of 8)*

The Explosion in Connectivity

- Network connectivity (Internet connectivity in particular) has exploded over the last twenty years.
  - Enterprises were fairly simple.
    - A perimeter, a network, and a data center containing servers
    - Desktop computers accessing those services from within a closed network
  - Today, the architecture is complex.
    - Mobile devices , cloud services using federated credentials
    - Corporate infrastructures operated by third-party providers
- Network complexity has exploded.
  - Everything is interconnected in a myriad of ways.
- With the rise of mobile, cloud, and the "Internet of things," everything is connected.
- Complex and sophisticated devices are vulnerable to countless glitches, bugs, and exploits that can turn them from useful appliances into malicious tools.
- In an all-connected world, the functionality is amazing, but the security challenges are daunting.
- Managing, protecting, and defending this complexity are extremely difficult, if not impossible.

Why Cyberintrusions Succeed *(3 of 8)*

Consolidation of Enterprise IT

- Twenty years ago, highly-trained and experienced administrators performed IT functions.
- Today the functions are scripted and automated.
  - Administrators can now manage ten or a hundred times as many computers rather than a relatively few computers.
  - Enterprise data centers can now contain thousands or tens of thousands of computers vs. a hundred servers.
  - Opportunities for mistakes and glitches have grown significantly.
- Modern data centers with cloud services, virtual networking, virtual storage, and virtual computing add to the protection challenge.
  - Layers of virtualization and abstraction add complexity.
  - Specialized administration areas are difficult to understand, troubleshoot, and protect.
- Legacy data centers had a server administrator who was the **one** point of contact for server and services protection.
  - In a virtualized environment, successful server administration depends on multiple administrators for network, storage, virtualization, servers, and applications.
  - Achieving proper configurations across all layers of the computing environment is difficult and complex, and it requires collaboration.
- If attackers get control of the IT power that is in the hands of a small number of people, they can use the enterprise's own tools against itself.

Why Cyberintrusions Succeed *(4 of 8)*

Defeat of Protective Controls/Failure of Detective Controls

- Before discussing the Defeat of Protective Controls and the Failure of Detective Controls, it is important to understand the types of cybersecurity controls used to mitigate enterprise risks.
- Cybersecurity controls help reduce ***confidentiality***, ***integrity***, or ***availability*** risks by
  - reducing risk probability;
  - reducing risk impact;
  - detecting occurrences of risk incidents;
  - collecting evidence to support security evaluations and incident investigations; and
  - providing validation that risks are being mitigated adequately.
- Cybersecurity control types include the following:
  - ***Preventive Controls***
    - Block the threat and prevent incidents from occurring altogether
  - ***Detective Controls***
    - Detect when the threat has transpired
    - Generates alerts that can then be acted upon
  - ***Forensic Controls***
    - Collect records of activities related to the threat
    - Can be used to produce artifacts to support the following:
      - The operation of detective controls
      - Investigations of incidents
      - Audits of controls to verify their operation and effectiveness
  - ***Audit Controls***
    - Investigate the following:
      - Presence of the threat
      - Incidents associated with the threat
      - Operation of controls that mitigate the risk

Why Cyberintrusions Succeed *(5 of 8)*

Defeat of Preventive Controls

- Much of cybersecurity has involved blocking undesired activities and preventing them from executing.
- The preventive approach sounds good in principle, but it has its limitations.
- Establishing preventive controls is like putting up a network of fences and then assuming the fences are working as designed without ever checking them.
- Advanced attackers have consistently succeeded in defeating or working around preventive controls to accomplish their objectives.
- Preventive controls are riddled with vulnerabilities, holes, bugs, and poor configurations.
- Enterprises *must assume* preventive controls will, at best, *only slow down* an attacker.
- Eventually, even the strongest preventive controls may be defeated by a skilled and patient attacker.
- Does the above commentary mean preventive controls have failed altogether? Of course not!
- However, it does mean such controls have limits—***successful cyberdefense needs more than prevention!***

Why Cyberintrusions Succeed *(6 of 8)*

Failure of Detective Controls

- Detective controls are supposed to raise alerts or alarms when malicious activity occurs in their vicinity, based on recognizing known patterns of malicious behavior or software.
- Systemic detective control failures involve (1) lack of incident detection and (2) overloading cybersecurity personnel with potential incident alarms, most of which are false alarms or simply noise.
- First, in many cases, detection is not even happening.
  - Most IT systems can log activity, but the activity is often in the form of cryptic text files or event codes that require significant expertise to decipher.
  - Consequently, many enterprises have *little to no visibility* of activity taking place within their systems.
  - Enterprises must integrate these logs, correlate across them, and then use the data to alert on activity patterns that are or may be malicious.
- Second, even when enterprises have set up their systems to alert them on potentially malicious behavior, it is easy to become buried in alerts.
  - With terabytes of data and thousands of servers, there can be hundreds or thousands or even millions of events per day calling for investigation.
  - In practice, a cyber analyst can thoroughly investigate perhaps a dozen events in a single day.
  - When people become overwhelmed with data, the enterprise is just as blind as it was when it had nothing.

Why Cyberintrusions Succeed *(7 of 8)*

Compliance over Capability

- Ironically, many of the companies involved in credit card breaches had been recently certified as complying with the Payment Card Industry Digital Security Standards (PCI_DSS).
- Given this situation, it appears compliance certification against established standards does not necessarily correlate with breach resistance.
  - First, standards must necessarily focus on the presence or absence of technologies or controls, but it is hard for standards to specify the level of resistance of those technologies or controls to deliberate attack by skilled attackers.
    - We can ask if a firewall is present or if network traffic is being filtered, but how do we expand compliance specifications to determine if the firewall is properly configured to stop a deliberate attack?
    - The cybersecurity industry is still relatively immature compared to other industries with regard to the establishment of repeatable and auditable standards for effectiveness.
  - Second, the requirement for standards compliance can take enterprise resources away from "real cybersecurity."
    - Compliance standards incentivize leadership to focus on checking the box to meet standards and receive certification vs. modeling cybersecurity threats and building effective defenses.
    - Once an enterprise is certified as compliant, it can then fall back on the compliance certification if something goes wrong, shielding itself from liability or accusations of negligence.
- Evidence suggests compliance frameworks are not having their intended effect and may need to be upgraded to correlate better with cyberdefense effectiveness against real-world cyberattack scenarios.

Why Cyberintrusions Succeed *(8 of 8)*

The Gap in Cybersecurity Effectiveness

- The graphic suggests that perhaps cyberattacks are improving faster than cyberdefenses, resulting in a gap in effectiveness.
- Unfortunately, gradually improving cyberdefenses may be losing ground over time.
- Modern cybersecurity architecture consists, in part, of secured networks, firewall protections, and anti-virus on endpoints.
- Modern cybersecurity architecture does not seem to be holding up well against cyberattacks.
- Maintaining the defenses of ten years ago is an increasingly daunting task given the
  - complexity of devices;
  - exploding size of IT architectures;
  - interconnections among partners, vendors, and customers;

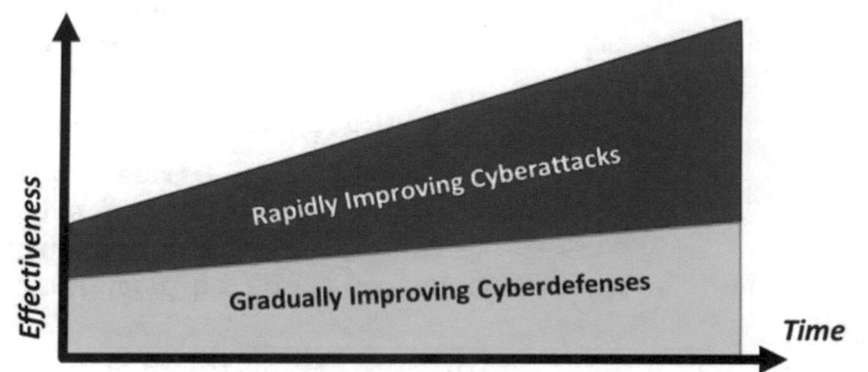

  - bring-your-own-device (BYOD); and
  - cloud services.
- Meanwhile, cyberattackers and the technologies they use are only getting better.
- As cyberdefenses are upgraded, attackers continue to find and exploit gaps and vulnerabilities.
- The result is a consistent arms race between attackers and defenders.
- It may be time to embrace a new cybersecurity mindset.

A New Cybersecurity Mindset *(1 of 3)*

- **Determined attackers will eventually penetrate any and all defenses.**
- Intelligent attackers will adjust their attacks to work around the defenses they encounter.
- Therefore, defenders must not place all of their focus on attempting to stop the attacker because stopping a determined attacker is impossible.
  - Enterprise defenses must value delay and detection.
  - An attack that is detected can be stopped, while an attack that is not detected will progress until it eventually succeeds.
  - Defenders can usually stop a discovered attack before the attack accomplishes its objective.
- Defenses must be architected to create defensible areas where detection can occur after attacks begin but before they succeed.
  - Active defenders monitor and patrol these areas to find attacker activities.
  - Defenders analyze attacker activities to understand what attackers are doing, where they are coming from, and so on.
  - Defenders repel attacks after they are detected but before they can succeed.
  - Defenders improve defenses to make future attacks more difficult.
- Analogy—How Protection Is Performed in the Physical World
  - It is impossible to perfectly protect physical assets from harm or theft.
  - Physical protection is designed to detect and delay attacks until authorities can arrive.
  - Locks, gates, alarms, cameras, guards, and authorities all work together as a system to provide "good enough" protection.

A New Cybersecurity Mindset *(2 of 3)*

- The graphic delineates four **next-generation cyberdefense axioms** that can help cyberdefenders be more effective against intelligent attackers.

1. **Assume an intelligent attacker will eventually defeat all defensive measures.**
   a) An intelligent attacker is not going to walk into defenses as they are designed.
   b) An attacker is going to seek to find the easiest, fastest, and potentially cheapest attack.
   c) Enterprises must look at themselves from the attacker's perspective and design defenses accordingly.

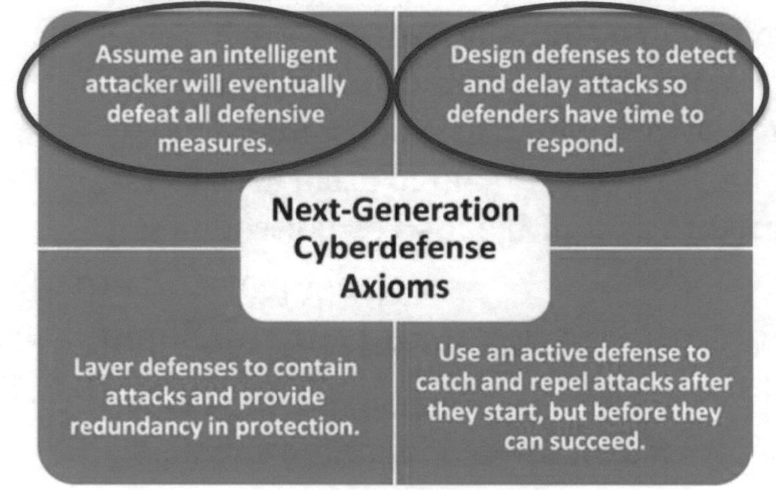

2. **Design defenses to detect and delay attacks so defenders have time to respond.**
   a) Prevention will inevitably fail or be defeated.
   b) When preventive controls fail or are defeated, defenses should detect the attack and delay attackers long enough for defenders to respond.
   c) Detection must be designed to catch real attacks and not overload defenders with *noise* from false positives.

A New Cybersecurity Mindset *(3 of 3)*

3. **Layer defenses to contain attacks and provide redundancy in protection.**
   a) Design defenses so initial incursions, particularly in Internet-facing systems such as web servers or endpoints, can be detected when they first occur.
   b) Have additional layers of protection around the databases, file servers, and security infrastructures the attackers are really targeting.
   c) For the most critical information assets, ensure defenders have multiple opportunities to detect and respond to attacks before the attacks can succeed, and test those defense regularly.

4. **Use an active defense to catch and repel attacks after they start, but before they can succeed.**
   a) Active defense involves real people who monitor IT systems and respond to intrusions when they occur.
   b) The incident response team must diagnose attacks and repel them before the attackers can achieve their objectives.

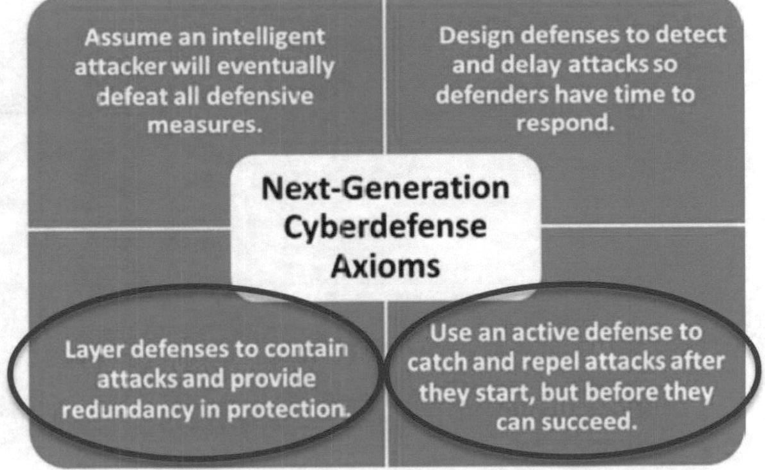
Assume an intelligent attacker will eventually defeat all defensive measures.
Design defenses to detect and delay attacks so defenders have time to respond.
Next-Generation Cyberdefense Axioms
Layer defenses to contain attacks and provide redundancy in protection.
Use an active defense to catch and repel attacks after they start, but before they can succeed.

   c) When attacks are not being detected, defense teams should be actively hunting for signs of attacker activity and seeking to improve prevention, detection, and response capabilities.

- Cybersecurity professionals
  - need to achieve partial security, rather than doing everything perfectly all the time; and
  - must work with the business to implement enterprise defenses that are effective relative to the business's activities.

An Effective Enterprise Cybersecurity Program *(1 of 5)*

- *How is this new cybersecurity mindset turned into* an effective *enterprise cybersecurity program?*
- Enterprises must pause and consider what the elements of an enterprise cybersecurity program are—*policy, programmatics, IT life cycle,* and *assessments.*

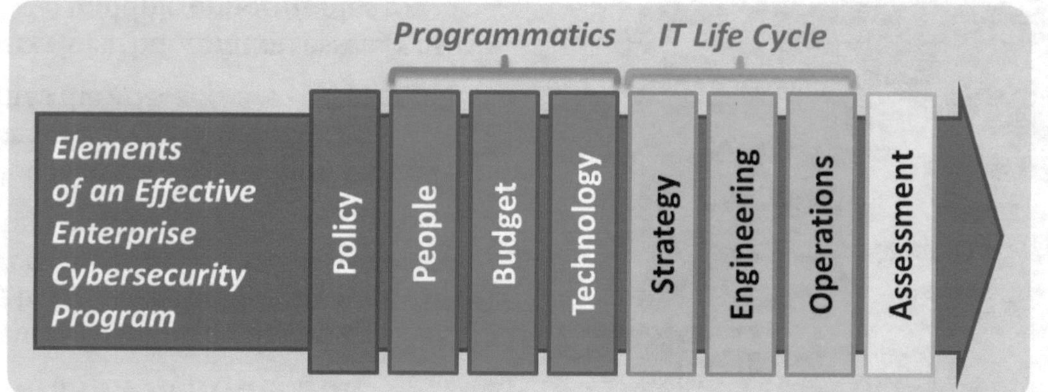

- Not only do these elements need to be coordinated, but they also need to be integrated to work well together.

An Effective Enterprise Cybersecurity Program *(2 of 5)*

- For an enterprise cybersecurity program to be effective, all elements must
  - be part of a common roadmap
  - be well-coordinated; and
  - work effectively together.
- Otherwise, critical cybersecurity pieces fall into the gaps and are missed.
  – *Having the right policy is a necessary start.*
    - However, if the technology to implement the policy is not deployed, then the policy will not be effective.

  – *Having the right technology deployed is great.*
    - However, if the operational processes are not in place to operate and maintain the technology after deployment, then the technology will not be effective.
- If the enterprise cannot constantly assess its status and cybersecurity effectiveness to keep up with rapidly changing threats, then the program is going to fall quickly behind.

An Effective Enterprise Cybersecurity Program *(3 of 5)*

- The graphic depicts the necessary elements needed for an effective enterprise cybersecurity program.

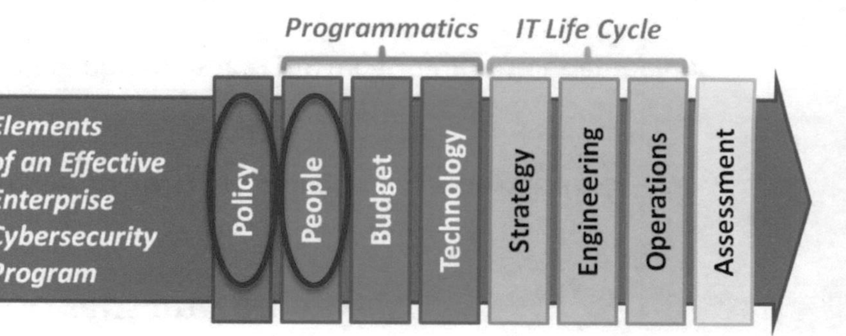

1. ***Policy***
   a) Staffing, budget, technology, and operations must trace to written policy that directs what is to be protected and to what degree as well as what the consequences are for violations.
   b) This traceability is the foundation of the entire cybersecurity program.
   c) Policy includes standards, guidelines, procedures, and baselines for the entire enterprise.

2. ***People***
   a) This element organizes the people responsible for cybersecurity.
   b) These people may report to different departments of IT, operations, cybersecurity, compliance, or internal audit.
   c) People must be carefully organized so their authority, responsibility, and expertise are all in harmony with each other.
   d) Organizational lines of authority and responsibility must be carefully considered, along with organizational interfaces where departments must collaborate.

An Effective Enterprise Cybersecurity Program *(4 of 5)*

3. ***Budget***
   a) Allocation of resources to pay for deploying, operating, and maintaining the cybersecurity technologies and operational processes making up the enterprise cybersecurity program must be well thought out.
   b) The amount of money allocated to each cybersecurity item must be adequate for the functional area to be effective.

4. ***Technology***
   a) The size, complexity, and speed of modern IT dictate that cybersecurity cannot be accomplished manually.
   b) Cybersecurity technologies protect the enterprise by providing for prevention, detection, logging, response, and audit capabilities.
   c) The right technologies, well deployed and properly maintained, are essential to success.

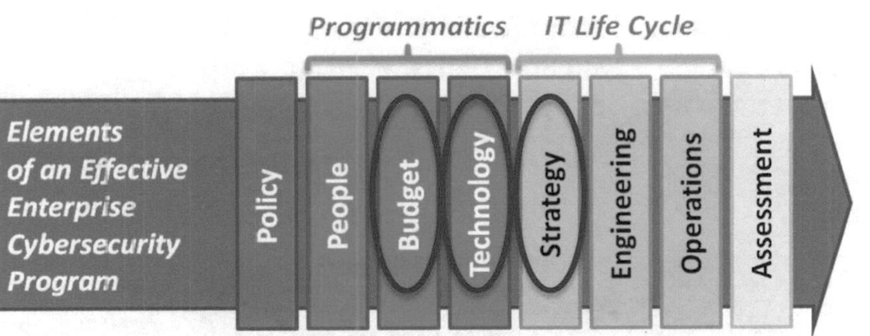

5. ***Strategy***
   a) Effective strategy ensures the technologies are well coordinated so they work together as integrated systems.
   b) Integration applies both to (1) cybersecurity technologies themselves and (2) cybersecurity technologies being well coordinated with the whole of the IT enterprise.
   c) Strategic disconnects can render technologies ineffective, impair enterprise productivity, or dramatically increase operational costs.

An Effective Enterprise Cybersecurity Program *(5 of 5)*

6. ***Engineering***
   a) Proper engineering ensures technologies are (1) properly selected to meet requirements, (2) configured and deployed, and (3) supported so they continue to meet initial and new requirements over their life cycles.
   b) It also ensures deployed systems are "fit for purpose" and "fit for use" for as long as they are needed and used.

7. ***Operations***
   a) Security technologies must be operated to stay effective.
   b) Other security operational processes such as policy exception management must also be performed.
   c) If cybersecurity is not maintained on an ongoing basis, it will become ineffective over time.

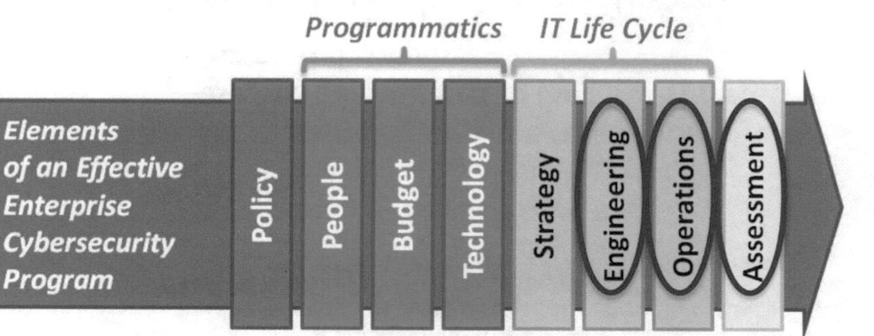

8. ***Assessment***
   a) Assessment tools evaluate the effectiveness of the enterprise's risk mitigations, cybersecurity capabilities, and operational processes.
   b) Assessment includes (1) reporting status against legal, regulatory, and compliance requirements, and (2) ensuring enterprise cybersecurity measures up to the requirements of thwarting real-world cyber adversaries.

Rest of Study Guide

- The remainder of this study guide presents a new *Enterprise Cybersecurity Framework* for managing a cohesive enterprise cybersecurity program in a well-coordinated and integrated manner.

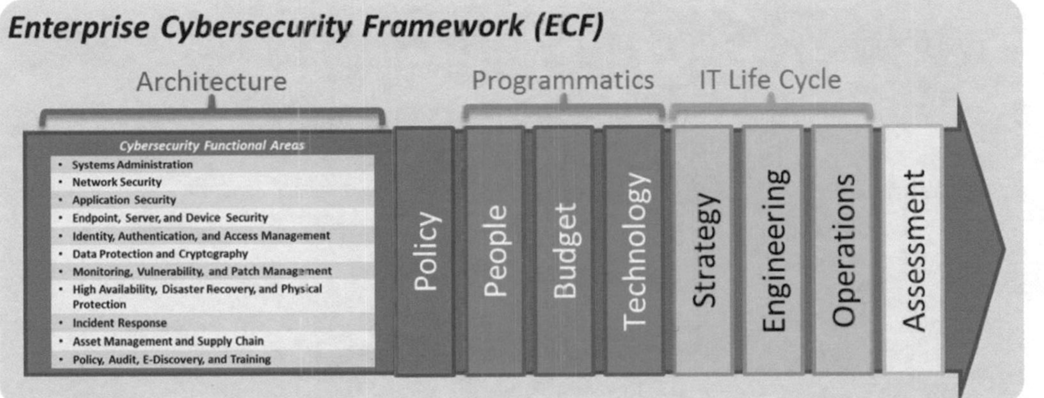

- The *Enterprise Cybersecurity Framework* is field-tested and field-proven for managing cyberdefenses against the most dangerous nation-state attackers.
  - Enterprise cybersecurity is organized into functional areas.
  - Functional areas are then used to delegate and coordinate policy, programmatics, IT life cycle, and assessments in a coherent fashion.
- Cybersecurity leadership can spend less time on integration and more time on strategy.
- Practitioners can build a cyberdefense that is flexible, cost-effective, comprehensive, and, above all, effective against today's modern cyberthreats and tomorrow's envisioned cyberthreats.

CHAPTER 2

Meeting the Cybersecurity Challenge

S. E. Donaldson et al., *Enterprise Cybersecurity Study Guide*, https://doi.org/10.1007/978-1-4842-3258-3_2

Overview *(1 of 2)*

- This chapter describes
  - how an enterprise successfully defends itself against cyberattacks;
  - the challenges in building an effective cyberdefense;
  - some of the current major approaches to address these challenges;
  - some of the difficulties with these approaches; and
  - a different technique for dealing with these challenges.
- *What makes up an effective enterprise cybersecurity program?*
  - Not just about technology
  - Not just about defenses
  - Not just about compliance frameworks, checklists, or simply a passing grade on an audit
- The graphic depicts a combination of factors required to protect an enterprise.

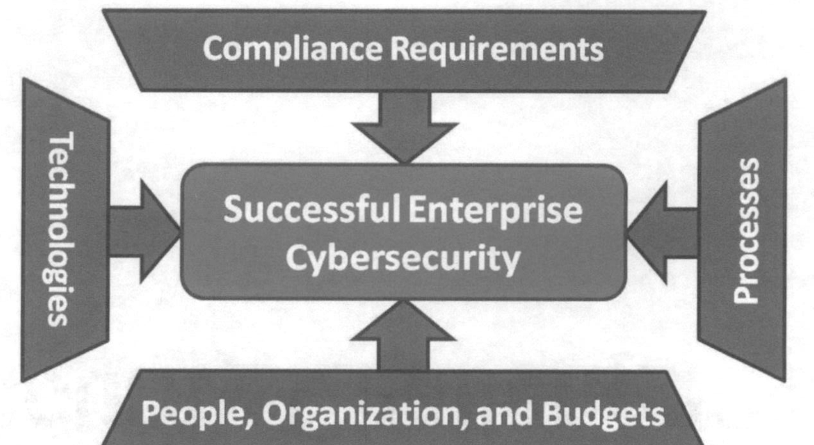

- ***An effective enterprise cybersecurity program*** protects the enterprise in a cost-effective manner that balances technology, processes, people, organization, budgets and external compliance requirements, all while supporting the business mission as much as possible.

Overview *(2 of 2)*

- ***People, organization, and budgets*** are the foundation of a successful cybersecurity program.
  - Everything begins with ***people*** because they make the program succeed or fail.
  - CISO ***organizes*** cybersecurity people so individuals and teams clearly understand their responsibilities.
    - Control Objectives for Information and Related Technology (COBIT)
    - Information Technology Infrastructure Library (ITIL)
    - Responsible, Accountable, Consulted, and Informed (RACI)
  - CISO makes the business case for the cybersecurity budget; if an enterprise does not fund cybersecurity, then it is not important.
- ***Processes and technologies*** work together, but they can also be opposed to each other.
  - Deployed processes should account for how technology is going to be (re-)configured.
    - Processes deployed without technology seldom endure.

  - Deployed technology should account for how people are going to operate it.
    - Technology deployed without processes seldom stays working for long.
- ***Compliance requirements*** are a double-edged sword.
  - Requirement: There is external validation that security measures are in place and working.
  - Reality: There is only a loose connection between compliance and security.
  - Compliance is good, but must not be the only cyberdefense objective.

Topics

- Cybersecurity Frameworks
- The Cybersecurity Process
- Cybersecurity Challenges
- The Risk Management Process
- Cybersecurity Controls
- Cybersecurity Capabilities
- Cybersecurity and Enterprise IT
- An Enterprise Cybersecurity Architecture

Cybersecurity Frameworks *(1 of 2)*

Representative Frameworks

- There are a number of excellent cybersecurity frameworks that
  - provide a methodology for talking about cybersecurity; and
  - help ensure important elements of protection and defense are considered for incorporation into an enterprise's cybersecurity efforts.

(ISC)² Common Body of Knowledge 10 security domains	ISO 27001 / 27002 v2013 114 controls in 14 domains	NIST SP800-53v4 224 controls in 18 families	Council on Cyber Security Critical Security Controls - 20 controls
1. Access Control 2. Telecommunications and Network Security 3. Information Security Governance and Risk Management 4. Software Development Security 5. Cryptography 6. Security Architecture and Design 7. Security Operations 8. Business Continuity and Disaster Recovery Planning 9. Legal, Regulations, Investigations, and Compliance 10. Physical (Environmental) Security	1. Information Security Policies 2. Organization of Information Security 3. Human Resource Security 4. Asset Management 5. Access Control 6. Cryptography 7. Physical and Environmental Security 8. Operations Security 9. Communications Security 10. System Acquisition, Development, and Maintenance 11. Supplier Relationships 12. Information Security Incident Management 13. Information Security Aspect of Business Continuity Management 14. Compliance	1. Access Control 2. Awareness and Training 3. Audit and Accountability 4. Security Assessment and Authorization 5. Configuration Management 6. Contingency Planning 7. Identification and Authentication 8. Incident Response 9. Maintenance 10. Media Protection 11. Physical and Environmental Protection 12. Planning 13. Personnel Security 14. Risk Assessment 15. System and Services Acquisition 16. System and Communications Protection 17. System and Information Integrity 18. Program Management	1. Inventory of Devices 2. Inventory of Software 3. Secure Configurations for Computers 4. Continuous Vulnerability Assessment and Remediation 5. Malware Defenses 6. Application Software Security 7. Wireless Device Control 8. Data Recovery Capability 9. Security Skills Assessment and Training 10. Security Configurations for Network Devices 11. Network Ports, Protocols, and Services 12. Control of Administrative Privileges 13. Boundary Defense 14. Security Audit Logs 15. Need-to-Know Access Control 16. Account Monitoring and Control 17. Data Loss Prevention 18. Incident Response Capability 19. Secure Network Engineering 20. Penetration Testing and Red Team Exercises

Cybersecurity Frameworks *(2 of 2)*

Commonalities of Cybersecurity Frameworks

- ***Functional Areas***
  - Frameworks divide the enterprise and its protection into a number of functional areas (also known as domains, families, control areas, and control objectives).
  - Generally, there are between 10 and 20 functional areas.
- ***Risk Management***
  - Allows enterprise to identify what protections are needed.
  - Based on an objective evaluation of its assets, threats against those assets, vulnerabilities in the protection of those assets, and risks resulting from the threats being analyzed against vulnerabilities.
  - Considers risk mitigations, either reducing risk probability or risk severity.
- ***Security Controls***
  - Purpose is to reduce the probability or the severity of a risk.
  - Some security controls can also serve to detect the exploitation of the risk or to collect forensic data to support later investigations.
- ***Mechanism for Audits, Evaluations, and Validations***
  - Mechanism helps to determine the presence or absence of controls described in the framework.
  - Sometimes mechanism is done through documented standards for evaluation.
  - Sometimes mechanism is done through checklists for auditing.
  - Many frameworks contain evaluation guidance.

The Cybersecurity Process *(1 of 3)*

- Major frameworks contain some method of a cybersecurity process that practitioners can use to implement their organization's cybersecurity program.
- The graphic depicts the National Institute of Standards and Technology (NIST) process.[1]
  - It is one of the more comprehensive documented processes for implementing an enterprise cybersecurity program.
  - It is freely available.
  - Each process step lists corresponding references that provide additional detail and guidance.

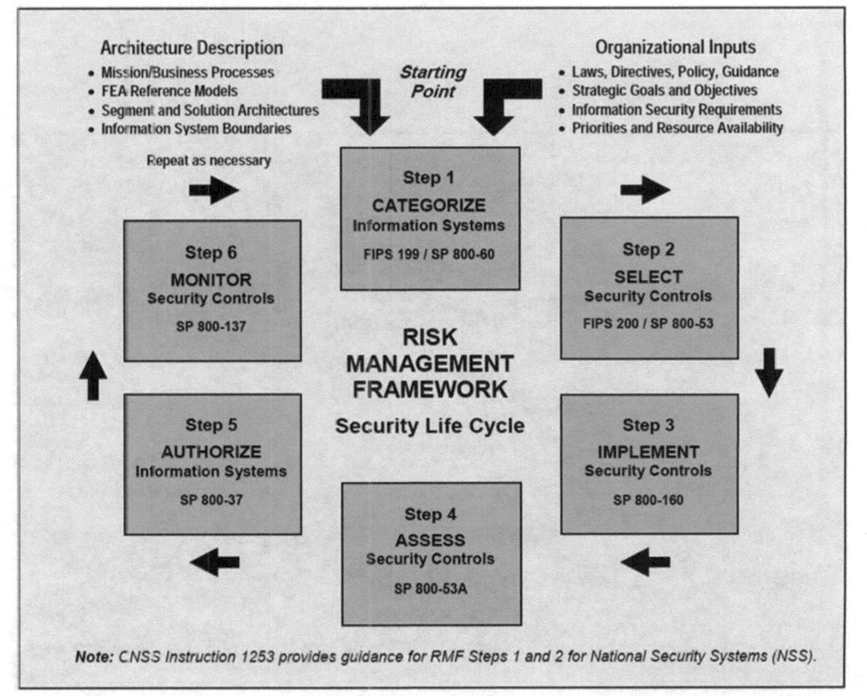

[1]Graphic taken from *Special Publication 800-53 Revision 4*, National Institute of Standards and Technology, 2013.

The Cybersecurity Process *(2 of 3)*

- ***Step 1***—Categorizes the information systems according to the "potential impact of loss"
- ***Step 2***—Selects the security controls for each information system
- ***Step 3***—Implements the security controls and security configurations for enterprise systems
- ***Step 4***—Assesses the security controls to ensure controls
  - Were implemented correctly
  - Operate as intended
  - Meet the security objectives and requirements
- ***Step 5***—Authorizes the information systems for operation based on
  - Validation of the security controls
  - An overall risk assessment considering the benefits of the system against its potential risks
- ***Step 6***—Monitors the security controls to ensure they remain effective over time

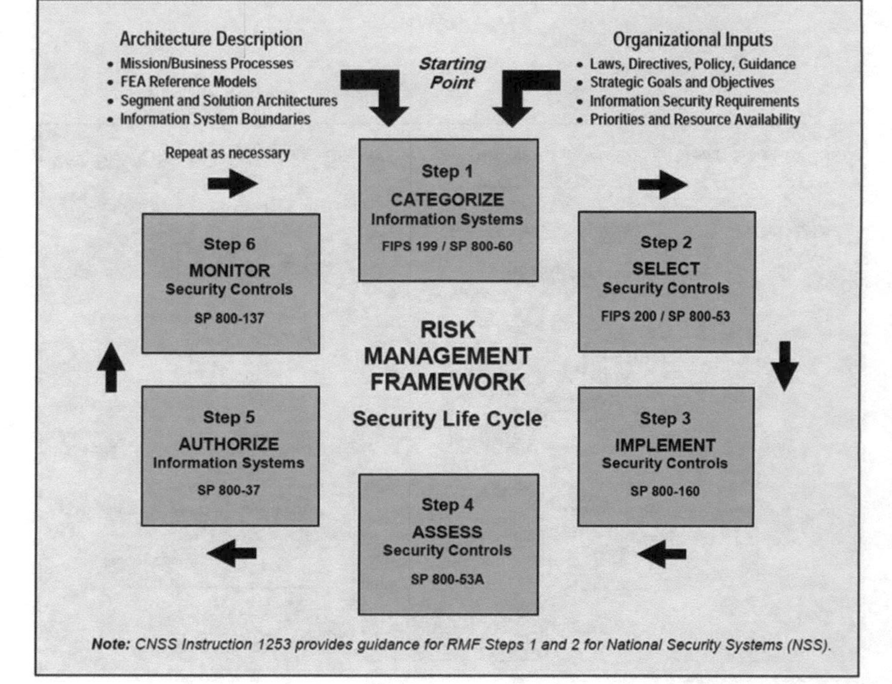

The Cybersecurity Process *(3 of 3)*

Referenced Documents

- **CNNS Instruction 1253**: *Security Categorization and Control Selection for National Security Systems*
- **FIPS 199**: *Standards for Security Categorization of Federal Information and Information Systems*
- **SP 800-60**: *Guide for Mapping Types of Information and Information Systems to Security Categories*
- **FIPS 200**: *Minimum Security Requirement for Federal Information Systems*
- **SP 800-53**: *Security and Privacy Controls for Federal Information Systems and Organizations*
- **SP 800-160**: *Systems Security Engineering*
- **SP 800-53A**: *Guide for Assessing the Security Controls in Federal Information Systems and Organizations*
- **SP 800-37**: *Guide for the Security Certification and Accreditation of Federal Information*
- **SP 800-137**: *Information Security Continuous Monitoring (ISCM) for Federal Information Systems and Organizations*

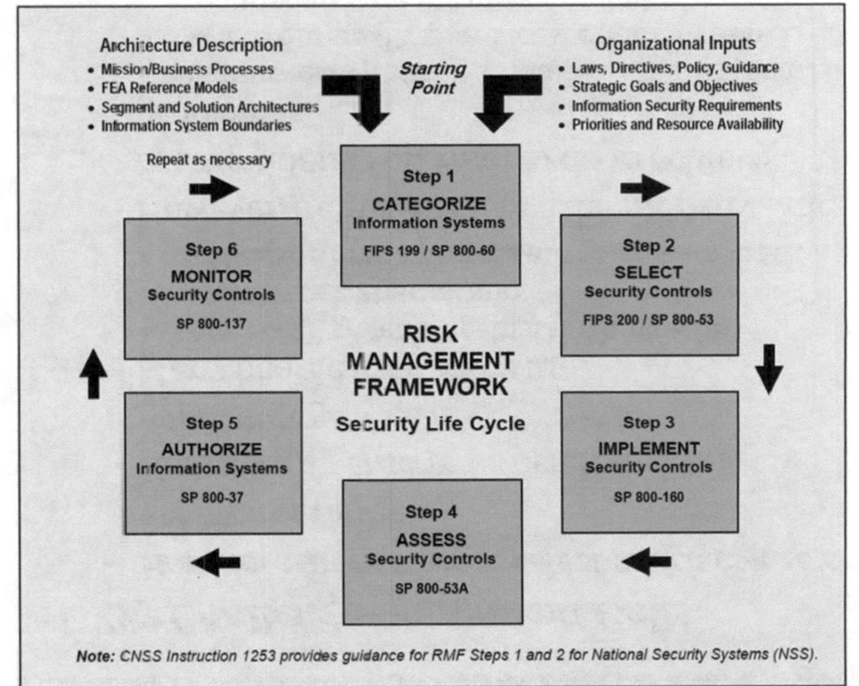

Cybersecurity Challenges *(1 of 3)*

*NIST Special Publication 800-53 Revision 4**

- ***1st Challenge—Scalability***
  - *The six-step process is fine for a single computer, but what happens when a single IT system has a hundred computers in it?*
  - *How is a single systems administrator, who is trying to get everything set up, going to get all the paperwork done, especially when that person is already over budget and behind schedule on the deployment project?*
  - Often, the security process languishes until management ends up exempting the security process simply to get things operational in time.
  - The cybersecurity industry needs a streamlined security process that
    - actually gets implemented, especially for modern, complex IT environments; and
    - abstracts the security process above the level of single computers and single servers to "systems" and "systems of systems."
- ***2nd Challenge—Judgment Calls***
  - *How does an enterprise* ***select*** *which controls are appropriate?*
  - *How does an enterprise determine what is* ***good enough****?*
  - Many people may agree to
    - protect IT systems against unknown, but anticipated, attacks; and
    - anticipate how attackers are going to operate.
  - However, frameworks give the industry little or no guidance on what to do to achieve protection.
    - Frameworks provide a "kitchen sink" approach where the smallest and least critical system is required to have the most onerous of security controls applied to it … don't want to skimp on security.
    - Often, these controls are arbitrarily applied and then incompletely implemented.
      - Produces crucial control protection gaps
      - Hard to identify, prioritize, and remediate gaps

**SSP 800-53r4 Security and Privacy Controls for Federal Information Systems and Organizations*

Cybersecurity Challenges *(2 of 3)*

NIST Special Publication 800-53 Revision 4

- ***3rd Challenge—Detective Controls***
  - There is significant effort describing control measures to prevent attacks from being successful.
  - There is relatively little effort talking about detecting and responding to attacks when they occur.
  - Preventive controls are good, but they will not actually stop a determined attack.
    - It is like having a good lock on your doors.
    - A determined attacker will spend about five minutes playing with the lock, and then simply go and break a window.
  - Greater attention needs to be paid to what happens after the window has been broken, instead of simply installing all of the different types of locks that can be put on the door.
- ***4th Challenge—Security Operations***
  - ***Control monitoring*** addresses some security operations aspects.
  - The primary process focuses on ***maintaining preventive*** controls, not ***monitoring detective*** controls to catch attacks in real time.
  - At the time of writing, a few mainstream frameworks focus on security operations to
    - monitor security controls;
    - capture events;
    - detect incidents;
    - investigate those incidents; and
    - respond to incidents and repel the attackers.
  - Recognizing the importance of monitoring and detective controls is a transition that is still "in progress" for major frameworks.

Cybersecurity Challenges *(3 of 3)*

NIST Special Publication 800-53 Revision 4

- ***5th Challenge—Unfulfillable Requirements***
  - Security control frameworks frequently place requirements on products and technologies that simply “cannot be fulfilled.”
  - Meetings with product vendors often result with hemming and hawing about how the product “can” be placed into a secure configuration, which may result in useful features being disabled.
  - Cybersecurity personnel then conduct investigations of third-party products to address the gap by enhancing the original product with additional protections, logging, or monitoring features.
  - Investigation may find third-party products, but solutions may be overkill for the need, excessively complex to maintain, and unaffordable.
  - Finally, there will be an effort to negotiate the security requirement in order to do the paperwork to pass an audit.
  - Reality is the control is not effective as it needs to be.
- General Comments
  - Mainstream security architectures represent an excellent body of work.
  - The five cybersecurity challenges presented leave room for some new ideas and a more pragmatic approach.

The Risk Management Process *(1 of 4)*

- The graphic depicts a simplified risk management process that can be adapted for specific enterprise needs.
- The process involves a systematic analysis to determine
  - where an enterprise may have compromises;
  - consequences of those compromises; and
  - ways to reduce the probability or severity of those compromises.

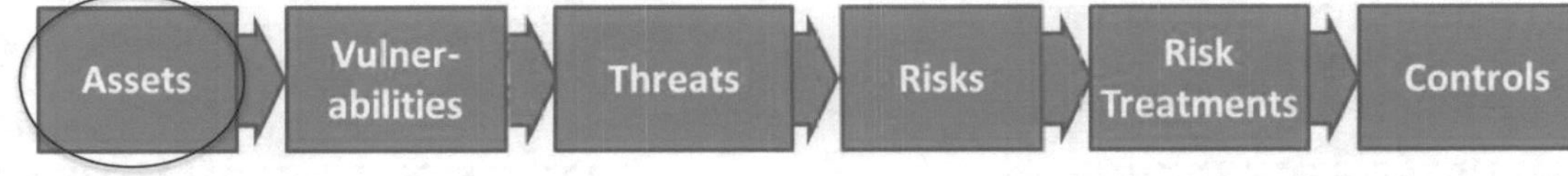

- ***Assets***
  - ***Personnel*** are people in the organization who bring their own knowledge and abilities.
  - ***Facilities*** are the locations where people work, along with their the tools and equipment.
  - ***Processes*** are the procedures whereby the organization operates and the systems it uses to accomplish its goals.
  - ***Information*** is the proprietary, customer, or business data held by the enterprise.
  - **All** assets must be protected.

The Risk Management Process *(2 of 4)*

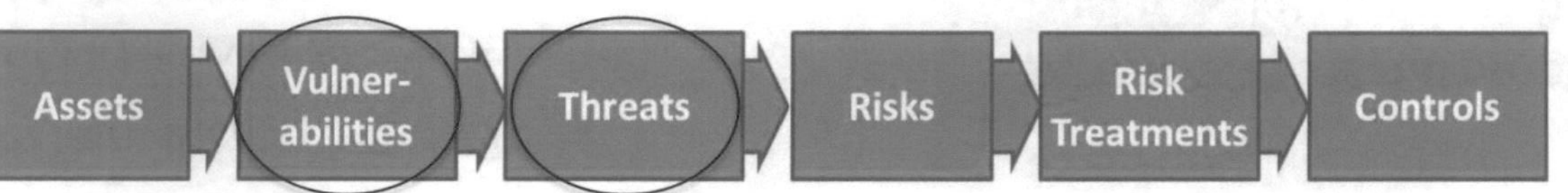

- ***Vulnerabilities***
  - Vulnerabilities are ways the assets can be compromised.
    - For example, a facility vulnerability may be where one side of the facility is adjacent to an abandoned building.
    - For example, a vulnerability for a business process may be that it relies on an extremely unreliable IT system.
  - IT systems vulnerabilities can be further characterized in terms of ***CIA***:
    - ***Confidentiality*** protects the secrecy of data.
    - ***Integrity*** protects data from unauthorized changes.
    - ***Availability*** makes IT systems and the data the systems host available to those who need the data when it is needed.

- ***Threats***
  - Threats are ways in which vulnerabilities can be exploited to cause damage to the asset.
  - They can be natural or man-made, accidental or deliberate, random or deterministic.
  - Considering threats is one of the most creative steps in the process.
    - Involves a lot of Murphy's Law thinking (*What can possibly go wrong?*)
    - Helpful to think about threats in terms of how they would affect the CIA of the enterprise's information and information systems

The Risk Management Process *(3 of 4)*

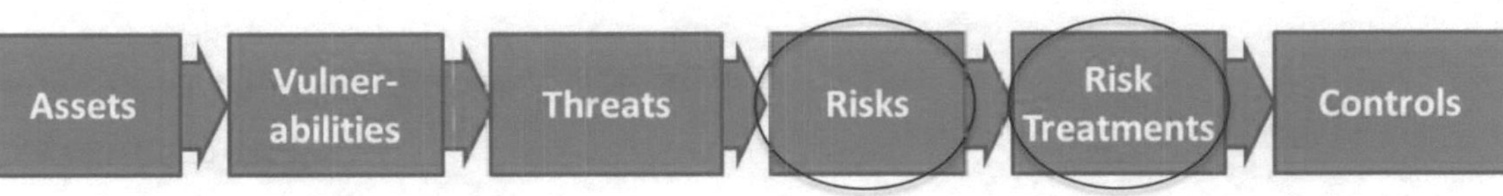

- ***Risks***
  - By ***combining*** vulnerabilities with threats, risks can be identified.
  - Threats against well-protected areas generally produce ***a low level of risk***.
  - Threats against not-well-protected areas generally produce ***a risk that must be considered***.
  - Identifying and evaluating risks is fundamentally a judgment call with challenges.
    - ***Underestimating a risk*** because vulnerability is underestimated
    - ***Missing a risk*** because a particular threat scenario is not considered
  - As will be discussed, identifying and evaluating risk challenges can be simplified by using ***security scopes*** to group risks and handle them in aggregate.
- ***Risk Treatments***
  - ***Avoid*** risk by eliminating the vulnerability or the threat.
  - ***Mitigate*** risk by reducing the probability that it will occur or the impact when it does occur.
  - ***Share*** the risk by introducing a third party—such as an insurance company—that will compensate the enterprise in the event the risk occurs.
  - ***Retain*** risk where the enterprise simply accepts the possibility the risk may occur and deals with consequences when they happen; self-insurance is a good example.

The Risk Management Process *(4 of 4)*

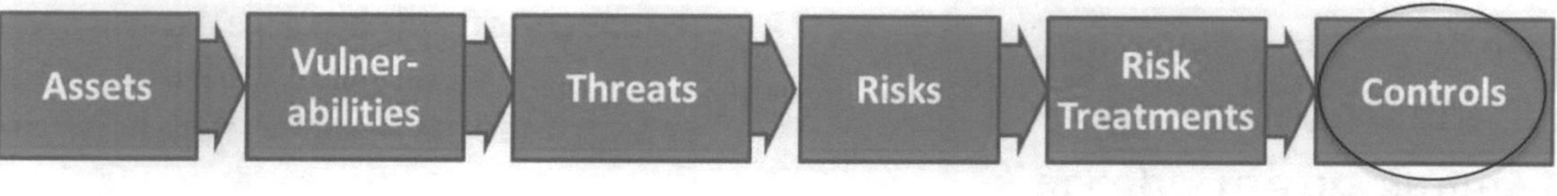

- ***Controls***
  - Can ***reduce the probability*** the risk will occur or make it more difficult for attackers to execute on the risk
  - Can ***reduce the impact*** when the risk does occur, perhaps limiting the amount of damage that occurs
  - Can ***detect the occurrence*** of the risk happening
    - Allows for active responses to contain the damage
    - Helps reduce the potential exposure
  - Can ***collect evidence***
    - Shows the operation of security controls
    - Detects failures of the controls
    - Supports investigations after an incident has occurred

Vulnerabilities, Threats, and Risks *(1 of 2)*

- The graphic depicts the next level of detail of the risk management process.
  - Note that the CIA factors span vulnerabilities, threats, and risks.
- For information assets, the enterprise should consider vulnerabilities, threats, and risks in terms of the CIA factors, rather than considering each one separately.
- ***Confidentiality*** is the protection of data that should be access-controlled and not widely disseminated.
  - *What vulnerabilities are there?*
  - *How can confidentiality be breached?*
  - *What would be the resulting data loss?*
  - *What threats (accidental or deliberate) could cause data loss?*
  - *When combining vulnerabilities and threats, what are the risks regarding confidentiality?*

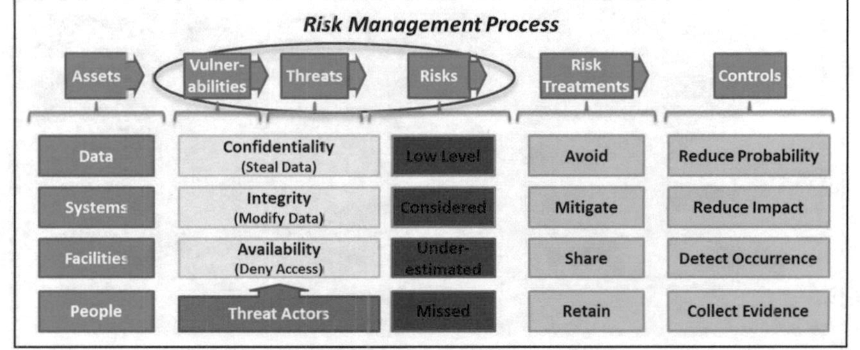

Vulnerabilities, Threats, and Risks *(2 of 2)*

- ***Integrity*** involves data being consistent from the time it is entered into a system to the time it is later retrieved.
  - Does not sound very interesting, except when the data being modified is about money or a transaction involving money
  - Risk analysis surrounding integrity identifies
    - where integrity is important;
    - consequences of an integrity violation; and
    - threats that could result in those consequences
- ***Availability*** involves information and information systems being available when needed.
  - Threats to availability include the following:
    - Systems being temporarily unavailable, but otherwise unimpaired
    - Systems being completely destroyed or corrupted beyond recovery
  - Generally, availability concerns are driven by business considerations of negative financial impacts vs. availability maintenance and recovery costs

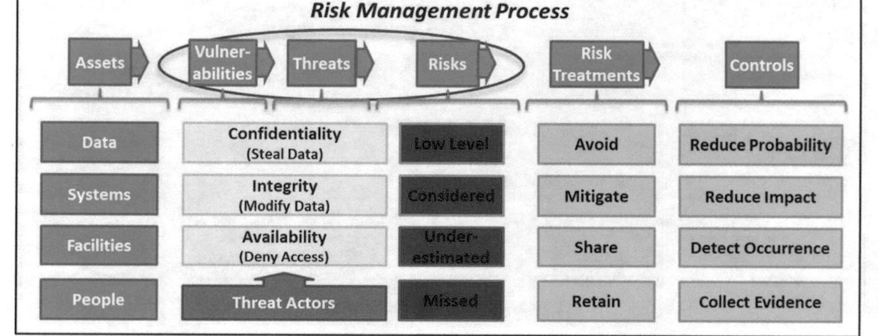

Risk Analysis and Mitigation *(1 of 2)*

Reducing the Probability and/or Impact of an Incident (1 of 2)

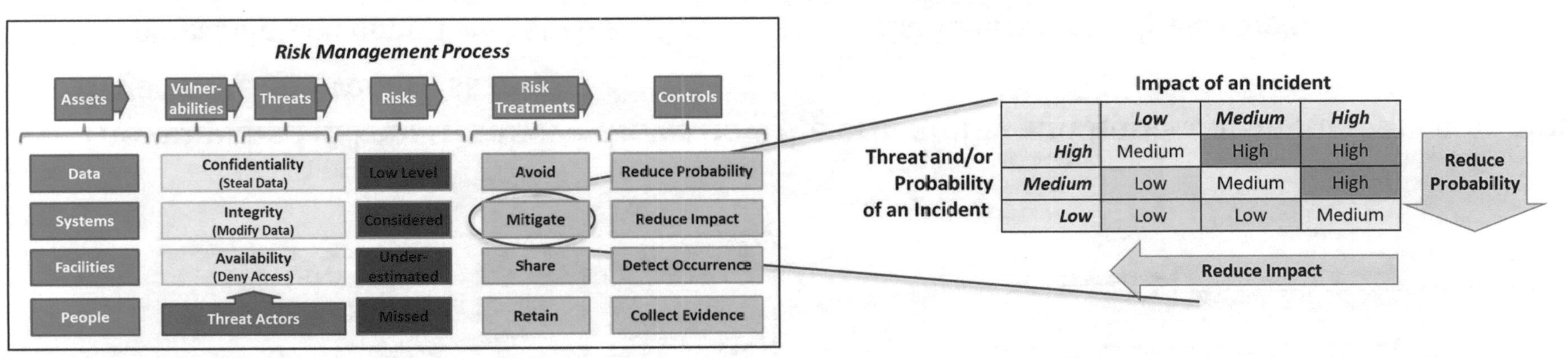

	Low	Medium	High
High	Medium	High	High
Medium	Low	Medium	High
Low	Low	Low	Medium

- Once the CIA risks have been identified, risk mitigation can be considered and often gets the most attention of the risk treatments.
- Risk analysis is needed before risk mitigation can be implemented.
- Risk is characterized in terms of magnitude— high, medium, or low.
  - Can be broken out into more gradations
  - Can be broken into a numeric scale
  - Can be thought of in terms of ***probability*** of occurring and the ***impact*** if the risk occurs

Risk Analysis and Mitigation *(2 of 2)*

Reducing the Probability and/or Impact of an Incident *(2 of 2)*

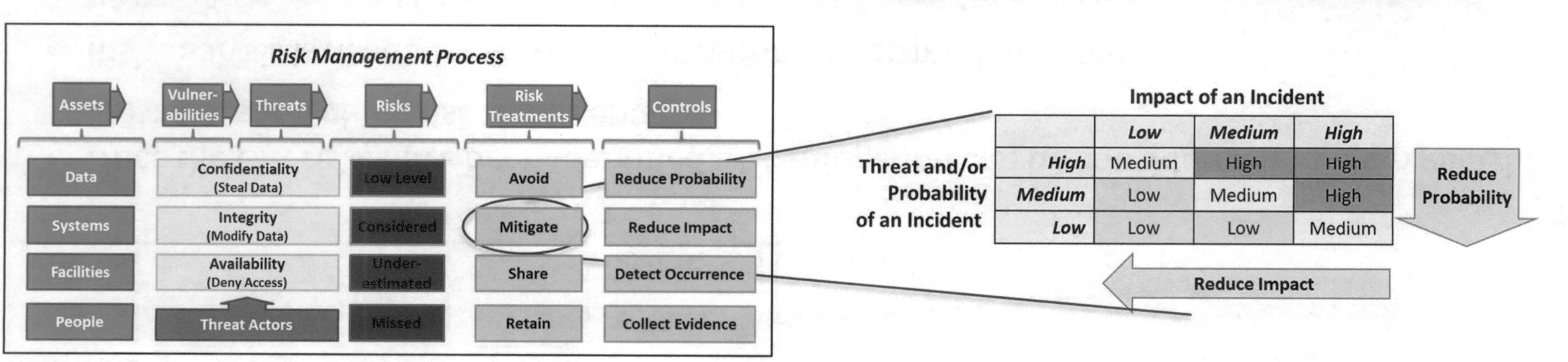

	Low	Medium	High
High	Medium	High	High
Medium	Low	Medium	High
Low	Low	Low	Medium

- The simplified risk matrix above shows how the probability and impact of an incident combine to generate an overall risk level.
  - If probability and impact are both high, then the overall risk level is probably also ***high***.
  - If the probability and impact are both low, then the overall risk level is probably also ***low***.
  - If the probability of risk is low, but the impact is high, the overall risk level is most likely ***medium***.
  - If the probability of risk is high, but the impact is low, the overall risk is most likely ***medium***.

Cybersecurity Controls *(1 of 5)*

Context

- Controls help mitigate enterprise confidentiality, integrity, or availability risks.
  - Reduce risk probability and risk impact
  - Detect occurrences of incidents involving the risk
  - Collect evidence to support evaluations and incident investigations related to the risk
- This study guide defines a *security control* as "consisting of security capabilities or audit activities that are applied to an IT system or business process to prevent, detect, or investigate specific activities that are undesirable, and respond to those activities when they occur."

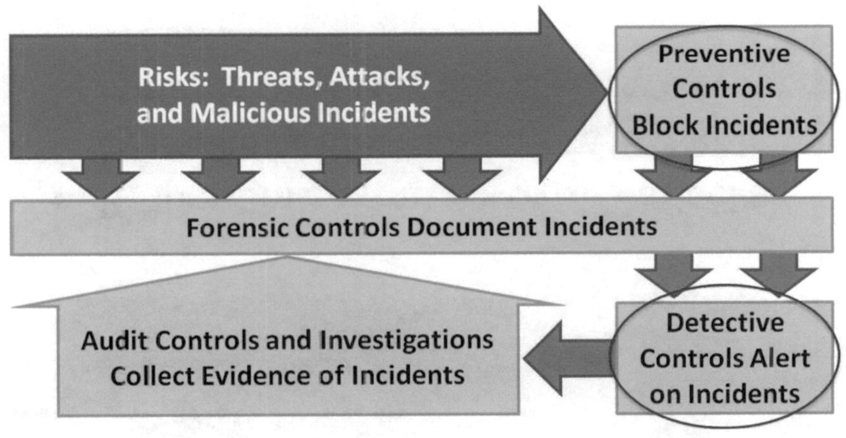

- The graphic shows types of cybersecurity controls.
  - ***Preventive Controls***: Block the threat and prevent incidents from occurring altogether
  - ***Detective Controls***: Detect when the risk has transpired and generate alerts that can then be acted upon

Cybersecurity Controls *(2 of 5)*

- ***Cybersecurity control types (continued)***
  - ***Forensic Controls***: Collect records of activities related to the risk; can be used to produce artifacts to support the operation of detective controls, investigations of incidents, and audits of controls to verify their operation and effectiveness
  - ***Audit Controls***: Investigate for the presence of the risk, incidents associated with the risk, and the operation of controls that mitigate the risk
- Traditionally, enterprises have given disproportional consideration to preventive controls—for example, firewalls that block unwanted protocols—at the expense of other controls.
- However, modern threats such as Advanced Persistent Threats (APTs) are designed to get around preventive controls and turn the enterprise against itself.

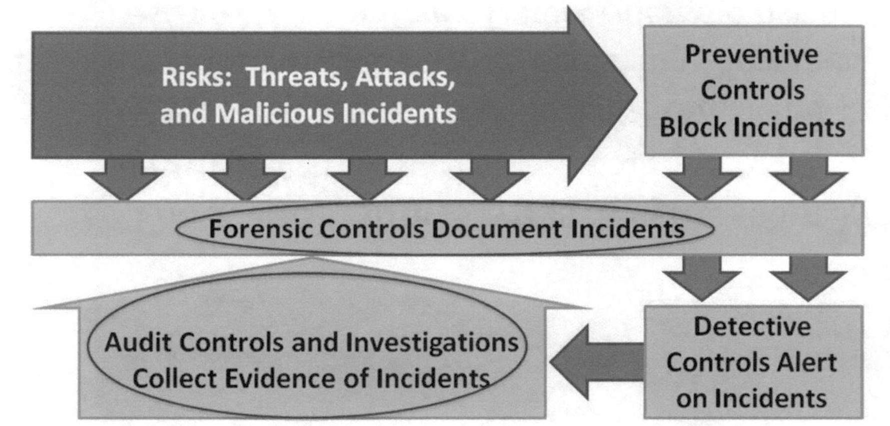

- Responding to threats of APT attacks by enacting more and more preventive controls can bring about its own set of problems.

Cybersecurity Controls *(3 of 5)*

- The graphic compares the security control types by showing how each type of control represents a trade-off among multiple factors including cost of deployment, operation, and impact on continuing operations.
- ***Preventive Cybersecurity Controls***
  - Get lots of attention because they block attacks and incidents—preventing successful attacks
  - Unless configured in conjunction with corresponding detective controls, not generally good at detecting attacks
  - Can have a high operational impact (costs) because they may also prevent legitimate users from doing their jobs

	Cybersecurity Control Types			
Characteristics	***Preventive***	***Detective***	***Forensic***	***Audit***
Block Attacks?	Good	Medium	Poor	Poor
Detect Attacks?	Poor	Good	Poor	Medium
Operational Impact	High	Low	Low	Low
Investigate Attacks?	Poor	Medium	Good	Good
Cost to Implement	High	Medium	Medium	Low
Cost to Operate	Medium	High	Low	Medium
Flexibility	Poor	Poor	Medium	Good

  - While generally inexpensive to operate once they are operational, can be expensive to implement because of their complexity
  - Can be difficult to modify in response to rapidly changing situations

Cybersecurity Controls *(4 of 5)*

- ***Detective Cybersecurity Controls***
  - Generally get shortchanged, but their importance is trending upward
  - Unlike preventive controls, cheap to implement and have little operational impact on the enterprise
  - Can be expensive to operate as alerts have to be investigated
  - Can be significantly less expensive overall than the lost productivity from aggressive preventive controls
  - Essentially is cheaper overall to allow people do whatever they want, alert them when they do wrong, and then deal with it
    - A real-world analogy is law enforcement trying to prevent crimes.
    - Only a small range of potential crimes are actively prevented.
    - Law enforcement is aggressive in pursuing and punishing crimes after they actually occur.

	Cybersecurity Control Types			
Characteristics	***Preventive***	***Detective***	***Forensic***	***Audit***
Block Attacks?	Good	Medium	Poor	Poor
Detect Attacks?	Poor	Good	Poor	Medium
Operational Impact	High	Low	Low	Low
Investigate Attacks?	Poor	Medium	Good	Good
Cost to Implement	High	Medium	Medium	Low
Cost to Operate	Medium	High	Low	Medium
Flexibility	Poor	Poor	Medium	Good

- ***Forensic Cybersecurity Controls***
  - Not very good at actively detecting or blocking attacks
  - Absolutely critical to investigating attacks successfully after they have occurred
  - Relatively cheap to operate once they are in place
  - Provide economical way to implement parts of the security equation without significant investments

Cybersecurity Controls *(5 of 5)*

- ***Audit Cybersecurity Controls***
  - Almost the exact opposite of preventive controls
    - Preventive controls are effective at stopping attacks, albeit with considerable operational impact.
    - Audit controls have almost no operational impact, but they also don't stop much in the way of attacks.
  - Low-cost, unobtrusive, and agile
  - Frequently the only way to find attacks that have defeated the preventive controls
  - Not "exotic" but deserve respect and consideration in an enterprise's security architecture
  - A simple audit can often find problems that have been lurking for months or years, despite all the other controls

	Cybersecurity Control Types			
Factors	***Preventive***	***Detective***	***Forensic***	***Audit***
Block Attacks?	Good	Medium	Poor	Poor
Detect Attacks?	Poor	Good	Poor	Medium
Operational Impact	High	Low	Low	Low
Investigate Attacks?	Poor	Medium	Good	Good
Cost to Implement	High	Medium	Medium	Low
Cost to Operate	Medium	High	Low	Medium
Flexibility	Poor	Poor	Medium	Good

- General Comments
  - The graphic provides a partial list of evaluation factors to consider.
  - When looking at security technologies, it is useful to evaluate them
    - in terms of what types of control functionality they primarily provide; and
    - to understand how the different control objectives are going to be achieved.
  - Ideally, all four control types are designed and operated in parallel, thus supporting each other.

Cybersecurity Capabilities *(1 of 2)*

- NIST describes the idea of security capability as an abstraction.[2]
  - "Security capabilities can address a variety of areas that can include, for example, technical means, physical means, procedural means, or any combination thereof ..."
  - "It is important for organizations to have the ability to describe key security capabilities needed to protect core organizational missions/business functions ..."
  - "This [security capability construct] simplifies how the protection problem is viewed conceptually ..."
  - "In essence, using the construct of security capability provides a shorthand method of grouping security controls that are employed for a common purpose or to achieve a common objective ..."
  - "This [security capability construct] becomes an important consideration, for example, when assessing security controls for effectiveness ..."
- This study guide defines, in part, a *security capability* as "a process or technology that enables the organization to perform a specific security control."
  - For example, a firewall capability makes it possible to implement
    - preventive controls for network access control;
    - detective controls for network traffic alerting;
    - forensic controls for network traffic logging; and
    - audit controls for validating network security and looking for intrusions.
- An enterprise's security capabilities, both procedural and technological, form the foundation for its cybersecurity program.

[2]Adapted from NIST SP 800-53 Revision 4

Cybersecurity Capabilities *(2 of 2)*

- ***Security Capability***
  - Is as simple as a person following a procedure on a set schedule or in response to a predefined event
  - Is as complex as a sophisticated technology component that spans the enterprise and provides many features in support of many different controls
  - Can be further defined, in part, as "providing for the auditing, logging, detection, or prevention of a particular type of malicious behavior"
  - Can be either procedural or technological
- ***Procedural Security Capabilities***
  - Are capabilities that are delivered by having a person follow a procedure on a set schedule or in response to an action
  - Are most likely an enterprise's most powerful capabilities
  - Don't scale like a piece of technology due to the limits of human skills and abilities
  - Actual security against a professional attacker is almost entirely dependent on people, not technology
- ***Technological Security Capabilities***
  - Are provided by technologies that are installed into the enterprise's infrastructure
  - May be provided by a single technology ("block" an attack and "alert" on attack)
  - May provide security capabilities across multiple functional areas
  - Are powerful because once they are deployed, they tend to "just work" (until they break or stop)
  - Involve "buying stuff" and deploy "neat technology"
  - Need to be engineered, deployed, managed, and monitored carefully to live up to their potential

Cybersecurity and Enterprise IT *(1 of 4)*

Context

- Regardless of the specific technologies, enterprise IT provides services to deliver information to support the business whether
  - the business is large or small;
  - services are delivered using mainframes, microcomputers, servers, or cloud services; or
  - information delivery is from a single room, over a private network, over dial-up terminals, or over the Internet.
- General IT architecture involves the Internet, which complicates cybersecurity protection.
- Every host on the Internet is only one hop away from every other host, including malicious hosts operated by potential attackers.

- From architectural and strategic perspectives, the graphic illustrates the various enterprise IT components and how they are generally connected to the Internet.
  - Endpoint devices consist of customer, Internet organization, and internal organization devices.
  - Enterprise infrastructure consists of application servers, database servers, and systems administration and monitoring.

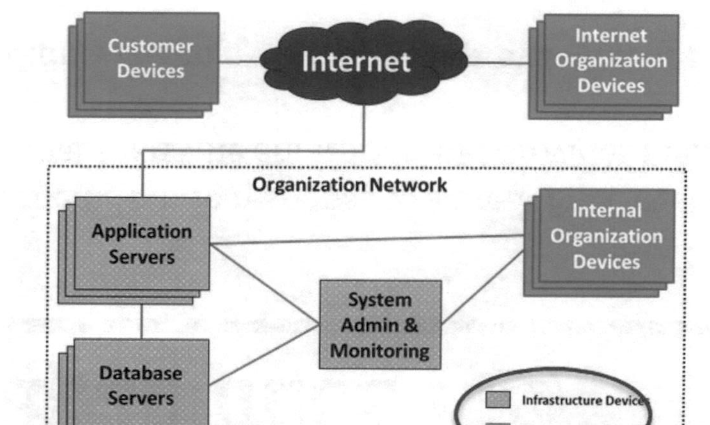

Cybersecurity and Enterprise IT *(2 of 4)*

Endpoints *(1 of 2)*

- ***Customer Devices***
  - If a business involves interacting with customers over a network, then their devices are an important part of the overall IT architecture.
  - *Why worry about customer devices?*
  - *What if every single customer device is malicious and can attack the enterprise?*
  - *From a cybersecurity perspective, how would an enterprise interact with their customers?*
  - *If a customer's computer is actively using the enterprise's data to attack the enterprise, would the enterprise trust the customer?*
  - Many people say, "It depends."
  - Customer devices need to be considered when an enterprise implements its cybersecurity controls and capabilities.

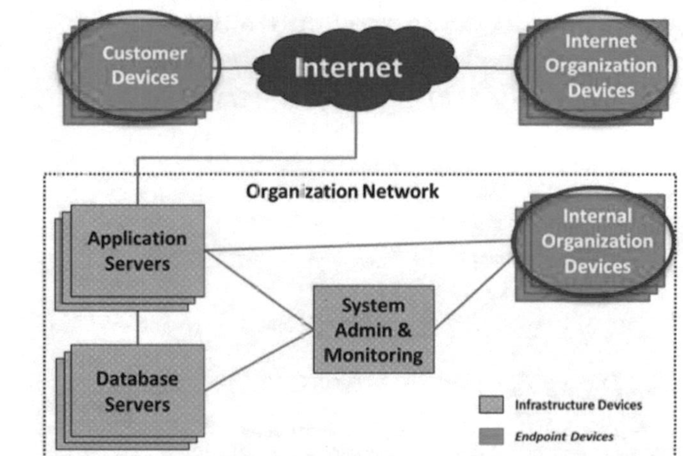

Cybersecurity and Enterprise IT *(3 of 4)*

Endpoints *(2 of 2)*

- ***Organization Devices***
  - Devices that connect to the enterprise over a ***public network***—for example, the Internet
    - Depending upon enterprise policies, these devices may be company-owned computers, personal computers, mobile devices, or Bring Your Own Device (BYOD).
    - The reality is the majority of organizations are going to allow some of their employees to connect to enterprise resources over an open network.
  - Devices that connect to the enterprise over an ***internal network***—for instance, enterprise intranet
    - Good news—the enterprise likely has more control over these devices than the myriad of customer and organizational devices connecting over an open network.

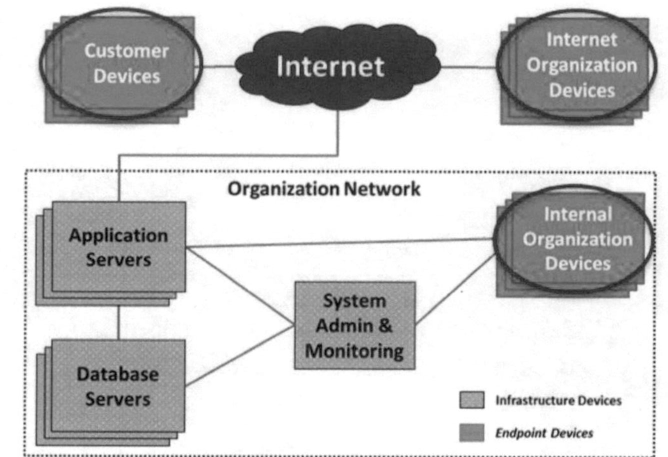

- Bad news—unless the enterprise tolerates a lot of operational headaches, control is likely spotty due to personal, customer, vendor, and other devices occasionally connecting to the enterprise network.
- These potential connections jeopardize the enterprise's efforts to control and protect the integrity of what is internal.

Cybersecurity and Enterprise IT *(4 of 4)*

IT Infrastructure

- Enterprise IT infrastructure consists of three components that should all work together as a coherent and coordinated system:
  - ***Application servers*** deliver business applications enabling the generation of business value.
  - ***Database servers*** contain the business's data.
  - ***Systems administration and monitoring*** channels manage and monitor the infrastructure.
- In some cases, the data and the applications may actually be hosted on a single component, but most often the two are separate.
- Systems administration and monitoring provides IT personnel with the ability to monitor and manage the enterprise; without this capability the enterprise may be unmanageable.

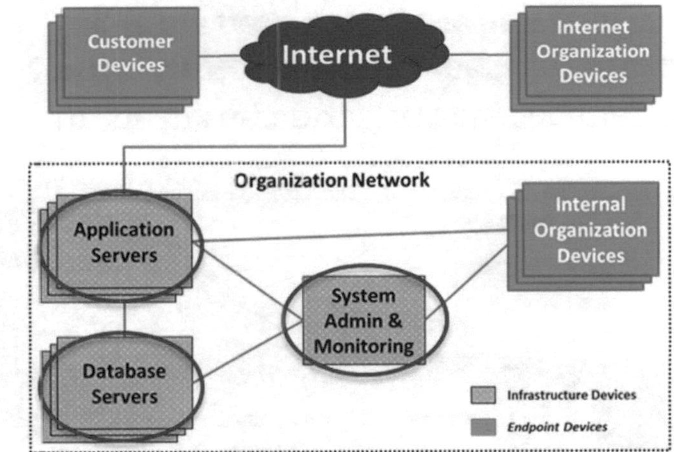

- It is helpful to consider these IT functionalities when considering the various ways that attackers seek to penetrate the infrastructure and accomplish their goals.
- Protections can be applied around the networks, endpoints, applications, databases, and systems administration functionalities.

Emplacing Cyberdefenses *(1 of 2)*

- Enterprise cybersecurity involves hardening the various components and connections so each component is more difficult to compromise.
- It sounds simple, but it isn't.
  - The more complex the enterprise is, the more complex the security is.
  - Complexity begets complexity.
- The graphic illustrates a notional enterprise and shows how security hardening can be applied to each enterprise IT component, including accounts, hosts, inter-host communications, and the organization network perimeter.
  - ***Internet organization devices*** should be protected from compromise even while they are connected to the Internet and other trusted networks.
  - The line connecting the Internet to the ***organization network*** is another security boundary where cybersecurity protections should be applied.

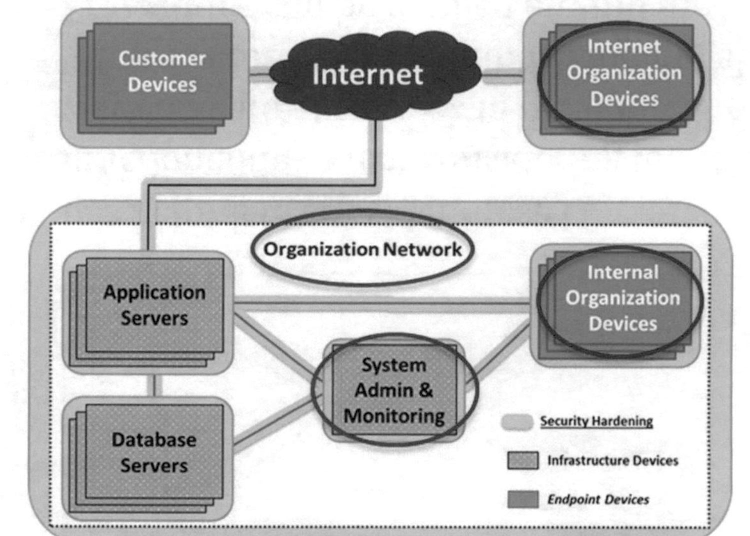

  - Inside the organization network, the ***internal organization devices***, which are already inside the network, can be powerful attack vectors if they are compromised by an attacker.
  - ***Systems administration and monitoring*** is probably the most important element to be protected as its compromise can be used to disable or bypass most of the other cybersecurity defenses.

Emplacing Cyberdefenses *(2 of 2)*

- ***Database servers*** are where the enterprise data resides and they must be protected.
  - Confidentiality protects the secrecy of data.
  - Integrity protects data from unauthorized changes.
  - Availability makes IT systems and the data they host available when and where they are needed.
- ***Application servers*** provide enterprise services and they must be protected.
  - Servers must be externally facing while also providing access to enterprise data for legitimate and authorized users.
- ***Customer devices*** that access enterprise resources are almost impossible to protect.
  - Security status must always be considered in an enterprise's security architecture.

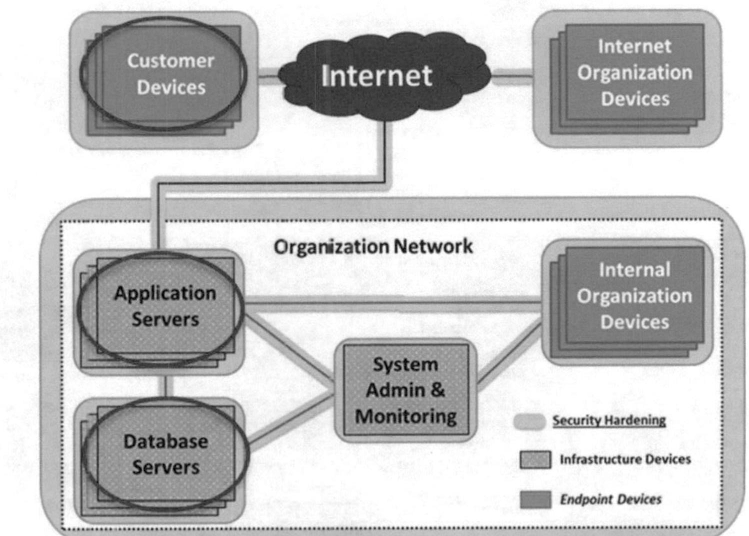

- General Comments
  - The graphic illustrates a basic architecture—applications, databases, servers, clients—used by an enterprise's security infrastructure.
  - An actual architecture will end up containing more components than this basic architecture example.

How Cyberdefenses Interconnect *(1 of 3)*

- The graphic illustrates an ***enterprise attack graph*** that shows
  - how different cybersecurity components interact with each other; and
  - how individual cybersecurity component defenses depend on each other.
- An enterprise can use the attack graph methodology to envision conceptually what these interdependencies look like.
- Following is an example attack scenario statement:

  To compromise organizational data, an attacker can compromise the (1) network and steal the data, (2) cryptography and steal the data in transit, (3) systems administration and take control of the servers hosting the data, or (4) applications hosting the data and use them to obtain the data.
- Attack scenario statements cause the enterprise to step back and examine the big picture of how an enterprise really works.

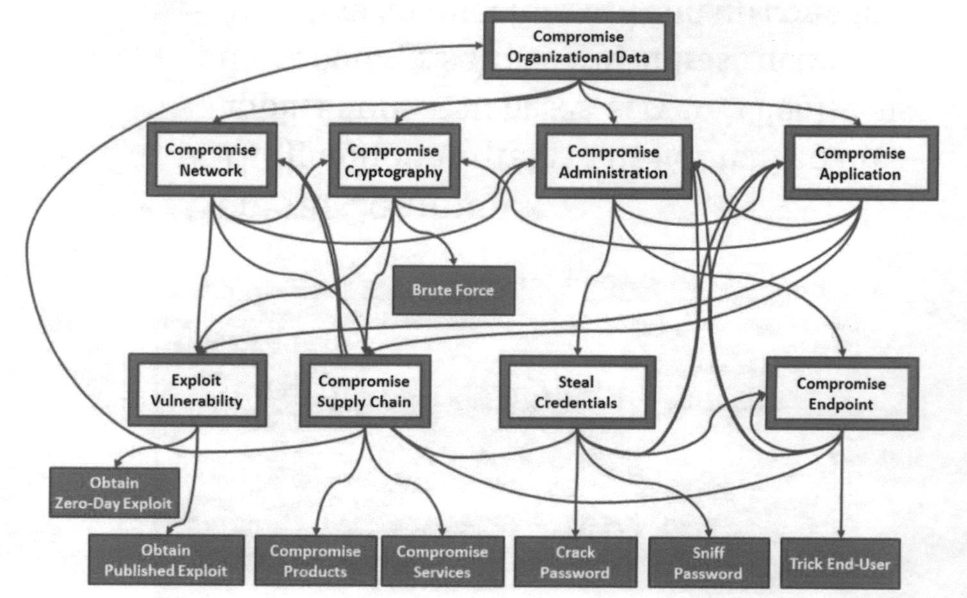

How Cyberdefenses Interconnect *(2 of 3)*

- The example attack graph represents an attack scenario statement for an entire enterprise.
  - Although the graph looks somewhat like "spaghetti ball," it shows that all the enterprise security components connect with and depend on each other.
  - Every aspect of the enterprise's security ultimately depends on every other aspect.
  - Consequently, a breach anywhere in the enterprise can eventually be exploited to compromise the entire enterprise
- Due to the interdependency of enterprise IT and cybersecurity components,
  - attackers can start with an exploit almost anywhere; and
  - eventually attackers expand the initial exploit to get compete control.

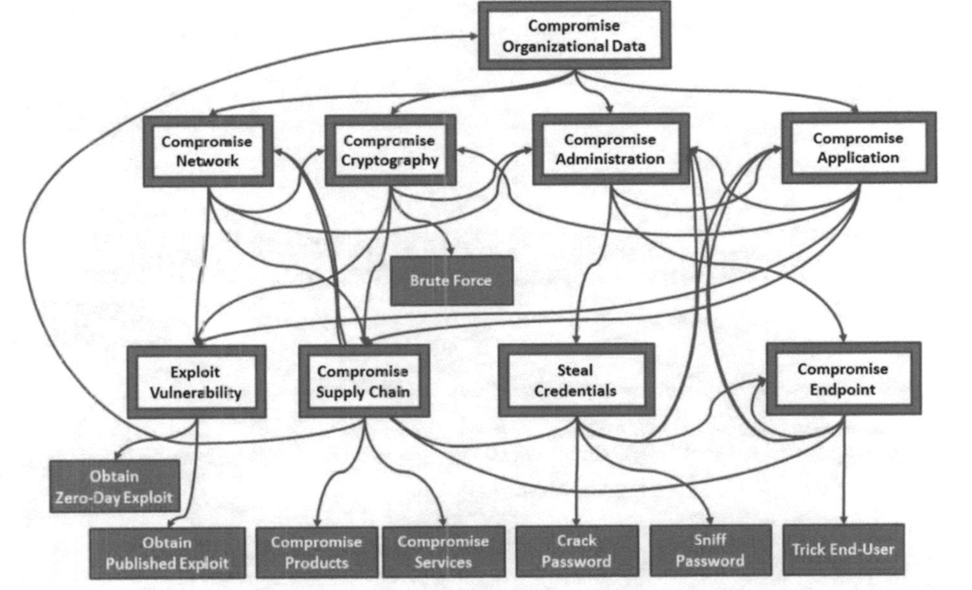

How Cyberdefenses Interconnect *(3 of 3)*

- While disconcerting, this connectivity and dependency should not be dismaying.
- An enterprise
  - needs to appreciate the complexity of enterprise security as a system; and
  - understand how enterprise defenses actually stop attacks.
- Enterprise cybersecurity defenses
  - slow the attack down;
  - add steps to the attack;
  - increase the enterprise's chances of catching the attack before it is completely successful;
  - make the attack process more difficult, expensive, and time-consuming; and
  - give defenders time to detect and respond to the intrusion.

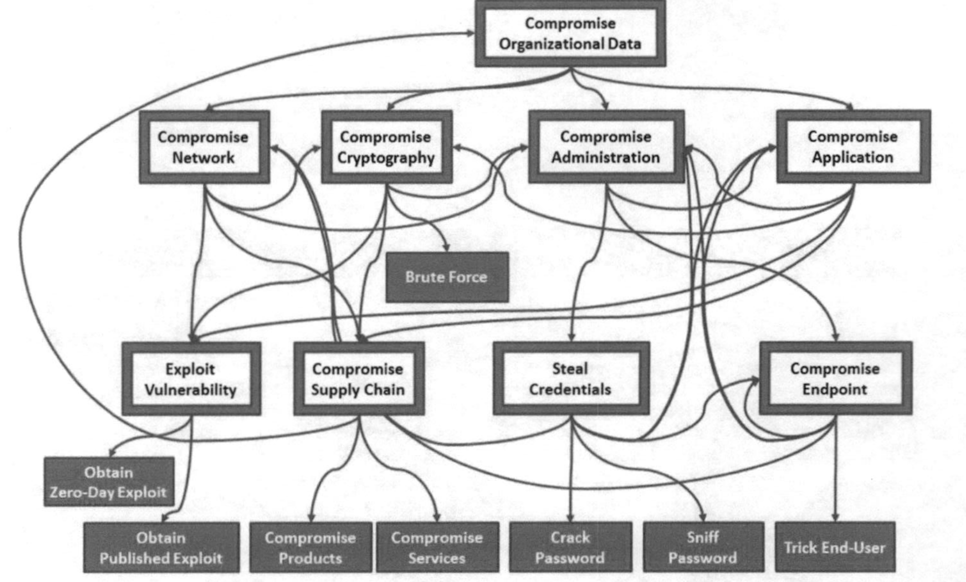

An Enterprise Cybersecurity Architecture *(1 of 4)*

Context

- To be effective, a cybersecurity architecture should achieve the following objectives:
  - Cover the full breadth of cybersecurity so nothing is left out
  - Align people, processes, budgets, and controls into a single framework so they are well-coordinated
  - Organize cybersecurity capabilities and controls into functional areas so they can be managed more easily
  - Account for the interdependence of controls and capabilities on each other across functional areas
  - Be simple enough so it can be managed and briefed at a high level
- The graphic represents a new ***enterprise cybersecurity architecture.***
  - Defined by ***cybersecurity functional areas*** covering the technical and operational breadth of enterprise cybersecurity

Enterprise Cybersecurity Architecture *(Cybersecurity Functional Areas)*	
Systems Administration	Monitoring, Vulnerability, and Patch Management
Network Security	High Availability, Disaster Recovery, and Physical Protection
Application Security	Incident Response
Endpoint, Server, and Device Security	Asset Management and Supply Chain
Identity, Authentication, and Access Management	Policy, Audit, E-Discovery, and Training
Data Protection and Cryptography	

- ***Cybersecurity Functional Areas***
  - Relatively independent from each other
  - Align well with how staff, expertise, and responsibilities are distributed in an organization utilizing the IT management frameworks such as the following:
    - ITIL (IT Infrastructure Library)
    - COBIT (Control Objectives for Information and Related Technology)
  - Enable IT leadership to unify technologies, staff, and corresponding budget into a coherent cybersecurity program
- Overall cybersecurity posture depends equally on the performance of all the functional areas.

An Enterprise Cybersecurity Architecture *(2 of 4)*

- This new ***enterprise cybersecurity architecture***
  - manages the capabilities that deliver preventive, detective, audit, and forensic controls to the enterprise;
  - provides for consistent management of security capabilities;
  - assists in prioritizing security capability deployment, maintenance, and upgrades over time;
  - provides strong accountability and good alignment of strategy, staffing, budget, and technology to meet the organizational security needs;
  - is designed to be flexible and scalable from a small enterprise up to a large enterprise; and
  - provides an extensible mechanism for adjusting cyberdefenses over time in response to changing cyberthreats.

Enterprise Cybersecurity Architecture *(Cybersecurity Functional Areas)*	
Systems Administration	Monitoring, Vulnerability, and Patch Management
Network Security	High Availability, Disaster Recovery, and Physical Protection
Application Security	Incident Response
Endpoint, Server, and Device Security	Asset Management and Supply Chain
Identity, Authentication, and Access Management	Policy, Audit, E-Discovery, and Training
Data Protection and Cryptography	

- ***Cybersecurity Functional Areas***
  - ***Systems Administration*** provides for secure administration of enterprise infrastructure and security systems, and protects systems administration channels from compromise.
  - ***Network Security*** provides for security of enterprise networks, their services, and access to them from the Internet and internally connected devices.

An Enterprise Cybersecurity Architecture *(3 of 4)*

- ***Cybersecurity Functional Areas (continued)***
  - ***Application Security*** provides for the security of enterprise applications using security technologies that are appropriate to and tailored for the protection of those applications and their communications.
  - ***Endpoint, Server, and Device Security*** provides for the protection of endpoints, servers, and devices that access enterprise data, and protects them from compromise.
  - ***Identity, Authentication, and Access Management*** provides for identification, authentication, and access control throughout the identity life cycle including provisioning, re-certification, and de-provisioning.
  - ***Data Protection and Cryptography*** provides for the protection of data stored in the enterprise and the use of cryptographic technologies to perform that protection. It also supports other operations such as authentication, non-repudiation, and data integrity.

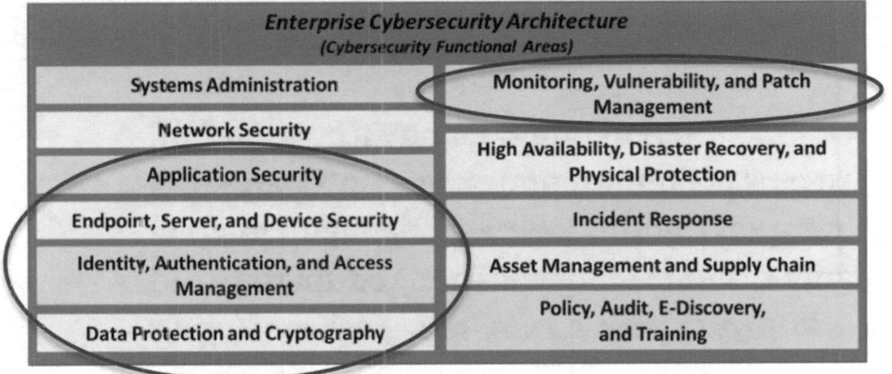

  - ***Monitoring, Vulnerability, and Patch Management*** provides for the regular monitoring of security infrastructure, scanning, and analysis of vulnerabilities in that infrastructure, and management of patches and workarounds to address those vulnerabilities.

An Enterprise Cybersecurity Architecture *(4 of 4)*

- ***Cybersecurity Functional Areas (continued)***
  - ***High Availability, Disaster Recovery, and Physical Protection*** provides for the protection of availability in the enterprise, including making systems highly available, recovering from disasters, and physically protecting facilities, people, systems, and data.
  - ***Incident Response*** provides for the investigation, response, and recovery of incidents that are identified through monitoring of the enterprise.
  - ***Asset Management and Supply Chain*** provides for the accounting of enterprise assets, procurement information associated with them, their life cycles, changes, and ensuring orderly and secure disposal without compromise of enterprise data or security.

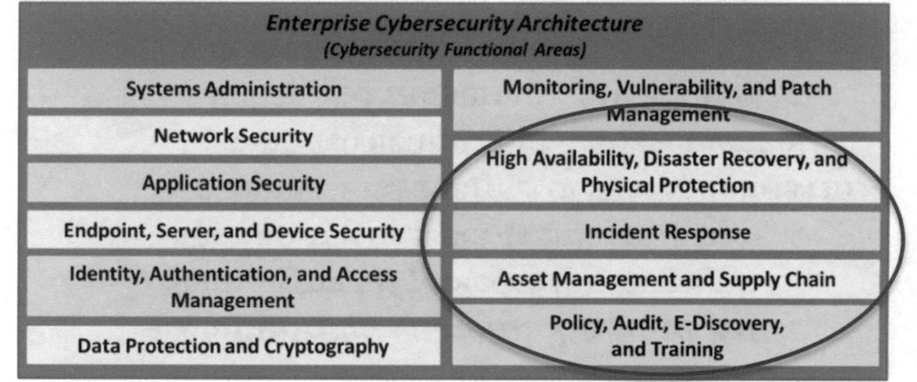

  - ***Policy, Audit, E-Discovery, and Training*** provides for policy oversight of controls and audit of their effectiveness, support for legal e-discovery activities, and training of staff in proper security policies and practices

Part II: A New Enterprise Cybersecurity Architecture

- Chapter 3: Enterprise Cybersecurity Architecture
- Chapter 4: Implementing Enterprise Cybersecurity
- Chapter 5: Operating Enterprise Cybersecurity
- Chapter 6: Enterprise Cybersecurity and the Cloud
- Chapter 7: Enterprise Cybersecurity for Mobile and BYOD

CHAPTER 3

Enterprise Cybersecurity Architecture

S. E. Donaldson et al., *Enterprise Cybersecurity Study Guide*, https://doi.org/10.1007/978-1-4842-3258-3_3

Overview *(1 of 2)*

- This chapter describes an architecture consisting of ***cybersecurity functional areas*** used to organize and manage enterprise cybersecurity.
- Each functional area is described using the following characteristics:
  - Definition
  - Goal / Objectives
  - Threat Vectors
  - Capabilities
- As the cyberthreat evolves, so will specific functional areas and corresponding capabilities.

Enterprise Cybersecurity Architecture *(Cybersecurity Functional Areas)*
• Systems Administration
• Network Security
• Application Security
• Endpoint, Server, and Device Security
• Identity, Authentication, and Access Management
• Data Protection and Cryptography
• Monitoring, Vulnerability, and Patch Management
• High Availability, Disaster Recovery, and Physical Protection
• Incident Response
• Asset Management and Supply Chain
• Policy, Audit, E-Discovery, and Training

Overview *(2 of 2)*

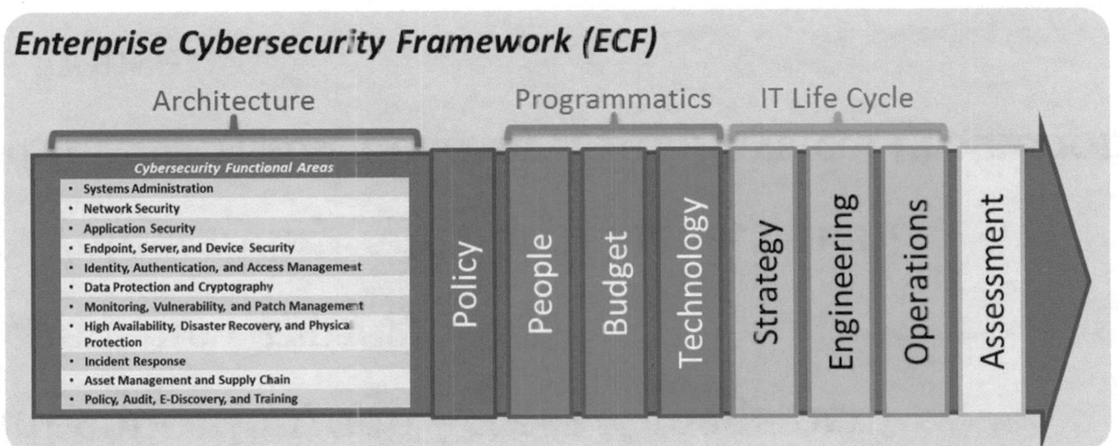

Organizing a cybersecurity program around the ***cybersecurity functional areas*** delineated in this presentation provides an enterprise with an underlying ***architecture*** for an extensible cybersecurity framework to protect against evolving cyberthreats.

Topics

- Systems Administration
- Network Security
- Application Security
- Endpoint, Server, and Device Security
- Identity, Authentication, and Access Management
- Data Protection and Cryptography
- Monitoring, Vulnerability, and Patch Management
- High Availability, Disaster Recovery, and Physical Protection
- Incident Response
- Asset Management and Supply Chain
- Policy, Audit, E-Discovery, and Training

Systems Administration *(1 of 3)*

- ***Definition***
  - Provides secure administration of enterprise and security infrastructures by protecting systems administration (SA) channels from compromise
  - ***Probably most important functional area*** because if it is compromised, an attacker can easily disable and bypass rest of enterprise security
- ***Goal / Objectives***

  Protect the enterprise's administrative channels from being used by an adversary

  - ***Preventive*** objective is to (1) make it harder for attackers to get SA control, (2) slow down attackers so they are easier to catch, and (3) make it easier to catch attacks when they occur.
  - ***Detective*** objective focuses on detecting attacks against SA channels and attempts at malicious SA activity.
  - ***Forensic*** objective focuses on creating detailed audit logs of all privileged SA activities.
  - ***Audit*** objective focuses on generating artifacts and evidence that SA is not malicious in the enterprise.

Systems Administration *(2 of 3)*

- ***Threat Vectors***
  - SA credentials and computers
  - Computing infrastructure (virtualization, storage, and so on)
  - SA infrastructure (enterprise computer management, patch management, other systems, and so forth)
  - Monitoring systems that have administrative access to the enterprise
  - Local computer administrative accounts to move from one computer to another
- ***Capabilities***
  - Make it harder for attackers to get administrative access
  - Make attackers easier to detect and stop if they get control
  - Isolate command and control networks and protocols
  - Provide cryptographic protection for system administrators
  - Allow for auditing of SA activities to detect attacks

Systems Administration *(3 of 3)*

- ***Representative Capabilities***
  - Bastion Hosts
  - Out-of-Band (OOB) management
  - Network Isolation
  - Integrated Lights-Out (ILO), Keyboard Video Mouse (KVM), and Power Controls
  - Virtualization and Storage Area Network (SAN) Management
  - Separation of Administration from Services
  - Multifactor Authentication for Systems Administrators
  - Administrator Audit Trail(s)
  - Command Logging and Analytics

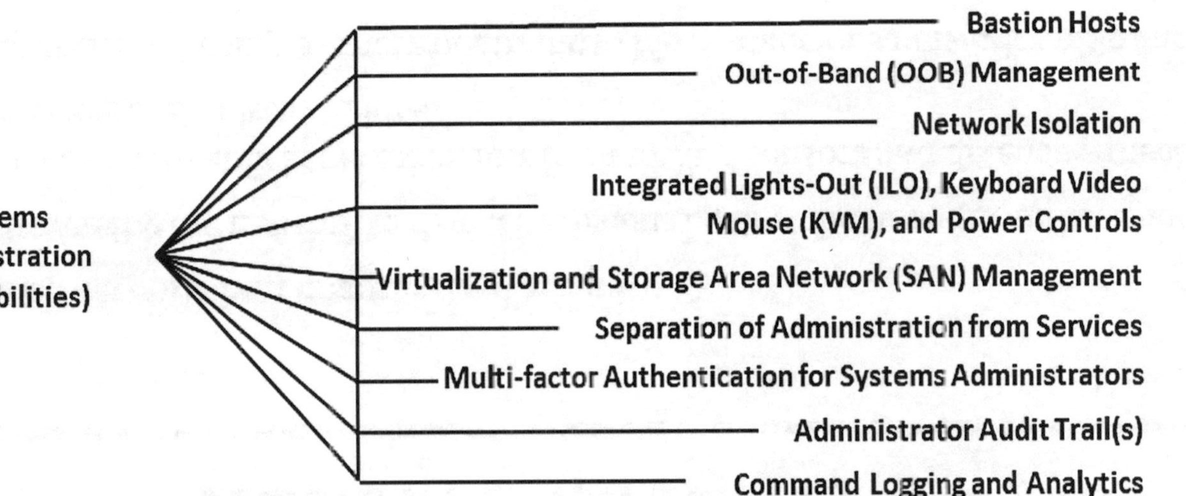

Network Security *(1 of 3)*

- ***Definition***
  - Protects enterprise network from unauthorized access
  - Examines data traversing the network to detect intrusions against the network and connected computers
  - Is used to channel user and attacker activity, routing it toward sensors and defensive mechanisms and away from weaknesses and vulnerabilities
  - Involves filtering and monitoring the network traffic to block malicious network traffic and detect attacker network traffic
- ***Goal / Objectives***

  Protect the enterprise's network from use or attack by an adversary
  - ***Preventive*** objective is to block or channel malicious traffic.
  - ***Detective*** objective is to monitor and analyze network traffic.
  - ***Forensic*** objective is to log information about network traffic.
  - ***Audit*** objective is to analyze network traffic to identify malicious activity or generate artifacts indicating lack of malicious activity.

Network Security *(2 of 3)*

- ***Threat Vectors***
  - Outbound network connections from servers or clients on the internal network
  - Network connections of Internet-facing servers
  - Internal networks where attackers move laterally between computers inside the enterprise
  - Network infrastructure components to gain entry to the enterprise or to bypass other security measures
- ***Capabilities***
  - Preventive, detective, forensic, and audit functions
  - Not "silver bullets" that satisfy all cybersecurity requirements
  - Can block, detect, and intercept many potential attacks

Network Security *(3 of 3)*

- ***Representative Capabilities***
  - Switches and Routers
  - Software Defined Networks (SDN)
  - Domain Name System (DNS) and Dynamic Host Configuration Protocol (DHCP)
  - Network Time Protocol (NTP)
  - Network Service Management
  - Firewall and Virtual Machine Firewall
  - Network Intrusion Detection/Network Intrusion Prevention System (IDS/IPS)
  - Wireless Networking (Wi-Fi)
  - Packet Intercept and Capture
  - Secure Sockets Layer (SSL) Intercept
  - Network Access Control (NAC)
  - Virtual Private Networking (VPN) and Internet Protocol Security (IPSec)
  - Network Traffic Analysis (NTA)
  - Network Data Analytics (NDA)

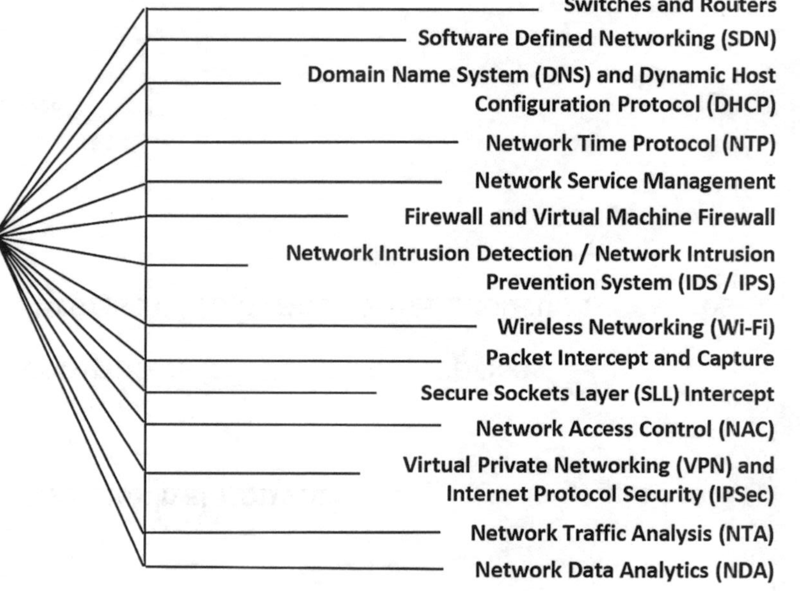

Application Security *(1 of 3)*

- ***Definition***
  - Involves security measures that are specific to certain applications or protocols running within the enterprise
  - Protects applications accessible from the Internet with security
  - Operates alongside network security
  - Includes e-mail security, application-aware firewall features, database gateways, and forward web proxies
  - Helps prevent attacks that exploit application vulnerabilities or application communication protocols
- ***Goal / Objectives***

  Protect the enterprise's applications from use or attack by an adversary
  - ***Preventive*** objective is to block exploitation of applications and application communications protocols from malicious use.
  - ***Detective*** objective is to detect compromises of applications and attempts to exploit them for malicious purposes.
  - ***Forensic*** objective is to log data about application activities that can be used for audits and investigation of incidents.
  - ***Audit*** objective is for auditors to be able to collect evidence and artifacts that suggest the applications are safe and not being used or manipulated by attackers.

Application Security *(2 of 3)*

- ***Threat Vectors***
  - E-mail messages that may contain attachments that attempt to exploit vulnerabilities
  - Web browsers and web plug-ins
  - Enterprise server applications (web application servers)
  - Flaws in in-house enterprise applications
- ***Capabilities***
  - Additional protections to many enterprise applications that are tailored to them specifically
  - Commercially-available solutions include e-mail filtering, web proxies, web application firewalls, and database firewalls

Application Security *(3 of 3)*

- ***Representative Capabilities***
  - E-Mail Security
  - Webshell Detection
  - Application Firewalls
  - Database Firewalls
  - Forward Proxy and Web Filters
  - Reverse Proxy
  - Data Leakage Protection (DLP)
  - Secure Application and Database Software Development
  - Software Code Vulnerability Analysis (including source code verification and bug tracking)

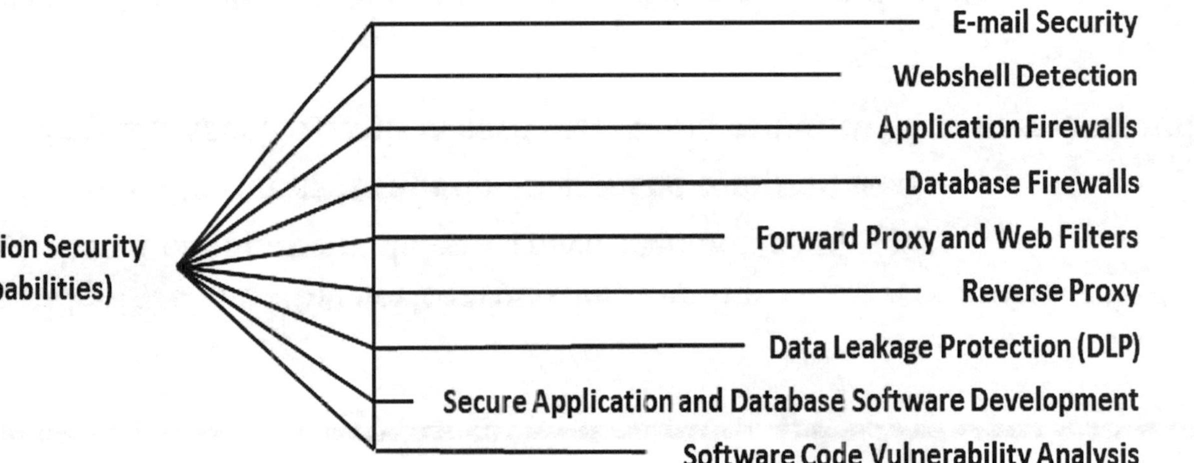

Endpoint, Server, and Device Security *(1 of 3)*

- ***Definition***
  - Involves protecting endpoint computing devices (personal computers, servers, and mobile devices) from attack and detecting when those endpoint defenses have been breached
  - Reduces the probability that the enterprise's endpoints will be compromised
  - Deploys protection tailored to specific needs of each computing platform. "One sizes **does not** fit all."
- ***Goal / Objectives***

  Prevent attackers from taking administrative control of computing devices
  - The overall goal is to detect attempts to maliciously use these devices.
  - The objectives include facilitating investigation of incidents when compromises of systems or data are suspected.
  - ***Preventive*** objective is to make endpoints, servers, and devices hard to compromise. Endpoint security centers on ***hardening*** operating systems so they are difficult to breach and exploit.
  - ***Detective*** objective is to alert the enterprise about malicious software and attempts to exploit the operating system so defenders can identify systems that are either compromised or under attack.
  - ***Forensic*** objective is to log device activities securely so there is an audit trail for investigations. Forensics may include complete imaging of systems for detailed forensic analysis.
  - ***Audit*** objective involves analyzing logs to identify malicious activity or to create artifacts indicating the absence of malicious activity on audited systems.

Endpoint, Server, and Device Security *(2 of 3)*

- ***Threat Vectors***
  - Unlimited ways to take control of an endpoint
  - Operating system vulnerabilities
  - Unpatched vulnerabilities–zero-day attacks
  - Enterprise software products
  - Administrative credentials
  - Malicious software on app stores
- ***Capabilities***
  - Endpoint security, server security, and device security may need to be considered separately due to the differences in how they are used; there may be some common security capabilities.
  - Capabilities include hardened computer images, computer policies, endpoint security suites (anti-virus, anti-malware, host firewall and intrusion detection) and polices for access controls, privilege management, auditing, and forensics.
  - Mobile devices generally require their own sets of tools and technologies.
  - BYOD may not have features needed for enterprise protection.

Endpoint, Server, and Device Security *(3 of 3)*

- ***Representative Capabilities***
  - Local Administrator Privilege Restrictions
  - Computer Security and Logging Policies
  - Endpoint and Media Encryption
  - Computer Access Controls
  - Forensic Imaging Support for Investigations
  - Virtual Desktop/Thin Clients
  - Mobile Device Management (MDM)
  - Anti-Virus/Anti-Malware
  - Application whitelisting
  - In-Memory Malware Detection
  - Host Firewall and Intrusion Detection
  - "Gold Code" Software Images
  - Security Technical Implementation Guides (STIGs)
  - Always-On Virtual Private Networking (VPN)
  - File Integrity and Change Monitoring

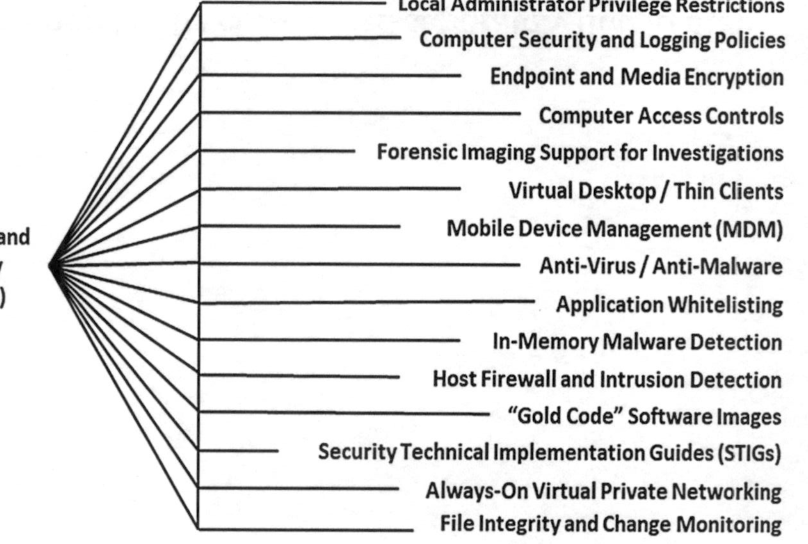

Identity, Authentication, and Access Management *(1 of 4)*

- ***Definition***
  - Supports all other security functional areas by providing answers to the following questions:
    - Who is accessing enterprise IT systems?
    - How are they identified?
    - What can they access once they are authenticated?
  - ***Identity management*** helps to ensure accounts and accesses are provisioned, de-provisioned, and periodically re-certified according to enterprise policies.
  - ***Authentication*** helps to ensure appropriate technologies are used to positively identify users who are accessing enterprise systems.
  - ***Access management*** helps to ensure that privileges are provisioned and de-provisioned according to least privilege and that users do not have privileges exceeding their roles.

Identity, Authentication, and Access Management *(2 of 4)*

- ***Goal / Objectives***

  Ensure only authorized people can access enterprise resources while people, resources, and permissions change over time

  - ***Preventive*** objective is to make it harder for attackers to gain access to enterprise resources by impersonating legitimate users.
  - ***Detective*** objective is to alert the enterprise on credential or permission abuse and identify when accounts are being attacked or have been compromised.
  - ***Forensic*** objective is to log account activity that can be data-mined and correlated with other enterprise events to identify attack patterns.
  - ***Audit*** objective involves analyzing logs to create artifacts and gather evidence if accounts and permissions are being abused.

Identity, Authentication, and Access Management *(3 of 4)*

- ***Threat Vectors***
  - Credential abuse
  - Accounts that are no longer used or maintained, but have not been removed from enterprise
  - Credentials to legitimate accounts used, in part, to escalate attacker privileges
  - Weak authentication methods or protocols allow impersonation of legitimate users
  - Weaknesses in privilege management allow regular user accounts to obtain administrative or other super-user privileges
- ***Capabilities***
  - Center around managing the full identity and access life cycle that can be complex and cost millions of dollars
  - Require a careful balance between automation and manual procedures

Identity, Authentication,and Access Management *(4 of 4)*

- ***Representative Capabilities***
  - Identity Life Cycle Management
  - Enterprise Directory
  - Multifactor Authentication
  - Privilege Management and Access Control
  - Identity and Access Audit Trail and Reporting
  - Lightweight Directory Access Protocol (LDAP)
  - Kerberos, RADIUS, 802.1x
  - Federated Authentication
  - Security Assertion Markup Language (SAML)

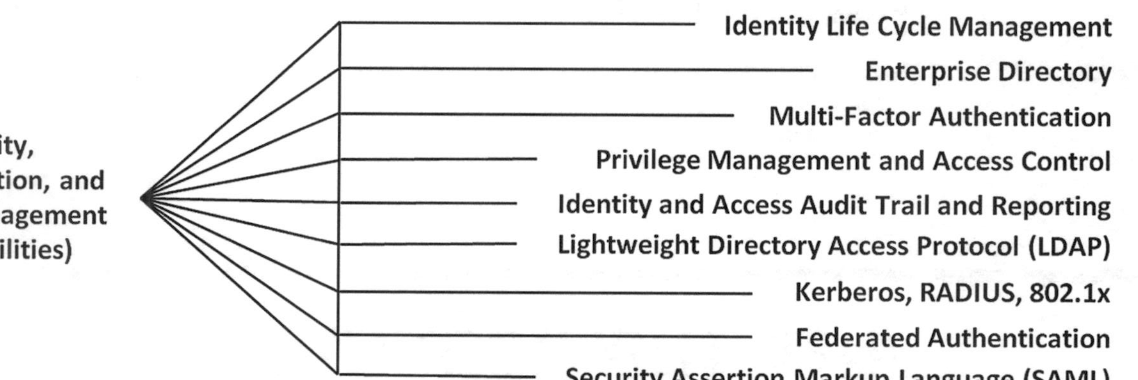

Data Protection and Cryptography *(1 of 3)*

- ***Definition***
  - Protects data at rest and in transit
  - Provides for strong authentication and non-repudiation for messages and data
  - Supports message identity and authenticity
- ***Goal / Objectives***

  Protect the confidentiality and integrity of data using such techniques such as encryption and digital signatures
  - ***Preventive*** objective involves protecting the confidentiality and integrity of enterprise data by using cryptographic technologies.
  - ***Detective*** objective involves monitoring enterprise cryptographic use to detect weak cryptography or cryptographic breaches when they occur.
  - ***Forensic*** objective involves tracking the cryptography used in the enterprise and logging what algorithms and keys are used to support later investigations.
  - ***Audit*** objective involves collecting information on the cryptography and keys that are used and their strengths, and ensuring they meet enterprise requirements for strength and protection.

Data Protection and Cryptography *(2 of 3)*

- ***Threat Vectors***
  - Encrypted web sessions either into or out of an enterprise
  - Attacker-encrypted enterprise data used to demand a ransom for the keys to decrypt the data
  - Weak cryptography
  - Passwords
  - Keys to strong cryptography
  - "Code signing" certifications
  - Unencrypted stolen data (at rest or in transit)
- ***Capabilities***
  - Require three things to be accomplished correctly:
    - Cryptography algorithms must be chosen that are secure and stay secure for the life of the protected data.
    - Cryptographic keys must be chosen and protected from compromise.
    - Application of cryptography must be carefully coordinated with the overall life cycle of the data to be protected.
  - Decrypt data and protect decrypted data by other means so it can be used when needed

Data Protection and Cryptography *(3 of 3)*

- ***Representative Capabilities***
  - Secure Sockets Layer (SSL) and Transport Layer Security (TLS)
  - Digital Certificates (Public Key Infrastructure [PKI])
  - Key Hardware Protection (Smart Cards, Trusted Platform Modules [TPMs], and Hardware Security Modules [HSMs])
  - One-Time Password (OTP) and Out-of-Band (OOB) Authentication
  - Key Life Cycle management (including key rotation)
  - Digital Signatures
  - Complex Passwords
  - Data Encryption and Tokenization
  - Brute Force Attack Detection
  - Digital Rights Management (DRM)

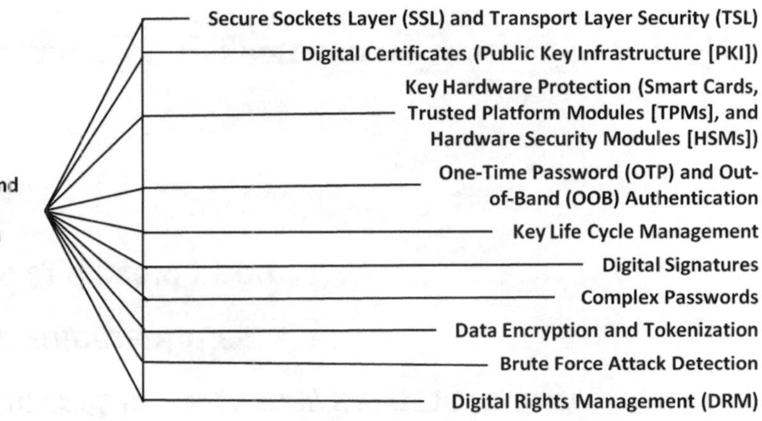

Monitoring, Vulnerability, and Patch Management *(1 of 3)*

- ***Definition***
  - Monitors the status of the enterprise's security
  - Maintains security over time by identifying and patching vulnerabilities as they become known
  - Supports operational processes by identifying and patching vulnerabilities
  - Monitors security systems so security alerts can be detected and acted upon
- ***Goal / Objectives***

  Understand how security changes over time
  - ***Preventive*** objective is to ensure vulnerabilities are compensated for and patched before they can be exploited by attackers.
  - ***Detective*** objective involves monitoring all enterprise security automation systems to detect incidents.
  - ***Forensic*** objective involves logging event and incident information to be correlated, cross-checked, and investigated.
  - ***Audit*** objective involves centrally collecting forensic data to be analyzed by auditors and investigators.

Monitoring, Vulnerability, and Patch Management *(2 of 3)*

- ***Threat Vectors***
  - Attack methods that are not detected, or detected by unmonitored systems and are invisible to defenders
  - Exploit of software vulnerabilities during the time window when they become known and before they can be patched enterprisewide
  - Exploit of vulnerabilities in software components that are not centrally managed or patched
  - Zero-day exploits
  - Compromise of security or logging infrastructure to block or delete records of attacker activities
  - Lack of cross-correlation of attacker activities
- ***Capabilities***
  - Focus on maintaining the enterprise's security on an ongoing basis and actively detecting incidents against enterprise security systems
  - Collect and analyze logging data
  - Process data to identify events of interest
  - Identify specific incidents that require investigation and remediation
  - Scan the enterprise infrastructure and computers to identify vulnerabilities in software or configuration so identified vulnerabilities can be remediated
  - Help ensure the ongoing patching of commercial products to keep them current with the latest security fixes and enhancements

Monitoring, Vulnerability, and Patch Management *(3 of 3)*

- ***Representative Capabilities***
  - Operational Performance Monitoring
  - System and Network Monitoring
  - System Configuration Change Detection
  - Privilege and Access Change Detection
  - Log Aggregation
  - Data Analytics
  - Security Information and Event Management (SIEM)
  - Network and Computer Vulnerability Scanning
  - Penetration Testing
  - Patch Management and Deployment
  - Rogue Network Device Detection
  - Rogue Wireless Access Point Detection
  - Honeypots/Honeynets/Honeytokens
  - Security Operations Center (SOC)

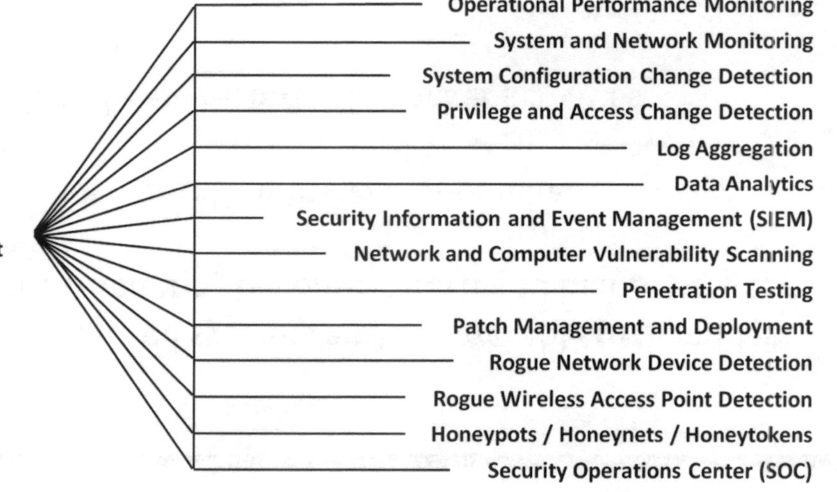

High Availability, Disaster Recovery, and Physical Protection *(1 of 3)*

- ***Definition***
  - Provides the enterprise's primary protection against threats to availability
  - Leverages HADRPP capabilities for protection against all types of hazards to availability, not just cyberattacks
  - Provides cost-effective business continuity capabilities measured in terms of recovery point objectives (RPO) and recovery time objectives (RTO)
- ***Goal / Objectives***

  Satisfy business requirements for continuity of operations in the face of adversity
  - Rather than discuss this functional area in terms of preventive, detective, forensic, or audit objectives, it makes more sense to discuss it in terms of the enterprise's reaction capabilities.
  - ***Overall objective*** is to ensure enterprise has ability to ***respond*** to wide range of potential adverse situations.
  - Perhaps most importantly, an enterprise needs to consider how these reaction capabilities might serve the enterprise in the event of a cyberattack.

High Availability, Disaster Recovery, and Physical Protection *(2 of 3)*

- ***Threat Vectors***
  - Adversities, whether they come from regular mechanical wear and tear, natural circumstances that are outside of anyone's control, or human-led activities that are either negligent or malicious
  - Scheduled maintenance when systems are taken offline
  - Regular wear and tear or hard-to-predict circumstances that result in enterprise systems failing
  - Cyberattack impacts to the integrity of IT systems such as backup systems or disaster recovery systems
  - Loss of a primary data center
  - A deliberate attack (act of war or a sophisticated criminal act) resulting in the physical destruction or impairment of facilities required for operations
- ***Capabilities***
  - Center on making IT systems more robust and having the same data in multiple locations
  - Protect the physical devices and storage containing enterprise data and systems
  - Primarily about availability, but also consider data confidentiality and integrity

High Availability, Disaster Recovery, and Physical Protection *(3 of 3)*

- ***Representative Capabilities***
  - Clustering
  - Load Balancing, Global Server Load Balancing (GSLB)
  - Network Failover, Subnet Spanning
  - Virtual Machine Snapshots and Cloning
  - Data Mirroring and Replication
  - Backups and Backup Management
  - Off-Site Storage
  - Facilities Protection
  - Physical Access Controls
  - Physical Security Monitoring

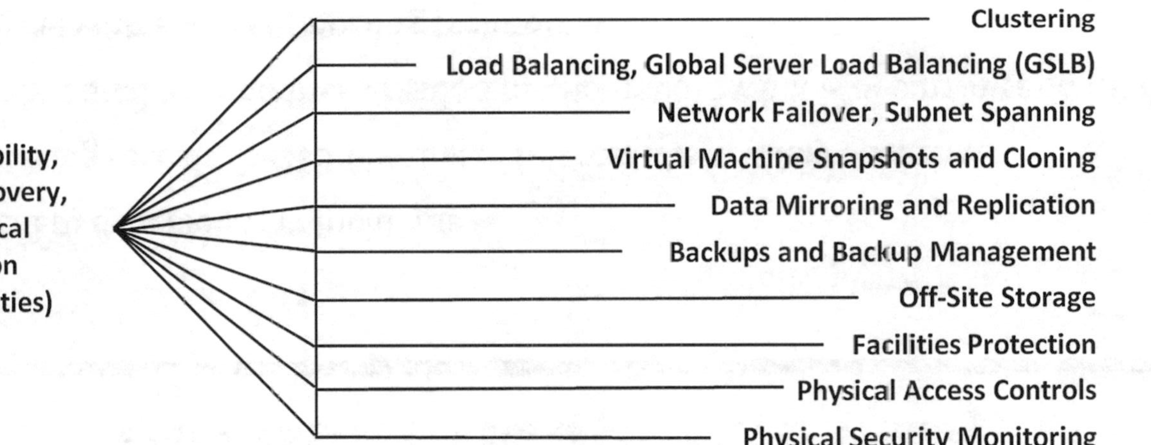

Incident Response *(1 of 4)*

- ***Definition***
  - Capability to respond to cybersecurity incidents
  - Occurs when monitoring reveals that something of interest has actually occurred
  - Consists of further alert analysis and investigation to understand what is occurring and its significance
  - Is primarily procedural with some supporting technology
  - Does not protect enterprise from attack
  - Gives the enterprise the ability to respond to attacks
  - Is a multistep process consisting of investigating, reporting, containing, and ultimately remediating the incident
  - Includes operational disruptions, security incidents, deliberate attacks, natural and man-made disasters, and mistakes/accidents

Incident Response *(2 of 4)*

- ***Goal / Objectives***

  Provide for timely response when security incidents are identified

  – ***Overall objective*** is to reduce the enterprise's vulnerability while simultaneously repelling the attack.

  – ***Overall objective*** includes clearly defining ***formal communication channels*** and lines of authority.

  – ***Overall objective*** includes defines ***processes for assessing the situation*** so the enterprise understands when a situation is "snowballing" and overwhelming the enterprise's initial response.

  – ***Overall objective*** includes knowing the ***limits of the enterprise's crisis response capabilities*** and the potential losses of service due to exceptional severe circumstances.

  – When the enterprise is operating in a degraded state, it is critical to have a ***security reserve*** to protect the enterprise.

Incident Response *(3 of 4)*

- ***Threat Vectors***
  - No enterprise incident-response process coordinated ahead of time
  - Poor coordination between operational and security personnel
  - Failure to feed indicators of compromise (IOCs) back to the monitoring and detection process
  - Incident remediation process fails to adequately strengthen defenses that were breached
  - Deliberate attackers leveraging the incident response (for example, attackers force the enterprise into an incident response mode and then manipulate and disable security features)
  - Failure to account for regulatory or legal requirements on reporting and disclosure that can result in financial, legal, or public relations penalties
- ***Capabilities***
  - Enable the enterprise to respond to incidents effectively and efficiently
  - May include technologies that greatly assist with the forensic investigations needed to track down and catch stealthy attackers
  - May be fundamentally procedural in nature

Incident Response *(4 of 4)*

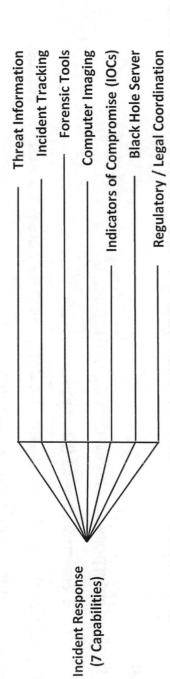

- ***Representative Capabilities***
  - Threat Information
  - Incident Tracking
  - Forensic Tools
  - Computer Imaging
  - Indicators of Compromise (IOC)
  - Black Hole Server
  - Regulatory/Legal Coordination

Asset Management and Supply Chain *(1 of 3)*

- ***Definition***
  - Involves tracking enterprise assets and the origin of the assets
  - Accounts for the IT enterprise assets throughout their life cycle
  - Has appropriate level of confidence assets are doing what they are supposed to be doing
  - Prerequisite for endpoint and server security controls
  - Helps ensure assets are accounted for during their life cycle and made compliant with enterprise policies when they are put into service
  - Helps ensure assets are properly disposed of or protected when assets are finally disposed at the end of their life cycle
- ***Goal / Objectives***

  Ensure the enterprise knows what IT assets it has and manage supply chain risks from acquisition through operation through disposal
  - ***Overall objective*** is to ensure operational staff follow proper procedures that are supported by various technical capabilities.

Asset Management and Supply Chain *(2 of 3)*

- ***Threat Vectors***
  - Attacker's ability to place components in the enterprise without those components being noticed
  - Unauthorized changes or reconfiguration of systems
  - Compromised products provided by suppliers
  - Supplier ecosystem that is not protected as well as the enterprise
  - Disposed electronics that were not properly sanitized, revealing enterprise information
- ***Capabilities***
  - Ensure enterprise assets are accounted for over their life cycle, are made compliant with enterprise policies, and are properly disposed at end of life
  - Ensure assets are obtained from trustworthy suppliers

Asset Management and Supply Chain *(3 of 3)*

- ***Representative Capabilities***
  - Asset Management Database
  - Configuration Management Databases (CMDB)
  - Change Management Databases
  - Software Inventory and License management
  - Supplier Certification Processes
  - Secure Disposal, Recycling, and Data Destruction

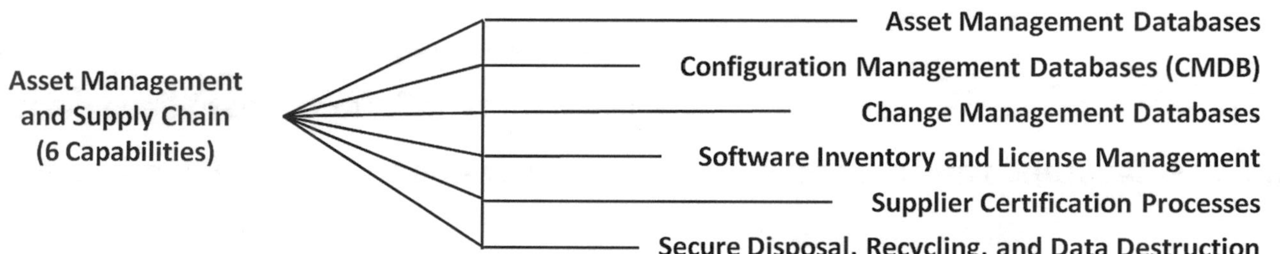

Policy, Audit, E-Discovery, and Training *(1 of 3)*

- ***Definition***
  - Deals with governance and security oversight functions
  - Includes mapping security controls to meet compliance requirements, along with some secondary functions regarding personnel security and privacy concerns
  - Sets the organizational strategy for all other functional areas (policy)
  - Periodically reviews other functional areas for compliance (audit)
  - Oversees
    - External reporting requirements
    - Audit program of preventive, detective, and monitoring controls
    - Interfaces with the legal department to support e-discovery
    - Training for employees, IT, and security personnel
  - Home of the Chief Information Security Officer (CISO)
- ***Goal / Objectives***

  Address the people, policy, regulatory, and compliance aspects of enterprise cybersecurity
  - Control of enterprise processes and capabilities
  - Management of programmatic and personnel issues associated with process and capability deployment

Policy, Audit, E-Discovery, and Training *(2 of 3)*

- ***Threat Vectors***
  - Consist of gaps that result in processes or capabilities being neglected, causing security risks
    - Security management
    - Compliance management
    - Personnel security
    - Training and accountability
- ***Capabilities***
  - Provide oversight of controls and audit of their effectiveness, support for legal e-discovery activities, and training of staff in proper security policies and practices
  - Account for compliance requirements and mapping security controls to meet those requirements
  - Oversee the security control audit program that periodically reviews preventive, detective, and monitoring controls to verify their operation and effectiveness

Policy, Audit, E-Discovery, and Training *(3 of 3)*

- ***Representative Capabilities***
  - Governance, Risk, and Compliance (GRC) with Reporting
  - Compliance and Control Frameworks (SOX, PCI, others)
  - Audit Frameworks
  - Customer Certification and Accreditation (C&A)
  - Policy and Policy Exception Management
  - Risk and Threat Management
  - Privacy Compliance
  - E-Discovery Tools
  - Personnel Security and Background Checks
  - Security Awareness and Training

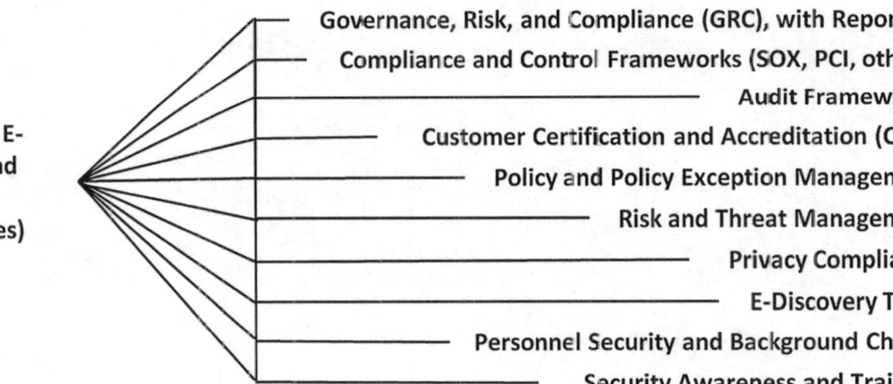

CHAPTER 4

Implementing Enterprise Cybersecurity

S. E. Donaldson et al., *Enterprise Cybersecurity Study Guide*, https://doi.org/10.1007/978-1-4842-3258-3_4

Overview

- This chapter describes ***how to implement*** an enterprise cybersecurity program by
  - organizing personnel;
  - integrating cybersecurity into the IT system life cycle;
  - defining security policies and scopes;
  - selecting security controls and technologies; and
  - considering overall security effectiveness.
- Procedural and technological capabilities
  - Deliver the security controls needed to mitigate risks
  - Can be organized into enterprise cybersecurity functional areas

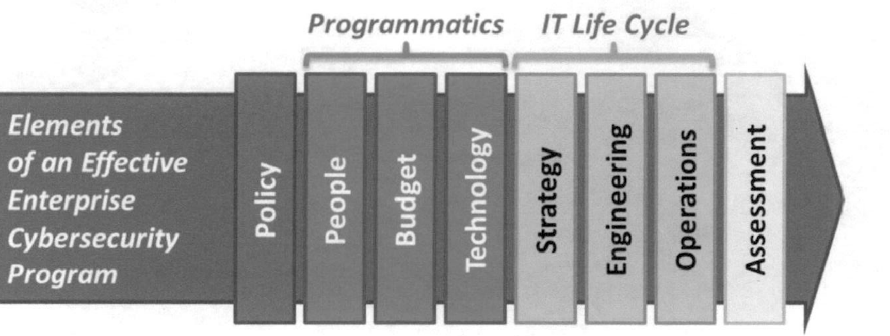

- The graphic delineates the necessary elements needed for an effective ***enterprise cybersecurity program.***
- Not only do these elements need to be well coordinated, but they also need to be integrated and work well together.

Topics

- IT Organization
- IT System Life Cycle
- Defining Security Policies
- Defining Security Scopes
- Identifying Security Scopes
- Selecting Security Controls
- Selecting Security Capabilities
- Selecting Security Technologies
- Considering Security Effectiveness

IT Organization *(1 of 6)*

Context

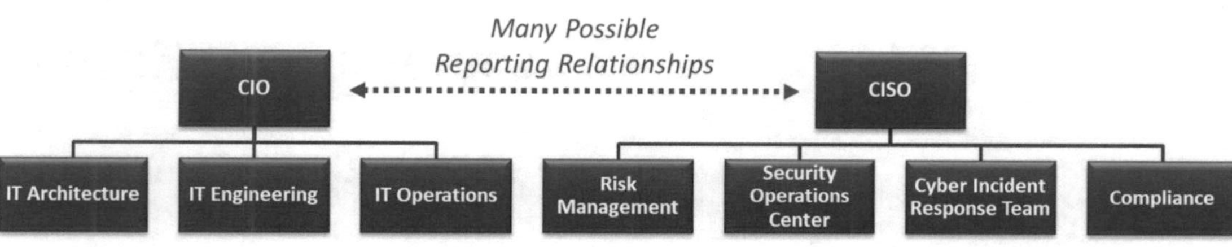

- Organizing people is the first step in protecting an enterprise from cyberattacks.
- Organization has significant impacts that provide valuable information:
  - What is easy to accomplish
  - What is hard to accomplish
  - Where the functions and disjunctions exist in an organization
- IT management frameworks suggest three major IT functions that often report to the Chief Information Officer (CIO):
  - IT Architecture
  - IT Engineering
  - IT Operations
- Security sub-functions generally report to the Chief Information Security Officer (CISO).
  - Risk Management
  - Security Operations Center
  - Cyber Incident Response Team
  - Compliance
- The graphic depicts these functions and sub-functions (also known as teams or departments) in a notional organization chart.

IT Organization *(2 of 6)*

Many Possible Reporting Relationships

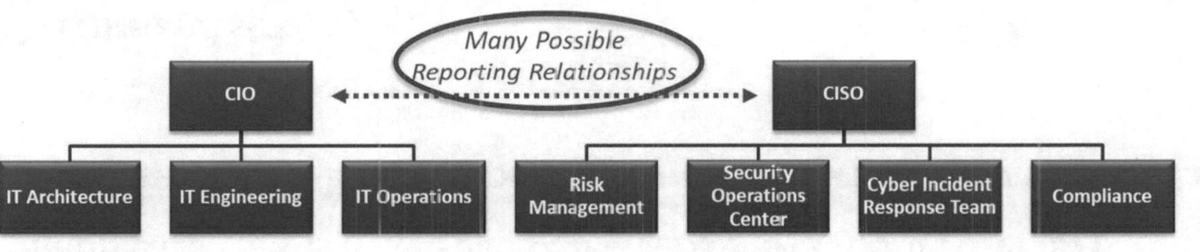

- The CIO and CISO's reporting relationship is a complex question with no one "correct" answer.
- In some organizations, the CIO and CISO are peers and both report to senior leadership.
- In other organizations, the CISO reports to the CIO.
- In yet other organizations, the CIO reports to the CISO.
- Each reporting arrangement has trade-offs in regard to how cybersecurity conflicts get escalated and at what level business decisions are made to accept cybersecurity risks or mitigate them in some manner.

IT Organization *(3 of 6)*

Chief Information Officer (CIO) *(1 of 2)*

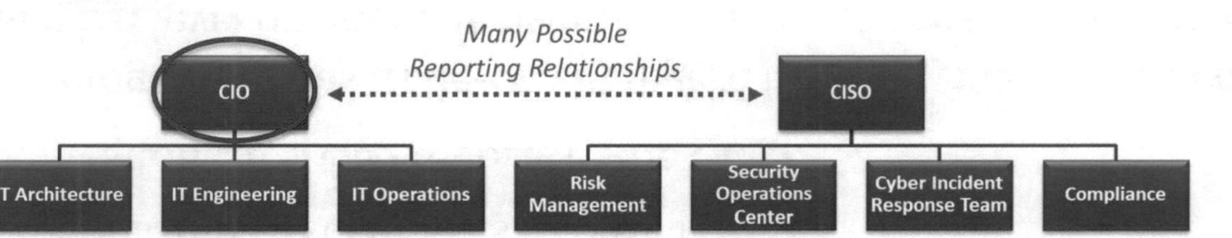

- The ***CIO*** is the ultimate enterprise authority for IT and has authority over other IT functions.
  - Sometimes, one or more of the subordinate functions is in a separate organization.
  - There may be multiple CIO levels where each CIO has some authority over an organizational component.
  - Multiple CIOs often have dotted-line relationships to an enterprise CIO with overall authority.
- IT Architecture
  - Guides IT architecture and strategy
  - Coordinates with other departments to align technology with the business
  - Conducts multi-year planning
  - Manages strategic vendor and technology relationships

IT Organization *(4 of 6)*

Chief Information Officer (CIO) *(2 of 2)*

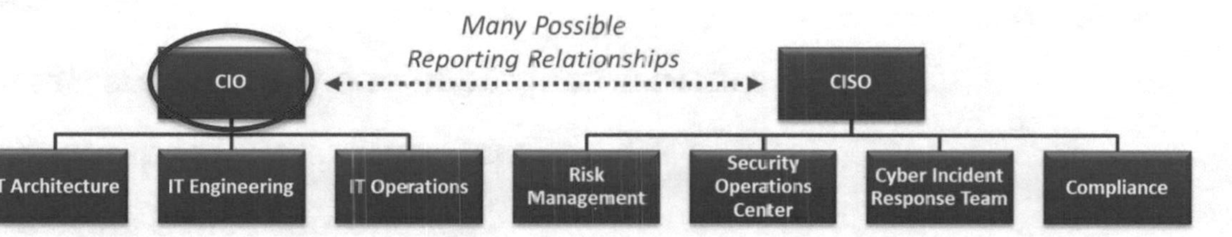

- IT Engineering
  - Designs, deploys, maintains, and retires enterprise technologies
  - Is often separate from IT Operations to reduce costs and ensure accountability
  - Introduces challenges in regard to staff agility and career progression with separation
- IT Operations
  - Operates IT technologies cost-effectively using Service Level Agreements (SLAs)
  - Frequently separated from engineering
  - Does not provide agility to "design solutions on the fly" or respond quickly to changing situations
  - Works well for managing operation costs, formalizing operational process, and achieving high levels of system reliability and stability

IT Organization *(5 of 6)*

Chief Information Security Officer (CISO) *(1 of 2)*

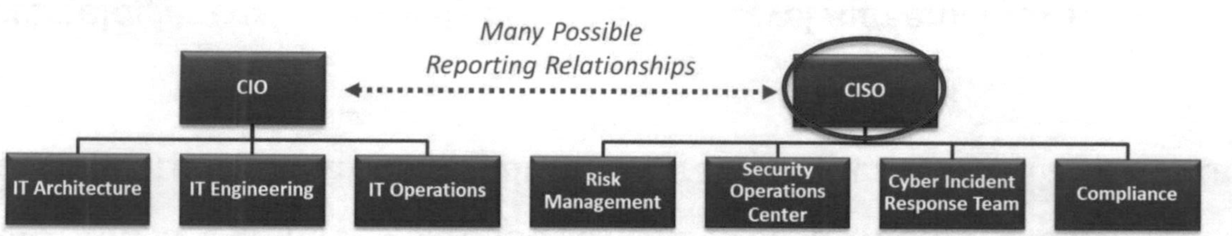

- The ***CISO*** is the ultimate enterprise authority for cybersecurity.
  - Directs cybersecurity policy
  - Oversees cybersecurity policy compliance
  - Has a role throughout the IT system life cycle
  - Has its own strategy, engineering, and operations activities
- Risk Management
  - Evaluates assets, vulnerabilities, threats, and risks
  - Defines policies to manage risks
  - Engages with IT projects to identify and manage risks due to enterprise changes

IT Organization *(6 of 6)*

Chief Information Security Officer (CISO) (2 of 2)

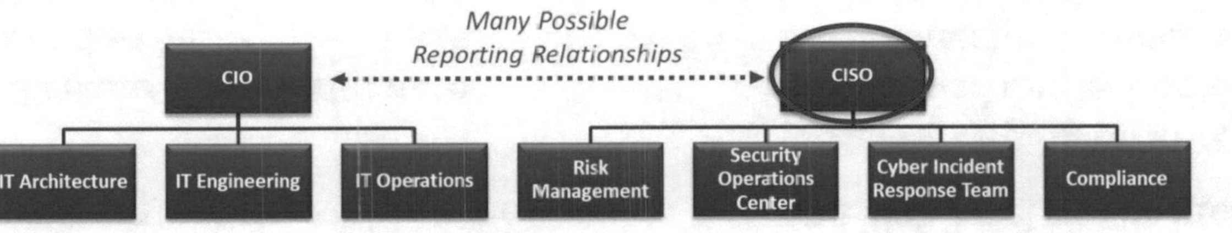

- Security Operations Center (SOC)
  - Involves operating security controls and services on an ongoing basis
  - Maintains the security for the enterprise
  - Identifies cyber incidents when they occur
- Cyber Incident Response Team
  - Responds to cybersecurity incidents and supervises their investigation and remediation
  - May employ outside experts for specialized skill sets
- Compliance
  - Collects security infrastructure and operations artifacts that provide evidence the security controls and policies are operating as intended
  - "Maps" the artifacts to external compliance requirements and regulatory standards to demonstrate enterprise compliance

IT System Life Cycle *(1 of 4)*

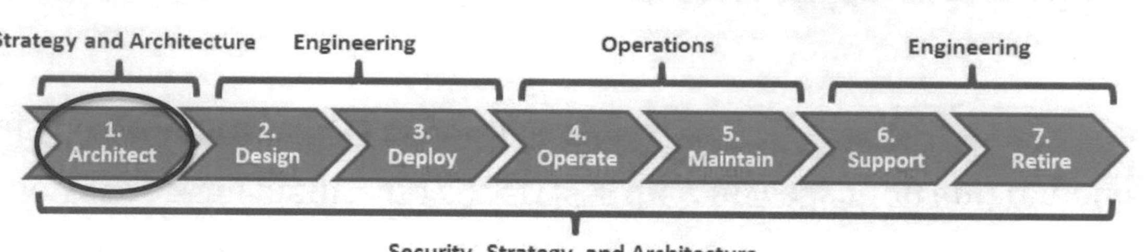

- The graphic illustrates a notional IT life cycle.
  - Adapted from Information Technology Infrastructure Library (ITIL)
  - Indicates IT departments responsible for the stages
  - Starts with Architecture and transitions to Design, Deploy, and so on.
- The IT system life cycle spans the stages systems go through during their lifetime.

- The ***Architect Stage*** involves
  - selecting preferred vendors and applicable technological standards;
  - developing long-term technology roadmaps and high-level system architectures;
  - engaging the engineering department to ensure available technologies can work within the architectural guidelines; and
  - staying engaged throughout the life cycle to monitor significant architectural changes that might impact technology roadmaps.

IT System Life Cycle *(2 of 4)*

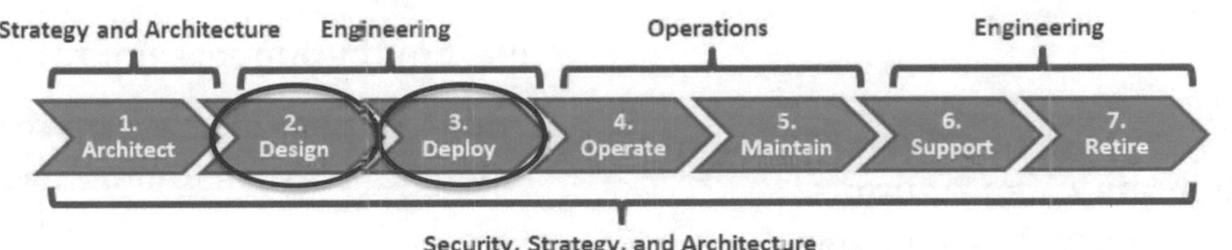

- The ***Design Stage*** involves
  - turning the defined system architecture into a functional system design;
  - defining business and technical requirements;
  - working with vendors to get bids, evaluate proposals, and test technologies;
  - determining the best balance of project cost, schedule, and performance;
  - working with the security department to identify security requirements;
  - conducting risk analysis for the new system or service; and
  - specifying a "detailed design."

- The ***Deploy Stage*** involves
  - transforming the detailed design into a functioning system and deploying the system into an IT environment;
  - issuing purchase orders to procure components or services;
  - installing servers and software (if required);
  - configuring components and services;
  - creating "as-built" documentation, operating procedures, and manuals to get ready for operational use; and
  - ensuring security configurations meet security requirements.

IT System Life Cycle *(3 of 4)*

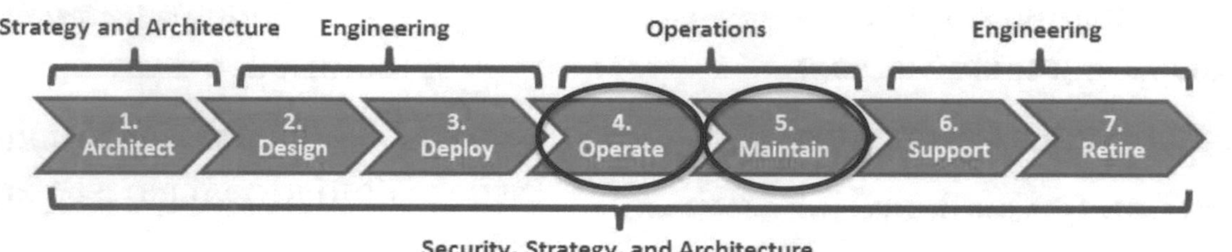

- The ***Operate Stage*** involves
  - shaking out procedures and ensuring the system or service is performing as expected;
  - meeting service-level agreements;
  - managing and reducing operational costs over time;
  - collecting extensive metrics to document the system or service costs and operations; and
  - identifying opportunities for fine-tuning and streamlining over time.

- The ***Maintain Stage*** involves
  - keeping the system or service operating at a steady-state level on an ongoing basis;
  - making minor system or service changes, also known as enhancements; and
  - patching, implementing routine upgrades, refreshing hardware, and updating vendor services.

IT System Life Cycle *(4 of 4)*

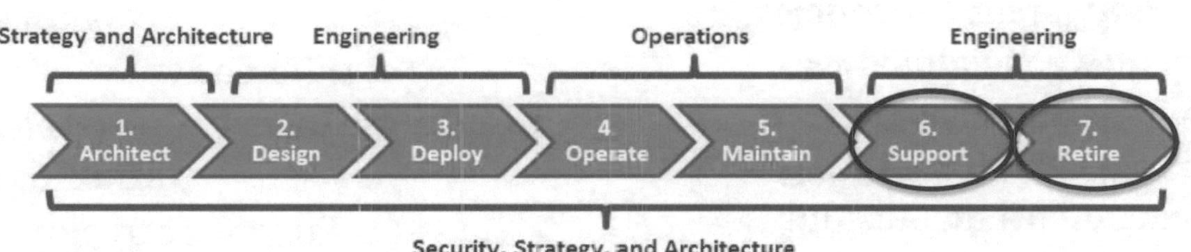

- The ***Support Stage*** involves
  - providing "warranty" service to address defects identified during system or service standup;
  - supporting the system or service on an ongoing basis by addressing "problems" identified and formally documented by operations;
  - analyzing problems, performing business analysis, and determining best engineering/ business alternatives; and
  - deferring or accepting alternatives given the enterprise priorities.
- The ***Retire Stage*** involves
  - retiring the system or service at the end of its useful life because it is
    - no longer needed;
    - superseded by another capability;
    - no longer cost-effective to operate; and
    - no longer secure enough to meet organizational standards.
  - consulting with all interested parties on the decision to retire system or service via a formal process; and
  - updating enterprise records so that the retired system or service is "off the books."

Defining Security Policies

- Security policies identify the assets to be protected and the protection afforded those assets:
  - What is protected
  - Who is responsible for the protection
  - How well the protection is to be performed
  - What the consequences are for protection failure
- Policies should be unambiguous, well-organized, well-maintained, and balanced between security and business needs.
- The graphic depicts the security documentation pyramid.
  - ***Policy*** is a high-level statement of principle or course of action governing enterprise information security.
  - ***Standards*** are documents specifying measures for behavior, processes, configurations, or technologies to be used for enterprise cybersecurity.

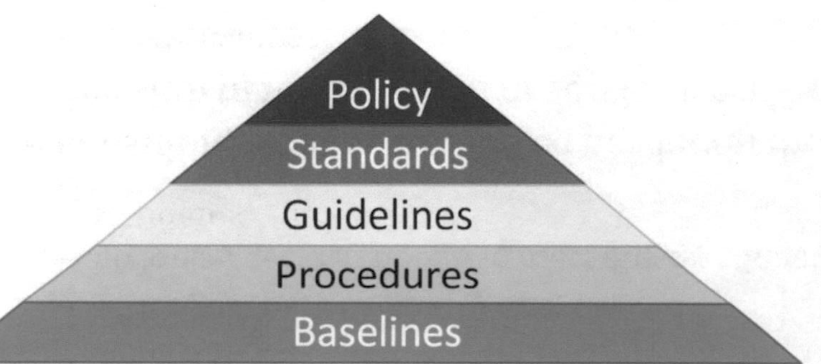

  - ***Guidelines*** are documents providing non-authoritative guidance on policy and standards for use by subordinate organizations.
  - ***Procedures*** are a set of documents describing step-by-step or detailed instructions for implementing or maintaining security controls.
  - ***Baselines*** are specific configurations for technologies and systems designed to provide easy compliance with the established policy, standards, guidelines, and procedures.

Defining Security Scopes *(1 of 5)*

Context *(1 of 2)*

- NIST provides detailed guidance on performing risk-management activities within the NIST Risk Management Framework (RMF).
- The remainder of this chapter focuses on **Step 1**: **CATEGORIZE Information Systems.**
- According to NIST,

  "Conducting initial risk assessments brings together the available information on threat sources, threat events, vulnerabilities, and predisposing conditions—thus enabling organizations to use such information to categorize information and information systems based on known and potential threats to and vulnerabilities in organizational information systems and environments in which those systems operate. (NIST 800-30 rev 1)"

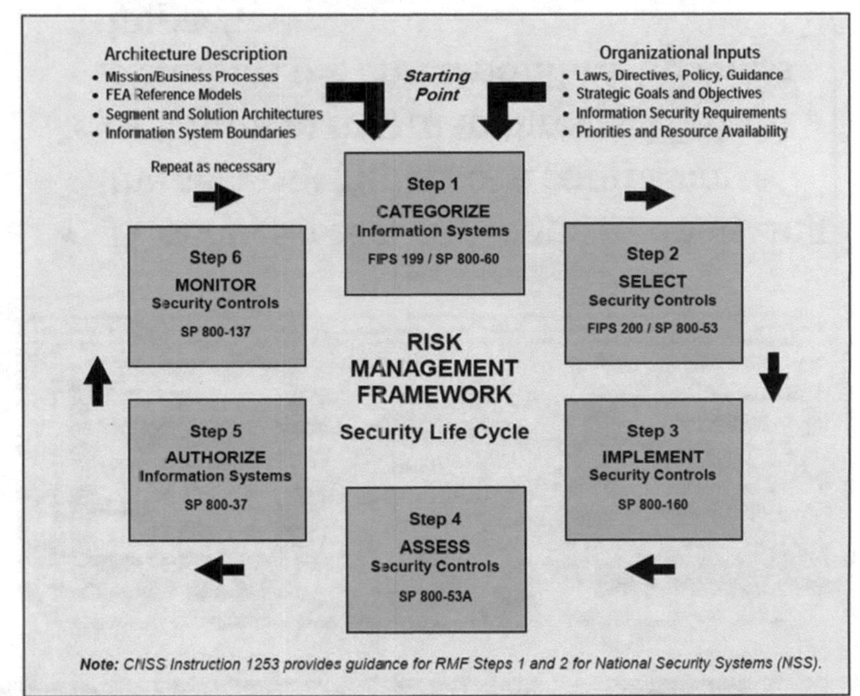

- The NIST risk management framework security life cycle provides a process for implementing an enterprise cybersecurity program.

Defining Security Scopes *(2 of 5)*

Context *(2 of 2)*

- Practitioners interpret NIST's guidance as applying to a ***single*** server or computer system.
- However, NIST's guidance can be applied at a higher level of abstraction where a single set of analysis is applied to ***entire sets*** of computers and their networks.
- This study guide refers to such a grouping of systems and networks as a ***security scope***.
  - Groups together assets and security controls around a common business impact caused by a common set of threats
  - Is a collection of IT systems where the systems have similar risk profiles and share a common business impact due to a security incident

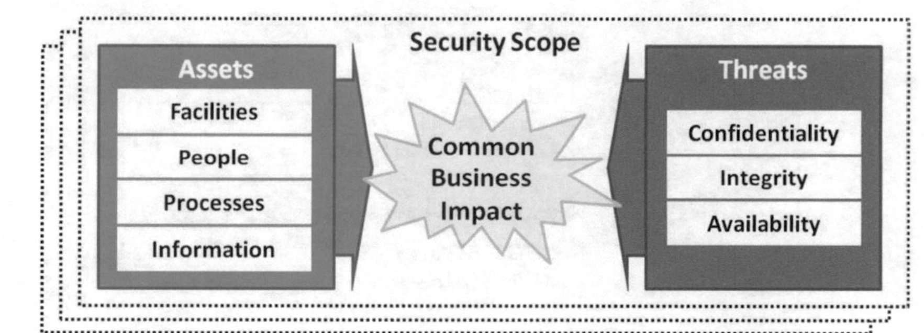

- IT defines a security scope by analyzing the security impact of a compromise or failure in regard to threats. IT also examines the corresponding business impact.
  - Compromise of enterprise administrative systems might be in one security scope.
  - Compromise of transaction processing systems might be in a different scope.

Defining Security Scopes *(3 of 5)*

The Eight Types of Security Scopes (1 of 2)

- The business impact is the ***dominating factor*** when identifying security scopes.

  1. A ***non-critical security scope*** is where none of the three security factors is critical and there is tolerance for failures of all three factors (for example, business administrative systems).
  2. A ***confidentiality critical scope*** is where data needs to be protected from breach or disclosure, but integrity and availability are not major concerns (such as employee data).
  3. An ***integrity critical scope*** is where data integrity is of concern, but confidentiality and availability are not major concerns (for instance, internal financial systems).

Security Scope Type	Confidentiality (Steal Data)	Integrity (Modify Data)	Availability (Deny Access)
1. Non-Critical	Low/Med	Low/Med	Low/Med
2. Confidentiality Critical	High	Low/Med	Low/Med
3. Integrity Critical	Low/Med	High	Low/Med
4. Availability Critical	Low/Med	Low/Med	High
5. Confidentiality Non-Critical	Low/Med	High	High
6. Integrity Non-Critical	High	Low/Med	High
7. Availability Non-Critical	High	High	Low/Med
8. All Factors Critical	High	High	High

4. An ***availability critical scope*** is where systems need to be highly available, and confidentiality and integrity are not major concerns (such as public-facing web sites).

Defining Security Scopes *(4 of 5)*

The Eight Types of Security Scopes (2 of 2)

5. A ***confidentiality non-critical scope*** is where availability and integrity are critical, but confidentiality is not (for example, an enterprise directory).

6. An ***integrity non-critical scope*** is where confidentiality and availability are critical, but integrity is not (security scope is rarely used).

7. An ***availability non-critical scope*** is where confidentiality and integrity are critical, but availability is not (for example, customer account data where data must be carefully protected, but temporary outages are acceptable).

Security Scope Type	Confidentiality (Steal Data)	Integrity (Modify Data)	Availability (Deny Access)
1. Non-Critical	Low/Med	Low/Med	Low/Med
2. Confidentiality Critical	High	Low/Med	Low/Med
3. Integrity Critical	Low/Med	High	Low/Med
4. Availability Critical	Low/Med	Low/Med	High
5. Confidentiality Non-Critical	Low/Med	High	High
6. Integrity Non-Critical	High	Low/Med	High
7. Availability Non-Critical	High	High	Low/Med
8. All Factors Critical	High	High	High

8. An ***all-factors critical scope*** is where CIA are all critical and there is little tolerance for failures (for example, online transaction processing systems such as Amazon.com).

Defining Security Scopes *(5 of 5)*

Considerations in Selecting Security Scopes

- Selecting security scopes is an approximate process.
- Factors other than confidentiality, integrity, and availability (CIA) factor into the process.
  - Differing needs for CIA of systems and their data
  - The business impact of a failure or breach
  - Distinct patterns with regard to vulnerabilities, threats that exploit those vulnerabilities, and the probabilities and impacts of exploitations
  - Production vs. non-production environments
  - Most of these factors considered during NIST's assessment process
  - One of the most important considerations when conducting this analysis is to keep the analytical process at a high level and not too detailed.

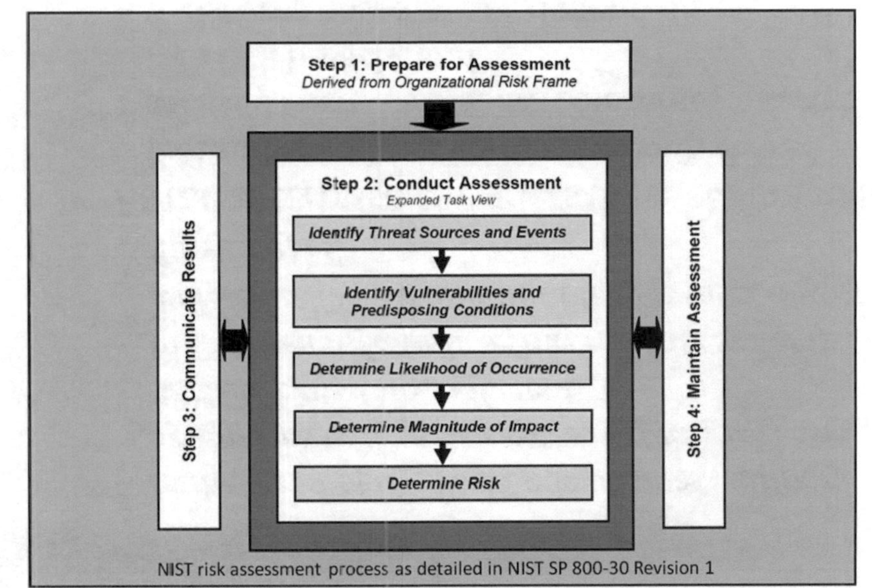

NIST risk assessment process as detailed in NIST SP 800-30 Revision 1

  - An enterprise of 1,000 servers shouldn't have 1,000 security scopes; the enterprise should have between three and five scopes.

Identifying Security Scopes *(1 of 6)*

Context

- Identifying security scopes establishes enterprise boundaries and compartments that are logical points for managing security.
- The general process for selecting security scopes can be reduced to the four steps shown in the graphic.
- This simplified process provides an enterprise with business statements that characterize the consequences of a breach, compromise, or failure.
  - *If these systems fail, our business will be unable to generate revenue.*
  - *In the event of a breach, our customer data will be compromised and our entire business placed in jeopardy.*
  - *In the event of a failure, our business support operations will be disrupted, driving up costs and making us less efficient.*
  - *In the event of a failure, our security systems will be ineffective and unable to protect any of the rest of IT.*
- As the enterprise considers these statements,
  - it intuitively identifies systems with shared security postures that are commonly affected by a CIA breach; and
  - it discerns how systems depend on each other, creating webs of interconnected systems that need to be treated similarly.
- The identification process is imperfect, the results will not be clear-cut, and the overall security design needs to address exceptions and gaps.

Identifying Security Scopes *(2 of 6)*

Security Scopes for the Typical Enterprise (1 of 3)

- Many enterprises have approximately five security scopes to consider that cover their server, user, and security infrastructure environments.
- The graphic shows five typical security scopes that can be used as a starting point when identifying security scopes.
- ***Security and Systems Administration***
  - If an attacker gets control of an enterprise's authentication, network security, system management, or other security infrastructure, the defense of the enterprise will experience "game over."
  - These systems are often shared across the entire enterprise and all systems to include customer-facing systems.
  - This security scope needs to be secured at the same or higher level as all security scopes depending upon it.

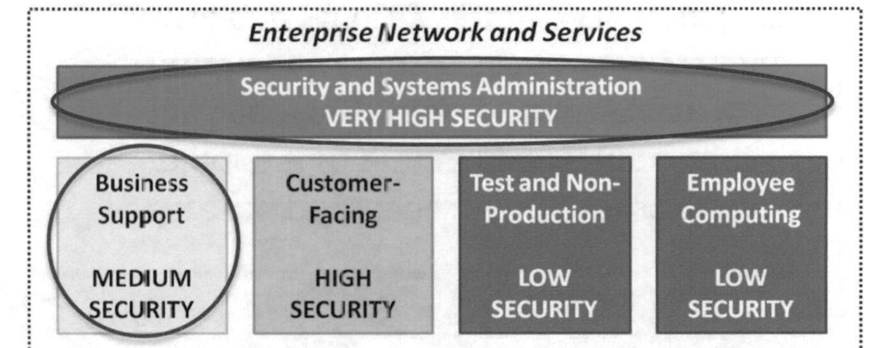

- ***Business Support***
  - This scope contains systems supporting the business operation that do not directly generate revenue, such as e-mail, financial, and payroll systems.
  - Consider a payroll system and a credit card processing system. What are the business impacts of systems going down?
    - Payroll = people don't get paid
    - Credit card = enterprise cannot generate revenue
    - These systems have different business impacts if they fail and consequently, may have different risk profiles and security scopes.

Identifying Security Scopes *(3 of 6)*

Security Scopes for the Typical Enterprise (2 of 3)

- ***Customer-Facing***
  - These systems are used to run the business.
  - Without these systems the business is unable to generate revenue.
  - In an e-commerce business, these systems can be the majority of IT.
  - In a manual business, there may be only a few or even none of these systems.
  - It is important to consider which IT systems result in an immediate loss of revenue and group them together into a security scope, if practical.
- ***Test and Non-Production***
  - These systems are the supporting systems that are critical in the long run, but non-critical in the short run.

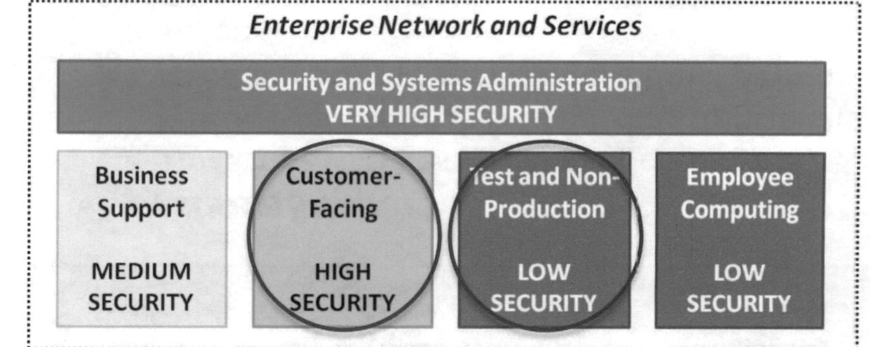

  - An enterprise looks at how these systems interact with production systems and weighs the benefits of simply putting them in the production security scope with its more stringent security vs. the benefits of having them in a lower-security environment.
  - Enterprise needs to watch out for the "gotchas" that occur when non-production systems are part of the path-to-production or when they are handling copies of production data.

Identifying Security Scopes *(4 of 6)*

Security Scopes for the Typical Enterprise (3 of 3)

- ***Employee Computing***
  - If an enterprise allows its employees to surf the web from enterprise computers and receive e-mail from the Internet, then it is strongly recommended giving the employee computing its own security scope.
  - The enterprise simply is not able to protect Internet-connected employees as well as the rest of the enterprise.
  - If the enterprise allows those employees to interact with the other security scopes (for example, systems administration) from these computers, then the enterprise needs to engineer protections to ensure employee breaches cannot be exploited.
- Based on the enterprise analyses, enterprises can add or remove security scopes as appropriate.

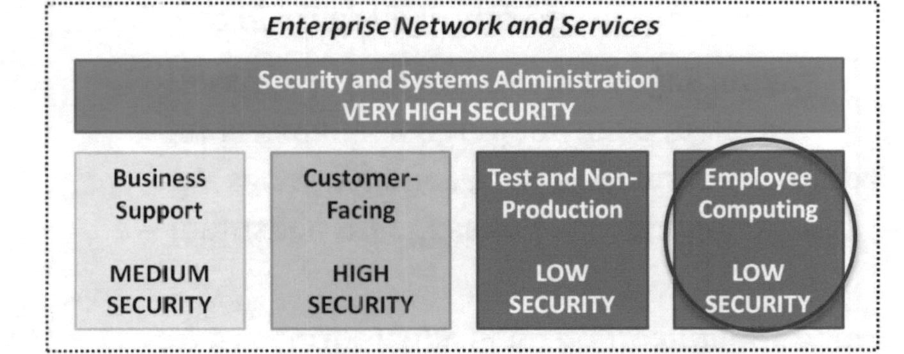

Identifying Security Scopes *(5 of 6)*

Considerations in Selecting Security Scopes (1 of 2)

- It is important to identify the number of security scopes that is "just right."
  - Having few security scopes simplifies an enterprise's security policy and engineering.
  - Having more security scopes gives the enterprise fine-grained control over its security policies and their application to different parts of the enterprise.
- Some general guidance on balancing these factors and selecting scopes include the following:
  - Systems must be well matched with the policy of the security scope in regard to confidentiality, integrity, and availability protections.
  - It is OK for the scope's security level to exceed the needs of a particular system in scope, but it is not acceptable for the system's needs to exceed the security of the scope.
  - Security policies are applied to all computers in a security scope at an approximately equal level.
  - It must be practical and acceptable to apply the security policy to all systems in the scope, and available technology must make it possible to implement that policy today.
  - The operational trade-offs of the security policy must be acceptable to most of the computers in the scope.

Identifying Security Scopes *(6 of 6)*

Considerations in Selecting Security Scopes (2 of 2)

- If there are a lot of operational requirements for greater agility, less configuration control, or lower cost operation and the security trade-offs are acceptable, consider segmenting those systems off into a separate security scope with a more relaxed policy.
- Interfaces between scopes become logical points for segmentation within the enterprise, and such interfaces are both logical choke points for policy enforcement and also potential attack vectors.

- Enterprise IT supporting computer systems bridge security scopes, and it is difficult to identify which scope such systems should reside in.
- Scopes have dependencies and connections where deliberate attacks can gain footholds in less-secure scopes and use these scopes to target more-secure scopes.
- Path-to-production systems are a common example of this phenomenon, especially when they host copies of production data.
- Security architecture needs to account for compensating controls to protect against these potential attack vectors.
- It is important to recognize the process is imperfect.

Selecting Security Controls *(1 of 3)*

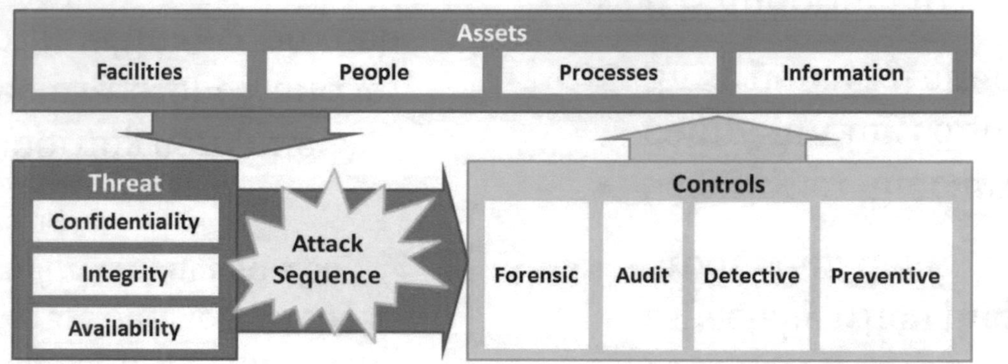

- Once the enterprise selects its security scopes, the next step is to identify the controls needed in those scopes.
- Start by re-visiting enterprise assets and threats, and the attack sequence against those assets from the threats.
- The graphic shows the selected controls (forensic, audit, detective, preventive) disrupting the attack sequence.
- The selected controls enable the enterprise to investigate, document, detect, and block attacks while they are in progress.

Selecting Security Controls *(2 of 3)*

- To select the best controls, the enterprise considers the attack sequence.

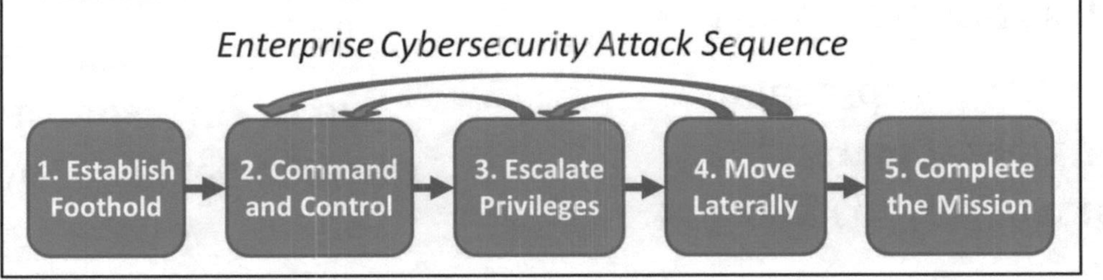

- A security controls completes a sentence that goes something like this:

  "When an attacker … , we respond by … "

  – When an attacker *sends a user a malicious e-mail message*, we respond by *intercepting that message and preventing it from getting to our users.*

  – When an attacker *attempts to steal administrator credentials*, we respond by *thwarting the theft by requiring two-factor authentication.*

  – When an attacker *installs malware on a server*, we respond by *blocking unauthorized software using whitelisting.*

  – When an *attacker attempts to control compromised internal resources*, we respond by *intercepting and blocking the malicious command and control network traffic.*

  – When an attacker *follows the attack sequence*, we respond by *having detective controls that detect attack patterns and alert us to their presence so we can engage and defeat them.*

Selecting Security Controls *(3 of 3)*

- Security controls are designed in sequence so attacks
  - leave a forensic trail;
  - can be picked up by an audit;
  - cause alerts that can be detected; and
  - are blocked, where possible.
- Business analysis is used to help determine the level of control protection as not all attack activities warrant blocking.
- As much as possible, selected controls should generate a forensic log to be examined during an investigation.
- The enterprise's goal is to give itself multiple opportunities to catch attackers and ensure any attack leaves a robust audit trail.
- Most important—if the enterprise blocks the attack with a preventive control, the enterprise wants to ensure it detects the attack first.
- Detection alerts the operation department that an attack is underway so the attack can be repelled before the attack is successful.
- Enterprises need to understand security is an "arms race."
- Every control that detects or blocks an attack can possibly be circumvented or defeated.
- The overall goal is to have multiple opportunities to catch the attack so that individual controls do not have to be 100% successful to be effective.

Selecting Security Capabilities *(1 of 3)*

- After building a library of security controls, the next step is to select the capabilities the enterprise needs to implement those controls.
- Building a controls library and selecting capabilities is an iterative process.
- As capabilities are identified, new controls may also be identified.
- The goal is to capture and record the high-level relationships among the most important components, without getting buried in minutia.

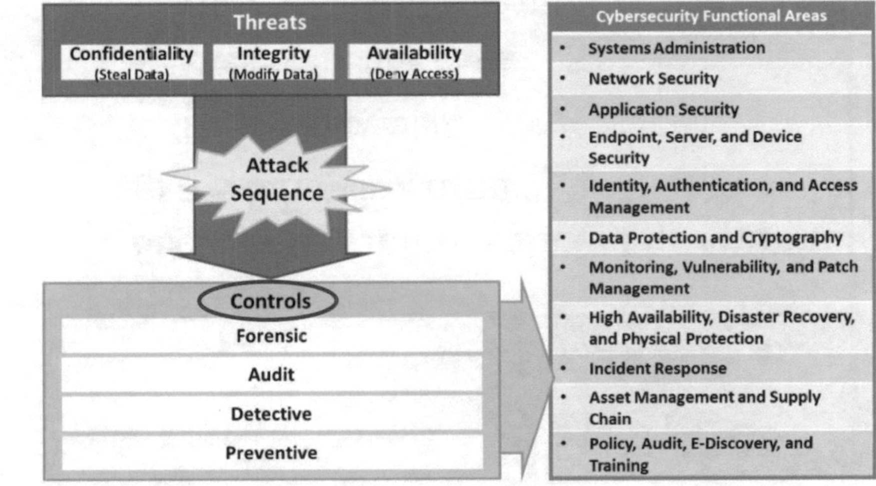

- The graphic illustrates how the controls connect to the cybersecurity functional areas.
- As the enterprise identifies controls needed to disrupt the attack sequence, it should organize the supporting capabilities by functional areas.

Selecting Security Capabilities *(2 of 3)*

- Functional areas
  - help to manage and operate the controls and corresponding capabilities in a coherent manner; and
  - should be approximately equal in importance in regard to the controls and capabilities contained in them, and their cybersecurity effectiveness.
- If the enterprise control design results in one or more functional areas being largely ignored, then there are probably controls missing that should be considered.

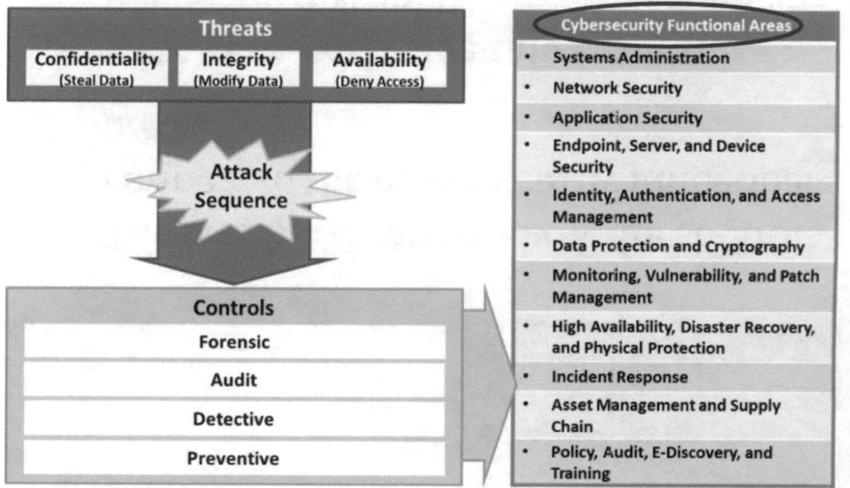

- Security capabilities should be examined in the following terms:
  - Their deployment
  - Their operating costs
  - The potential impact the capabilities have on enterprise IT operations and productivity

Selecting Security Capabilities *(3 of 3)*

- Some capabilities can support multiple controls.
  - Anti-virus capabilities can block malicious software and also alert when malicious software has been detected.
- It can be beneficial to consider forensic, audit, and detective controls before simply deploying preventive controls since detecting and investigating a targeted attack can be just as important as disrupting it.
- Security controls can be achieved through technological means or through procedural means.

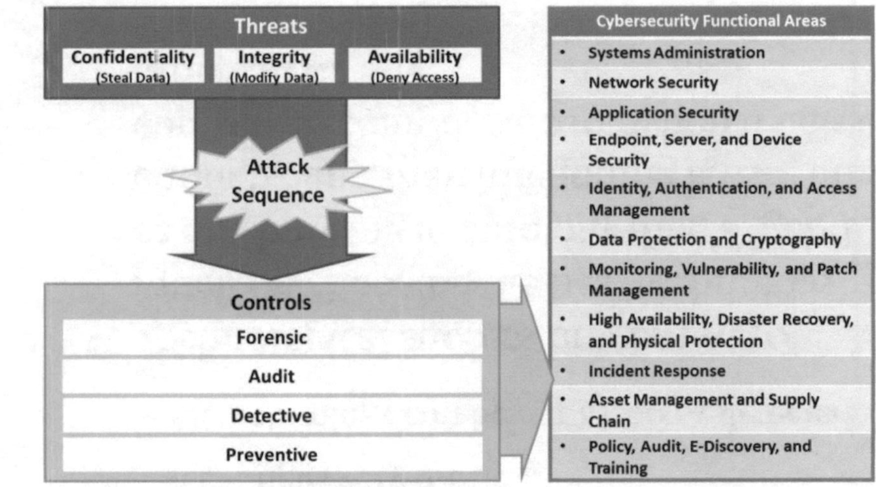

- In many ways, the cheapest way to achieve a control on short notice is through a manual process that is consistently followed, not a sophisticated technology.
- Manual processes have issues, but they should not be discounted prematurely.

Selecting Security Technologies *(1 of 2)*

- Once an enterprise selects its security capabilities, the next step is to decide if the controls are achieved through procedural or technological means.
- Whether to use procedural or technological means to achieve security capabilities is a business decision.
- The graphic shows security controls and capabilities can potentially be achieved by technological or procedural means.
- If technological means are chosen, then the corresponding technologies need to be selected.
- Security practitioners tend to prefer technological capabilities.

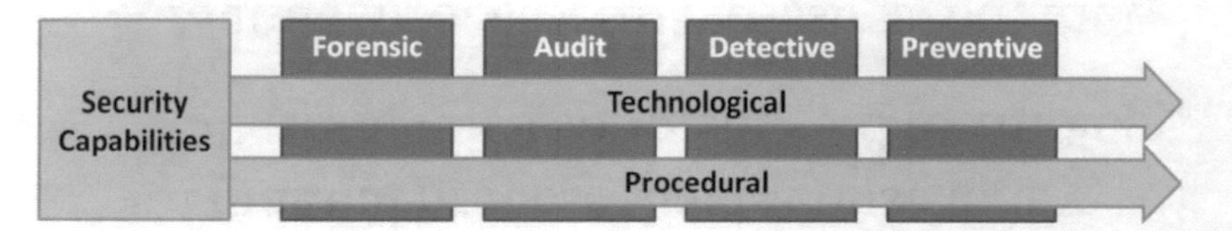

- At the business level, the technology is largely irrelevant.
  - It changes very quickly.
  - All technology can be bypassed or defeated.
- Technological success hinges not so much on choosing the best technology as on choosing technology that is "good enough," and then integrating it with other controls to compensate for when it fails or is defeated.

Selecting Security Technologies *(2 of 2)*

- Technology that is 99% effective
  - is only marginally better than technology that is 90% effective if the enterprise has a way of catching the attackers who can defeat the technology; and
  - is just as ineffective as technology that is 90% effective if an attacker figures out how to defeat it.
- Success is all about using combinations of capabilities and technologies to catch and defeat 100% of intrusions when they occur, not 90% or even 99%.
- Achieving this degree of success requires more than a single technology by itself.
- To achieve 100% success, it is important not to discount the power of procedural capabilities.
- People
  - are still better than computers at recognizing malicious patterns when their occur; and
  - are capable of having conversations with other people to figure things out.
- Even the best machine-learning technologies eventually rely on people to look at the pattern to determine if it is malicious or not.
- Do not discount the power of people to provide detection, investigation, and response.

Considering Security Effectiveness *(1 of 4)*

- To determine security architecture effectiveness, the enterprise considers the overall attack domain and cyberattack threats against the enterprise security scopes.
  - ***First attack***
    - Is not blocked by preventive controls or caught by detective controls
    - Leaves a forensic trail
  - ***Second attack***
    - Is not blocked by preventive controls or caught by detective controls
    - Found during periodic security audits
    - Includes many insider attacks

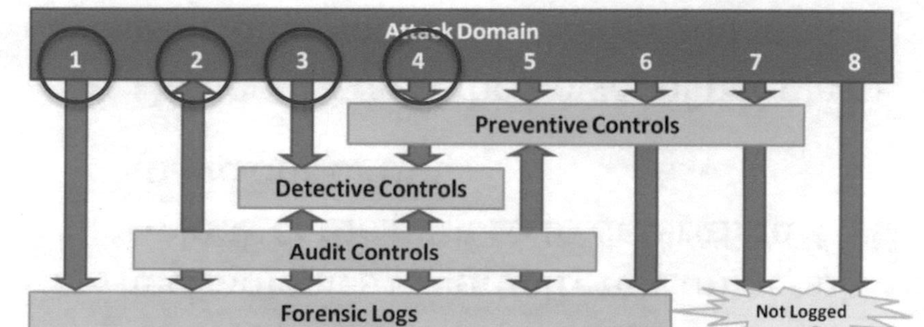

  - ***Third attack***
    - Is not blocked by preventive controls
    - Generates alerts on detective controls
    - Needs defense to be a robust and timely incident response capability
  - ***Fourth attack***
    - Is blocked by preventive controls and alerts on detective controls
    - Generates forensic logs picked up during audits
    - Requires defenses to be at their strongest because defenses not only block the attack but also alert defenders to what is going on

Considering Security Effectiveness *(2 of 4)*

– ***Fifth attack***

- Is blocked by preventive controls
- Does not alert on detective controls
- Generates forensic logs picked up during audits
- Is dangerous because attackers are blocked, but defenders are not alerted
- Gives attackers time to find ways around preventive controls before audits reveal them

– ***Sixth attack***

- Is blocked by preventive controls and generates forensic logs
- Not detected by detective controls
- Not picked up in security audits
- Is dangerous because attackers are blocked, but defenders are not alerted

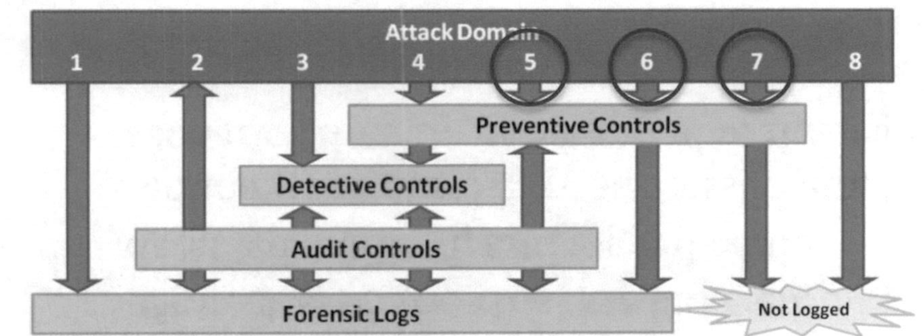

– ***Seventh attack***

- Is blocked by preventive controls, but is otherwise not detected
- Includes many attacks against Internet-facing firewalls due to the sheer volume of firewall logs generated and the challenges in retaining those logs
- Is vital to ensure these types of attacks, when they get past preventive controls, are blocked and detected by other controls further inside the defensive perimeter

Considering Security Effectiveness *(3 of 4)*

- ***Eighth attack***
  - Is not blocked and is not detected
  - Is most **dangerous** since attackers succeed without leaving a trace
  - Is important that defenses are designed with redundancy so this attack's success is not fatal to the enterprise

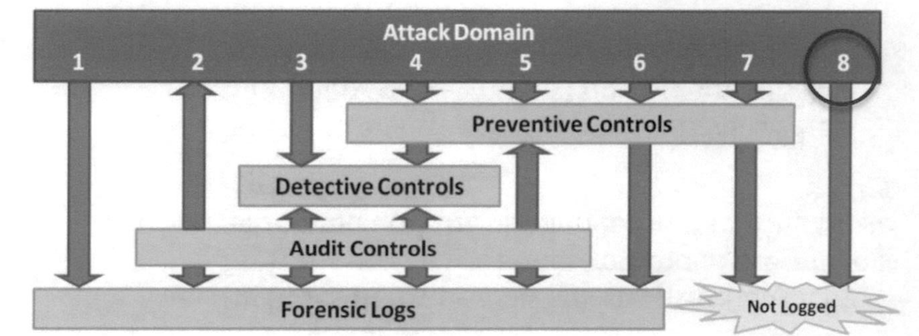

- These attack scenarios show that the overall security posture comes down to how much of the potential attack domain falls into each of these eight scenarios.
- A weak defense allows many attacks to succeed, while a good defense thwarts many attacks.
- An important objective of an enterprise's defense is to maximize the number of attack scenarios that are blocked, detected, audited, and logged while reducing the number of successful attack scenarios that are not stopped or detected.

Considering Security Effectiveness *(4 of 4)*

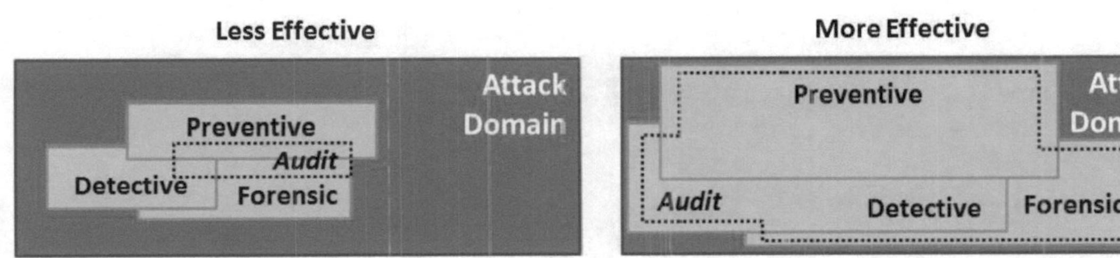

- Less effective security covers a smaller portion of the potential attack domain with preventive, detective, audit, and forensic controls.
- More effective security covers a larger portion of the potential attack domain.
- The enterprise can use this risk analysis process to drive the control design process.
- The enterprise can try to envision attack scenarios where attackers defeat its preventive controls without being detected.
  - Often such attacks are insider attacks and credential abuse.
  - Enterprise defense architectures often assume credentialed users on internal network are legitimate users and not attackers.
  - Experience has shown internal attacks are the most difficult type of attacks to detect and defeat.

CHAPTER 5

Operating Enterprise Cybersecurity

S. E. Donaldson et al., *Enterprise Cybersecurity Study Guide*, https://doi.org/10.1007/978-1-4842-3258-3_5

Overview *(1 of 2)*

- This chapter examines the enterprise cybersecurity operational processes.
- The graphic depicts the 17 major operational processes and 14 major information systems that support cybersecurity operations in the 11 functional areas.
- This chapter explains how they all work together to operate an effective cybersecurity program.
- Organizationally, security
  - does not have to be in charge of all cybersecurity operational processes; and
  - does need to have a role in ensuring processes are present, operating properly, and satisfying enterprise security objectives.

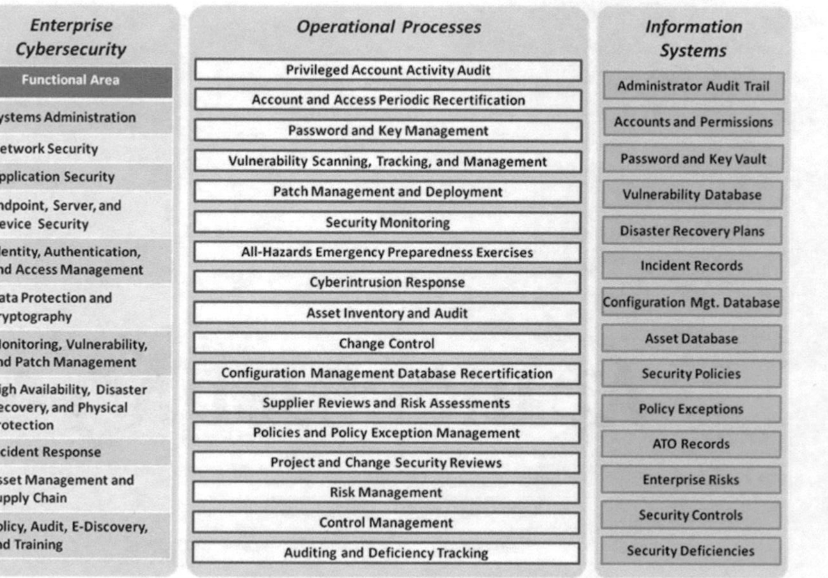

- Enterprise security without security operations is unlikely to hold up long against a deliberate attacker, so security operations are critical to achieving successful enterprise cybersecurity.

Overview *(2 of 2)*

Cybersecurity Functional Areas
Cybersecurity Operational Processes
Supporting Information Systems
Cybersecurity Functional Areas
Systems Administration
Network Security
Application Security
Endpoint, Server, and Device Security
Identity, Authentication, and Access Management
Data Protection and Cryptography
Monitoring, Vulnerability, and Patch Management
High Availability, Disaster Recovery, and Physical Protection
Incident Response
Asset Management and Supply Chain
Policy, Audit, E-Discovery, and Training
• Privileged Account Activity Audit
• Account and Access Periodic Re-certification
• Password and Key Management
• Security Monitoring
• Patch Management and Deployment
• Vulnerability Scanning, Tracking, and Mgt.
• All-Hazards Emergency Preparedness Exercises
• Cyberintrusion Response
• Supplier Reviews and Risk Assessments
• Config. Mgt. Database Re-certification
• Change Control
• Asset Inventory and Audit
• Auditing and Deficiency Tracking
• Control Mgt.
• Risk Management
• Project and Change Security Reviews
• Policies and Policy Exception Mgt.
• Incident Records
• Administrator Audit Trail
• Accounts and Permissions
• Password and Key Vault
• Incident Records
• Security Controls
• Enterprise Risks
• Vulnerability Database
• Enterprise Risks
• Vulnerability Database
• Config. Mgt. Database
• DR Plans
• Incident Records
• Vulnerability Database
• Enterprise Risks
• Enterprise Risks
• Asset Database
• Security Controls
• Config. Mgt. Database
• Config. Mgt. Database
• Asset Database
• Asset Database
• Security Controls
• Security Deficiencies
• Incident Records
• Enterprise Risks
• Security Controls
• Security Controls
• Enterprise Risks
• ATO Records
• Enterprise Risks
• ATO Records
• Policy Exceptions
• Security Policies

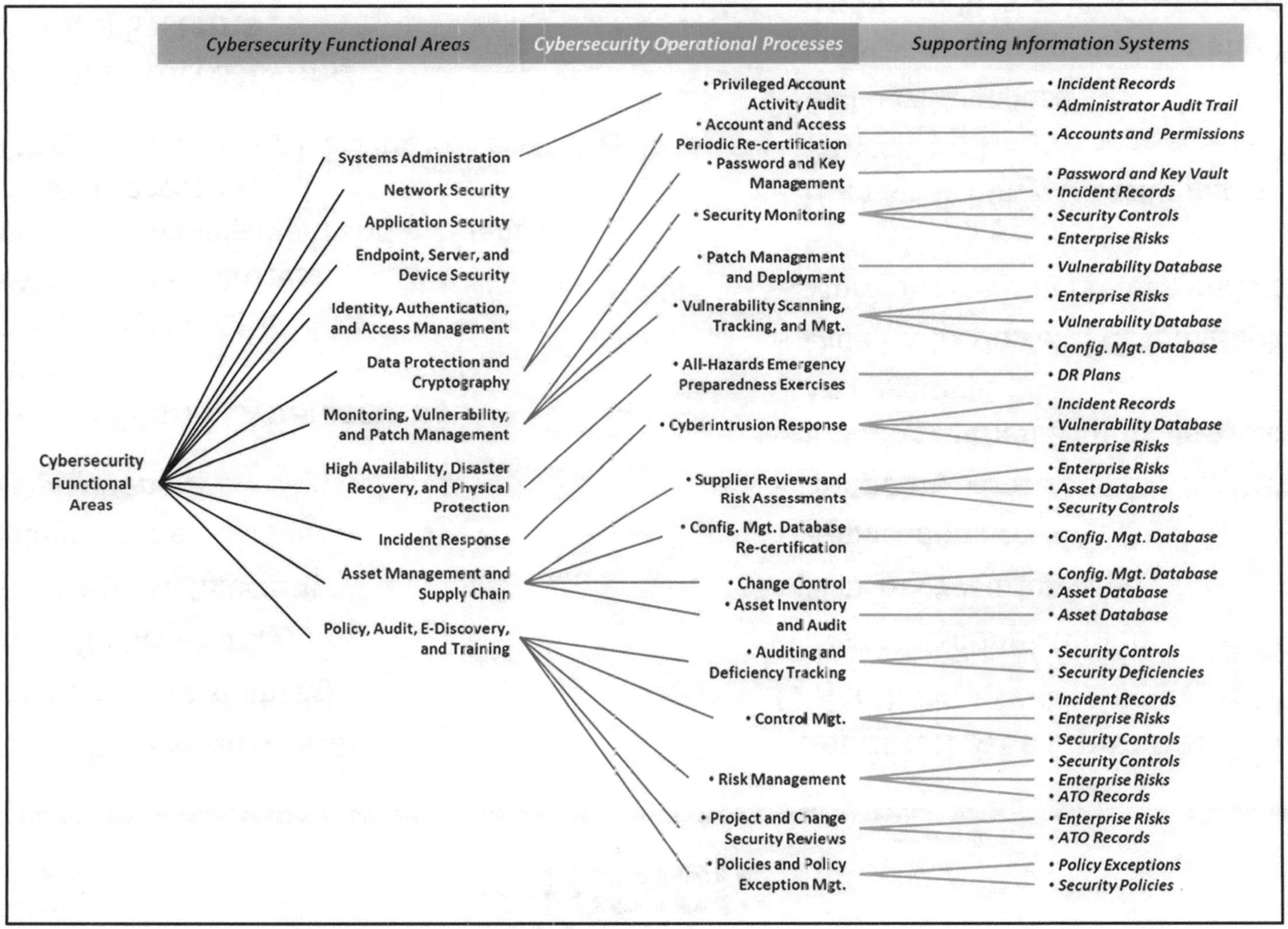

Topics

- Operational Responsibilities
  - Business (CIO, Customers)
  - Security (Cybersecurity)
  - (IT) Strategy/Architecture
  - (IT) Engineering
  - (IT) Operations
- High-Level IT and Cybersecurity Processes
  - IT Operational Process
  - Risk Management Process
  - Vulnerability Management and Incident Response Process
  - Auditing and Deficiency Tracking Process
- Operational Processes and Information Systems
  - Cybersecurity Operational Processes
  - Supporting Information Systems
- Functional Area Operational Objectives
  - Systems Administration
  - Network Security
  - Application Security
  - Endpoint, Server, and Device Security
  - Identity, Authentication, and Access Management
  - Data Protection and Cryptography
  - Monitoring, Vulnerability, and Patch Management
  - High Availability, Disaster Recovery, and Physical Protection
  - Incident Response
  - Asset Management and Supply Chain
  - Policy, Audit, E-Discovery, and Training

Operational Responsibilities *(1 of 3)*

- The graphic shows the various organizations that have security responsibilities and how those responsibilities are allocated across the seven-stage IT life cycle.
- Generally, cybersecurity operations involve leveraging processes and technology across departments to maintain the enterprise's security posture over time.
- For example, (IT) operations primarily support stages 4, 5, and 6; however, it also provides support and coordinates with the other departments and corresponding responsibilities.

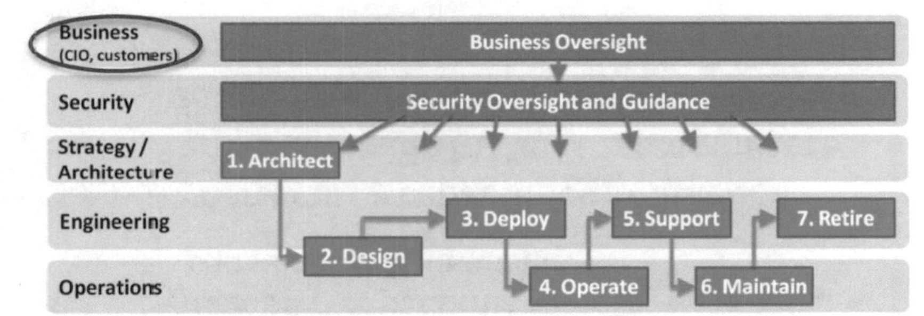

- ***Business (CIO, customers)***
  - Provides business oversight in regard to cybersecurity operations
  - Adjudicates risk decisions and security vs. operational trade-offs that involve tough calls on what level of risk is acceptable—that is, what is best for the business

Operational Responsibilities *(2 of 3)*

- ***Security (Cybersecurity)***
  - Generally under the Chief Information Security Officer (CISO)
  - Provides guidance across all departments
  - Responsible for ensuring security processes are in place and operating
  - May either perform cybersecurity processes itself or hold other teams responsible for them
  - Cybersecurity department often consists of teams to include the following:
    - ***Risk Management*** performs risk analysis and management.
    - ***Security Operations Center (SOC)*** provides for security monitoring and incident identification.

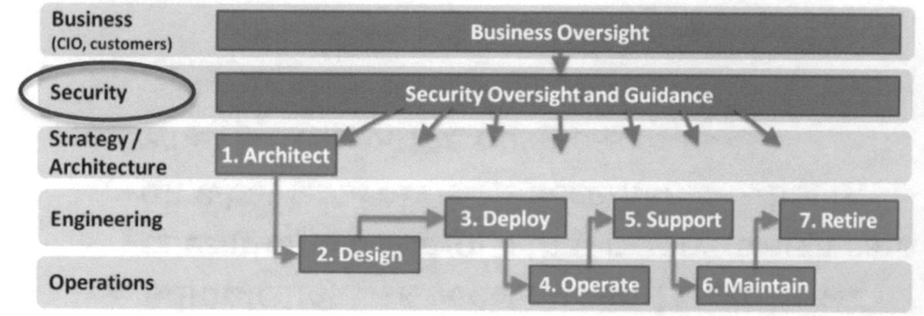

    - ***CyberIntrusion Response Team (CIRT)*** provides for incident response.
      - CIRT may also stand for "Cybersecurity Incident Response Team."
    - ***Compliance*** performs reporting for external compliance requirements.
  - Cybersecurity capabilities or functions frequently reside in the IT teams and are "dotted-line" accountable to the CISO office.

Operational Responsibilities *(3 of 3)*

- ***(IT) Strategy/Architecture***
  - Is involved in a number of security operational processes
  - Ensures system architectures are consistent with the enterprise strategy and overall architecture, including vendor and technology selection
  - From strategy and architecture perspectives, is responsible for risk management and policy review
- ***(IT) Engineering***
  - Has significant role in security operational processes to design security capabilities and controls that are effective and cost-effective
- ***(IT) Operations***
  - Is responsible for enterprise IT operations and has significant responsibility for security operational processes

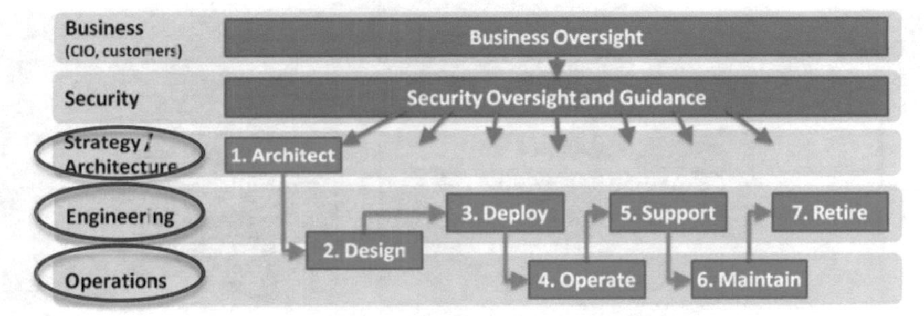

- However, cybersecurity department maintains oversight of the security operations and ensures security is not compromised for operational expediency
- This separation of responsibilities ensures that when there is a conflict between *cybersecurity operations* and *IT operations*, the conflict gets escalated to the CIO level so it can be resolved as a business decision

High-Level IT and Cybersecurity Processes *(1 of 13)*

Context

- CISO maintains a number of enterprise operational processes to maintain an effective cybersecurity posture.
- The following four *high-level* IT and cybersecurity processes set the context for this process discussion:
  - IT Operational Process
  - Risk Management Process
  - Vulnerability Management and Incident Response Process
  - Auditing and Deficiency Tracking Process

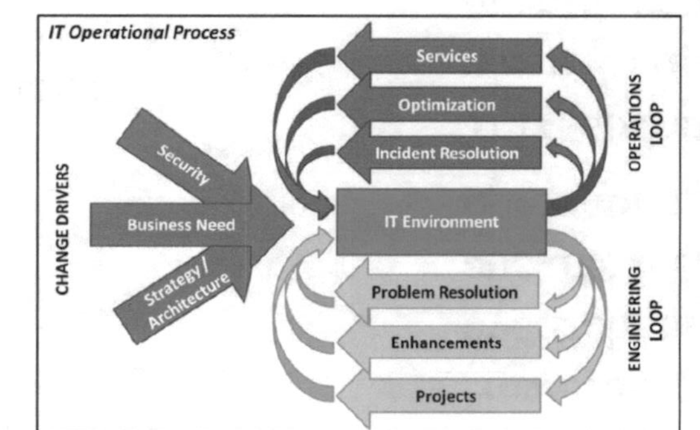

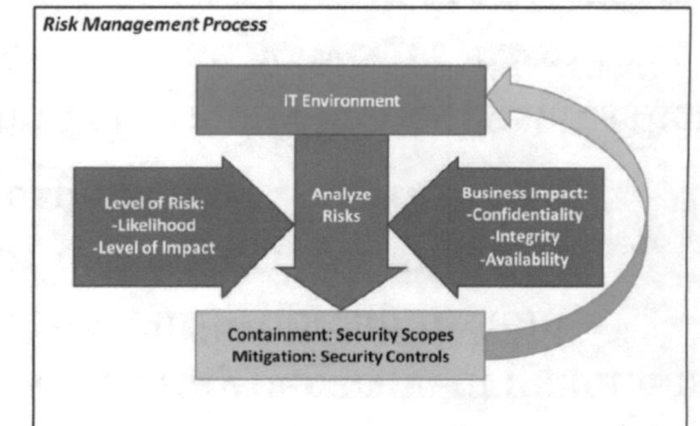

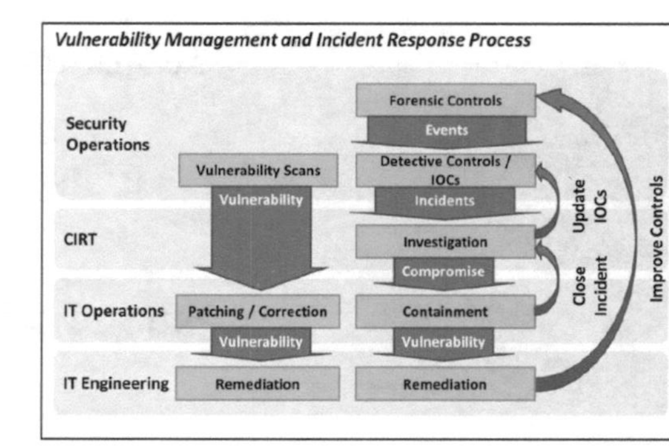

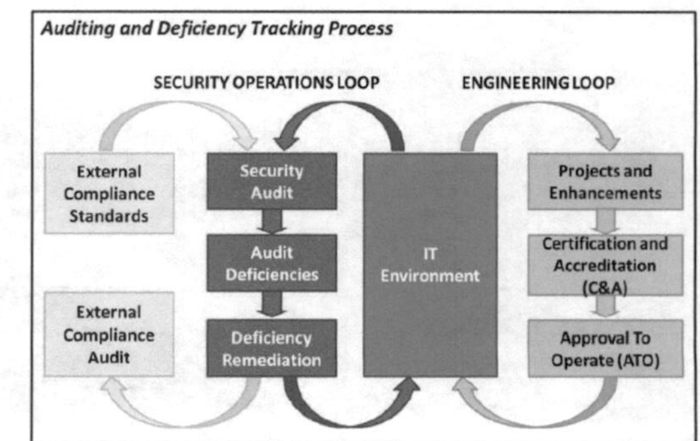

High-Level IT and Cybersecurity Processes *(2 of 13)*

IT Operational Process *(1 of 3)*

- The graphic depicts the fundamental IT operational process.
- ***Change drivers*** influence the IT environment via business need, security, strategy, and architecture.
- ***Business needs*** drive the execution of two "loops" that operate and change the IT environment, namely, the ***operations*** and ***engineering loops***.
- The IT operational process is at the core of many IT functions, including many of the security functions supporting IT operations and engineering.

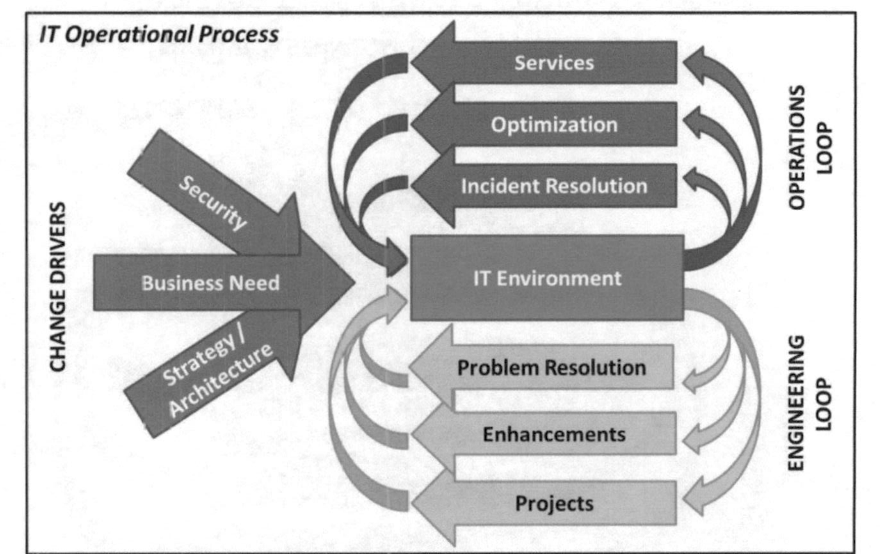

High-Level IT and Cybersecurity Processes *(3 of 13)*

IT Operational Process *(2 of 3)*

- ***Services***
  - Involves delivering IT services, both on a continuous basis and on an as-requested bases
  - Is most often associated with operations
- ***Optimization***
  - Involves performing relatively minor tasks and "tweaks" to improve the efficiency and effectiveness of IT operations
  - Can be a fine line between optimization and engineering changes
  - Usually involves changes that improve efficiency or performance without changing (1) service delivered, (2) software installation, or (3) addition or removal of servers or computers

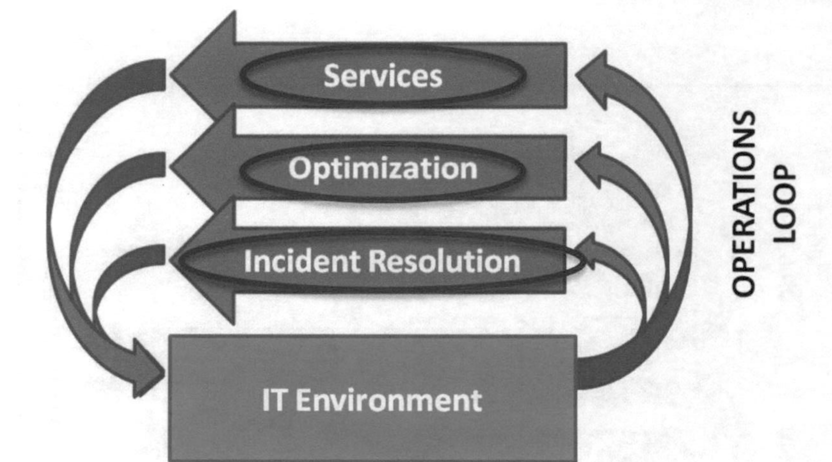

- ***Incident Resolution***
  - Involves solving problems with IT environment where a deficiency occurs that must be resolved to restore normal operations
  - May affect a single user or it may affect an entire system or service
  - IT operations captures incidents and tracks them through resolution

High-Level IT and Cybersecurity Processes *(4 of 13)*

IT Operational Process *(3 of 3)*

- ***Problem Resolution***
  - Responds to IT infrastructure problems
  - Addresses software bugs that impact operations and requires vendor support
  - IT operations identifies IT environment problems such as (1) system does not perform as designed or (2) flaws are identified in design that require redesign or re-engineering to correct them
- ***Enhancements***
  - Are relatively minor changes to IT environment to improve service quality, reduce cost, or enable new services
  - Are different from projects because they are generally performed within operations and maintenance budgets vs. a dedicated budget or formal schedule
  - Are low-cost efforts not requiring significant management oversight

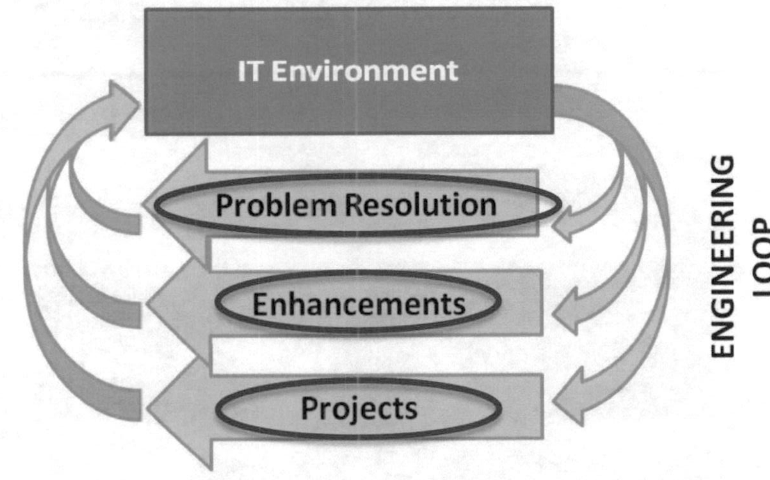

- ***Projects***
  - Are major changes to IT environment to deliver new services, retire legacy services, deploy new technologies, or make major upgrades to existing capabilities or services
  - Are distinct from enhancements because they have dedicated budgets, schedules, and management oversight to ensure they are successful

High-Level IT and Cybersecurity Processes *(5 of 13)*

Risk Management Process

- Is one of the most fundamental processes of the cybersecurity effort
- Requires collaboration among cybersecurity and other departments
- Identifies risks to the business, the consequences of those risks, and appropriate risk mitigations
- Starts with the business analyzing the potential risks to the IT environment assets in terms of confidentiality, integrity, and availability—*What are potential business impacts?*
- Evaluates identified risks with regard to their likelihood and level of impact
- Determines overall risk level for a specific threat (likelihood + impact)

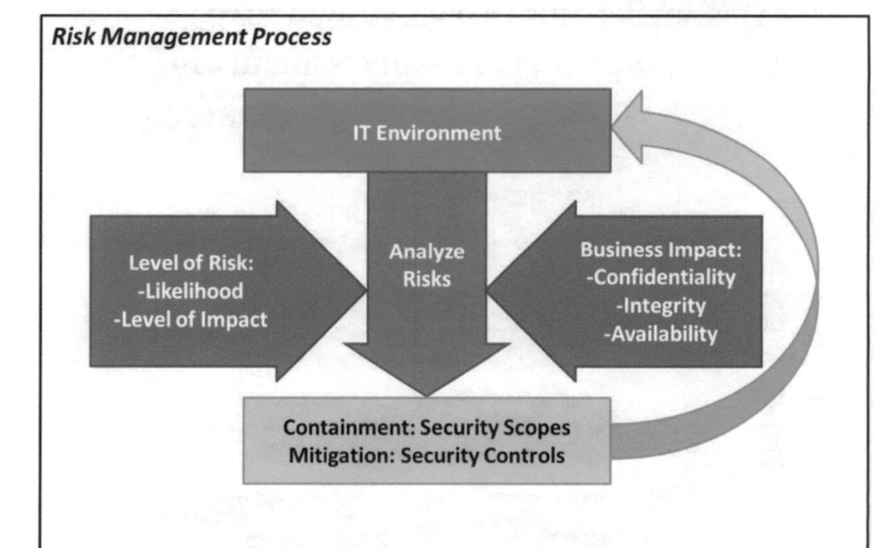

- Cybersecurity determines
  - containment (security scopes) for subsequent protection; and
  - mitigation (security controls) to reduce risk likelihood and impact.

High-Level IT and Cybersecurity Processes *(6 of 13)*

Vulnerability Management and Incident Response Process *(1 of 5)*

- Process is really two processes side-by-side:
  - Vulnerability Management (left-side track of graphic)
  - Incident Response (right-side track of graphic)
- ***Vulnerability Management***
  - Security Operations usually initiates process.
  - Security team ensures
    - vulnerability management process is performed; and
    - its quality and quantity are not compromised in the interest of other IT priorities.
  - Includes the following high-level steps:
    - Vulnerability Scans
    - Patching and Correction
    - Remediation
- ***Vulnerability Scans***
  - Performed by IT security against enterprise IT systems to identify vulnerabilities (missing patches, configuration failures)

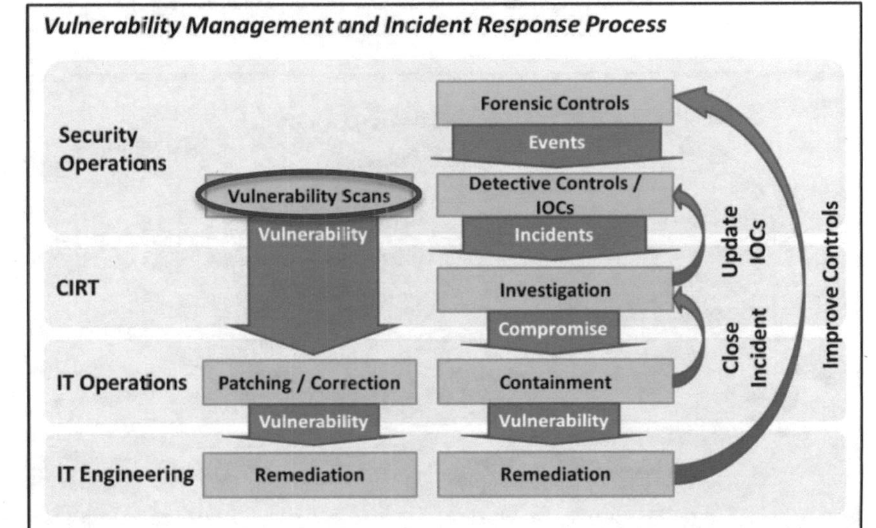

  - Performed on as many IT systems as possible by using automated tools
  - Scanning priority given to production and public-facing systems connected to the Internet
  - Produce a list of vulnerabilities and remediation recommendations

High-Level IT and Cybersecurity Processes *(7 of 13)*

Vulnerability Management and Incident Response Process (2 of 5)

- ***Patching / Correction***
  - Performed by IT operations
  - Involves following guidance from the vulnerability scans to remediate as much vulnerability as possible
  - Timely fixes occasionally hindered by compatibility issues, service level agreements, or other business
  - Can involve non-trivial system changes that are passed to engineering
- ***Remediation***
  - Performed by IT engineering when remediation requires redesign, re-engineering, or other engineering capabilities

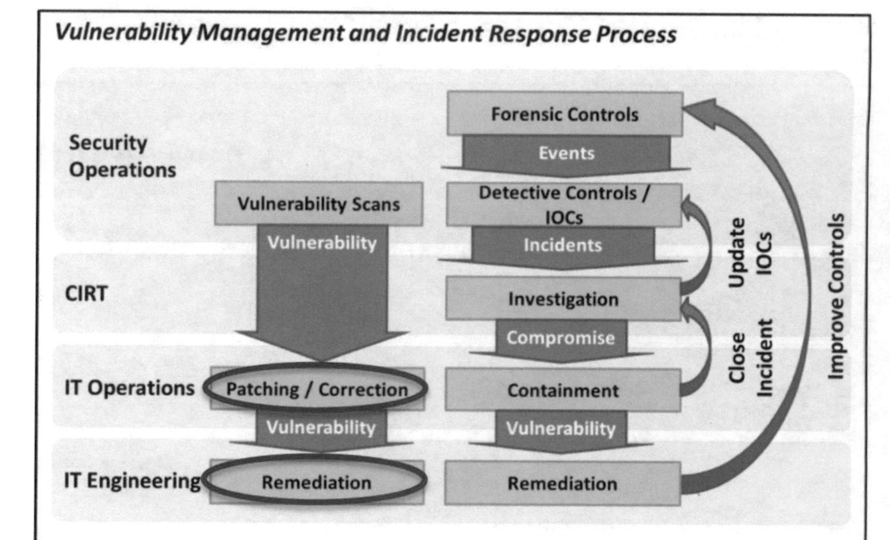

  - IT security tracks vulnerabilities that require engineering actions until
    - they are successfully mitigated;
    - compensating controls are put in place; and
    - risk is handled by business leadership.

High-Level IT and Cybersecurity Processes *(8 of 13)*

Vulnerability Management and Incident Response Process *(3 of 5)*

- ***Incident Response***
  - The right-side track of the graphic represents the incident response process, which is initiated by IT security.
  - Incident response is passed to IT operations and engineering until the situation can be resolved and remediated.
  - Remediation includes patching and sometimes re-engineering.
  - Incident response includes the following high-level steps:
    - Forensic Controls
    - Detective Controls and Indicators of Compromise (IOC)
    - Investigation
    - Containment
    - Remediation

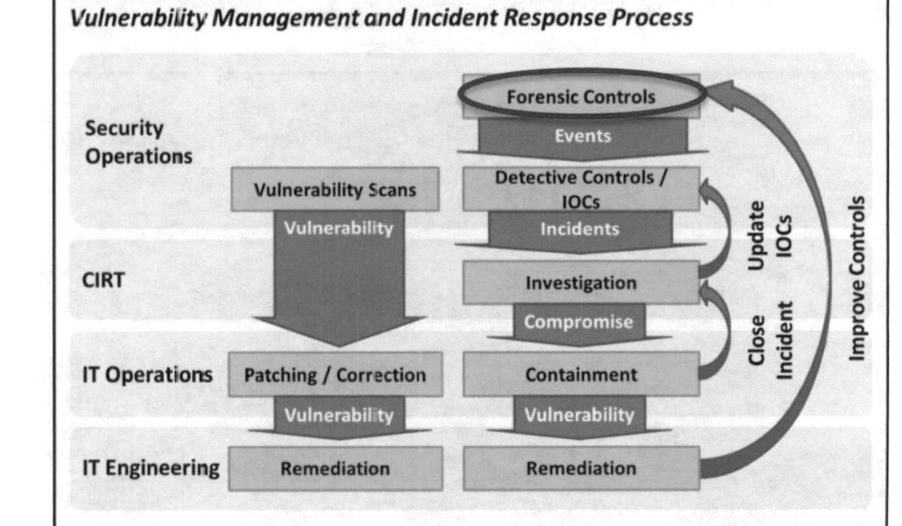

- ***Forensic Controls***
  - Logs enterprise events and makes them available for automated processing and review
  - Is starting point for the incident process since it is primarily from these events that incidents are identified

High-Level IT and Cybersecurity Processes *(9 of 13)*

Vulnerability Management and Incident Response Process *(4 of 5)*

- ***Detective Controls and Indicators of Compromise (IOCs)***
  - Applied to forensic controls and logs to identify incidents from the events
    - Pattern matches
    - Event cross-correlation
    - Multivariable analysis
    - Artificial intelligence
  - Will have some measure of false positives (control triggers that are false alarms) and false negatives (controls fail to trigger)
  - Designed to minimize both sets of negatives
  - Produce a list of incidents to be investigated
- ***Investigation***
  - Performed by CIRT
    - Determines extent of incident
    - Identifies computers, accounts, and networks

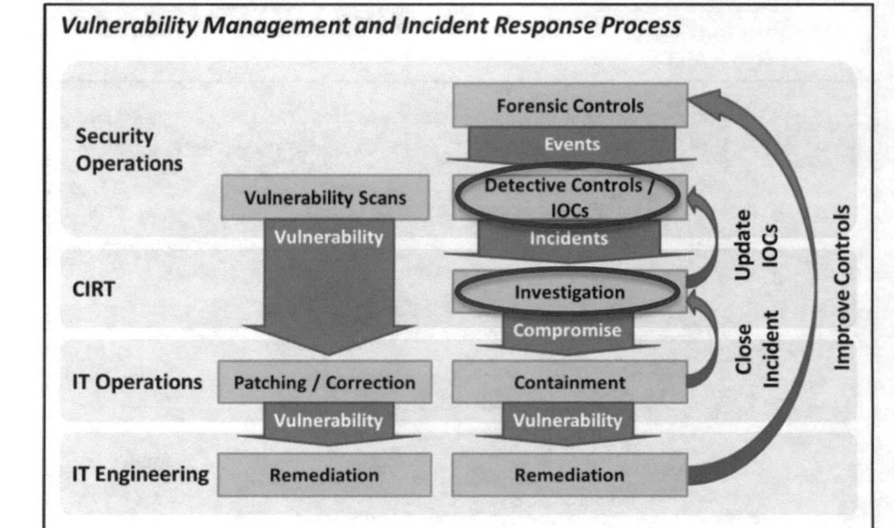

  - Generates IOCs to feed back into the detective controls to identify more computers, accounts, and networks
  - Provides output that is an assessment of compromise and its impact on enterprise

High-Level IT and Cybersecurity Processes *(10 of 13)*

Vulnerability Management and Incident Response Process *(5 of 5)*

- ***Containment***
  - Performed by IT operations team to contain the incident and restrict it from spreading further
  - Involves denying the adversary the use of compromised machines, accounts, and networks so they can no longer operate in the enterprise and the actual cleanup can begin
  - Produces a list of vulnerabilities that were exploited by the attackers and need to be remediated to prevent the same attack from occurring again
- ***Remediation***
  - Performed by IT engineering to harden the enterprise against future attacks

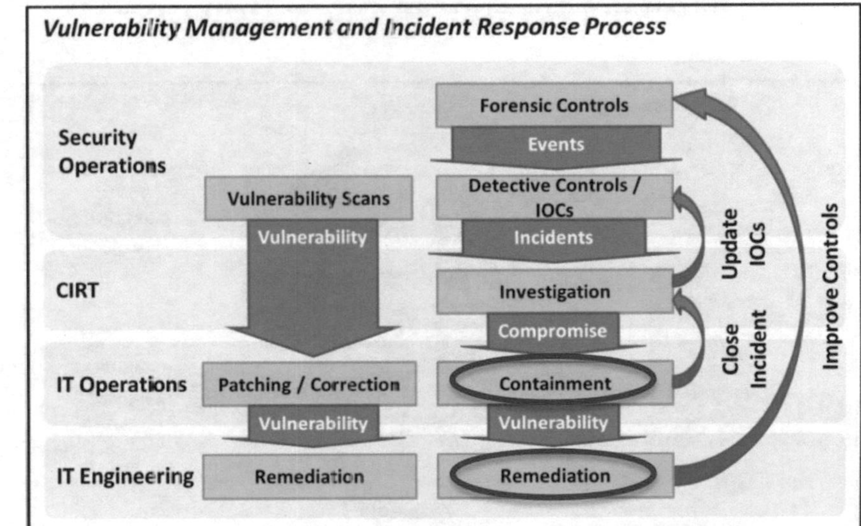

  - Can be quite significant
    - Strengthening preventive controls
    - Improving forensic, detective, and audit controls to improve detection, response, and future remediation
  - May result in cybersecurity projects lasting months or years after the initial incident is resolved

High-Level IT and Cybersecurity Processes *(11 of 13)*

Auditing and Deficiency Tracking Process (1 of 3)

- Involves two tracks that run somewhat in parallel and are subsets of the overall IT operations loop
  - Security operations loop (left-hand side track of graphic)
  - Engineering loop (right-hand side track of graphic)
- ***Security Operations Loop***
  - Security Operations Loop includes periodic audits of the IT environment to ensure security controls are present and operating as designed.
  - Security audits may be internally driven or externally driven.
  - Likely there may be multiple security audits over the course of a year to satisfy different audit requirements.
  - Security audits also may also be a part of general security maintenance, independent of regulatory compliance.

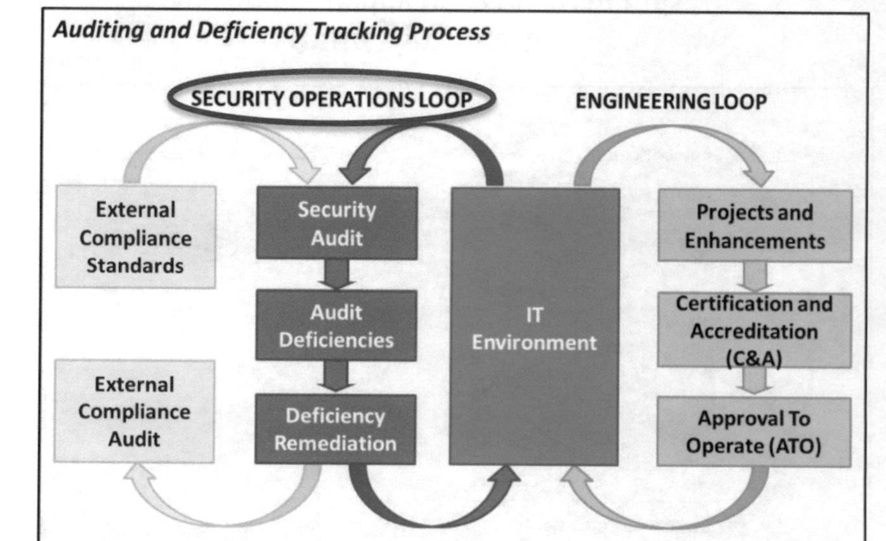

- Security audits include the following high-level steps:
  - External Compliance Standards
  - Security Audit
  - Audit Deficiencies
  - Deficiency Remediation
  - External Compliance Audit

High-Level IT and Cybersecurity Processes *(12 of 13)*

Auditing and Deficiency Tracking Process (2 of 3)

- ***External Compliance Standards***
  - These standards are inputs to audit for external compliance.
  - "Internal-use-only" audits use external standards, frameworks, or internal cybersecurity control documentation.
- ***Security Audit***
  - Initiated by security operations to examine the operation of controls
  - Triggered by schedule (monthly, quarterly, annual), an event, or external requirement
  - Examines cybersecurity controls to determine their effectiveness

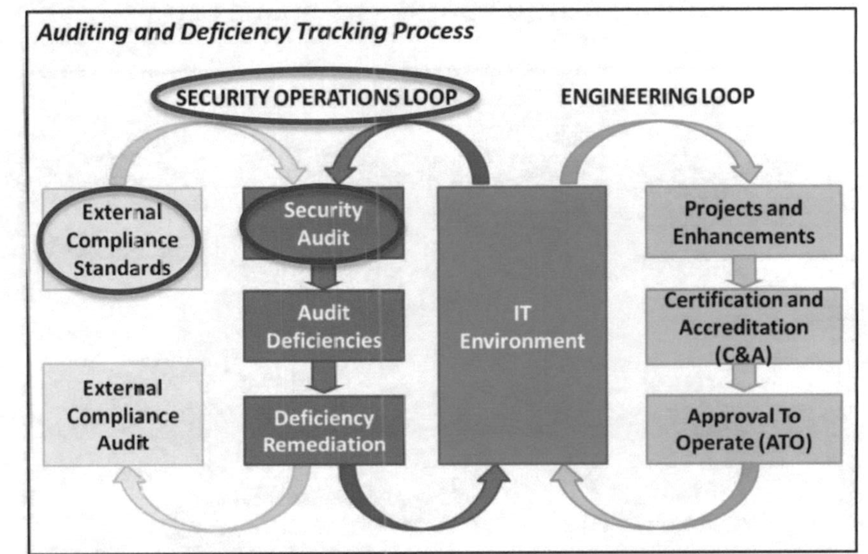

  - For preventive controls, audit involves testing to ensure behavior that is supposed to be blocked is actually blocked.
  - For detective and forensic controls, audit involves creating incidents to ensure incidents are detected or sampling logs to search for expected incident detections.

High-Level IT and Cybersecurity Processes *(13 of 13)*

Auditing and Deficiency Tracking Process *(3 of 3)*

- ***Audit Deficiencies***
  - Deficiencies are identified via audit process and formally tracked through resolution.
  - When identified by external auditors, deficiencies often require explanation or follow-up testing.
  - Sometimes deficiencies are not really defects or are the result of control operating as designed, but not doing what auditors expect.
- ***Deficiency Remediation***
  - Remediation corrects deficiencies so that controls function as designed.
  - Sometimes audits reveal design deficiencies requiring engineering involvement or non-trivial investment to correct.
- ***External Compliance Audit***
  - Results are obtained from the audit process as required.

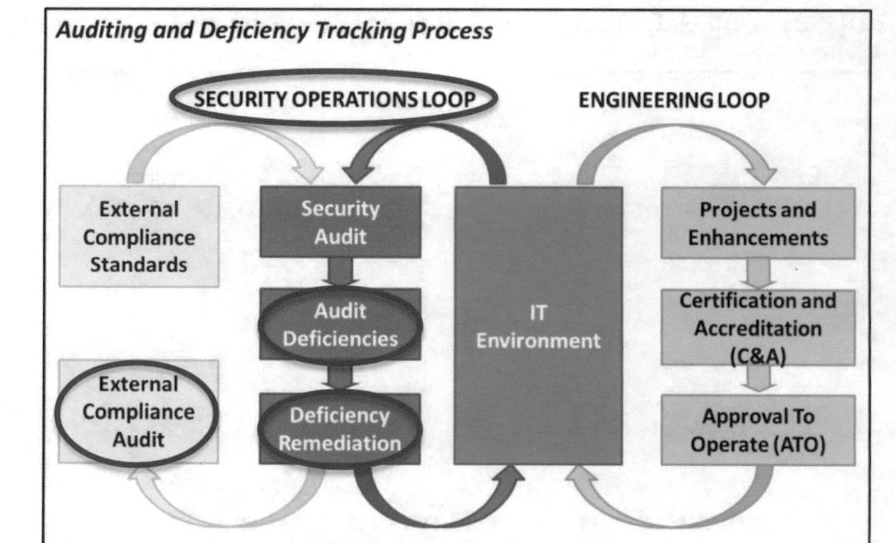

  - With a well-designed control framework, it is possible to conduct a single internal cybersecurity audit that generates results satisfying multiple external compliance requirements, even when external audits use different control frameworks.

Operational Processes and Information Systems

Context

- The previous section described four high-level IT and cybersecurity processes:
  - IT Operational Process
  - Risk Management Process
  - Vulnerability Management and Incident Response Process
  - Audit and Deficiency Tracking process
- The above four high-level processes can be further decomposed into 17 cybersecurity operational processes, as shown in the the graphic.
- This section *introduces* these 17 cybersecurity operational processes that are essential to the proper operation of enterprise cybersecurity.
- Appendix B contains a *detailed* description of the processes.

Cybersecurity Operational Processes

- Privileged Account Activity Audit
- Account and Access Periodic Recertification
- Password and Key Management
- Vulnerability Scanning, Tracking, and Management
- Patch Management and Deployment
- Security Monitoring
- All-Hazards Emergency Preparedness Exercises
- Cyberintrusion Response
- Asset Inventory and Audit
- Change Control
- Configuration Management Database Recertification
- Supplier Reviews and Risk Assessments
- Policies and Policy Exception Management
- Project and Change Security Reviews
- Risk Management
- Control Management
- Auditing and Deficiency Tracking

Operational Processes *(1 of 6)*

- ***Privileged Account Activity Audit***
  - Audit involves manually auditing system administration activities for the most sensitive accounts.
  - Not all administrative accounts need to be subject to this level of scrutiny.
  - Accounts that have enterprisewide access and the ability to turn off or bypass security logging should be subject to audit and other controls to detect any attempt at misuse.
- ***Account and Access Periodic Recertification***
  - This process involves managing accounts and accesses throughout their life cycles, from creation through assignment and removal of permissions, periodic recertification, and retirement.
  - It is important that recertification or a similar method be used to ensure accounts and access that are no longer needed are removed in a timely fashion.

Cybersecurity Operational Processes

- Privileged Account Activity Audit
- Account and Access Periodic Recertification
- Password and Key Management
- Vulnerability Scanning, Tracking, and Management
- Patch Management and Deployment
- Security Monitoring
- All-Hazards Emergency Preparedness Exercises
- Cyberintrusion Response
- Asset Inventory and Audit
- Change Control
- Configuration Management Database Recertification
- Supplier Reviews and Risk Assessments
- Policies and Policy Exception Management
- Project and Change Security Reviews
- Risk Management
- Control Management
- Auditing and Deficiency Tracking

Operational Processes *(2 of 6)*

- ***Password and Key Management***
  - This process involves managing enterprise keys throughout their life cycle, from creation through storage, rotation, recertification, and retirement.
  - Organizational passwords (those used for service accounts and external accounts) should be treated as keys and stored securely throughout their life cycle.
- ***Vulnerability Scanning, Tracking, and Management***
  - This process involves periodically scanning enterprise IT systems for vulnerabilities.
  - Identified vulnerabilities are tracked until they are patched or otherwise remediated.
  - Vulnerabilities that cannot be easily mitigated may result in enterprise risks that are tracked long-term.
- ***Patch Management and Deployment***
  - This process involves patching enterprise systems to resolve security vulnerabilities, resolve operational problems, or stay current on vendor product patches.

Cybersecurity Operational Processes

- Privileged Account Activity Audit
- Account and Access Periodic Recertification
- Password and Key Management
- Vulnerability Scanning, Tracking, and Management
- Patch Management and Deployment
- Security Monitoring
- All-Hazards Emergency Preparedness Exercises
- Cyberintrusion Response
- Asset Inventory and Audit
- Change Control
- Configuration Management Database Recertification
- Supplier Reviews and Risk Assessments
- Policies and Policy Exception Management
- Project and Change Security Reviews
- Risk Management
- Control Management
- Auditing and Deficiency Tracking

Operational Processes *(3 of 6)*

- ***Patch Management and Deployment (continued)***
  - This process has two main tracks: (1) routine patch deployments and (2) emergency patching to resolve urgent problems.
  - Emergency patching requires management oversight to adjudicate the risk of patching without adequate testing vs. the security or operational risk of waiting for the normal process.
- ***Security Monitoring***
  - Security Monitoring involves monitoring security systems for alerts related to potential security incidents.
  - Alerts feed into the incident response process when incidents are identified and confirmed.
  - There is an important feedback loop where false alerts are identified and alerts are constantly tuned to reduce false alerts.
- ***All-Hazards Emergency Preparedness Exercises***
  - This process involves testing emergency preparedness processes in context of potential hazards, including natural disasters, man-made situations, accidents, and cyberintrusions.

Cybersecurity Operational Processes

- Privileged Account Activity Audit
- Account and Access Periodic Recertification
- Password and Key Management
- Vulnerability Scanning, Tracking, and Management
- Patch Management and Deployment
- Security Monitoring
- All-Hazards Emergency Preparedness Exercises
- Cyberintrusion Response
- Asset Inventory and Audit
- Change Control
- Configuration Management Database Recertification
- Supplier Reviews and Risk Assessments
- Policies and Policy Exception Management
- Project and Change Security Reviews
- Risk Management
- Control Management
- Auditing and Deficiency Tracking

Operational Processes *(4 of 6)*

- ***All-Hazards Emergency Preparedness Exercises (continued)***
  - Goal is to establish a robust set of emergency procedures that can be used to handle a variety of situations affecting enterprise information systems, facilities, or people.
- ***Cyberintrusion Response***
  - Involves responding to cyberintrusions when they occur and tracking them through to containment and ultimate remediation.
- ***Asset Inventory and Audit***
  - This process involves inventorying enterprise IT assets to ensure IT properly accounts for all assets.
  - Assets that are not tracked cannot be secured.
- ***Change Control***
  - Ensures enterprise changes are properly authorized and reviewed prior to implementation
  - Includes formal approvals to operate new IT systems and tracking enterprise risks associated with vulnerabilities that are not remediated prior to deployment of operational system
  - May also be able to detect unauthorized changes so they can be investigated

Cybersecurity Operational Processes

- Privileged Account Activity Audit
- Account and Access Periodic Recertification
- Password and Key Management
- Vulnerability Scanning, Tracking, and Management
- Patch Management and Deployment
- Security Monitoring
- All-Hazards Emergency Preparedness Exercises
- Cyberintrusion Response
- Asset Inventory and Audit
- Change Control
- Configuration Management Database Recertification
- Supplier Reviews and Risk Assessments
- Policies and Policy Exception Management
- Project and Change Security Reviews
- Risk Management
- Control Management
- Auditing and Deficiency Tracking

Operational Processes *(5 of 6)*

- ***Configuration Management Database Re-Certification***
  - Involves periodically reviewing configuration documentation to identify discrepancies between enterprise system configuration records and actual configurations deployed and operating
  - Ensures identified discrepancies are properly reviewed and remediated
- ***Supplier Reviews and Risk Assessments***
  - Involve reviewing the IT supply chain to assess cybersecurity risk from a supplier perspective
  - Ensure mitigations are in place to protect against potentially compromised service providers or products
- ***Policies and Policy Exception Management***
  - Involves maintaining the enterprise cybersecurity policies and standards
  - Involves tracking and managing exceptions to those policies and standards when they are required

Cybersecurity Operational Processes

- Privileged Account Activity Audit
- Account and Access Periodic Recertification
- Password and Key Management
- Vulnerability Scanning, Tracking, and Management
- Patch Management and Deployment
- Security Monitoring
- All-Hazards Emergency Preparedness Exercises
- Cyberintrusion Response
- Asset Inventory and Audit
- Change Control
- Configuration Management Database Recertification
- Supplier Reviews and Risk Assessments
- Policies and Policy Exception Management
- Project and Change Security Reviews
- Risk Management
- Control Management
- Auditing and Deficiency Tracking

Operational Processes *(6 of 6)*

- ***Project and Change Security Reviews***
  - These reviews involve modifying the IT project and change processes to include security reviews and approvals prior to going live.
  - Process is tricky to get right so security is involved but does not become an obstacle to progress.
- ***Risk Management***
  - Involves identifying risks to the enterprise IT environment and its assets, and then identifying controls to mitigate those risks
- ***Control Management***
  - Involves maintaining the enterprise security controls to ensure they stay relevant over time and effectively utilize available security technologies and capabilities
- ***Auditing and Deficiency Tracking***
  - Involves auditing the IT environment to find cybersecurity controls' deficiencies and tracking those deficiencies until they can be resolved or remediated

Cybersecurity Operational Processes

- Privileged Account Activity Audit
- Account and Access Periodic Recertification
- Password and Key Management
- Vulnerability Scanning, Tracking, and Management
- Patch Management and Deployment
- Security Monitoring
- All-Hazards Emergency Preparedness Exercises
- Cyberintrusion Response
- Asset Inventory and Audit
- Change Control
- Configuration Management Database Recertification
- Supplier Reviews and Risk Assessments
- Policies and Policy Exception Management
- Project and Change Security Reviews
- Risk Management
- Control Management
- Auditing and Deficiency Tracking

Supporting Information Systems *(1 of 5)*

Context

- The graphic lists supporting information systems enabling the cybersecurity operational processes.
- Depending upon enterprise needs and its level of complexity and maturity, systems may be simple (spreadsheets, word processing documents, or paper files) or sophisticated (major enterprise applications with supporting databases).
- The cybersecurity department is responsible for ensuring these information systems are present and operating within the IT environment.
- The remainder of this section provides a brief explanation of each system and its significance to enterprise security.

Information Systems

- Administrator Audit Trail
- Accounts and Permissions
- Password and Key Vault
- Vulnerability Database
- Disaster Recovery Plans
- Incident Records
- Config Mgt Database
- Asset Database
- Security Policies
- Policy Exceptions
- ATO Records
- Enterprise Risks
- Security Controls
- Security Deficiencies

Supporting Information Systems *(2 of 5)*

- ***Administrator Audit Trail***
  - Involves tracking privileged administrator activities so such activities can be audited
- ***Accounts and Permissions***
  - Will most likely be obtained from supporting information systems, such as enterprise directories and identity/access management systems
- ***Password and Key Vault***
  - This information system tracks organizational accounts and passwords.
  - It is ideal for this information to be maintained using highly secure vault technology that provides access controls and audit trails; less than ideal is using a spreadsheet to track this information.
  - These organizational accounts/passwords are the "keys to the kingdom" and should be correspondingly well-protected.
- ***Vulnerability Database***
  - Tracks vulnerabilities identified through vulnerability scans and other automated methods
  - Tracks vulnerabilities against the associated IT assets
  - Tracks business decisions associated with what is done for each vulnerability

Supporting Information Systems *(3 of 5)*

- ***Disaster Recovery Plans***
  - Plans include contingency plan for a wide range of disaster scenarios to include natural disasters and severe cybersecurity events.
  - IT staff members need to now where the plans are and when/how to use them.
- ***Incident Records***
  - Track enterprise cybersecurity incidents
  - Identify the assets involved in the incidents, threats that caused the incidents, vulnerabilities exploited, and containment and mitigation performed to resolve the incidents
  - Track the risks associated with attack, and help with understanding patterns of threats and vulnerabilities affecting the enterprise
- ***Configuration Management (CM) Database***
  - This information system ties into the asset database to keep track of high-level configuration attributes of systems.
  - CM database and the asset database are essential for identifying IT assets and understanding the business impact of cybersecurity events involving IT assets.
- ***Asset Database***
  - Is most likely to be automated
  - Keeps track of the IT assets in the enterprise
  - Tracks vendors, servers, computers, networking equipment, software, and so on

Supporting Information Systems *(4 of 5)*

- ***Security Policies***
  - These policies represent enterprise security policies and standards, which are the foundation of risk management.
- ***Policy Exceptions***
  - This information system addresses the fact that "for every rule there is an exception."
  - Exceptions to policies and standards need to be tracked so they can be periodically re-evaluated and eventually mitigated.
  - Otherwise, the enterprise runs the risk of exceptions becoming the rule and policies becoming meaningless.
- ***Approval to Operate (ATO) Records***
  - When new IT systems are placed online, it is important to document their risks.
  - This information system records the business decision to operate the system.
  - System owners document and retain the performance, cost, and risk of system operation.
  - The records should be periodically revisited as standards and threats evolve.

Supporting Information Systems *(5 of 5)*

- ***Enterprise Risks***
  - Tracks risks in terms of threats and consequences to confidentiality, integrity, and availability (CIA)
    - For example, a risk might state, "An attacker steals credit card data and causes financial damages and a regulatory violation."
    - Mitigations then center on deploying security controls to reduce the probability or impact of the risk.
- ***Security Controls***
  - This information system tracks the enterprise's active security controls and is essential to being able to validate security so it can be audited for compliance.
  - A challenge is that security control lists cannot be so large that no one can comprehend them.
  - The goal is to a strike the balance of having a controls list that is sufficiently high level while containing sufficient detail to be auditable.
- ***Security Deficiencies***
  - Tracks security deficiencies identified in the course of security audits through to remediation
  - Tracks risks associated with deficiencies
  - Tracks deficiencies against the affected assets and security controls

Functional Area Operational Objectives *(1 of 13)*

Context

- This section describes the operational objectives of enterprise cybersecurity, grouped by functional area.
- The graphic illustrates how the functional areas, operational processes, and supporting information systems can be unified to achieve successful enterprise cybersecurity operations.
- Each functional area's primary operational objective is to maintain its capabilities to deliver the enterprise's preventive, detective, forensic, and audit controls.
- Most functional areas host one or more operational processes that are supported by one or more supporting information systems.

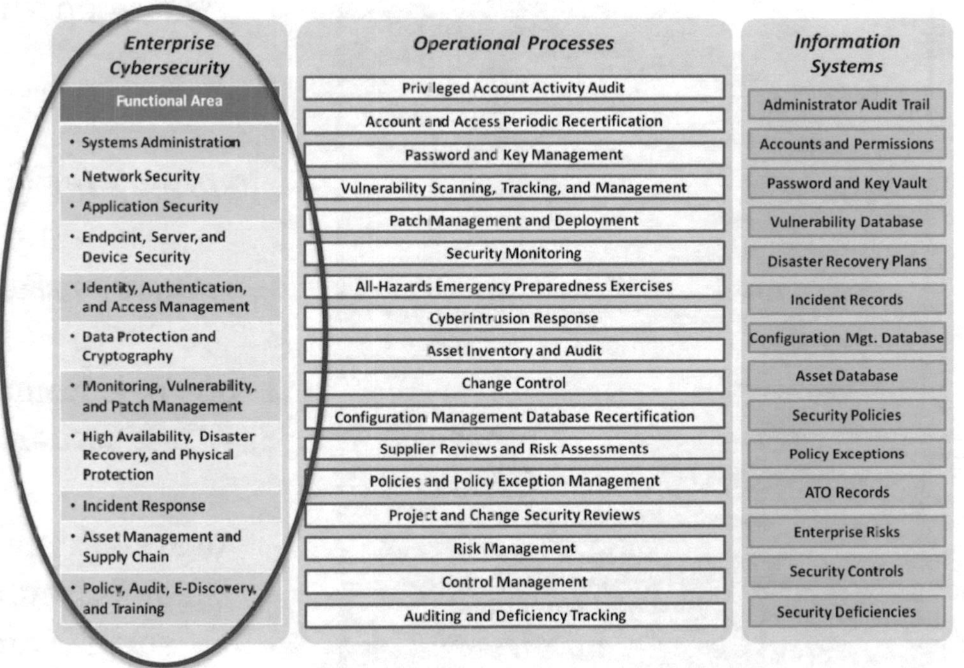

- The rest of this section describes the functional area operational objectives.

Functional Area Operational Objectives *(2 of 13)*

- ***Systems Administration***
  - Has primary operational of ensuring that secure systems administration capabilities are operating to protect systems administration channels from exploitation by attackers who gain access to enterprise networks
  - Uses a combination of preventive, detective, forensic, and audit controls—all working together through automated and manual processes
  - Hosts the following operational process: *Privileged Account Activity Audit*
  - Accesses the following information systems: (1) *Administrator Audit Trail* and (2) *Incident Records*
- ***Network Security***
  - Has primary operational objective of preventing, detecting, and documenting illicit activity targeting the enterprise
  - Achieves objective by using a large number of capabilities to provide preventive, detective, forensic, and audit controls affecting communications among enterprise computers and the Internet

Cybersecurity Functional Areas
• Systems Administration
• Network Security
• Application Security
• Endpoint, Server, and Device Security
• Identity, Authentication, and Access Management
• Data Protection and Cryptography
• Monitoring, Vulnerability, and Patch Management
• High Availability, Disaster Recovery, and Physical Protection
• Incident Response
• Asset Management and Supply Chain
• Policy, Audit, E-Discovery, and Training

Functional Area Operational Objectives *(3 of 13)*

- ***Network Security (continued)***
  - Needs to provide the following high-level capabilities to accomplish primary objective:
    - A ***perimeter*** that connects the enterprise to the Internet while also protecting vulnerable systems inside the enterprise from external exploitation
    - ***Segmentation*** within the enterprise to protect business functions with different security needs from each other and to contain incidents
    - ***Inspection*** of external access to internal systems to identify unauthorized access or malicious network traffic
    - ***Support*** for incident investigation and response so incidents can be quickly analyzed, contained, and remediated when they occur
- ***Application Security***
  - Has primary operational objective of preventing, detecting, and documenting illicit activity in enterprise applications
  - Focuses on the capabilities, limitations, vulnerabilities, and security controls specific to particular enterprise applications, including e-mail, web servers, databases, and custom-built software

Cybersecurity Functional Areas
• Systems Administration
• Network Security
• Application Security
• Endpoint, Server, and Device Security
• Identity, Authentication, and Access Management
• Data Protection and Cryptography
• Monitoring, Vulnerability, and Patch Management
• High Availability, Disaster Recovery, and Physical Protection
• Incident Response
• Asset Management and Supply Chain
• Policy, Audit, E-Discovery, and Training

Functional Area Operational Objectives *(4 of 13)*

- ***Endpoint, Server, and Device Security***
  - Has primary operational objective of preventing, detecting, and documenting attacks and compromises of enterprise computers and computing devices
  - Focuses on the operating systems and software installed on these systems
  - Hardens above systems so they are difficult to compromise, detects compromises when they occur, and documents compromises and security control activities so they can be investigated after the fact
  - Involves keeping the capabilities supporting it operational and maintaining those capabilities according to vendor specifications and best practices
- ***Identity, Authentication, and Access Management***
  - Has primary operational objective of managing identities and accesses within the enterprise throughout their life cycle—from instantiation through retirement
  - Involves regular re-certification so unused identities and accesses can be de-provisioned in a timely fashion

Cybersecurity Functional Areas
• Systems Administration
• Network Security
• Application Security
• Endpoint, Server, and Device Security
• Identity, Authentication, and Access Management
• Data Protection and Cryptography
• Monitoring, Vulnerability, and Patch Management
• High Availability, Disaster Recovery, and Physical Protection
• Incident Response
• Asset Management and Supply Chain
• Policy, Audit, E-Discovery, and Training

Functional Area Operational Objectives *(5 of 13)*

- ***Identity, Authentication, and Access Management (continued)***
  - Frequently uses automation (such as identity management technology and enterprise directories), but not required, especially in smaller organizations
  - Is successful if it results in an effective role-based access control and "least-privilege" provisioning with minimum amount of unnecessary accounts and accesses lingering and posing a cybersecurity threat
  - Hosts the following operational process: *Account and Access Periodic Recertification*
  - Accesses the following information systems: *Accounts and Permissions*
- ***Data Protection and Cryptography***
  - Has primary objective of protecting, detecting, and documenting activities surrounding enterprise data and keys
  - Is data-focused and includes technologies such as digital rights management, digital watermarking, and pattern recognition
  - Tracks data flows within the enterprise
    - What data is going where
    - How data is protected

Cybersecurity Functional Areas
• Systems Administration
• Network Security
• Application Security
• Endpoint, Server, and Device Security
• Identity, Authentication, and Access Management
• Data Protection and Cryptography
• Monitoring, Vulnerability, and Patch Management
• High Availability, Disaster Recovery, and Physical Protection
• Incident Response
• Asset Management and Supply Chain
• Policy, Audit, E-Discovery, and Training

Functional Area Operational Objectives *(6 of 13)*

- ***Data Protection and Cryptography (continued)***
  - Includes cryptographic capabilities: encryption, signature, authentication, key management, password management (since passwords are also keys)
  - Is successful if it results in effective use of data protection and cryptographic capabilities to protect the enterprise data, detect misuse of that data, and document data and cryptographic activities for investigation and audit as required
  - Hosts the following operational process: *Password and Key Management*
  - Accesses the following information systems: *Password and Key Vault*
- ***Monitoring, Vulnerability, and Patch Management***
  - Primary operational objective is to operate the enterprise security detective controls on an ongoing basis.
  - Many of the major functions required to maintain and operate the security systems fall under this functional area.

Cybersecurity Functional Areas
• Systems Administration
• Network Security
• Application Security
• Endpoint, Server, and Device Security
• Identity, Authentication, and Access Management
• Data Protection and Cryptography
• Monitoring, Vulnerability, and Patch Management
• High Availability, Disaster Recovery, and Physical Protection
• Incident Response
• Asset Management and Supply Chain
• Policy, Audit, E-Discovery, and Training

Functional Area Operational Objectives *(7 of 13)*

- ***Monitoring, Vulnerability, and Patch Management (continued)***
  - Major functions include the following:
    - ***Patch management***—maintaining enterprise information systems in a secure state
    - ***Vulnerability management***—detecting and remediating vulnerabilities when they occur
    - ***Security monitoring***—monitoring the environment on an ongoing basis to detect intrusions when they occur
  - Is successful if operation results in effective monitoring and security maintenance on an ongoing basis.
  - Functional area can include scans for rogue computers and network connections, penetration tests if they are regularly scheduled, and advanced detection capabilities such as honeypots and honeynets.
  - If an enterprise has a security operations center (SOC), its operation falls under this functional area.
  - Functional area hosts the following operational processes: (1) *Vulnerability Scanning, Tracking, and Management*, (2) *Patch Management and Deployment*, and (3) *Security Monitoring*.

Cybersecurity Functional Areas
• Systems Administration
• Network Security
• Application Security
• Endpoint, Server, and Device Security
• Identity, Authentication, and Access Management
• Data Protection and Cryptography
• Monitoring, Vulnerability, and Patch Management
• High Availability, Disaster Recovery, and Physical Protection
• Incident Response
• Asset Management and Supply Chain
• Policy, Audit, E-Discovery, and Training

Functional Area Operational Objectives *(8 of 13)*

- ***Monitoring, Vulnerability, and Patch Management (continued)***
  - Functional area accesses the following information systems: (1) *Vulnerability Database*, (2) *Incident Records*, (3) *Configuration Management Database*, and (4) *Enterprise Risks*.
- ***High Availability, Disaster Recovery, and Physical Protection***
  - Has primary operational objective to be able to recover rapidly from operational disruption through redundancy, backups, and physical protection of data, equipment, personnel, and facilities.
  - Functional area includes not only the IT technologies required to meet service level agreements, but also more dramatic capabilities required to recover from natural and man-made disasters.
  - *Resiliency* is the operative term for this functional area:
    - Makes business resistant to all types of adversity
    - Gives enterprise tools and options when things go wrong and failures occur

Cybersecurity Functional Areas
• Systems Administration
• Network Security
• Application Security
• Endpoint, Server, and Device Security
• Identity, Authentication, and Access Management
• Data Protection and Cryptography
• Monitoring, Vulnerability, and Patch Management
• High Availability, Disaster Recovery, and Physical Protection
• Incident Response
• Asset Management and Supply Chain
• Policy, Audit, E-Discovery, and Training

Functional Area Operational Objectives *(9 of 13)*

- ***High Availability, Disaster Recovery, and Physical Protection (continued)***
  - Capabilities are designed and combined in an integrated fashion so they can be leveraged to support each other through
    - shared procedures;
    - shared technologies; and
    - common training.
  - This functional area provides disaster recovery capabilities that are critical to robust incident response against advanced threats.
  - This functional area provides physical protection and access to information systems to prevent physical destruction and compromise of information systems.
  - Successful operation results in the enterprise meeting its service-level agreements on an ongoing basis and having robust capabilities to protect and recover from losses of data, systems, personnel, or facilities.
  - Functional area hosts the following operational process: *All-Hazards Emergency Preparedness Exercises.*
  - Functional area accesses the following information systems: *Disaster Recovery Plans.*

Cybersecurity Functional Areas
• Systems Administration
• Network Security
• Application Security
• Endpoint, Server, and Device Security
• Identity, Authentication, and Access Management
• Data Protection and Cryptography
• Monitoring, Vulnerability, and Patch Management
• High Availability, Disaster Recovery, and Physical Protection
• Incident Response
• Asset Management and Supply Chain
• Policy, Audit, E-Discovery, and Training

Functional Area Operational Objectives *(10 of 13)*

- ***Incident Response***
  - Has primary operational objective of preparing for and responding to security incidents when they occur
  - Includes threat analysis to gain intelligence on what types of incidents should be detected and prepared for
  - Is important for this functional area to have methods for obtaining external assistance and "surge support" when it is required as a fixed staff can quickly be overwhelmed
  - Is successful if it results in security incidents being quickly identified, investigated, contained, and remediated within the enterprise environment
  - Hosts the following operational process: *Cyberintrusion Response*
  - Accesses the following information systems: (1) *Vulnerability Database* and (2) *Incident Records*
- ***Asset Management and Supply Chain***
  - Has primary operational objective of tracking the assets, configurations, technologies, and vendors used in the enterprise IT environment throughout the asset life cycle

Cybersecurity Functional Areas
• Systems Administration
• Network Security
• Application Security
• Endpoint, Server, and Device Security
• Identity, Authentication, and Access Management
• Data Protection and Cryptography
• Monitoring, Vulnerability, and Patch Management
• High Availability, Disaster Recovery, and Physical Protection
• Incident Response
• Asset Management and Supply Chain
• Policy, Audit, E-Discovery, and Training

Functional Area Operational Objectives *(11 of 13)*

- ***Asset Management and Supply Chain (continued)***
  - Includes maintaining information to (1) ensure the secure procurement of IT assets, (2) track the assets throughout their life cycle, and (3) ensure their secure destruction at the end of that life cycle
  - Is responsible for a number of IT operational databases critical not only to enterprise security, but also to successful enterprise IT operations in general
  - Is successful if it results in the enterprise being able to track its vendors, technologies, assets, their configuration, and changes through their life cycle
  - Hosts the following operational process: (1) *Asset Inventory and Audit*, (2) *Change Control*, (3) *Configuration Management Database Recertification*, and (4) *Supplier Reviews and Risk Assessments*
  - Accesses the following information systems: (1) *Configuration Management Database*, (2) *Asset Database*, (3) *Enterprise Risks*, and (4) *Security Controls*

Cybersecurity Functional Areas
• Systems Administration
• Network Security
• Application Security
• Endpoint, Server, and Device Security
• Identity, Authentication, and Access Management
• Data Protection and Cryptography
• Monitoring, Vulnerability, and Patch Management
• High Availability, Disaster Recovery, and Physical Protection
• Incident Response
• Asset Management and Supply Chain
• Policy, Audit, E-Discovery, and Training

Functional Area Operational Objectives *(12 of 13)*

- ***Policy, Audit, E-Discovery, and Training***
  - Has primary operational objective of operating the office of the CISO or director of cybersecurity and ensuring the performance of the scheduled and unscheduled cybersecurity activities within the enterprise
  - Includes
    - Risk management functions
    - Development of security policy and architecture
    - Performance of security screening and training for employees and contractors
    - Reporting on security status and posture
    - Audit of security functions
    - Answering e-discovery requests
    - External coordination and reporting on cybersecurity status, posture, and compliance
  - Operates many of the administrative cybersecurity information systems that do not logically fit within one of the other functional areas (such as security awareness)

Cybersecurity Functional Areas
• Systems Administration
• Network Security
• Application Security
• Endpoint, Server, and Device Security
• Identity, Authentication, and Access Management
• Data Protection and Cryptography
• Monitoring, Vulnerability, and Patch Management
• High Availability, Disaster Recovery, and Physical Protection
• Incident Response
• Asset Management and Supply Chain
• Policy, Audit, E-Discovery, and Training

Functional Area Operational Objectives *(13 of 13)*

- ***Policy, Audit, E-Discovery, and Training (continued)***
  - Is successful if it results in a coherent cybersecurity policy, posture, training, good coordination across other functional areas, and the cybersecurity program representing itself effectively to external auditors, evaluators, and regulatory bodies
  - Hosts the following operational process: (1) *Policies and Policy Exception Management*, (2) *Project and Change Security Reviews*, (3) *Risk Management*, and (4) *Audit and Deficiency Tracking*
  - Accesses the following information systems: (1) *Incident Records*, (2) *Security Policies*, (3) *Policy Exceptions*, (4) *Approval to Operate (ATO) Records*, (5) *Enterprise Risks*, (6) *Security Controls*, and (7) *Security Deficiencies*

Cybersecurity Functional Areas
• Systems Administration
• Network Security
• Application Security
• Endpoint, Server, and Device Security
• Identity, Authentication, and Access Management
• Data Protection and Cryptography
• Monitoring, Vulnerability, and Patch Management
• High Availability, Disaster Recovery, and Physical Protection
• Incident Response
• Asset Management and Supply Chain
• Policy, Audit, E-Discovery, and Training

CHAPTER 6

Enterprise Cybersecurity and the Cloud

S. E. Donaldson et al., *Enterprise Cybersecurity Study Guide*, https://doi.org/10.1007/978-1-4842-3258-3_6

Overview

- This chapter examines how the cloud is transforming the way businesses everywhere approach building IT solutions.
  - Rather than hiring technical staff to build data centers and configure servers, businesses are outsourcing these functions "to the cloud."
  - Businesses are procuring applications, platforms, and computing capacity.
- Cloud enables new levels of business agility.
  - Small startups have access to computing and application capabilities that were once considered "supercomputing."
- Transition to the cloud has its own set of challenges.
  - Cybersecurity practitioners still struggle to effectively secure on-premise computers and servers.
  - Cybersecurity protection has transformed from one of building high walls into something requiring more nuance and a new type of understanding.
- This chapter describes how an enterprise manages and operates cybersecurity when its computing and applications are in the cloud.

Topics

- Introducing the Cloud
- Cloud Protection Challenges
  - Developer Operations (DevOps)
  - Developer Security Operations (DevSecOps)
  - Scopes and Account Management
  - Authentication
  - Data Protection and Key Management
  - Logging, Monitoring, and Investigations
  - Reliability and Disaster Recovery
  - Scale and Reliability
  - Contracts and Agreements
- Planning Enterprise Cybersecurity for the Cloud

Introducing the Cloud *(1 of 4)*

Context

- NIST provides an industry-recognized definition of "the cloud" in their special publication 800-145.
- NIST also provides a discussion of challenges with cloud environments in their special publication 800-146.
- The graphic depicts a version of the NIST reference model.[1]

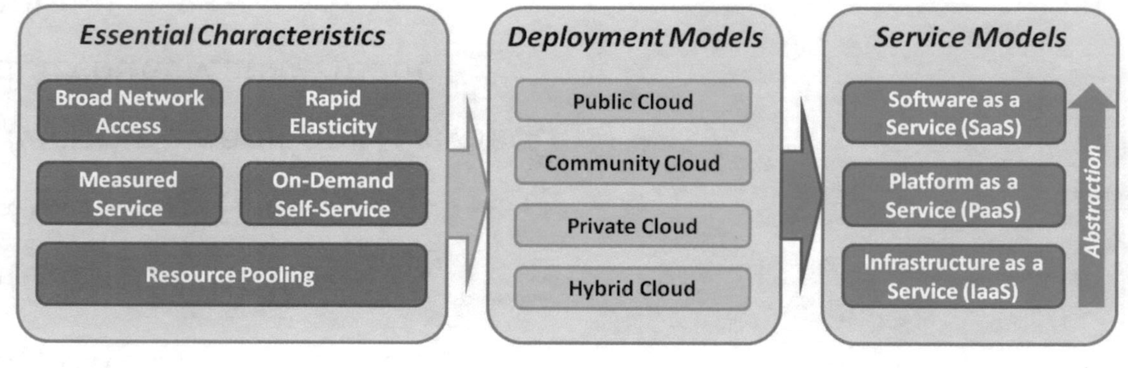

[1]National Institute of Standards and Technology Special Publication 800-145, Peter Mell and Timothy Grance, September 2011.

Introducing the Cloud (2 of 4)

Five Essential Characteristics

- ***Broad Network Access***
  - Means services are delivered via a network—most often the Internet
  - Is accessible from a wide range of network-connected devices, such as via a web browser
- ***Rapid Elasticity***
  - Means resources and capabilities can be increased or decreased quickly in response to changing demands
  - Presents what appears to be almost unlimited capacity to the end user
- ***Measured Service***
  - Refers to all aspects of service delivery—including storage, bandwidth, computing capacity, and application activity
  - Is measured for reporting and potential charge-back to both the provider and the customer

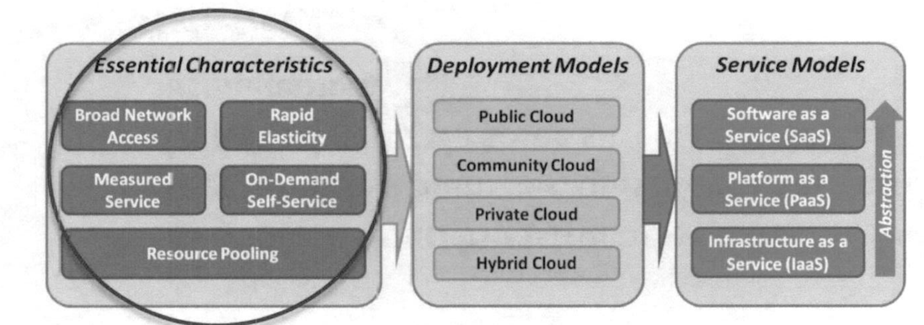

- ***On-Demand Self-Service***
  - Means the customer of the cloud service can unilaterally provision capabilities and capacity without requiring significant human interaction or coordination
- ***Resource Pooling***
  - Means all of these capabilities are delivered from a shared resource pool that supports multiple customers in a multitenant arrangement
  - Ensures capabilities are isolated among customers so individual customers only have visibility of resources allocated to them

Introducing the Cloud *(3 of 4)*

Deployment Models

- ***Public Cloud***
  - Is a cloud solution provided by a service provider for the general public
  - Has no restrictions on who may procure and use its services
- ***Community Cloud***
  - Is a cloud solution provided for a restricted community of organizations, usually as a shared service or jointly contracted arrangement
  - May be provided by a public cloud provider on its public infrastructure, but with certain restrictions on its configuration and authorized users
- ***Private Cloud***
  - Is a cloud solution built and operated by a single organization for its exclusive use

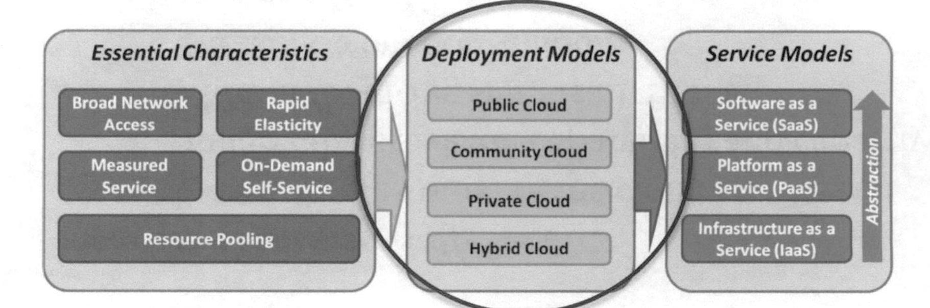

  - May locate cloud infrastructure on the organization's premises, or it may be provided by a third party via some sort of contractual arrangement
- ***Hybrid Cloud***
  - Is a combination of two or more of the previous arrangements, bound together using technology or standards so they function as an integrated system

Introducing the Cloud *(4 of 4)*

Service Models

- ***Software as a Service (SaaS)***
  - SaaS is the highest level of abstraction, where the entire software application—such as sales management, financial system, or database—is delivered "on demand" to the customer over the network from the provider.
  - Customers simply accesses the application using a web browser or other network client application.
- ***Platform as a Service (PaaS)***
  - PaaS is a lower level of abstraction, where the service provider delivers the underlying computing platform, such as operating systems.
  - Customers have full control to install their own applications and data onto the platform.

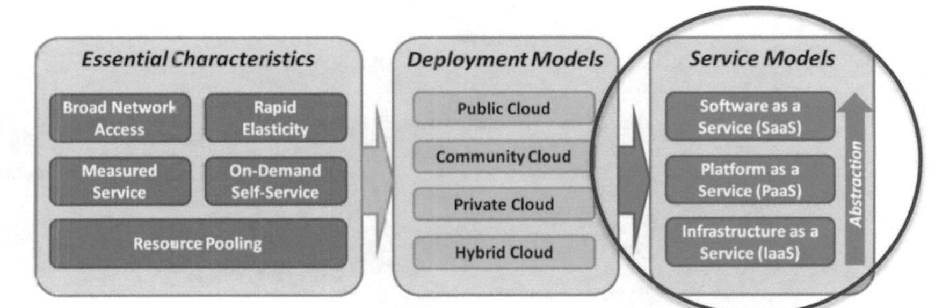

- ***Infrastructure as a Service (IaaS)***
  - IaaS is the lowest level of abstraction, where the cloud provider delivers the computing infrastructure—including storage, hardware, and network connectivity.
  - Customers have full freedom to install and configure whatever operating systems, application software, and data onto that infrastructure that they please.

Cloud Protection Challenges *(1 of 11)*

Context

- Moving enterprise IT to the cloud may or may not improve cybersecurity compared to operating it in a private network and datacenter.
- Improving cybersecurity with cloud computing depends, in part, on enterprise size and security maturity vs. the cloud provider's size and security maturity.
- Cloud providers have the same challenges securing their systems that enterprises have.
  - Shifting schedules and priorities
  - Resource constraints
  - Finding and retaining talented security professionals
- Cloud providers have several advantages.
  - A consolidated, standardized infrastructure
  - Ability to "design once and replicate many" for security solutions
  - Simplicity due to standardized offerings and centralized management

Cloud Protection Challenges *(2 of 11)*

High-Level Cybersecurity Considerations

	Small Customer	*Large Customer*
Small Cloud Provider	When both organizations are small, security will likely be slightly better at the cloud provider than the customer, due to standardization across multiple customers and the provider's own motivation to protect its reputation and grow its business.	A small cloud provider likely will not be able to secure data as well as the customer can on its own. On the other hand, cloud provider may be considerably cheaper and more flexible than customer's own services.
Large Cloud Provider	A small customer will most likely see a security increase with a large cloud provider, compared to the size and sophistication of the security controls they could build and maintain themselves.	Security is likely a toss-up between large cloud provider and large customer. Both have the ability to secure data well. Provider has the advantage of scale and standardization, while customer has the advantage of knowing which data is most critical and the motivation to protect it effectively.

- Small cloud providers have many of the same strengths and challenges as a small business.
- Likewise, large cloud providers have many of the same strengths and challenges as a large business.
- However, large customer enterprises doing business with small cloud providers should be cautious because the business cybersecurity may be better than the cloud provider's cybersecurity.

- Moving to the cloud presents a number of challenges
  - Developer operations (DevOps) and developer security operations (DevSecOps)
  - Scopes and account management
  - Authentication
  - Data protection and key management
  - Logging, monitoring, and investigations
  - Reliability and disaster recovery
  - Scale
  - Contracts and agreements

Cloud Protection Challenges *(3 of 11)*

Developer Operations (DevOps) and Developer Security Operations (DevSecOps) *(1 of 2)*

- ***DevOps and DevSecOps***
  - DevOps and DevSecOps provide an agile, cloud-based environment for software developers.
  - Software developers are responsible for the life cycle of their products.
    - Software development ➤ Path to production ➤ Operations
  - New IT paradigms dramatically increase the speed and tempo of service updates and fixes to problems.
- ***DevOps***
  - DevOps makes server operating systems and system configuration "part of the code" and manages them in the same manner and with the same tools and procedures as the other software DevOps is maintaining.
  - Security becomes one more part of the software codebase, and changes to security configurations are coded into the scripts used to build the computing environment and configure the servers.
- ***DevSecOps***
  - Cybersecurity becomes more about code and is integrated into systems in a cloud environment.
    - Scripts used to build servers
    - Scripts used to configure servers
    - Scripts used to install applications
    - Actual software code running on the applications
  - Cybersecurity team members may have to update their skill sets to build scripts.

Cloud Protection Challenges *(4 of 11)*

Developer Operations (DevOps) and Developer Security Operations (DevSecOps) *(2 of 2)*

- This paradigm shift also means cybersecurity team members may have to change their methods of incentivizing developers to comply with security policies.
- Since anyone with a cloud account can stand up a server, install an application, and start running code on the platform, cybersecurity may not be able to use traditional "gates" to review cybersecurity and enforce cybersecurity policies.
- Instead, the cybersecurity team may have to switch to a more passive method:
  - Review cybersecurity after the fact and then provide feedback to developers and management on significant cybersecurity deficiencies
- Rather than being a "gatekeeper," cybersecurity may need to be more of a "scorekeeper," giving cloud development teams feedback via "security scores" and "penalty flags" so business leaders can identify and consider cybersecurity concerns.

Cloud Protection Challenges *(5 of 11)*

Scopes and Account Management

- Challenge
  - In a cloud environment, developers can access the cloud and create hundreds of servers, platforms, or applications quickly.
  - If the developer's credentials are compromised, the same servers, platforms, or application instances can all be compromised or destroyed as equally quickly.
  - In a complex environment, questions of scope can become complicated quickly.
- Response
  - Use concept of "Blast Radius" to limit the potential compromise caused by a single developer account.
  - "Network of Trust" organizes cloud accounts and services so a single compromise cannot bring down the entire enterprise (in other words, "watertight compartments").
  - Compartmentalization may include the following:
    - Isolation by a business unit or development team
    - Separation of sandbox, development, and production environments
    - Separation of primary and alternate sites
    - Isolation of high-availability nodes
- By ensuring different people and teams manage different scopes, the enterprise can guard against a single breach or failure being disastrous.

Cloud Protection Challenges *(6 of 11)*

Authentication

- Cloud service is often delivered over an open network, and users and administrators must access the system and services through the network.
  - Authentication credentials are the only things protecting their access.
  - Enterprise may be only one username and password from the entire service being compromised.
  - To protect against this possibility, the enterprise needs the strongest possible protection for administrative accounts, including network-based protections and multistep or multifactor authentication, if such protections are available.
- Another authentication challenge is account life cycle and access management.
  - Some cloud providers allow federated authentication to enable users to use their enterprise credentials to access the cloud service.
  - Federated authentication can allow the enterprise to manage permissions and access controls from within its enterprise directory.
  - Federated authentication can increase cybersecurity risk if enterprise credentials are compromised.
  - Balanced solutions may involve using federation in conjunction with strong authentication.

Cloud Protection Challenges *(7 of 11)*

Data Protection and Key Management

- When using a cloud service, data is residing on someone else's computer in someone else's facility.
- Protection of data is at the mercy of someone else's enterprise operational procedures and supply chain.
- Data stored in a cloud provider's environment needs to be protected.
  - Data encryption is possible, but must be carefully designed and deployed.
  - Data needs to be encrypted to protect against an attacker, but it needs to be accessible by legitimate users.
  - Encryption keys need to be positioned so they are accessible only for legitimate users.
  - When customers rely on cloud provider's encryption, customers need to ask about provider's key rotation plan and processes for key escrow and recovery.
- When analyzing cloud key management, customers should ask the following questions:
  - *What cryptographic algorithms and key strengths does the provider support?*
  - *Does the cloud provider have the ability to generate and store cryptographic keys for its customers?*
  - *Does the cloud provider have the ability to use keys provided by the customer?*
  - *What capabilities does the cloud provider have to rotate keys on an automatic or semiautomatic basis?*
  - *What support does the cloud provider have for an enterprise re-key scenario?*
- Enterprises must balance their design of key management strategies carefully.
  - If keys to the encrypted data are lost, the data is as good as lost.
  - Data needs to be protected without being endangered.

Cloud Protection Challenges *(8 of 11)*

Logging, Monitoring, and Investigations

- Logging, monitoring, and investigations have to do with the enterprise's ability to record, detect, and investigate cybersecurity incidents within its cloud provider services.
  - Cloud customers need the ability to investigate cybersecurity incidents within their cloud services.
  - Cloud providers need to provide logging, monitoring, and investigation capabilities.
  - Potential lack of availability of logs sharply limits the customer's ability to create detective controls on its cloud services.
  - Incident detection and response start with logging of activity in the cloud environment so incidents can be detected.
  - Cloud customers should understand what cloud provider logs are available and how those logs record activity.
- Customers should ask questions about key attributes:
  - *Do logs record all activity in the cloud environment from the cloud provider's perspective?*
  - *Are activities performed through application programming interfaces logged so customers can match up calls made from their software with activities performed by the cloud provider?*
  - *Do the logs differentiate activities that are performed programmatically through application interfaces from activities that are performed manually through consoles or web interfaces?*
  - *Do the logs differentiate between activities performed on behalf of a server or application and activities performed on behalf of a person?*
- Good logging may be an afterthought for cloud providers and is a potential risk customers should consider.

Cloud Protection Challenges *(9 of 11)*

Reliability and Disaster Recovery

- Cloud providers are highly motivated to provide the best possible service.
  - Service outages can have dire consequences to provider reputation and business.
  - Providers have complex, interconnected systems undergoing constant changes and upgrades and a relatively small number of people manage environment changes.
  - Providers are subject to the same challenges of human frailty and fallibility as any organization.
  - Providers will make mistakes.
- Cloud providers have the IT challenges of a normal enterprise (people changing roles, hardware failing, software patching and upgrading, and constant pressure to reduce costs and increase revenue).
- Providers manage challenges on their schedule and not their customer's schedule (quarterly financial closing) and timing can be an issue (North America vs. Europe).
  - Provider changes could be problematic for certain customers.
  - Providers will not be aware of customer activities, such as quarterly financial closings.
- When the provider has an outage, customers may have little recourse and there may be few provider penalties.
  - Cloud contracts may provide little protection or remuneration in the event of service outages.
  - Customers need to think about extended outages and provider failures.
- Customers should have solid contingency plans.

Cloud Protection Challenges *(10 of 11)*

Scale and Reliability

- ***Scale***
  - Scale is a fundamental factor for cloud services.
  - Service consolidation into a cloud provider can be more efficient.
    - Bus more efficient than a car.
    - Train more efficient than a bus.
  - Large-scale systems are less agile than smaller-scale systems.
    - Car starts up faster than bus.
    - Bus starts up faster than train.
  - Scale of provider's customer base can take cloud provider longer to troubleshoot and repair simple problem because provider is simultaneously solving problem for tens, hundreds, or thousands of customers.
- ***Reliability***
  - In general, the provider is more reliable and stable than on-premise enterprise systems.
  - When providers fail, they can fail spectacularly.
  - Unplanned outages that would result in only an hour of downtime for an enterprise on its own—hardly a business disaster—can result in ten times more downtime for a provider.
  - Without considerable contingency capabilities, an enterprise may be down until provider recovers.
- Enterprise cloud architecture should be designed to be resilient.
  - Multiple providers at multiple locations
  - Unexpected failures handled without losing transactions

Cloud Protection Challenges *(11 of 11)*

Contracts and Agreements

- By using a cloud provider, an enterprise takes technical problems—storage management, network configuration, maintenance—and makes them contractual in nature.
- Providers write contracts to provide desired services while protecting themselves from liability to the greatest extent possible allowed by market and regulations.
- Enterprise needs to ensure contract provides desired features and protections.
- Enterprise needs to have some contingency plans without dependencies on cloud providers.
- Enterprise needs to perform risk assessments and consider contingency, insurance, and disaster recovery options to fill in gaps between enterprise needs and provider services.
- Questions to consider:
  - *What happens if the cloud provider simply disappeared from the face of the earth?*
  - *Will the cloud provider have all of the enterprise's customer, financial, or billing information?*
  - *Will the enterprise be able to restore this data from backups to an operational system or to another cloud service provider?*

Planning Enterprise Cybersecurity for the Cloud *(1 of 11)*

Systems Administration

How is an enterprise's cybersecurity program affected by its use of cloud services?

- Systems administrators frequently do their work using regular usernames and passwords, just like ordinary users.
- Secure systems administration may be severely impaired when using cloud services.
- To compensate for this potential situation, there are some actions an enterprise can do to protect its cloud systems administration:
  - If available, employ two-factor authentication for privileged accounts.
  - If not available, change passwords frequently and review reports of failed logon attempts.
  - Use network protection where privileged accounts can only be used from certain IP addresses or address ranges, or via a virtual private network connection.
  - Regularly audit privileged account activity logs for unusual patterns or malicious activity.

Planning Enterprise Cybersecurity for the Cloud *(2 of 11)*

Network Security

How is an enterprise's cybersecurity program affected by its use of cloud services?

- Cloud providers often provide basic firewalling or load balancing for systems, but few additional networks security services are offered.
- Provider has own network security infrastructure for protection and detection; it is unusual for customers to get visibility into provider's network security operations, events, alerts, or logs.
- Limitations may hamper customer's ability to do investigations requiring analysis of network traffic.

- Customer considerations include
  - network isolation for specific enterprise systems;
  - the fact that PaaS and IaaS may provide greater security options than SaaS;
  - host-based firewalls, intrusion detection/prevention, packet capture, and signature detection; and
  - network-based access controls and access to clients in certain countries.

Planning Enterprise Cybersecurity for the Cloud *(3 of 11)*

Application Security

How is an enterprise's cybersecurity program affected by its use of cloud services?

- With SaaS, application-level security configuration is up to the cloud provider.
- With PaaS and IaaS, the customer has the ability to put in place application-level security, which can include extensive detection capabilities.
- Provider will have access to customer's platform and storage. Customer should maintain tight control over the "path to production" to detect any unauthorized software changes.
- Every aspect of system configuration can become a script managed by the developers (see DevOps).
- Such scripts include network configuration, endpoint security, identify and authentication configuration, and so on.
- Enterprise needs to consider how to manage code, code configuration controls, and software path to production.

Planning Enterprise Cybersecurity for the Cloud *(4 of 11)*

Endpoint, Server, and Device Security

How is an enterprise's cybersecurity program affected by its use of cloud services?[2]

- With ***SaaS***, customers do not have control over how cloud provider configures and protects its servers, but customers can ask about protection.
- With ***PaaS***, customers have more ability to configure server security, but options may be limited and lead to certain risks.
- With ***IaaS***, customer security options are almost unlimited regarding hosts and operating systems.

- Major constraint is the fact that the servers reside on the Internet and may be accessible from the customer's internal network and security services.
- Enterprise can compensate for this situation by connecting cloud systems to the enterprise network via a point-to-point, always-on, virtual private network.
- Such connectivity gives systems access to the enterprise's internal services (that is, security). Be careful connectivity does not become a backdoor.

[2]This functional area is primarily about server security.

Planning Enterprise Cybersecurity for the Cloud *(5 of 11)*

Identity, Authentication, and Access Management

How is an enterprise's cybersecurity program affected by its use of cloud services?

- Public cloud services are connected to the Internet; user accounts are used to connect to these services.
- Protection of the services is primarily through identity, authentication, and access management of the user accounts.
- Multistep or multifactor authentication provides a dramatic increase in security over username and password authentication.
- Federated authentication simplifies authentication and the account management process, but it can add risk if accounts are compromised.
- Another security concern involves identity life cycle and de-provisioning.
  - *When people leave the organization, who removes their accounts and permissions on cloud services?*
- In the absence of an automated process, periodic manual audits should be performed to clean up orphan accounts and excessive permissions.

Planning Enterprise Cybersecurity for the Cloud *(6 of 11)*

Data Protection and Cryptography

How is an enterprise's cybersecurity program affected by its use of cloud services?

- Data protection is critical for cloud services; it is difficult to "get it right."
- Enterprises need to carefully review the cloud provider.
  - Cryptography standards, algorithms, and key strengths to help ensure encryption is not obsolete or inadequate—annual audits required
  - Key management: understand where encryption keys are stored, how they are protected, how they are accessed, and how they are rotated

- Hardware Security Module (HSM) services protecting cryptographic keys can be extremely effective at ensuring physical protection of keys, but they require significant expertise to deploy and maintain properly.
- Cryptographic keys need to be backed up to avoid a disaster recovery situation where the enterprise cannot decrypt its data.
- Digital signatures can be used for data integrity (detecting unauthorized changes to logs, transactions, and so on), but not for data confidentiality (stealing data).

Planning Enterprise Cybersecurity for the Cloud *(7 of 11)*

Monitoring, Vulnerability, and Patch Management

How is an enterprise's cybersecurity program affected by its use of cloud services?

- Functional area is largely depends on whether the cloud service is SaaS, PaaS, or IaaS.
- With ***SaaS***, monitoring, vulnerability, and patch management are entirely up to the cloud provider and should be transparent to the customers; customers have few options.
- With ***PaaS***, customers have control over the applications running on the platform; have the ability and responsibility to monitor, scan, and patch the applications to maintain their security.
- With ***IaaS***, customers have full control over system at the operating systems level and above, and they have the ability to monitor, scan, and patch the systems.
- Customers need thorough logs of all activities against the cloud environment (user account, originating system, request interface).
- For monitoring, provider may be able to feed some logs into customer systems for the sake of monitoring and incident response.
- Providers may make application interfaces so customers can connect to cloud service logs programmatically.

Planning Enterprise Cybersecurity for the Cloud *(8 of 11)*

High Availability, Disaster Recovery, and Physical Protection

How is an enterprise's cybersecurity program affected by its use of cloud services?

- Cloud provider determines the physical location and protection of cloud resources.
- Customers may have option to select cloud provider facilities.
- Customers can protect themselves.
  - Customers ***must*** have a solid disaster recovery plan for worst-case scenario, in which provider disappears and takes their infrastructure, software, applications and data.
  - Worst-case scenario plan must include
    - recovery point objectives (RPO) (how recently data is backed up); and
    - recovery time objectives (RTO) (how long it would take to stand up contingency operations).
  - Customers may choose to implement high-availability solutions that span multiple cloud providers.
- *Resiliency* should be a central tenet to a customer's cloud solution design.

Planning Enterprise Cybersecurity for the Cloud *(9 of 11)*

Incident Response

How is an enterprise's cybersecurity program affected by its use of cloud services?

- Even with cloud services, there is still a need for an incident response capability.
- Monitoring and investigating cloud services for security incidents can be considerably more difficult than with a traditional network perimeter.
- Detection capabilities should cover the most expected attack scenarios against the cloud service, particularly, stolen credentials and compromised servers; logs should record cloud service activity.
- Enterprise's Security Operations Center (SOC) should
  - have access to cloud service logs; and
  - practice common incident scenarios.
- Enterprises should meet periodically with cloud provider to discuss threat scenarios, incidents the provider is seeing, and joint protections.

Planning Enterprise Cybersecurity for the Cloud *(10 of 11)*

Asset Management and Supply Chain

How is an enterprise's cybersecurity program affected by its use of cloud services?

- Cloud services transform a technology challenge—standing up and deploying storage, computing, operating systems, and applications—into a supply chain challenge.
- Challenge involves establishing a contract with a supplier to deliver a service and manage assets associated with service in the context of cybersecurity that mitigates the enterprise's major risks.
- Enterprise should treat cloud service provider contract as a risk management exercise where cybersecurity risks are considered in terms of the cybersecurity functional areas.
  - *What protections are provided?*
  - *How do the protections fit into the enterprise's overall cybersecurity plan? Is there a worst-case disaster recovery plan?*
- Enterprise needs to perform cost-benefit analysis on security trade-offs and other related costs associated with breaches.

Planning Enterprise Cybersecurity for the Cloud *(11 of 11)*

Policy, Audit, E-Discovery, and Training

How is an enterprise's cybersecurity program affected by its use of cloud services?

- When using cloud services subject to regulation or external standards, the enterprise should consider the services in the context of those regulations or standards.
  - Some services may be better suited for one standard (export control) than another standard (health care).
  - An enterprise may need to use more than one provider to satisfy regulatory requirements.
- Cloud services may run afoul of other internal cybersecurity policies such as requirements for strong authentication, network protection, or encryption.
  - Careful risk analyses should be performed.
  - Analyses may result in policy exceptions or deployment of compensating preventive, detective, forensic, or audit controls.
- Just because a service is being provided by a cloud provider does not remove the service from enterprise's policies, procedures, or security capabilities.
  - Procedures for audits, re-certification, penetration tests, and so forth, apply to cloud services just as they do for internally hosted IT capabilities.
  - Enterprise cybersecurity leadership must ensure policies and activities include cloud services.
  - Business leaders need to understand how to apply these polices to cloud services.

CHAPTER 7

Enterprise Cybersecurity for Mobile and BYOD

S. E. Donaldson et al., *Enterprise Cybersecurity Study Guide*, https://doi.org/10.1007/978-1-4842-3258-3_7

Overview *(1 of 2)*

- The graphic depicts functional architecture of typical mobile devices and Bring Your Own Devices (BYODs).
- These devices impact how enterprises think about their IT.
  - With multiprocessing, graphical user interface, and gigabytes of memory at our fingertips 24 hours a day, the face of IT is changing almost daily.
  - These devices come in all shapes and sizes, such as notebooks, tablets, and cellular phones.
- This personal computing power arrives at a time enterprises are moving services onto the Internet and computing into the cloud.

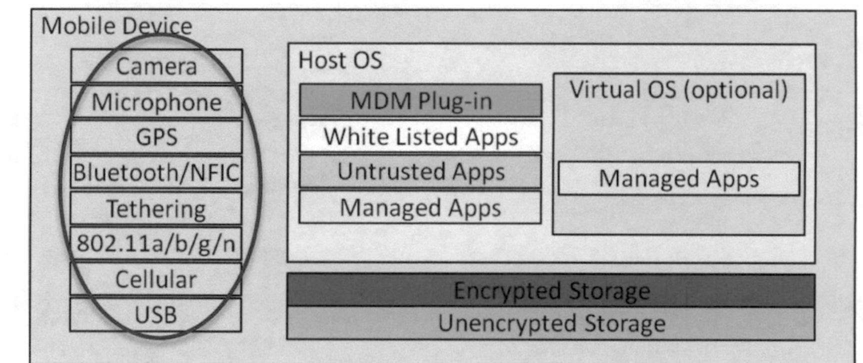

- Frequently, personal devices are as good or better than those purchased or issued by the enterprise.
- At the same time, many people have one or more computing devices at home and want to use those devices for work.

Overview *(2 of 2)*

- Enterprises need to embrace the fact that their data is going to be accessed from such devices.
  - Internet-savvy employees want to use their latest and greatest devices.
  - Organizations want employees to always be connected and able to be productive at home and on the road.
  - Cost of equipping employees with the latest technology rapidly becomes prohibitive.
- Given that mobile devices and BYODs are here to stay, it is important to figure out how to protect enterprise data in the face of this reality.

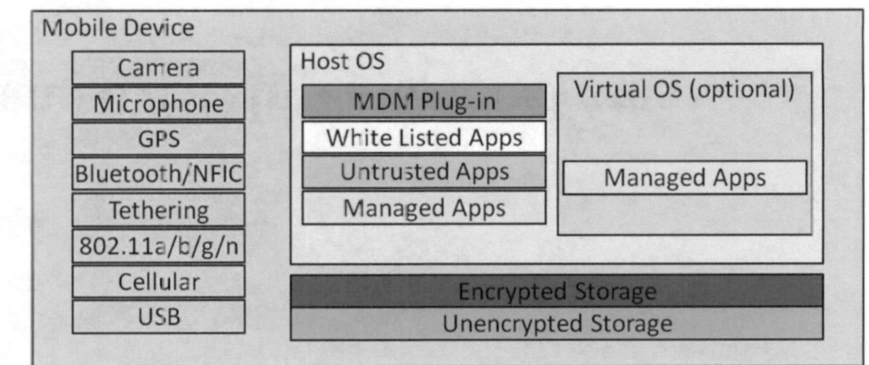

- This chapter describes
  - mobile and BYOD security challenges; and
  - how an enterprise cybersecurity program should manage protection of these devices.

Topics

- Introducing Mobile and BYOD
- Challenges with Mobile and BYOD
  - Legal agreements for data protection
  - Personal use and personal data
  - The mobile platform
  - Sensors and location awareness
  - Always-on and always-connected
  - Multifactor authentication
  - Mobile device management
- Enterprise Cybersecurity for Mobile and BYOD by Functional Area

Introducing Mobile and BYOD *(1 of 3)*

- For the most part, mobile and BYOD are different types of endpoint computing devices that are not owned or managed by the enterprise.
- The National Institute of Standards and Technology (NIST) defines a mobile device as having the following characteristics:
  - A small form factor
  - At least one wireless network surface
  - An operating system that is "not a full-fledged desktop or laptop operating system"
  - Applications available through multiple methods
- Mobile devices may have characteristics that may include one or more of the following characteristics:
  - Wireless personal area network, such as Bluetooth
  - Wireless interfaces for voice communication, such as cellular

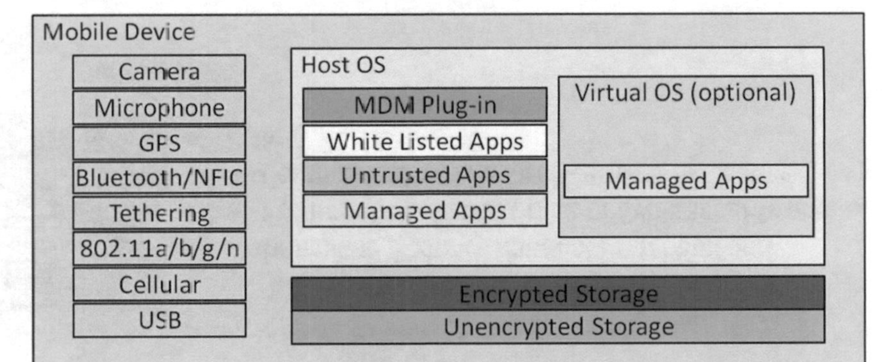

  - Global positioning system for location
  - One or more cameras or video recording devices
  - Removable media storage
- From a cybersecurity perspective, mobile devices present the following concerns:
  - Lack of physical security controls
  - Use of untrusted mobile devices, networks, applications, and content
  - Interaction with other systems
  - Use of location services

Introducing Mobile and BYOD *(2 of 3)*

- To address these mobile concerns, the US Federal CIO Council created a detailed mobile security reference architecture that describes strategies for managing such protections in the federal computing environment.
- The graphic depicts the Council's ***mobile security reference architecture*** that accounts for the mobile and BYOD security challenges in great detail.

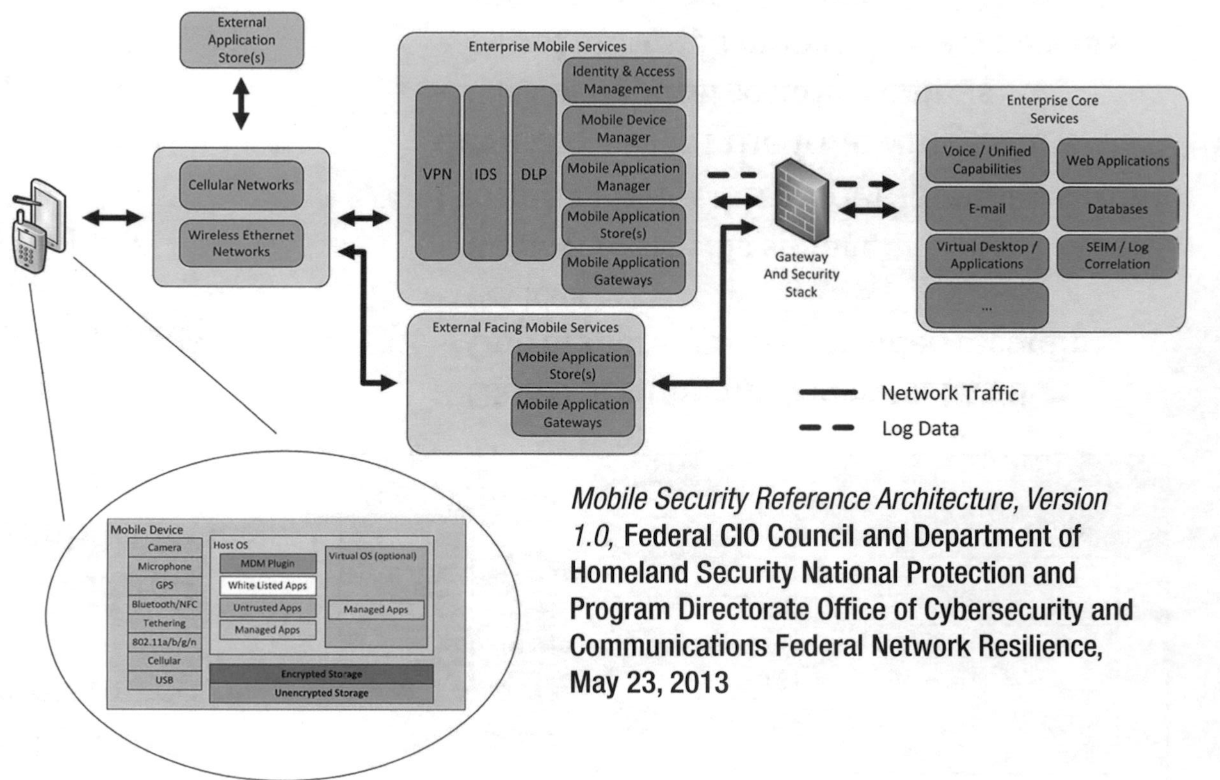

Mobile Security Reference Architecture, Version 1.0, **Federal CIO Council and Department of Homeland Security National Protection and Program Directorate Office of Cybersecurity and Communications Federal Network Resilience, May 23, 2013**

Introducing Mobile and BYOD *(3 of 3)*

- If an enterprise already allows access to its resources from home computers, through Internet-connected services, cloud services, or a virtual private network (VPN), then the enterprise is already facing personal device challenges.
- Much of what people can do with mobile computing is exactly the same as what they can do with personal computers.
- Challenges of protecting the enterprise data on these devices are just as great as if the devices were within the enterprise.
- Mobile computing only makes these challenges more distressing because the data is residing on devices that are
  - everywhere;
  - dropped;
  - stolen; and
  - misplaced.

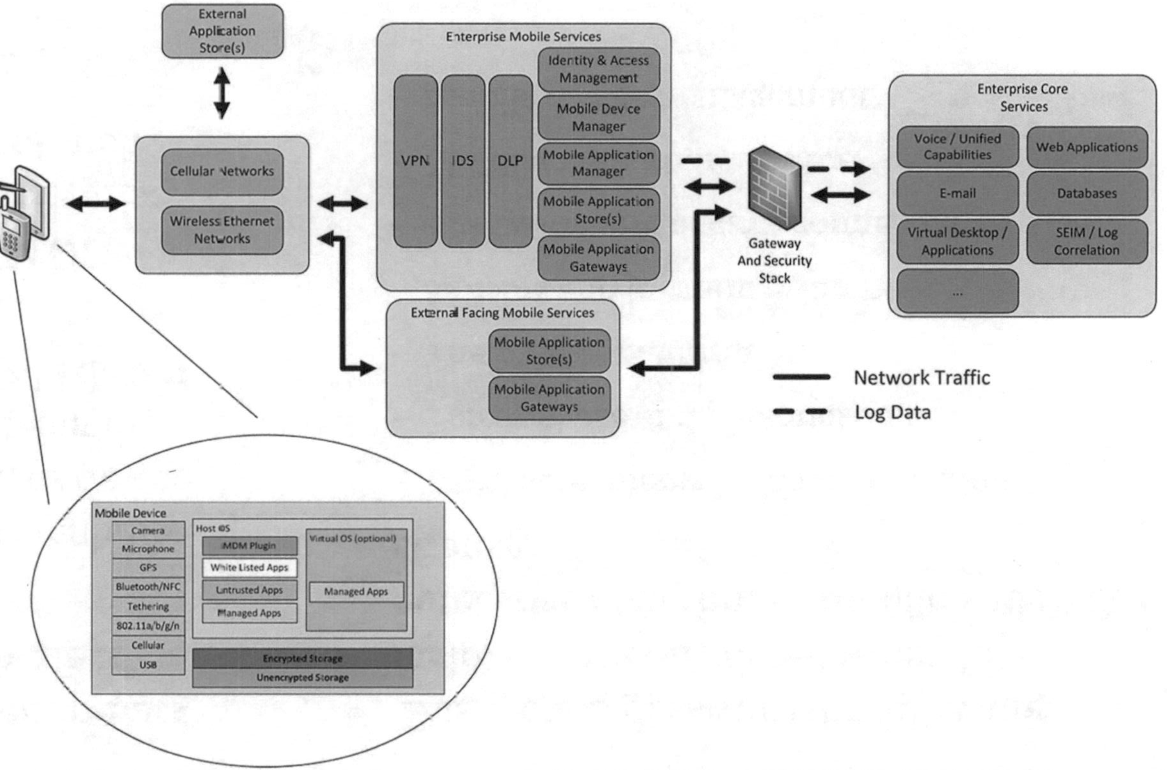

- The Federal CIO Council mobile security conceptual architecture shows the components of common mobile devices and who they might be managed by and interact with.

Challenges with Mobile and BYOD *(1 of 8)*

Context

- Mobile devices and BYOD are endpoints, and there is no such thing as "perfect" endpoint security.
- An enterprise can reduce the probability that any given endpoint, server, or device gets compromised while increasing the probability that the enterprise will detect the compromised endpoint.
- Personally owned mobile and BYOD devices are not owned by the enterprise, thus increasing the probability of such devices getting compromised.
- This section describes the following factors to be considered when an enterprise plans out its mobile and BYOD strategy:
  - Legal agreements for data protection
  - Personal use and personal data
  - The mobile platform
  - Sensors and location awareness
  - Always-on and always-connected
  - Multifactor authentication
  - Mobile device management

Challenges with Mobile and BYOD *(2 of 8)*

Legal Agreement for Data Protection

- One of the first data protection factors to consider is a legal one.
  - What happens when enterprise data is stored on devices that do not belong to the enterprise?
- The enterprise needs to consider this question, not only for mobile and BYOD devices, but also in terms of home personal computers, personally owned thumb drives, portable hard drives, and recordable media such as CDs or DVDs.
- For the most part, when enterprise data is copied to non-enterprise devices, data protection agreements need to be in place with employees and contractors.
- Such agreements may be hard to enforce in practice, but are needed for legal standing to protect the data after it is copied from organizational computers.
- Agreements help the enterprise deploy data protection technologies, such as remote wipe, onto non-enterprise devices.

Challenges with Mobile and BYOD *(3 of 8)*

Personal Use and Personal Data

- Mobile and BYOD devices are going to be used for personal and business use.
- Consequently, an enterprise cannot treat them as if they belong only to the organization.
- If an enterprise deploys data protection technology on the devices, then the enterprise needs to consider potential impacts on stored personal data.
- For the most part, such deployment tends to work OK in practice.
  - If a systems administrator accidently wipes an organizational device, the organization is liable for the damage and ultimately bears the cost of it.
  - On the other hand, what if the action accidentally deletes someone's personal information that is irreplaceable? What is the liability here?
  - These are some of the factors that need to be considered before accidents occur so everyone's expectations are managed.

Challenges with Mobile and BYOD *(4 of 8)*

The Mobile Platform

Strength

- Operating systems are generally designed for users not to have "root" access that would allow them to customize the operating system itself.
- Restriction makes these platforms more resistant to many types of attacks.

Challenge

- If the operating system privilege protection is defeated or if users undermine the device by "rooting" their phone, there is not as much recourse to protect the device as there is with more mature desktop operating systems.

Strength

- Mobile device vulnerabilities reflect poorly on carriers who sell these devices, so they are motived to protect devices well.

Challenge

- Carriers "turn over" mobile devices at a rapid rate and seldom provide patches or updates after the first year or so.

Strength

- Mobile devices use "App Stores" that screen applications to ensure minimal level of security protection and non-malicious behavior.

Challenge

- "App Stores" can lull users into a false sense of security.

Put all of these factors together and mobile as a platform is fundamentally neither more nor less secure than the personal computers that we are all familiar with. ... It's just different ...

Challenges with Mobile and BYOD *(5 of 8)*

Sensors and Location Awareness

- A significant distinction between mobile devices and desktop computing is the multitude of sensors in most mobile smartphone devices.
  - Sensors include light sensors, orientation sensors, fingerprint scanners, cameras, microphones, and GPS receivers.
  - It is not easy to tell or control when sensors are operating.
  - It is not easy to tell or control what sensor data is being collected.
  - Sensors might gain unintended access to proprietary information.
- Enterprises may not want employees to carry devices due to the possibility of sensor data being recorded—either deliberately or accidentally.
- Such data may be used against the enterprise or its employees.
- Sensors may be extremely useful; however, protecting them from potential misuse is extremely difficult.

Challenges with Mobile and BYOD *(6 of 8)*

Always-On and Always-Connected

- As opposed to PCs and desktops, ***many*** mobile devices have cellular radios that enable them to connect ***from*** almost anywhere all the time.
- Connectivity poses cybersecurity challenges, so enterprises should consider them ***always-on*** and ***always-connected*** unless the radios have been explicitly turned off using "airplane mode" or a similar feature.
- A robust mobile device sensor suite is able to transmit constantly.
  - What it sees and where it is to anyone who wants to know
  - Known ***without*** the device owner's knowledge or consent
- A compromised mobile device becomes a rogue device via a public network that is always watching and listening, and could be reporting to anyone at any time.
- Since the mobile device is connected through a public network, it is not protected by network security capabilities or controls.

Challenges with Mobile and BYOD *(7 of 8)*

Multi-Factor Authentication

- Challenge
  - Many strong authentication technologies (for exmaple, smart cards and USB tokens) are not directly compatible with mobile devices.
  - Multifactor authentication strategies must be expanded to accommodate mobile endpoints.
  - The enterprise can consider alternative form factors, such as software certificates and one-time-password (OTP) tokens.
- Challenge
  - Two-factor authentication technologies often use the mobile device as the second factor.
  - The enterprise needs to consider how the mobile device, being both the security token and the endpoint, affects the overall multifactor authentication.
  - Frequently, if the mobile device is compromised, then the multifactor authentication will be defeated as well.
  - The enterprise may need to consider alternative forms of strong authentication or compensating in other ways, such as anomaly detection or adaptive authentication.

Challenges with Mobile and BYOD *(8 of 8)*

Mobile Device Management (MDM)

- MDM software suites provide management of mobile devices and enterprise data stored on them.
- Capabilities include the following:
  - Device inventory and accounting
  - Malware scanning and detection
  - Encrypted storage of enterprise data on device
  - Protected “sandbox” for enterprise applications to run
  - Secure application stores for enterprise-approved software
  - Monitoring of device sensor use, including camera, microphone, and GPS
  - Remote “wipe” capability if the device is lost or stolen
- An enterprise often wants theses capabilities on ***all*** its endpoints and computers, not just its mobile devices.
- For personal devices, employees may not be willing to allow their devices to be managed in this way, regardless of the potential benefits.

Enterprise Cybersecurity for Mobile and BYOD *(1 of 11)*

Systems Administration

- Systems administration should be performed from enterprise-owned assets.
- Potential benefits of allowing systems administrators to perform their duties from mobile devices do not outweigh the security risks.
- If enterprise allows systems administration from unmanaged mobile or BYOD devices, it should consider the following mitigations:
  - Strong authentication for Sysadmin via tokens separate from the mobile devices they use for administration
  - Device recognition and fingerprinting for mobile and BYOD endpoints authorized for systems administration

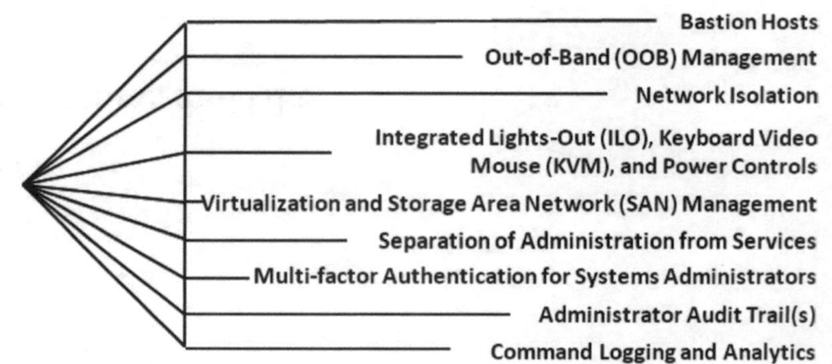

  - Virtual Private Networking connections for Sysadmin activities—enterprise can monitor devices
  - Increased logging and auditing of Sysadmin activities for rogue activity
  - Network-level anomaly detection to catch Sysadmin connections from unauthorized hosts or patterns and tools known to be malicious

Enterprise Cybersecurity for Mobile and BYOD *(2 of 11)*

Network Security

- Mobile and BYOD devices generally get their connectivity from outside the enterprise.
- Such devices are not protected by the enterprise's network "perimeter" when accessing the Internet.
- If the devices are compromised and interacting with external command-and-control networks or botnets, the enterprise will not know.
- However, an enterprise's network will be able to see device traffic when the traffic comes in from the Internet.
- Enterprise can look for evidence of compromise (for example, unusual connection patterns from unexpected locations).
- For more privileged activities, an enterprise may want to require such devices to create a Virtual Private Network (VPN) into the enterprise network.

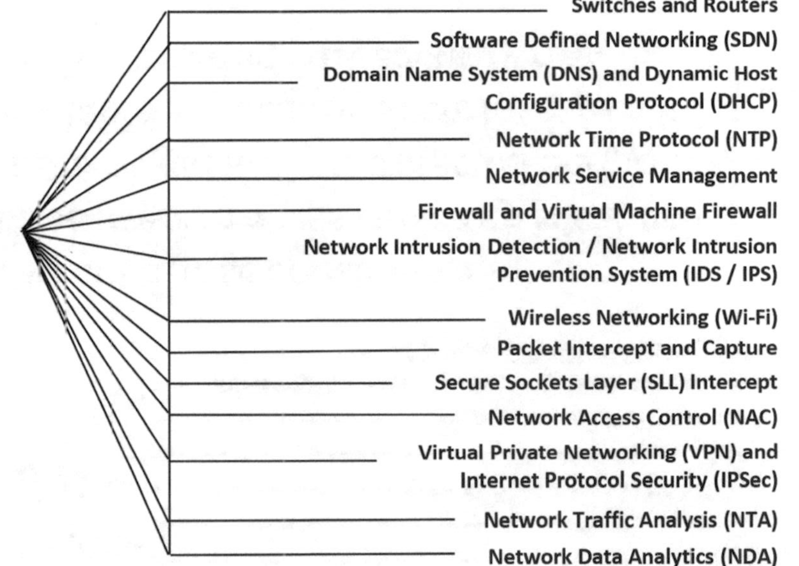

- Devices are treated as if they are inside of the network.
- Enterprise can see all traffic in and out of devices.
- Enterprise network defenses can monitor device network activity for malicious patterns and command-and-control traffic.

Enterprise Cybersecurity for Mobile and BYOD *(3 of 11)*

Application Security

- For specific-use cases, an enterprise may be able to leverage application security capabilities to compensate for mobile and BYOD security challenges.
- Generally, application security technologies that protect consumer-facing systems can apply just as well to enterprise users on mobile and BYOD devices.
- Some of these application security techniques and capabilities can also be used on applications that would not normally be public-facing, such as e-mail or financial systems.

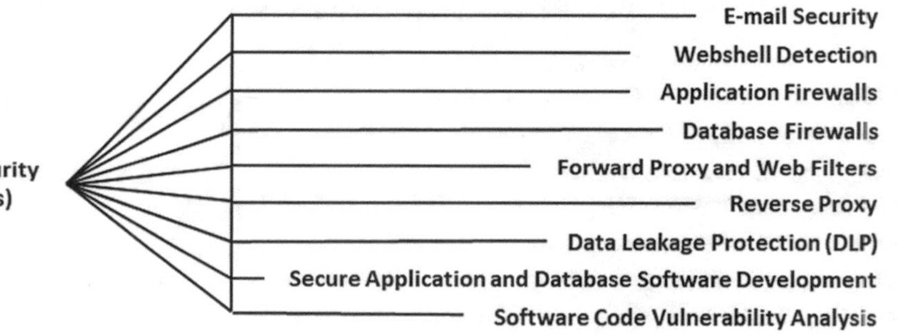

- When an enterprise considers allowing enterprise users to access these applications from unmanaged and unprotected endpoints, then available application security capabilities may be able to reduce the security risk.
- These systems can be protected from potentially anomalous activities by enterprise users on mobile or BYOD devices.

Enterprise Cybersecurity for Mobile and BYOD *(4 of 11)*

Endpoint, Server, and Device Security

- This functional area is the ***most*** impaired when users are on mobile or BYOD devices.
- With the exception of mobile device management (MDM) technologies, many enterprise tools are not applicable to personally owned computing devices.
- MDM can provide outstanding protection of enterprise apps and data while still allowing personal use of devices.
- Endpoint security software (anti-virus, firewall, and intrusion detection) may be licensed for BYOD devices.
- Remote access systems can enforce the presence of endpoint security software when machines connect to enterprise networks, reducing the probability of compromise to internal networks.
- Virtual desktops, thin clients, and "to-go" operating systems that boot from portable media provide secured, trusted endpoints for enterprise network connectivity.

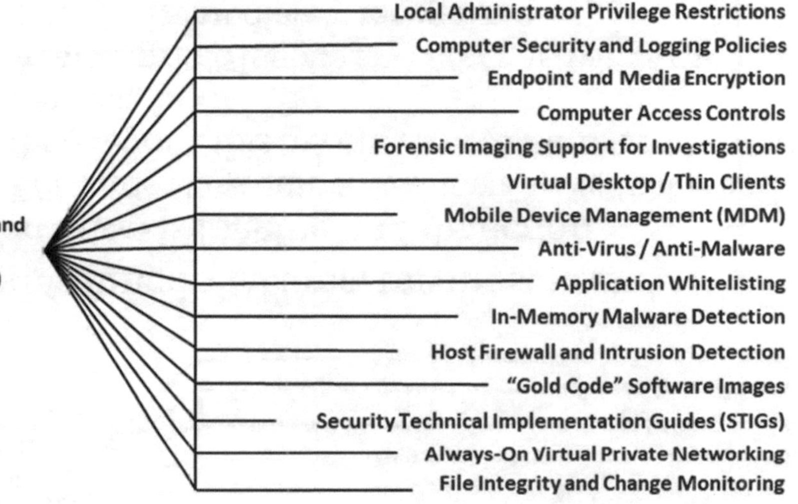

- Don't underestimate the power of policy.
  - Specifies what activities and data can and cannot be performed on mobile and BYOD devices (for example, handling of removable media and encryption of data in transit or rest).
  - Provides a legal basis for punitive actions when negligent behavior occurs.

Enterprise Cybersecurity for Mobile and BYOD *(5 of 11)*

Identity, Authentication, and Access Management

- Strong authentication protects accounts from being compromised even when privileged credentials are used from compromised endpoints or mobile devices.
- Even strong authentication cannot protect against *session hijacking* attacks where attackers wait for the users to authenticate using their credentials and then send commands through that authenticated session.
- Session hijacking can be very effective, particularly with applications such as electronic banking.

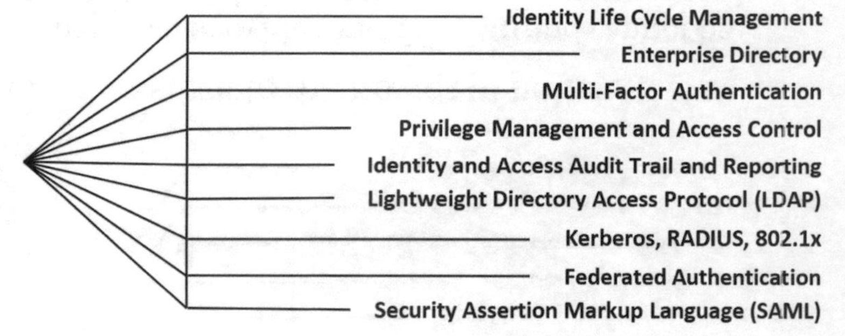

- In this functional area, the most useful protection is logging and detection.
  - Enterprise logs authentication and activities and then reports this information to the user after the fact.
  - Inappropriate logons and other activities can often be immediately recognized.
- Controlling access is effective by minimizing potential consequences of compromised endpoints and compromised credentials.

Enterprise Cybersecurity for Mobile and BYOD *(6 of 11)*

Data Protection and Cryptography

- This function has the ***most untapped potential*** with regard to securing personal computing devices used for enterprise purposes.
- In the future, secure elements on mobile and BYOD devices will store credit cards, payment information, and user identities in such a way that such information can be securely used over the Internet.
- Protection capabilities include the following:
  - Trusted platform module (TPM) that stores device certificates to authenticate "trusted" BYOD devices
  - Cryptographic tokens (smart cards or one-time-password generators) that provide strong, multifactor authentication, even from untrusted endpoints

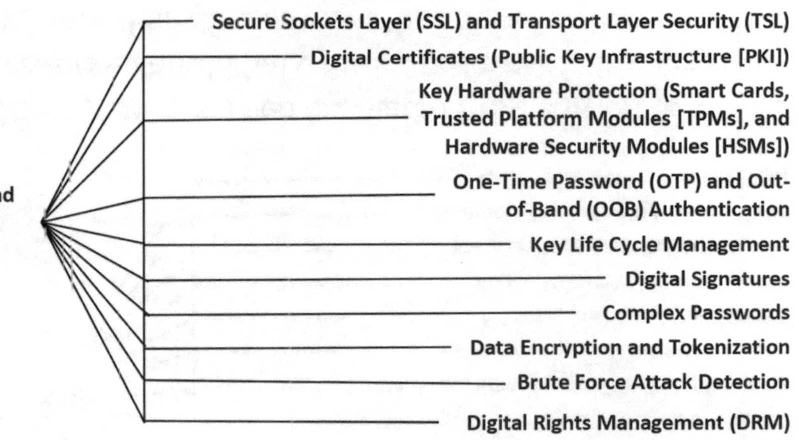

  - Secure sockets layer (SSL) and transport layer security (TLS) protocols to protect from snooping when using untrusted public networks (cellular and Wi-Fi hotspots)
- This functional area is still immature, but it has tremendous potential for enterprise use of mobile and BYOD devices.

Enterprise Cybersecurity for Mobile and BYOD *(7 of 11)*

Monitoring, Vulnerability, and Patch Management

- An enterprise is not going to be able to monitor mobile or BYOD endpoints for signs of attack or intrusions.
- However, an enterprise can monitor the enterprise infrastructure for signs of compromised mobile, BYOD, or enterprise-managed endpoints.
- ***Endpoints will be compromised.***
- Mobile and BYOD monitoring
  - Internet-facing systems, including Virtual Private Network (VPN) connections, should have monitoring in place to detect unusual connection patterns.
  - Internal networks should detect and identify unmanaged computing devices connecting to the network.
  - Depending upon network sensitivity, such devices should be sent to guest networks or otherwise isolated from the most sensitive internal infrastructure.

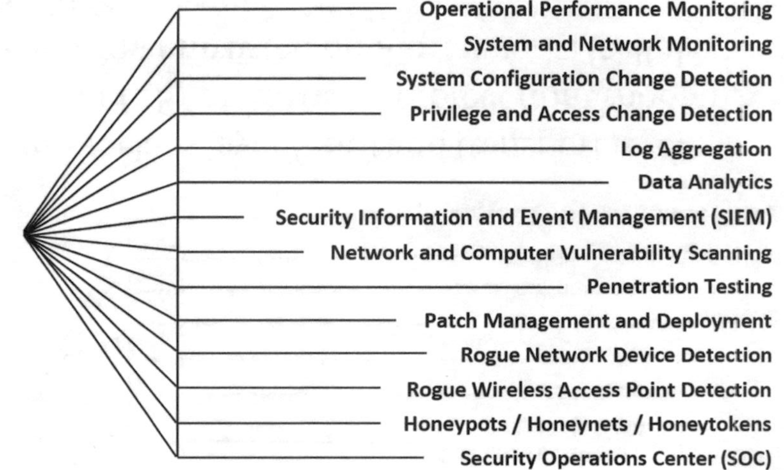

  - Guest networks, even if isolated from corporate networks, should have the same level of intrusion and malware detection as any other network.
- An enterprise must make sure that when cybersecurity systems detect malware from guest, mobile, or BYOD devices, the corresponding response is fast enough to catch the devices before they leave the building.

Enterprise Cybersecurity for Mobile and BYOD *(8 of 11)*

High Availability, Disaster Recovery, and Physical Protection

- Mobile and BYOD devices frequently have little to no physical protection.
- The reality is these devices will be lost or compromised.
- ***Mission-critical data and processing should never reside on such devices.***
- If such data does reside on the devices, strong contingency plans are needed.
- An enterprise should consider the physical security challenges for any type of personal computing device and use the same techniques and technologies to compensate for all the potential loss scenarios.
- Desktop computers are stolen from offices every now and then.

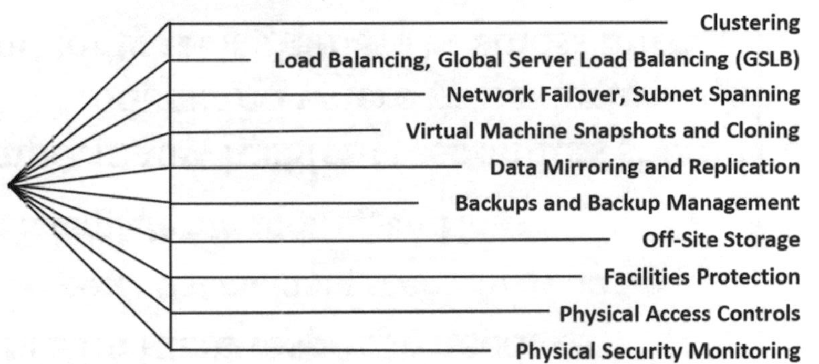

- Laptops are frequently lost or stolen.
- Personal computers and mobile devices are subject to the same situations.
- An enterprise should treat all of these possibilities as being on a continuum of physical protection challenges and use the same techniques and technologies for all these potential loss scenarios.

Enterprise Cybersecurity for Mobile and BYOD *(9 of 11)*

Incident Response

- The incident response process extends from the initial attack investigation, containment, remediation, and a post-incident IT environment with permanent security control enhancement to prevent a recurrence.
- When an enterprise introduces mobile and BYOD devices, some devices will be lost or stolen and potential data will be lost due to unencrypted media and devices.
- Enterprise incident response needs to include procedures to investigate anomalies stemming from mobile or BYOD access to corporate resources from internal networks or the Internet.

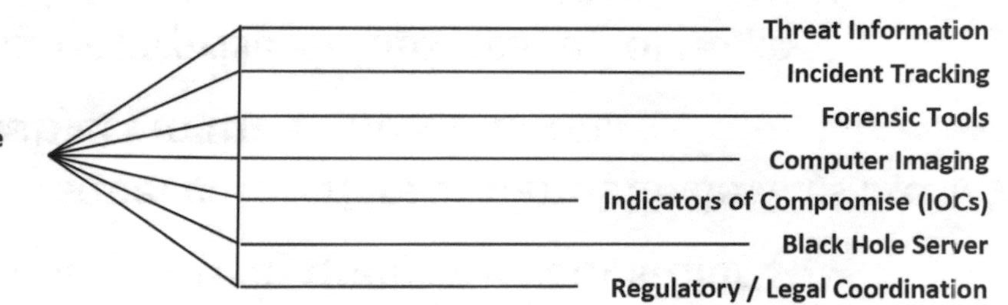

- Enterprise incident response needs to
  - consider potential incident scenarios; and
  - obtain adequate monitoring and logs.
- Most importantly, incident responders should be trained to understand where these devices are used and for what legitimate business purposes.
- Across the enterprise, everyone needs to be trained on mobile device security policy and safe usage considerations.

Enterprise Cybersecurity for Mobile and BYOD *(10 of 11)*

Asset Management and Supply Chain

- Since mobile and BYOD devices are frequently personally owned, they are not going to be easily accounted for in normal enterprise asset management and supply chain processes.
- To mitigate mobile and BYOD security risks,
  - enterprise supplier managers should identify if there are some mobile and BYOD suppliers that are unacceptable for certain purposes;

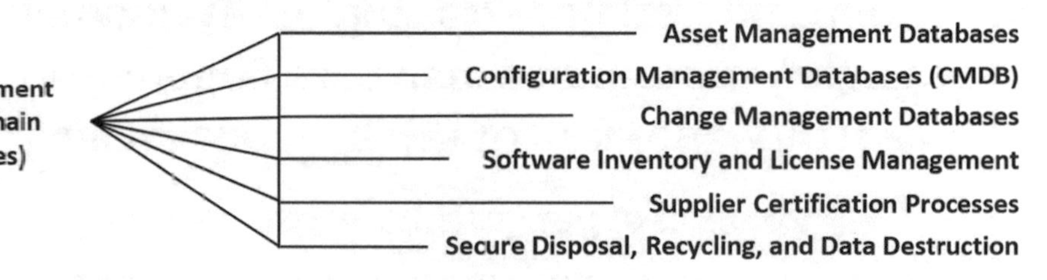

  - such information should be incorporated into policies and procedures and possibly be incorporated into and enforced by network and application controls; and
  - when personal devices are trusted for higher levels of access (systems administrators), such devices should be certified for use and tracked as if they were enterprise devices.

Enterprise Cybersecurity for Mobile and BYOD *(11 of 11)*

Policy, Audit, E-Discovery, and Training

- This functional area is the ***most important*** for mobile and BYOD devices because it serves as the starting point for all other enterprise protection efforts, technical or otherwise.
- Enterprise mobile and BYOD policy should include the following:
  - What business activities and data are
    - Acceptable without any limitations
    - Acceptable with limitations
    - NOT acceptable
  - Rules for protection of enterprise data stored on personal devices, at rest, in-transit, and on portable media such as thumb drives and recordable CDs or DVDs
  - Guidance on investigation of known or suspected breaches of policy

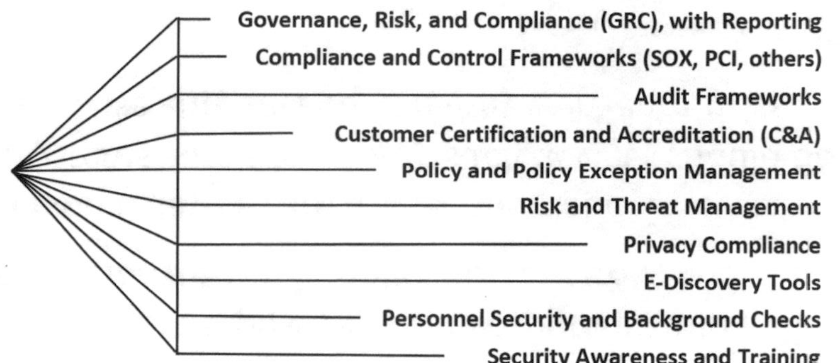

  - Consequences for violation of policies
  - Guidance on training related to policies
- Policies should apply to everyone who may be handling such data and devices, including temporary employees, vendors, and contractors.
- When training is not practical for certain personnel (vendors and contractors), then policies can be incorporated into a "data protection agreement and end-user device policy."

Part III: The Art of Cyberdefense

- Chapter 8: Building an Effective Defense
- Chapter 9: Responding to Incidents
- Chapter 10: Managing a Cybersecurity Crisis

CHAPTER 8

Building an Effective Defense

S. Donaldson et al., *Enterprise Cybersecurity Study Guide*, https://doi.org/10.1007/978-1-4842-3258-3_8

Overview

- A good cybersecurity architecture alone is not going to stop cyberattackers who are targeting an enterprise and attempting to defeat its cyberdefenses.
- Cyberdefense capabilities need to be applied in ways that disrupt, detect, delay, and defeat targeted cyberattacks.
- This chapter describes
  - the art of cyberdefense;
  - how to apply enterprise cybersecurity capabilities to counter unknown, but anticipated, advanced threats;
  - the sequence of steps attackers will take; and
  - practical challenges involved with deploying a program that is effective while also being cost-effective.

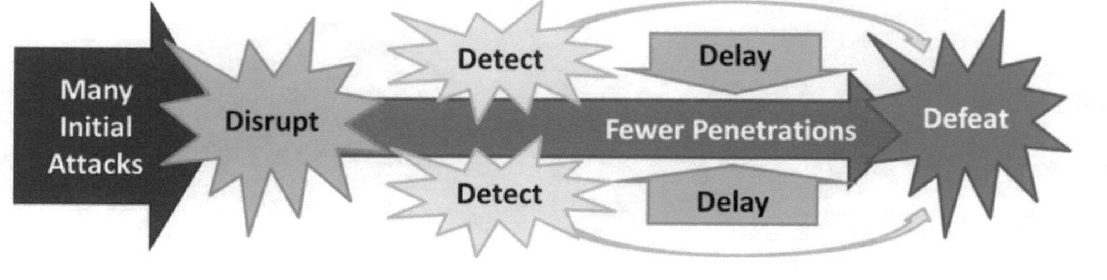

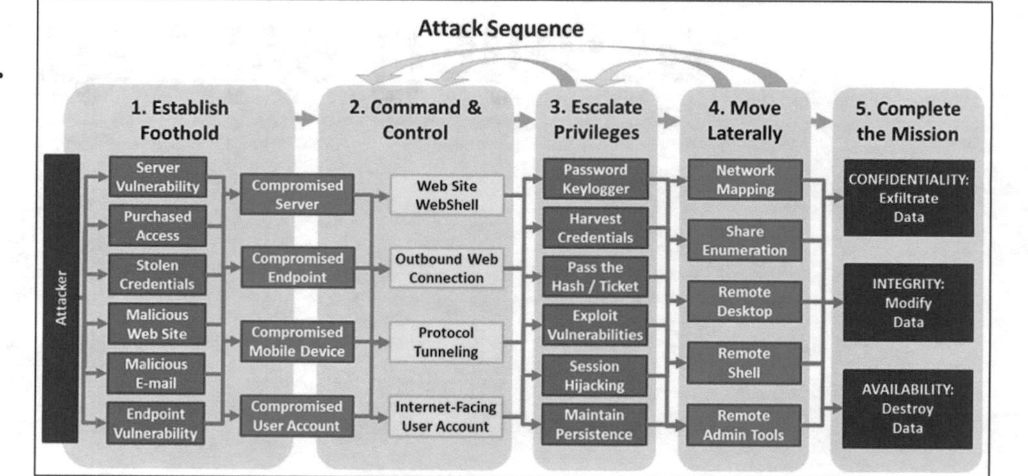

Topics

- Attacks Are as Easy as 1, 2, 3!
- Enterprise Attack Sequence in Detail
- Why Security Fails Against Advanced Attacks
- Business Challenges to Security
- Philosophy of Effective Defense
- Elements of an Effective Cyberdefense

Attacks Are as Easy as 1, 2, 3!

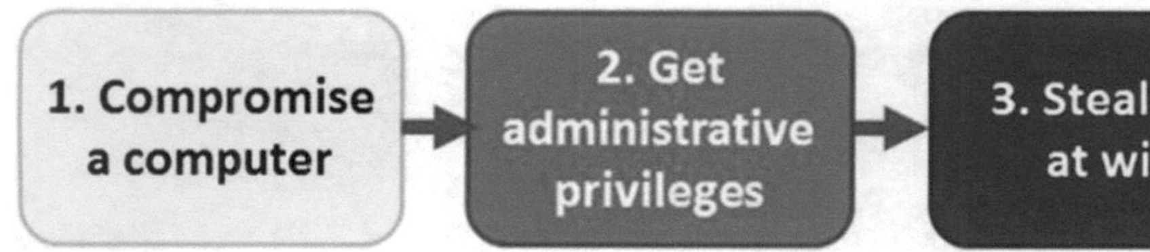
1. Compromise a computer
2. Get administrative privileges
3. Steal data at will!

- From a single compromised endpoint computer inside the targeted enterprise network, attackers can exploit common vulnerabilities to gain administrative privileges.
  - Flaws are inevitable.
  - Systems malfunction.
  - People make mistakes.
  - Defenders do not detect the attackers on the inside.
- Attackers will eventually succeed in obtaining administrative privileges, regardless of the defenses.
- Attackers can use such privileges to access, modify, or destroy whatever data they choose.
- ***Cybersecurity Goal****—Make advanced attacks more challenging than 1, 2, 3!*
- Deploying both preventive and detective controls can make the attackers' job more difficult.

Enterprise Attack Sequence in Detail *(1 of 6)*

Context

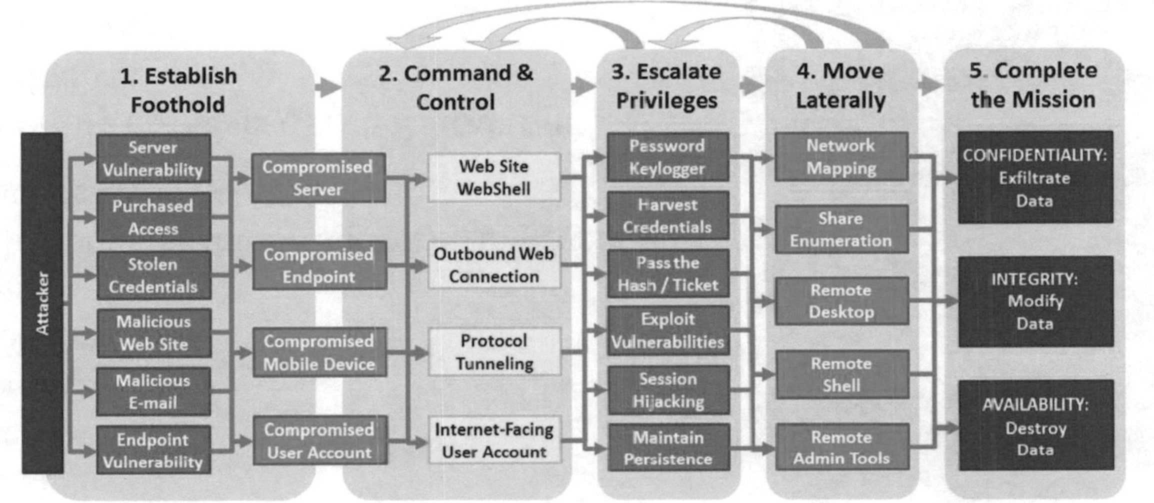

- Targeted attacks methodically work through victim defenses.
- The attack sequence gives defenders opportunities to successfully defend the enterprise by tracing the attack backward and identifying the data attackers might want to steal, modify, or destroy.
- Attackers might target data on servers, on endpoints, over the network, in backups, or on its customers' or business partners' systems.
- Attack steps are not always executed exactly in sequence.
- This process does not deal with distributed denial of service attacks.

Enterprise Attack Sequence in Detail *(2 of 6)*

Attack Sequence Step 1—Establish Foothold

- Foothold gives the attacker the ability to access enterprise resources and is often obtained by the following:
  - Server vulnerability
  - Purchased access
  - Stolen credentials
  - Malicious web sites
  - Malicious e-mail
  - Endpoint vulnerabilities (home networks, improperly configured public Wi-Fi networks)
- Foothold generally consists of the following:
  - Compromised server
  - Compromised endpoint
  - Compromised mobile device
  - Compromised user account
- From the foothold, attacker moves on to the next attack step.

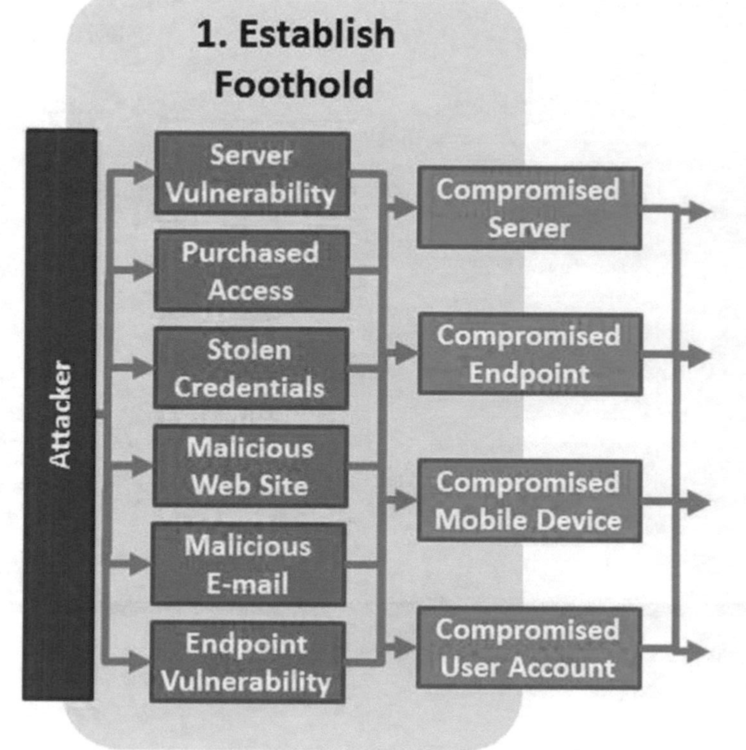

Enterprise Attack Sequence in Detail *(3 of 6)*

Attack Sequence Step 2—Establish Command and Control

- From the foothold, the attacker can execute commands.
- Attacker may escalate privileges or move laterally before establishing command and control (C^2).
- Generally, attacker establishes C^2 connectivity sooner rather than later to manually control the activities within the victim systems.
- Main C^2 methods include the following:
  - Web site webshell
  - Outbound web connections
  - Protocol tunneling
  - Internet-facing user accounts
- With C^2, the attacker can install and operate additional malware and tools beyond those used to establish the foothold, obtain additional privileges, and move laterally.

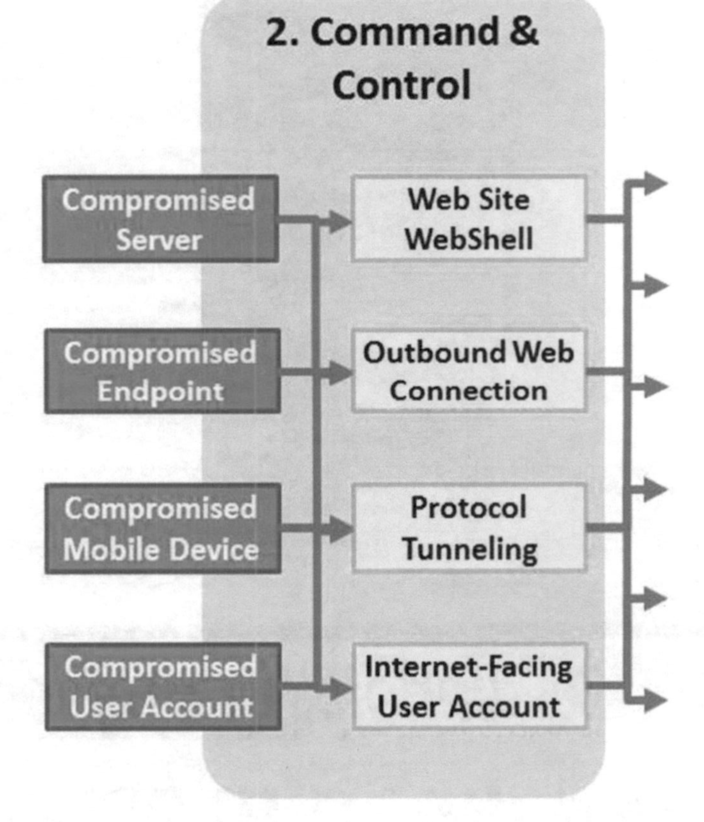

Enterprise Attack Sequence in Detail *(4 of 6)*

Attack Sequence Step 3—Escalate Privileges

- By escalating privileges, attackers can take control of additional servers and endpoints closer to the attack goal.
- Escalating privileges can involve gaining control of systems administration accounts that have permissions to log on to a large numbers of machines.
- Common escalation techniques include the following:
  - Password keylogger
  - Harvest credentials
  - Pass-the-hash or pass-the-ticket
  - Exploit vulnerabilities
  - Session hijacking
  - Maintain persistence
- Generally attacker goes through several cycles of privilege escalation and lateral movement.

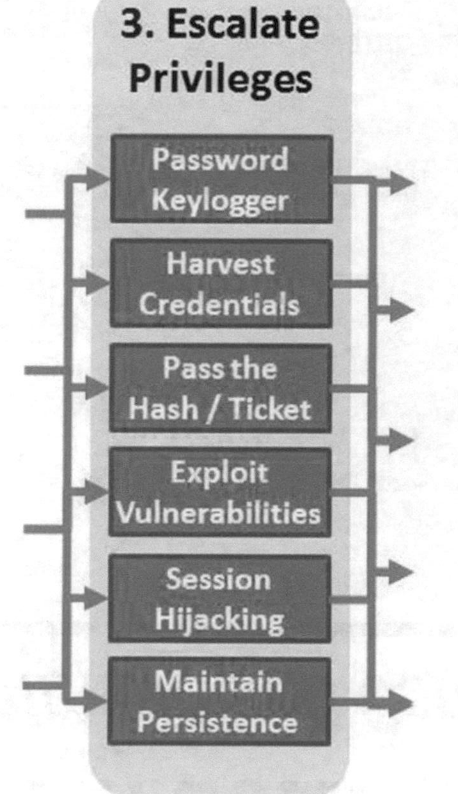

Enterprise Attack Sequence in Detail *(5 of 6)*

Attack Sequence Step 4—Move Laterally

- Attacker moves from computer to computer to expand the foothold.
  - For example, go from a regular user computer to endpoint administrator privileges to file server to e-mail administrator to e-mail server to domain administrator to enterprise domain controller servers ...
- Moving laterally includes the following:
  - Network mapping, share enumeration
  - Remote desktop, remote shell
  - Remote administration tools
- Attacker moves around and may not install malware on all systems touched.
- If attacker has control of privileged network accounts, attacker may switch to using systems administration tools already built into computer operating systems and permitted on the network.
- Attacker may get control of the enterprise without the enterprise's knowledge.

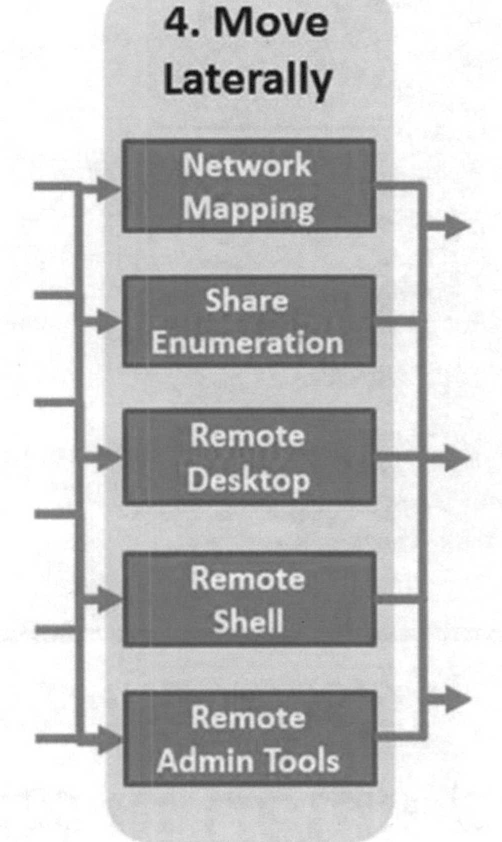

Enterprise Attack Sequence in Detail *(6 of 6)*

Attack Sequence Step 5—Complete the Mission

- Completing the attack mission includes the following:
  - ***Confidentiality***: Steal data, which might include logon credentials, credit card numbers, and financial or health care accounts for identity theft.
  - ***Integrity***: Modify data, which might include changing records to steal money by either altering financial records or using compromised credentials to access financial institution online and move money out of victim accounts.
  - ***Availability***: Destroy data, which might include (1) ransomware that encrypts victim's data and is used for blackmail, (2) denial-of-service attacks that render the enterprise's Internet services inaccessible, or (3) availability attack to distract defenders or cover up the attack after the real heist has been completed.
- After this step, the victim is left to pick up the pieces and figure out what just happened.
- Many victims do not even know that the attack has taken place until weeks or months later.

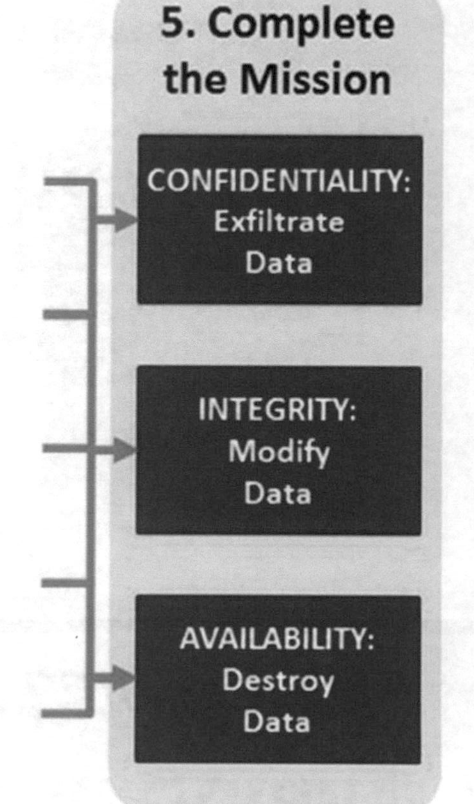

Why Security Fails Against Advanced Attacks *(1 of 5)*

Context

- *Why can't IT simply stop attacks from gaining a foothold in the first place?*
- *Why can't computers be secure against attacks?*
- *Why are complex operating systems impossible to secure perfectly for an extended period of time?*

- Answers are complex and include the following *technical* challenges:
  - The failure of endpoint security
  - The "Inevitability of 'the Click'" challenge
  - Systems administration hierarchy
  - Escalating attacks and defenses

Why Security Fails Against Advanced Attacks *(2 of 5)*

Technical Challenge 1—The Failure of Endpoint Security

- Modern operating systems are too large and complex to be fully protected.
- Security statistically reduces the percentage of compromised endpoints, but cannot eliminate them altogether.
- Endpoints are always susceptible to being compromised.

- Rules of thumb for # of compromised endpoints

Home Computers
1 / 10

Enterprise Computers
1 / 100

Enterprise Servers
1 / 1,000

Why Security Fails Against Advanced Attacks *(3 of 5)*

Technical Challenge 2—The "Inevitability of 'the Click'"[1]

- With only six messages in an e-mail phishing campaign, there is an 80% chance one recipient will click on an attachment or link related to e-mail.
- Large enterprises send thousands or millions of e-mail messages.
- The probability of at least "one click" in an e-mail phishing campaign increases significantly as more e-mails are sent during the campaign.
- ***Conclusion #1***—Enterprise endpoints and servers *will be* compromised.

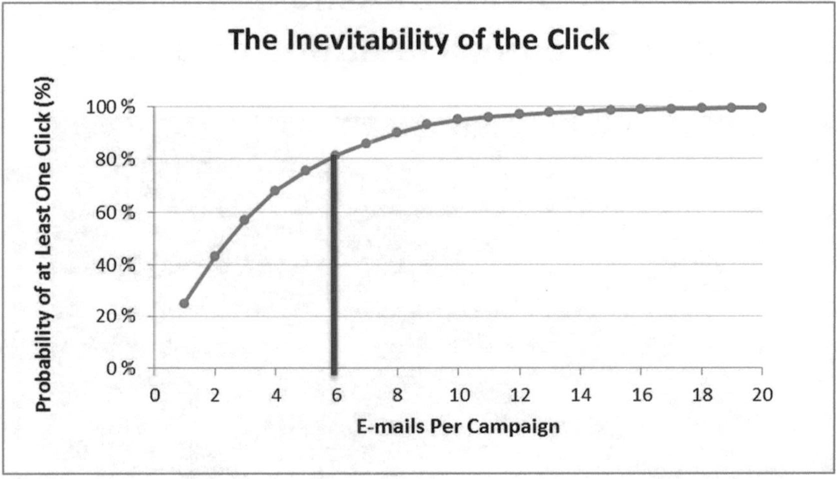

- ***Conclusion #2***—Enterprise must layer its defenses so endpoints mostly likely to be compromised first are not the most critical ones.

[1]Verizon Data Breach Investigations Report, 2013.

Why Security Fails Against Advanced Attacks *(4 of 5)*

Technical Challenge 3—Systems Administration Hierarchy

- Data center applications are complex and difficult to protect well.
- Application functions
  - are layered upon each other;
  - can be connected to the network;
  - often allow privileged access through systems administration account usernames and passwords; and
  - further down the stack can generally bypass security of layers above.
- Data center layers are often network-connected along with computer hardware intergrated Lights-Outs (iLO) interfaces.

Application	Administration
End User	User Credentials
Application	App Admin
Database	DB Admin
Network & Net Security	Network Admin
Operating System	OS Admin
Drivers	Suppliers
Virtualization (if present)	VM Admin
Firmware / BIOS	ILO / KVM Admin
Hardware	Physical Access
Hardware Security Module / Crypto	Crypto Access

More Dangerous Attacks

Systems Administrator Accounts

- When an endpoint gets compromised, the attacker has an opportunity to access the enterprise's systems administration channels and bypass most of the enterprise security measures.

Why Security Fails Against Advanced Attacks (5 of 5)

Technical Challenge 4—Escalating Attacks and Defenses

- For every defensive capability, there is a corresponding attacker tool, technique, or procedure.
- There is no ***perfect*** or ***unbreakable*** defense.
- Real-world attacks often use relatively simple attack methods.
  - Viruses
  - Spear phishing
  - Published vulnerabilities
  - Credential theft
  - Web site compromise

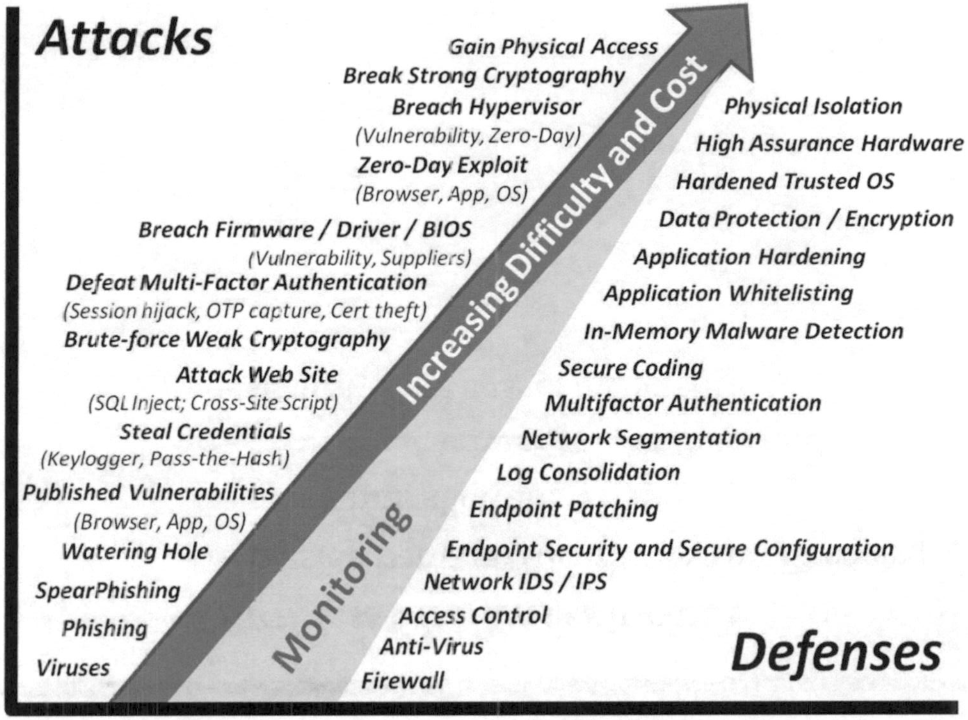

- Even with data encryption, high-assurance hardware, and physical isolation, enterprises remain open to more basic formats of attack.

Business Challenges to Security *(1 of 5)*

Context

- In addition to technical challenges of building effective enterprise defenses, what are the associated business challenges?
- Security programs fail, in part, due to business considerations rather than technical considerations.
- For an enterprise security program to be effective, the enterprise needs to understand its business and properly phrase its security needs in terms of *business costs* and *business value*.

- ***Business Challenges*** include
  - tension between security and productivity;
  - maximum allowable risk;
  - security effectiveness over time; and
  - security total cost of ownership.

Business Challenges to Security *(2 of 5)*

Business Challenge 1—Tension Between Security and Productivity

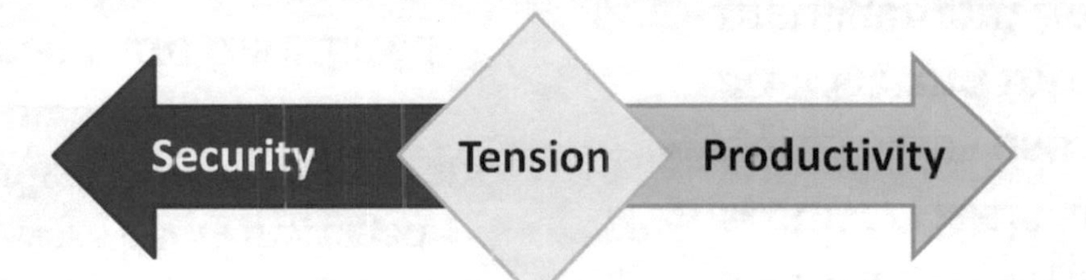

- ***Security*** and ***productivity*** are often diametrically opposed.
- Security measures tend to drive up costs, slow down progress, and add steps.
- Vendors often claim their security technology is seamless and invisible to users, but it requires installation, upgrades, and operation.
- It is almost impossible to add security to an enterprise without impacting productivity in some way.
- Technologies limiting access to systems and data require an ongoing effort to grant and revoke accesses on an ongoing basis.
- Productivity is impacted when people cannot do their jobs while waiting for access.
- Costs can be relatively small, but if a company makes $1B per year, reducing productivity by 1% costs the company $10M in lost productivity.
- The costs of security are offset by the costs of incidents that occur when security fails, but these amounts are difficult to estimate.

Business Challenges to Security *(3 of 5)*

Business Challenge 2—Maximum Allowable Risk

- Enterprises continually try to minimize costs to include security.
- Budget cuts often drive security to reduce costs and operate uncomfortably close to a cybersecurity disaster.
  - ***Green Zone***: Security budget may be bloated and probably needs to be cut.
  - ***Yellow Zone***: Security budget is about right, but enterprise feels somewhat uncomfortable regarding the security risks being managed.
  - ***Red Zone***: Security budget may be too low and can result in multiple breaches.
- Since some security costs are mandated by regulation, why would there be pressure to reduce security costs?
- Money spent on security is money taken away from growth, profits, or shareholders.

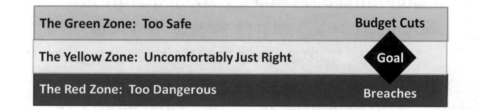

The Green Zone: Too Safe — Budget Cuts
The Yellow Zone: Uncomfortably Just Right — Goal
The Red Zone: Too Dangerous — Breaches

- Cutting the security budget and balancing security capabilities against risks encompass the concept of maximum allowable risk (in other words, how much security risk is acceptable?).
- Enterprises use metrics (such as probes, attacks, and intrusions), in part, to show management how the security risks are being stopped/mitigated.
- Metrics help everyone understand how close the enterprise is operating to a potential cybersecurity disaster.

Business Challenges to Security *(4 of 5)*

Business Challenge 3—Security Effectiveness over Time

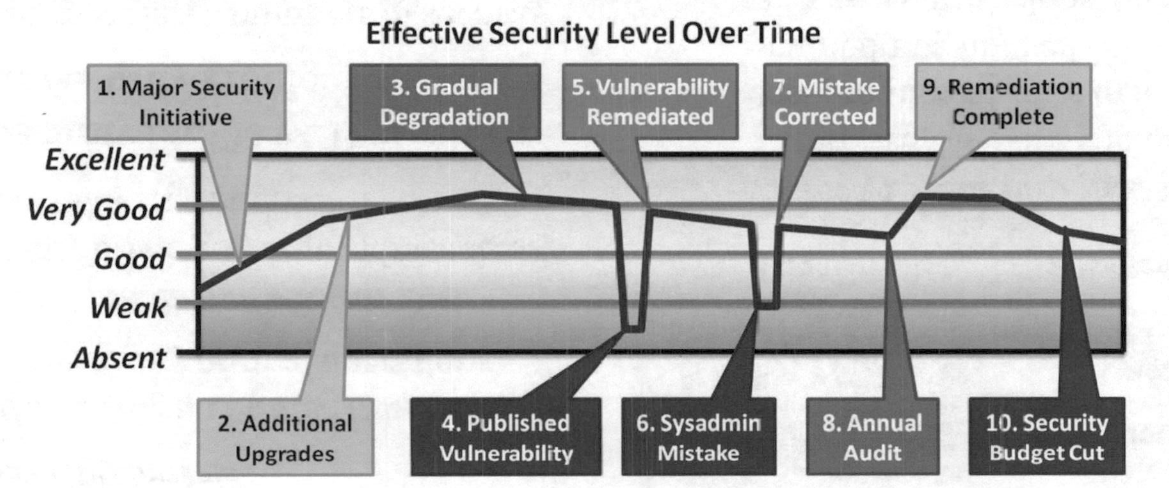

- An enterprise's security posture effectiveness is not static and is subject to factors within and outside of its control.
- Emerging vulnerabilities, setbacks, and mistakes impact security effectiveness.
- Audits/projects identify and remediate security program issues.

Business Challenges to Security *(5 of 5)*

Business Challenge 4—Security Total Cost of Ownership

- Total Cost of Ownership (TCO) consists of multiple cost components.
  - Installing, maintaining, and operating enterprise *security controls*
  - Maintaining/initiating an *incident response* capability and restoring normal operations
  - Remediating *lost productivity* due to not having necessary privileges, requesting access, or processing policy exceptions.
- Prevention Security Profile vs. Detection and Response Security Profile
  - ***Prevention*** suggests large numbers of security controls resulting in large amounts of lost productivity due to requesting permissions, re-certifying accesses, and interacting with security controls.

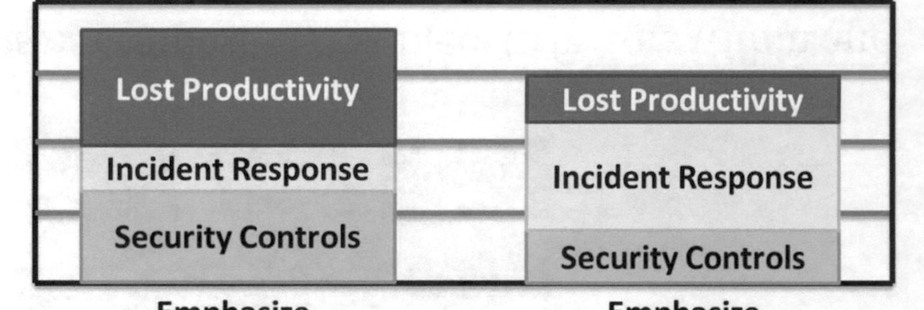

  - ***Detection and response*** suggest the enterprise will have cheaper controls and less lost productivity due to fewer personnel maintaining firewall rules or re-certifying accesses permissions, but they will require more incident response resources.
- It is important for an enterprise to consider TCO when evaluating its cybersecurity program.

Philosophy of Effective Defense *(1 of 8)*

Context

- *What makes up an effective cybersecurity program?*
- *How do defenses work in the physical world, law enforcement, and warfare?*
- *What real-world defense examples can IT incorporate into an effective cybersecurity defense?*
- Nowhere outside of IT do people rely exclusively on technologies such as walls, doors, and gates to stop attackers.
- Perhaps this physical world observation is a hint as to what an enterprise needs to do when implementing an effective cybersecurity program.
- Defense examples include the following:
  - Mazes vs. minefields
  - Disrupt, detect, delay, defeat
  - Cybercastles
  - Nested defenses

Philosophy of Effective Defense *(2 of 8)*

Defense Example 1—Mazes Vs. Minefields (1 of 2)

- What is more scary, a maze or a minefield?
  - Many people enjoy navigating a maze.
  - No one wants to walk across a minefield.
- Enterprise IT defenses often look like mazes.
  - Firewalls block network traffic.
  - Network protocols use accounts for authentication.
  - Access controls restrict who can see individual IT systems.
  - Like neighbor fences, such defenses amuse determined attackers who have tools and techniques for every defense.
  - Attackers can see every obstacle clearly and have time to figure out a way around it.
- Minefields look like a walk across a field, but the mines cannot be seen.
  - If there are enough mines, the probability of safely walking across the field is slim.
  - Attackers do not know which steps are safe and which ones are not safe.
  - An attack is significantly more challenging.

Photo credit: Floresco Productions/Getty Images.

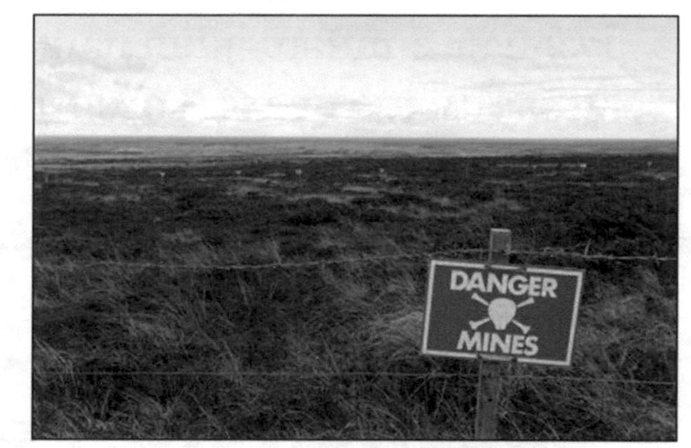

Photo credit: Charlie Bishop/Getty Images.

Philosophy of Effective Defense *(3 of 8)*

Defense Example 1—Mazes Vs. Minefields (2 of 2)

- When an enterprise only contains preventive controls, attackers eventually figure out a way to defeat each control.
- Detection provides an opportunity to respond to the attackers and repel them.
- Combining preventive and detection controls
  - slows attackers down;
  - gives enterprise more time to detect and respond to the attack before it is successful; and
  - leverages the advantages of both mazes and minefields.

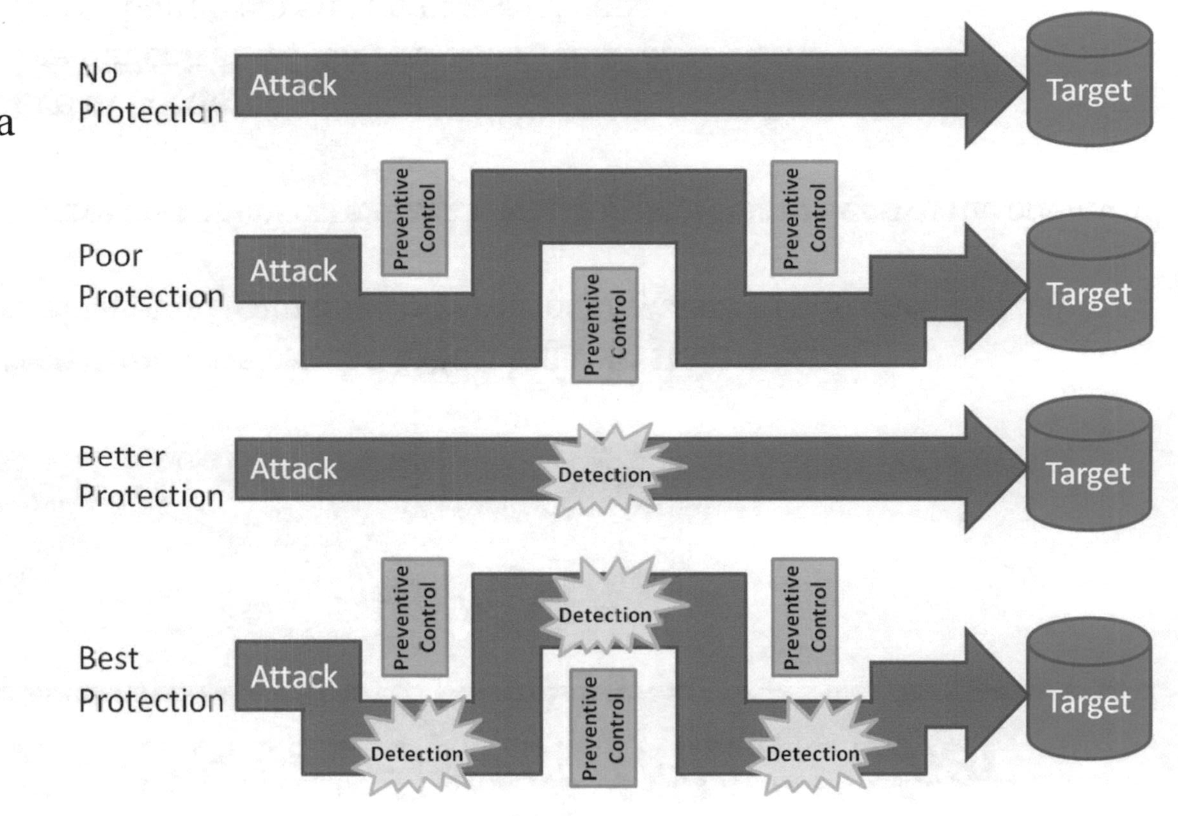

Philosophy of Effective Defense *(4 of 8)*

Defense Example 2—Disrupt, Detect, Delay, Defeat

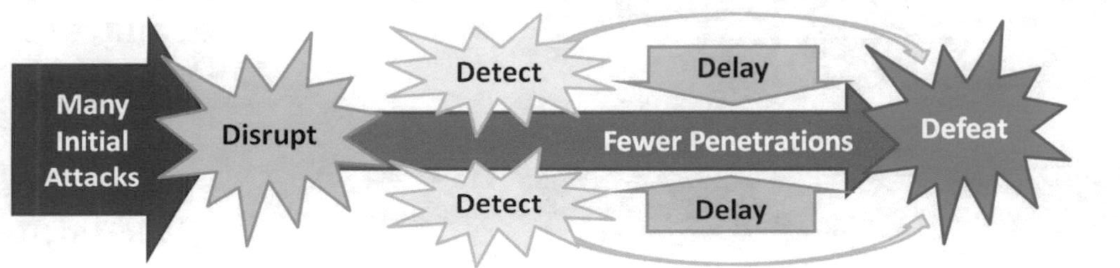

- US Army *Field Manual 100-5, Operations*, makes the following two statements:
  - The purpose of the defense is to "retain ground, gain time, deny the enemy access to an area, and damage or defeat attacking forces."
  - "A successful defense consists of reactive and offensive elements working together to deprive the enemy of the initiative."
- Consider the four Ds of an effective cyberdefense.
  1. ***Disrupt*** attacks to make them more difficult and deter less-determined attackers.
  2. ***Detect*** attacks so defenders can learn about them and prepare a response.
  3. ***Delay*** attacks in progress via obstacles requiring attackers spend time working around them.
  4. ***Defeat*** attacks as quickly as possible and before they can accomplish their objectives.
- Defeating cyberattacks involves removing the attackers from the enterprise and sending them back to their starting point.
- It is unlikely an enterprise will be able to catch the attackers.

Philosophy of Effective Defense *(5 of 8)*

Defense Example 3—Cybercastles

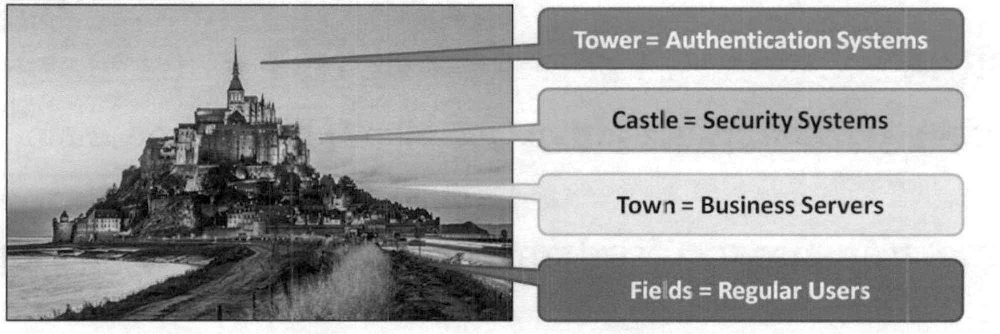

Photo credit: Jimmy Nilsson/EyeEm/Getty Images.

Enterprise defenses can be viewed in terms of security zones with progressively increasing security.

1. ***Fields*** were where the food was grown, but were almost completely indefensible. Attackers traveled across the fields at will, but such travel did not guarantee a successful attack. Fields are like business computers that are almost impossible to defend.
2. ***Town*** was better protected than the fields by a fence or low wall, which was easily scaled. Town is where commerce occurred. Town is like the enterprise business servers.
3. ***Castle*** was designed for protection with high walls and layers of defenses. The person who controlled the castle protected the town. Castle is like the enterprise security systems where most key business occurs.
4. ***Tower*** was designed, along with enclaves and keeps, to be the place where the weapons were stored and battles were fought, even when the initial castle defenses were breached. If defenders controlled the tower, enclaves, and keeps, they could eventually retake the castle, town, and fields. The tower is like enterprise authentication systems that enable an enterprise to beat back attackers who have taken control of everything else. Once an enterprise loses control of authentication systems , its position is extremely precarious.

Philosophy of Effective Defense *(6 of 8)*

Defense Example 4—Nested Defenses (1 of 3)

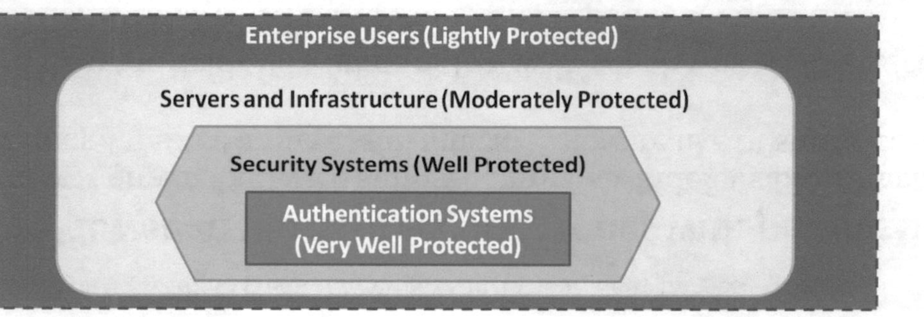

- During cybersecurity defense planning, the enterprise can establish four security zones with corresponding security scopes.
  - In some cases, the four zones are simply different parts of a single enterprise security scope.
- Security controls may be tailored to balance the need for security with the business need for operational flexibility.
  - This approach integrates security policy, network segmentation, endpoint protection, and other capabilities to deliver appropriate protection to different enterprise zones.
- The nested security perimeter forces the attackers to penetrate progressively better protected perimeters to take control of the enterprise.

Philosophy of Effective Defense *(7 of 8)*

Defense Example 4—Nested Defenses (2 of 3)

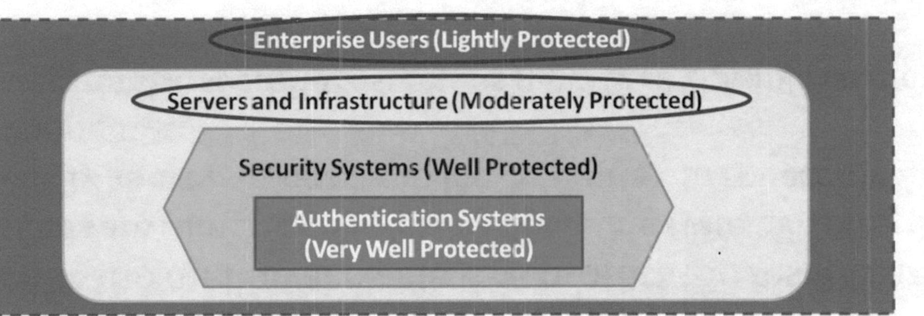

- ***Enterprise users*** are like medieval town fields where most of the productivity takes place and are the hardest to protect.
  - Key protection challenges include users surfing the Web, receiving e-mail, taking laptop computers home or on the road, and allowing mobile or BYOD devices.
  - Detecting compromised user endpoints and containing them before they can do significant damage may be significantly easier and cheaper than trying to harden them from compromise in the first place.
- ***Servers and infrastructure*** are like the medieval town where most of the enterprise business and commerce lie.
  - These systems are the ones most worth investing to protect.
  - However, these systems are moderately difficult to protect because of the large amount of activity, upgrades, and connectivity.

Philosophy of Effective Defense *(8 of 8)*

Defense Example 4—Nested Defenses (3 of 3)

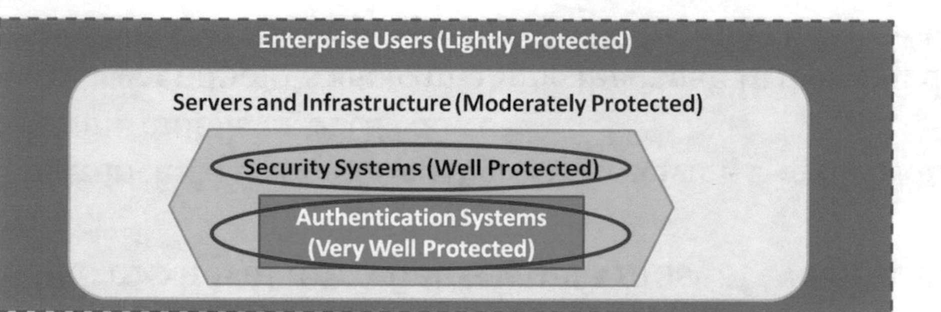

- ***Security systems*** are like the medieval castle that protect the rest of the enterprise.
  - When the security systems are running on the same operating systems, using the same accounts with the same network connectivity as everything else in the enterprise, they become no harder to hack than any enterprise servers or endpoints.
  - Smart attackers will compromise security systems as quickly as possible so they can take control of the rest of the enterprise.
- ***Authentication systems*** are like the castle tower with centralized authentication.
  - The authentication systems are the keys to the kingdom.
  - With control of the systems, attackers can issue themselves credentials, grant permissions to the created credentials, and take permissions away from legitimate system administrators.
  - Authentication systems must be treated as if they cannot be compromised. Any breach of their integrity must be detected and dealt with immediately.

Elements of an Effective Defense *(1 of 8)*

Context

- *What is the goal of an effective cyberdefense?*
- Simply stated, the goal is to take the onus of perfection off of the defender and push it back onto the attacker, where it belongs.
- With an ***ineffective*** cyberdefense, the defender has to do everything perfectly to protect the enterprise.
- With an ***effective*** cyberdefense, the attacker has to do everything perfectly to attack the enterprise.
- Defensive techniques that are particularly effective at disrupting, detecting, delaying, and defeating common attacks to include the following:
  - Network segmentation
  - Strong authentication
  - Detection
  - Incident response
  - Resiliency

Elements of an Effective Defense *(2 of 8)*

Effective Defensive Technique 1—Network Segmentation *(1 of 2)*

- Network segmentation
  - It is the oldest effective defensive technique.
  - It has been used for decades to protect classified military and civilian network.
  - Stuxnet attack demonstrated that even isolated, air-gapped networks can be attacked.
- Segmentation and network isolation
  - They make the attackers' job orders of magnitude more difficult than attacking a monolithic, fully connected, and unmonitored internal network.
  - In ***legacy networks***, Internet-facing DMZ servers are isolated, but everything else is in a single "trusted zone."
  - In ***fully segmented networks***, each major function is isolated from the others.
- In general, the network segmentation model should be as follows:
  - Nested (cybercastle analogy)
  - Integrated into the enterprise security scope architecture (risk assessments)

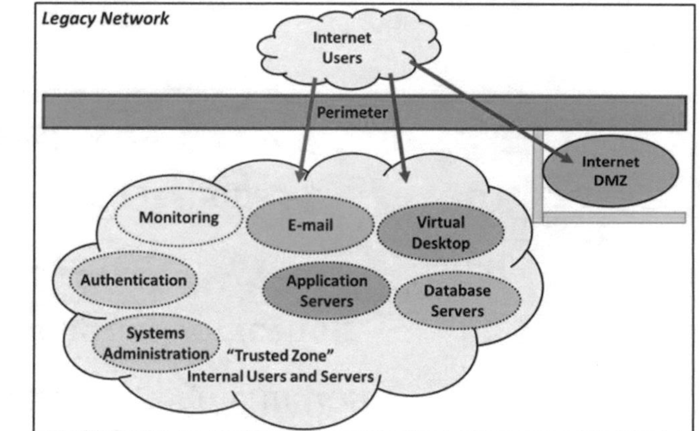

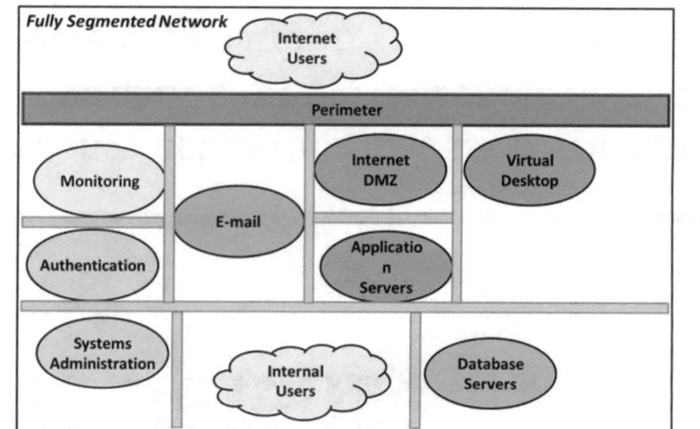

Elements of an Effective Defense *(3 of 8)*

Effective Defensive Technique 1—Network Segmentation (2 of 2)

- Systems in different security scopes should be segmented at the network layer.
- In between network segments, the enterprise should have its full range of network protection capabilities such as firewalls, IDS/IPS sensors, network recorders, and data leakage protection technologies.
- Well-segmented networks
  – allow legitimate network traffic to follow straightforward patterns that are easy to protect; and
  – allow traffic to follow patterns that can be monitored so security can respond to malicious patterns.
- The best defense is the one that detects the attackers and alerts defenders so they can respond.

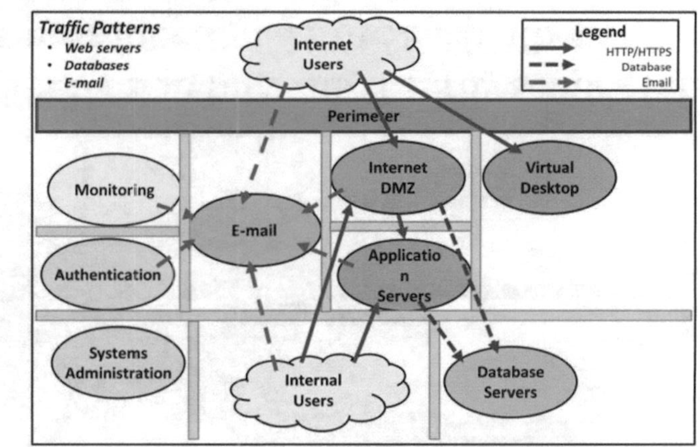

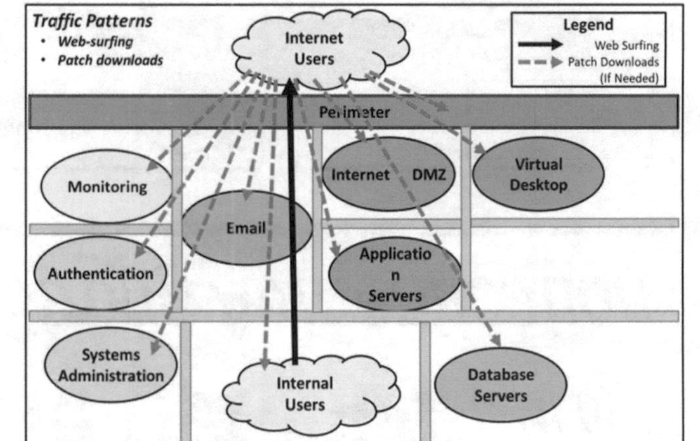

Elements of an Effective Defense *(4 of 8)*

Effective Defensive Technique 2—Strong Authentication

- Traditional authentication
  - Consists of a username and password
  - Relatively easy for attacker to find such credentials
- Strong authentication
  - Involves users proving who they are over a network or on enterprise computers by combining ***something they have*** with ***something they know***
  - Requires the attacker to physically steal the token used for secondary authentication or clone the token
- Is strong authentication foolproof?
  - Absolutely not!
  - Subject to "session hijacking" where attackers take control of the user's computer and then wait for the user to log on before sending illicit commands
  - Overall significantly reduces the odds of a user's credentials being used without the user's consent or knowledge

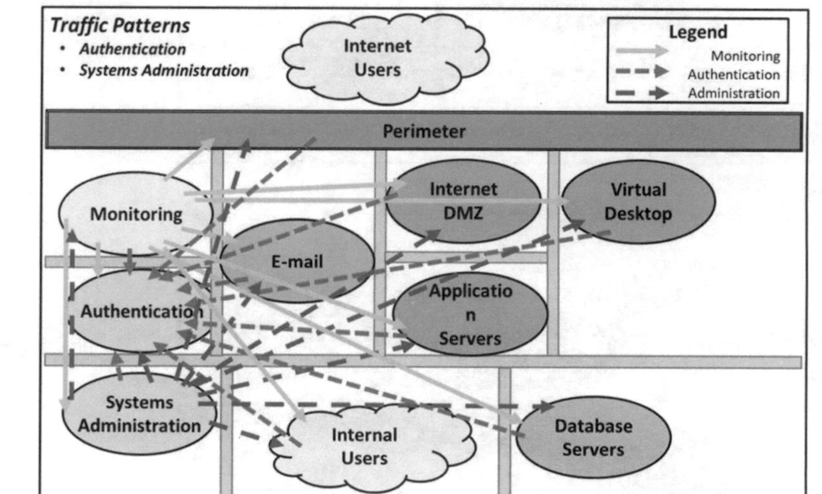

- Segmentation protects security scopes (and business functions) from each other.
- Network security methods can detect attacker attempts to move laterally across the segmented network.
- Strong authentication coupled with solid network segmentation contributes to an effective cyberdefense.

Elements of an Effective Defense *(5 of 8)*

Effective Defensive Technique 3—Detection *(1 of 2)*

- In many cases, an enterprise may not care if an attacker gains control of a single enterprise system or a single user account from the Internet or even inside the environment—particularly over a short period of time.
- What makes these attacks insidious is the following:
  - If the attacks are allowed to progress for hours or days or weeks or months, undetected and unchecked
  - If attackers gain control of enterprise systems administration systems
- If the enterprise simply blocks attackers, they will continue to pound on enterprise defenses over time until they can get around the block.
- Given enough time, attackers will eventually defeat every obstacle the enterprise can put in their way.
- Design enterprise controls focus on detecting the adversary activity first, and then preventing it. In other words, think of the ***Audit First Design Methodology***.
- Just as a minefield is most effective when the mines are arranged in haphazard, unpredictable patterns, an enterprise's ***detective*** controls are most effective when they are somewhat arbitrary and hard to predict.

Elements of an Effective Defense *(6 of 8)*

Effective Defensive Technique 3—Detection *(2 of 2)*

- Simple, but effective, detection rules include the following:
  - On segmented network
    - Detect port and network scans that extend from one segment to the next.
    - Detect systems administration protocols such as secure shell or remote desktop when they originate from servers.
  - For privileged accounts
    - Send administrators a daily report showing all the computers where their accounts were used, along with an admonition to report any suspected account abuse.
  - Alert
    - on the use of network administration tools or scanning tools from workstations such as ping or traceroute;
    - on the use of highly privileged network or service accounts on machines outside of the datacenter;
    - on changes to static web content on Internet-facing servers;
    - on outbound web connections other than patch downloads from Internet-connected servers; and
    - on protocol anomalies in standard web traffic such as domain name service or simple mail transfer protocol.
- The goal of detection is to look at the attack sequence and design detection to alert multiple times before an advanced attack can succeed.

Elements of an Effective Defense *(7 of 8)*

Effective Defensive Technique 4—Incident Response

- Some cyberattackers penetrate cyberdefenses no matter how well the defenses are designed, implemented, or maintained.
- Detecting cyberattackers is not going to save an enterprise if it does not have anyone
  - responding to those alerts;
  - investigating them to filter out false positives to identify the real attacks; and
  - repelling those attacks so that business can continue.
- Incident response can be done by
  - an enterprise response team that is always on standby; and
  - a third party who is kept on retainer or otherwise engaged.
- It is critical the enterprise perform incident response to repel attacks when they occur and send the attackers back to their starting points.

Elements of an Effective Defense *(8 of 8)*

Effective Defensive Technique 5—Resiliency

- Perhaps the most important property of an effective cyberdefense is resiliency.

  "Resiliency is the enterprise's ability to withstand attacks that successfully compromise endpoints, servers, and accounts without those attacks resulting in the attackers gaining complete control. "
- *Resiliency* means the following:
  - Defenders have ability to dynamically respond to cyberattacks by containing them, remediating them, or isolating them
  - Attacker's plan is disrupted and defenders have time and room to maneuver in response to the attack.
- Resiliency includes the ability to
  - rapidly ***rebuild*** compromised servers or endpoints;
  - ***reset*** user credentials and obtain detailed logs of user account activity of accounts that may have been compromised;
  - rapidly ***restore*** data or applications from backups that are known to be good and free of infection or malware; and
  - ***isolate*** sections of the enterprise, or even the entire enterprise, from the Internet so attackers lose the ability to control their foothold.
- Resiliency gives defenders options in an incident response (that is, agility) that makes it possible for defenders to outmaneuver their attackers.
- Defenders can take control of the situation, achieve rapid containment, and remediate incidents before adversaries gain administrative control and complete their objective.

CHAPTER 9

Responding to Incidents

S. E. Donaldson et al., *Enterprise Cybersecurity Study Guide*, https://doi.org/10.1007/978-1-4842-3258-3_9

Overview

- Some cyberattackers penetrate cyberdefenses no matter how well the defenses are designed, implemented, and maintained.
- ***Enterprise endpoints and servers will be compromised.***
- Generally, an enterprise can accept a number of ***minor*** cyberincidents provided they are contained before ***significant*** damage is done.
- Responding to these incidents (in other words, incident response) and the corresponding costs are part of modern cyberenvironments.
- Enterprises need to embrace this reality and deal with compromised systems as quickly and cheaply as possible.
- This chapter describes
  - an enterprise incident response process to deal with a detected cyberattack; and
  - what type of enterprise support is needed to respond to an incident.

Topics

- An Incident Response Process

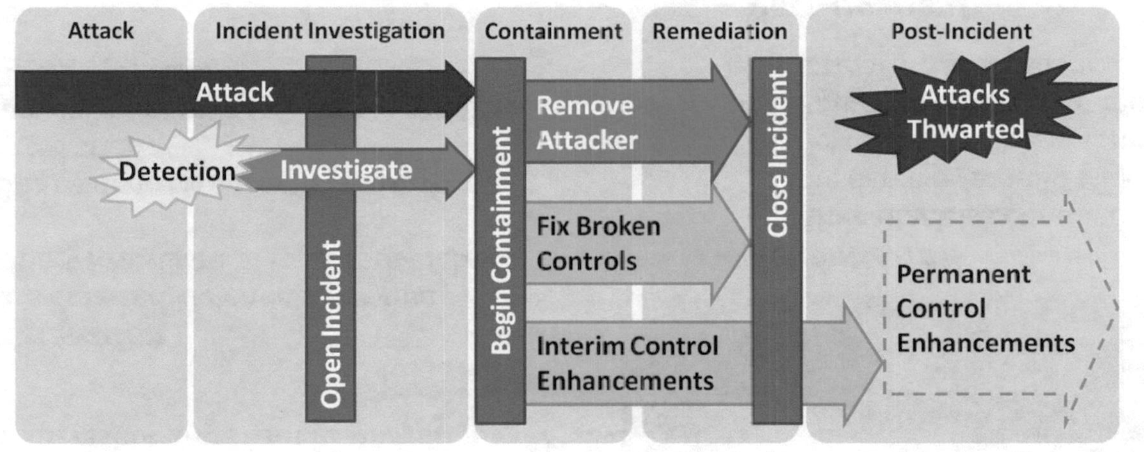

- Supporting the Incident Response Process

Incident Response Process *(1 of 15)*

Context *(1 of 2)*

- High-Level Sequence of Events
  - ***Attack***
    - Attack can be as simple as a computer getting infected with a virus.
    - It can also be as elaborate as a multi-phased attack.
  - ***Incident Investigation***
    - Once attack is detected, defenders respond with preliminary investigation to filter out false positives.
    - Corroborating evidence is collected to verify sensor reported attack.
    - Once verified, defenders formally start enterprise's incident response process.
  - ***Containment***
    - Once the extent of the attack is understood, containment begins.
    - Objectives include removing the attacker, fixing broken cybersecurity controls, and emplacing interim security fixes that should make it more difficult for the attacker to get in again.

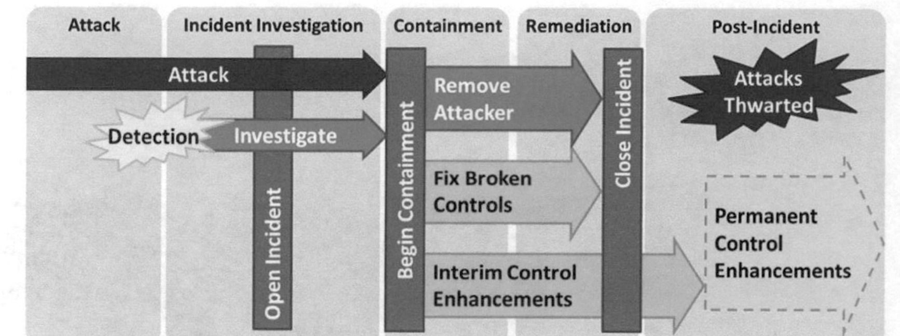

  - ***Remediation***
    - After attack is contained, defenders remediate the damage, rebuild affected systems, clean up defaced web sites, and restore normal operations.
    - At the conclusion of remediation, the enterprise formally closes out incident.
  - ***Post-Incident***
    - After the initial incident is remediated, follow-on attacks by the same attacker using the same tools, techniques, and procedures should be thwarted or at least rapidly detected and defeated.
    - Additional controls put in place may lead to long-term permanent security enhancements or strengthened controls.

Incident Response Process *(2 of 15)*

Context *(2 of 2)*

- At the next level of detail, incident response can be embodied in a ten-step process.
  - *Step 1: Identify the Incident*
  - *Step 2: Investigate the Incident*
  - *Step 3: Collect Evidence*
  - *Step 4: Report the Results*
  - *Step 5: Contain the Incident*
  - *Step 6: Repair Gaps or Malfunctions*
  - *Step 7: Remediate Compromised Accounts, Computers, and Networks*
  - *Step 8: Validate Remediation and Strengthened Security Controls*
  - *Step 9: Report the Conclusion of the Incident*
  - *Step 10: Resume Normal IT Operations*

Incident Response Process *(3 of 15)*

Step 1—Identify the Incident

- *How does an enterprise know a security incident has occurred?*
  - Enterprise security monitoring system generates an alert.
  - Users notice something wrong with enterprise IT systems.
  - The enterprise name shows up on the front page of the news!
- Regardless, the incident response process needs to be engaged.
- Incident response is a formal mechanism for declaring an incident and initiating the process.
- Everyone involved in the process needs to
  - know that a security incident is taking place; and
  - understand how the process should be prioritized in relation to other responsibilities.
- Generally, supporting security incidents should be a close second priority behind maintaining normal operations and services, but ahead of system improvements, upgrades, or audits.
- This situation is challenging because staff members are normally 100% engaged in supporting operations.
- *Who is in charge?*
  - Notionally, with full backing of CIO, IT Security is in charge.
  - CIO makes tough calls allocating resources.
- When a security incident is declared, IT Security goes from having an enterprise-supporting role to having a leading role.
- Resolving incident will likely have operational impacts.

Incident Response Process *(4 of 15)*

Step 2—Investigate the Incident *(1 of 3)*

- Simple investigations involve a single computer, account, network address, or piece of malware.
- Complex investigations can involve hundreds of systems and take months to complete.
- Investigation team maintains four lists to track the following Indicators of Compromise (IOCs):
  - ***Computers*** in the internal IT environment that were compromised, including personal computers, servers, and infrastructure systems
  - ***Networks accounts*** on the internal network that were compromised or used by attackers, including regular user accounts, privileged systems administrator accounts, and service accounts used by applications to communicate with each other
  - ***Tools, techniques, and procedures (TTPs)*** used to conduct the attack, including viruses, malware, remote controller programs, and operating system tools such as secure shell and remote desktop
  - ***Internet locations*** used by the attackers to control systems on the inside or to receive exfiltrated data

Incident Response Process *(5 of 15)*

Step 2—Investigate the Incident *(2 of 3)*

- The graphic depicts the IOC Cycle that investigators can use to help identify the full scope of the incident.
- ***Computers***
  - Inspect a computer that generated an alert from anti-virus or some type of malware activity
- ***Network Accounts***
  - Analyze the computer and identify user accounts that were used from that computer
  - Track the use of the accounts across the network
  - Identify non-legitimate uses of those accounts

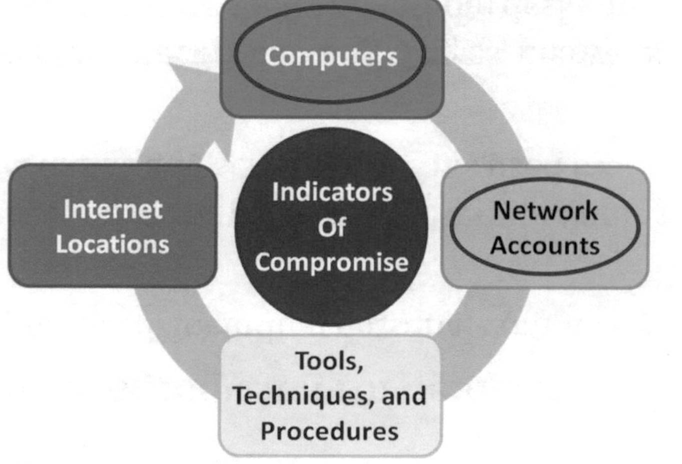

Incident Response Process *(6 of 15)*

Step 2—Investigate the Incident *(3 of 3)*

- ***Tools, Techniques, and Procedures (TTPs)***
  - Analyze the malware and identify hash signatures of the files involved or specific strings of software
  - Search the rest of enterprise for malware
  - Also look for network communications patterns that are distinct to the software involved (Such patterns are particularly useful when attackers are using operating system tools that are already built into the system.)
- ***Internet Locations***
  - Analyze the computer and its network connections
  - Look for web connections to the Internet or evidence of protocol tunneling to Internet addresses

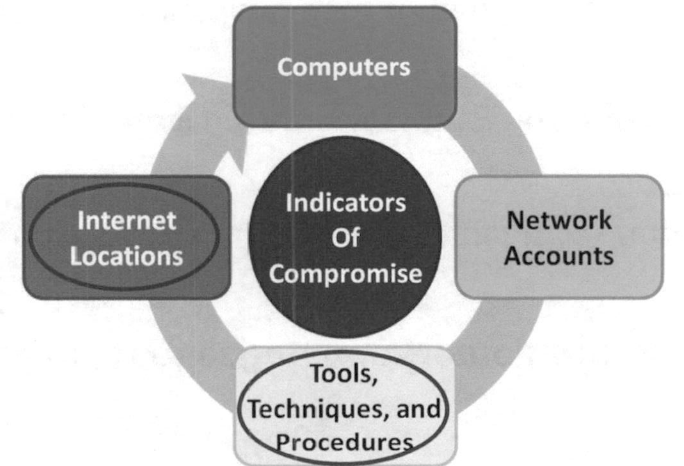

- Each time the IOC Cycle is performed, more computers, network accounts, TTPs, or Internet locations related to the incident may be found.

Incident Response Process *(7 of 15)*

Step 3—Collect Evidence

- The systems involved in cyberincidents are often governed by laws, regulations, or industry standards that require formal reporting or other procedures.
  - May be necessary to formally collect evidence and maintain chains of custody for evidence
  - May need internal auditors, external auditors, or law enforcement authorities
- Regulatory frameworks that might trigger formal evidence collection requirements in the United States include the following:
  - ***Personal Card Industry (PCI)***: Regulates data including credit card numbers and sometimes online banking information
  - ***Personally Identifiable Information (PII)***: Regulates data regarding personal identification and identity, regulated by United States privacy laws
  - ***Health Insurance Portability and Accountability Act (HIPAA)***: Regulates data containing personal health information
  - ***International Traffic In Arms Regulations (ITAR)***: Regulates technologies that are export-controlled by the United States Department of State
  - ***Sarbanes-Oxley (SOX)***: Regulates financial data for public companies related to company finance and financial results reporting

Incident Response Process *(8 of 15)*

Step 4—Report the Results

- Investigators report to enterprise management on what is going on and what the plan is for going forward.
- If investigators engage external services to assist in the investigation, then they will likely issue a formal report outlining what malware they found and evidence they collected.
- Report content should include the following information:
  - ***Timeline*** of what is known about the attack, including the first infection, lateral movements, and the time of discovery
  - ***Regulatory impact*** of affected computers and data so that enterprise management understands evidence collection and regulatory reporting requirements
  - ***Business impact*** of the attack, including how current business is being affected and how future business may be affected by the remediation process
  - ***Incident resolution plan*** to remove the attackers from the enterprise, strengthen defenses, and restore normal operations
  - ***Technical data*** about the attack, including computers, accounts, network addresses, and malware involved in the attacker activities
- Enterprise management needs to make decisions and provide guidance on executing the incident resolution plan.

Incident Response Process *(9 of 15)*

Step 5—Contain the Incident

- Containment
  - Is first step in incident remediation
  - Blocks computers, tools, accounts, and network addresses from being used by attackers
  - Must be carefully thought through to avoid a "whack-a-mole" scenario where attack continues to spread at the same time the enterprise tries to contain it
  - Needs to avoid a situation where attackers know they have been detected and contained because, if attackers know, they can change their methods and become invisible again
- Containment generally consists of the following actions:
  - ***Computers*** that have been compromised are disconnected from the network or malware is removed from them so it can no longer run.
  - ***Attackers' software tools*** are detected and blocked from running on enterprise computers.
  - ***User and service accounts*** that have been compromised are disabled or their credentials changed so they can no longer be used by the attackers.
  - ***Internet locations*** being used by the attackers are blocked so they can no longer be used to communicate with computers inside the network.

Incident Response Process *(10 of 15)*

Step 6—Repair Gaps or Malfunctions

- Once the incident is contained,
  - perhaps the ***most important step*** is to identify security deficiencies that allowed the incident to occur and close those deficiencies;
  - the enterprise may not be able to fix every deficiency, but it needs to strengthen security enough so the original attack will not succeed if the attackers come back and try it again;
  - some desired security enhancements may take more time or money than is available; and
  - residual risks will need to be managed until the risks can be remediated.
- Some key steps in repairing the enterprise security controls include the following:
  - ***Analyze attack sequence*** to understand how the attack occurred, what steps were involved in it, and where the enterprise can disrupt, detect, delay, and defeat future attacks.
  - ***Identify controls*** that are in place or can be put in place quickly to catch the attack should it occur again.
  - ***Emphasize detection*** to ensure the enterprise can detect future attacks while they are in progress and before they can be completed or cause significant damage.
  - ***Consider training*** to protect against attack vectors and methods that rely on user behaviors and mistakes such as clicking on links in phishing e-mails.

Incident Response Process *(11 of 15)*

Step 7—Remediate Compromised Accounts, Computers, and Networks

- Once the security controls are repaired,
  - the enterprise can proceed with remediating affected computers, accounts, and network components to bring them back to normal operations;
  - malware needs to be thoroughly eradicated; and
  - potential backdoors need to be cleaned up and closed off.
- Some key remediation steps include the following:
  - ***Change account credentials*** and passwords so they are no longer available to attackers
  - ***Wipe and rebuild*** affected computers, where possible, while being careful not to move infection from the old system to the new one
  - ***Manually clean up*** systems where wiping and rebuilding is too labor-intensive or disruptive to be practical
  - ***Restore data*** from backups, where necessary

Incident Response Process *(12 of 15)*

Step 8—Validate Remediation and Strengthen Security Controls

- Once remediation takes place,
  - security personnel need to validate the remediation activities to ensure they were performed correctly;
  - validation is needed because often security directs IT to take remediation actions, but before actions are completed, another crisis comes up and remediation gets put on the back burner or forgotten; and
  - validation is needed to close out the incident.
- Validation involves the following:
  - ***Checking computers*** to ensure affected computers are remediated (for example, rebuilding or cleaning up computers to remove malware and tools used in the attack)
  - ***Checking user accounts*** to ensure affected accounts are remediated (such as changing the password)
  - ***Checking network configuration*** to ensure network blocks or other changes are properly documented so they can be sustained
  - ***Checking security controls*** to ensure a future attack of the same type will be detected and disrupted
  - ***Checking regulator requirements*** to ensure necessary requirements are complied with and reports filed, if necessary
  - ***Identifying future actions*** as part of long-term strengthening of the enterprise security posture
  - ***Conducting an after-action review*** to understand what went well with the incident response process, what went poorly, and how the process can be improved going forward

Incident Response Process *(13 of 15)*

Step 9—Report the Conclusion of the Incident *(2 of 2)*

- The incident response team provides enterprise management with a final report to close out the incident.
  - The report documents the major incident details and supports future incident responses and investigations.
  - The report helps enterprise understand attack vectors and scenarios and provides valuable input to future cyberdefense planning efforts.
  - The final report can follow the same basic outline as the initial report, except all known facts are included.
- Key elements of the final report include the following:
  - ***Major differences*** from initial report, including initial "facts" that turned out to be incorrect or assumptions that turned out false
  - ***Timeline*** of the attack and remediation sequence, including dates and times of
    - Initial attacker activity
    - Initial discovery of breach
    - Major incident response activities including beginning and completion of containment, remediation, and validation activities
    - Times of day, which should be referenced against an appropriate time zone to prevent confusion

Incident Response Process *(14 of 15)*

Step 9—Report the Conclusion of the Incident *(2 of 2)*

- Key elements of the final report include the following (continued):
  - ***Regulatory impact*** of the incident, as well as any changes in regulatory impact and reporting that occurred during the investigation
  - ***Technical data*** about the attack, including lists of computers, accounts, network addresses, and malware involved in the attack activities
  - ***After-action report*** describing what went well with the incident response, what went poorly, and what lessons were learned
- It is OK if final report contradicts the initial report in many places.
  - Frequently, initial reports contain inaccuracies due to challenges of collecting good information during a crisis.
  - This reality does not necessarily reflect poorly on the incident team's efforts; it's just a matter of fact caused by the realities and confusion of the crisis.

Incident Response Process *(15 of 15)*

Step 10—Resume Normal IT Operations

- Things should be back to normal and systems should be fully operational.
- ***Temporary risk mitigation*** activities (for example, manual security controls, manual audits and checks) may still be ongoing.
- The enterprise needs to be cautious that such temporary measures do not become permanent.
- ***Permanent risk mitigation*** activities (for example, security control enhancements, system hardening) will likely be on-going for some time after the incident is resolved.

Support the Incident Response Process *(1 of 2)*

- Incident response involves many supporting cybersecurity capabilities to include the following:
  - ***Detection:*** If an enterprise cannot detect intrusions, it will not be able to start the incident response process.
  - ***Key Detection Capabilities***
    - Privileged activity monitoring
    - Network intrusion detection
    - Traffic analysis and data analytics
    - Data leakage protection
    - Anti-virus software
    - In-memory malware detection
    - Rogue network device detection
    - Event correlation
  - ***Investigation***: Investigation requires solid forensic capabilities across a wide variety of systems.
  - ***Key Forensic Capabilities***
    - Endpoint logging policies and forensic imaging support
    - Network packet intercept and capture
    - Firewall and IDS logging
    - Administrator audit trails
    - Forensics and e-discovery tools
    - Threat intelligence
    - Indicators of compromise
    - Network activity patterns across the entire network's critical connectivity links

Support the Incident Response Process *(2 of 2)*

- ***Remediation***: Remediation requires the ability to move faster than the attackers and remove them from the enterprise faster than they can maneuver to avoid removal.
- ***Key Remediation Capabilities***
    - Multi-factor authentication for administrators
    - Network service management
    - Application whitelisting
    - Identity life cycle management
    - Rapid computer imaging
    - Patch management and deployment
    - High availability and disaster recovery capabilities

- Incident response
    - Is not just about a single enterprise cybersecurity functional area or capability
    - Involves leveraging all functional areas and appropriate capabilities to mount an effective response when incidents occur

CHAPTER 10

Managing a Cybersecurity Crisis

S. E. Donaldson et al., *Enterprise Cybersecurity Study Guide*, https://doi.org/10.1007/978-1-4842-3258-3_10

Overview

- *When does a cybersecurity incident become a crisis?*
  - When it impacts entire enterprise
  - When it requires activation of disaster recovery plans
- For example, it becomes a crisis when a single compromised server becomes ten compromised servers, then a hundred, and pretty soon the entire data center is infected, damaged, or worse.
  - Saudi Aramco in 2012: Shamoon virus infected ~ 30,000 of its Windows-based machines.
  - Sony Pictures Entertainment in 2014: Malware stole huge amounts of confidential data.
  - In addition, smaller incidents happen every day outside of the public eye.
- This chapter describes
  - how things change when a crisis occurs;
  - how enterprises behave under the duress of a crisis situation; and
  - techniques for restoring IT during a crisis while simultaneously strengthening cybersecurity to protect against an active attacker who may hit the enterprise at any moment.

Topics

- Devastating Cyberattacks and "Falling Off the Cliff"
- Keeping Calm and Carrying On
- Managing the Recovery Process
- Recovering Cybersecurity and IT Capabilities
- Ending the Crisis
- Being Prepared for the Future

Devastating Cyberattacks and "Falling Off the Cliff" *(1 of 5)*

Context

- A cybercrisis begins with a devastating cyberattack impacting an enterprise's ability to function or deliver revenue-generating services.
  - Stuxnet attack impairing Iranian nuclear program
  - 2014 attack on a German foundry's blast furnace resulting in extensive physical damage
- Many devastating cyberattacks involve attackers gaining complete ***administrative control*** of victim network.
- Unfortunately, many enterprises structure their security in a manner that attackers can gain administrative control relatively easily.
- Devastating cyberattacks and potential impacts can be characterized as follows:
  - The Snowballing Incident
  - Falling Off the Cliff
  - Reporting to Senior Enterprise Leadership
  - Calling for Help

Devastating Cyberattacks and "Falling Off the Cliff" *(2 of 5)*

The Snowballing Incident

- The true magnitude of a devastating cyberattack may not be visible initially.
- Cyberattack starts like any other incident.
  - For example, an anti-virus alert or a logon fail with an administrator credential.
- As investigators analyze the incident and start correlating it across the enterprise, the incident's impact expands.
  - An administrator account is being used inappropriately throughout the enterprise.
  - Malware is discovered on critical application servers, systems administration servers, or authentication servers.
  - A piece of malware—once it is identified as such—is present on a significant portion of the enterprise's computers.
  - A large number of enterprise computers are communicating with an external command-and-control server.
  - Once the right signatures are loaded into network security systems, the enterprise realizes malicious communications are taking place throughout the enterprise network.
- The snowball gets bigger and bigger ...

Devastating Cyberattacks and "Falling Off the Cliff" *(3 of 5)*

Falling Off the Cliff

- As the investigation proceeds, the enterprise realizes this incident is
  - not a small incident to be cleaned up in a day; and
  - a "big deal." (The enterprise is in "big trouble.")
- Investigators refer to this situation as ***falling off the cliff***.
- As the crisis snowballs, the enterprise's ability to respond to it diminishes.
  - The incident includes most, if not all, servers in the system, along with the consoles used to control them.
  - Most computers are compromised.
  - Most of the enterprise's disaster recovery plans are not going to work because the attacker is in control.
  - The enterprise is still uncertain as to what the attacker can or cannot do.
- The enterprise needs to be careful not to let the attacker in control know the enterprise
  - knows what is going on; and
  - is about to kick the attacker out.
- The attacker might react and do something extremely destructive.
- Cybersecurity staff should be cautious regarding their communications.
  - Face-to-face and telephonic communications are preferred.
  - Messaging, e-mail, and other collaboration tools can be compromised and tip off the attackers.

Devastating Cyberattacks and "Falling Off the Cliff" *(4 of 5)*

Reporting to Senior Enterprise Leadership

- As the enterprise understands the cyberattack's magnitude, it is time to report the situation to senior leadership.
- Initial reports are most likely incorrect and do not accurately portray what it will take to resolve the situation.
- Report needs to present clearly the magnitude of the knowns, unknowns, threats, and risks.
- Key reporting points include
  - what is known so far;
  - what is not known so far;
  - what is understood about the attacker;
  - what will be required to stabilize the situation;
  - what will be required to resolve the situation; and
  - what help should be called in immediately to start the response.

Devastating Cyberattacks and "Falling Off the Cliff" *(5 of 5)*

Calling for Help

- Once senior enterprise leadership understands the magnitude of the cyberattack, leadership and employee channels will be consumed to
  - keep organized around the situation; and
  - maintain accurate status for leadership.
- Enterprises staffed for "normal" operations seldom have the bandwidth to handle additional reporting.
- Areas that may require help include the following:
  - ***Strategy, Architecture, and Planning***
    - Advising leaders on the big picture for crisis
    - Providing leaders with templates based on experience so leaders do not start from scratch
  - ***Investigating the Incident***
    - Understanding the magnitude of the crisis, affected accounts, computers, networks, and malware
    - Collecting information for remediation
  - ***Strengthening Cybersecurity***
    - Reinforcing security capabilities so attackers will not be able to counterstrike while they are being removed or after remediation
  - ***Rebuilding IT***
    - Reconstituting affected IT systems
    - Restoring impacted business operations
  - ***Tracking Status***
    - Keeping track of crisis activities
    - Accurately reporting activities to leadership
    - Facilitating discussions to understand and make risk-based decisions
    - Trading off operational risk with cybersecurity risk
- ***Calling for help*** takes the pressure off regular employees so they remain focused on staying in control of the situation and making decisions.

Keeping Calm and Carrying On *(1 of 12)*

Context

- As the magnitude of the crisis unfolds, people will be afraid for their
  - jobs,
  - careers, and
  - livelihoods.
- Many people will look for mistakes that may have led to the situation becoming a crisis.
- It is critically important for leadership to keep calm and hold second-guessing in check.
- Everyone needs to stay focused on the problems and finding solutions.

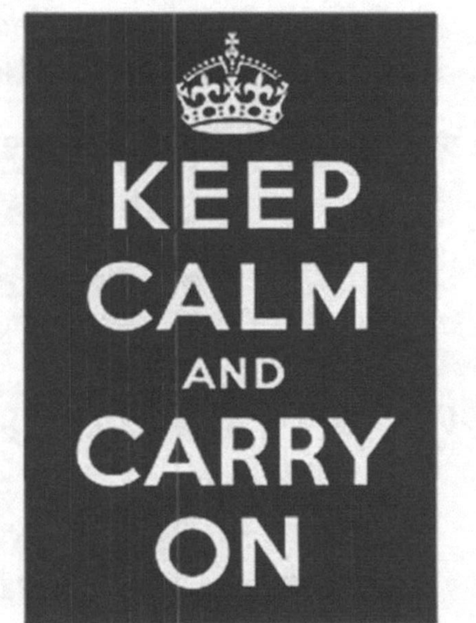

This poster was developed in Great Britain as part of the preparation for World War II, but it was not widely distributed at the time.

The British government kept it in storage for use in case of a devastating German attack.

It was rediscovered in 2000 and has since become quite popular.

Keeping Calm and Carrying On *(2 of 12)*

Playing Baseball in a Hailstorm

A cyberattack crisis is like playing a game of baseball while it is hailing baseballs.

- Keeping calm becomes more difficult as a crisis unfolds.
- Established communications channels become overloaded, along with corresponding leadership.
- Using the baseball analogy, everyone quickly becomes overwhelmed.
  - Leaders spend most of their time in meetings.
  - Leaders spend little of their time synthesizing reports, setting up assignments, or delegating tasks.
- Consequently, “the ball gets dropped” everywhere in the organization.
  - Normal processes of reporting and delegating become ineffective.
  - Usual communications channels of e-mails, voicemails, and meetings break down.
- In a crisis, the enterprise needs to change its method of operations (including support contractors) if it is to manage the crisis effectively.

Keeping Calm and Carrying On *(3 of 12)*

Communications Overload

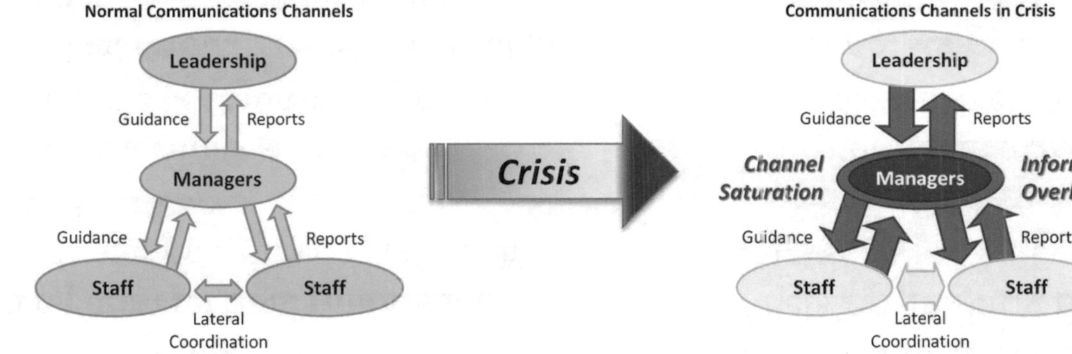

- As the situation becomes a crisis,
  - regular communications channels become saturated;
  - managers become overloaded by status information, requests for support, and guidance from leadership; and
  - communications overload seriously undermines the ability to accurately assess the situation.

- To improve the situation, staff and contractors can
  - rely more on lateral communication to coordinate among themselves, which takes pressure off of managers who don't have time for lateral communications.
  - spend more time synthesizing their reports into formats that managers need rather than simply giving them raw data.
  - elicit the guidance and requirements they need from managers rather than waiting for such information.

Keeping Calm and Carrying On *(4 of 12)*

Decision-Making Under Stress *(1 of 2)*

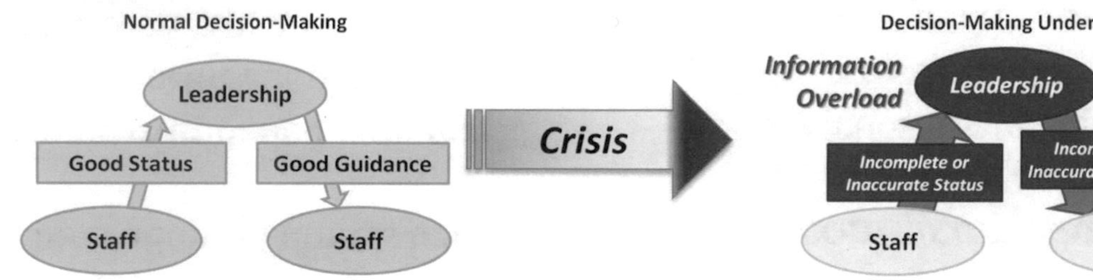

- As the crisis situation unfolds,
  - confusion in reports and status information can have an extremely detrimental effect on management effectiveness;
  - incomplete and inaccurate status can dramatically impede decision-making; and
  - incomplete and inaccurate status can result in incomplete and inaccurate management guidance.

- Several factors contribute to difficult decision-making during a crisis.
  - ***First***, status reports are incomplete, do not contain the right data in the right format, or are not summarized in the right way for decision-makers to properly handle the data.
  - ***Second***, some status reports are inaccurate or get distorted as the reports get passed through multiple layers of management.
  - ***Third***, overwhelmed leadership misses important facts or performs inadequate analysis or synthesis of the facts, resulting in faulty decisions.

Keeping Calm and Carrying On *(5 of 12)*

Decision-Making Under Stress *(2 of 2)*

- To assist decision-makers in getting the best possible status and making the best decisions, remember the following factors:
  - Accurate decision-making requires accurate data regarding the status, ***not opinions***, about the status.
    - Accurate Data = Four of five servers have been rebuilt and the fifth one will be ready tomorrow.
    - Opinion = Most of the servers are done and the rest will be done soon.
    - Opinions do not synthesize well into combined reports for key decision-makers.
  - Accurate data or status information will not always be available and frequently decisions will have to be made with incomplete information.
    - This situation is one of the most difficult situations for managers.
    - Talented leaders can make "gut" choices in the absence of accurate data.
    - Such choices will be revisited after the fact; that is, there will be an after-action review.
    - Leaders need to capture and document their assumptions when making key decisions.
  - Inaccurate status information is absolutely toxic to good decision-making.
    - When different enterprise departments maintain their own status and the statuses do not match, senior leadership must spend valuable time de-conflicting the reports.
    - Bad status can result in wasted time and delays in decision-making.
    - Worst of all are decisions and guidance that are wrong due to inaccurate situational awareness.

Keeping Calm and Carrying On *(6 of 12)*

Asks Vs. Needs: Eliciting Accurate Requirements and Guidance

- Staff and contractors should ask intelligent questions to help ensure the
  - status they are giving is accurate and actually needed; and
  - guidance they are receiving is actually the appropriate guidance.
- It is not unusual for staff members to send up a situation status report and expect certain guidance based on that status, only to get contrary guidance.
  - This situation occurs because the original status was distorted going up the chain of command.
  - It can also occur because the resulting guidance got distorted coming back down.
- Staff and contractors who recognize these disconnects can question the communications and address the distortions to help the enterprise make smart decisions.
- To help with clarification, staff and contractors need to following these recommendations:
  - ***First***, they need to have a conversation with management about what status management is looking for and what the resulting status actually *means*. In other words, what does management want to measure that accurately *reflects* the goal to be achieved and the corresponding progress toward the goal?
  - ***Second***, they need to have conversations with management when they receive guidance for action. They need to ask follow-up questions to understand better what management really wants (deliverables) to avoid wasting time doing the wrong thing.
  - ***Third***, they should elicit accurate deliverable requirements, particularly in contract situations where requirements are at the heart of the contract (for example, giving customer sample requirements to approve, disapprove, or correct to make it easier for management to provide concrete guidance). In other words, they need concrete guidance and *get everyone on the same page*.

Keeping Calm and Carrying On *(7 of 12)*

The Observe Orient Decide Act (OODA) Loop

- US Air Force Colonel John Boyd (1927–1997) developed the Observe Orient Decide Act (OODA) loop to describe how fighter pilots perform in combat.
- Enterprises can apply this model when they make decisions.
- The four steps are as follows:
  - ***Observe***: Collect status from personnel "on the ground" and synthesize the status into a coherent picture for decision-makers
  - ***Orient***: Analyze the situation and prepare to make the decision; may involve processing status data into "actionable intelligence" and preparing plans and alternative courses of actions for decision-makers
  - ***Decide***: decide on a course of action and break decisions down into their contingent parts so teams can take actions based on the decision

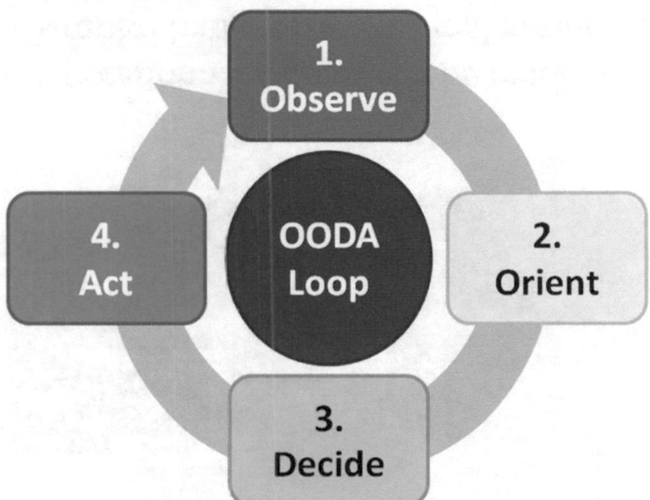

  - ***Act***: execute the decisions by repositioning resources and executing procedures (in other words turn the decision into actions, and observe the results and impacts ... then cycle begins again)
- If an enterprise can operate faster than the cyberattacker's OODA loop, then the cyberattacker will be forever "one step behind" and unable to respond effectively to the enterprise's actions.

Keeping Calm and Carrying On *(8 of 12)*

Establishing Operational Tempo *(1 of 2)*

- The OODA theory maps directly to enterprise crisis operations.
  - Information collection
  - Decision-making
- The theory states that reports and decisions have to be synchronized so that there is time to observe the results of decisions before making new decisions to continue moving forward.
- Making decisions at an accelerated rate requires that reporting, meetings, and coordination all take place at an accelerated rate as well.
- This synchronization defines the enterprise's ***operational tempo***.
- The pace of decision-making depends on the time required for each OODA step.

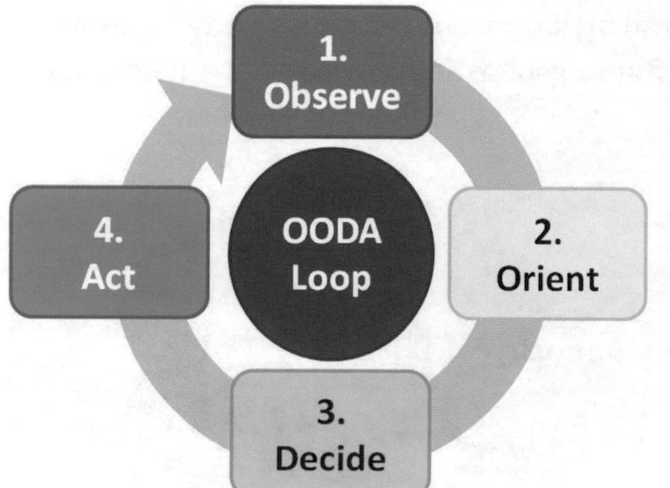

- Operational changes can be made hourly by simply changing operational parameters.
- Staffing changes can take weeks to execute (hiring, training, and so on).
- Engineering changes can take days, weeks, months, or years (re-tooling, testing, and so forth).
- Strategy shifts can take months or years to observe and orient before making key decisions.

Keeping Calm and Carrying On *(9 of 12)*

Establishing Operational Tempo *(2 of 2)*

- In a crisis, faster OODA loops may be required (for instance, hours vs. days).
- Normal business operations often revolve around a *weekly* tempo of reports and decision-making.
  - At low levels, there may be daily, or even hourly, "huddles" to make sure everyone is on the same page and problems are dealt with quickly.
  - Staff and teams may meet weekly to coordinate.
  - Strategic management layers may meet monthly, quarterly, or annually.
- Crisis business operations tend to be compressed due to urgency of the situation.
  - Every hour is used to its maximum to make progress against threat.
  - Crisis operational tempo tends to be *daily*.
- Even with daily reporting and guidance, there are delays and it can take several days for

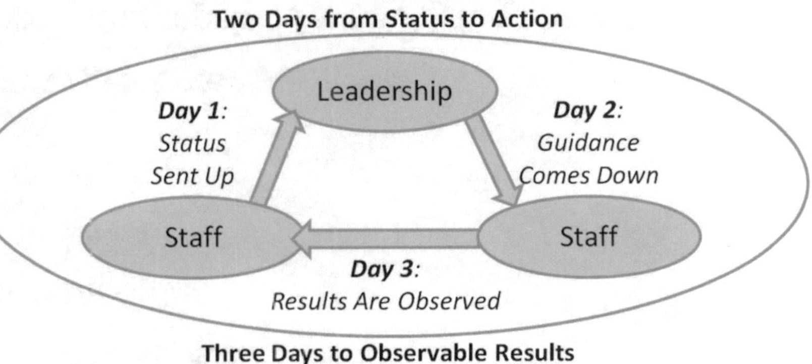

  - status to travel up the hierarchy;
  - decisions to travel down the hierarchy; and
  - the impacts of the decisions to be observed and reported back up.
- Traditional meetings often don't keep pace with a crisis; the crisis requires alternative methods, procedures, and tools to co-locate observers, analysts, and decision-makers (for example, war rooms and crisis operations centers).

Keeping Calm and Carrying On *(10 of 12)*

Operating in a Crisis Mode *(1 of 3)*

- During a crisis, it is helpful for an enterprise to think about the following key crisis factors:
  - ***Planning***: It is important for an enterprise to have a crisis recovery plan.
  - ***Process***: An enterprise needs to establish a process for the recovery effort.
  - ***Prioritization***: The next challenge is to prioritize recovery efforts.
  - ***Parallelism***: An enterprise may have a lot of resources at its disposal.
  - ***Sequencing***: It helps to ensure recovery happens in the right order.
- ***Crisis Factor: Planning***
  - Does not need to be elaborate
  - Needs to have some agreement on where to go and how to get there
  - Establishes initial operating capability (IOC) and full operating capabilities (FOC) targets
  - Needs to get everyone "on the same page" to help manage the chaos
  - Can be refined and detailed as crisis unfolds so everyone gets required information
  - Can occur "just in time" along with everything else in the recovery process

Keeping Calm and Carrying On *(11 of 12)*

Operating in a Crisis Mode *(2 of 3)*

- ***Crisis Factor: Process***
  - Reduces ad hoc communications and enables teams to interface smoothly
  - Should contain the following elements:
    - Regularly scheduled meetings for reporting, coordination, and issue discussion
    - Standardized formats for reports and requests
    - Supporting capabilities such as telephone bridges, document repositories, request trackers, and workspaces
    - A room where people can go to for information, a whiteboard containing important announcements, a telephone bridge, or a request line staffed by support personnel
- ***Crisis Factor: Prioritization Factor***
  - Tends to be difficult because everyone wants everything recovered immediately and IT systems that are nonfunctional have critical business consequences
  - Lacks enough resources to do everything simultaneously
  - Requires tough decisions
  - Turns IT discussions about technical priorities and dependencies into discussions about business priorities so leadership can make informed decisions

Keeping Calm and Carrying On *(12 of 12)*

Operating in a Crisis Mode *(3 of 3)*

- ***Crisis Factor: Parallelism Factor***
  - Organizes the resources so they are working at maximum efficiency
  - Requires minimizing resources tripping over each other while waiting for interdependencies among teams and systems
  - Plans recovery activities by keeping available resources fully utilized at all times, thereby avoiding time spent waiting on interdependencies
  - Requires a delicate balance between parallelism and prioritization
- ***Crisis Factor: Sequencing Factor***
  - Avoids having critical resources sitting idle while they are waiting for other pieces of the enterprise to recover
  - Builds IT system layers in correct order to deliver capabilities
    - Networking, storage, computing, operating systems, applications, Internet connectivity, and clients
  - Tests IT systems late in the recovery process due to the time required for all pieces to be integrated
  - Establishes an initial operating capability (IOC) vs. full operating capabilities (FOC) so recovery can continue in parallel across multiple tracks

Managing the Recovery Process *(1 of 7)*

Context

- The CIO looked around at his staff as the gravity of the situation sank in … the attackers had complete control, and the enterprise was entirely at their mercy.

"So, what do we do now?"

The CISO leaned forward and replied, *"Now we fight!"*

- What does an enterprise need to do in a cybersecurity crisis to regain control of the situation, rebuild impaired systems, and recover lost business functionality?
  - Engaging in Cyber Hand-to-Hand Combat
  - "Throwing Money at Problems"
  - Identifying Resources and Resource Constraints
  - Building a Resource-Driven Project Plan
  - Maximizing Parallelism in Execution
  - Taking Care of People

Managing the Recovery Process *(2 of 7)*

Engaging in Cyber Hand-to-Hand Combat

- The beginning of a *cyberattack* crisis is not the end of the *cyberbattle*, which generally consists of the following phases:
  - ***Stealth***: In the beginning, attackers often have stealth on their side as they move slowly and carefully to avoid setting off enterprise defenses.
  - ***Discovery***: After enterprise defenders discover the attack, they should move carefully to avoid tipping their hand and letting the attackers know the enterprise is aware of the attack. Defenders analyze the attack sequence to understand the extent of the attack and consider defensive and remediation options.
  - ***Containment and Remediation***: Now the game is on. Defenders attempt to contain the attack and remediate affected systems. Mistakes and oversights allow the attackers to retain their foothold or retake it after they are first repelled.
  - ***Counterattack and Battle***: After the initial remediation, attackers may attempt to regain control of the enterprise. Attackers now know the defenders are on to them, so they often switch tactics. Speed and tenacity are all-important now as the cyberbattle may wage back and forth for days, weeks, months, or even years.
  - ***Entrenchment and Stabilization***: Eventually, the situation stabilizes, with one party emerging victorious. Generally, defenders regain control of the enterprise. Sometimes, attackers outmaneuver the defense and disappear inside of unmonitored IT systems, thus retaining their foothold on an ongoing basis. Other times, the business disruption required for complete eradication may be too great and the attackers continue to have access to noncritical systems.
- For cybersecurity personnel in the midst of battle, it feels like cyber "hand-to-hand combat" as attackers take over accounts, computers, servers, and networks. The process is grueling and exhausting.

Managing the Recovery Process *(3 of 7)*

"Throwing Money at Problems"

- In a crisis, money may be the only lever an enterprise really has to deal with problems and take pressure off of overburdened staff and teams.
  - ***Buy Experience***: Bring in service providers to help with planning, investigation, cybersecurity improvements, IT rebuilding, and status tracking to free up employees so they can provide leadership and strategy
  - ***Buy Services***: Buy supplemental services while enterprise IT systems are offline during the recovery process
  - ***Buy Capacity***: Buy excess capacity on a temporary basis during the rebuilding process as some systems may be held as evidence for criminal investigations or to provide capacity to support parallel rebuilding
  - ***Buy Capability***: Negotiate with vendors for "sampler platter" licensing contracts that enable the enterprise to use the vendors' full range of products, and to rapidly test and discard options without getting bogged down in contract and licensing negotiations; for the long term, only keep the capabilities that are ultimately needed
  - ***Buy Contingencies***—Hedge against potential failures and uncertainties during the rebuilding process to guard against big problems becoming showstoppers
- Money can be used to obtain expertise, services, software, and equipment to give the recovery effort options and flexibility.

Managing the Recovery Process *(4 of 7)*

Identifying Resources and Resource Constraints

- An early step in the recovery process is identifying the resources available for the recovery effort, which ones are going to be critical, and which ones are going to be overtaxed, such as
  - ***Leadership and Project Management***: Leadership and project management quickly become saturated in a crisis situation and need whatever useful relief they can get.
  - ***Incident Response and Forensics***: Few enterprises have in-house incident response teams that are staffed to handle an incident of any magnitude.
  - ***Cybersecurity Engineering***: Efforts to shore up cyberdefenses in the wake of a breach will likely exceed the capacity of the existing team; such expertise is critical for proceeding.
  - ***IT Infrastructure and Backups***: As rebuilding efforts get underway, critical infrastructure elements—such as networking, firewalls, storage, computing, and backup systems—become bottlenecks to progress and system recovery.
  - ***IT Support and Help Desk***: If major changes are performed to endpoints or enterprise applications, IT support staff quickly become overwhelmed in supporting impacted employees who are unable to work effectively.
- As these resource constraints are identified, planners can hedge against them by obtaining additional resources, lining up contingency resources, or exploring alternative approaches.

Managing the Recovery Process *(5 of 7)*

Building a Resource-Driven Project Plan

- The result of the recovery planning effort is a ***resource-driven*** project plan vs. a ***normal*** project plan.
  - Resource-driven projects are designed around primary constraints—time and available resources.
  - The goal is to ensure all resources are gainfully employed at their maximum level so the rebuilding process goes as quickly as possible.
- The highest-priority project should be overlaid onto the resources first—part of critical path.
- Lower-priority projects are sequenced later with the understanding that they will spend time waiting for the resources needed to execute successfully.
- High-priority, mid-priority, and low-priority projects are laid out and sequenced.
- Low-priority projects are worked on an “if-time-is-available” basis until higher priority efforts are completed.

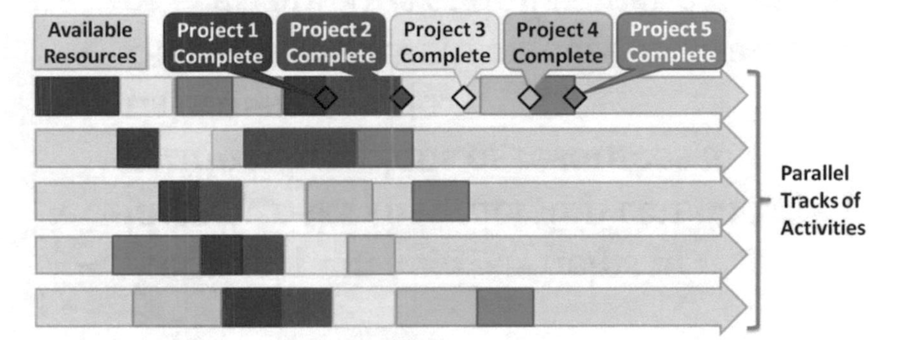

- The graphic depicts how five projects can be overlaid onto available resources so the highest-priority project completes first.
- It also depicts the projects progressing linearly; the reality is much more complex and iterative.
- Projects can be performed out of sequence to compress overall project schedule, but risk goes up.
- “Keep calm and carry on” while remembering that in a crisis you never have the resources you need to do everything you want.

Managing the Recovery Process *(6 of 7)*

Maximizing Parallelism in Execution

- A resource-driven plan strives to optimize available resources to get the most important recovery activities completed first to help the business recover as quickly as possible.
- As the plan is executed, the ***critical path*** jumps around among the different teams as each team's activities become critical to the rebuilding process.
- Teams that have resource constraints may be disproportionally represented on the critical path.
- Teams include leadership, incident response, cybersecurity, IT infrastructure, and IT support teams.
- In a highly parallelized rebuilding effort, the critical path can jump around among the different parallel tracks.

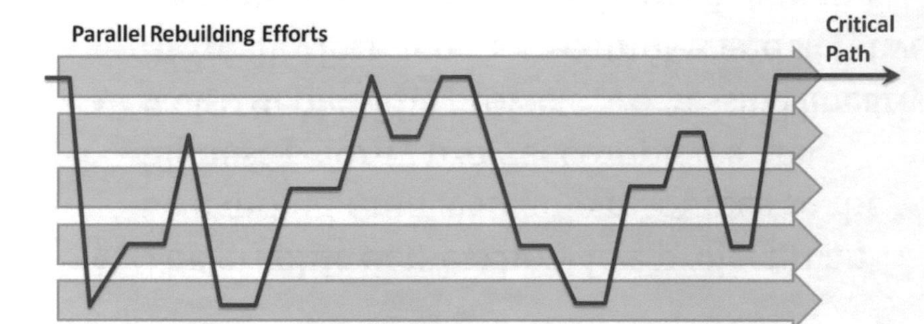

- A critical path analysis helps to identify risks so leadership can line up contingency plans or resources to keep risks manageable.
- Delays in recovery can cost thousands or even millions of dollars per day in lost productivity.
- Business leaders need to calculate the cost of lost productivity so that they can make smart investments to reduce the real or potential costs of such delays.

Managing the Recovery Process *(7 of 7)*

Taking Care of People

- During a crisis, there are periods where people dive in and give up their nights and weekends to deal with the crisis, but such efforts are difficult to sustain.
- Leadership needs to establish a sustainable pace for the overall effort (probably a marathon, not a sprint) that is in effect 24 hours a day, 7 days a week.
- Establishing a pace includes
  - identifying key decision-makers (such as CIO and CISO) who do not need to be available 24/7, but who are available to make decisions at critical times;
  - Getting personnel backups (for example, deputies and senior direct reports) so that key decision-makers can get the rest and breaks they need to be able to stay on top of things; and
  - arranging shifts, relief schedules, and vacations.
- Management should watch out for the technical people who are consulted on ***every project*** or who are the ***sole source*** of institutional knowledge on key systems.
- When such technical people are identified, leadership should consider the following:
  - ***First***, ensuring these people are incentivized to stay through the recovery process
  - ***Second***, ensuring they have some relief by assigning colleagues or consultants to assist them
  - ***Third***, watching their work schedules and making sure they are given breaks when opportunities arise
- Leadership should establish work schedules to ensure everyone gets time off with some regularity.
- Leadership can support morale with inexpensive activities (for example, catered food) to help everyone stay productive.

Recovering Cybersecurity and IT Capabilities *(1 of 10)*

Context

- As the recovery process gets moving, there will likely be two parallel tracks occurring.
  - Remediation and strengthening the cybersecurity situation
  - Restoration of damaged IT capabilities

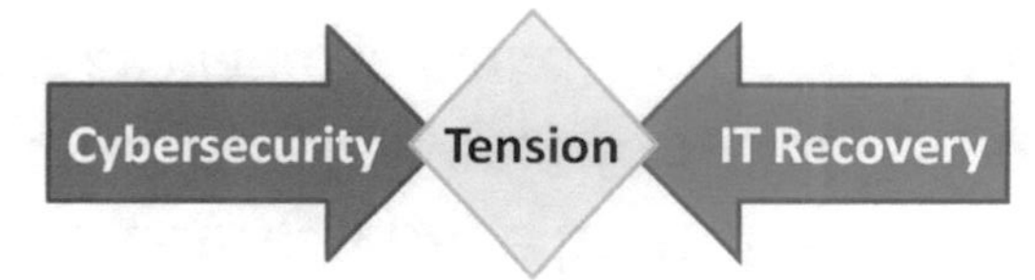

- Cybersecurity improvements in controls (particularly preventive controls) can often interfere with the rapid rebuilding of compromised IT systems.
- Consequently, these two parallel tracks may be in tension with one another.

- *How can an enterprise deal with this tension?*
  - Building the Bridge While You Cross It
  - Preparing to Rebuild and Restore
  - Closing Critical Cybersecurity Gaps
- Establishing Interim IT Capabilities
  - Conducting Prioritized IT Recovery and Cybersecurity Improvements
  - Establishing Full Operating Capabilities for IT and Cybersecurity
  - Considering Cybersecurity Vs. IT Restoration
  - Preparing for Maximum Allowable Risk
- Leadership must carefully manage this tension to ensure IT does not jeopardize the recovery process by undermining cybersecurity protections.

Recovering Cybersecurity and IT Capabilities *(2 of 10)*

Building the Bridge While You Cross It

- "Building Airplanes in the Sky"[1]
  - Construction workers build an airplane while it is in flight.
  - Workers parachute off the completed airplane at the end.
  - Analogy: Complex systems present building and deployment challenges, particularly when the systems are needed immediately or are operational throughout the project.
- "Building the bridge while you cross it" is a similar analogy for the relationship between cybersecurity and IT recovery during an extensive rebuilding effort.
  - Cybersecurity needs to protect IT.
  - Cybersecurity also relies on IT to provide the enterprise with networks, storage, and computing needed to deliver cybersecurity protective capabilities.
  - If cybersecurity gets ahead of IT, it will deploy security capabilities that IT cannot use, thus getting in the way of the IT recovery process.
  - If cybersecurity falls too far behind IT, the IT systems will be deployed without the cybersecurity protections the systems need to be safe.
- Cybersecurity needs to protect IT as systems are built, but cybersecurity also relies on those systems to support IT.
- Cybersecurity and IT efforts need to be carefully synchronized so that IT functionality and cybersecurity protection both come online together.

[1]Electronic Data Systems television advertisement, 2000.

Recovering Cybersecurity and IT Capabilities *(3 of 10)*

Preparing to Rebuild and Restore (1 of 2)

- A balanced strategy for rebuilding considers the following questions:
  - What will it take to disrupt the attackers?
  - What will it take to deny the attackers the ability to operate in the IT environment?
  - What will it take to regain cybersecurity control?
  - What will it take to recover impaired business IT capabilities?
  - What is the minimum amount of cybersecurity necessary before proceeding with the IT recovery process?
  - How can cybersecurity enhancements be phased so cybersecurity and business recovery can proceed together?
  - What if the attackers counterattack in the middle of the recovery process?
  - What is at risk if cybersecurity gets defeated while the recovery is in progress?
  - What is the business's tolerance for risk in the overall recovery effort while balancing business impairment, IT recovery, and cybersecurity?

Recovering Cybersecurity and IT Capabilities *(4 of 10)*

Preparing to Rebuild and Restore *(2 of 2)*

- Generally, the resulting plan should use a phased approach to start the recovery without making the situation worse.
  - ***First***, critical cybersecurity controls are shored up enough to remove attackers from the enterprise, or at least deny them administrative control.
  - ***Second***, interim IT capabilities are established so the business can continue functioning.
  - ***Third***, more extensive IT recovery is performed in parallel with more extensive cybersecurity improvements. These two tracks run in parallel, ***building the IT bridge while cybersecurity crosses it***. This approach is used to establish initial operating capabilities for IT and cybersecurity functions in parallel.
  - ***Fourth,*** as the situation stabilizes and the business regains functionality, initial operating capabilities are matured into full operating capabilities, with full capacity, high availability, redundancy, and disaster recovery as needed by the business.
- The strategy helps allow recovery while enabling the enterprise to proceed with an agreed-upon balance of business, IT, and cybersecurity risk.

Recovering Cybersecurity and IT Capabilities *(5 of 10)*

Closing Critical Cybersecurity Gaps

- First recovery steps:
  - ***Repel attackers*** actively inside the enterprise environment
  - ***Close critical cybersecurity gaps*** so that attackers cannot interfere with recovery process
- It is not realistic to think cybersecurity can be immediately brought ***up to par***.
- Small, incremental steps may be taken to deny attackers administrative control or keep them out of critical infrastructure.
  - Use of air-gapped systems and networks
  - Establishment of multi-factor authentication on critical system accounts
- Initial key actions to consider in the recovery process include the following:
  - ***Disrupt attacker communications channels*** so attackers cannot control malware inside the enterprise that might be left over from before the attack
  - ***Protect critical systems administrator accounts*** with multifactor authentication, rapidly changing passwords, or extensive auditing
  - ***Protect critical security servers*** through patching, hardening, network isolation, or monitoring
  - ***Isolate key infrastructure*** onto separate network segments with restrictive firewall rules
  - ***Use application whitelisting or monitoring*** to detect unauthorized changes on key and/or vulnerable systems
  - ***Establish 24/7 monitoring and altering*** to detect and respond to future attacker activity

Recovering Cybersecurity and IT Capabilities *(6 of 10)*

Establishing Interim IT Capabilities

- While cybersecurity gaps are being closed, IT can simultaneously start preparing IT capabilities to replace lost capabilities and support the recovery process.
- Options depend, in part, on the severity of what was lost and the long-term IT strategy.
  - ***Transition production IT data and services*** to development or staging systems that were unaffected by the attack
  - ***Recover IT servers from backup*** and bring them back to operation as they were before the attack
  - ***Recover IT data from backups*** and rebuild affected servers as they were before the attack
  - ***Migrate IT functions to cloud services***, either on a temporary or a permanent basis
  - ***Accelerate otherwise planned upgrades to IT systems*** and roll out upgraded systems
  - ***Use manual workarounds***, such as pen and paper or personal computer tools, rather than enterprise applications
- Combinations of these approaches can work well.
- Don't underestimate the value of manual workarounds that work fine on a temporary basis and free up critical IT talent to focus on recovering important IT systems.

Recovering Cybersecurity and IT Capabilities *(7 of 10)*

Conducting Prioritized IT Recovery and Cybersecurity Improvements

- Once critical cybersecurity gaps are addressed and interim IT capabilities are established, the recovery effort begins in earnest.
  - ***Prioritize activities*** based on business needs
  - ***Break up recovery into multiple phases of IT capabilities*** so that initial operating capability (IOC) is delivered quickly and full operating capability (FOC) is delivered later
  - ***Use limited resources*** to deliver the greatest amount of IT functionality in the least amount of time
- In parallel with the IT recovery, the enterprise will most likely make improvements to cybersecurity capabilities.
  - Ensure recovered IT systems are adequately protected from current attackers or other more advanced attackers in the future
  - Plan carefully so improvements don't interfere with recovery activities
  - Break up improvements into IOC and FOC phases to effectively use limited engineering, deployment, and support resources

Recovering Cybersecurity and IT Capabilities *(8 of 10)*

Establishing Full Operating Capabilities for IT and Cybersecurity

- With the completion of IT recovery and cybersecurity upgrades, the IOC is established for the majority of functions damaged or loss due to the crisis.
- The enterprise should be able to resume ***normal*** operations as it was conducted before the crisis.
- Work remains to achieve FOC and remove limitations associated with capacity, redundancy, high availability, disaster recovery, or security.
- Schedule, budget, or resource constraints impact the FOC timeline, which can takes months or even years.
- Systems may operate in a "high-risk" configuration until required budget is available.
- While uncomfortable, decisions and trade-offs are appropriate to balance the business, IT, and cybersecurity risks involved.

Recovering Cybersecurity and IT Capabilities *(9 of 10)*

Cybersecurity Versus IT Restoration

- Throughout the recovery process, there will likely be an ***active tension*** between cybersecurity and IT.

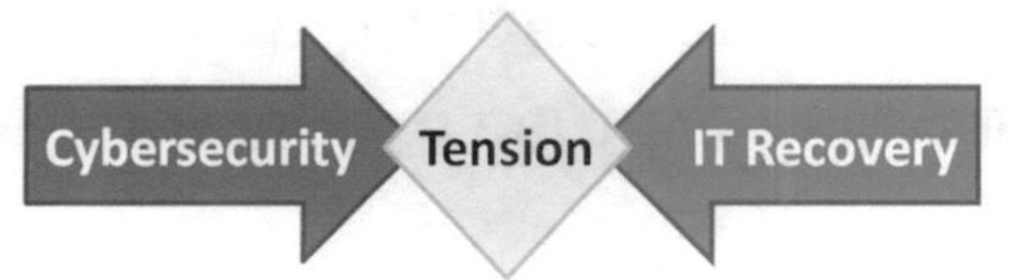

- Cybersecurity controls inevitably get in the way of IT personnel recovering systems and rebuilding IT capabilities.
- To maintain a balance between these recovery activities, it is important the enterprise embraces this tension and maintains open communications channels on ***what is working*** and ***what is not working***.
- There is no one right answer—only a delicate balance.

- What actions can the enterprise take to maintain this balance?
  - ***Educate IT staff*** on the purpose of cybersecurity controls that interfere with their work and let everyone know that management understands how the controls impact productivity
  - ***Ensure cybersecurity staff understands*** the operational impact of cybersecurity controls and plans ahead for alternatives should this impact becomes untenable
  - ***Have leadership regularly monitor*** the productivity impact of cybersecurity controls and be prepared to execute contingency plans if necessary
  - ***Have cybersecurity be proactive*** about what they are doing and why
- IT staff will be more supportive, contribute to solutions, and come to their own conclusions that the chosen controls are the least adverse alternatives.

Recovering Cybersecurity and IT Capabilities *(10 of 10)*

Maximum Allowable Risk

- Throughout the recovery process, business, IT, and cybersecurity leaders need to ensure all aspects of the recovery are performed at the same overall risk level.

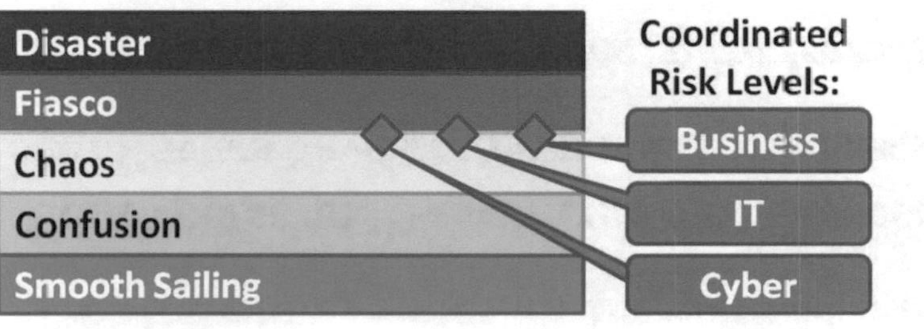

- Depending on the severity of the original crisis, an enterprise's tolerance for risk may vary.
  - If the crisis was minor, the enterprise appetite for risk in the recovery may also be low.
  - If the crisis was catastrophic, the enterprise appetite for risk in the recovery could be very high.
- Leadership should constantly monitor risk to ensure the risk levels stay as well coordinated as possible.
- The primary business driver is speed.
  - Business leadership will likely push IT and cybersecurity to move at the maximum speed possible to get recovery done securely without resulting in spectacular failure.
  - Business impairment may be worth thousands or millions of dollars a day.
  - When such costs are high, the business appetite for risk in the name of speed will likely be quite high.
- Challenge is translating these risk factors into business decisions so that leaders can make the best-informed decisions possible.

Ending the Crisis *(1 of 5)*

Context

- As the expression goes, “This too shall come to pass.”
- The enterprise eventually reaches a point where it is no longer operating in crisis.
- This transition generally happens at different times for different teams.
- Some personnel—*particularly cybersecurity personnel*—stay in crisis mode long after most employees have gotten back to business as usual.
- *How does an enterprise deal with transitioning from crisis to “normal” operations?*
  - Resolving the Crisis
  - Declaring the Crisis Remediated and Over
  - After-Action Review and Lessons Learned
  - Establishing a “New Normal” Culture

Ending the Crisis *(2 of 5)*

Resolving the Crisis

- Generally, a crisis winds down through four recovery phases as different parts of the enterprise return to ***normal*** operations:
  - ***Regular Employees***: The first phase occurs when basic enterprise functions are restored, often using interim or contingency capabilities. Interestingly, for most regular employees, this first milestone marks the conclusion of the crisis since the impact to their ability to do their jobs is largely mitigated.
  - ***Corporate Staff***: The second phase occurs when the most important enterprise IT systems are recovered to initial operating capability (IOC). At this point, business personnel (corporate staff) are able to get back to work using their normal processes.
  - ***IT Staff***: The third phase occurs when IT systems are fully restored back to full operating capability (FOC). At this point, IT staff can get back to a regular schedule of system maintenance, updates, and improvements.
  - ***Cybersecurity Staff***: The fourth phase occurs when cybersecurity improvements are completed and cybersecurity staff can "relax" and get back to their business as usual.

Ending the Crisis *(3 of 5)*

Declaring the Crisis Remediated and Over

- At some point during the four recovery phases, enterprise leadership is able to declare the crisis remediated and over.
- *Why is it important to declare the crisis remediated and over?*
  - ***First***, employees need to understand the crisis is over and the expectation for them *to go the extra mile* is no longer present. Employees can get back to a normal work-life balance, take care of families and households, and enjoy vacations.
  - ***Second***, there may be policies and procedures put in place specifically for the crisis that need to either be returned to *normal* or permanently adjusted into part of the *new normal.*
  - ***Third***, often crisis situations are funded and accounted for separately from normal business operations so they can be tracked as *one-time events* or may even be paid for separately by insurance. The costs associated with the crisis need to be accounted for and the end of those expenses must be clearly delineated.
- There is no hard-and-fast rule when the crisis is declared remediated and over, but generally it is some time between the third and fourth phases.

Ending the Crisis *(4 of 5)*

After-Action Review and Lessons Learned

- When the crisis is declared complete,
  - leadership should get together and make a list of lessons learned—not a huge list, but a candid list of what went well and what went poorly; and
  - lessons learned will help the enterprise handle the next crisis a little better
  - lessons learned are important inputs into strategic culture shifts that will persist long after the original crisis is resolved, establishing a "new normal" culture
- The after-action review should include lessons in successes and failures regarding the following:
  - Balancing of operations vs. cybersecurity and recovery
  - Task organization and coordination
  - Performance of technologies, procedures, and techniques
  - Performance of teams and organizations
  - Performance of partners and contractors
  - Recovery costs and cost-savings opportunities

Ending the Crisis *(5 of 5)*

Establishing a "New Normal" Culture

- Every crisis has a lasting impact on an enterprise.
- The challenge is to leverage the crisis to
  - make strategic adjustments to the enterprise culture, emphasizing computer and information security more greatly than in the past; and
  - translate those cultural changes into a "new normal."
- Concrete and visible changes include the following:
  - Greater willingness among business leaders to trade-off cost and productivity in the name of cybersecurity
  - Greater security of endpoint devices and computers at the expense of functionality
  - Restrictions on the use of personal computing devices and conducting enterprise business from home or other locations
  - Greater emphasis on using enterprise devices inside of controlled facilities to do critical work
  - Greater discipline among IT staff to focus on protecting enterprise systems and servers
  - Employee awareness training on cybersecurity concerns and potential threats

Being Prepared for the Future

"Disasters happen, and they happen to everyone ... eventually."

- ***Contingency planning*** reduces time in the "Orient" and "Decide" phases of the OODA loop.

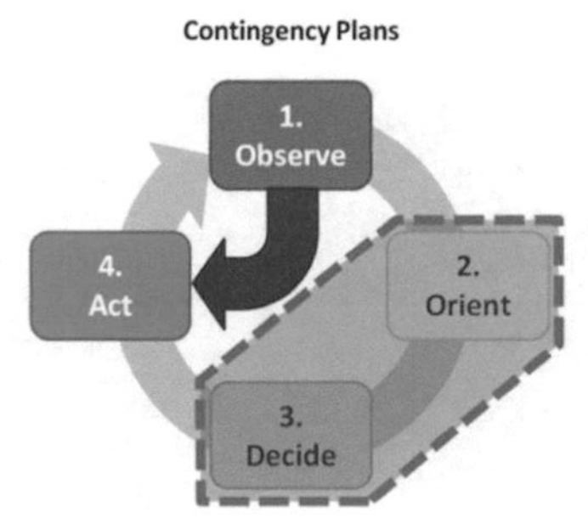

- When contingency scenarios are well-defined ahead of time, staff can go straight from "Observe" to "Act"; this helps to minimize wasted time.
- Such planning is critically important for incident rapid response scenarios. Specific attack scenarios can be worked out ahead of time along with response procedures to isolate affected accounts, computers, networks, and servers so that attacks can be stopped before they get out of control.

- ***Disaster recovery resources*** reduces time in the "Decide" and "Act" phases of the OODA loop.

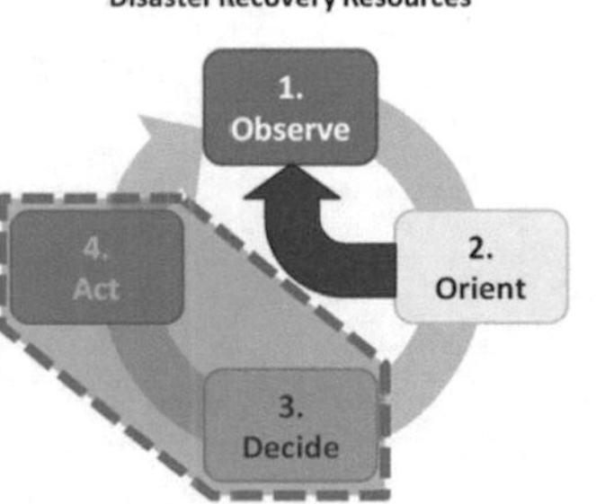

- When disaster recovery resources can be brought to fruition quickly in a future crisis, staff can go straight from "Orient" to "Observe"; this helps to determine if the resources have their intended effect.
- Resources may be offsite backups, contingency systems, or cloud services that are pre-coordinated and prepared ahead of time.
- Realistic training and tabletop exercises provide insight on how to operate in a crisis and what capabilities are needed.

Part IV: Enterprise Cyberdefense Assessment

- Chapter 11: Assessing Enterprise Cybersecurity
- Chapter 12: Measuring a Cybersecurity Program
- Chapter 13: Mapping Against Cybersecurity Frameworks

CHAPTER 11

Assessing Enterprise Cybersecurity

S. E. Donaldson et al., *Enterprise Cybersecurity Study Guide*, https://doi.org/10.1007/978-1-4842-3258-3_11

Overview

- This chapter discusses several things related to auditing and assessing an enterprise's cybersecurity program.
  - How auditing is used to evaluate enterprise cybersecurity
  - How audits should be used to drive the cybersecurity control design process
  - How enterprise cybersecurity can be systematically evaluated using four levels of assessment detail
  - How deficiency tracking is an integral component of any formal auditing or assessment process
- Audits and assessments can be conducted by internal or external assessors.
  - Can be risk-based, threat-based, framework-based, or control-based
  - Should be a formal part of a successful enterprise cybersecurity program
- Without periodic and objective assessment, the cybersecurity program will eventually suffer due to the atrophy that naturally occurs over time.

Topics

- Cybersecurity Auditing Methodology
- Cybersecurity Audit Types
- "Audit First" Design Methodology
- Enterprise Cybersecurity Assessments
- Audit Deficiency Management

Cybersecurity Auditing Methodology *(1 of 5)*

Context

- *What is a cybersecurity audit?*

  "An ***audit*** is a process whereby a person checks an automated system or operational process to ensure that it is operating properly."
- The graphic depicts a cybersecurity audit process.
  - Analyzing the ***records*** generated by the system or process
  - Collecting ***evidence*** of proper operation from those records
  - Compiling evidence into ***artifacts*** to support the audit
  - Compiling artifacts and conclusions into ***audit results***
- ***Audit results*** document what was done during the audit and what was found from the audit, including identified deficiencies and their eventual remediation.

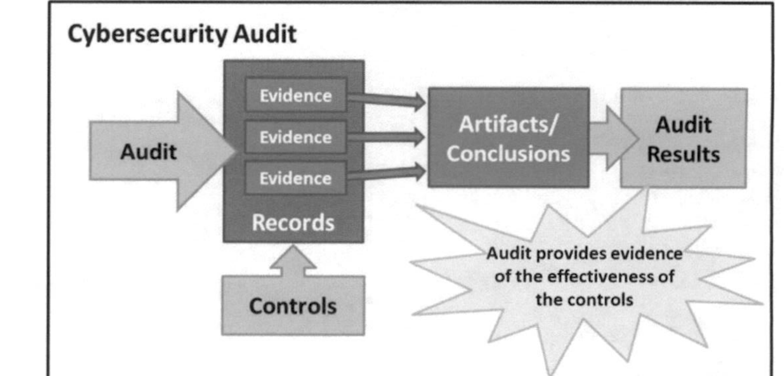

- Auditing Methodology Topics
  - The Challenge of Proving Negatives
  - Cybersecurity Audit Objectives
  - Cybersecurity Audit Plans
  - Audit Evidence Collection
  - Audit Artifacts
  - Audit Results
  - Deficiency Tracking and Remediation
  - Reporting and Records Retention

Cybersecurity Auditing Methodology *(2 of 5)*

- ***The Challenge of Proving Negatives***
  - The goal of the auditor is to collect evidence that ***proves*** nothing bad or unexpected occurred during the audit period.
  - Inductive reasoning suggests it is ***not possible*** to prove the ***absence of something***.
  - If malicious or negligent activity generates ***records***, then those records can be searched for evidence of such malicious or negligent activity, or its absence.
  - If auditors collect ***evidence of something not taking place***, then such evidence gives a basis for reasonably concluding that it may not exist.
  - *How thorough does the checking need to be?*
    - Financial records may require checking every transaction because fraud may be only in a single record.
    - Other records may only require spot-checking.
  - Generally, audits collect evidence from available records to indicate the proper operation of security controls.

- ***Cybersecurity Audit Objectives***
  - The cybersecurity audit planning process starts with audit objectives that can be phrased in terms of a sentence.
    - *I want my audit to indicate that__is occurring; or*
    - *I want my audit to indicate that__is NOT occurring.*
  - Example audit objectives:
    - *I want my audit to indicate that my web servers are functioning properly and serving up the correct pages.*
    - *I want my audit to indicate that attackers are NOT abusing my systems administrator accounts.*
    - *I want my audit to indicate that my IT systems are compliant with Sarbanes-Oxley regulations.*
    - *I want my audit to indicate that my confidential customer data is not being inappropriately accessed.*

Cybersecurity Auditing Methodology *(3 of 5)*

- ***Cybersecurity Audit Plans***
  - The graphic depicts a cybersecurity audit process that identifies what evidence is helpful to prove the audit objective.
  - Desired evidence must be compared to what evidence is available from IT systems' audit trails and logs, or manual processes' records.
  - The cybersecurity audit planning process includes the following activities:

1. Auditor analyzes the ***audit objective*** to understand what information is needed to satisfy the objective(s).
2. Auditor determines the ***desired evidence*** that supports the audit objective(s).
3. Auditor analyzes the ***available records*** to see what logs and information are available for analysis.

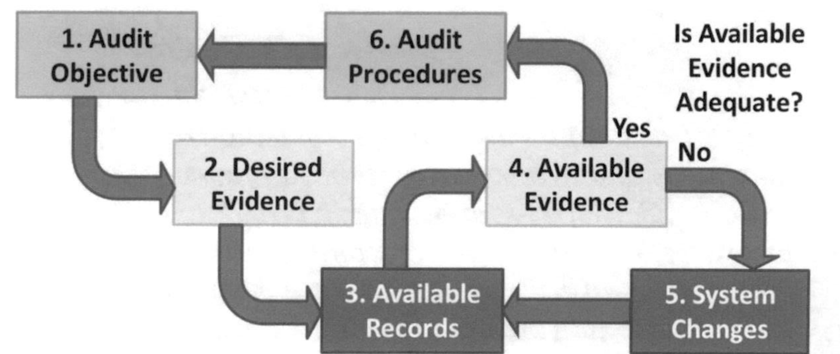

4. The available evidence comes from the ***available records***. The auditor analyzes the available evidence to determine if it will be adequate for satisfying the audit objective(s).
5. If the available evidence is not adequate, ***system changes*** (automated or manual) may need to be made to increase or change the available logs and evidence.
6. Finally, the auditor constructs ***audit procedures*** to analyze the available evidence in order to satisfy the audit objective(s).

Cybersecurity Auditing Methodology *(4 of 5)*

- ***Audit Evidence Collection***
  - Specifies what records are to be analyzed
  - Specifies the processes for analyzing the records
  - Defines key information such as record sources, points of contact, and sample sizes
  - Specifies sample sizes and statistical analysis methods to be used
- ***Audit Artifacts***
  - Answer the "because" question regarding the audit

    We believe systems administrator accounts are not being compromised BECAUSE we looked at systems administrator activity for 50% of the administrators over a two-week period and did not find any anomalies.
  - Make up the data behind the second half of the above sentence (that is, after *BECAUSE*)
  - Are copied out of logs and then stored with the audit and are subject to the data retention rules that apply to the rest of the audit

Cybersecurity Auditing Methodology *(5 of 5)*

- ***Audit Results***
  - Are compiled together for reporting to management and must be actionable
  - Identify what was audited and the findings, including deficiencies to be remediated
  - Are summarized to management in terms of their business impact or level of concern
  - Contain enough supporting information to be used by security practitioners to respond to and remediate the deficiencies
- ***Deficiency Tracking and Remediation***
  - May be outside the audit process, but should be formally tracked and reported to management
  - May be deferred for specific deficiencies that are not cost-effective to remediate; such deficiencies should be treated as enterprise risks
- ***Reporting and Records Retention***
  - Should include the audit report and supporting artifacts
  - Should comply with regulatory requirements per regulation or independent auditors, or retained like other business and financial records
  - May not make sense to report on deficiency remediation as part of original audit since it can take weeks or months to complete after the original audit is completed and reported
  - Regularly scheduled audits should brief deficiency remediation at the start of the next regularly scheduled audit

Cybersecurity Audit Types *(1 of 3)*

- The graphic depicts three common cybersecurity audit types:
  - A ***threat audit*** (also known as *hunting*) analyzes cyberthreats and then audits for evidence that those threats are occurring in the IT environment.
    - Looks for evidence of the threat targeting the confidentiality, integrity, or availability of enterprise's IT systems and data
    - Actively searches (hunts) for intruder and attacker activities using latest intelligence on intruder/attacker tactics, techniques, and procedures (TTP)

  - An ***assessment audit*** involves analyzing a set of requirements and assessing the cybersecurity controls pertaining to those requirements.
    - Generally conducted against regulatory requirements, external standards, or industry frameworks, or in regard to defenses against specific cybersecurity threats
    - Determines if controls are countering threats or complying with regulations or standards
    - Identifies which controls are countering the threats or complying with regulations or standards
    - Evaluates the effectiveness of those controls in satisfying requirement or countering the threat

Cybersecurity Audit Types *(2 of 3)*

– A ***validation audit***, unlike the other two audits, starts with the enterprise security controls and evaluates each control's effectiveness compared to its design and documented requirements.

- Evaluates if those controls are actually performing effectively
- Is used to improve cybersecurity control operation and design
- Can also be mapped back to external regulations or standards to demonstrate compliance

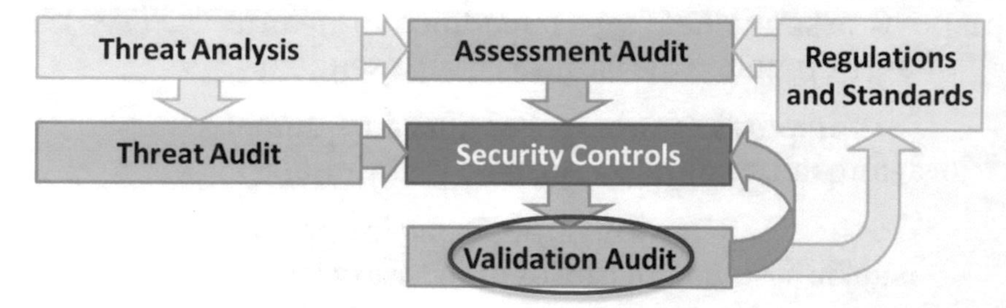

- Cybersecurity audits should follow a consistent methodology starting with audit objectives and ending with an audit report.
- Defining cybersecurity audit methodology can be non-trivial, especially for a complex cybersecurity environment.

Cybersecurity Audit Types *(3 of 3)*

- This table summarizes the three types of cybersecurity audits in terms of their inputs and outputs.

Audit Type	***Input***	***Output***
Threat	List of threats and attacker tactics, techniques, and procedures (TTPs).	For each threat, evidence of the threat being conducted against the enterprise or not.
Assessment	List of regulatory requirements to be complied with, standards to be adhered to, or threats to be countered.	For each requirement, standard, or threat, identification of the controls that pertain to them, whether they are preventive, detective, logging, or audit in nature, and analysis of their status and efficacy.
Validation	List of enterprise IT security controls.	For each control, a report on its nature and effectiveness compared to its documented requirements.

- Different audit types can be combined into a single audit activity.

"Audit First" Design Methodology *(1 of 5)*

Context *(1 of 2)*

- When designing cybersecurity defenses, security practitioners may jump straight to preventive controls vs. audit, forensic, or detective controls.
- Preventive controls
  - Can be cheap to operate
  - Use exciting "new" technology
  - Enable practitioners to make definitive statements about security
    - *We have blocked that behavior.*
    - *They won't be able to do that.*
  - Often introduce new vulnerabilities and dependencies on other IT systems that may be poorly understood
- Enterprise cybersecurity is NOT a point solution or collection of point solutions.
- Smart attackers target preventive control vulnerabilities and dependencies to defeat controls.
- A ***preventive-control-first*** approach results in a set of complex interdependencies that are often poorly understood, yet represent the foundation of the enterprise's security.
- Unfortunately, enterprise cybersecurity can end up simply being ***security by obscurity*** until an attacker comes along and figures out how to bypass everything.
- Security practitioners can address this reality by thinking about preventive controls ***last*** instead of ***first***.

"Audit First" Design Methodology *(2 of 5)*

Context *(2 of 2)*

- The graphic depicts the ***"Audit First" Design Methodology*** for thinking about preventive controls last, after considering other control types.

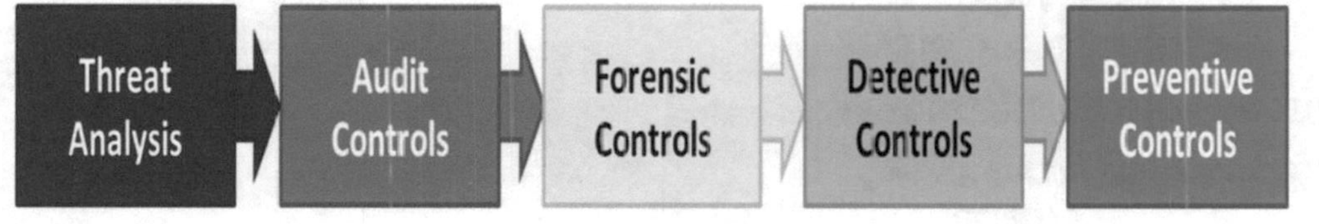

- Start with a threat analysis and then design controls to counter those threats.
- Simply stated, let security audits help drive the design of the enterprise's cyberdefenses.

"Audit First" Design Methodology *(3 of 5)*

- ***Threat Analysis***
  - Used to determine the enterprise's various security scopes[1]
  - Identifies CIA threats to the enterprise's data and IT systems in terms of threat impacts and indicators

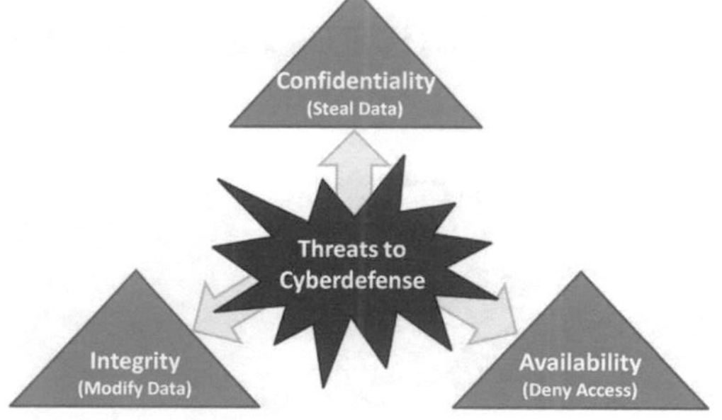

  - Considers the threats that are *most likely* and *most dangerous* or a *combination of both* (Not *every* single possible threat with such consideration is overwhelming.)
  - Prioritizes threats and risks just as an enterprise does with physical security considerations by addressing the greatest risks first

- ***Audit Controls***
  - After the threat analysis, the next step is to design threat audit controls that search for threat activities
  - If an enterprise's concern is loss of confidentiality, the security team might ask the following questions:
    - *How would the enterprise manually search the IT systems to identify that a confidentiality breach has occurred?*
    - *What evident would the attacker leave?*
  - If an enterprise's concern is loss of integrity, the team might ask:
    - *What evidence would be left when data was changed inappropriately?*
    - *How would the enterprise investigate a data change incident to prove that data has been changed?*
  - If an enterprise's concern is loss of availability, the team could ask:
    - *How would the enterprise differentiate an availability loss due to system failure from one caused by a malicious attack?*

[1]Security scopes group together assets and controls around a shared business impact caused by a common set of threats against confidentiality, integrity, or availability (CIA).

"Audit First" Design Methodology *(4 of 5)*

- ***Forensic Controls***
  - Forensic investigation involves analyzing logs, files, and sometimes program code to understand *attacker* activities and methods.
  - When conducting a threat audit, an enterprise generally
    - discovers little of the information needed to find confidentiality, integrity, or availability breaches against its systems;
    - gains insight regarding the information it *needs to collect* to protect itself using, in part, forensic controls; and
    - discovers the forensic controls effort may require significant upgrades to IT systems.
  - Many real-world environments are deficient in logging the right data.
  - It is important to resist the temptation to log everything; collect the information necessary to investigate likely attacks or support actual investigations.
  - Data logging should extend across all of the 11 enterprise cybersecurity functional areas.

- ***Detective Controls***
  - Effective logging, when in place, can be used to find attacker activity and help design detective controls that alert on suspected attacker activity.
  - If controls generate lots of false positives, they are not useful.
    - Alerts that are constantly ignored are of little use.
    - Detection does not need to be perfect to be effective.
  - A security information and event management (SIEM) system or *big data logging* may be helpful to do cross-correlation and enable more sophisticated alerting.
  - The goal is to ensure the most dangerous attacks trigger an alert when an attack occurs.
    - For example, firewalls alerting on internal port scans, versus scans originating from the Internet
  - Detective controls tend to have a small impact on business operations and can be deployed (or removed) aggressively vs. preventive controls.
  - When combined with forensic controls, detective controls give enterprise ability to know when the attacks occur and stop them.

"Audit First" Design Methodology *(5 of 5)*

- ***Preventive Controls***
  - Block undesired activities and prevent them from occurring
  - Are often considered primary controls to the detriment of audit, forensic, and detective controls
  - Are generally the most disruptive to business to emplace and operate
    - Each control requires a process for getting access or bypassing the block when required by the enterprise (for example, firewall exception and access management process)
  - Characteristics of *useful* preventive controls include
    - blocking behaviors that would be *noisy* with detection alone, reducing investigation costs;
    - deploying or operating controls that do not cost too much, particularly in terms of business disruption caused by the block;
    - not introducing significant new vulnerabilities; and
    - blocking attacks and detecting attacks in progress.

- ***Letting Audits Drive Control Design***
  - Helps enterprise design controls to effectively detect attacker activities while reducing the disruption to business operations

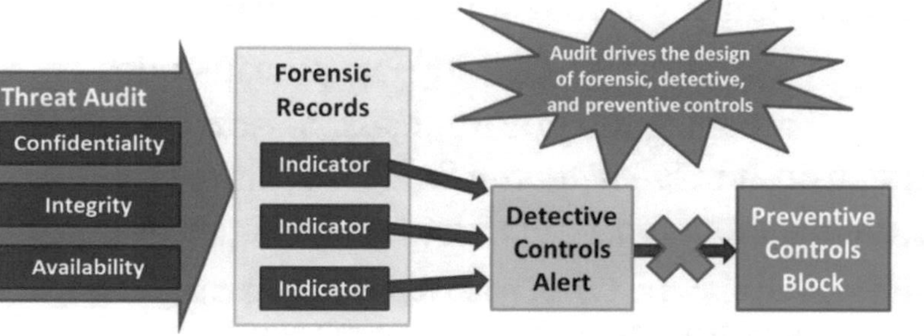

  - Identifies the most likely threats to enterprise IT confidentiality, integrity, or availability via Threat Audit
  - Searches for attacks that have occurred and collects the necessary supporting evidence
  - Identifies what forensic records are needed to log incidents and Indicators of Compromise (IOCs)
  - Creates detective and then preventive controls

Enterprise Cybersecurity Assessments *(1 of 9)*

Context *(1 of 3)*

- An enterprise cybersecurity program organized into functional areas lends itself to an assessment methodology that can be executed at different levels of detail.
- The remainder of this section describes how to do a multi-level enterprise cybersecurity assessment organized around the cybersecurity functional areas.
- **Level 1 Assessment:** *Focus on Risk Mitigations*
  - Analyzes the risks to the enterprise and the threats against the confidentiality, integrity, and availability of IT systems and data; identifies the ***most likely*** and ***most dangerous*** threat vectors
  - Examines attack sequences for those threats and enterprise defensive capabilities to disrupt, detect, delay, and defeat those attacks
- **Level 2 Assessment:** *Focus on Functional Areas*
  - Evaluates the 11 enterprise cybersecurity functional areas, as well as security operations, at a high level
  - Quickly identifies the functional areas that are most likely to be exploited

Enterprise Cybersecurity Assessments *(2 of 9)*

Context *(2 of 3)*

- **Level 3 Assessment:** *Focus on Security Capabilities*
  - Assesses in detail 113 enterprise cybersecurity capabilities and 17 operational processes (described in this study guide)
  - Aggregates results into overall enterprise cybersecurity assessment that can be used to prioritize areas for improvement
- **Level 4 Assessment:** *Focus on Controls, Technologies, and Processes*
  - Assesses the controls, technologies, and manual processes that deliver the enterprise's cybersecurity capabilities
  - Identifies specific recommendations for tuning, adjustments, or remediation to improve their operational effectiveness
- Assessments (internal or external) should be performed within the security scopes identified in the cybersecurity planning process.

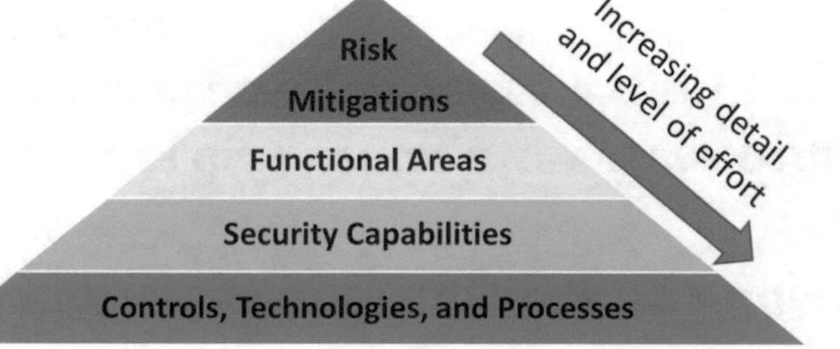

Enterprise Cybersecurity Assessments *(3 of 9)*

Context *(3 of 3)*

- This top-down assessment approach differs from control-based cybersecurity assessments.
  - It looks at cybersecurity functional areas and capabilities rather than focusing on the individual controls.
  - It provides remediation and prioritization guidance rather than producing results containing dozens or hundreds of recommendations with little guidance on how to manage remediation.
  - ***It finds the forest for the trees*** by organizing results into 11 cybersecurity functional areas for remediation delegation.
- Quantitative methods can be used to calculate assessment scores and can be combined into various measurement indices to indicate the entire enterprise's cybersecurity effectiveness.

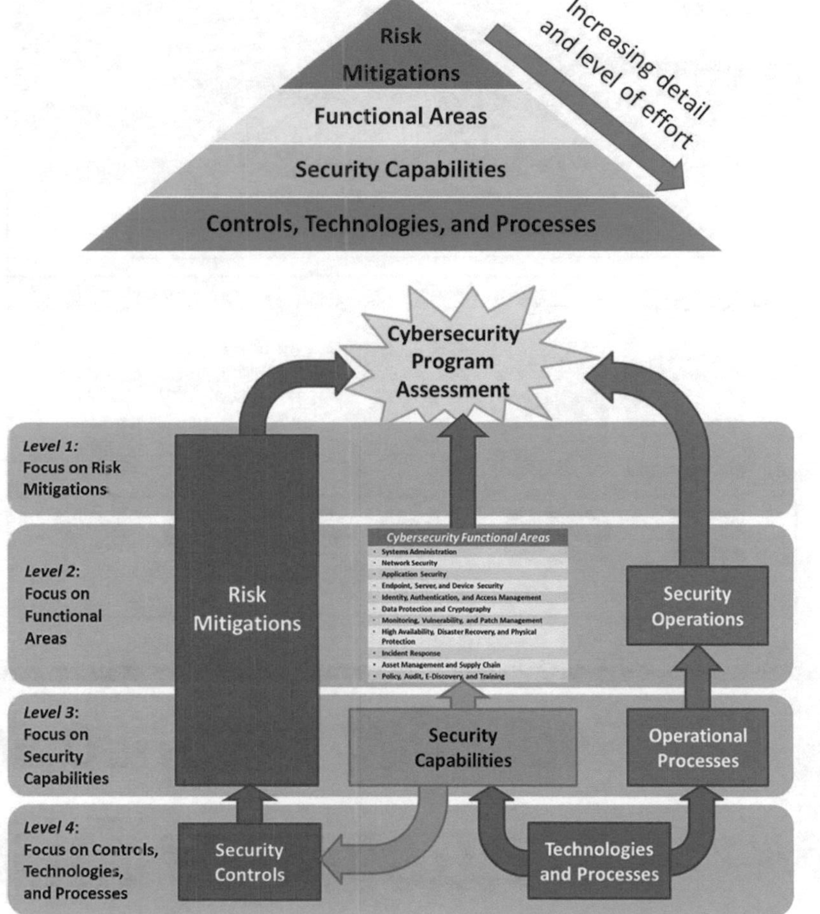

Enterprise Cybersecurity Assessments *(4 of 9)*

Level 1 Assessment: Focus on Risk Mitigations (1 of 2)

- This assessment starts with the ***risk management process*** to identify threats to the security scope and then considers those threats in terms of their ***attack sequence steps***.
- ***Level 1 Assessment Activities*** include
  - identifying threats and business impacts on *confidentially, integrity*, and *availability;*
  - identifying the *most likely* and *most dangerous* threats to the security scope;
  - analyzing the threats to understand the attack sequences that attackers would follow;
  - assessing security controls that log, detect, or block those attack sequences in terms of their ability to reduce the probability or impact of attacks completing each step of the attack sequence; and
  - if possible, investigating security control logs to see if attacks have occurred or are occurring and may be escaping detection.

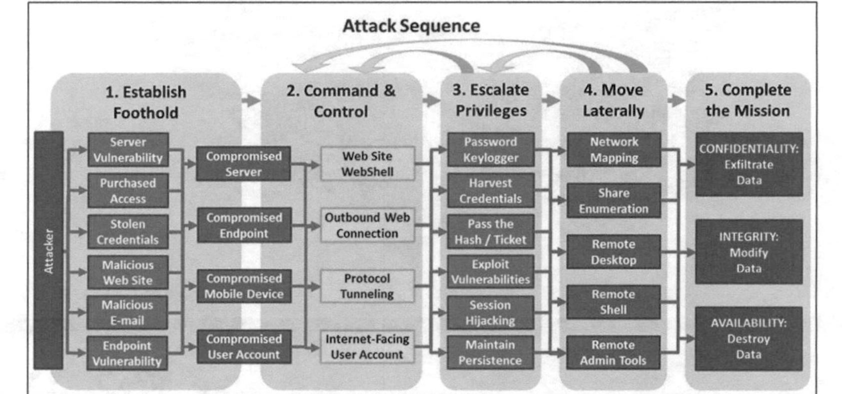

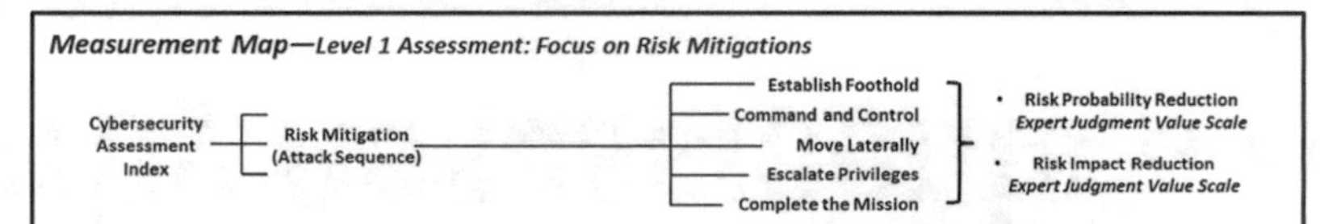

Enterprise Cybersecurity Assessments *(5 of 9)*

Level 1 Assessment: Focus on Risk Mitigations *(2 of 2)*

- ***Level 1 Assessment Outputs*** include the following:
  - List of highest-level risks and threats
  - Documentation of attack sequences
  - Security controls that apply to attack sequences
  - Assessment score

Enterprise Cybersecurity Assessments *(6 of 9)*

Level 2 Assessment: Focus on Functional Areas

- Level 2 Assessment builds upon Level 1 Assessment and considers the following:
  - Level 1 risk mitigations
  - Cybersecurity posture of functional areas
  - Operational process (that is, Security Operations)
- ***Level 2 Assessment Activities*** include
  - using Level 1 Assessment to identify security scopes and evaluate risk mitigations against the enterprise cybersecurity attack sequence;
  - evaluating functional areas and security operations in terms of *effectiveness* and *comprehensiveness* for each security scope;
  - capturing evaluated results for all the functional areas and security operations (strongest to weakest);
  - identifying how to improve by considering people, organization, budgets, processes, technologies, and capabilities for weakest areas; and
  - considering overall security posture compared to the security requirements of the scope.
- ***Level 2 Assessment Outputs*** include
  - an evaluation of each functional area and an identification of the weakest functional areas.

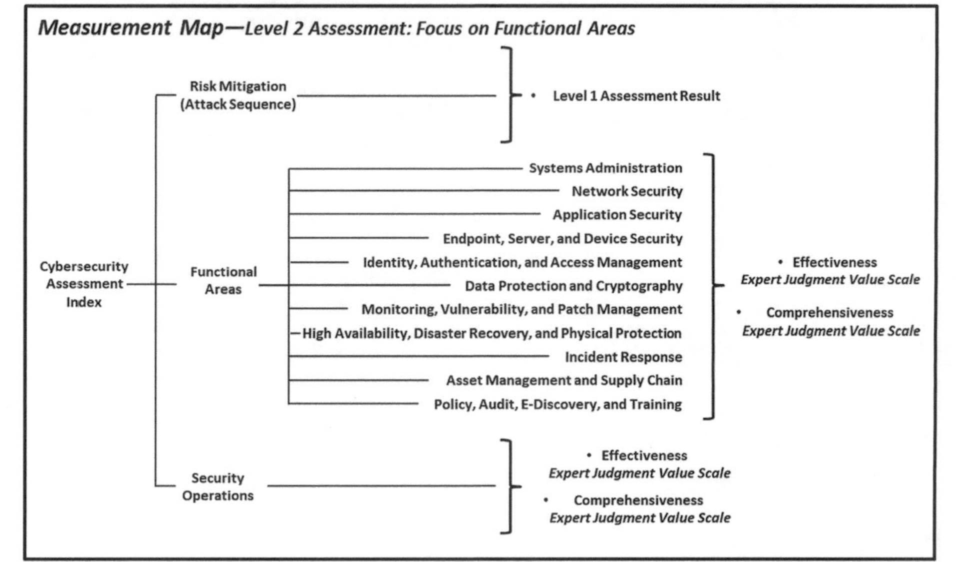

Enterprise Cybersecurity Assessments *(7 of 9)*

Level 3 Assessment: Focus on Security Capabilities (1 of 2)

- Level 3 Assessment goes into greater detail by considering the individual capabilities within each functional area, as well as by examining each of the 17 operational processes.
- For each capability and operational process, this assessment evaluates their *maturity* and *utilization*.
- This assessment can be used to develop action plans to improve specific functional areas.
- There is an excellent balance of assessment efforts vs. actionable results.
- ***Level 3 Assessment Activities*** include
  - using Level 1 Assessment to identify security scopes and evaluate risk mitigations against the enterprise cybersecurity attack sequence; and
  - identifying the functional areas to be evaluated and corresponding cybersecurity capabilities.

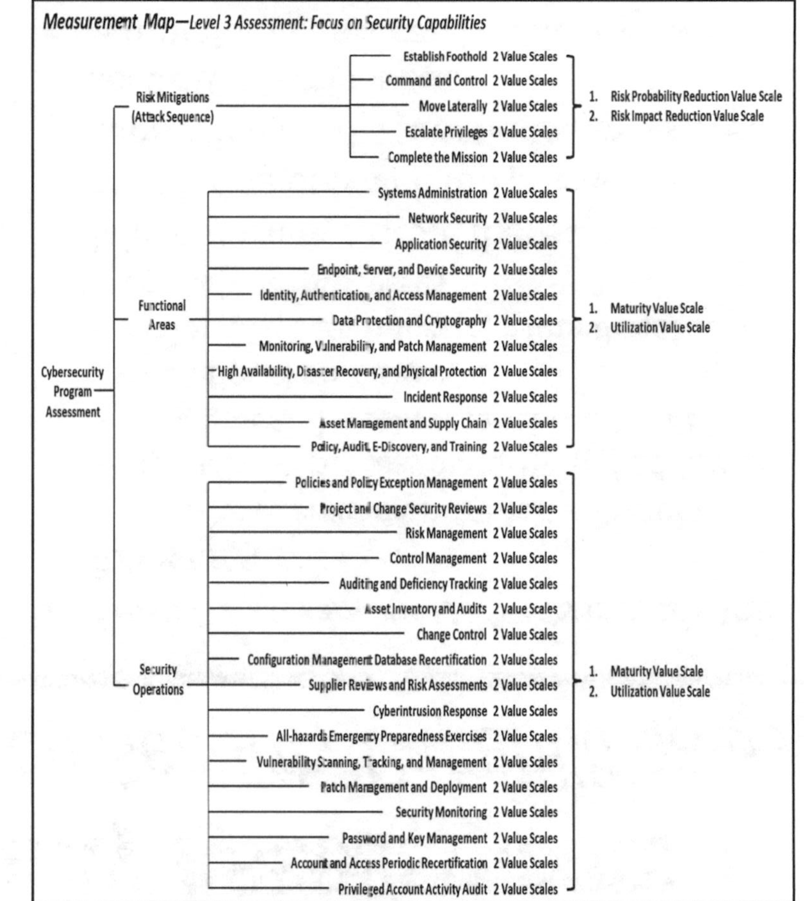

Enterprise Cybersecurity Assessments *(8 of 9)*

Level 3 Assessment: Focus on Security Capabilities (2 of 2)

- ***Level 3 Assessment Activities (continued)***
  - For a complete assessment, all capabilities in all functional areas should be evaluated, in addition to all operational processes.
  - For each functional area's capabilities, security teams examine the technologies and processes that deliver the capability to evaluate the cybersecurity's ***maturity*** (how well it works) and ***utilization*** (how consistently it is being used).
  - This functional area capability examination evaluates how well the capability ***delivers*** security to the enterprise.
  - For each operational process, assessors analyze its ***maturity*** (how well it works) and ***utilization*** (how consistently it is being used).
  - This operational process examination evaluates how well the operational process ***helps*** the enterprise operate its cybersecurity.
- ***Level 3 Assessment Outputs*** include the following:
  - Functional area maturity and utilization
  - Operational process maturity and utilization
  - Strongest and weakest capabilities and operational processes
  - Action plans for improving functional areas and operational processes
- It is important to note there is not a perfect correlation between the presence of capabilities and a functional area's overall security effectiveness.
- A functional area can be effective without having all the cybersecurity capabilities.
- A functional area can have many of its cybersecurity capabilities present and utilized; however, if they are not configured properly, they can be ineffective or neutralized by a deliberate attacker.

Enterprise Cybersecurity Assessments *(9 of 9)*

Level 4 Assessment: Focus on Controls, Technologies, and Processes

- Level 4 Assessment focuses on the following:
  - Controls (preventive, detective, forensic, and audit)
  - Technologies
  - Supporting processes
- Can be limited to a single functional area or even just a set of cybersecurity capabilities, their supporting technologies and process, or the security controls they support
- Can be useful when evaluating deficient functional areas in order to identify tuning opportunities and cost-effective capability improvements
- ***Level 4 Assessment Activities*** include
  - identifying the functional areas, capabilities that are of interest, and the supporting controls, technologies, and processes;

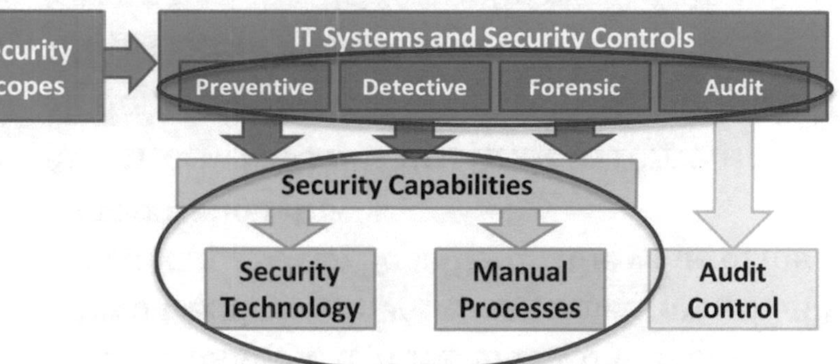

  - examining them to identify issues with their effectiveness, configuration, or operation; and
  - aggregating resulting recommendations into comprehensive change proposals for updating controls, technologies, or processes to make them more effective.
- ***Level 4 Assessment Outputs*** include
  - specific recommendations to improve the effectiveness of each control, technology, or process that was considered; and
  - recommendations that are technology-specific and actionable.

Audit Deficiency Management *(1 of 2)*

- Deficiencies and deficiency tracking are important components of the auditing process and must not be shortchanged or ignored just because the audit is over.
- *What is a deficiency?*
  - A situation where a capability, process, technology, or control does not function as it was designed and documented
  - Indication that overall enterprise security is not as effective as one would expect upon a simple review of documentation
  - Revelation when actual performance of capabilities, processes, or technologies is not what was expected when they were tested
- Deficiencies
  - Important because they undermine, or even completely nullify, the enterprise security that should be present through the various controls and capabilities
  - The ***fine print*** that needs to be appended to any discussion of the business value of the security controls and capabilities found to be deficient

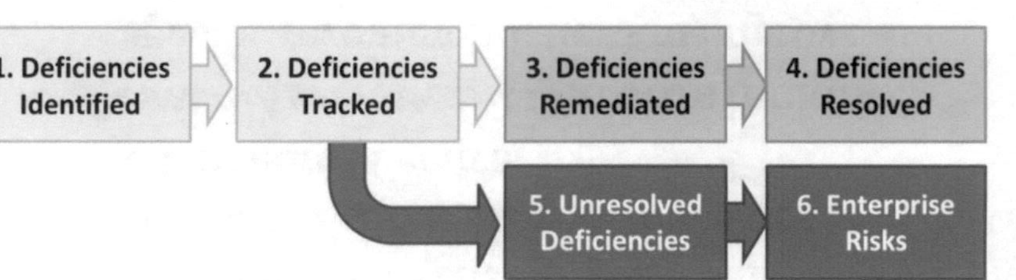

- The graphic depicts a deficiency tracking process.
  - When deficiencies are identified, a simple process can be followed to track and resolve them.
  - With tracking, follow-up, and timely remediation, an enterprise can benefit from the value of the overall audit process.
- An enterprise ***does not*** have to remediate all deficiencies, but an enterprise shouldn't simply ***ignore*** them either.
- Enterprise should formally track deficiencies as part of its overall risk management process so that deficiencies do not slip through the cracks.

Audit Deficiency Management *(2 of 2)*

- ***Audit Deficiency Management Activities*** include
  - identifying the deficiencies through an audit or formal testing;
  - recognizing that capability, process, technology, or control is not as effective as it should be and must be considered in the context of overall enterprise risk.
  - tracking identified deficiencies until they are disposed—employees departing, laptops getting lost, or other routine changes should not result in the deficiency list being lost;
  - remediating deficiencies so things get back to working as expected;
  - documenting remediated and resolved deficiencies;
  - considering deficiencies (for example, > 1-year old) unresolved unless there is an enterprise-approved mitigation plan and documenting these deficiencies for future audits (for instance, 75% effective, which may be acceptable); and

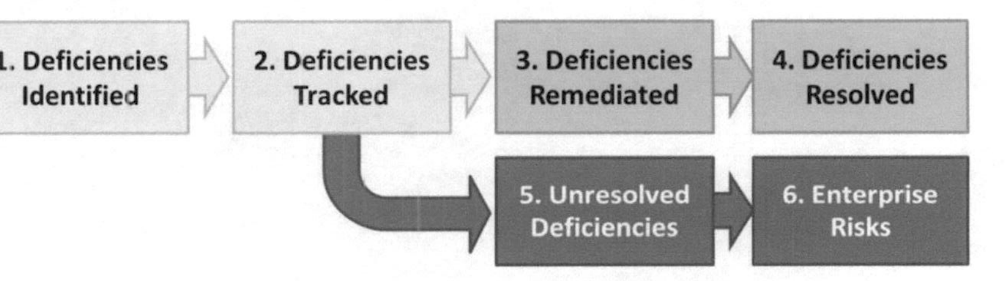

- ***Audit Deficiency Management Outputs*** include
  - identified deficiencies,
  - remediated and resolved deficiencies,
  - no resolved deficiencies; and
  - patterns of repeat deficiencies and remediation
- In general, whether audits are regularly scheduled control validations, externally performed assessments, or internal threat audits, it is critical the audit findings, deficiencies, and recommendations be tracked through to completion.
- Enterprises benefit from the audit process with tracking, follow-up, and timely remediation.

CHAPTER 12

Measuring a Cybersecurity Program

S. E. Donaldson et al., *Enterprise Cybersecurity Study Guide*, https://doi.org/10.1007/978-1-4842-3258-3_12

Overview

- People often measure things because somebody—some edict or some policy—stipulates that things should be measured.
- Unless measurement's role is thought through, it can degenerate into a meaningless exercise.
  - Measuring lengths down to the nearest sixteenth of an inch with a ruler that contains only quarter-inch marks.
  - Measuring things without measurement context; measurements are not taken for the purpose of answering specific questions.
  - Expressing measurements in a language the intended audience cannot understand, in effect, a ***foreign*** language.
- ***Measurement for measurement's sake is a waste of time and money.***
- This chapter
  - describes how to measure the effectiveness of ongoing enterprise risk mitigation and security operations;
  - offers guidance on how to measure the effectiveness of cybersecurity functional areas and their associated capabilities in everyday terms familiar—*and therefore meaningful*—to the enterprise; and
  - describes ***expert judgment*** and ***observed data*** measurement approaches.
- Regardless of the measurement approach, an enterprise measurement program needs to produce results that support informed business decisions.

Topics

- Cybersecurity Measurement
- Cybersecurity Program Measurement
- Visualizing Cybersecurity Assessment Scores
- Cybersecurity Measurement Summary

Cybersecurity Measurement *(1 of 2)*

- *How does an enterprise measure cybersecurity?*
  - There is no shortage of assessment frameworks that
    - focus on business processes or security controls;
    - provide guidance on how to judge process, or control presence or compliance; and
    - generally do not include guidance on how to score or measure the effectiveness of the security controls.
- For example, an enterprise evaluates its cybersecurity program against a control framework.
  - 80% of controls are present and functioning.
  - *Is the cybersecurity good?*
  - *Or are the 20% of the controls that are missing the ones that the attackers are exploiting to steal the enterprise's data?*
- Control frameworks used to measure cybersecurity programs pose challenges because they
  - are often designed around programs achieving 100% *compliance*, else they are deficient;
  - do not provide much guidance on how to prioritize remediation for noncompliance; and
  - do not provide much guidance on how to prioritize maintenance of security controls to ensure the most important controls stay operational.

Cybersecurity Measurement *(2 of 2)*

- Another framework challenge has to do with quantifying cybersecurity measurements.
  - *How does an enterprise score itself when it is trying to determine the effectiveness of its security controls?*
    - When using frameworks with lots of controls,
      - the enterprise can count how many controls are effective, ineffective, or absent, and they can score the program based on various ratios.
    - When there are fewer controls,
      - the enterprise may need to consider some shades of gray and give partial control scores based on how well they are implemented or how effectively they are used.
    - When some controls are more important than others,
      - the enterprise may need to weight scores to account for more important controls carrying more weight in the overall evaluation.
- Measurement challenges are non-trivial and contribute to the uncertainty in trying to get useful, actionable results from a cybersecurity program evaluation.

Cybersecurity Program Measurement

- The graphic depicts a cybersecurity program measurement approach that leverages (1) risk mitigations, (2) functional areas, and (3) ongoing security operations.

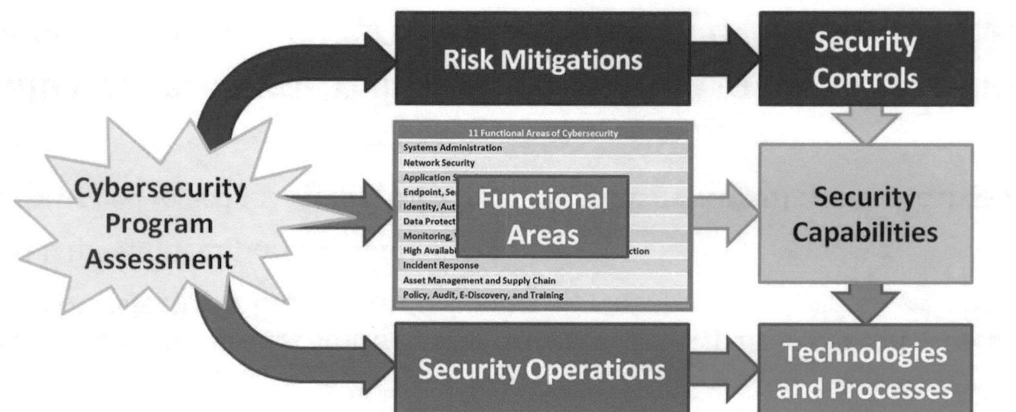

- This approach also encompasses the corresponding (1) security controls, (2) security capabilities, and (3) technologies and processes.

Object Measurement Example *(1 of 12)*

Context

- Object Measurement (OM) is a methodology that can be used to measure an enterprise cybersecurity program and produce actionable results.

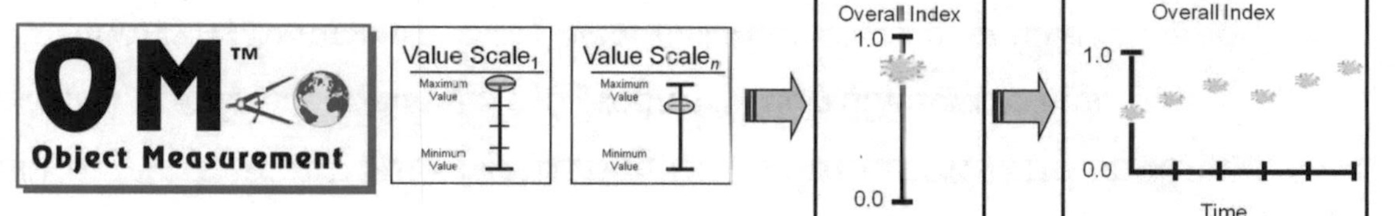

- Generally, OM consists of six steps.
  - Step 1: Define the ***questions*** to be asked
  - Step 2: Select ***appropriate objects*** to measure
  - Step 3: For each object, define the ***object characteristics*** to measure
  - Step 4: For each characteristic, create a ***value scale***
  - Step 5: ***Measure*** each object characteristic using the value scales
  - Step 6: Calculate the ***overall index*** (e.g., Cybersecurity Program Assessment Index)
- The following example assessment illustrates how OM is used to measure enterprise cybersecurity program effectiveness.

Object Measurement Example *(2 of 12)*

OM Step 1: Define the question(s) to be answered

- For this example assessment, the ***question*** is:

  For the selected security scope, how effective is the enterprise's cybersecurity program against cyberattacks?

- An enterprise can use various measurement approaches to measure cybersecurity.
  - ***Expert judgment assessment*** is frequently used in real-world assessments, and will be demonstrated in this example along with techniques for managing its limitations and challenges.
    - The challenge is that different evaluators can produce widely different results.
    - Results are not always reproducible across different environments or at different times.
  - ***Observed data*** associated with the cybersecurity processes or security controls can also be used.
    - Results are generally more objective, more reproducible, and less subject to individual opinions, knowledge, experience, or judgment.
- For this measurement example, an ***expert judgment assessment*** is described and demonstrates how to reduce its intrinsic challenges.

Object Measurement Example *(3 of 12)*

OM Step 2: Select appropriate objects to measure

- Measurements can be done with different levels of detail and fidelity (in other words, various assessment scopes), allowing for quick, *high-level* assessments or *thorough, detailed* assessments.
  - ***Level 1—Focus on Risk Mitigations***: Measure Risk Mitigations
  - ***Level 2—Focus on Functional Areas***: Measure Risk Mitigations + Functional Areas + Security Operations
  - ***Level 3—Focus on Security Capabilities***: Measure Risk Mitigations + Security Capabilities + Security Operations
  - ***Level 4—Focus on Controls, Technologies, and Process***: Measure Security Controls + Technologies + Processes
- The assessment scope is a portion of the enterprise's environment where a security compromise will have a business impact.

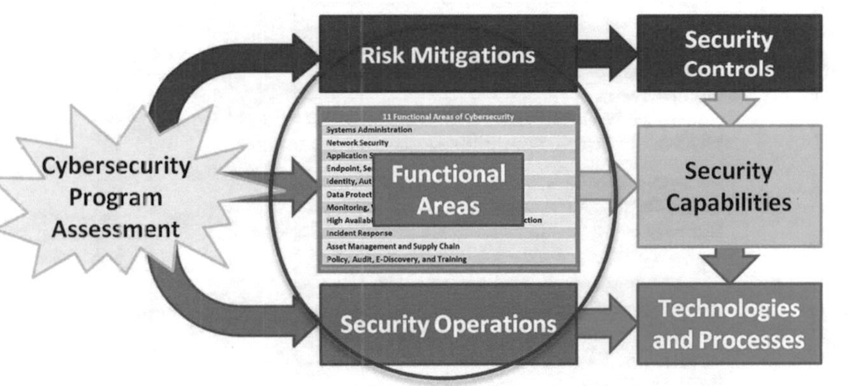

- Within well-defined scopes, systems work together to maintain a particular security posture to defend against a business impact.
- Scope is frequently defined based on regulatory, statutory, or liability requirements.
- This example expert judgment assessment is a Level 2 Assessment.
- ***Appropriate objects*** to measure are
  - risk mitigations,
  - functional areas, and
  - security operations.

Object Measurement Example *(4 of 12)*

OM Step 3: For each object, define the object characteristics to measure

- For this example assessment, the ***object characteristics*** to be measured are shown in the right-hand column of the figure.
  - **Risk Mitigations (Attack Sequence)**
    - Establish Foothold
    - Command and Control
    - Etc.
  - **Functional Areas**
    - Systems Administration
    - Network Security
    - Etc.
  - **Security Operations**
    - Policies and Policy Exception Management
    - Project and Change Security Reviews
    - Etc.

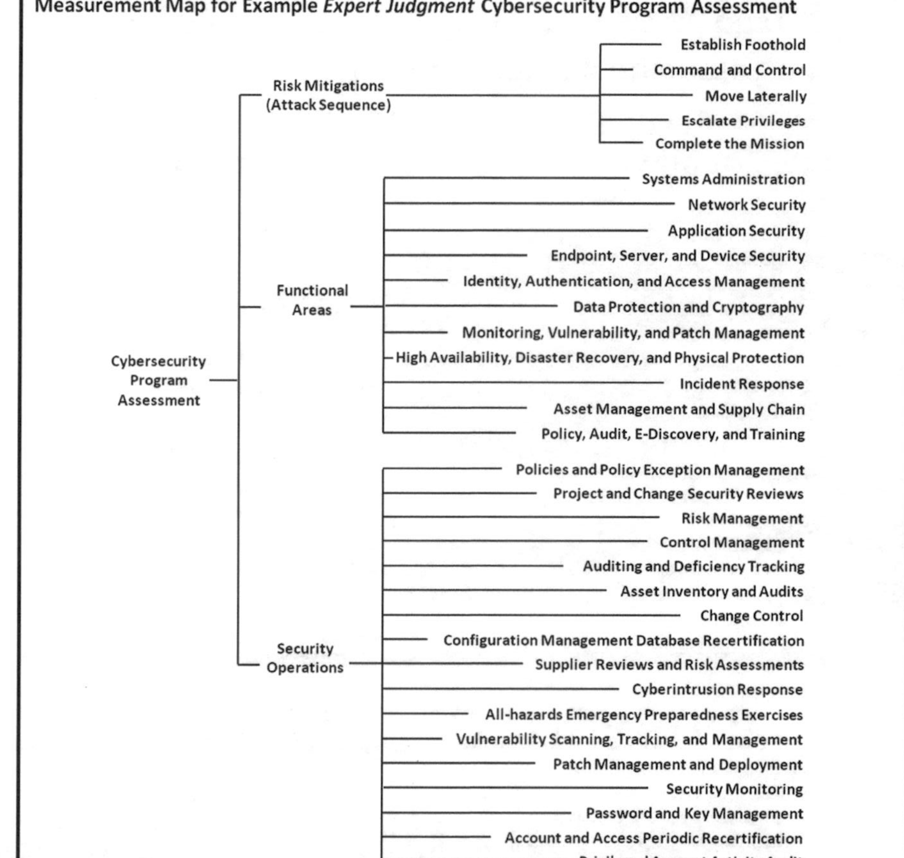

Object Measurement Example *(5 of 12)*

OM Step 4: For each characteristic, create a value scale (1 of 6)

- Value scales help associate an enterprise vocabulary (that is, language) with measurement.
- The challenge is to establish value scales to make ***meaningful*** measurements.
- *Meaningful* means "the enterprise uses the measurements to determine whether and where cybersecurity needs to be improved."
- OM value scale types include *discrete, binary*, and *sliding*.

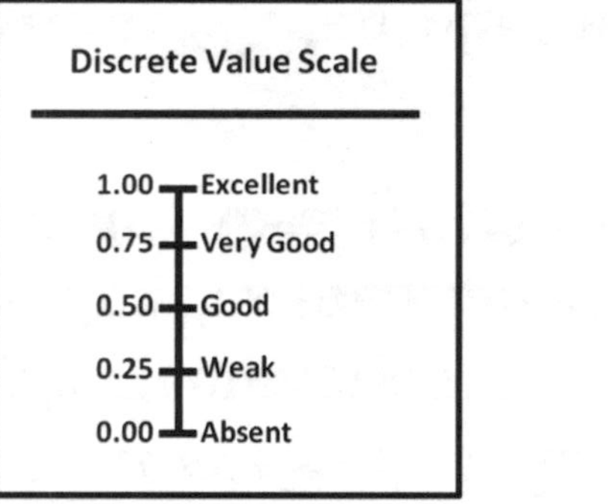

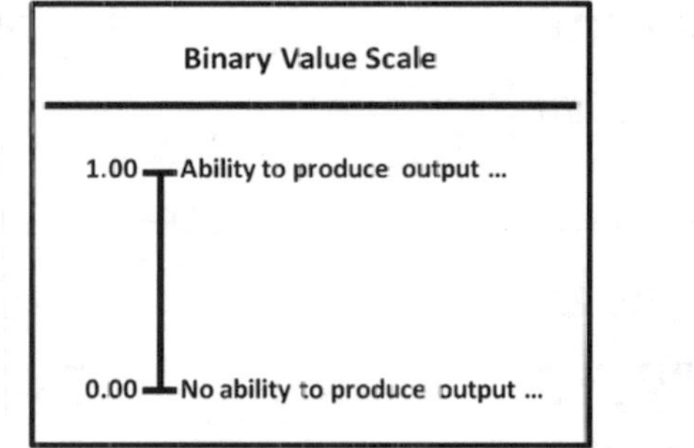

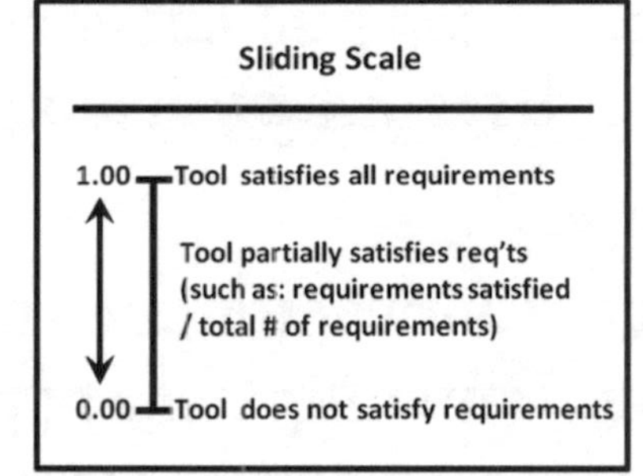

- Value scales have a minimum and maximum numeric value, along with a plain-language description on the tick-mark labels.
- The numeric range of values is not restricted to zero (0.00) to one (1.00) and can accommodate any numeric range.

Object Measurement Example *(6 of 12)*

OM Step 4: For each characteristic, create a value scale (2 of 6)

- ***Discrete value scales*** allow for *distinct interim* numeric values and corresponding tick-mark labels (for example, 0.00 = Absent; 0.25 = Weak, and so on).
- ***Binary value scales*** are often used to measure *on/off* or *yes/no* or *desired behavior/lack of desired behavior*.
- ***Sliding value scales*** measure a *minimum* numeric value, a *partial* numeric value based on a ratio, and a *maximum* numeric value.
- Value scale tick-mark labels need to be defined in everyday enterprise language to aid in communicating measurement results.
- *Note:* There is ***no one set of terms*** (that is, numeric values and tick-mark labels) that defines value scales.
- The enterprise decides what terms define its value scales.

Object Measurement Example *(7 of 12)*

OM Step 4: For each characteristic, create a value scale (3 of 6)

- For this example assessment, the ***expert judgment value scales*** to be used are listed in the right-hand column of the figure and subsequently explained in detail.
  - Mitigations
    - Risk Probability Reduction
    - Risk Impact Reduction
  - Functional Areas
    - Effectiveness
    - Comprehensiveness
  - Security Operations
    - Maturity
    - Utilization

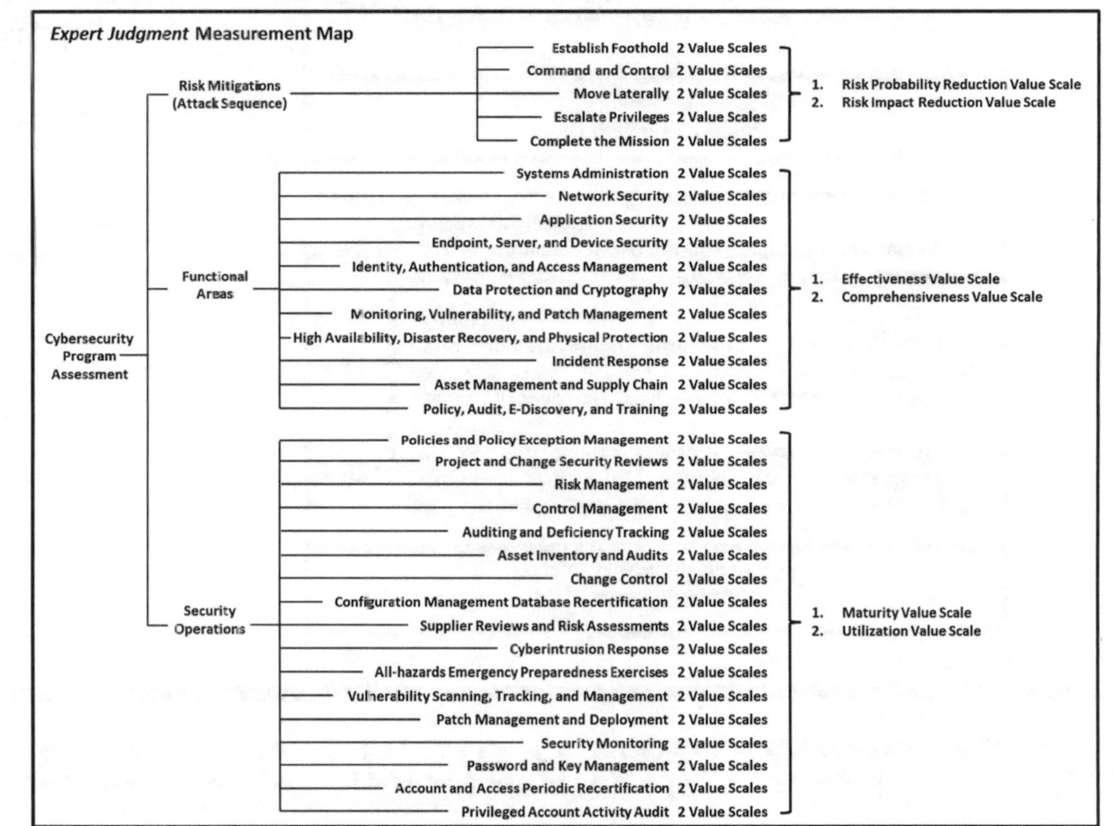

Object Measurement Example *(8 of 12)*

OM Step 4: For each characteristic, create a value scale (4 of 6)

- An enterprise can gauge its ***risk mitigation*** efforts based on two dimensions.
  - ***Risk Probability Reduction***
    - 1.00—High probability reduction
    - 0.50—Medium probability reduction
    - 0.00—Low probability reduction
  - ***Risk Impact Reduction***
    - 1.00—High impact reduction
    - 0.50—Medium impact reduction
    - 0.00—Low impact reduction
- If an enterprise is significantly reducing the *probability* and the *impact* of the *risk*, then the enterprise's security can be considered very good or excellent.

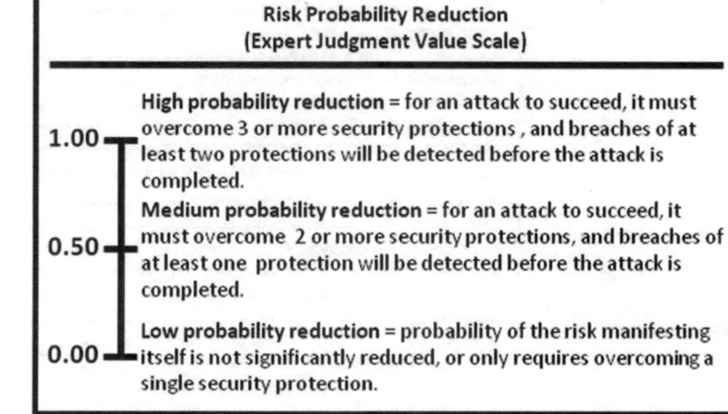

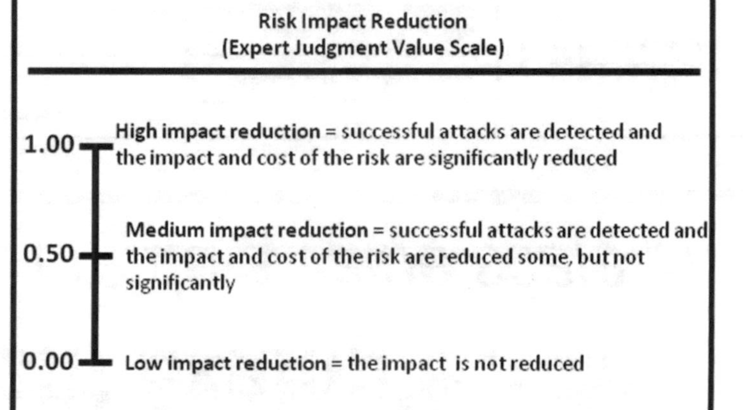

Risk Impact Reduction
(Expert Judgment Value Scale)
1.00
High impact reduction = successful attacks are detected and the impact and cost of the risk are significantly reduced
0.50
Medium impact reduction = successful attacks are detected and the impact and cost of the risk are reduced some, but not significantly
0.00
Low impact reduction = the impact is not reduced

Object Measurement Example *(9 of 12)*

OM Step 4: For each characteristic, create a value scale (5 of 6)

- An enterprise can gauge its ***functional areas*** based on two dimensions.
  - ***Effectiveness*** measures how effective the functional area is in protecting the enterprise and mitigating cybersecurity risks.
    - 1.00—High effectiveness
    - 0.50—Medium effectiveness
    - 0.00—Low effectiveness
  - ***Comprehensiveness*** measures how comprehensively the functional area is used to protect the security scope.
    - 1.00—High comprehensiveness
    - 0.50—Medium comprehensiveness
    - 0.00—Low comprehensiveness

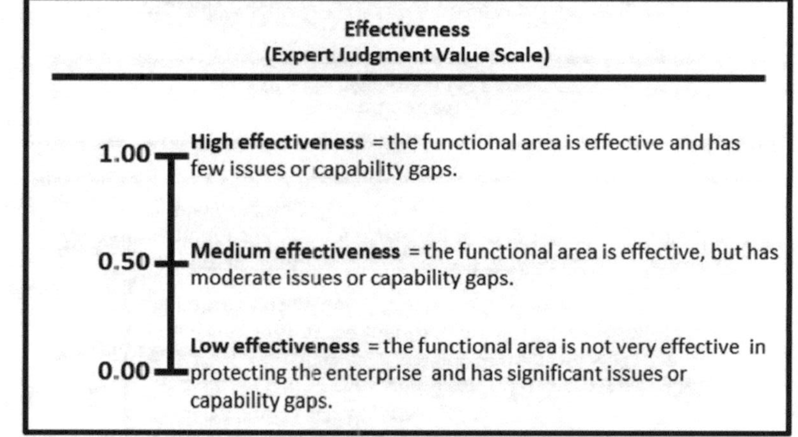
Effectiveness
(Expert Judgment Value Scale)
1.00
High effectiveness = the functional area is effective and has few issues or capability gaps.
0.50
Medium effectiveness = the functional area is effective, but has moderate issues or capability gaps.
0.00
Low effectiveness = the functional area is not very effective in protecting the enterprise and has significant issues or capability gaps.

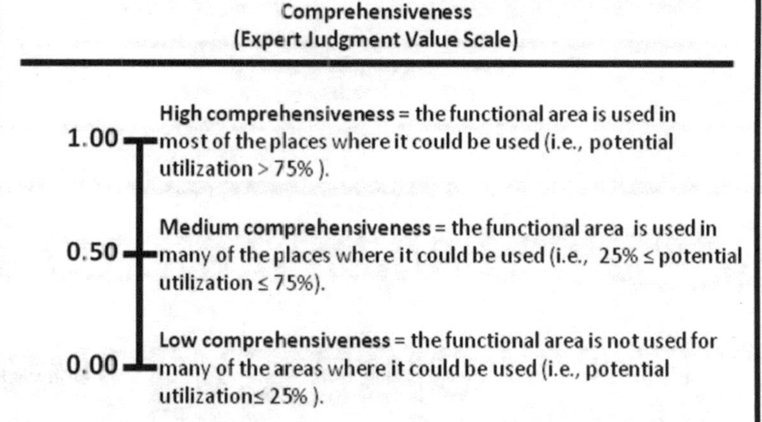
Comprehensiveness
(Expert Judgment Value Scale)
1.00
High comprehensiveness = the functional area is used in most of the places where it could be used (i.e., potential utilization > 75%).
0.50
Medium comprehensiveness = the functional area is used in many of the places where it could be used (i.e., 25% ≤ potential utilization ≤ 75%).
0.00
Low comprehensiveness = the functional area is not used for many of the areas where it could be used (i.e., potential utilization≤ 25%).

Object Measurement Example *(10 of 12)*

OM Step 4: For each characteristic, create a value scale (6 of 6)

- An enterprise can gauge its ***security operations*** based on two dimensions.
  - ***Maturity*** measures how well implemented the security operations element is.
    - 1.00—High maturity
    - 0.50—Medium maturity
    - 0.00—Low maturity
  - ***Utilization*** measures how much the security operations element is used in the enterprise.
    - 1.00—High utilization
    - 0.50—Medium utilization
    - 0.00—Low utilization

Maturity
(Expert Judgment Value Scale)
1.00
High maturity = the security control element is fully operational and proven. Configuration and procedures are fully documented and performance specs for functionality are defined and validated by 3rd party experts.
0.50
Medium maturity = the security control element is partially operational, but unproven. Documentation and operational procedures are not complete or untested. There are minor limitations on functionality that are untested.
0.00
Low maturity = the security control element is barely or partially operational. There are severe limits on its functionality, durability, reliability or scalability.

Utilization
(Expert Judgment Value Scale)

1.00 — **High utilization** = the security control, capability, process or technology is being utilized for most of its intended purposes (i.e., potential utilization > 75%).

0.50 — **Medium utilization** = the security control, capability, process or technology is being utilized for many of its intended purposes (i.e., 25% ≤ potential utilization ≤ 75%).

0.00 — **Low utilization** = the security control, capability, process or technology is in pilot or only used by a small group (i.e., potential utilization ≤ 25%).

Object Measurement Example *(11 of 12)*

OM Step 5: Measure each characteristic using the value scales

- Assess the characteristics using the value scales and record the resulting raw measurement data.
- The graphic shows this assessment's example raw measurement data that represents an expert's judgment as expressed by the defined value scales.

Risk Mitigations/Attack Sequence	Risk Probability Reduction	Risk Impact Reduction
1. Establish Foothold	Low Risk Probability Reduction = 0.00	Low Impact Reduction = 0.00
2. Command and Control	Low Risk Probability Reduction = 0.00	Medium Impact Reduction = 0.50
3. Move Laterally	Low Risk Probability Reduction = 0.00	High Impact Reduction = 1.00
4. Escalate Privileges	Medium Risk Probability Reduction = 0.50	Medium Impact Reduction = 0.50
5. Complete the Mission	Medium Risk Probability Reduction = 0.50	High Impact Reduction = 1.00

Enterprise Cybersecurity Functional Areas	Effectiveness	Comprehensiveness
Systems Administration	Low Effectiveness = 0.00	Low Comprehensiveness = 0.00
Network Security	Low Effectiveness = 0.00	Medium Comprehensiveness = 0.50
Application Security	Medium Effectiveness = 0.50	Medium Comprehensiveness = 0.50
Endpoint, Server, and Device Security	High Effectiveness = 1.00	Medium Comprehensiveness = 0.50
Identity, Authentication, and Access Management	High Effectiveness = 1.00	High Comprehensiveness = 1.00
Data Protection and Cryptography	High Effectiveness = 1.00	Low Comprehensiveness = 0.00
Monitoring, Vulnerability, and Patch Management	High Effectiveness = 1.00	High Comprehensiveness = 1.00
High Availability, Disaster Recovery, and Physical Protection	High Effectiveness = 1.00	Medium Comprehensiveness = 0.50
Incident Response	High Effectiveness = 1.00	High Comprehensiveness = 1.00
Asset Management and Supply Chain	Low Effectiveness = 0.00	Low Comprehensiveness = 0.00
Policy, Audit, E-Discovery, and Training	Medium Effectiveness = 0.50	Medium Comprehensiveness = 5.00

Enterprise Cybersecurity Operational Processes	Maturity	Utilization
1. Policies and Policy Exception Management	Low Maturity = 0.00	Low Utilization = 0.00
2. Project and Change Security Reviews	Medium Maturity = 0.50	Medium Utilization = 0.50
3. Risk Management	High Maturity = 1.00	Medium Utilization = 0.50
4. Control Management	Medium Maturity = 0.50	Medium Utilization = 0.50
5. Auditing and Deficiency Tracking	Medium Maturity = 0.50	Medium Utilization = 0.50
6. Asset Inventory & Audits	High Maturity = 1.00	Medium Utilization = 0.50
7. Change Control	Medium Maturity = 0.50	Medium Utilization = 0.50
8. Configuration Management Database Recertification	Medium Maturity = 0.50	Medium Utilization = 0.50
9. Supplier Reviews and Risk Assessments	High Maturity = 1.00	Medium Utilization = 0.50
10. Cyberintrusion Response	Medium Maturity = 0.50	Low Utilization = 0.00
11. All-hazards Emergency Preparedness Exercises	Low Maturity = 0.00	Low Utilization = 0.00
12. Vulnerability Scanning, Tracking, and Management	Medium Maturity = 0.50	Low Utilization = 0.00
13. Patch Management and Deployment	High Maturity = 1.00	Medium Utilization = 0.50
14. Security Monitoring	High Maturity = 1.00	Low Utilization = 0.00
15. Password and Key Management	Medium Maturity = 0.50	Medium Utilization = 0.50
16. Account and Access Periodic Recertification	Medium Maturity = 0.50	Low Utilization = 0.00
17. Privileged Account Activity Audit	High Maturity = 1.00	Medium Utilization = 0.50

Object Measurement Example *(12 of 12)*

OM Step 6: Calculate the overall cybersecurity program assessment index using object measurement index equation

- *How effective is the enterprise cybersecurity in protecting against cyberattacks?*
- The graphic shows how the raw measurement data is input to an appropriate OM index equation to calculate the example expert judgment *indices.*
  - **RiskMitigations*Index*** = 0.55
  - **FunctionalArea*Index*** = 0.70
  - **SecurityOps*Index*** = 0.57
- Also, the three indices above can be aggregated into an *overall summary index.*
  - **CybersecurityProgramAssessment*Index*** = 0.64
- Appropriate people in the enterprise should meet to examine the measurements and discuss how to address the corresponding results.
- To support the discussion, the measurements need to be expressed in everyday terms that make sense to the enterprise so that leadership can make informed decisions.

RiskMitigations*Index* =

$$= \frac{\sqrt{0^2 + 0^2 + 0^2 + .5^2 + 0^2 + 1^2 + .5^2 + .5^2 + .5^2 + 1^2}}{\sqrt{10}}$$

$$= \frac{1.73}{3.16} = 0.55;$$ where number of Attack Sequence Steps measurements = 10

FunctionalArea*Index* =

$$= \frac{\sqrt{\begin{array}{c}0^2 + 0^2 + 0^2 + .5^2 + .5^2 + .5^2 + 1^2 + .5^2 + 1^2 + 1^2 + 1^2 + \\ 0^2 + 1^2 + 1^2 + 1^2 + .5^2 + 1^2 + 1^2 + 0^2 + 0^2 + .5^2 + .5^2\end{array}}}{\sqrt{22}}$$

$$= \frac{3.28}{4.69} = 0.70;$$ where number of Functional Areas measurements = 22

SecurityOps*Index* =

$$= \frac{\sqrt{\begin{array}{c}0^2 + 0^2 + .5^2 + .5^2 + 1^2 + .5^2 + .5^2 + .5^2 + .5^2 + .5^2 + 1^2 + .5^2 + \\ .5^2 + .5^2 + .5^2 + .5^2 + 1^2 + .5^2 + .5^2 + 0^2 + 0^2 + 0^2 + .5^2 + 0^2 + \\ 1^2 + .5^2 + 1^2 + 0^2 + .5^2 + .5^2 + .5^2 + 0^2 + 1^2 + .5^2\end{array}}}{\sqrt{34}}$$

$$= \frac{3.32}{5.83} = 0.57;$$ where the number of Security Operations Elements = 34

CybersecurityProgramAssessment*Index* =

$$= \frac{\sqrt{.55^2 + .70^2 + .57^2}}{\sqrt{3}}$$

$$= \frac{1.11}{1.73} = 0.64;$$ where number of Expert Judgment Indices = 3; all weighting factors = 1; all value scales range from 0 to 1.

Visualizing Cybersecurity Assessment Scores *(1 of 3)*

Cybersecurity assessment measurements can be visualized in a number of ways, but enterprises need to decide what makes the best sense for their organizational culture.

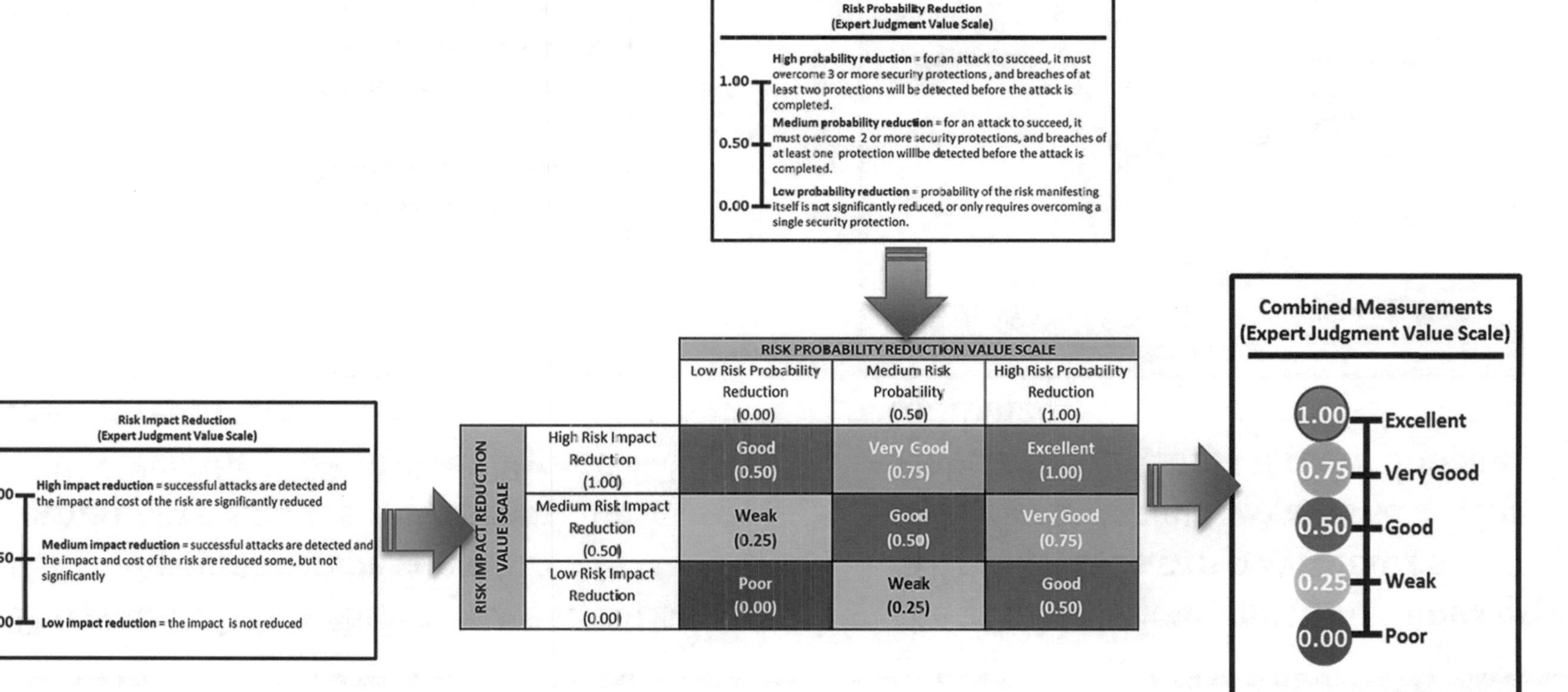

Visualizing Cybersecurity Assessment Scores *(2 of 3)*

- The graphic below shows how enterprise risk mitigations can be considered in terms of two expert adjustment value scales regarding risk probability and risk impact reduction.

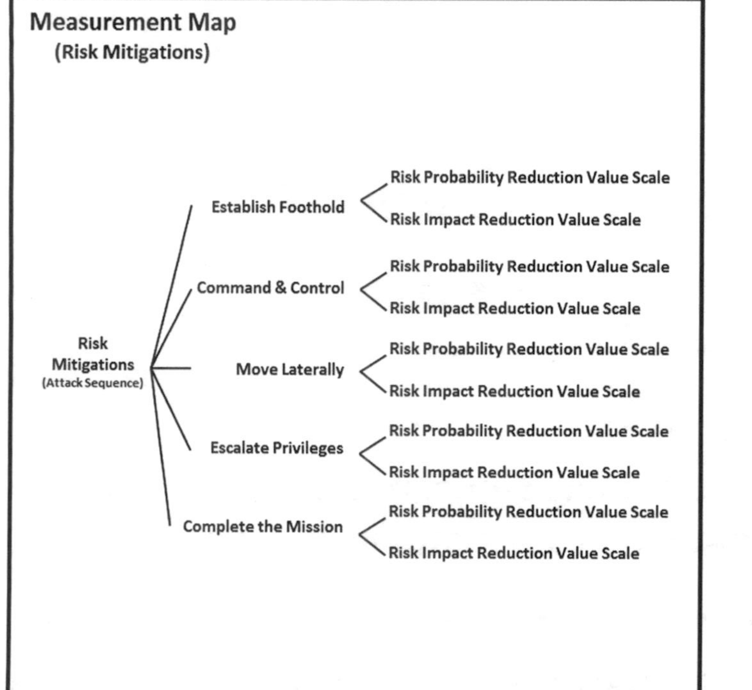

- The graphic below shows how enterprise risk mitigations can be visualized numerically when the value scales for probability and impact reduction are combined.

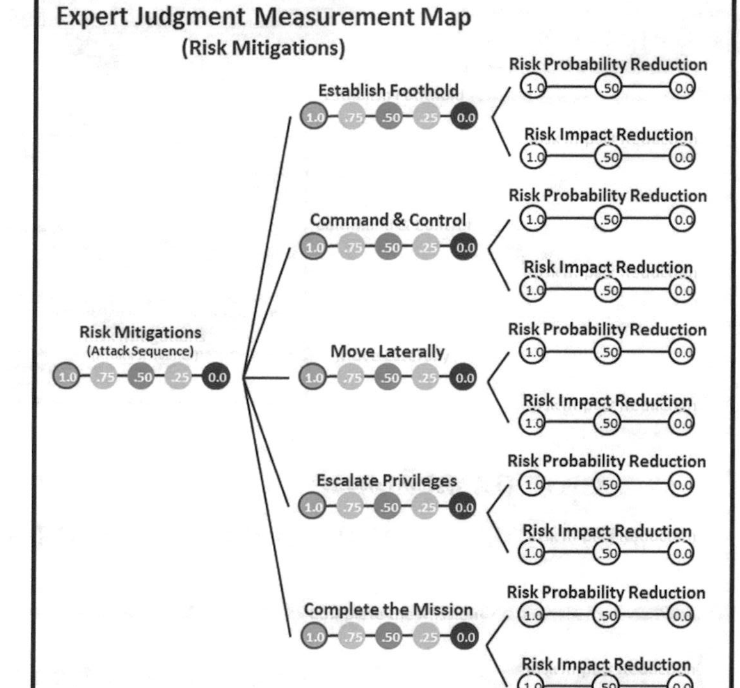

Visualizing Cybersecurity Assessment Scores *(3 of 3)*

- The graphic below shows what expert value judgments were recorded in terms of ***risk probability*** and ***risk impact reductions*** (ellipses) and the resulting metrics for the attack sequence steps (solid circles with numbers).

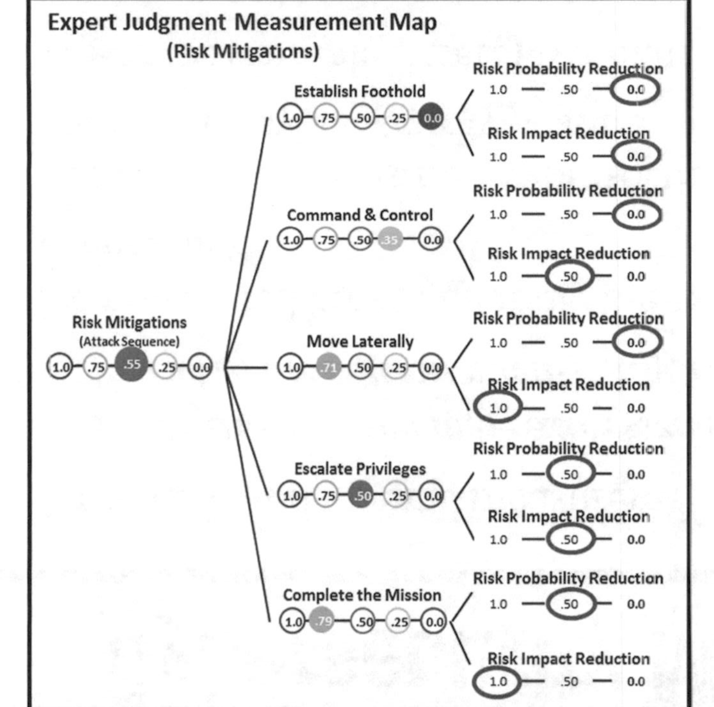

- The graphic below shows the overall combined risk mitigation metric (also known as **RiskMitigations*Index***) with a numeric value of 0.55, which was calculated with the Object Measurement. Index Equation

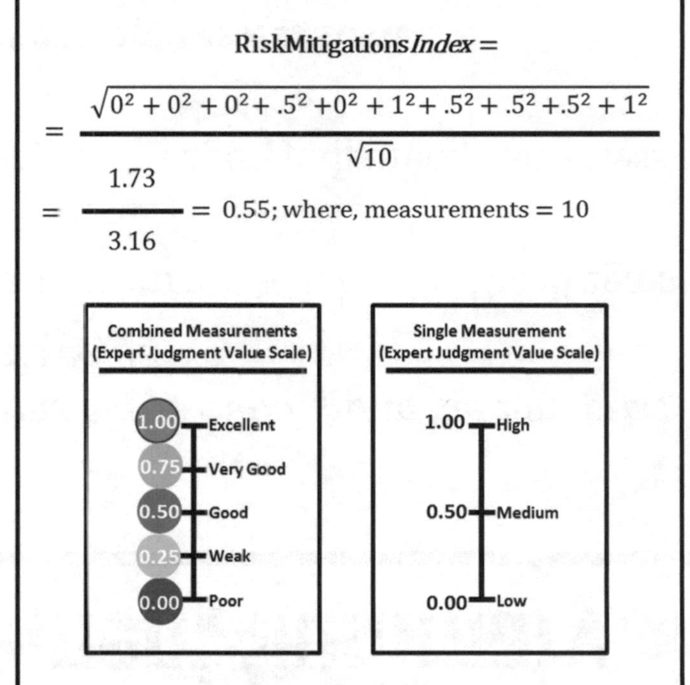

Cybersecurity Measurement Summary

- Presented fundamental measurement principle

  Measurements need to be expressed in everyday terms that are familiar to the enterprise; otherwise, the measurements may, at best, be of little value.

- Demonstrated how to quantify the extent to which an enterprise is defending itself against cyberattacks
- Focused on showing how cybersecurity experts, using their expert judgment, can assess an enterprise's cybersecurity posture
- Presented example expert judgment value scales for example assessment
- Introduced Measurement Map concept to visualize how value scales can be combined to help communicate how the assessment is defined
- Used example calculations to show how a collection of expert judgments can be combined into a single number called an ***index*** that gives enterprise management the means to chart a corrective action course to improve its cybersecurity posture
- Presented alternative visualizations of raw measurement data, combined expert measurement data, and overall combined metric

CHAPTER 13

Mapping Against Cybersecurity Frameworks

S. E. Donaldson et al., *Enterprise Cybersecurity Study Guide*, https://doi.org/10.1007/978-1-4842-3258-3_13

Overview *(1 of 3)*

- This chapter describes how an enterprise's cybersecurity program can be mapped against other cybersecurity frameworks such as the following:
  - (ISC)^2 Common Body of Knowledge (CBK)
  - ISO 27001/27002 Version 2013
  - NIST SP800-53 Revision 4
  - Council on CyberSecurity 20 Critical Security Controls (CSC 20) Version 5.1
- Reasons for such mapping include the following:
  - Many industries are regulated and must comply with regulations.
  - Similarly, cybersecurity programs must comply with regulatory cybersecurity requirements.
  - Compliance with such regulations and requirements needs to be demonstrable to independent auditors and regulators.
  - Enterprises need to report on the status of their cybersecurity programs against external frameworks to satisfy their own auditors or other internal business purposes.
  - Enterprises wish to crosswalk their cybersecurity program against an external framework to generate ideas for strengthening the enterprise's cybersecurity posture.
- Why not simply run an enterprise's cybersecurity program according to one of these frameworks?
  - Frameworks are not generally designed for running a comprehensive cybersecurity program.

Overview *(2 of 3)*

- This study guide describes a ***cohesive*** *enterprise cybersecurity framework* that integrates the following:
  - ***Architecture*** (a.k.a. Enterprise Cybersecurity Architecture) consisting of cybersecurity capabilities organized into functional areas that make capabilities easier to track, manage, and delegate
  - ***Cybersecurity policy*** designed to balance security needs against business priorities
  - ***Programmatics*** involving people, budget, and technology that are allocated to day-to-day operations and projects
  - ***IT life cycle*** aligned with IT departments responsible for strategy and architecture, engineering, and operations
  - ***Cybersecurity assessments*** that are conducted periodically to help prevent cybersecurity program obsolescence

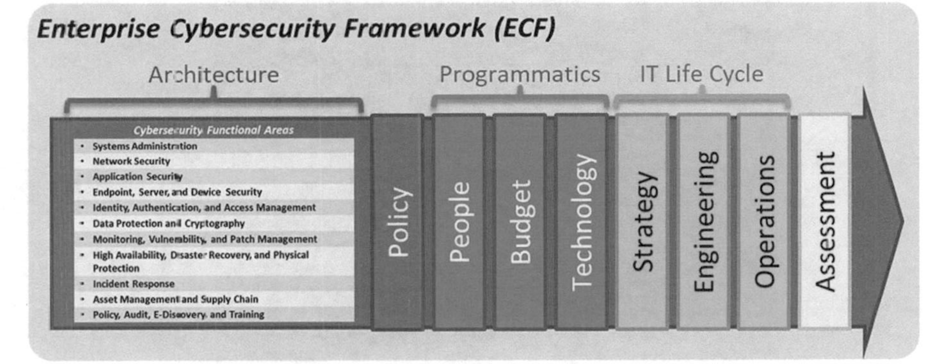

- The enterprise cybersecurity framework is pragmatic, realistic, and designed for battling today's cyberthreats as well as tomorrow's next-generation cyberthreats.

Overview *(3 of 3)*

- It is not uncommon for an enterprise to report against two, three, or more cybersecurity frameworks.
- This study guide's ***enterprise cybersecurity architecture*** is a convenient structure for cross-walking required regulatory reporting such as the following:
  - Sarbanes-Oxley regulations for financial systems
  - Heath Insurance Portability and Accountability Act (HIPPA) for medical systems
  - Payment Card Industry Data Security Standard (PCI DSS) for payment processing of credit cards
  - North American Electric Reliability Corporation Critical Infrastructure Protection (NERC CIP) regulations for energy generation systems
  - International Organization for Standardization (ISO) 27001 for general IT systems

Health Insurance Portability and Accountability Act (HIPAA) **Security Rule:** 22 Requirements in 5 Areas
Administrative Safeguards
1. Security Management Process
2. Assigned Security Responsibility
3. Workforce Security
4. Information Access Management
5. Security Awareness and Training
6. Security Incident Procedures
7. Contingency Plan
8. Evaluation
9. Business Associate Contracts and Other Arrangements
Physical Safeguards
10. Facility Access controls
11. Workstation Use
12. Workstation Security
13. Device and Media Controls
Technical Safeguards
14. Access Control
15. Audit Controls
16. Integrity
17. Person or Entity Authentication
18. Transmission Security
Organizational Requirements
19. Business Associate Contracts or Other Arrangements
20. Requirements for Group Health Plans
Policies and Procedures and Documentation Requirements
21. Policies and Procedures
22. Documentation

North American Electric Reliability Corporation (NERC) **Critical Infrastructure Protection (CIP) Cyber Security Version 5** 32 Cybersecurity Requirements in 10 Areas	
CIP-002	Critical Cyber Assets
CIP-003	Security Management Controls
CIP-004	Personnel and Training
CIP-005	Electronic Security
CIP-006	Physical Security
CIP-007	Systems Security Management
CIP-008	Incident Reporting and Response Planning
CIP-009	Recovery Plans for BES Cyber Assets
CIP-010	Configuration Changes and Vulnerability Assessments
CIP-011	Information Protection

Topics

- Looking at Control Frameworks
- Clearly Defining "Controls"
- Mapping Against External Frameworks
- One Audit, Many Results

Looking at Control Frameworks *(1 of 2)*

- A side-by-side comparison of this study guide's enterprise cybersecurity architecture is shown below alongside some major control frameworks.

Enterprise Cybersecurity Architecture 11 Functional Areas	**(ISC)² Common Body of Knowledge (CBK)** 10 Security Domains	**ISO 27001 / 27002 Version 2013** 114 Controls in 14 Domains	**NIST SP800-53 Revision 4** 224 Controls in 18 Families	**Council on CyberSecurity Critical Security Controls Version 5.1** 20 Controls and 182 Control Activities
1. Systems Administration 2. Network Security 3. Application Security 4. Endpoint, Server, and Device Security 5. Identity, Authentication, and Access Management 6. Data Protection and Cryptography 7. Monitoring, Vulnerability, and Patch Management 8. High Availability, Disaster Recovery, and Physical Protection 9. Incident Response 10. Asset Management and Supply Chain 11. Policy, Audit, E-Discovery, and Training	1. Access Control 2. Telecommunications and Network Security 3. Information Security Governance and Risk Management 4. Software Development Security 5. Cryptography 6. Security Architecture and Design 7. Security Operations 8. Business Continuity and Disaster Recovery Planning 9. Legal, Regulations, Investigations, and Compliance 10. Physical (Environmental) Security	1. Information Security Policies 2. Organization of Information Security 3. Human Resource Security 4. Asset Management 5. Access Control 6. Cryptography 7. Physical and Environmental Security 8. Operations Security 9. Communications Security 10. System Acquisition, Development, and Maintenance 11. Supplier Relationships 12. Information Security Incident Management 13. Information Security Aspect of Business Continuity Management 14. Compliance	1. Access Control 2. Awareness and Training 3. Audit and Accountability 4. Security Assessment and Authorization 5. Configuration Management 6. Contingency Planning 7. Identification and Authentication 8. Incident Response 9. Maintenance 10. Media Protection 11. Physical and Environmental Protection 12. Planning 13. Personnel Security 14. Risk Assessment 15. System and Services Acquisition 16. System and Communications Protection 17. System and Information Integrity 18. Program Management	1. Inventory of Devices 2. Inventory of Software 3. Secure Configurations for Computers 4. Continuous Vulnerability Assessment and Remediation 5. Malware Defenses 6. Application Software Security 7. Wireless Device Control 8. Data Recovery Capability 9. Security Skills Assessment and Training 10. Security Configurations for Network Devices 11. Network Ports, Protocols, and Services 12. Control of Administrative Privileges 13. Boundary Defense 14. Security Audit Logs 15. Need-to-Know Access Control 16. Account Monitoring and Control 17. Data Loss Prevention 18. Incident Response Capability 19. Secure Network Engineering 20. Penetration Testing and Red Team Exercises

- There are some commonalities: All five frameworks include access control and network or communications security; 4 of 5 frameworks include physical security; and so on.
- All the frameworks more or less cover the same topics.

Looking at Control Frameworks *(2 of 2)*

- Unlike other frameworks, this study guide's ***enterprise cybersecurity architecture*** is designed for *running* a comprehensive cybersecurity program.
- Architecture *organizes* cybersecurity controls by ***enterprise cybersecurity functional areas***.
- Functional areas *underlie* and *integrate* an ***enterprise cybersecurity program*** that includes the following:
  - Policy
  - Programmatics
  - IT Life Cycle
  - Assessment
- Functional areas provide the following:
  - Clear lines of delegation, responsibility, and accountability
  - Alignment of enterprise technologies and capabilities with people's skill sets

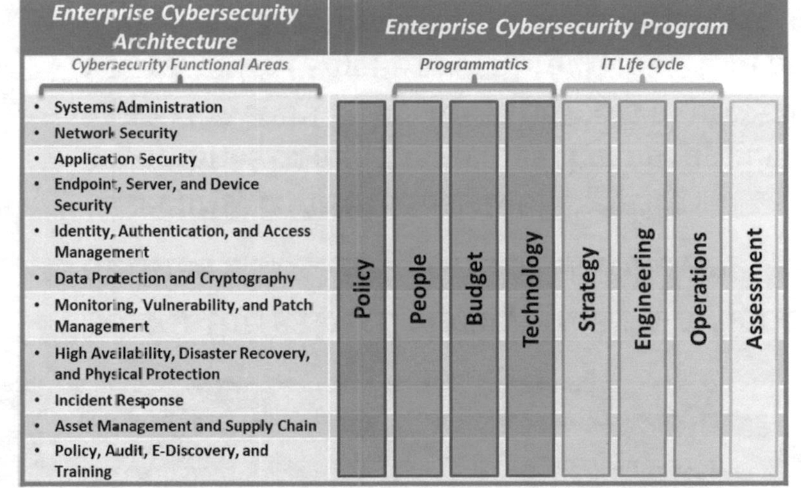

  - Efficient engineering, deployment, operation, auditing, and reporting of enterprise security capabilities
  - Crosswalk to required reporting against multiple regulatory requirements
- These combined features provide an easy-to-understand and practical enterprise cybersecurity architecture that adapts to the real world of evolving threat vectors.

Clearly Defining "Controls" *(1 of 2)*

- There is some confusion over exactly what various cybersecurity frameworks mean by an "IT security control."
- This confusion results in considerable room for interpretation and judgment in regard to auditing against these frameworks.
- Sometimes, what the frameworks call a "control," this study guide would call a "capability."
- Other times, the frameworks talk about "requirements," and it is up to individuals to identify what capabilities and controls would be needed to satisfy the requirements.

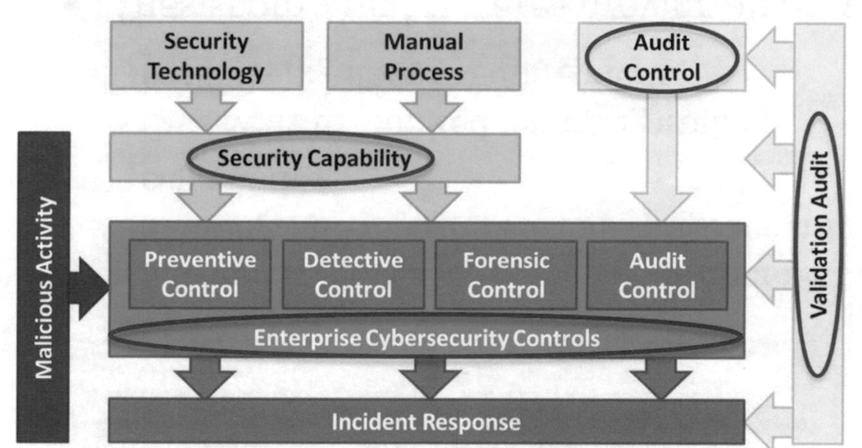

- So, for the sake of clarity, this study guide defines a security control as follows:

  "A security control consists of security capabilities or audit activities that are applied to an IT system or business process to prevent, detect, or investigate specific activities that are undesirable; an incident response is issued when those activities occur."

- The graphic depicts how enterprise cybersecurity controls fit with security capabilities and the various audit types.

Clearly Defining "Controls" *(2 of 2)*

- Security technologies or manual processes deliver enterprise security capabilities in terms of four types of security controls:
  - preventive, detective, forensic, and audit
- These controls can then trigger an incident response when potentially malicious behavior occurs.
- Audit activities deliver enterprise audit controls and periodic validation audits to ensure that everything is operating as designed.
- For a security control to be effective, the following five elements should be present:
  - A specific ***IT system*** or ***business process*** must be identified that contains information where the enterprise is concerned about its confidentiality, integrity, or availability.
  - A specific ***malicious activity*** against an IT system or business process must be identified.

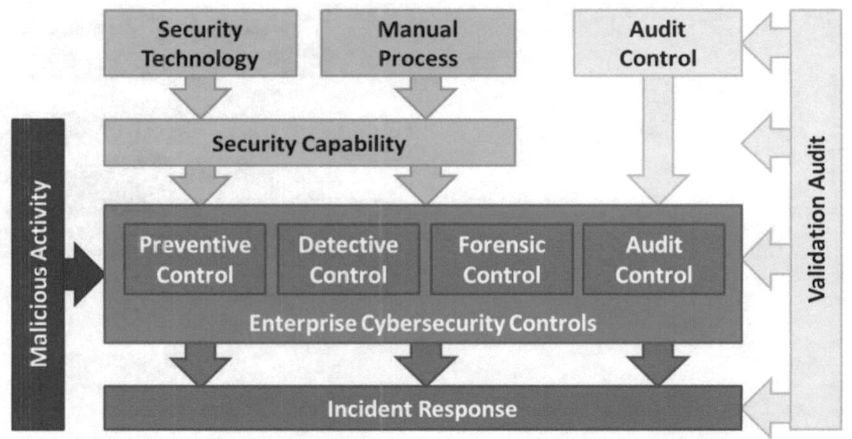

  - A ***security capability*** or ***audit control*** must be applied to an IT system or business process to restrict, delay, detect, or document the specific malicious activity that is of concern.
  - ***Incident responses*** must occur when malicious activities are detected.
  - ***Validation audits*** must occur periodically to ensure controls are effective and functioning properly.

Mapping Against External Frameworks *(1 of 7)*

Context

- An enterprise can use external cybersecurity frameworks in the following ways:
  - To help design an enterprise's cybersecurity program to comply with specific external standards
  - To validate an enterprise's cybersecurity program against those external standards
  - To give an enterprise ideas for cybersecurity capabilities and controls that may be of interest
- The graphic below depicts how external frameworks influence the selection of security scopes and controls for Threat, Assessment, and Validation audits.

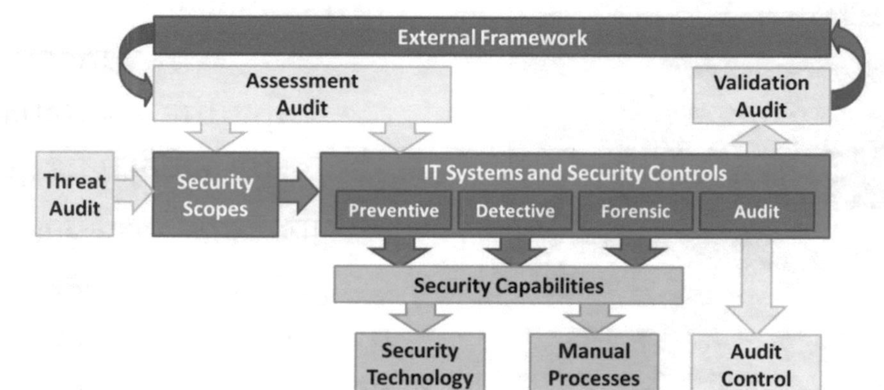

- External frameworks feed into the selection of enterprise security scopes and security controls that are delivered by ***security capabilities***, ***technologies***, ***manual processes***, and ***audit controls***.

Mapping Against External Frameworks *(2 of 7)*

Assessment Audit and Security Scopes

- Analyze how external framework controls and requirements apply to the enterprise
- Decide if the enterprise wants a *narrow scope* or *broad scope* application of the framework
  - ***Narrow scope***: Only IT systems and processes that are primarily involved in the external framework's scope are considered to be in-scope for the assessment; supporting systems and processes that are only indirectly involved in the assessed function are considered to be out-of-scope.
  - ***Broad scope***: IT systems that are primarily involved in the external framework's scope as well as supporting IT systems that are only indirectly involved are considered in-scope; scope can result in a large number of systems to be considered in-scope.
- Supporting security systems help determine security scope.

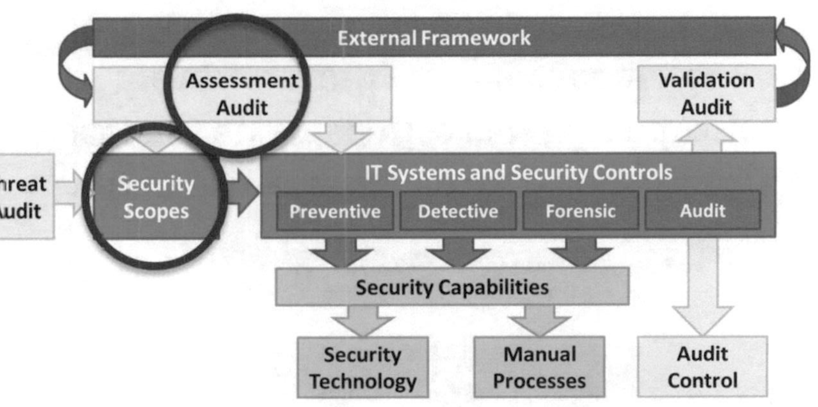

- If an enterprise security program is going to be validated by internal or external auditors, it is recommended the cybersecurity team meet with the auditors to mutually agree on whether a narrow scope or broad scope approach is necessary.
- It is important to determine which supporting security systems and process are to be considered in-scope for an assessment.

Mapping Against External Frameworks *(3 of 7)*

IT Systems and Security Controls

- An enterprise needs to identify the security controls appropriate to meet the external framework's requirements.
- Requirements have general guidance.
  - *"You shall have a firewall."*
  - *"Credit card data will be encrypted."*
  - For example, ISO 27001 and the HIPPA security rules provide rules to follow.
- Requirements may be very specific.
  - *"Application whitelisting technology will be used on servers."*
  - For example, Council on CyberSecurity 20 Critical Controls and HITECH provide rules to follow.
- Mandated controls depend upon the specifics of the framework being considered and the capabilities available to implement them.

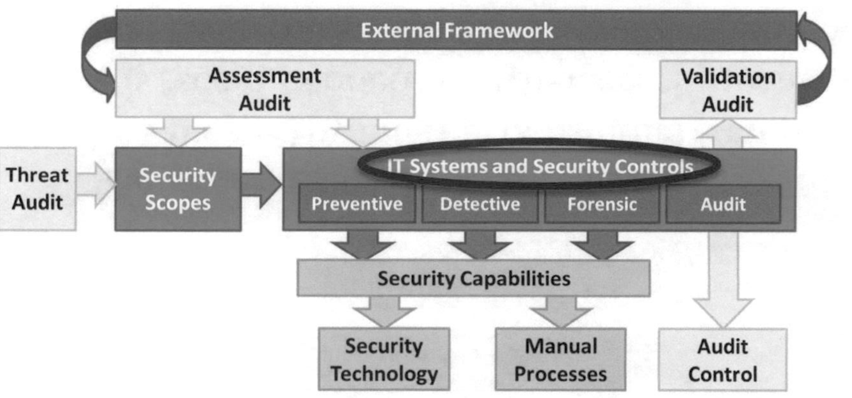

- When using frameworks where there is leeway, an enterprise can take advantage of the opportunity to select controls that work well in its environment and are economical to procure, deploy, and operate.
- Many cybersecurity frameworks have been established over the past two decades and are in common use today.

Mapping Against External Frameworks *(4 of 7)*

Balancing Prevention with Detection and Response

- Many popular frameworks focus primarily on preventive controls that block undesirable activities and give less attention to detective, forensic, and audit control alternatives.
- A prevention focus can lead to the following:
  - A false sense of security
  - Controls that are highly disruptive to legitimate business activities
- When an enterprise delivers the same level of security "in the background" without disrupting people's normal activities, it can be a significant win vs. security being a constant disruption to people doing their jobs.
- Enterprises can look at security control alternatives with the ***"Audit First" Design Methodology***.
- If an enterprise opts for detective, forensic, and audit control alternatives vs. preventive controls,

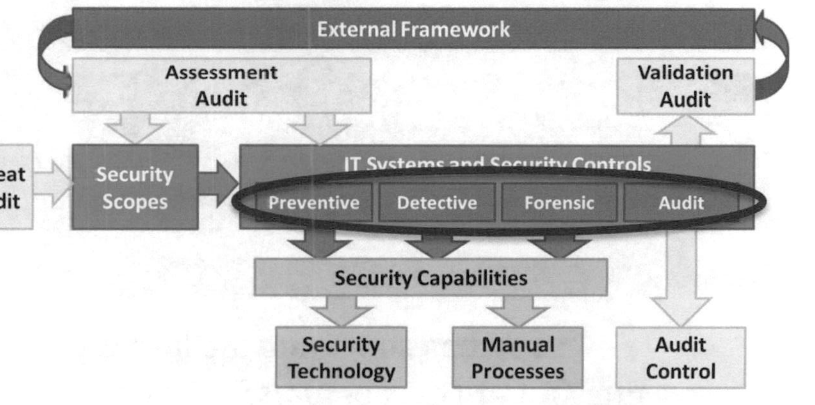

  - some negotiation between the cybersecurity team and auditors may be required with respect to how the enterprise protects itself; and
  - auditors may be thinking only of preventive controls and not give credit for other controls that are in place.
- An enterprise needs to work with its auditors to consider how passive controls (detective, forensic, and audit) can provide effective protection of IT assets and data.

Mapping Against External Frameworks *(5 of 7)*

Security Capabilities, Technologies, and Processes (1 of 2)

- Enterprises must identify the security capabilities, technologies, manual processes, and audit processes necessary to deliver the controls chosen.
- It is often faster and cheaper to set up a manual detective control or audit process than to install a new security technology.
- Where speed is of the essence, an enterprise can stand up "quick and dirty" controls until more permanent solutions can be put in place.
- Enterprises shouldn't underestimate the power of manual processes to protect on a temporary basis (months or years) until funding is available for long-term solutions.

- Some controls are manual and are no less valid than automated preventive and detective controls.
  - Maintaining paper or digital logs of activities
  - Auditing system logs to identify and investigate malicious activities

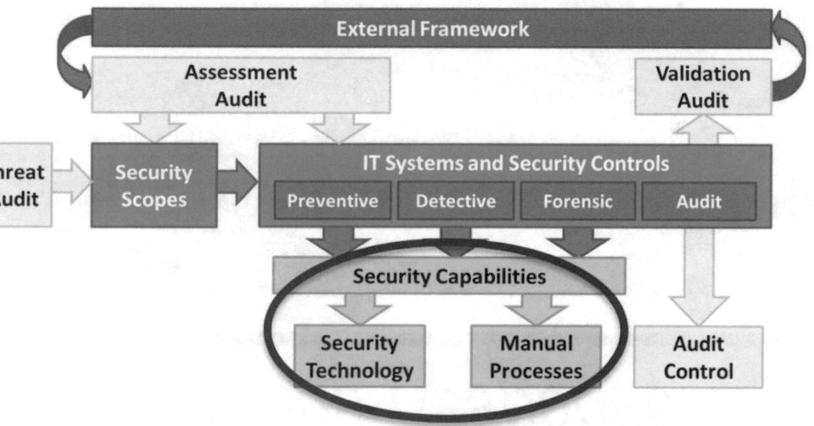

Mapping Against External Frameworks *(6 of 7)*

Security Capabilities, Technologies, and Processes (2 of 2)

- An enterprise should document manual processes.
  - What they are
  - Who should be doing them
  - Who is responsible for overseeing and maintaining them

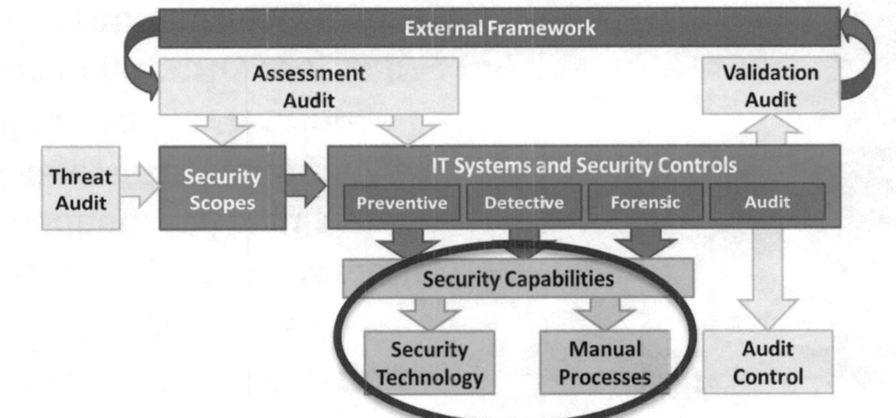

- If manual processes deliver the same functionality as automated technology, then an enterprise should give itself credit for having the capabilities.

Mapping Against External Frameworks *(7 of 7)*

Validation Audit and Reporting

- With enterprise controls in place, an enterprise should conduct validation audits of the cybersecurity program and report the results to internal and external auditors and regulators.
- *Note:* Validation and assessment audits should be conducted in a similar fashion.
- Once an enterprise's cybersecurity program is in place, the validation audit from one time period can serve as the assessment audit for the next time period.
- This audit sequence provides the enterprise with the inputs needed to make adjustments to the cybersecurity program over time.
- There are two validation audit reports.
  - External-facing audit report
  - Internal-facing audit report
- The ***external-facing audit report*** presents the results to external auditors and regulators.

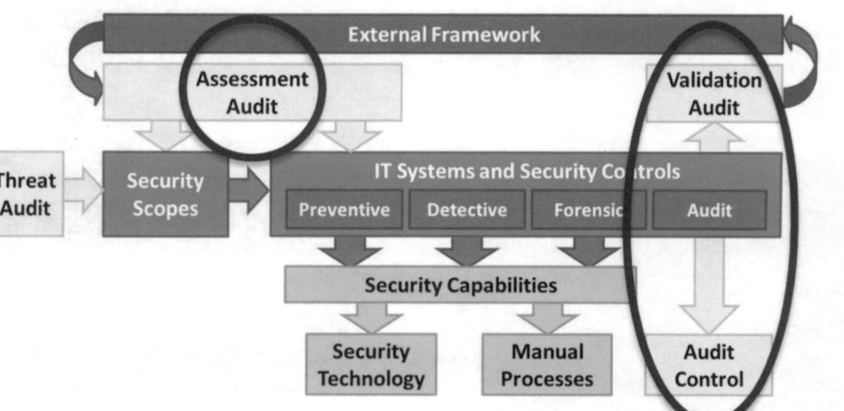

  - Lists the requirements of the framework to be audited
  - Explains how the cybersecurity program satisfies the requirements, any deficiencies identified during the audit, and the results of remediating those deficiencies
- The ***internal-facing audit report*** is an addendum to the external-facing report.
  - Contains internal-use-only recommendations for improving future security and audit results

One Audit, Many Results *(1 of 3)*

Context

- Enterprises are often required to report to multiple external frameworks where a number of controls are common to more than one framework.
- The graphic shows an approach for auditing the controls and reporting the audit results against the separate frameworks.

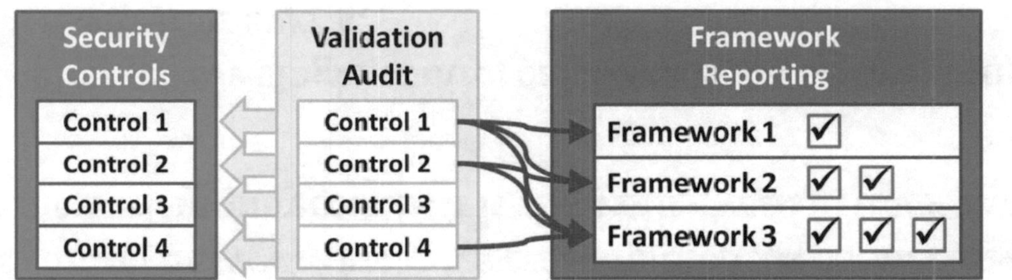

- Once controls are in place, validation audits can verify if the control framework was implemented. Then the results of those audits can be mapped and reported against multiple frameworks.
- The key to this reporting approach is separating the audit process from the security frameworks so the audit covers all controls and a superset of the framework requirements.

One Audit, Many Results *(2 of 3)*

Audit Reporting Mapping

- Audit results can be reported against various frameworks.
- If the enterprise's *control database* includes cross-references connecting controls to the applicable framework requirements, it is straightforward to track results to various frameworks.
- Using such cross-references, a single control can be referenced by multiple frameworks or different parts of a single framework.
- When the audit is complete, the enterprise follows these cross-references to build the report against the structure of each framework to be reported against.
- A simple database is able to show results against multiple frameworks across multiple audits.

One Audit, Many Results *(3 of 3)*

Deficiency Tracking and Management

- Audit deficiencies should be tracked against the controls they apply to and cross-referenced against the external frameworks for reporting purposes.
- The results, in part, provide input to substantial discussions about the materiality of deficiencies against framework compliance.
- A single deficiency may be material against one external framework, but immaterial against another framework.
- The key challenge is properly handling the delay between reporting the initial results of the audit and actually remediating the identified deficiencies.
  - Regularly scheduled audits looking at the same controls on a regular basis—for example, quarterly or annually—help to address this reporting delay challenge.
  - Deficiencies from the previous audit may become part of the kickoff for the next audit.
  - Enterprise management can then pay particular attention to deficiencies that are not remediated between audit, or that show up as recurring problems across multiple audit cycles.

Part V: Enterprise Cybersecurity Program

- Chapter 14: Managing an Enterprise Cybersecurity Program
- Chapter 15: Looking to the Future

CHAPTER 14

Managing an Enterprise Cybersecurity Program

S. E. Donaldson et al., *Enterprise Cybersecurity Study Guide*, https://doi.org/10.1007/978-1-4842-3258-3_14

Overview

- This chapter describes how the enterprise can use iterative assessments and prioritization to ***select***, ***plan***, ***resource***, and ***execute*** progressive improvements to its cybersecurity posture.
- The cybersecurity program utilizes the following management tools:
  - A framework for managing a cybersecurity program
  - A quantitative method for assessing the program and identifying strengths and weaknesses
  - Ongoing operations and cycles of improvements

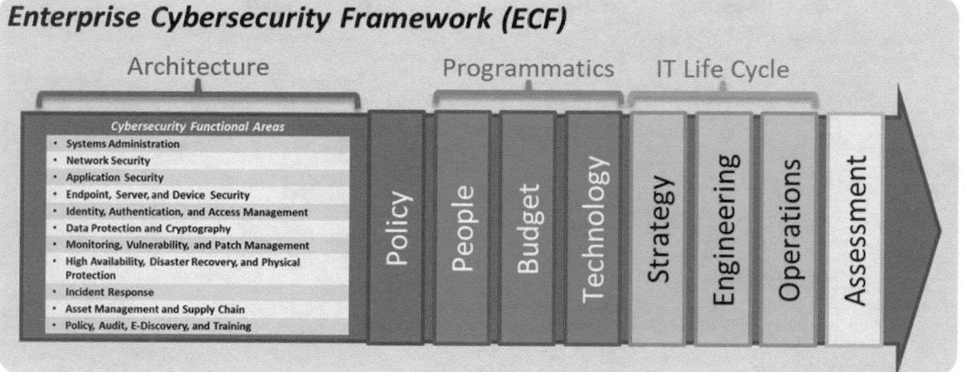

Topics

- Enterprise Cybersecurity Program Management
- Assessing Security Status
- Analyzing Enterprise Cybersecurity Improvements
- Prioritizing Improvement Projects
- Tracking Cybersecurity Project Results

Enterprise Cybersecurity Program Management *(1 of 13)*

Context

- Enterprise cybersecurity program management involves the following processes:
  - Risk management
  - Control management
  - Deficiency tracking
  - Process improvement
  - Measurement
- Enterprise cybersecurity program management also involves an ongoing cycle of the following:
  - Assessing threats and risks
  - Making progressive improvements to mitigate threats and risks
  - Collecting metrics from security operations

- This management process consists of the following major steps:
  1. Assess assets, threats, and risks
  2. Identify security scopes
  3. Assess risk mitigations, capabilities by functional area, and security operations
  4. Identify target security levels
  5. Identify deficient areas
  6. Prioritize remediation and improvements
  7. Resource and execute improvements
  8. Collect operational metrics
  9. Return to Step 1

Enterprise Cybersecurity Program Management *(2 of 13)*

Step 1: Assess Assets, Threats, and Risks

- ***Step 1*** involves assessing enterprise IT assets, threats, and risks.[1]
  - Considers the missions of potential attackers
    - Breach ***confidentiality***
    - Compromise ***integrity***
    - Disrupt ***availability***
  - Produces an output that is an understanding of the enterprise assets to be protected and the threats against those assets
    - Assets may be corporate data, customer data, or critical services such as power generation or healthcare delivery.

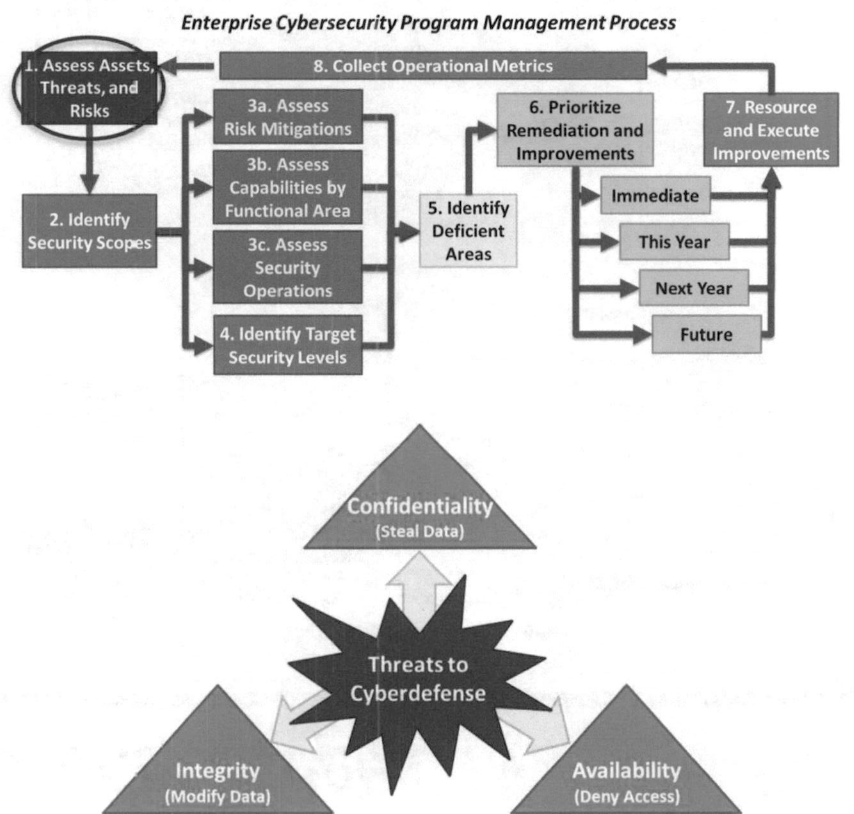

[1]See Chapter 4.

Enterprise Cybersecurity Program Management (3 of 13)

Step 2: Identify Security Scopes (1 of 2)

- ***Step 2*** groups the enterprise assets identified in Step 1 and groups the threats and risks against them into security scopes for protection.[2]
- Cybersecurity capabilities should be tied to security scopes.
  - Multiple scopes may use the same security capabilities.
  - Scope boundaries are important for ensuring the right levels of capabilities are employed in the right places.
  - Scopes enable the right balance between restrictive security and permissive operations must be achieved so that the enterprise can operate efficiently and effectively.

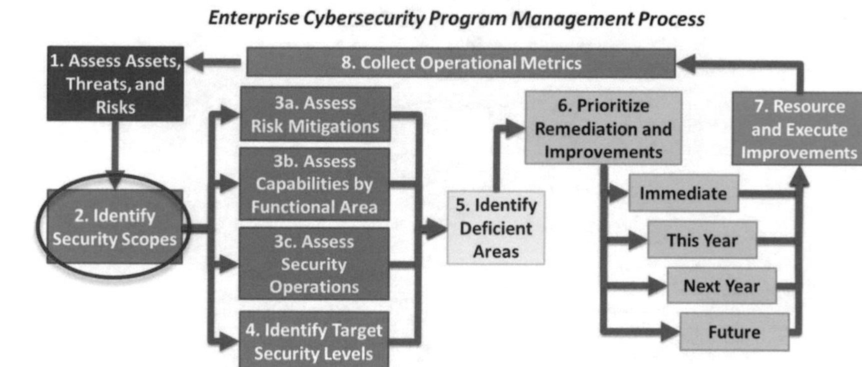

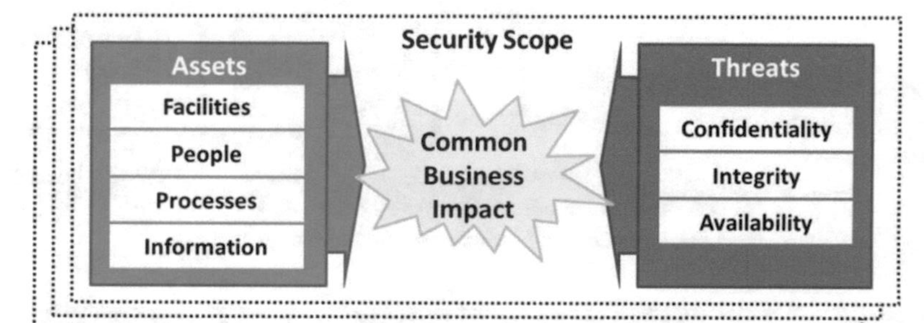

- Scopes are useful in identifying regulated data and systems for ensuring regulations are adhered to in a practical and economical manner.

[2]See Chapter 4.

Enterprise Cybersecurity Program Management *(4 of 13)*

Step 2: Identify Security Scopes (2 of 2)

- Challenges
  - Enterprise must keep track of which policies, rules, and controls apply to which scope, potentially increasing complexity.
    - Enterprise mitigates with a limited number of scopes aligned with the its regulatory obligations and cybersecurity architecture.
  - Systems that cross scope boundaries, such as data interconnects and systems administration consoles, present challenges.
    - Compensating controls may be necessary to ensure the interconnections do not become security vulnerabilities.
    - Allowing these systems to receive e-mail, surf the Web, and run office productivity applications may open them up to targeted attacks.

Enterprise Cybersecurity Program Management Process

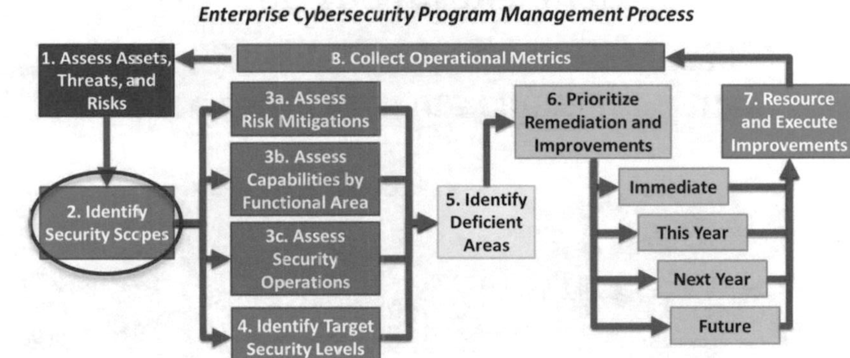

Security Scope Type	*Confidentiality (Steal Data)*	*Integrity (Modify Data)*	*Availability (Deny Access)*
1. *Non-Critical*	Low/Med	Low/Med	Low/Med
2. *Confidentiality Critical*	High	Low/Med	Low/Med
3. *Integrity Critical*	Low/Med	High	Low/Med
4. *Availcbility Critical*	Low/Med	Low/Med	High
5. *Confidentiality Non-Critical*	Low/Med	High	High
6. *Integrity Non-Critical*	High	Low/Med	High
7. *Availability Non-Critical*	High	High	Low/Med
8. *All Factors Critical*	High	High	High

- The goal, in part, is to ensure the defensive measures applied to each scope are appropriate and economical.

Enterprise Cybersecurity Program Management *(5 of 13)*

Step 3: Assess Risk Mitigations, Capabilities by Functional Area, and Security Operations (1 of 2)

- ***Step 3*** assesses the security of the security scope(s) in terms of the following:
  - ***Risk Mitigations***
    - Use the attack sequence to evaluate enterprise's ability to disrupt, detect, delay, and defeat attacks
    - Consider each potential attack scenario and then aggregate the results
  - ***Capabilities*** by functional area
    - Examine the 11 functional areas and calculate corresponding Object Measurement (OM) scores
    - Look out for functional areas that are deficient when compared to other functional areas
  - ***Security Operations***
    - Examine the 17 security operational processes
    - Assess the enterprise's ability to perform these processes to operate its cybersecurity systems

- Once the scores are calculated, they can be aggregated and compared for evaluation and further analysis.
- If a security scope is inadequately protected, then specific improvement activities can be considered.

Enterprise Cybersecurity Program Management *(6 of 13)*

Step 3: Assess Risk Mitigations, Capabilities by Functional Area, and Security Operations *(2 of 2)*

- The graphic depicts a potential ***measurement map*** to be used to assess
  - ***risk mitigations,***
  - ***capabilities*** by functional area, and
  - ***security operations.***
- The overall enterprise cybersecurity program assessment score can be tracked over time to show quantitatively how the cybersecurity posture evolves as improvements are implemented.

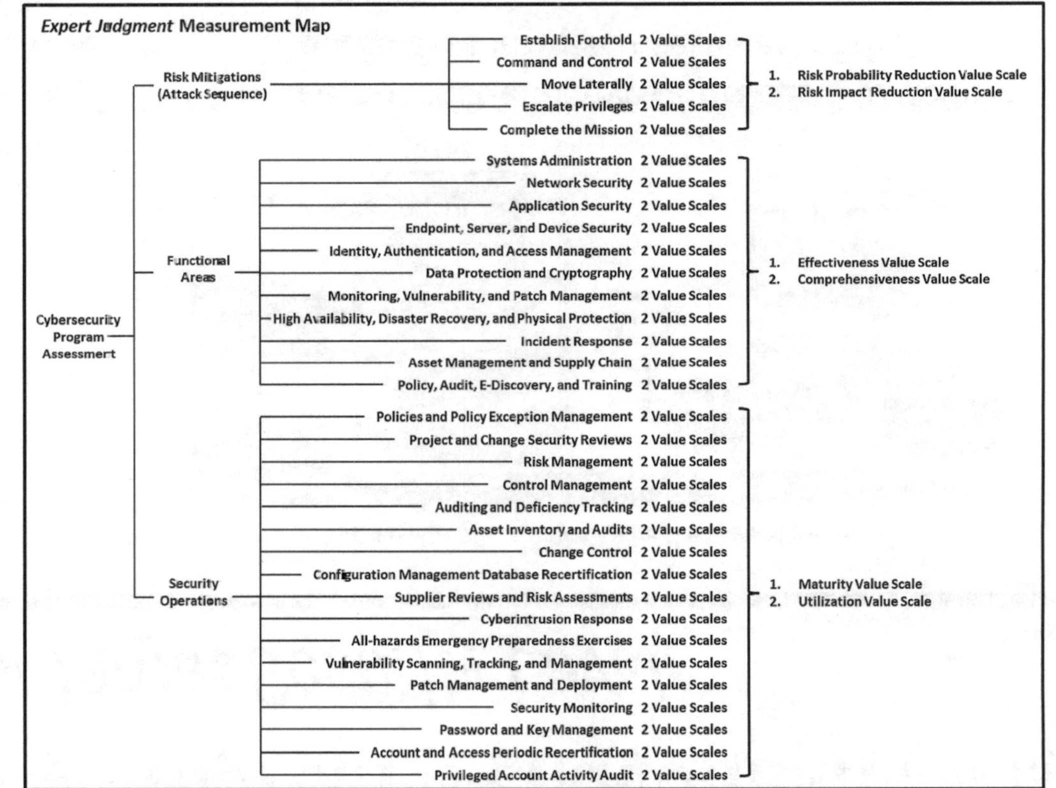

Enterprise Cybersecurity Program Management *(7 of 13)*

Step 4: Identify Target Security Levels

- For each security scope and associated assets, ***Step 4*** involves using the risk assessment methodology to identify the target security levels and understand if the scope's current security is adequate, inadequate, or even excessive.
- ***Target security level***
  - Represents the business tolerance for potential compromise within the scope
  - Is used to balance the severity of the threats with the business desire for flexibility and unobtrusive security that does not impeded business agility
- ***Security scopes***
  - Limit the number of systems and people who are subject to the most stringent security protection
  - Help prioritize cybersecurity resources toward the areas where they will deliver the greatest enterprise benefits
  - Simplify the cybersecurity process by reducing the attack surface of vulnerable systems

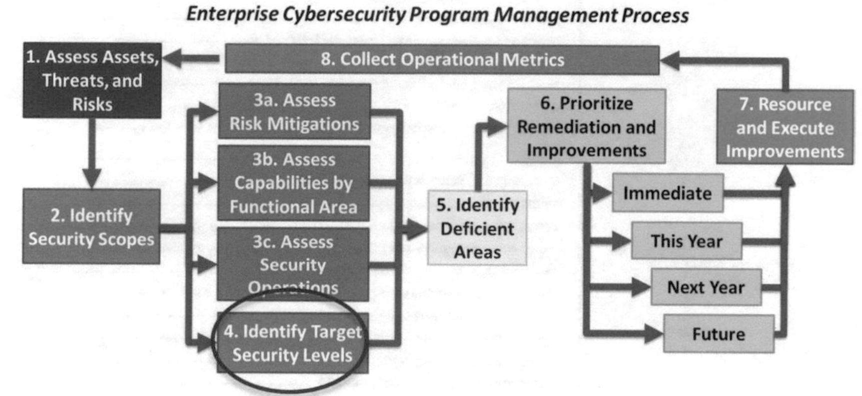

- It is not cost-effective or practical to deliver "perfect" security to every part of the enterprise.
- Different parts of the enterprise require different levels of protections and different preventive, detective, forensic, and audit controls.
- The security infrastructure requires the greatest level of protection so it can successfully protect the rest of the enterprise.

Enterprise Cybersecurity Program Management *(8 of 13)*

Step 5: Identify Deficient Areas

- ***Step 5*** identifies which areas are deficient and require improvements when compared to the target.
  - The target security level for the security scope may be too high or too low.
    - If additional security capabilities might be necessary, after considering the associated costs and potential operational trade-offs.
    - If a different security scope is required, the evaluation can be reconsidered.
  - Some functional areas are likely to stand out as being considerably weaker than other areas.
    - Weaker areas should be prioritized for improvements first since cybersecurity gaps are the most likely to be exploited by potential attackers.

  - After the most deficient functional areas are addressed, the next improvement phase involves bringing all areas up to the target level of security.
    - This phase often involves a comprehensive effort to improve risk mitigations, security capabilities, and security operations.
- At this point, the enterprise should understand its "as-is" cybersecurity posture.

Enterprise Cybersecurity Program Management *(9 of 13)*

Step 6: Prioritize Remediation and Improvements (1 of 2)

- ***Step 6*** prioritizes remediation and improvement efforts and is influenced by the following factors:
  - Bringing deficient functional areas up to target levels of security
  - Implementing improvements that rely on other improvements as prerequisites
  - Availability and skill levels of available staff and contractors
  - Cost of improvements
- The goal relies on the enterprise
  - addressing deficient enterprise cybersecurity functional areas first; and
  - working on bringing all functional areas up to the target cybersecurity level in a balanced manner.
- Improvements can be grouped into categories.
  - ***Immediate improvements*** that can be done immediately using readily available staff and budget

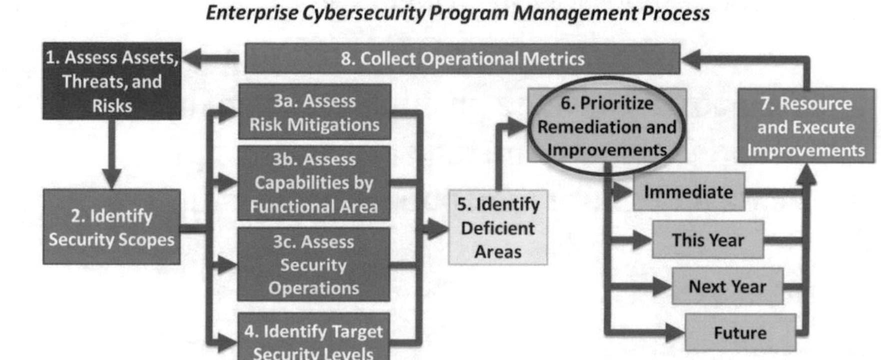

  - ***This-year*** improvements that can be done within the current year using resources that are obtainable in the year or after minor prerequisites or other dependencies have been addressed
  - ***Next-year*** improvements that should be done next year, after completing the immediate and this-year projects, and obtaining budgets, approvals, or satisfying other prerequisites
  - ***Future*** improvements that are a lower priority or will require obtaining budget, hiring staff, and so on

Enterprise Cybersecurity Program Management *(10 of 13)*

Step 6: Prioritize Remediation and Improvements *(2 of 2)*

- Improvements can be further prioritized and subgrouped.
- At the highest level, the groupings are helpful to start aligning cybersecurity priorities with business financial cycles so that work can be resourced and executed.
- Projects and tasks will move around on the priority lists.
- Having a "big picture" story to tell leadership is important.
  - Where the enterprise is
  - Where it is going
  - How it is going to get there

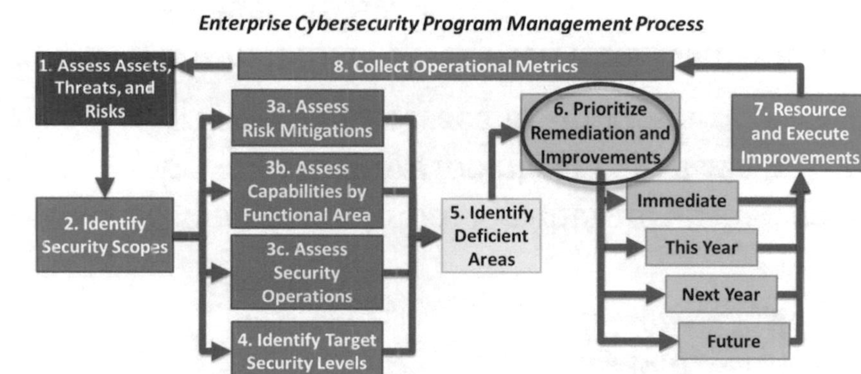

- Business leadership wants to understand that such prioritized improvements are not just spending money.
- Maintaining the cybersecurity strategy grouped into these categories simply makes it easier for security to manage and explain its priorities and plans to enterprise leadership.

Enterprise Cybersecurity Program Management *(11 of 13)*

Step 7: Resource and Execute Improvements

- ***Step 7*** involves the following tasks that are conducted in parallel against each category grouping of improvements:
  - For ***immediate*** improvements, cybersecurity leadership directs the work and supervises its progress.
  - For ***this-year*** improvements, cybersecurity leadership works on lining up resources, shuffling priorities, or completing prerequisites so that the actual improvement can start work within the current year.
  - For ***next*** and ***future*** improvements, cybersecurity leadership starts framing project plans and resource requirements so that they can be considered and budgeted in future fiscal years.

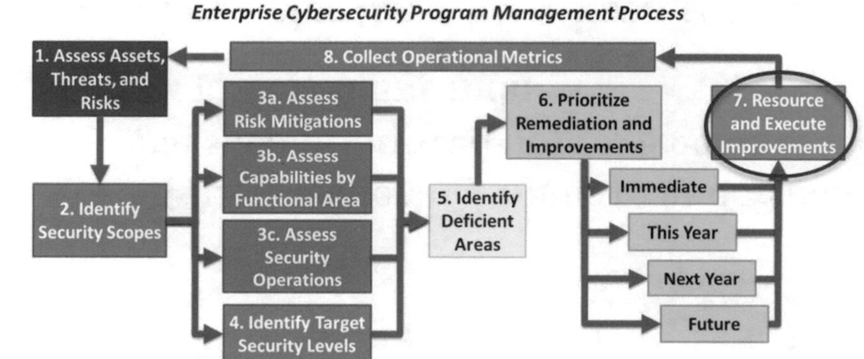

  - Many times, improvements are pushed back because they are too big or expensive to execute in a foreseeable timeframe.
  - It is helpful to break such improvements into smaller pieces.
  - Alternatively, it may help to link such improvements to other business needs to garner support from multiple departments.

Enterprise Cybersecurity Program Management *(12 of 13)*

Step 8: Collect Operational Metrics

- ***Step 8*** collects metrics as the enterprise executes it improvements and operates it security program.
- Metrics
  - Span all functional areas
  - Give particular attention to metrics measuring the signs of security incidents and near-incidents, or indicators of attacker activities indicating the presence of anticipated threats
  - Give enterprise leadership visibility into the following:
    - What threats are
    - Where threats are coming from
    - What can result if threats are not stopped
  - Even relatively crude metrics like "The enterprise was scanned a million times last month," can be useful if metrics are tracked and trended over time.
- Metrics are used in a variety of ways.[3]
  1. how external frameworks influence the selection of security scopes and controls for Threat, Assessment, and Validation audits.

Enterprise Cybersecurity Program Management Process

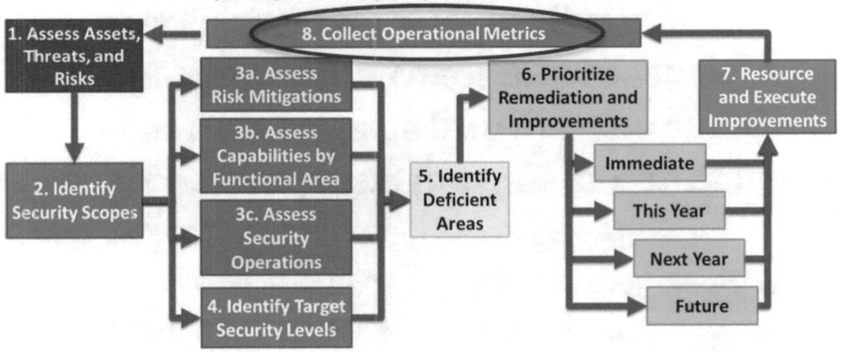

1. Assess Assets, Threats, and Risks
2. Identify Security Scopes
3a. Assess Risk Mitigations
3b. Assess Capabilities by Functional Area
3c. Assess Security Operations
4. Identify Target Security Levels
5. Identify Deficient Areas
6. Prioritize Remediation and Improvements
Immediate
This Year
Next Year
Future
7. Resource and Execute Improvements
8. Collect Operational Metrics

- In this study guide, "metric" means the following:
  - A standard or unit of measurement or formula used to quantify something, and/or
  - The values the standard or formula may assume
- Metrics are expressed in terms that make sense to the intended audience; otherwise, they may misconstrue results.
- Metrics need to have benchmarks.

[3]Adapted from *Successful Software Development*, 2nd Edition, by Scott E. Donaldson and Stanley G. Siegel (Prentice Hall, 2001).

Enterprise Cybersecurity Program Management *(13 of 13)*

Return to Step 1

- After collecting operational metrics, the cybersecurity program management process returns to Step 1 and the ***cycle*** repeats.
- Assess ➤ Prioritize ➤ Execute ➤ Operate
  - Should iterate multiple times each year
  - Updates its threat assessment
  - Takes stock of completed security improvements
  - Identifies new security improvements to implement
  - Lines up future security improvements for execution when resources become available
- As the cycle iterates, security projects move through the various priority categories until they are executed.
- Projects get inserted into the categories due to incidents, new threats, or IT projects requiring additional protections.

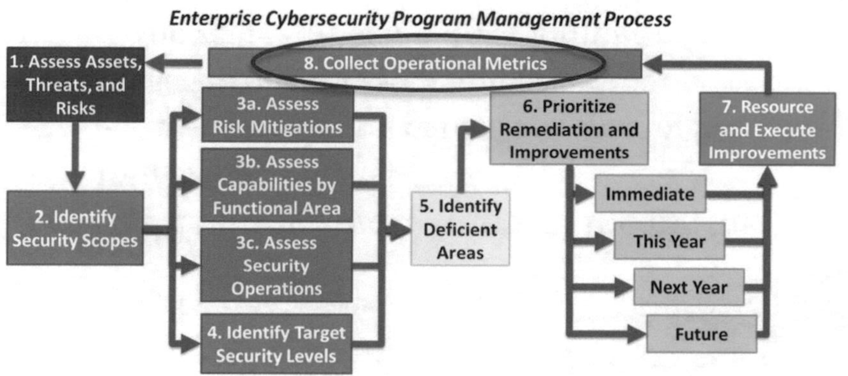

- Accommodating the day-to-day realities with new projects provides the enterprise a flexible framework for managing its overall cybersecurity program.
- This process provides the ability to report on immediate activities and the "big picture" strategy at any time.

Assessing Security Status *(1 of 7)*

Context

- After ***Step 1*** and ***Step 2***, ***Step 3*** assesses the overall security posture and status within each scope.
- The graphic depicts the next level of detail for assessing the enterprise's overall security posture.
- For each security scope, the enterprise
  - can consider if it needs to protect primarily ***confidentiality***, ***integrity***, or ***availability***;
  - considers the ***appropriate balance*** of preventive, detective, forensic, and audit controls to deliver the desired protection; and
  - has substantive discussions with business leaders to understand the proper balance of ***cybersecurity vs. business utility*** to deliver the most appropriate and cost-effective protection.

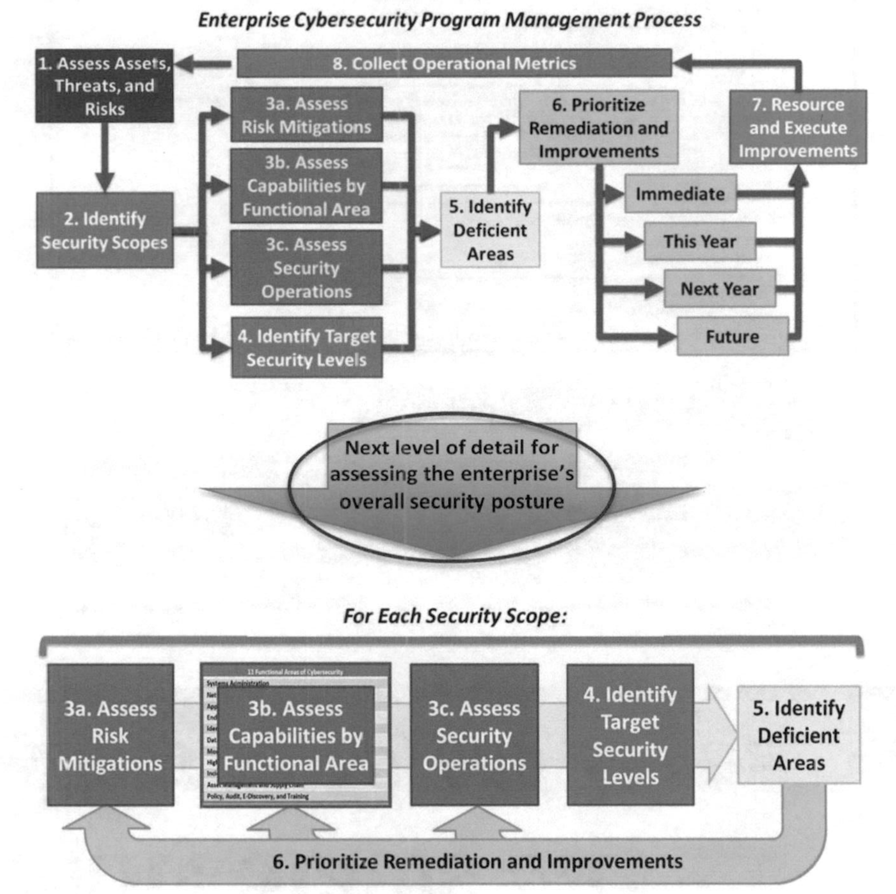

Assessing Security Status *(2 of 7)*

Cybersecurity Program Steps 3a, 3b, and 3c (1 of 2)

- ***Step 3a: Assessing Cybersecurity Risk Mitigations***
  - What is the effectiveness of risk mitigations within the security scope?
  - What are the abilities of the risk mitigations to disrupt the attack sequence of anticipated attacks?
  - Step 3a considers
    - the attacks to be countered;
    - the controls being deployed against the attack sequence; and
    - the effectiveness of the resulting mitigations.
  - Object Measurement methodology can be used to measure the effectiveness of these mitigations.
- ***Step 3b: Assessing Cybersecurity Capabilities by Functional Area***
  - Step 3b assesses the functional areas using Object Measurement methodology to calculate cybersecurity scores.
  - Functional area assessment scores are evaluated alongside the risk mitigations and security operations to determine, in part, the enterprise's overall cybersecurity posture.

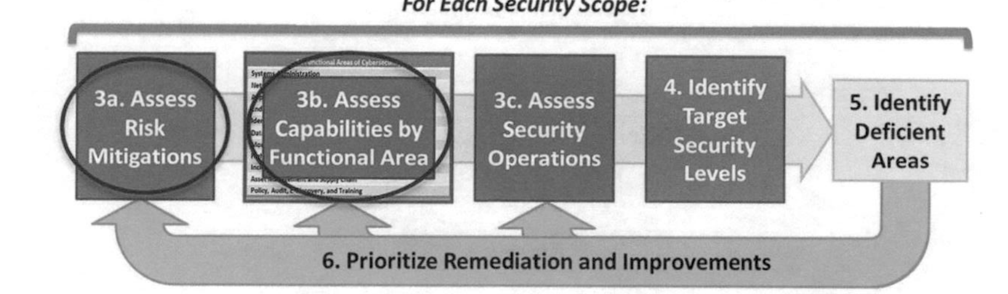

Measurement Map for Example *Expert Judgment* Cybersecurity Program Assessment

Cybersecurity Program Assessment
Risk Mitigations (Attack Sequence)
Establish Foothold
Command and Control
Move Laterally
Escalate Privileges
Complete the Mission
Functional Areas
Systems Administration
Network Security
Application Security
Endpoint, Server, and Device Security
Identity, Authentication, and Access Management
Data Protection and Cryptography
Monitoring, Vulnerability, and Patch Management
High Availability, Disaster Recovery, and Physical Protection
Incident Response
Asset Management and Supply Chain
Policy, Audit, E-Discovery, and Training
Security Operations
Policies and Policy Exception Management
Project and Change Security Reviews
Risk Management
Control Management
Auditing and Deficiency Tracking
Asset Inventory and Audits
Change Control
Configuration Management Database Recertification
Supplier Reviews and Risk Assessments
Cyberintrusion Response
All-hazards Emergency Preparedness Exercises
Vulnerability Scanning, Tracking, and Management
Patch Management and Deployment
Security Monitoring
Password and Key Management
Account and Access Periodic Recertification
Privileged Account Activity Audit

Assessing Security Status *(3 of 7)*

Cybersecurity Program Steps 3a, 3b, and 3c (2 of 2)

- ***Step 3c: Assessing Security Operations***
  - Step 3c assesses the 17 security operational processes and the 14 supporting information systems in terms of utilization and effectiveness.
  - Information Systems
    - Administrator Audit Trail
    - Accounts and Permissions
    - Password and Key Vault
    - Vulnerability Database
    - Disaster Recovery Plans
    - Incident Records
    - Configuration Management Database
    - Asset Database
    - Security Policies
    - Policy Exceptions
    - Authority To Operate Records
    - Enterprise Risks
    - Security Controls
    - Security Deficiencies
  - Object Measurement methodology can be used to score the processes and/or systems.

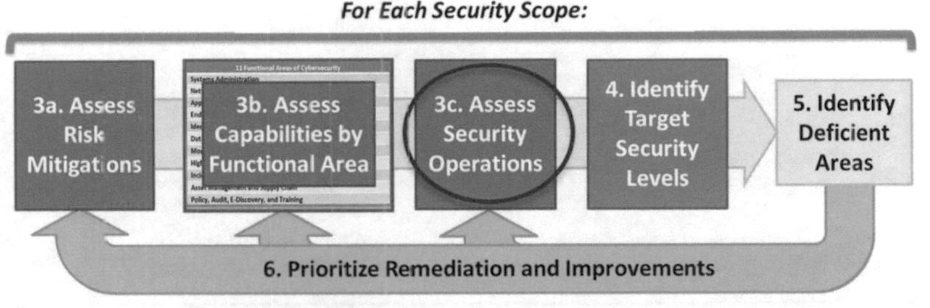

Measurement Map for Example *Expert Judgment* Cybersecurity Program Assessment

Cybersecurity Program Assessment

Risk Mitigations (Attack Sequence)
Establish Foothold
Command and Control
Move Laterally
Escalate Privileges
Complete the Mission

Functional Areas
Systems Administration
Network Security
Application Security
Endpoint, Server, and Device Security
Identity, Authentication, and Access Management
Data Protection and Cryptography
Monitoring, Vulnerability, and Patch Management
High Availability, Disaster Recovery, and Physical Protection
Incident Response
Asset Management and Supply Chain
Policy, Audit, E-Discovery, and Training

Security Operations
Policies and Policy Exception Management
Project and Change Security Reviews
Risk Management
Control Management
Auditing and Deficiency Tracking
Asset Inventory and Audits
Change Control
Configuration Management Database Recertification
Supplier Reviews and Risk Assessments
Cyberintrusion Response
All-hazards Emergency Preparedness Exercises
Vulnerability Scanning, Tracking, and Management
Patch Management and Deployment
Security Monitoring
Password and Key Management
Account and Access Periodic Recertification
Privileged Account Activity Audit

Assessing Security Status *(4 of 7)*

Cybersecurity Program Step 4: Identify Target Security Levels (1 of 2)

- ***Step 4*** identifies the target security level for a cybersecurity scope, based on the ***risk assessment process*** that considers
  - assets, threats, risks to scope, and potential attack sequences; and
  - balance between restrictive cybersecurity needs vs. flexible business agility needs to determine security controls.
- The graphic shows the analytical progression from assets to vulnerabilities to threats to treatments, and finally, to controls to mitigate risks (see Chapter 2).

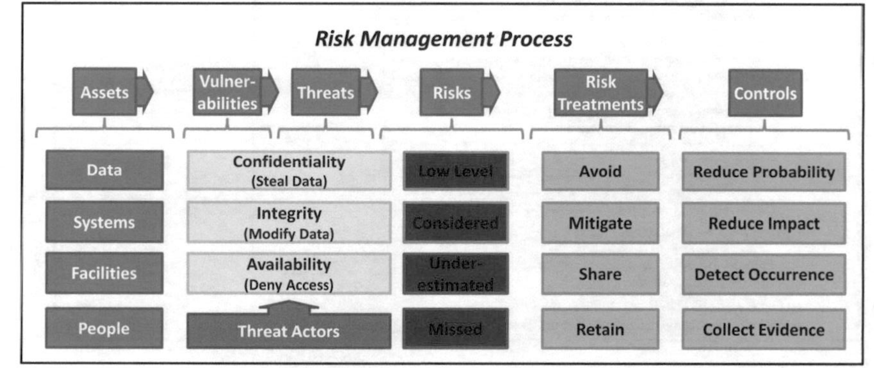

Assessing Security Status *(5 of 7)*

Cybersecurity Program Step 4: Identify Target Security Levels (2 of 2)

- One output can be a cybersecurity ***program assessment score*** that represents the ***assessed target security level*** for the security scope.
- Using Object Measurement, the assessed target security level can be represented as a ***single number*** (for example, 55%) for the entire scope.
- The graphic depicts one way to visualize this step's output.
  - Risk mitigations (aggregated score)
  - 11 functional areas (individual scores)
  - Security operations (aggregated score)
  - Dotted line represents the target cybersecurity program score at the 80% target security level

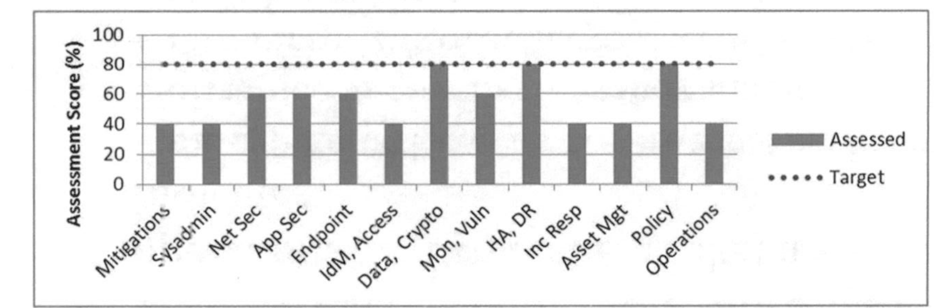

- The graphic also shows which cybersecurity areas are the strongest and weakest.

Assessing Security Status *(6 of 7)*

Cybersecurity Program Step 5: Identify Deficient Areas

- ***Step 5***: Once the scoring is completed and the results plotted or otherwise displayed, the cybersecurity areas that are most ***deficient*** should be apparent.
- The graphic shows the following cybersecurity areas standing out as being ***deficient*** relative to the overall average cybersecurity level of 55%:
  - Risk Mitigations—40%
  - Systems Administration—40%
  - Identity, Authentication, and Access Management—40%
  - Incident Response—40%
  - Asset Management—40%
  - Security Operations—40%
- The above cybersecurity areas are most likely to be related to security failures leading to successful cyberattacks.

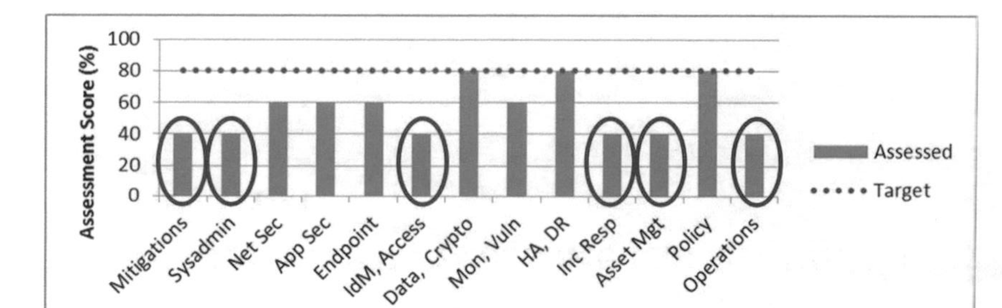

- The fact that risk mitigations and security operations are two of the weaker areas indicates:
  - the cyberattack sequences are most likely not disrupted as effectively as they should be; and
  - the enterprise's overall cybersecurity program is likely not being operated with adequate rigor to protect against deliberate or targeted attacks.

Assessing Security Status *(7 of 7)*

Cybersecurity Program Step 6: Prioritize Remediation and Improvements

- ***Step 6*** prioritizes the remediation and improvement efforts across all scopes.
- The cybersecurity improvements can be performed in two phases.
  - ***First***, deficient cybersecurity areas are addressed and brought up to the same cybersecurity level as the other areas.
  - ***Second***, all the cybersecurity areas are brought up to the target level together.
    - Improve risk mitigations by addressing projected attack sequences
    - Improve functional areas by adding security capabilities or improving their utilization
    - Improve security operations by implementing operational processes
- The overall enterprise cybersecurity program assessment score would change from 55% to 65%, and then to 80%.

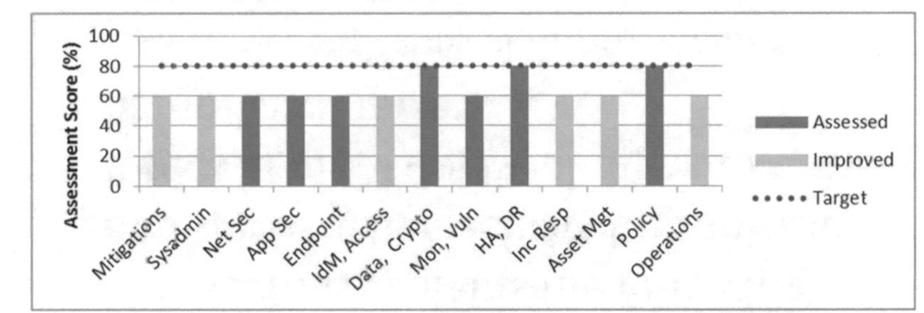

- In the above example, the ***first phase*** of improvements brings the most deficient areas up to the same level as the others.

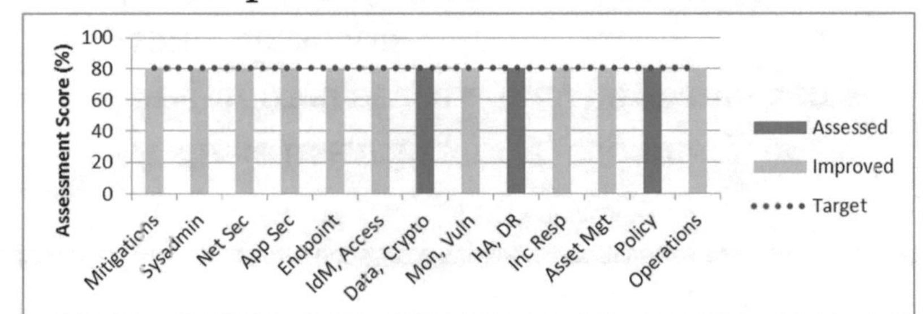

- In the above example, the ***second phase*** of improvements brings all cybersecurity areas up to the same target level.

Analyzing Enterprise Cybersecurity Improvements *(1 of 8)*

Context

- Cybersecurity Program Assessment
  - Assigns a quantitative measurement to cybersecurity
  - Helps with making business decisions regarding the relative value of different types of security investments
  - Helps in calculating which improvements will provide the biggest "bang for the buck"
  - Provides insight into which cybersecurity improvements will generate the greatest security improvement for the lowest cost
    - Projected program assessment score changes / Estimated improvement costs
- Challenges
  - Cybersecurity program assessment focuses on the security scope as the basic platform for analyzing security and security capabilities.
  - Most enterprises have multiple scopes.
  - A single risk mitigation, capability, or operational process may be shared across multiple scopes.
  - Consequently, the benefit of security improvements should be considered across multiple scopes as well.
- This section explains the following enterprise cybersecurity improvement topics in more detail, along with some helpful examples:
  - Considering Types of Improvements
  - Considering Threat Scenarios
  - Examining Cybersecurity Assessment Scores across Multiple Scopes
  - Considering Improvement Opportunities across Multiple Scopes
  - Considering "Bang for the Buck"

Analyzing Enterprise Cybersecurity Improvements *(2 of 8)*

Considering Types of Improvements

- In general, security improvements fall into three categories, depending upon the specific security area to be improved.
  - ***Risk mitigations*** should be the top improvement category if it scores poorly compared to other categories.
    - Focus on disrupting, detecting, delaying, and defeating known threats and their attack sequences
    - Require certain levels of security capabilities and operational processes
  - ***Security capabilities*** is the next category for improvement.
    - Address unknown threats, unanticipated attacks, defender mistakes, and attackers who use new technologies or innovative approaches
  - ***Security operations*** is the third category for improvement.
    - Required to make risk mitigations and security capabilities work in repelling attacks on an ongoing basis
- Cybersecurity improvements in the above categories improve the enterprise's cybersecurity posture.
- Calculating which improvements will generate the greatest security improvement for the lowest investment and in the least amount of time helps the enterprise make informed business decisions.

Analyzing Enterprise Cybersecurity Improvements *(3 of 8)*

Considering Threat Scenarios

- When thinking through attacker scenarios and corresponding risk mitigations, consider ***red-team exercises*** and ***penetration testing***.
- These techniques analyze enterprise defenses from the attacker's perspective to identify gaps in protection and vulnerabilities in defenses.
- Exercises can consider the following threat scenario elements:
  - What asset would be endangered (for example, credit card numbers that could be stolen)
  - Where the asset resides and when
  - Who has access to the asset
  - When and how an attacker might access the asset (for example, via the operating system, database, application, or user account levels)
  - Attack sequences for attackers to obtain access
  - Audit controls to log the access, if the access occurred
  - Detective controls to alert the enterprise when such access occurred
  - Preventive controls to block such access from occurring
- It is useful to bring in third parties to conduct a red-team review of enterprise scenarios, assumptions, and gaps to identify attack vectors the enterprise never considered.
- Another useful exercise is to have penetration testers actually exercise the scenarios.
  - Use the tools and techniques attackers might be expected to use
  - Use results to understand how preventive controls should block the attacks and how other controls should detect, log, and search for the attacks

Analyzing Enterprise Cybersecurity Improvements *(4 of 8)*

Examining Cybersecurity Assessment Scores Across Multiple Scopes (1 of 2)

- Most enterprises have multiple security scores.
  - Remember that cybersecurity program assessment scores are calculated within a single security scope.
- This reality adds complexity to the cybersecurity management effort.
- In an enterprise cybersecurity architecture, security scopes represent the following:
  - Separately managing the security posture of each scope:
    - assets, threats, and risks
    - risk mitigations applied to defend against attacks
    - cybersecurity capabilities and controls used to deliver risk mitigations
    - operational processes used to operate capabilities
  - Separately calculating cybersecurity assessment scores and target scores for each scope

- Frequently, there is significant sharing of cybersecurity capabilities across multiple scopes.
- Sharing is OK unless the cybersecurity capabilities allow attackers to exploit them to get from a lower-security scope to a higher-security scope.

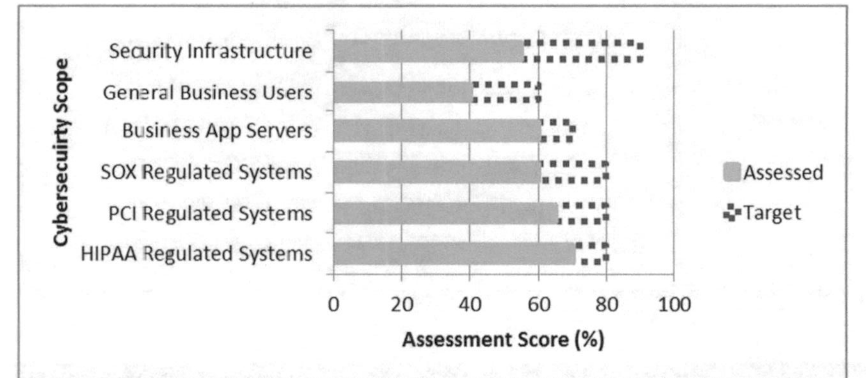

- The graphic depicts one way to visualize enterprise cybersecurity program ***assessment scores*** and ***target scores*** across multiple scopes.

Analyzing Enterprise Cybersecurity Improvements *(5 of 8)*

Examining Cybersecurity Assessment Scores Across Multiple Scopes (2 of 2)

- Considering the cybersecurity requirements associated with the hypothetical example, the enterprise might have the following six security scopes:
  - ***Security infrastructure*** that protects the data in the other five scopes
    - This infrastructure must be hardened to
      - resist attack;
      - detect breaches or failures of security;
      - provide a forensic trail for all security-related activities; and
      - be aggressively audited to ensure its ongoing integrity.
  - ***General business users*** who primarily use e-mail, desktop productivity tools, and web-based business applications for conducting general business
  - ***Business application servers*** that support the enterprise's business operations

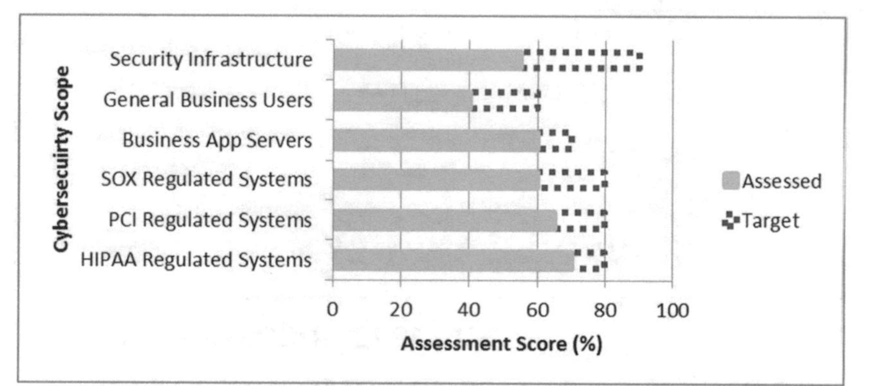

  - ***SOX regulated systems*** that support the business's reporting of financial results to the public stock markets and are subject to the Sarbanes-Oxley regulations regarding financial reporting integrity
  - ***PCI regulated systems*** that support the business's processing of credit cards and other payment mechanisms and are subject to the regulations of the Payment Card Industry (PCI)
  - ***HIPAA regulated systems*** that handle medical and personally identifiable information for the business

Analyzing Enterprise Cybersecurity Improvements *(6 of 8)*

Considering Improvement Opportunities Across Multiple Scopes

- When looking at cybersecurity scores across multiple scopes it is worthwhile to model and visualize the cybersecurity value of potential improvements.
- To assess the value, the enterprise
  - calculates its cybersecurity program assessment scores *before* and *after* the improvements; and
  - determines the amount the assessment scores change between the two assessments.

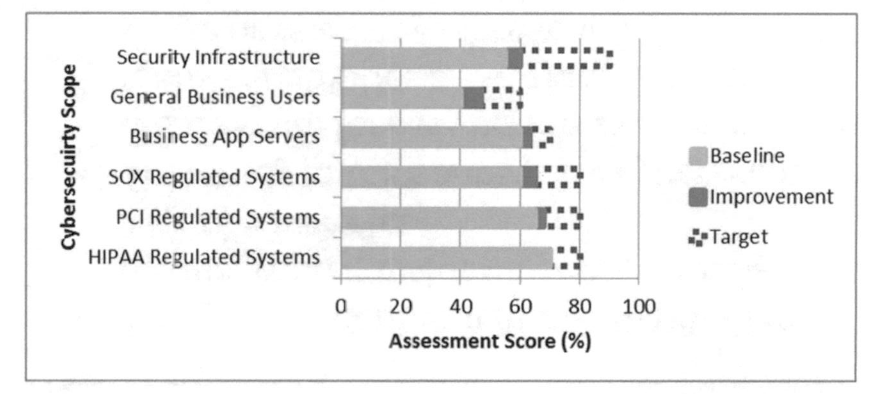

- The graphic provides an example of a before-and-after calculation.
- The proposed improvements impact five of the six security scopes.
- The total improvement value is calculated by adding up its impact across all scopes.

Analyzing Enterprise Cybersecurity Improvements *(7 of 8)*

Considering "Bang for the Buck" (1 of 2)

- It is important for leadership to make well-informed decisions regarding cybersecurity investments.
- Investments should consider the cost and time involved in deployment and operations compared to the impact the capability will have on the enterprise cybersecurity posture when deployed and operational.
- The challenge is spending thousands or millions of dollars and, at the end of the day, realizing that the huge investment only delivers a single or relatively few cybersecurity capabilities.
- ***Bottom line***: There are *no silver cybersecurity bullets* and the deployment of one or relatively few capabilities seldom makes the difference between overall cybersecurity success and failure against targeted attackers.

Cost / Complexity	Security Benefits: Low	Security Benefits: High
High	Poor Investments	Good Investments
Low	Tweaks	Quick Wins

- The graphic depicts a matrix of possible results when considering ***cost/complexity*** vs. ***security benefits***.
- This study guide's enterprise cybersecurity architecture focuses on the value of having many capabilities all working together vs. a single or relatively few capabilities.
- Security strategy should consider the cost and benefit of desired improvements and prioritize ***quick wins*** and ***good investments***.
- Lower-value ***tweaks*** should be delegated to technical staff and ***poor investments*** should be avoided altogether.

Analyzing Enterprise Cybersecurity Improvements *(8 of 8)*

Considering "Bang for the Buck" *(2 of 2)*

- The matrix shows potential improvements falling into four general categories.
  - ***Tweaks*** have low security benefits, but also low costs. Tweaks can be a time suck for leadership as they distract leadership from the high-value activities and investments, and should be delegated to junior staff.
  - ***Poor investments*** have high costs, but low security benefits. Unless these investment can be carefully managed to control the cost and ensure the potential benefits, these project should be avoided. In particular, poor investments can be a significant drain on leadership bandwidth, taking attention away from other opportunities with greater security value.

Cost / Complexity	*Security Benefits* Low	High
High	Poor Investments	Good Investments
Low	Tweaks	Quick Wins

- ***Quick wins*** have high security benefits and low cost and complexity. Enterprise leadership should be on the lookout for these opportunities and should give them high priority for implementation.
- ***Good investments*** have high security benefits, but also have high cost and complexity. Leadership must carefully consider and manage these investments to ensure they are successful. Making multiple *good investments* in a single fiscal year may require significant resources.

Prioritizing Improvement Projects *(1 of 3)*

- Cybersecurity improvement projects can be divided into four groups based on when they might take place.

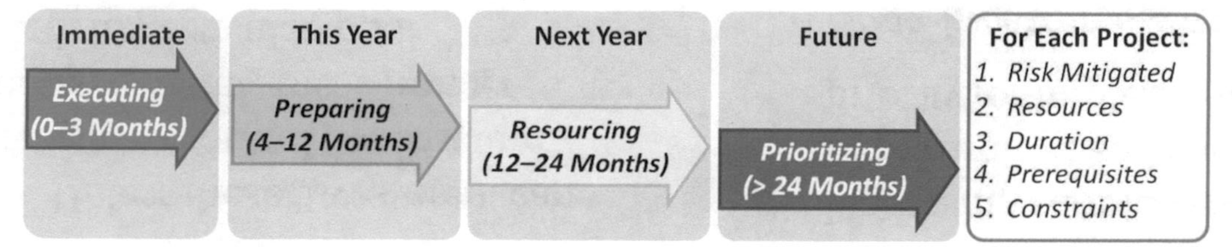

- It is seldom possible or practical for an enterprise to do all improvements at once.
- Improvements can be (1) prioritized based on value and cost, (2) sequenced based on dependencies, (3) resourced from limited available resources, and (4) influenced by internal and external constraints.
- Questions to consider when planning improvement projects:
  - *What is the risk to be mitigated by the project or its capabilities?*
  - *What is the project going to do to improve the enterprise's cybersecurity?*
  - *Are the required resources within both the budget and personnel expertise?*
  - *What is the duration of the project? A quarter? A year? Multiple years? Can the project be broken up into phases that are manageable and enable iterative success?*
  - *What are the prerequisites for the project? Dependency on other projects?*
  - *What are the constraints? Regulations? Audits?*

Prioritizing Improvement Projects *(2 of 3)*

- When combined, these four groups and their improvement projects constitute the enterprise's ***long-term*** cybersecurity improvement program and strategy.

- ***Immediate***: *Executing* projects executing now. Generally quick wins at low cost.
- ***This Year***: *Preparing* projects to be completed with the current fiscal year. Low cost, but may require investment. Moved to *executing* when ready to execute. Preparing includes technical prerequisites, vendor selections, or contract negotiations.
- ***Next Year***: *Resourcing* projects are not queued up within the current fiscal year. Focus is on refining plans. May need to execute sooner than originally planned.
- ***Future***: *Prioritizing* projects do not make sense to execute within current fiscal year and where resources are not available to plan them until the following fiscal year. Competing for priority alongside other business concerns and strategic investments.
- Using cybersecurity assessments and calculated assessment scores, leadership can show quantitatively how the enterprise cybersecurity posture is going to change to help prioritize the projects.

Prioritizing Improvement Projects *(3 of 3)*

- Over time, cybersecurity projects naturally migrate from one list to another.
  - Executing projects are completed.
  - Projects planned for this year move to execution.
  - As fiscal years transition, what was planned for next year transitions into executing for the current year.

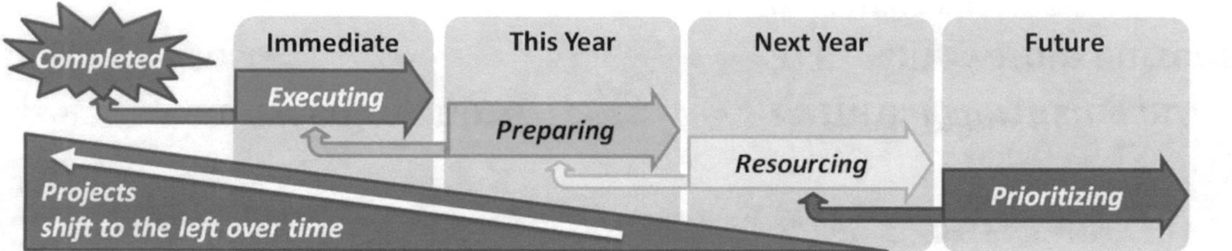

- The graphic above depicts this process of updating the enterprise's priorities.
- Generally, projects shift to the left, although sometimes shifting business priorities and limited available resources can cause projects to be deferred to later times as well.

Tracking Cybersecurity Project Results *(1 of 2)*

Visualizing Cybersecurity Program Assessment Scores

- Because a program assessment score is a quantitative measurement, it is well suited for managing cybersecurity status over time and visualizing that status graphically to inform leadership decision-making.
- The graphics can visualize the enterprise cybersecurity program via a Kiviat diagram or spider chart format.
- The shape of the filled-in areas reflects nicely the relationship among all the plotted assessment scores.
  - Initial Assessment = 55%
  - Updated Assessment = 65%
  - Target Security Level Achieved = 80%

Starting Security Level
Initial Assessment: 55%

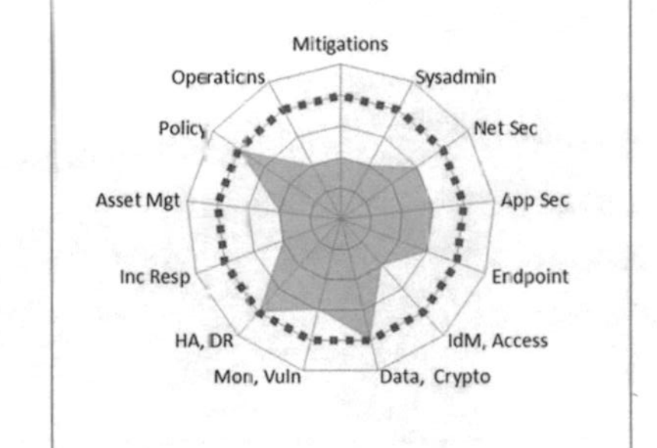

Deficient Areas Remediated
Updated Assessment: 65%

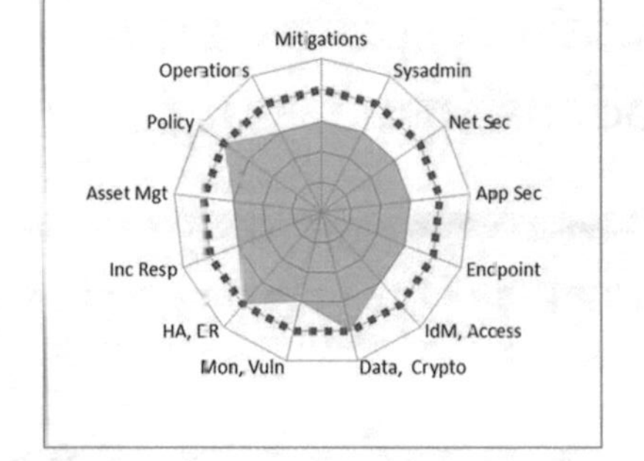

Target Security Level
Achieved: 80%

Assessed Security Level
Target Security Level

Tracking Cybersecurity Project Results *(2 of 2)*

Measuring Cybersecurity Program Assessment Scores Over Time

- Using assessment scores, the security posture for a cybersecurity scope can be reduced to a single number that can be tracked over multiple time periods to show quantitatively the impact of security investments.

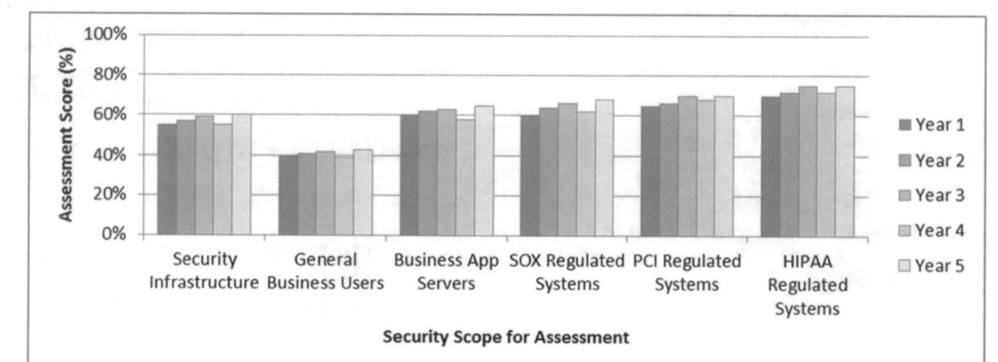

- The above figure depicts the assessment scores for six security scopes over a five-year period and shows trends of the enterprise's cybersecurity posture over time.
  - Security Infrastructure
  - General Business Users
  - Business Application Servers
  - SOX Regulated Systems
  - PCI Regulated Systems
  - HIPAA Regulated Systems
- Quantitative assessment methods, security scopes, and visualization techniques provide the enterprise with some of the tools it needs to delegate and manage its enterprise cybersecurity program.

CHAPTER 15

Looking to the Future

S. E. Donaldson et al., *Enterprise Cybersecurity Study Guide*, https://doi.org/10.1007/978-1-4842-3258-3_15

Overview

- This study guide describes a pragmatic framework for managing a cohesive enterprise cybersecurity program that
  - ties together ***architecture***, ***policy***, ***programmatics***, ***IT life cycle***, and ***assessments*** into a single framework.
  - aligns functional areas with real-world skills of cybersecurity professionals, and operational budgets, and cybersecurity technologies.
    - Functional areas enable easy delegation and reporting of status at an abstraction layer suitable for executive consumption.
    - Functional areas support the business decision-making process for strategy and prioritization.

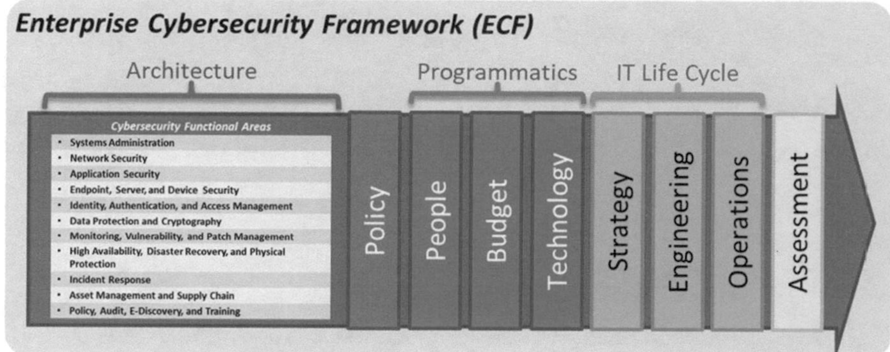

- While this framework may provide a successful cyberdefense today, attackers and defenders are not standing still.
- Cybersecurity challenges and technologies continue to evolve quickly.
- This chapter examines how this cybersecurity framework may evolve in the future.

Generations of Weapons Systems

Context *(1 of 3)*

- Jet fighters since WWII are often grouped into generations.
- Each generation represents a leap forward in capability and renders the previous generations obsolete.

Gen 1:
F-86 Sabre
(1949)

Gen 2:
F-8 Crusader
(1957)

Gen 3:
F-4 Phantom
(1960)

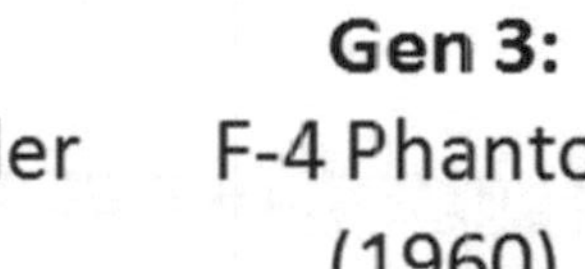

Gen 4:
F-15 Falcon
(1976)

Gen 5:
F-22 Raptor
(2005)

The F-15 has a claimed combat record of 101 victories and zero losses in actual air-to-air combat

Generations of Malware

Context (2 of 3)

- Malware can also be grouped into generations.
- Subsequent generations reflect increases in capability and threat.

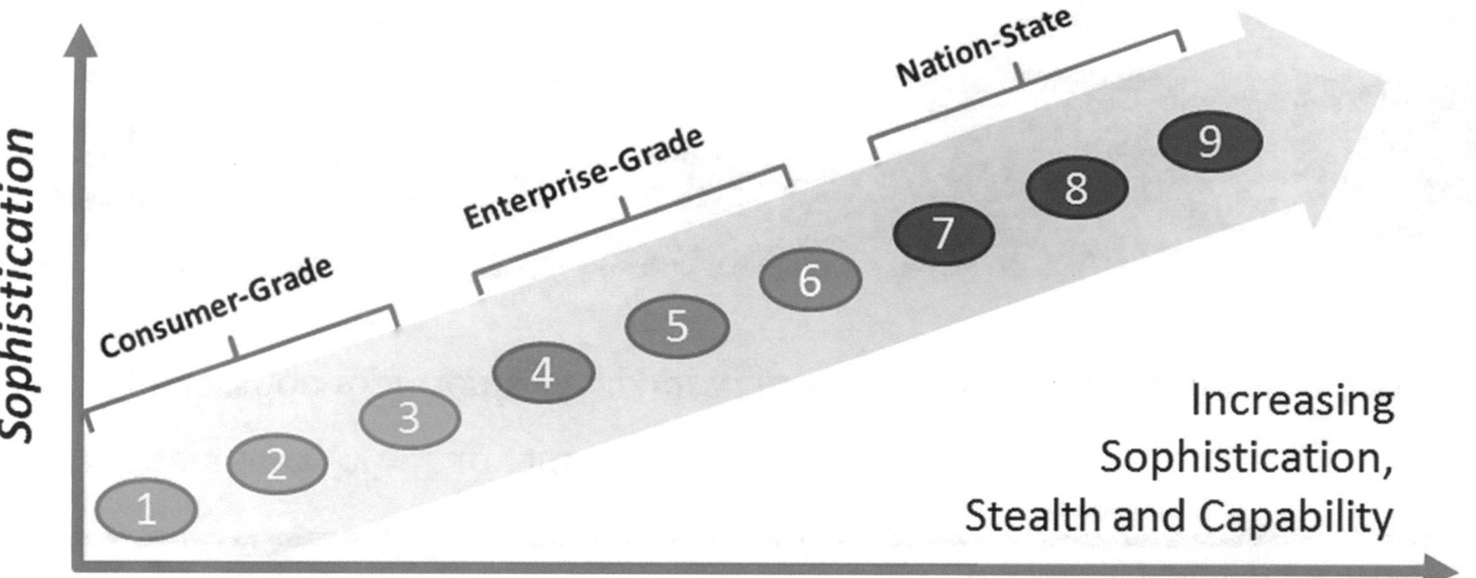

1. **Static Virus**
2. **Network-based Virus**
3. **Trojan Horse**
4. **Command and Control**
5. **Customized**
6. **Polymorphic**
7. **Intelligent**
8. **Autonomous and Polymorphic**
9. **Firmware and Supply Chain**

Generations of Cyberdefense

Context *(3 of 3)*

- Cyberattacks and defenses can be characterized as generations.

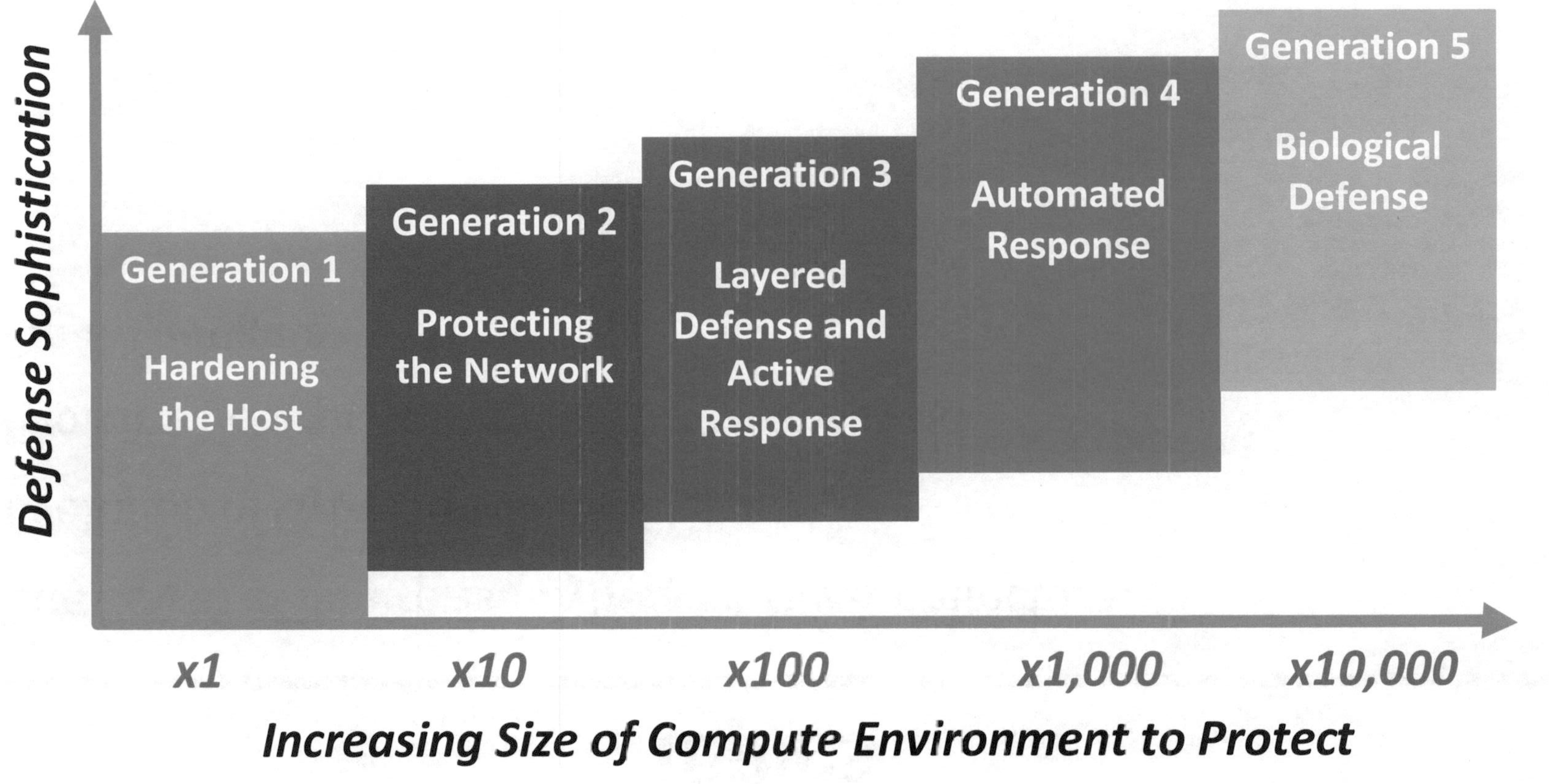

Topics

- The Power of Enterprise Cybersecurity Architecture
- Evolution of Cyberattack and Defense
- Evolving Enterprise Cybersecurity over Time
- Final Thoughts

The Power of Enterprise Cybersecurity Architecture *(1 of 2)*

- ***Policy***
  - Policy can be organized using enterprise cybersecurity functional areas.
  - Policy helps to ensure comprehensive coverage of enterprise cybersecurity with clear policy statements.
- ***People***
  - Functional areas align closely with actual skill sets of technical staff and team leaders.
  - Technical staff and cybersecurity leadership are positioned for success in their areas.
  - Functional areas also align well with typical organizational boundaries for matrixed teams where cybersecurity policy and enforcement might be separated from technical implementation and operations.

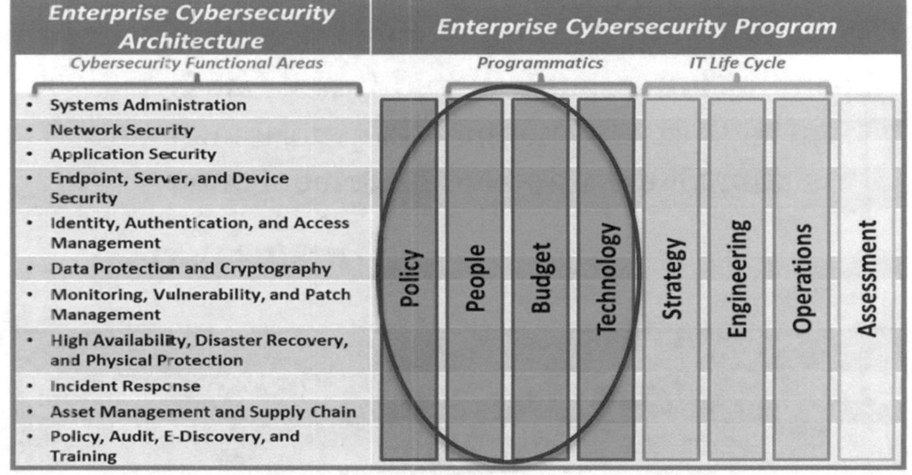

- ***Budget***
  - Functional areas align well with policy and organizational structures.
  - Cybersecurity leadership can allocate operational and project funding among functional areas to ensure people, budget, and technology are all coordinated.
- ***Technology***
  - Functional areas align well with the capabilities of many security technologies.

The Power of Enterprise Cybersecurity Architecture *(2 of 2)*

- ***Strategy***
  - Functional areas were designed with the IT Infrastructure Library (ITIL) framework in mind.
  - IT strategy and architecture can be planned using the functional areas to help ensure a well-integrated overall solution.
- ***Engineering***
  - Functional areas align well with typical engineering boundaries for system design, deployment, support, and retirement activities.
- ***Operations***
  - Cybersecurity operations can be performed in an integrated fashion across the functional areas to ensure all aspects of security operations are well coordinated.

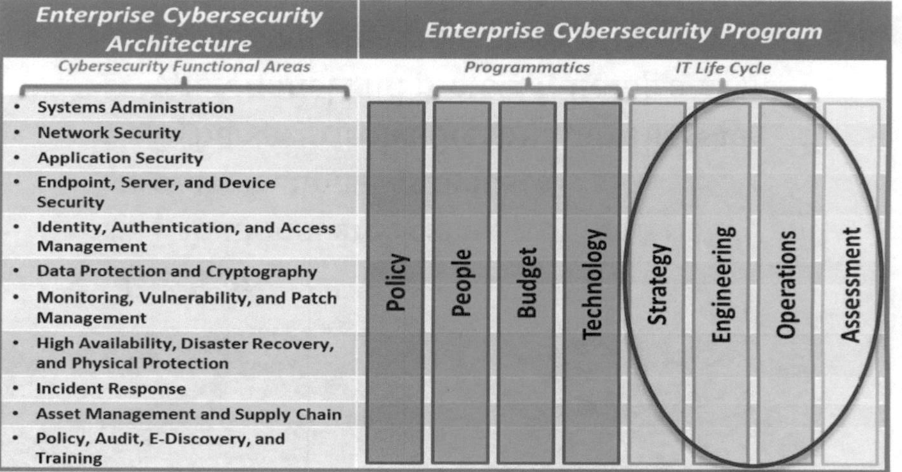

- ***Assessment***
  - Functional areas provide a straightforward framework for quantitatively assessing the cybersecurity program, measuring its quality over time, and reporting against external frameworks.

Evolution of Cyberattack and Defense *(1 of 9)*

Context

- Over time, attacker sophistication increases.
  - ***Casual Attackers***
    - Use professional attacker capabilities when they become mainstream
    - Use them for opportunistic ends
      - Disrupt operations
      - Explore private enterprises and their data
      - Make political statements
  - ***Professional Attackers***
    - Take nation-state attacker techniques and commercialize them for use on industrial scales
      - Espionage, Blackmail
      - Larceny, Identify Theft
  - ***Nation-State Attackers***
    - Have greatest amount of sophistication
    - Generally are the trailblazers of the most sophisticated and devastating cyberattacks
- Cyberattacks and cyberdefenses can be grouped into discrete generations of cybersecurity.

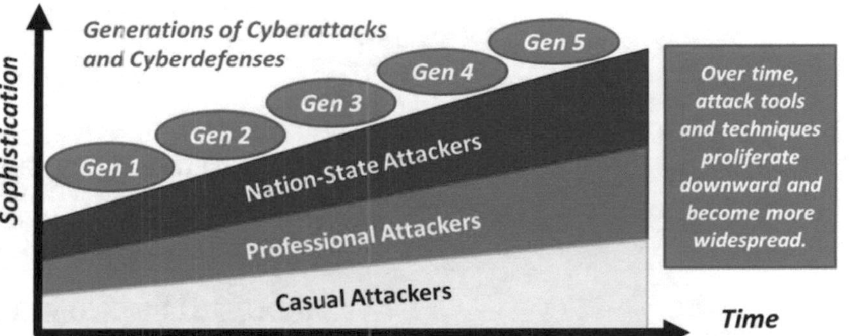

- Cyberattack generations represent a leap forward in capability that is ***almost completely effective*** against previous cyberdefense generations.
  - *Generation 1: Hardening the Host*
  - *Generation 2: Protecting the Network*
  - *Generation 3: Layered Defense and Active Response*
  - *Generation 4: Automated Response*
  - *Generation 5: Biological Defense*

Evolution of Cyberattack and Defense *(2 of 9)*

Before the Internet

- Before the Internet,
  - there was the Advanced Research Agency Network (ARPANET), but
  - the network was small and not designed with security in mind.
- As ARPANET got larger,
  - users started putting passwords on computers and networking protocols;
  - cybersecurity was not robust; and
  - "Good-fences-make-good neighbors" security was used as everyone was trusted.
- At the same time,
  - personal computers had little to no security; and
  - early viruses ran rampant propagating from machine to machine via "floppy disks" and other media.
- Since personal computerization was not interconnected and essentially being used as advanced typewriters and calculators, not much was at stake.

Evolution of Cyberattack and Defense *(3 of 9)*

Generation 1: Hardening the Host

Generation 1

Hardening the Host

Challenges

- Internet-connected systems and people operating those systems expanded and diversified outside military researchers and academic institutions
- Systems did not have significant security features
- Network service authentication primarily single-factor (usernames/passwords)

Attacks

- Originate from attacker computers
- Exploit insecure protocols
- Target unpatched host vulnerabilities

Defenses

- Security Technical Implementation Guides (STIGs)
- Host firewalls, intrusion prevention
- Regular vendor patches, air-gapping

Resulting Environment

- Increases in the numbers of Internet-connected systems
- Multi-user systems with large numbers of users

Evolution of Cyberattack and Defense *(4 of 9)*

Generation 2: Protecting the Network

Generation 2

Protecting the Network

Challenges

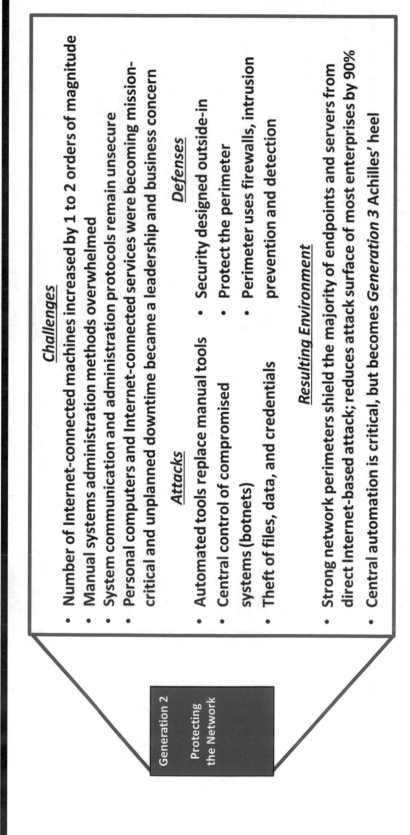

- Number of Internet-connected machines increased by 1 to 2 orders of magnitude
- Manual systems administration methods overwhelmed
- System communication and administration protocols remain unsecure
- Personal computers and Internet-connected services were becoming mission-critical and unplanned downtime became a leadership and business concern

Attacks

- Automated tools replace manual tools
- Central control of compromised systems (botnets)
- Theft of files, data, and credentials

Defenses

- Security designed outside-in
- Protect the perimeter
- Perimeter uses firewalls, intrusion prevention and detection

Resulting Environment

- Strong network perimeters shield the majority of endpoints and servers from direct Internet-based attack; reduces attack surface of most enterprises by 90%
- Central automation is critical, but becomes *Generation 3* Achilles' heel

Evolution of Cyberattack and Defense *(5 of 9)*

Generation 3: Layered Defense and Active Response

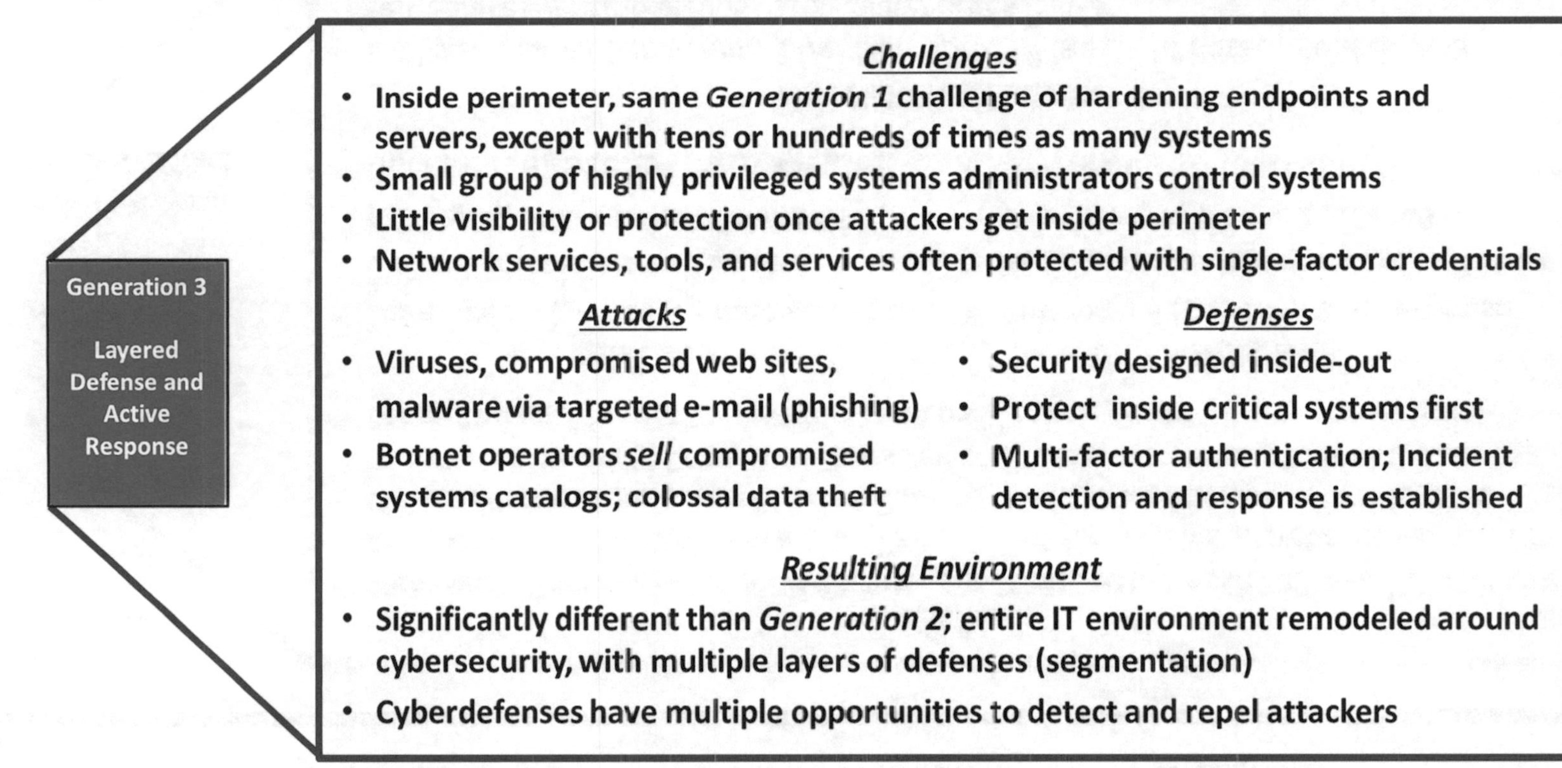

Generation 3
Layered Defense and Active Response
Challenges
Inside perimeter, same *Generation 1* challenge of hardening endpoints and servers, except with tens or hundreds of times as many systems
Small group of highly privileged systems administrators control systems
Little visibility or protection once attackers get inside perimeter
Network services, tools, and services often protected with single-factor credentials
Attacks
Viruses, compromised web sites, malware via targeted e-mail (phishing)
Botnet operators *sell* compromised systems catalogs; colossal data theft
Defenses
Security designed inside-out
Protect inside critical systems first
Multi-factor authentication; Incident detection and response is established
Resulting Environment
Significantly different than *Generation 2*; entire IT environment remodeled around cybersecurity, with multiple layers of defenses (segmentation)
Cyberdefenses have multiple opportunities to detect and repel attackers

Evolution of Cyberattack and Defense *(6 of 9)*

Generation 4: Automated Response

Generation 4

Automated Response

Challenges

- Numbers of network-connected systems continue to increase, with addition of the *Internet of things* with devices, appliances, and accessories all network-connected
- External business relationships continue to increase as cloud services are used
- Mobile computing / Bring Your Own Device (BYOD) complicate endpoint security
- Labor and cost for active detection and incident response (aggressive attacks)

Attacks

- Leverage social media / data analytics
- Customized malware escalates privileges; overwhelms defenders
- Defenders must prioritize responses

Defenses

- Automated detection and response
- Rapid containment and reconstitution of affected systems; 24x7x365
- Strict configuration control

Resulting Environment

- Looks similar to *Generation 3* but *Generation 4* is able to detect, contain and remediate cyberintrusions many, many times faster
- Automatically repelling attacks in real time is game-changing

Evolution of Cyberattack and Defense *(7 of 9)*

Generation 5: Biological Defense

Generation 5

Biological Defense

Challenges

- Complexity of enterprise IT architectures continues to be a problem
- Proliferation of vulnerable devices provides attackers footholds / stepping points
- Visibility and detection is ongoing challenge
- Automated detection and response *only* detects what it sees and *only* responds in predetermined ways

Attacks

- Install malware via zero-day and supply chain
- Evade detection due to autonomous and stealthy malware
- Act like insider attacks once inside

Defenses

- Distributed rather than centralized
- Use analytics to recognize behavioral anomalies; organized around data, not the host or perimeter

Resulting Environment

- Has a biological capability to detect and respond to sophisticated and stealthy cyberattacks
- As attacks adapt to evade defenses, the defenses adapt to keep up with attacks

Evolution of Cyberattack and Defense *(8 of 9)*

Cybergenerations Moving Down Market

- Cyberattack generations move ***down market*** over time.
- Cyberattack techniques become cheaper and more widely used over time.
- Generation 5 cyberattacks are solely in the domain of *advanced* nation-state attackers. However, it is realistic to expect that
  - five years from now, these techniques will be used by *other* nation-state attackers; and
  - ten years from now, these techniques might be used by *everyday professional cybercriminals*.

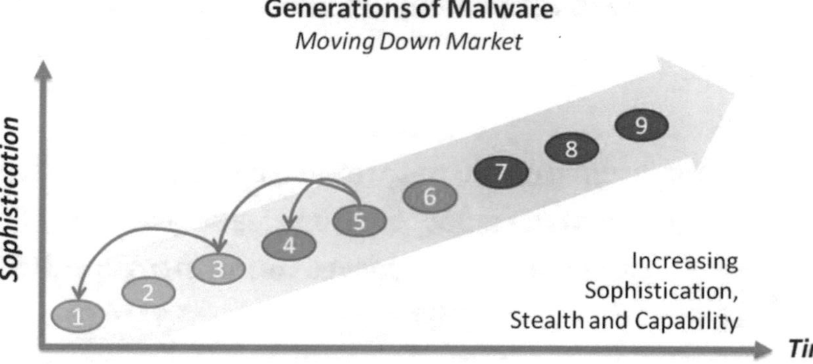

- Generation 3 cyberattacks that are causing trouble for commercial industries today were being commonly used by nation-state attackers only five years ago.
  - Five years from now, these cyberattack tools and techniques will likely be in the hands of *casual hackers*.
- Enterprises must be aware of these trends and try to stay ahead of them.

Evolution of Cyberattack and Defense *(9 of 9)*

Future Cybersecurity Evolution

- New generations of attacks will be extremely effective against older generations of defenses.
- Defenses ***cannot simply skip*** *a generation* and jump straight to advanced defensive techniques.
- Each successive generation of defenses ***builds upon*** the previous generation of defensive technologies.
- Most of today's compliance frameworks to assess cybersecurity effectiveness were designed around the Generation 2 model of perimeter defenses and endpoint protection.
- Such compliance models only go so far in thwarting professional attackers using Generations 3, 4, and 5 capabilities.
- Upgrading these frameworks is ***essential*** to confronting Generations 3, 4, and 5 attack techniques.

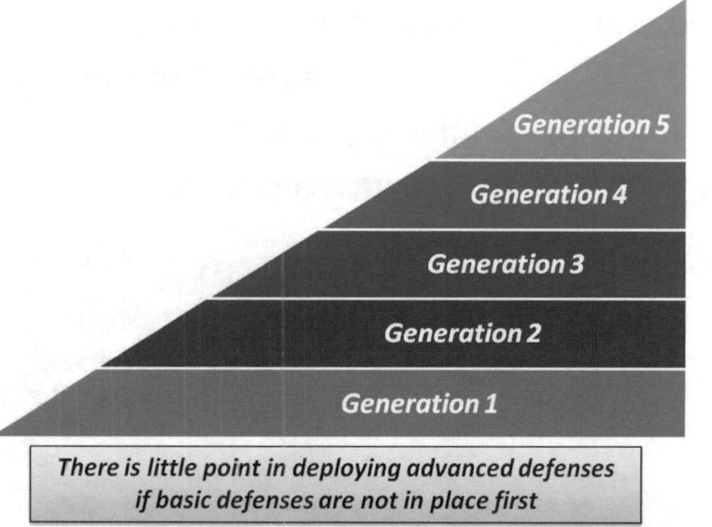

- Defenses build upon on another.
  - Generation 5: Host, Network, Detection, Response, Analytics
  - Generation 4: Host, Network, Detection, Response
  - Generation 3: Host, Network, Detection
  - Generation 2: Host, Network
  - Generation 1: Host

Evolving Enterprise Cybersecurity over Time *(1 of 6)*

Context

- Cybersecurity is constantly and rapidly evolving.
- An enterprise's cybersecurity architecture needs to keep pace with this evolution.
- This study guide's enterprise cybersecurity architecture is designed as a framework for managing a cybersecurity program over time.
- To date, the framework has proven itself to be effective while also accommodating changing situations and needs.

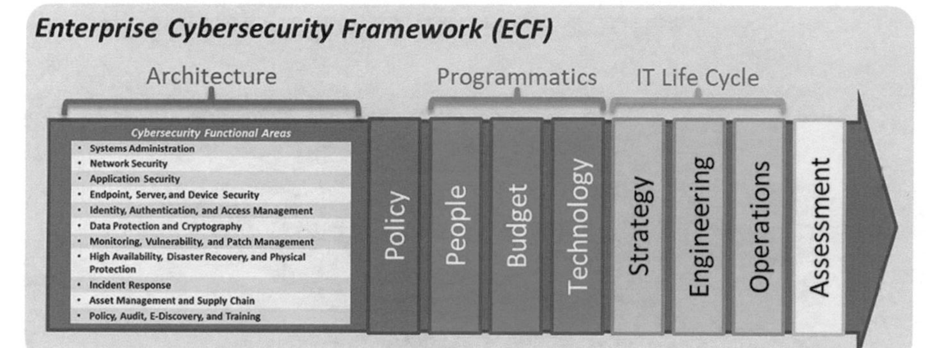

- In the future, the framework will continue to evolve and mature regarding the following factors:
  - Enterprise Cybersecurity Implementation Considerations
  - Tailoring Cybersecurity Assessments
  - Evolution of Enterprise Cybersecurity Capabilities
  - Evolution of Enterprise Cybersecurity Functional Areas

Evolving Enterprise Cybersecurity over Time *(2 of 6)*

Enterprise Cybersecurity Implementation Considerations

- Cybersecurity practitioners can use this study guide's framework to organize and measure
  - real-world cyberthreats,
  - cyberdefense capabilities, and
  - day-to-day cybersecurity operations.
- The framework is designed to
  - accommodate a wide spectrum of enterprise cybersecurity configurations;
  - manage and communicate challenges; and
  - summarize the richness and nuance of the underlying reality.
- The major goal is to
  - help enterprise leaders and practitioners represent real-world complexity effectively so that they can make informed strategic and tactical decisions.
- Implementation considerations include
  - functional areas that apply to a wide range of enterprise types, buy that may need to be modified to meet an enterprise's needs.

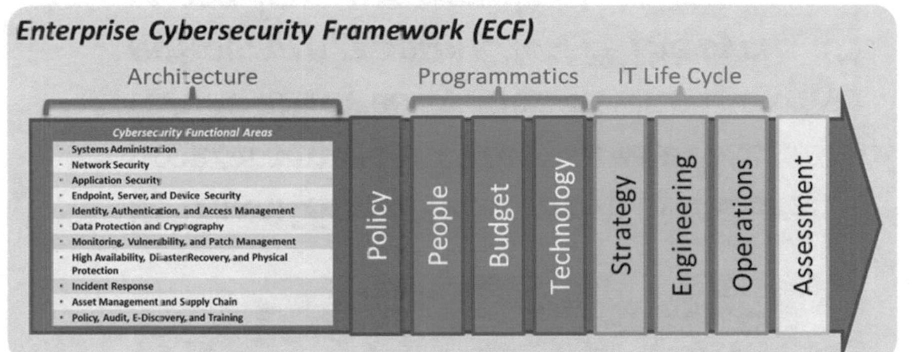

- Functional areas are ***approximately equal in importance*** so the enterprise does not rely too much on a single set of cybersecurity capabilities for enterprise protection.
- Enterprise cybersecurity capabilities are not and will never be perfectly complete; each enterprise should add, remove, or tailor capabilities as needed.
- Functional areas help align cybersecurity capabilities to policies, programmatics, IT life cycle, and assessments; however, the alignment should reflect how the enterprise prefers to operate.
- The framework is not perfect; however, it is comprehensive, integrated, and adaptable.

Evolving Enterprise Cybersecurity over Time *(3 of 6)*

Tailoring Cybersecurity Assessments *(1 of 2)*

- The enterprise cybersecurity framework works well for conducting a cybersecurity program assessment.
- By considering ***risk mitigations***, ***cybersecurity capabilities*** (grouped by functional areas), and ***security operations*** side-by-side, assessment results align closely with an enterprise's real-world cybersecurity effectiveness.
- By using a ***hierarchy*** of risk mitigations, functional areas, capabilities, and underlying technologies, assessments can be performed at numerous levels to provide high-level results quickly and detailed results progressively.

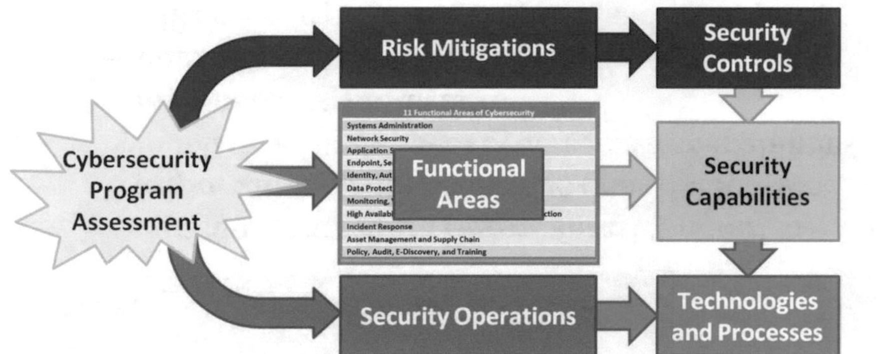

- By organizing an enterprise cybersecurity program into functional areas, assessment results are already aligned with the way ***policy***, ***programmatics***, ***IT life cycle***, and ***operations*** are organized.
- This alignment enables immediate delegation and assignment of resulting recommendations to appropriate teams for execution.

Evolving Enterprise Cybersecurity over Time *(4 of 6)*

Tailoring Cybersecurity Assessments (2 of 2)

- The cybersecurity capabilities presented are meant as a starting point for consideration.
  - New technologies may deliver new capabilities for cybersecurity.
  - Such information should be incorporated into an enterprise's cybersecurity framework for assessment and evaluation.
- Object Measurement can be used to quantitatively measure cybersecurity program effectiveness.

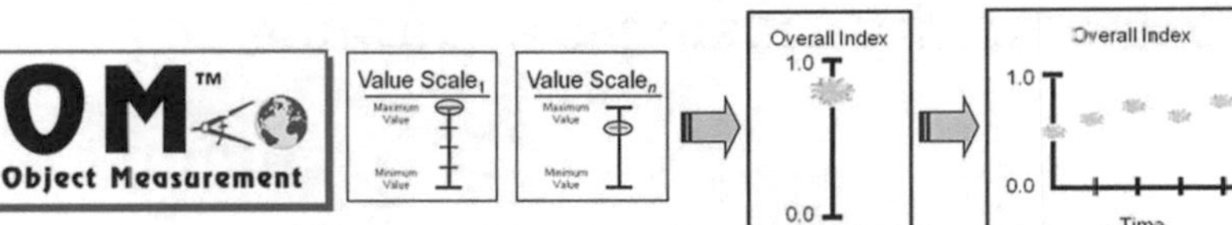

- This measurement approach provides a direct correlation between an enterprise's risk analysis and its level of protection.
- Value scales and resulting metrics help point to potential weaknesses that cyberattackers could use as attack vectors.

Functional Area	Capabilities	
Systems Administration (SA)	• Bastion hosts • Out-of-Band (OOB) management • Network isolation • Integrated Lights-Out (ILO), Keyboard Video Mouse (KVM), and power controls • Virtualization and Storage Area Network (SAN) management	• Separation of administration from services • Multi-factor authentication for Systems Administrators (SAs) • Administrator audit trail(s) • Command logging and analytics
Network Security (NS)	• Switches and routers • Software Defined Networking (SDN) • Domain Name System (DNS) and Dynamic Host Configuration Protocol (DHCP) • Network Time Protocol (NTP) • Network service management • Firewall and virtual machine firewall • Network Intrusion Detection / Network Intrusion Prevention System (IDS / IPS)	• Wireless networking (Wi-Fi) • Packet intercept and capture • Secure Sockets Layer (SSL) intercept • Network Access Control (NAC) • Virtual Private Networking (VPN) and Internet Protocol Security (IPSec) • Network Traffic Analysis (NTA) • Network Data Analytics (NDA)
Application Security (AS)	• E-mail security • Webshell detection • Application firewalls • Database firewalls • Forward proxy and web filters	• Reverse proxy • Data Leakage Protection (DLP) • Secure application and database software development • Software code vulnerability analysis
Endpoint, Server, and Device Security (ESDS)	• Local administrator privilege restrictions • Computer security and logging policies • Endpoint and media encryption • Computer access controls • Forensic imaging support for investigations • Virtual desktop / thin clients • Mobile Device Management (MDM) • Anti-virus / anti-malware	• Application whitelisting • In-memory malware detection • Host firewall and intrusion detection • "Gold code" software images • Security Technical Implementation Guides (STIGs) • Always-on Virtual Private Networking (VPN) • File integrity and change monitoring
Identity, Authentication, and Access Management (IAAM)	• Identity life cycle management • Enterprise directory • Multi-factor authentication • Privilege management and access control • Identity and access audit trail and reporting	• Lightweight Directory Access Protocol (LDAP) • Kerberos, RADIUS, 802.1x • Federated authentication • Security Assertion Markup Language (SAML)
Data Protection and Cryptography (DPC)	• Secure Sockets Layer (SSL) and Transport Layer Security (TLS) • Digital certificates (Public Key Infrastructure [PKI]) • Key hardware protection (Smart cards, Trusted Platform Modules [TPMs], and Hardware Security Modules [HSMs])	• One-Time Password (OTP) and Out-of-Band (OOB) authentication • Key life cycle management • Digital signatures • Complex passwords • Data encryption and tokenization • Brute force attack detection • Digital Rights Management (DRM)
Monitoring, Vulnerability, and Patch Management (MVPM)	• Operational performance monitoring • System and network monitoring • System configuration change detection • Privilege and access change detection • Log aggregation • Data analytics • Security Information and Event Management (SIEM)	• Network and computer vulnerability scanning • Penetration testing • Patch management and deployment • Rogue network device detection • Rogue wireless access point detection • Honeypots / honeynets / honeytokens • Security Operations Center (SOC)
High Availability, Disaster Recovery, and Physical Protection (HADRPP)	• Clustering • Load balancing, Global Server Load Balancing (GSLB) • Network failover, subnet spanning • Virtual machine snapshots and cloning • Data mirroring and replication	• Backups and backup management • Off-site storage • Facilities protection • Physical access controls • Physical security monitoring
Incident Response (IF)	• Threat information • Incident tracking • Forensic tools • Computer imaging	• Indicators of Compromise (IOCs) • Black hole server • Regulatory / legal coordination
Asset Management and Supply Chain (AMSC)	• Asset management databases • Configuration Management Databases (CMDB) • Change management databases	• Software inventory and license management • Supplier certification processes • Secure disposal, recycling, and data destruction
Policy, Audit, E-Discovery, and Training (PAET)	• Governance, Risk, and Compliance (GRC), with reporting • Compliance and control frameworks (SOX, PCI, others) • Audit frameworks • Customer Certification and Accreditation (C&A)	• Policy and policy exception management • Risk and threat management • Privacy compliance • E-Discovery tools • Personnel security and background checks • Security awareness and training

Evolving Enterprise Cybersecurity over Time *(5 of 6)*

Evolution of Enterprise Cybersecurity Capabilities

- It is difficult to envision today what cybersecurity capabilities might look like ten years in the future.
- The enterprise cybersecurity framework will continue evolving along with the strategic challenges of managing complexity in an increasingly interconnected world.
- Enterprise cybersecurity changes may include the following:
  - Valid security capabilities should be considered and added to the framework as necessary.
  - New security technologies may or may not fit easily into the existing functional areas.
  - A single technology may provide multiple capabilities falling into different functional areas; enterprises will need to decide where to house the technology.
  - Over time, security capabilities may merge into a single, integrated capability or split into multiple sub-capabilities.
  - Existing capabilities may be superseded by other capabilities, fall out of favor, or simply become obsolete.

Evolving Enterprise Cybersecurity over Time *(6 of 6)*

Evolution of Enterprise Functional Areas

- ***All*** of an enterprise's cybersecurity should be divided up into functional areas, and capabilities within those functional areas, so everything is accounted for and nothing is missed.
- Over time, the functional areas will continue to evolve.
  - As capabilities are added to the architecture, functional area definitions may need adjustments to continue providing clear lines of delineation for organizing policies, people, programmatics, IT life cycle, and assessments.
  - As cybersecurity technologies and practices evolve, there may be a marked shift in the importance of different functional areas.

Enterprise Cybersecurity Architecture *(Cybersecurity Functional Areas)*
• Systems Administration
• Network Security
• Application Security
• Endpoint, Server, and Device Security
• Identity, Authentication, and Access Management
• Data Protection and Cryptography
• Monitoring, Vulnerability, and Patch Management
• High Availability, Disaster Recovery, and Physical Protection
• Incident Response
• Asset Management and Supply Chain
• Policy, Audit, E-Discovery, and Training

  - The framework was designed to address the needs of Generations 3, 4, and 5 cyberdefenses, but cloud and BYOD are straining enterprise cybersecurity methodologies, technologies, and practices.
  - Innovations and paradigm shifts might prompt future adjustments.
  - Over time, the framework will need to evolve to remain relevant and effective.

Final Thoughts *(1 of 2)*

- This study guide presents a number of key ideas and methodologies for dealing with modern enterprise cybersecurity challenges.
  - Management techniques for facing those challenges
  - Coherent, integrated cybersecurity framework suitable for an enterprise ranging from a few dozen employees to hundreds of thousands of employees
  - Techniques for applying this cybersecurity program framework against modern adversaries
- Ideas and methodologies are not theoretical, but represent real-world experience and work across a wide range of enterprise situations.
  - Clients ranging from the US Federal Government to the US Department of Defense to commercial customers (small nonprofits to large multinationals)
- Organizing cybersecurity into functional areas makes it possible to manage most aspects of a cybersecurity program under one convenient and coherent framework.
  - Policy, people, budget, technology, architecture, engineering, operations, and assessments
- Cyberattack and cyberdefense generations provide a context for considering cyberthreats at a strategic level.
  - Technology evolves on a continuous basis, but it is helpful to use generation groupings to characterize different levels of cyberattack sophistication and the corresponding cyberdefenses.

Final Thoughts *(2 of 2)*

- The cybersecurity industry is in throes of a generational shift going from Generation 2 to Generation 3.
  - Within the next decade, a similar shift will occur to get to Generation 4 defenses, and then to Generation 5 defenses.
  - By the time Generation 5 defenses are commonplace, there will be 6th and 7th Generation attacks to defend against.
- As computers have risen in power and capability, and their capability has been multiplied through networking, the threats against these systems have risen as quickly as the capability.
- Computers and networked systems are becoming *mission critical*.
  - Airline and financial industries stop when their computers go down.
  - Over the next 20 years, this mission-critical reliance will occur in almost every area of business and government.
  - Over the next 30 years, computers will have to achieve a level of resilience where they do not go down, even in the face of severe crises from adversaries, criminals, or natural disasters.
- Looking back at the past 30 years of information technology, it is mind-boggling how information technology has transformed our lives.
  - Today's children cannot conceive of televisions that aren't large and flat, of typewriters that only put words on paper, or of mobile devices that don't have instant access to most knowledge on Earth.
- Let's work together to keep these machines and ourselves safe for the next 30 years.

Part VI: Appendices

- Appendix A: Sample Cybersecurity Policy
- Appendix B: Cybersecurity Operational Processes
- Appendix C: Object Measurement
- Appendix D: Cybersecurity Sample Assessment
- Appendix E: Cybersecurity Capability Value Scales

APPENDIX A

Sample Cybersecurity Policy

S. E. Donaldson et al., *Enterprise Cybersecurity Study Guide*, https://doi.org/10.1007/978-1-4842-3258-3_16

Context *(1 of 2)*

- Security policies identify the assets to be protected and the protection afforded those assets.
  - What is protected
  - Who is responsible for the protection
  - How well the protection is to be performed
  - What the consequences are for protection failure
- Policies should be unambiguous, well organized, well maintained, and balanced between security and business needs.
- The graphic depicts the security documentation pyramid.
  - ***Policy*** is a high-level statement of principle or course of action governing enterprise information security.

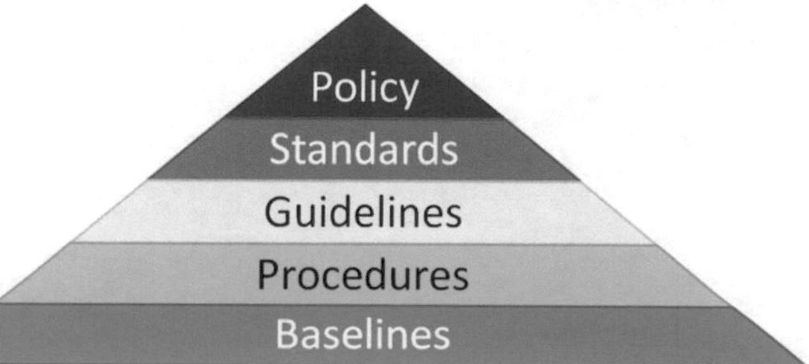

- ***Standards*** are documents specifying standards for behavior, processes, configurations, or technologies to be used for enterprise cybersecurity.
- ***Guidelines*** are documents providing non-authoritative guidance on policy and standards for use by subordinate organizations.
- ***Procedures*** are a set of documents describing step-by-step or detailed instructions for implementing or maintaining security controls.
- ***Baselines*** are specific configurations for technologies and systems designed to provide easy compliance with the established policy, standards, guidelines, and procedures.

Context *(2 of 2)*

- This appendix provides an example cybersecurity policy.
  - Can be used as starting point for organizing an enterprise's policies using enterprise cybersecurity functional areas
  - Can be well coordinated with enterprise's personnel, budgets, technologies, IT life cycle, and cybersecurity assessments
- Do not consider this example policy as the only way to do things or the best way to do things.
  - Standards and requirements change over time.
  - What makes sense today will change as technologies, standards, and best practices continue to evolve.
- Each enterprise is different and will need to develop and evolve a cybersecurity program that makes sense for the enterprise.

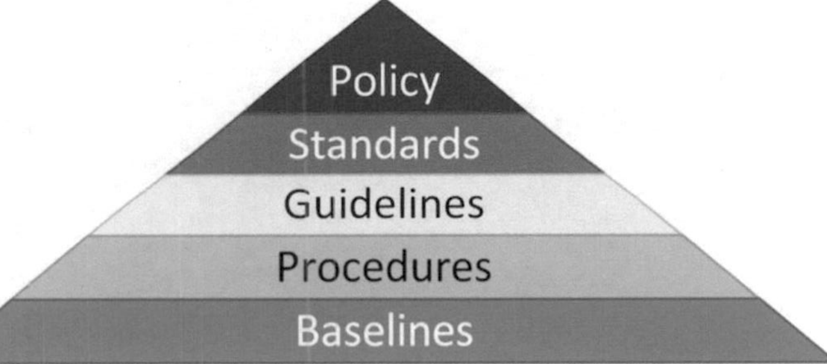

Enterprise Cybersecurity Architecture
(Cybersecurity Functional Areas)

- **Systems Administration**
- **Network Security**
- **Application Security**
- **Endpoint, Server, and Device Security**
- **Identity, Authentication, and Access Management**
- **Data Protection and Cryptography**
- **Monitoring, Vulnerability, and Patch Management**
- **High Availability, Disaster Recovery, and Physical Protection**
- **Incident Response**
- **Asset Management and Supply Chain**
- **Policy, Audit, E-Discovery, and Training**

Topics

- The Policy
  - Purpose
  - Scope and Applicability
  - Policy Statement
  - Compliance
  - Responsibilities
    - Chief Information Officer (CIO)
    - Chief Information Security Officer (CISO)
    - Managers
    - Employees
    - Contracted third parties, suppliers, temporary employees, and consultants
- Policy Guidance by Functional Area

The Policy *(1 of 3)*

- ***Purpose***
  - Delineates security requirements, roles, and responsibilities necessary to protect enterprise data and information from:
    - Unauthorized access
    - Inappropriate disclosures
    - Compromise
  - Reviewed and approved by enterprise senior management
  - Disseminated to employees and relevant external partners
  - The following parties provided input and reviewed content to ensure governing laws, regulations, and enterprise policies are appropriately incorporated
    - Chief Information Officer (CIO)
    - Chief Information Security Officer (CISO)
    - Chief Human Resources Officer (CHRO)
  - Defined in the context of the ownership of the enterprise (public vs. private) and legal regulatory requirements while taking into account industry security best practices
- ***Scope and Applicability***
  - Applicable to all employees, temporary employees, contractors, and enterprise subsidiaries
  - Must be used to assess third-party suppliers who sign a contract to provide business services to the enterprise
  - Must be used to assess the risk of conducting business
  - Reviewed and adjusted as needed on a periodic basis
- ***Policy Statement***
  - Compiles with all legal, regulatory, and contractual obligations regarding protection of enterprise data
  - Provides the authority to design, implement, and maintain security controls meeting enterprise standards
  - Ensures enterprise employees comply with the policy and undergo periodic training

The Policy *(2 of 3)*

- ***Policy Statement (continued)***
  - Informs employees that the enterprise monitors employee usage of information systems
  - Requires enterprise data be stored and manipulated on enterprise-provided information systems or contracted systems that comply with this policy
  - Implements a security incident reporting mechanism
- ***Compliance***
  - Lapses or failures may result in disciplinary action, such as removal or limiting access to systems, termination of employment, an so on.
  - Lack of compliance could have legal or regulatory ramifications with regard to federal, state, local, or international law.
  - Compliance is enforced through executing periodic assessments by enterprise security, internal / external audits, or self-assessments.
- ***Responsibilities***
  - *Chief Information Officer (CIO)*
    - Provides governance for enterprise IT systems and information with respect to security compliance with this policy
    - Publishes a common operating environment (COE) that defines infrastructure standards incorporating security policies
    - Reviews and approves any low-risk COE deviations or exceptions
    - Provides guidelines for on-and-off-network information systems with respect to maintaining an information security plan
  - *Chief Information Security Officer (CISO)*
    - Acts as primary custodian of the information security risk assessment process
    - Reports identified risk to the enterprise risk committee and other key stakeholders
    - Keeps the enterprise security policy and procedures current for both digital and physical assets

The Policy *(3 of 3)*

- ***Responsibilities (continued)***
  - *Chief Information Security Officer (CISO)*
    - Ensures identified system vulnerabilities are mitigated in a timely manner
    - Publishes up-to-date security standards
    - Acts as the incident lead during an active incident
    - Is responsible for submitting an incident root-cause report to management
    - Enforces compliance with enterprise security policies by conducting periodic security checks and audits
    - Oversees internal and external reporting requirements (SOX, SEC, incidents, HIPAA)
    - Interfaces with the legal department to support e-discovery
    - Implements security awareness and training campaigns
    - Supports due diligence process for vetting security quality of suppliers, products, and subsidiaries during mergers and acquisitions
  - *Managers*
    - Ensure compliance with enterprise's security policies by incorporating security into the IT lifecycle process.
    - Ensure employee security training is completed
    - Follow established incident reporting and escalation procedures
    - Periodically update standard operating procedures (SOPs) to ensure compliance with enterprise policy and procedures
  - *Employees*
    - Comply with enterprise security policy and procedures
    - Complete required security training
    - Follow established incident reporting and escalation procedures
    - Take reasonable care to protect their enterprise-provided equipment and access credentials
  - *Contracted third parties, suppliers, temporary employees, and consultants*
    - Must demonstrate they can meet and perform per enterprise policy and procedures
    - Provide the enterprise with required third-party audit reports as part of due care

Policy Guidance by Functional Area *(1 of 23)*

Systems Administration

- Provides management and administration of enterprise IT and cybersecurity systems.
  - If malicious actors compromise systems administration, they have access to enterprise data and information systems.
- Activities must include the following:
  - All systems administration activities at the application, data, and operating system levels shall require authentication, and all logons to these systems shall be logged for audit.
  - Systems administration protocols that are insecure or vulnerable to attack, including critical infrastructure of storage, computing, and data center management, shall only be used on isolated networks.
  - Systems Administrator
    - Accounts shall require multi-factor authentication before administrative access is granted.
    - Activities shall be monitored for signs of inappropriate activity.
    - Logons shall be recorded and audited periodically (for example, weekly).
    - Access control lists shall be verified periodically (for example, quarterly) to ensure least privilege and separation of duties.
    - Changes to access control lists shall be recorded and audited periodically (for example, weekly).
  - Security configurations shall be reviewed on a periodic basis (for example, annually), including re-validation of all policy exceptions.
  - Systems administration's preventive, detective, audit, and forensic controls shall be verified and tested for proper operation periodically (for example, at least annually).

Policy Guidance by Functional Area *(2 of 23)*

Network Security *(1 of 2)*

- Network security protects enterprise data and information from internal and external malicious actors.
- Activities must include the following:
  - Network and network security infrastructure, including routers, switches, and firewalls, shall be centrally managed; logons shall be logged for audit.
  - Network infrastructure administration activities shall be isolated from general business network traffic.
  - All administrative logons shall require credentials and multi-factor authentication.
  - Networks
    - Publicly accessed or not physically protected, networks, such as wireless networks, shall use access control to ensure only authorized users are permitted access.
    - Networks shall have measures in place to detect and block network traffic known to be malicious via protocols, payloads, sources, or destinations.
  - Access to
    - enterprise networks from the Internet shall require multi-factor authentication; and
    - privileged internal networks directly from the Internet shall not be permitted.
  - Network traffic
    - known to be malicious, either through automated or manual means, shall be blocked within a defined period, such as one business day of detection;
    - thought to be questionable and may be indicative of attacks shall be recorded and retained for a defined period of time (for example, 90 days) to permit analysis and investigation; and
    - known to be secure shall not be excluded from analysis to identify and block malicious activity.

Policy Guidance by Functional Area *(3 of 23)*

Network Security *(2 of 2)*

- Network
  - Infrastructure shall provide for basic services, such as host configuration, that shall be hardened to protect them from attack or compromise.
  - Configuration changes shall require approval and shall be logged for audit and investigation, as required.
  - Security configurations shall be reviewed on a periodic basis (for example, annually).
- All network policy configurations and exceptions shall be re-validated periodically (for example, annually).
- Network security's preventive, detective, audit, and forensic controls shall be verified and tested for proper operation periodically (for example, annually).

Policy Guidance by Functional Area *(4 of 23)*

Application Security

- Application security protects enterprise application systems from external and internal attacks and vulnerabilities.
- Activities must include the following:
  - Internet-facing application servers shall be protected from unauthorized configuration changes.
  - Configuration changes shall be logged and audited to catch the introduction of unauthorized "backdoors" into application systems.
  - Critical enterprise applications such as e-mail, voicemail, and web services must be configured to prevent and detect attacks and exploits of vulnerabilities.
  - For attacks and exploits that are not prevented or detected, adequate forensic logs much be maintained to permit audit and investigation after the fact.
  - Communication between application components shall require authentication and shall be performed using secure protocols when performed over networks.
  - Applications sensitive to
    - ***confidentiality*** concerns—processing data sensitive to breach—shall employ protection and detection to protect against data leakage;
    - ***integrity*** concerns—potential data changes with financial or other repercussions—shall employ data integrity protections such as digital signature and data modification audit trails; and
    - ***availability*** concerns shall employ high availability and rapid disaster recovery to protect them from internal or external denial of service attacks.
  - Applications
    - using custom source code shall be analyzed using static code analysis periodically (for example, at least quarterly), and all medium and higher vulnerabilities shall be addressed and remediated;
    - that are generally available on the Internet or internal networks shall be scanned for vulnerabilities periodically (for example, at least monthly), and all medium and higher vulnerabilities shall be addressed and remediated (for example, 90 days); and
    - found to be in violation of policy may be temporarily or permanently disconnected from Internet or enterprise network until remediated.

Policy Guidance by Functional Area *(5 of 23)*

Endpoint, Server, and Device Security *(1 of 2)*

- This functional area hardens and secures endpoints such as desktops, laptops, mobile devices, and servers using standard vendor-recommended security guides and builds.
- Activities must include the following:
  - Local administrator account passwords or keys shall be unique to each endpoint.
  - Enterprise endpoints shall be configured from master images that are configuration-controlled and protected from tampering, changes, or the introduction of authorized or malicious code.
  - Network-connected endpoint systems shall be configured to forward security logs—including administrator logon and security component configurations—to a central infrastructure for logging and correlation.
  - All portable and removeable endpoints shall have their built-in and removable media encrypted.
  - Personal computes and mobile devices, when used for enterprise work, must include the ability to remotely delete enterprise data from the system in the event of compromise.
  - Security infrastructure endpoints shall include the ability to detect and alert on changes to security configuration files within a set time (for example, 1 hour).

Policy Guidance by Functional Area *(6 of 23)*

Endpoint, Server, and Device Security *(2 of 2)*

- Endpoint systems
  - shall be configured for investigation of cyberincidents by installing forensic tools and configuration security logs to meet incident investigators' requirements;
  - shall be configured according to vendor-approved security guidelines for secure operating system installation and operation;
  - shall include endpoint protection to block and detect malicious software and network connectivity as appropriate for system security; and
  - that are involved in operating or managing cybersecurity functions for the enterprise shall have application whitelisting installed and configured for maximum restrictiveness.
- Servers directly connected to the Internet shall be scanned for operating system vulnerabilities using a credentialed vulnerability scanner periodically (for example, monthly) and remediated according to policy (for example, 30 days).
- Endpoints found to be in violation of policy may be temporarily or permanently disconnected from the enterprise network until the violation is remediated.
- Endpoint server and device security configurations shall be reviewed on periodic basis (for example, annually).
- ...

Policy Guidance by Functional Area *(7 of 23)*

Identity, Authentication, and Access Management *(1 of 3)*

- Access to enterprise systems shall require unique network identities and authentication to systems shall use approved means.
  - Such access shall provide for unique identification of the users and non-repudiation of their activities.
  - Accesses to data and systems shall be configured on an as-required basis according to need-to-know.
  - Accesses and online identities that are no longer required shall be removed on a timely basis.
- Activities must include the following:
  - All production enterprise systems shall use centralized identity provisioning and de-provisioning, and centralized access management where possible.
  - Cloud-based systems and Software-as-a-Service (SaaS) solutions used by the enterprise are subject to this policy as well as on-premise systems.
  - Identity systems
    - shall be protected at the same or greater level as the sensitivity of the enterprise application that they serve;
    - shall alert on suspected attacker activities, including using privileged accounts on non-privileged systems and patterns of excessive logons or logon attempts that may be malicious;
    - shall provide protective, detective, audit, and forensic controls governing all administrative changes to the identity system and identity life cycle actions—including account provisioning, de-provisioning, and changes—and permission provisioning, de-provisioning, and changes; and
    - shall support the protocols required for authentication and access control on enterprise on-premise and cloud-based systems, such as Kerberos, RADIUS, LDAP, X.509 certificates, and SAML.
  - Electronic identities and permissions
    - held by non-employees shall be sponsored by at least one employee and re-certified periodically (for example, 90 days).

Policy Guidance by Functional Area *(8 of 23)*

Identity, Authentication, and Access Management *(2 of 3)*

- Activities must include the following (continued):
    - Electronic identities and permissions used by computer systems (service accounts) shall be sponsored by at least one employee and re-certified on a periodic basis, such as 90 days, or be de-provisioned.
    - Electronic identities no longer needed shall be de-provisioned with a set time period (for example, 180 days).
    - Access permissions no longer needed shall be removed with a set time period (for example, 90 days).
  - Multi-factor authentication shall be supported for access to enterprise systems and applications from untrusted networks such as the Internet, and for all uses of privileged systems administrator accounts on all networks.
  - Authentication failures shall not reveal information about user names, passwords, permissions, or authentication methods.
  - Identity, authentication, and access management security configurations shall be reviewed on a periodic basis (for example, annually).
  - Failed logons shall include a delay so no more than five failed logons can be performed within one hour.
    - More than ten failed logon attempts on a single account shall generate an alert requiring investigation before the account may be used.
  - Security configurations and policy exceptions shall be reviewed periodically (for example, annually).

Policy Guidance by Functional Area *(9 of 23)*

Identity, Authentication, and Access Management *(3 of 3)*

- Activities must include the following (continued):
  - Passwords, when they are used for authentication, shall be subject to the following policy requirements:
    - Passwords
      - should be at least 12 characters long;
      - must contain uppercase, lowercase, and a number or a special character;
      - should not contain internal repetitions to allow them to meet length requirements (PasswordPassword 1); and
      - should not be displayed in clear text during the login process.
  - Active user passwords
    - must be changed periodically (for example, 90 days) and the past ten passwords must be unique; and
    - shall not be written down on paper or stored in unencrypted computer files.
  - Passwords internal to systems and not used interactively by users must be changed periodically (for example, annually) and the past ten passwords must be unique.
  - System account passwords shall be physically protected in a locked safe.
    - If stored electronically on network-accessible systems, such storage shall be encrypted and access-controlled.
    - If a single electronic system contains more than 100 system passwords, user access to it shall require multi-factor authentication.
  - When passwords must be generated and transmitted, such transmission shall be by encrypted means, or given verbally over the telephone.
    - Only one-time passwords may be transmitted over insecure channels.
  - Password security configuration shall be reviewed on a periodic basis (for example, annually), including re-validation of all policy exceptions.
  - Password management preventive, detective, audit, and forensic controls shall be verified and tested for proper operation periodically (for example, annually).

Policy Guidance by Functional Area *(10 of 23)*

Data Protection and Cryptography (1 of 2)

- Data protection and cryptography are essential to achieving
  - strong authentication, non-repudiation, and the protection of confidentiality and integrity of data at rest and in transit; and
  - protection of enterprise data and identities adequate to resist current and projected attacks.
- Activities must include the following:
  - Sensitive data transmission shall be protected—using Secured Sockets Layer (SSL), Transport Layer Security (TLS), Internet Protocol Security (IPSec), or equivalent secure protocols—on internal protected networks and insecure networks such as the Internet.
  - Encryption modules, algorithms, and protocols shall meet US National Institute of Standards and Technology (NIST) requirements as documented in approved Federal Information Processing Standards (FIPS) documents.
  - Cryptography used for more sensitive operations may need to resist an attacker with $100,000 worth of computing power.
  - Password policy shall be set using cryptographic principles based upon the amount of entropy required and the ability of brute-force attacks to be detected or delayed.
    - Design password complexity and rotation policy so attackers have less than 1% chance of successfully guessing a password within its usable lifetime.
    - Passwords with longer lifetimes shall require commensurately greater complexity to resist brute-force attacks.
  - Published cryptographic vulnerabilities (such as Heartbleed) shall be remediated within a set period (for example, 30 days) of publication, or compensating preventive or detective controls shall be put place so attempted exploits are blocked or at least detected.

Policy Guidance by Functional Area *(11 of 23)*

Data Protection and Cryptography *(2 of 2)*

- Activities must include the following (continued):
  - Encryption keys shall be centrally escrowed and retained for a period of time (for example, seven years) after the date of last use.
  - All non-public enterprise data at rest shall be either physically protected in a locked facility or container, or encrypted using cryptographic keys that are separate from the data, such as a strong password or encryption token.
  - Data encryption shall include adequate logging separate from the media itself to permit investigators to validate that lost media was, in fact, encrypted at the time of loss.
  - Strong and multi-factor authentication shall use cryptographic methods to make authentication resistant to keylogging, replay, session hijacking, and brute-force attacks.
    - Methods include digital certificates, one-time passwords, and secure cryptographic modules for storing persistent keys.
  - Persistent keys used for strong authentication or persistent encryption shall be protected using Hardware Security Modules (HSMs), Trusted Platform Modules (TPMs), secure elements, or smart cards that resist physical and logical attacks to extract the keys.
  - Session encryption (such as that used by SSL, TLS, or IPSec) does not require hardware protection, except where session compromise would pose an enterprise risk.
  - Data protection and cryptography modules, algorithms, protocols, and security configurations shall be reviewed on a periodic basis (for example, annually), including re-validation of all policy exceptions.
  - Data protection and cryptography preventive, detective, audit, and forensic controls shall be verified and tested for proper operation on a periodic basis (for example, at least annually).

Policy Guidance by Functional Area *(12 of 23)*

Monitoring, Vulnerability, and Patch Management (1 of 3)

- Monitoring of account activity and security incidents relies on robust logging of activities and alerting that catches potentially malicious activities.
  - Such monitoring shall be able to detect violations of security policies, procedures, and active attacks when they occur.
  - Timely detection of malicious activities aids in preventing or containing malicious actions before damage can be performed.
- Vulnerability and patch management reduce exposure to attacks by tracking and remediating vulnerabilities in a timely fashion, and by patching systems to reduce their exposure to attack.
- Activities must include the following:
  - Enterprise systems and cloud services
    - shall be monitored for performance and availability if delivering business-critical functions so that failures can be detected within a set period of time (for example, 30 minutes) of their occurrence; and
    - shall forward their logs to a central system for correlation and analysis, or shall provide for in-place analysis and alerting that ties in with enterprise incident detection and investigation services.
  - Log entries shall be synchronized to Coordinated Universal Time (UTC) or a clearly delineated global time zone so the times when events occur are clearly presented to investigators.
  - Security audit logs
    - must clearly tie user activity in the information system to named user or service accounts;
    - must be protected from tampering;
    - shall be made available to support investigations for a set period of time (for example, one year) after the event is logged; and
    - that are related to public company financial activities shall be retained for a set period of time (for example, seven years) after the event is logged.

Policy Guidance by Functional Area *(13 of 23)*

Monitoring, Vulnerability, and Patch Management *(2 of 2)*

- Activities must include the following (continued):
  - Networks shall be monitored to detect rogue or malicious devices connecting to them.
  - Wireless networks shall be configured to detect attacks and rogue wireless access points.
  - Cybersecurity may use detective technologies such as honeypots, honeynets, and honeytokens to detect attacker exploits of vulnerabilities and identify attacker tools, techniques, and procedures (TTPs).
  - System security monitoring shall feed into a central system for correlation that is monitored 24/7 to detect security incidents.
    - Security logs shall be monitored for activities known or suspected to be malicious.
    - Security alerts shall be generated within a set period of time (for example, 30 minutes) of such activity occurring.
  - New applications and servers shall be vulnerability-scanned, and all medium or high vulnerabilities shall be addressed prior to their becoming operational.
  - Enterprise applications that are generally available on the Internet or enterprise internal networks shall be scanned for vulnerabilities using a credentialed vulnerability scanner on a periodic basis (for example, monthly).
    - All medium or higher operating system vulnerabilities shall be addressed or remediated within a set period of time, such as 30 days, upon discovery.
    - For sensitive systems with significant business impact, this remediation window may be shorter—as little as one day.
  - Servers directly connected to the Internet
    - Servers shall be scanned for operating system vulnerabilities using a credentialed vulnerability scanner on a periodic basis (for example, monthly).
    - All medium or higher operating system vulnerabilities shall be addressed or remediated with a set period of time (for example, 30 days) upon discovery.
    - For sensitive systems with significant business impact, this remediation window may be shorter—as little as six hours.

Policy Guidance by Functional Area *(14 of 23)*

Monitoring, Vulnerability, and Patch Management (3 of 3)

- Activities must include the following (continued):
  - Cybersecurity shall ensure that applications and systems in violation of vulnerability remediation policy are disconnected from the Internet and enterprise networks until remediation is performed and validated.
  - Vendor-provided patches shall be evaluated and installed as recommended by vendors.
    - Vulnerabilities relating to missing patches shall be handled as per vulnerability policy.
    - When security patches cannot be installed for operational reasons, mitigating preventive and detective controls shall be employed to keep the overall risk acceptable.
  - The system owner is responsible for patching.
    - Automated systems may be used to simplify patch deployment.
    - Limitations to such automated systems must be compensated for using manual techniques to ensure that security vulnerabilities are addressed in a timely manner.
  - Detective controls shall be configured to detect attacker exploits of known vulnerabilities when this configuration is technically possible.
  - Internet-facing and user networks shall be penetration-tested on a periodic basis, such as annually, to identify vulnerabilities related to real-world attacker techniques.
  - Monitoring, vulnerability, and patch management are essential.
    - Security configurations shall be reviewed on a periodic basis, such as annually, including re-validation of all policy exceptions.
    - Preventive, detective, audit, and forensic controls shall be verified and tested for proper operation on a periodic basis, such as at least annually.

Policy Guidance by Functional Area *(15 of 23)*

High Availability, Disaster Recovery, and Physical Protection *(1 of 3)*

- Enterprise IT services, systems, servers, and data shall be
  - protected from losses of availability related to system failure, physical destruction, and accidental or malicious incidents; and
  - configured with adequate redundancy and protection to meet business needs and cost-effective service delivery in the event of accidental or deliberate incidents targeting their availability.
- Activities must include the following:
  - Availability
    - Revenue-generating systems must have at least 99.99% availability.
    - Other business IT systems must have at least 99.9% availability.
    - Supporting infrastructure may be subject to high-availability requirements as needed by the business.
  - Recovery Point Objectives (RPO) in the event of natural or man-made disaster
    - Revenue-generating and business financial systems must be able to recover all committed transactions with customers or vendors that have financial consequences.
    - Other business IT systems must be able to recover data up into the day previous to the incident (daily backup).
  - Recovery Time Objectives (RTO) in the event of natural or man-made disaster
    - Revenue-generating business functions must be able to recover and achieve initial operating capability within a specific time (for example, seven days).
    - Business financial systems must be able to recover to initial operating capability within a specific time (for example, 45 days).
    - Other business IT systems must be able to recover to initial operating capability within a specific time (for example, 90 days).

Policy Guidance by Functional Area *(16 of 23)*

High Availability, Disaster Recovery, and Physical Protection *(2 of 3)*

- Activities must include the following (continued):
  - Recovery Time Objectives (RTO) in the event of natural or man-made disaster
    - Planning shall consider the time required for rebuilding affected servers, in addition to the time required for restoring affected data.
  - Major system upgrades and configuration changes must include adequate backups to "roll back" the changes within the *availability*, *recovery point*, and *recovery time* requirements.
  - Backup data
    - shall be sufficiently protected physically and logically so that natural or man-made disasters will not result in the destruction of both the primary copy and the backup;
    - that is taken offsite shall be encrypted, and the keys to that data shall be sufficiently protected from loss or compromise so that data can be recovered even in the event of catastrophic loss.
  - Theft or loss of any enterprise-furnished equipment must be reported to the incident response team as soon as possible.
  - Enterprise-sensitive data printed on paper or other material must be physically protected in a locked room or cabinet.
  - Enterprise facilities and data centers
    - These centers shall include physical protection, monitoring, and detective controls to protect personnel and equipment from harm and accidents.
    - Sensitive data and systems handling personnel and equipment in an unencrypted fashion shall be protected using double-barrier protection and need-to-know access controls.
    - Third-party access to the data center must be approved by the data center operations supervisor and guests must be escorted during the visit.
    - When automated physical access controls are used at facilities, the access logs shall be
      - maintained for a specific time (for example, one year) to support investigations by audit, security, legal, and law enforcement personnel; and
      - monitored 24/7 to detect intrusions and intrusion attempts.

Policy Guidance by Functional Area *(17 of 23)*

High Availability, Disaster Recovery, and Physical Protection *(3 of 3)*

- Activities must include the following (continued):
  - – Backup media, replication processes, and snapshot procedures must be tested periodically (for example, at least annually) to verify their proper operation.
  - – Disaster recovery and service continuity plans must be tested using a drill, rehearsal, or tabletop practical exercise periodically (for example, every two years) to ensure their effectiveness.
  - – Physical security risk assessments must be conducted for all data centers, server rooms, and server closets on a periodic basis (for example, annually).
  - – High availability, disaster recovery, and physical protection
    - Configurations shall be reviewed on a periodic basis (for example, annually), including re-validation of all policy exceptions.
    - Preventive, detective, audit, and forensic controls shall be verified and tested for proper operation on a periodic basis (for example, annually).

Policy Guidance by Functional Area *(18 of 23)*

Incident Response *(1 of 2)*

- A security incident is any malicious event (perceived or real) performed against the enterprise's data or information systems.
  - Such incidents can originate inside the enterprise (insider threat), in external entities, or in the surrounding environment.
  - When a cybersecurity-related incident is reported, the incident response team takes charge of the incident and matrixes with the appropriate resources to investigate and remediate the situation.
- Activities must include the following:
  - Incident response team shall
    - track cybersecurity threats against the enterprise;
    - inform cybersecurity and IT leadership of threats that pose new or previously unknown risk to the enterprise; and
    - propose potential mitigations.
  - All information systems supporting enterprise business systems must have a documented incident response process.
  - Incident response processes must have clearly defined roles and responsibilities, and may leverage shared services that are centrally operated by cybersecurity.
  - For major incidents, a single leader must be designated for the duration of the incident.
    - Coordinates containment of the incident
    - Reduces the impact
    - Ensures remediation
    - Keeps all stakeholders informed of the status
  - Suspected incidents shall be investigated according to a set schedule (example timeframes):
    - ***Critical*** alerts shall be investigated within one hour of their detection.
    - ***High*** alerts shall be investigated within 12 hours of their detection.
    - ***Medium*** alerts shall be investigated within 24 hours of their occurrence.
    - ***Low*** or ***routine*** alerts shall be investigated within two business days of their occurrence.

Policy Guidance by Functional Area *(19 of 23)*

Incident Response (2 of 2)

- Activities must include the following (continued):
  - All incidents shall be documented to capture the originating alert or event, results of investigation, and remediation and conclusion.
  - Confirmed incidents shall have their root cause investigated, identified, and documented.
  - Incident documentation shall be retained for a specific period (for example, seven years after conclusion).
  - Incident investigation teams shall
    - have the tools and permissions they need to investigate accounts, computers, and networks involved in malicious activity; and
    - have the ability to directly or by request disable and remediate accounts, computers, and networks as necessary to contain and resolve the incident.
  - The cybersecurity department shall
    - oversee contractual, regulatory, or legal obligations related to incidents;
    - identify incidents with contractual, regulatory, or legal implications; and
    - bring to bear the appropriate resources to ensure that contractual, regulatory, and legal obligations related to those incidents are met.
  - The enterprise shall have anonymous methods for employees to report security policy violations or suspected security incidents without fear of reprisal.
  - Incident response configurations shall be reviewed on a periodic basis (for example, annually), including re-validation of all policy exceptions.
  - Incident response preventive, detective, audit, and forensic controls shall be verified and tested for proper operation on a periodic basis (for example, at least annually).

Policy Guidance by Functional Area *(20 of 23)*

Asset Management and Supply Chain (1 of 2)

- Asset management is the accounting of all enterprise assets (hardware and software).
  - It is critical this information be kept up-to-date to support IT operation and handling of cybersecurity incidents.
- A supply chain management program covers both products and services to include the following:
  - Security assessment
  - Periodic re-assessments
  - Inclusion of supplier information in the asset management database
- Activities must include the following:
  - All software and hardware assets shall be assigned to an enterprise system with a primary and alternative employee point of contact.
  - A centralized asset management system shall be utilized to track all enterprise hardware and software assets from their acquisition through to their disposal.
  - A centralized configuration and change management system shall be utilized to
    - track configurations of enterprise hardware and software systems;
    - track the approval of changes to those configurations; and
    - detect unauthorized changes when they occur.
  - Software licenses and software utilization in the enterprise shall be tracked so that
    - software licenses can be matched to utilization;
    - software license compliance can be ensured; and
    - unauthorized software in the enterprise can be identified and remediated.
  - As part of the system acquisition, cybersecurity shall review and approve vendors and suppliers, with associated risks identified and accepted or mitigated.
  - Hardware and software assets retired from service shall be properly disposed by
    - removal of assets from asset and configuration databases;
    - release of software licenses and termination of software and hardware support contracts; and
    - sanitization or destruction of hardware persistent storage (flash and hard drive storage) to protect enterprise data.

Policy Guidance by Functional Area *(21 of 23)*

Asset Management and Supply Chain (2 of 2)

- Activities must include the following (continued):
  - Persistent storage media, including flash drives, portable media, hard drives, and device-embedded storage (such as copiers and voicemail appliances with data storage features), shall be sanitized of enterprise data using the following:
    - Physical destruction
    - Data cleaning
    - Data scrubbing
    - Data encryption methods so that data may not be recovered after disposal
  - Data disposal methods shall be validated periodically (for example, annually) to ensure their effectiveness.
  - Data encryption methods shall be validated to ensure the encryption strength is adequate to protect data for a set period (for example, ten years) following disposal.
  - Loss or unintended disposal of equipment or disclosure of data shall be reported as a cybersecurity incident.
  - Hardware and software assets shall be inventoried periodically (for example, annually), with all associated points of contact validated and updated as necessary.
  - Hardware, software, and service provider risk evaluations shall be reviewed and updated periodically (for example, annually) or when changes occur that materially affect the security posture.
    - Cyberincidents or breaches
    - Mergers
    - Divestitures
    - Bankruptcies
    - Foreign acquisitions
  - Asset management and supply chain configurations shall be reviewed periodically (for example, annually), including re-validation of all policy exceptions.
  - Asset management and supply chain preventive, detective, audit, and forensic controls shall be verified and tested for proper operation periodically (for example, at least annually).

Policy Guidance by Functional Area *(22 of 23)*

Policy, Audit, E-Discovery, and Training (1 of 2)

- Security governance is paramount for the smooth functioning of the enterprise cybersecurity program.
  - Maintenance of enterprise cybersecurity policies
  - Periodic audits of controls and protections
  - Support for legal e-discovery activities
  - Training of cybersecurity personnel, employees and contractors in proper cybersecurity practices and techniques
- Activities must include the following:
  - Enterprise cybersecurity policy shall be approved by business leadership with inputs from key stakeholders.
    - Business leadership
    - Legal
    - Contractual
    - IT
    - Cybersecurity departments
  - A formal security forum shall be established to enable key stakeholders to discuss security matters on a regular basis and document policy changes or enhancement recommendations.
  - Enterprise shall
    - track cybersecurity risks and their potential consequences;
    - report on cybersecurity risks and their mitigation on a periodic basis (for example, quarterly);
    - employ tools to provide the following:
      - overall cybersecurity governance
      - risk management
      - compliance reporting so all contractual, regulator, statutory and legal requirements can be met;
    - comply with all contractual, regulatory, statutory, and legal requirement as they are stipulated:
      - Sarbanes-Oxley (SOX), Payment Card Industry (PCI), and Health Insurance Portability and Accountability Act (HIPAA)
      - regulations relating to privacy of employee and customer data; and
    - comply with all requests for e-discovery originating from the legal department.
      - Requests shall be documented.
      - Documentation shall be retained for a set period (for example, seven years).

Policy Guidance by Functional Area *(23 of 23)*

Policy, Audit, E-Discovery, and Training (2 of 2)

- Activities must include the following (continued):
  - Exceptions to cybersecurity policies shall be documented, tracked, and re-certified on a periodic basis (for example, annually).
  - Policy exceptions that are not re-certified shall be removed and the policy enforced.
  - The enterprise shall comply with customer and internal requirements for information system Certification and Accreditation (C&A), as specified in customer contracts and internal Memorandum of Understanding (MOUs).
  - The enterprise shall ensure all employees receive annual training on cybersecurity concerns and obligations.
  - Employees in positions of trust, including executives and systems administrators, shall receive additional training.
    - Suitable to their roles
    - Risks associated with those roles
    - Their obligation to provide additional protection of enterprise and customer data
  - The enterprise shall audit *all* cybersecurity preventive, detective, audit, and forensic controls on a periodic basis (for example, annually) to ensure their proper design and operation.
  - Policy, audit, e-discovery, and training programs shall be reviewed on a periodic basis (for example, annually), including re-validation of all policy exceptions.
  - Policy, audit, e-discovery, and training preventive, detective, audit, and forensic controls shall be verified and tested for proper operation on a periodic basis (for example, at least annually).

APPENDIX B

Cybersecurity Operational Processes

S. E. Donaldson et al., *Enterprise Cybersecurity Study Guide*, https://doi.org/10.1007/978-1-4842-3258-3_17

Overview

- To maintain an effective cybersecurity posture, the Chief Information Security Officer (CISO) should maintain a number of ***cybersecurity operational processes***.
- As suggested by the graphic, this appendix describes a set of such processes and their ***supporting information systems***.
- While this list is not all-inclusive, it includes important processes for effective cybersecurity.
- These processes are usually operated from within ***enterprise functional areas***.
- Processes cross over organizational and technological boundaries so they are somewhat manual and procedural.

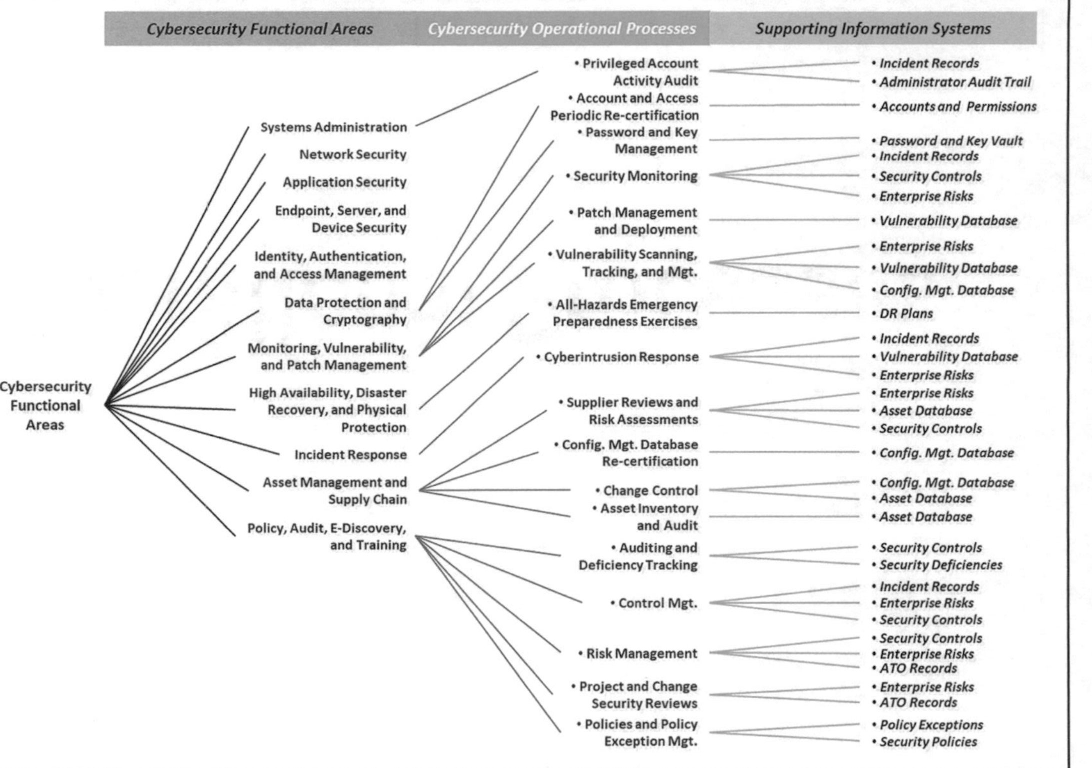

Topics

1. Policies and Policy Exception Management
2. Project and Change Security Reviews
3. Risk Management
4. Control Management
5. Auditing and Deficiency Tracking
6. Asset Inventory and Audit
7. Change Control
8. Configuration Management Database Re-certification
9. Supplier Reviews and Risk Assessments
10. Cyberintrusion Response
11. All-Hazards Emergency Preparedness Exercises
12. Vulnerability Scanning, Tracking, and Management
13. Patch Management and Deployment
14. Security Monitoring
15. Password and Key Management
16. Account and Access Periodic Re-certification
17. Privileged Account Activity Audit

Policies and Policy Exception Management

- This process maintains enterprise policies and exceptions to those policies.
  - Enterprises may be good at establishing and maintaining processes, but managing exceptions to policies tends to be more problematic.
  - Enterprises need to ensure policy exceptions are formally approved and re-certified.
  - Security leadership needs to observe policy exceptions carefully so the "exception does not become the rule."

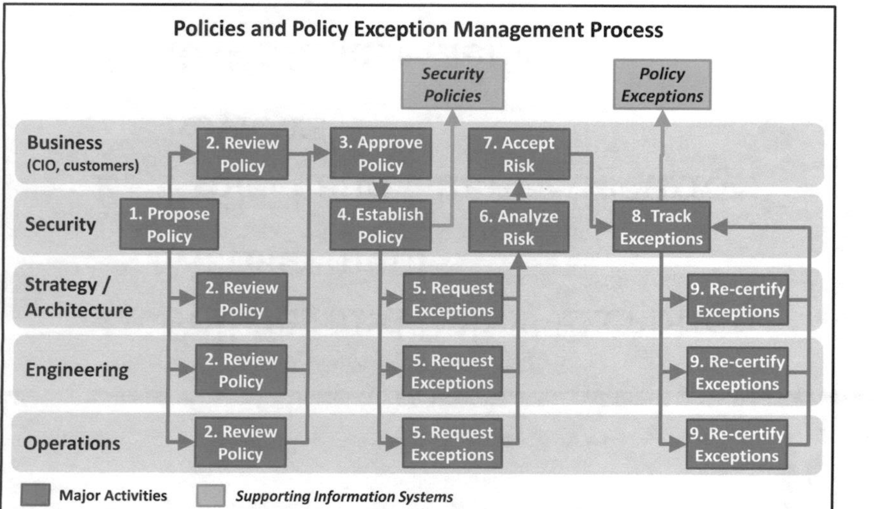

1. ***Propose Policy***: Security team proposes a policy be created.
2. ***Review Policy***: Business leadership, strategy/architecture, engineering, and operations review the policy to ensure it is reasonable and supports the business.
3. ***Approve Policy***: Business leadership approves the policy after it has been reviewed and revised, as needed, to balance risk with business needs.
4. ***Establish Policy***: Security team integrates policy with rest of the security policies and established methods for monitoring and enforcing policy. Policies should be periodically reviewed and updated. This sub-process is not shown in the graphic.
5. ***Request Exceptions***: Strategy/architecture, engineering, and operations teams may find they need exceptions to the policy.
6. ***Analyze Risk:*** When exceptions are requested, security team analyzes the risk associated with the exceptions and reports that risk to business leadership.
7. ***Accept Risk***: Business leadership balances the business value with the associated risk to make a business decision on approving the exception and accepting the associated risk.
8. ***Track Exceptions***: Security team tracks approved exceptions and ensures they are periodically re-certified.
9. ***Re-certify Exceptions***: Requesters are required to periodically re-certify their exceptions to ensure the exception need still exists and the risk is still acceptable.

Project and Change Security Reviews

- This process involves cybersecurity in enterprise projects and changes.
  - Process ensures, in part, that IT systems are designed and deployed with cybersecurity capabilities "baked in" to the best extent possible and that they are practical.
  - Process should be integrated into the larger system development life cycle process and can be part of the management gates.

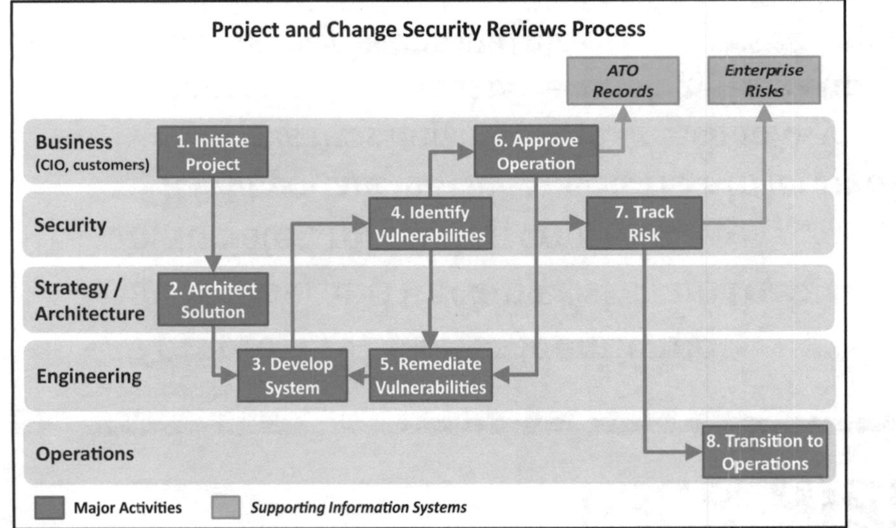

1. ***Initiate Project***: In response to a business need, the business leadership initiates a project for a new system or an existing system change.
2. ***Architect Solution***: In context of the overall enterprise, the strategy and architecture team architects the solution, in part, by identifying technologies and standards that comprise the solution. The team factors security policies and standards into the solution.
3. ***Develop System***: Next, the engineering team develops the system or change, taking the architecture and security standards into consideration. The engineering team designs the system by balancing performance, security, and cost requirements, as well as other constraints.
4. ***Identify Vulnerabilities***: During the system design process, security reviews the proposed design and identifies vulnerabilities. They are defined in terms of threats and business consequences that result in confidentiality, integrity, or availability (CIA) losses.
5. ***Remediate Vulnerabilities***: As vulnerabilities are identified, the system is engineered to reduce the potential threats and negative business consequences. Sometimes, mitigating the vulnerabilities may not make business sense.
6. ***Approve Operation***: Business leadership considers the identified vulnerabilities and corresponding business risks. If the risks are too great, engineering needs to modify the system design to acceptable risk levels. Once the business leadership accepts the risk, they grant and document the approval to operate (ATO).
7. ***Track Risk***: Security team then documents the residual risks in the enterprise risk database. Documentation includes threat scenarios and associated business impacts on CIA.
8. ***Transition to Operations***: Once the system is approved to operate and residual risks are accounted for, the system can be transitioned to operations.

Risk Management

- This process involves identifying, analyzing, and tracking risks and their associated mitigating controls.
  - It is important the CISO tracks risks in terms of their business impact, not their technology impact; risks should be technology-agnostic.
  - Technology factors into the risk process as vulnerabilities are identified and exploited by attackers; associated business risks can increase and possibly require additional mitigations.

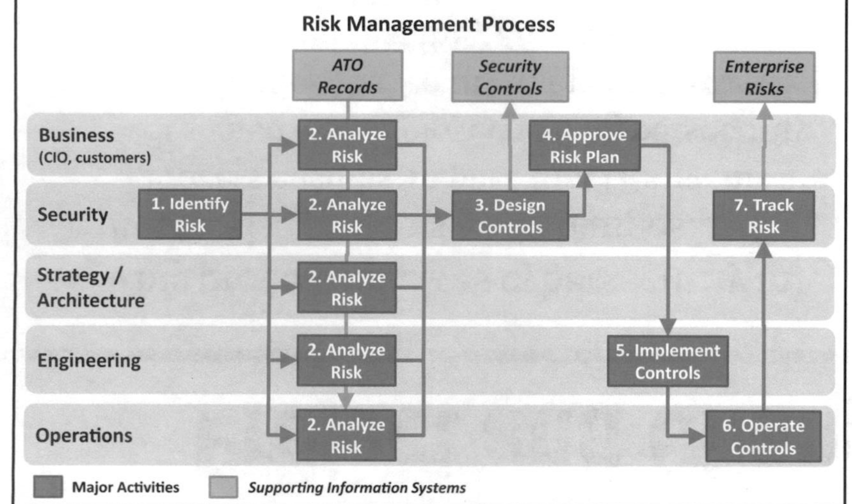

1. ***Identify Risk***: Security team starts the process by identifying risk. In the event of a risk re-certification or review, this activity may involve taking an existing risk and initiating the process to review it.
2. ***Analyze Risk***: Next, all departments analyze risk from their perspectives. The departments evaluate the importance/consequences of the risk and potential mitigations.
3. ***Design Controls***: Security team works with engineering to design controls to mitigate the risk, either by ***reducing its probability*** or ***reducing its impact***. In some instances, the best business decision may be to accept the risk as is without mitigation.
4. ***Approve Risk Plan***: Business leadership reviews the risk and the planned mitigation measures to ensure the risk plan balances performance, security, and cost to serve the needs of the business.
5. ***Implement Controls***: Once the risk plan is approved, engineering implements the controls and prepares them for production. Engineering is involved in the control design to ensure the planned controls are actually achievable.
6. ***Operate Controls***: After the controls are designed and implemented, operations takes responsibility for the day-to-day activities.
7. ***Track Risk***: Finally, the security team tracks the risk, along with its associated mitigating controls, via the enterprise risks database.

Control Management

- This process involves identifying and tracking enterprise security controls.
  - Tracking controls are helpful because they allow management to track how security resources are being allocated to mitigate risks while preserving business value.
  - A good control identifies the risk it mitigates, whether it is ***reducing the probability*** or the ***reducing the impact*** of the risk, and who is doing what to deliver mitigation.
  - It is helpful to tie this process to incident management process so controls are developed to mitigate risks related to real-world cyberincidents.

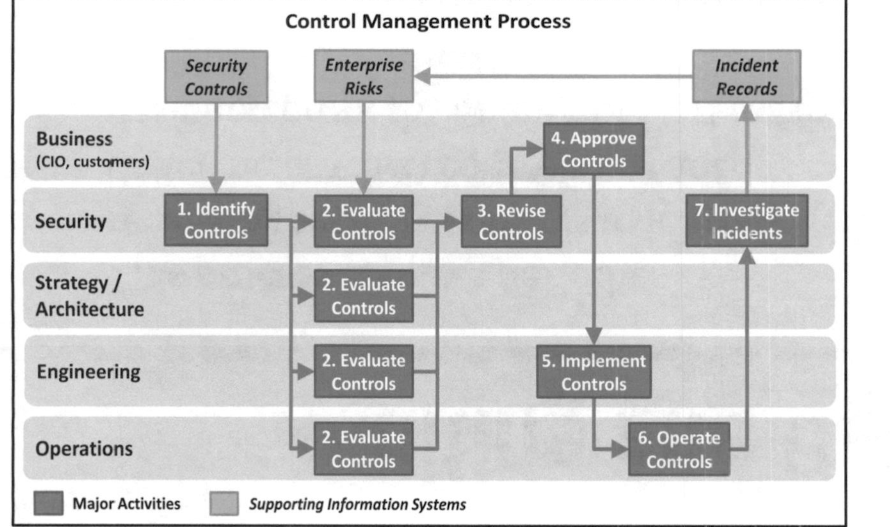

1. ***Identify Controls***: Security team identifies the controls to be considered, which either come from the risk management process (in other words, identifies new controls) or a review of existing controls.
2. ***Evaluate Controls***: Next, security, strategy and architecture, engineering, and operations consider each of the controls from their perspectives. Generally, business leadership does not need to be involved.
3. ***Revise Controls***: Security team works with engineering to create, update, or modify the controls based on the results of the evaluation process.
4. ***Approve Controls***: Business leadership reviews the revised controls in light of the risk and potential business impact to ensure performance, security, and cost are appropriately balanced to serve the needs of the business.
5. ***Implement Controls***: Once the business leadership approves the revised controls, engineering implements the controls and prepares them for production. Engineering is involved in the control design to ensure the planned controls are actually achievable.
6. ***Operate Controls***: After the controls are designed and implemented, operations takes responsibility for the day-to-day activities.
7. ***Investigate Incidents***: During operation, the controls will generate security incidents that will require security to conduct an investigation.

Auditing and Deficiency Tracking

- This process involves periodically reviewing security controls to identify deficiencies when controls are not designed properly, or are not working as designed.
  - Audits are essential to maintaining controls.
  - Audit types include self-audit, internal audit, and external audit.

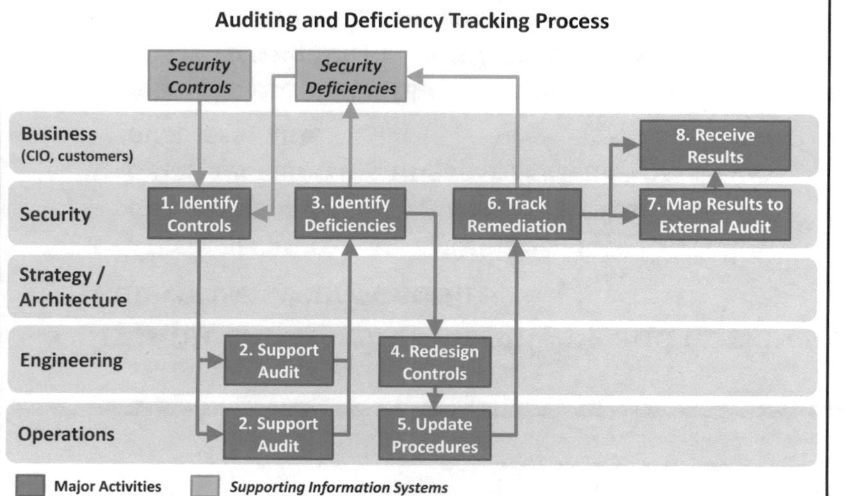

1. ***Identify Controls***: Security team identifies the controls to be audited. Seldom will a single audit consider all controls; most likely an audit is a subset of all controls. Note that for internal and external audits, the process is directed by a department outside of IT, but it should still be facilitated through the security office.
2. ***Support Audit***: Engineering and operations personnel support the audit by answering questions on the design and operation of the control.
3. ***Identify Deficiencies***: During the course of the audit, security documents and tracks deficiencies.
4. ***Redesign Controls***: In response to deficiencies, engineering may have to redesign or modify the controls.
5. ***Update Procedures***: In response to deficiencies and control redesign, operations may have to update their procedures for operating the controls or improve the execution of the procedures that are already in place.
6. ***Track Remediation***: Security tracks the changes to the controls or their operation and works with the audit team to determine if the changes constitute adequate remediation of the deficiency. Note that not all deficiencies are resolved successfully; sometimes it may make better business sense to simply accept the deficiency.
7. ***Map Results to External Audits***: For audits that are performed against an external standard such as NIST, PCI, or HIPAA, security maps the audit results from the internal controls to the requirements of the external framework.
8. ***Receive Results***: Senior leadership receives the audit results. In situations where deficiencies are accepted and not resolved, senior leadership weights in on the business sense of such decisions.

Asset Inventory and Audit

- This process involves tracking / auditing IT assets to ensure the enterprise assets actually present match the assets believed to be present.
  - A wide range of assets are tacked, including physical computers and technology equipment, licensed software, and key and security measures.
  - Finance generally requires capitalized assets to be tracked for depreciation purpose; for IT security purposes, other assets are tracked as well.
  - Frequency of audits is dependent, in part, on the asset type, value, and asset security.

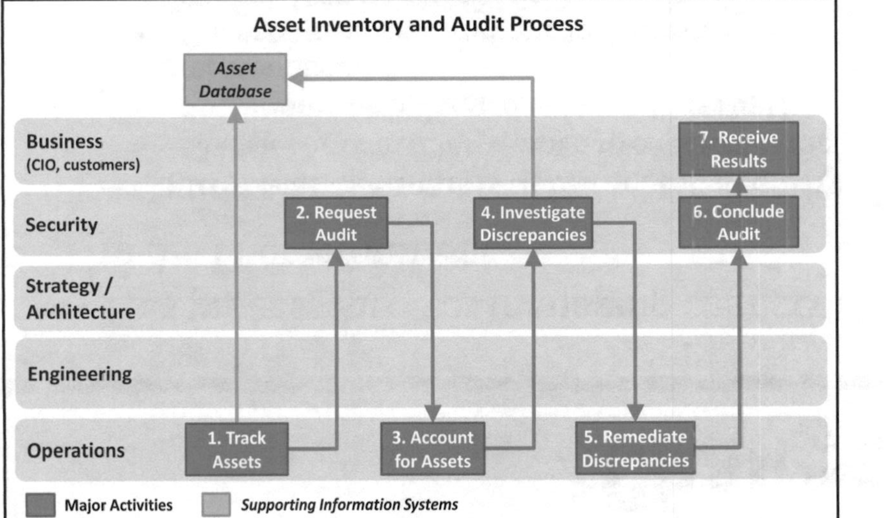

1. ***Track Assets***: Operations tracks assets throughout their life cycle, from acquisition to disposal.
2. ***Request Audit***: Security initiates the audit process by requesting it. The process is often on a regular schedule (for example, annually) or as a rolling audit where partial inventories are done monthly or quarterly.
3. ***Account for Assets***: Under security's supervision, operations audits assess by identifying discrepancies.
4. ***Investigate Discrepancies***: When discrepancies are found, security tracks them and attempts to determine if the reasons for the discrepancies are a process problem or an execution problem.
5. ***Remediate Discrepancies***: When discrepancies are investigated, operations remediates the discrepancies so the actual inventory matches the asset database content.
6. ***Conclude Audits***: Security concludes the audit by compiling the results of what was audited, what discrepancies were found, and how the discrepancies are remediated. The report includes valuing the cost of the discrepancies. Cost values are important in making business decisions in response to the audit.
7. ***Receive Results***: Senior leadership receives the audit results and makes business decisions, which might include changing processes, investing in asset management technology, or disciplining employees for not following procedures.

Change Control

- This process involves managing changes to the IT environment.
  - Control Management is of interest to security.
    - Changes are carefully planned to ensure they do not introduce unplanned vulnerabilities to IT environment.
    - Changes that occur without authorization or approval can be signs of deliberate attack.
  - Change control process helps ensure smooth IT operations.

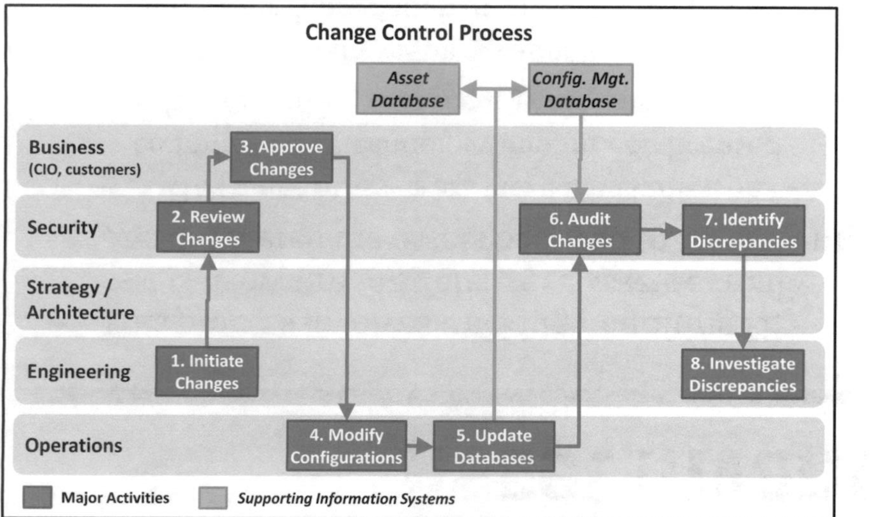

1. ***Initiate Changes***: Engineering initiates this process. Ideally, changes are documented and tracked through a change management system (not shown).
2. ***Review Changes***: Security should have an opportunity to review changes prior to their approval.
3. ***Approve Changes***: By considering the business value of the proposed change in regard to operations, security risk, and cost, business leadership approves all changes prior to implementation and execution.
4. ***Modify Configurations***: Once business approves the change, operations modifies the configuration in accordance with established procedures.
5. ***Update Databases***: After operations completes the changes (or in conjunction with executing the changes), operations updates asset and configuration management databases to document the change.
6. ***Audit Changes***: As part of the change completion process, security audits the change to ensure what was actually changed matches the documentation.
7. ***Identify Discrepancies***: Audit may identify discrepancies where what was changed does not match the documentation. These discrepancies are particularly common when automated systems are used to constantly scan for unauthorized changes. Discovered discrepancies should be treated as security incidents for investigations.
8. ***Investigate Discrepancies***: When discrepancies are identified, engineering and operations work with security to investigate the discrepancies and determine what happened.

Configuration Management Database Re-Certification

- This process involves periodically auditing system configurations against the configuration management database to verify that system configurations match the database.
  - Unplanned changes, debugging and troubleshooting, and attacker activity can result in configuration discrepancies that need to be resolved periodically.
  - Security should review the changes to ensure that discrepancies are not the result of attacker activity.

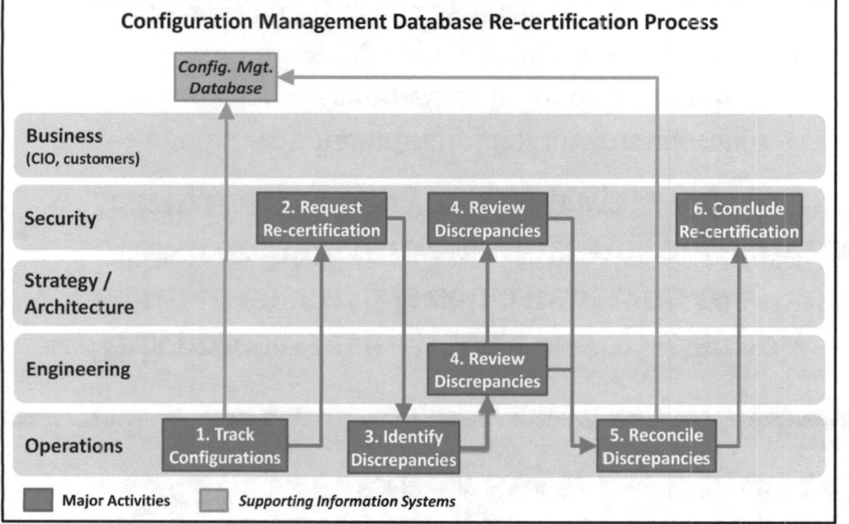

1. ***Track Configurations***: Operations tracks configurations as a normal course of business and formal change control.
2. ***Request Re-certification***: Security initiates the re-certification process, which is done on a routine schedule (for example, quarterly or annually), in response to an identified discrepancy, or to support other audit activities.
3. ***Identify Discrepancies***: Operations reviews system configurations compared to the database and identifies discrepancies where the configurations do not match the database.
4. ***Review Discrepancies***: Engineering and security review discrepancies to determine if the discrepancies are evidence of malicious activity or represent an engineering or security risk.
5. ***Reconcile Discrepancies***: Operations reconciles the discrepancies with what is in operation (that is, configuration management database). This reconciliation may involve either updating the database or updating the configuration so they both match. Obviously, if the configuration is to be changed, proper change control procedures must be followed.
6. ***Conclude Re-certification***: After all discrepancies have been reviewed, security concludes the re-certification. This activity may include tracking the re-certification results to identify systemic and process problems over time.

Supplier Reviews and Risk Assessments

- This process reviews the enterprise supply chain to ensure it is consistent with the overall architecture and does not pose undue risk to enterprise cybersecurity.
  - Supplier risks include supplier location, foreign government or competitor influences, supplier vulnerabilities, regulatory compliance, and supplier access to enterprise IT systems.
  - Suppliers must be periodically reviewed and their security assessments updated in light of threats.

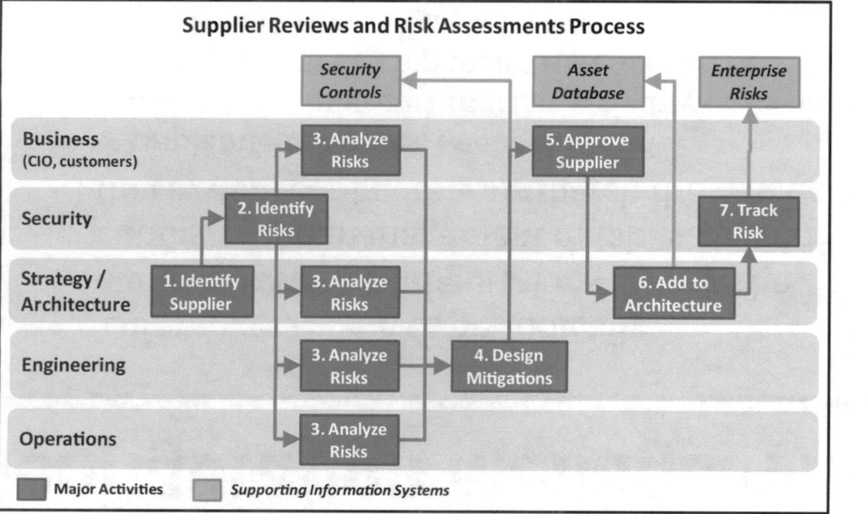

1. ***Identify Supplier***: Architecture team identifies suppliers for consideration. Strategy and architecture have visibility on all major enterprise suppliers to ensure suppliers and their technologies are consistent with the overall enterprise architecture.
2. ***Identify Risks***: Security team evaluates the supplier risk, considering how the supplier interacts with the enterprise. Do suppliers have access to enterprise networks, or supply hardware, software, or services? Identifying risks considers a wide range of potential threat scenarios related to CIA.
3. ***Analyze Risks***: Business leadership, strategy / architecture, engineering, and operations analyze the supplier risk to understand the potential impact should it manifest itself.
4. ***Design Mitigations***: Engineering collaborates with security (not shown in the graphic) to design mitigations to reduce the probability or the impact of those supplier risks, if possible and warranted.
5. ***Approve Supplier***: Business leadership formally approves the supplier risk mitigations by considering the business impact, risks, mitigations, and costs involved.
6. ***Add to Architecture***: Strategy and architecture add approved suppliers, along with any risk assessment caveats, to the enterprise architecture.
7. ***Track Risks***: Security tracks the risks associated with the approved suppliers.

Cyberintrusion Response

- This process is used to investigate identified incidents, contain the breach or instruction, and restore normal business operations.
  - The process is central to a modern, responsive cyberdefense, and it is led by the security CyberIncident Response Team (CIRT).
  - CIRT works with engineering and operations throughout the process.

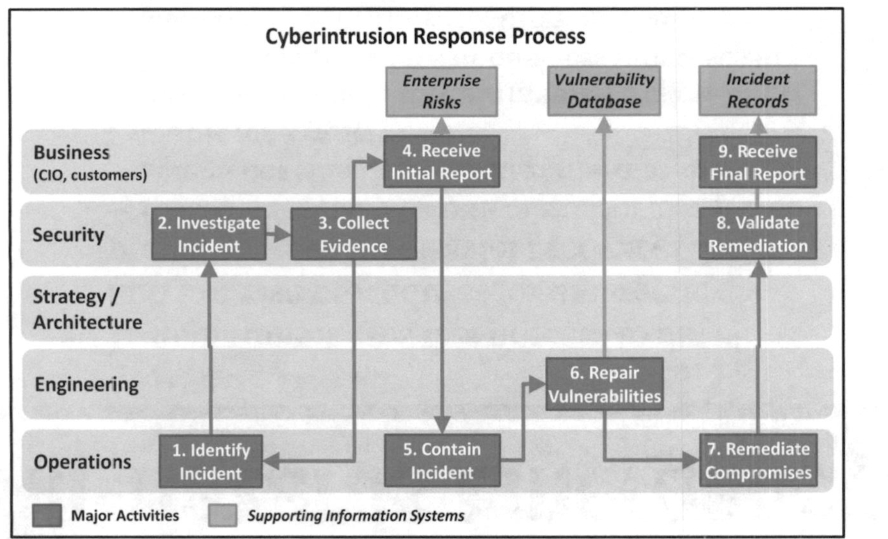

1. ***Identify Incident***: Operation team identifies a security incident has occurred. Identification includes reviewing and investigating alerts from monitoring systems and conducting searches for suspected attacker activities based on known patterns.
2. ***Investigate Incident***: Security investigates and tracks the identified incident and identifies the tools, techniques, and procedures used in the attack. Scope often expands as more hosts, accounts, and networks are identified as being involved.
3. ***Collet Evidence***: Security collects evidence that may be used by law enforcement, but may also be of interest to auditors and regulators.
4. ***Receive Initial Reports***: Security reports the status of the incident to business management. Status covers the business impact in terms of breaches of CIA, as well as the anticipated business impact due to the remediation. Business leadership, along with security, updates the enterprise risks to document how enterprise was exploited.
5. ***Contain Incident***: Operations moves forward to contain the incident to stop the attackers from being able to operate in the enterprise environment and limit further damage.
6. ***Repair Vulnerabilities***: Vulnerabilities exploited by the attackers are identified and remediated as well as possible. Engineering tracks vulnerabilities that cannot be repaired immediately and considers alternative mitigating controls.
7. ***Remediate Compromises***: Operations remediates and restores the attacked assets (for example, computers, user accounts, and networks) back to normal operation.
8. ***Validate Remediation***: Security validates the remediation activities to ensure the incident has been contained, vulnerabilities have been repaired, and compromised assets remediated.
9. ***Receive Final Report***: IT department fully documents the incident and covers the business impact, explains what the incident means going forward, and recommends actions to strengthen defenses.

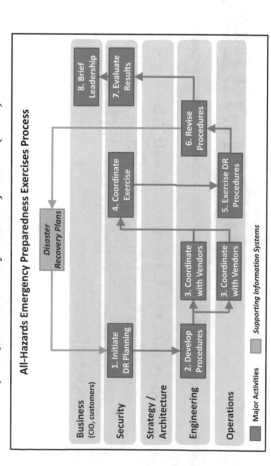

All-Hazards Emergency Preparedness Exercises

- IT department uses this process to develop and exercise procedures for emergency preparedness and disaster recovery (DR).
  - Procedures should be generalized for all types of emergency situations (all-hazards) and should be usable for a variety of crises.
  - Procedures should include manual workarounds, failover of applications or business processes to alternate sites or infrastructures, and restoration of data and applications from backups.
  - For information systems, availability DR should be considered in terms of recovery point objectives (RPO) and recovery time objectives (RTO).

1. ***Initiate Disaster Recovery (DR) Planning***: Security team ensures DR plans are maintained and periodically updated. Team initiates exercise process periodically (for example, annually).
2. ***Develop Procedures***: Engineering develops or updates the DR procedures that cover a wide range of possible failure scenarios. Particular attention is paid to personnel factors to ensure success is not dependent on any one person.
3. ***Coordinate with Vendors***: IT DR system procedures are highly dependent on underlying technology capabilities. Engineering and operations develop procedures in close coordination with vendors.
4. ***Coordinate Exercise***: When draft procedures are ready, security team coordinates an exercise to test and practice the procedures. The scale of the exercise is based, in part, on cost, schedule, and business impact factors.
5. ***Exercise DR Procedures***: Operations teams lead the practice of the DR procedures, as documented in the plans. Exercise can be a simple procedures walkthrough, a tabletop mock drill, or a full failover.
6. ***Revise Procedures***: Based on exercise results, if needed, engineering leads the revision of the DR procedures and plans.
7. ***Evaluate Results***: Security compiles the exercise results to be reported to business leadership.
8. ***Brief Leadership***: Security briefs business leadership on exercise results, highlighting the business risks posed by disaster scenarios and the parameters for recovery point objectives (RPO) and recovery time objectives (RTO).

Vulnerability Scanning, Tracking, and Management

- This process is relatively straightforward and involves using tools to scan for vulnerabilities in network-connected systems.
  - Vulnerabilities allow attackers to disable systems, disrupt their operation, modify data, or in the worst case take full control of those systems to access the enterprise and its data.
  - Not all vulnerabilities can be patched or remediated.
  - Security team considers overall enterprise risks to understand how unresolved vulnerabilities potentially impact the CIA of critical data.

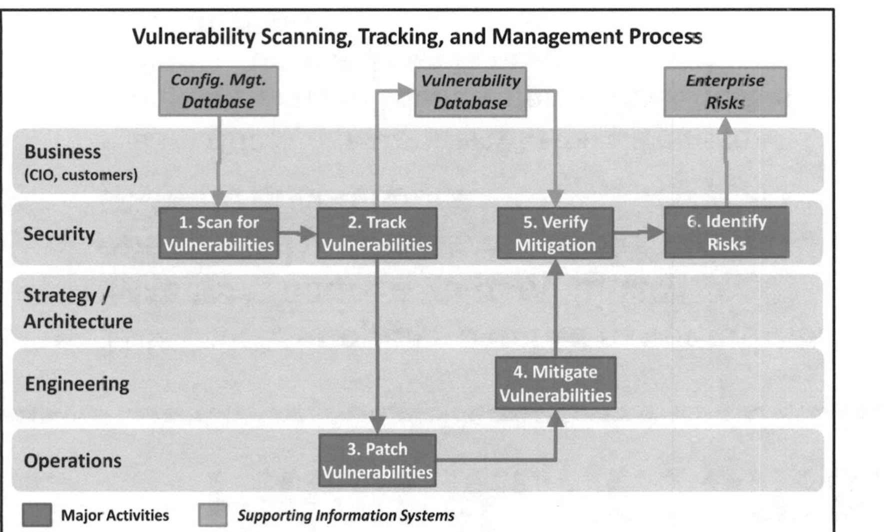

1. ***Scan for Vulnerabilities***: Security team initiates vulnerability scans. Traditionally, operations performs this activity, but security team ensures scanning is being conducted on a regular basis. Scanning is done using automated tools, although manual procedures can be followed as well.
2. ***Track Vulnerabilities***: Security tracks identified vulnerabilities for remediation. Some vulnerabilities may need to be accepted; in those cases, mitigating controls should be considered.
3. ***Patch Vulnerabilities:*** For many vulnerabilities, the fix is as simple as installing a patch or performing a re-configuration.
4. ***Mitigate Vulnerabilities***: Engineering mitigates vulnerabilities that cannot be simply patched or addressed. Mitigation may be through preventive controls that make the vulnerability harder to exploit or detective controls to catch exploits when they occur.
5. ***Verify Mitigation***: When engineering performs mitigation, the security team is consulted to verify the mitigation will be effective and perform as desired.
6. ***Identify Risks***: Security considers the business impacts of the vulnerabilities, their remediation, and any mitigation performed. It then uses that information to update the list of enterprise risks, as necessary.

Patch Management and Deployment

- This process deploys patches to operational systems to address vulnerabilities, operational problems, or simple routine software maintenance.
  - It is critical for enterprises to have a patch management and deployment process that is tightly integrated into IT operations and maintenance.
  - This process needs to allow for the occasional deployment of unscheduled, emergency patches.

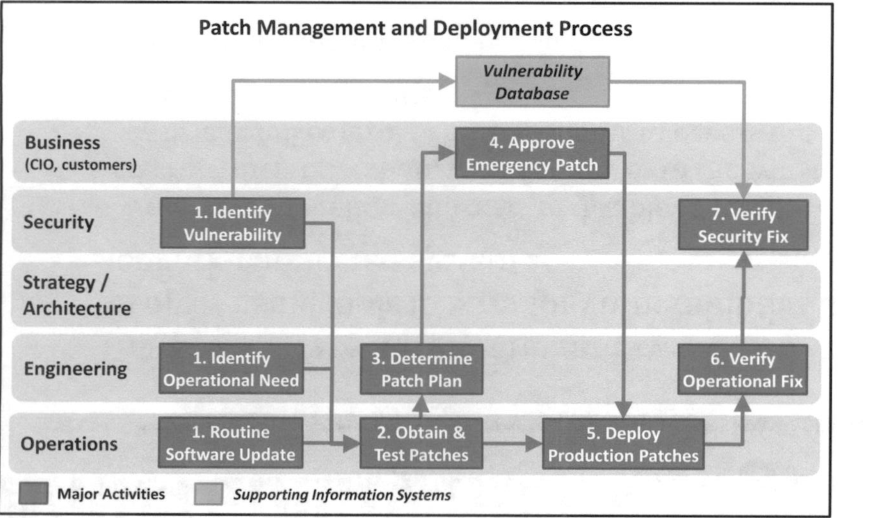

1. ***Identify Vulnerability, Operational Need, or Routine Software Update***: Security identifies the need for a patch: security vulnerability, an operational problem, or routine software patches from vendor. First, two patch needs may necessitate non-routine, "emergency" patching.
2. ***Obtain and Test Patches***: Operations obtains the software patches and ensures their legitimacy and compatibility with the systems to be patched.
3. ***Determine Patch Plan***: For emergency patches, engineering reviews the patches to ensure adequate testing is performed and the operational or security risk warrants deploying the patch outside of the routine patching process. The patch plan includes back-out and contingency procedures.
4. ***Approve Emergency Patch***: For emergency patches, business leadership makes the final decision to patch outside of normal procedures, evaluating the overall business risk.
5. ***Deploy Production Patches***: Upon approval, operations proceeds with the patching either using normal operating procedures and maintenance windows, or using the emergency patch plan prepared by engineering.
6. ***Verify Operational Fix***: For emergency patches in particular, engineering reviews the system post-patching to verify the system is operating as expected.
7. ***Verify Security Fix***: For security patches, security reviews the system post-patching to verify the security vulnerabilities of concern have been adequately addressed.

Security Monitoring

- This process is one of the most fundamental enterprise security processes and is a "must-have" for countering modern threats.
  - Process involves designing alerts triggered by likely adversary activity and then using those alerts to identify incidents in the environment.
  - Process should be ongoing, not only to monitor systems and identify incidents, but also to continually refine the alerts to reduce false positives and search for new indicators of compromise (IOC).

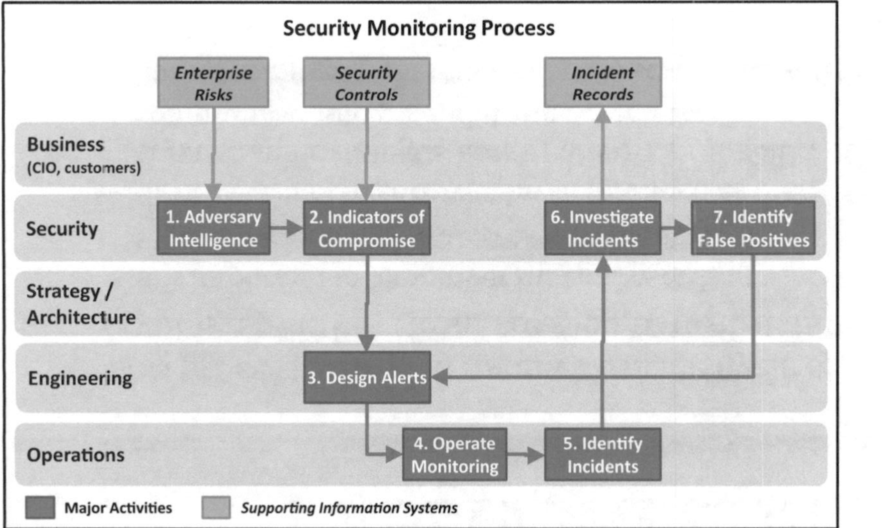

1. ***Adversary Intelligence***: Security needs to understand the adversary threats that should be detected. Threats are considered in terms of the assets they affect and the business consequences should the threats occur. For deliberate attackers, the attackers' tools, techniques, and procedures are considered, if known.
2. ***Indicators of Compromise (IOC)***: From the threat scenarios, security can determine IOC that would indicate attacker activity or events. These indicators may be as simple as an anti-virus alert, or may be sophisticated patterns that can be identified with a correlating log system. These indicators may be automated indicators obtained from an external service or internally deployed analytics technologies.
3. ***Design Alerts***: Based on IOC, engineering designs alerts to be triggered when those indicators are present. The alerts are designed to have a high fidelity, while also to minimize the numbers of "false positives."
4. ***Operate Monitoring***: Alerts are then passed on to IT operations that uses the monitoring capability to detect the alerts when they occur. During daily operations, the alerts are periodically tested to ensure they are functioning properly.
5. ***Identify Incidents***: As monitoring detects alerts, security evaluates these alerts to identify incidents for investigation. A single incident may come from multiple alerts, just as a single alert may be related to multiple incidents. The difference here is that incidents are manually created, while alerts are usually automated.
6. ***Investigate Incidents***: Operations hands off detected incidents to the incident response team, which then follows the cyberintrusion response process to investigate and resolve the incident.
7. ***Identify False Positives***: Some incidents may turn out to be false positives after investigation. Too many false positives may prompt the IT department to modify the alerts to reduce the amount of unnecessary alerting and investigation.

Password and Key Management

- This process is used to manage the life cycle of cryptographic keys from creation to destruction.
  - It is important to remember that passwords are essentially keys that are easy to write down.
  - Keys have life cycles driven by factors such as their cryptographic strength, usage patterns, probability of compromise, and potential attack vectors.
  - Strong cryptographic keys (and passwords) can still be compromised.
  - Detecting compromised keys can be extremely difficult, if not impossible.

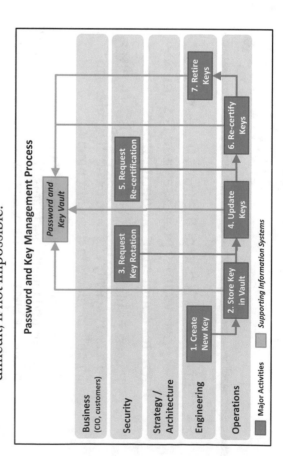

Password and Key Management Process

Password and Key Vault

Business (CIO, customers)

Security

3. Request Key Rotation

5. Request Re-certification

Strategy / Architecture

Engineering

1. Create New Key

7. Retire Keys

Operations

2. Store Key in Vault

4. Update Keys

6. Re-certify Keys

Major Activities

Supporting Information Systems

1. ***Create New Key***: Engineering or operations creates a new key or password. Note this process primarily refers to organizational keys or passwords, although personal accounts can be managed this way if there is a compelling business need.

2. ***Store Key in Vault***: Once the key is created, it is archived for protection. Key can be retrieved and changed when necessary.

3. ***Request Key Rotation***: Keys must be rotated in accordance with security policy. This activity should be audited on a periodic basis.

4. ***Update Keys***: As keys are rotated or otherwise updated, operations updates the key vault to reflect the new key material or password value.

5. ***Request Re-certification***: Security should periodically request re-certification of keys to ensure the keys are still needed and the people responsible for the keys have access to the keys.

6. ***Re-certify Keys***: Key re-certification ensures the keys are still needed, people responsible for the keys have access to the keys, and the corresponding information is up-to-date.

7. ***Retire Keys***: Engineering retires keys at the end of the life cycle or when the system using them is retired.

Account and Access Periodic Re-certification

- This process is used to manage the life cycle of enterprise accounts and permissions.
  - Generally, accounts and accesses are granted when they are needed, so provisioning seldom presents a problem.
  - What is a problem is de-provisioning, where accounts and accesses that are no longer needed are released in a timely fashion.
  - De-provisioning is primarily a function of identity and access management technologies, which are critically important in large organizations.
  - Without these technologies, the same results can be achieved via periodic re-certification / audit of accounts and access to ensure they are de-provisioned, and to check that the most critical privileges are not abused.

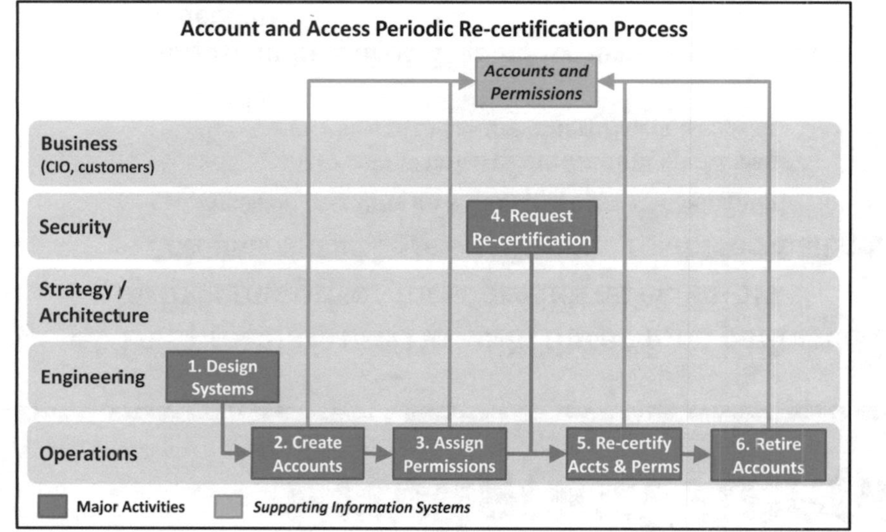

1. ***Design Systems***: Accounts and accesses generally stem from systems that utilize them and the people who need access to those systems. Engineering designs and deploys systems along with associated accounts and access permissions.
2. ***Create Accounts***: Once there are systems that require accounts, operations creates account for access to those systems.
3. ***Assign Permissions***: Operations assigns account permissions for enterprise systems to allow people access. There are three general levels of system permissions.
   - ***Administrators***—Ability to install and configure the computer, database, or application
   - ***Operators***—Ability to manipulate the data, but cannot change application
   - ***Users***—Have unprivileged access to the application and data
4. ***Request Re-certification***: Security ensures accounts and permissions are periodically re-certified so unused account and permissions can be removed. The more decentralized the enterprise is, the harder re-certification process will be.
5. ***Re-certify Accounts and Permissions***: Operations conducts the re-certifications and keeps tracks of accounts and permissions so they can be re-certified in a timely manner.
6. ***Retire Accounts***: Operations de-provisions accounts and accesses that are not longer needed.

Privileged Account Activity Audit

- This process is used to audit the actions performed by the enterprise's most privileged accounts.
  - Accounts should be selected using a risk-based method.
    - Focus on accounts for which there are few safeguards
    - Focus where compromise of the account could result in the compromise of the entire enterprise or a signification portion
  - Robust audit trail of all activities using these accounts is needed.
  - If accounts are compromised, the audit trail cannot be simply "turned off" without being detected.

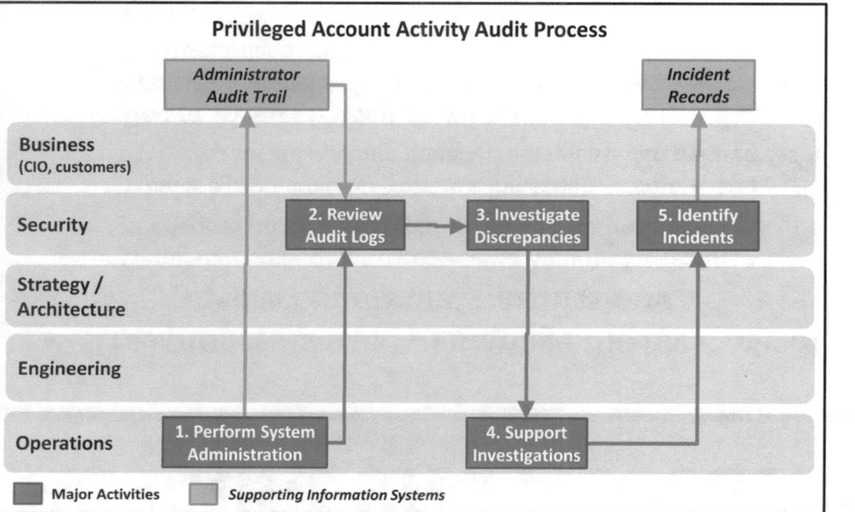

1. ***Perform Systems Administration***: Operations performs systems administration activities that generate, in part,
   - an audit trail of all activities using the privileged accounts; and
   - alerts for security to review certain activities.
2. ***Review Audit Logs***: Security team reviews the activity audit logs, which may reference change records and the configuration management database. Note it is helpful for operations to also get the audit logs so they can perform their own review.
3. ***Investigate Discrepancies***: Security investigates activities that are suspicious or outside of normal patterns. Note that, while it is helpful to enable operations staff to conduct their own review and investigation to properly mitigate insider threats, it is necessary to have a separate team also performing these investigations.
4. ***Support Investigations***: Operations needs to support the investigation process. While they are instrumental in supporting these investigations, it is important to ensure they are not self-auditing, either.
5. ***Identify Incidents***: Investigations that turn up discrepancies generate incidents for follow-up by the CyberIncident Response Team (CIRT), through the cyberintrusion response process.

APPENDIX C

Object Measurement

S. E. Donaldson et al., *Enterprise Cybersecurity Study Guide*, https://doi.org/10.1007/978-1-4842-3258-3_18

Fundamental Principles *(1 of 4)*

- An enterprise wants to protect itself from cybersecurity attacks that are constantly morphing.
- Consequently, *successful enterprise cybersecurity* is a continual improvement exercise designed to address the evolving cyberthreats.
- Measurement is a means for effecting enterprise cybersecurity improvement.
- People often think of cybersecurity
  - from a single perspective such as a manager, technologist, or cybersecurity expert;
  - in terms of a function such as systems administration, network security, or data protection and cryptography; or
  - in terms of a capability such as network isolation, network traffic analysis, or digital certificates.
- However, measuring enterprise cybersecurity effectiveness involves multiple dimensions.
- Mathematical and scientific disciplines often handle multidimensional quantities with entities known as *vectors*.
  - Physics uses vectors to describe many quantities such as displacement, velocity, and acceleration.

Fundamental Principles *(2 of 4)*

- To illustrate from the list of physics quantities, the change in position of a particle is called a *displacement.*
  - When we go to work in the morning, we *displace* ourselves from our home to our place of work.
  - This displacement can be represented as an arrow on a map drawn from home to work.
  - The graphic depicts this displacement concept in one, two, and *n* dimensions.
- Simply stated, the calculated vector ***length*** combines multiple dimensions into a single quantity or ***index***.

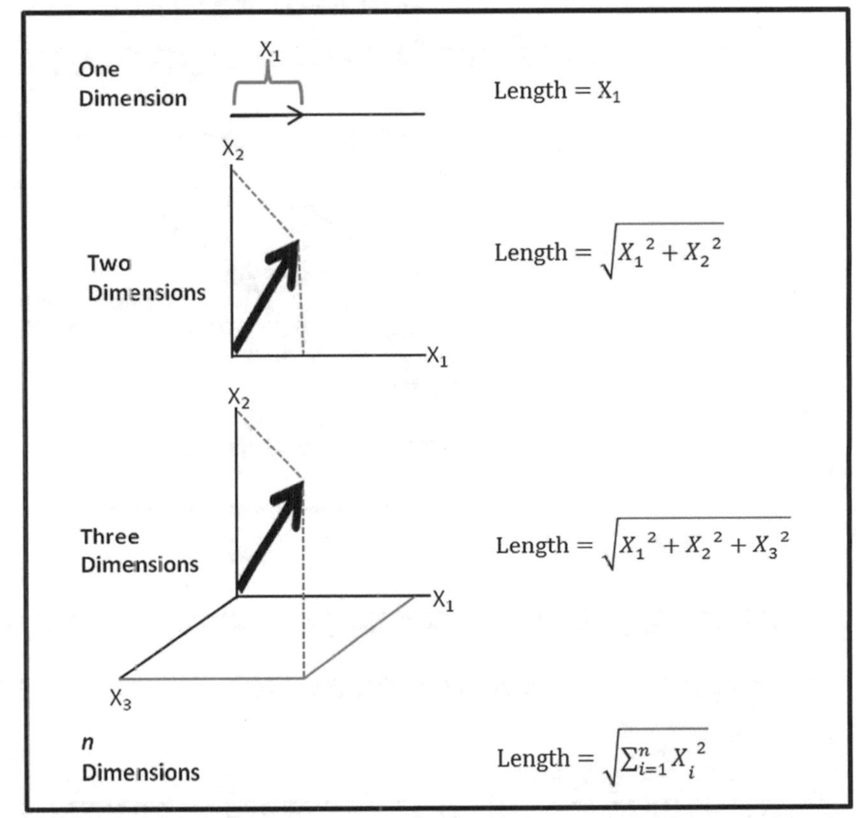

Fundamental Principles *(3 of 4)*

- Object Measurement (OM) uses this notion of an index to measure enterprise cybersecurity effectiveness.
  - The left-hand side of the graphic depicts how OM uses the notion of a vector to derive an overall index.
  - The right-hand side depicts a corresponding example, cybersecurity effectiveness index (CSE*Index*), based on three cybersecurity functional areas.

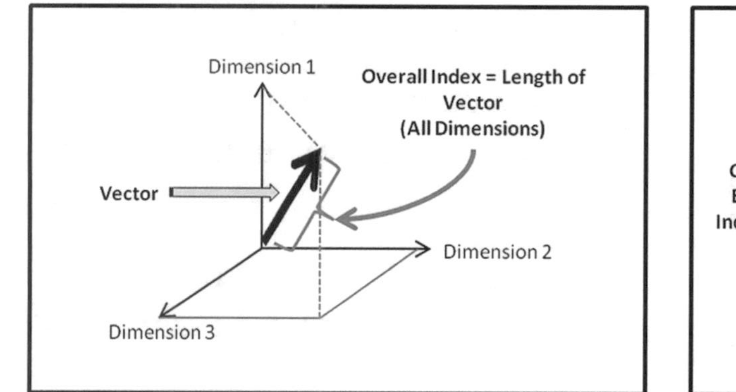

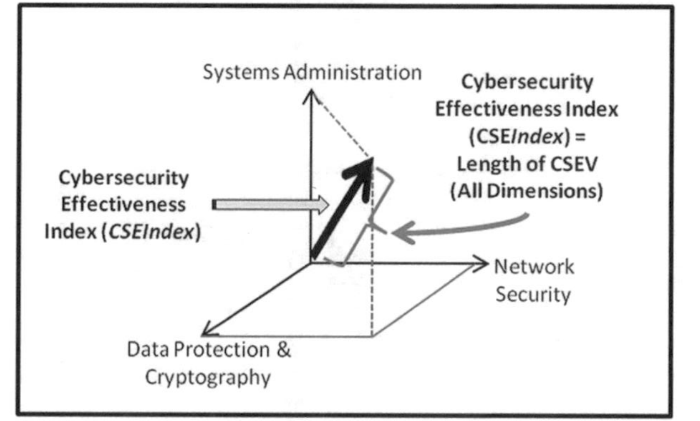

- It is acknowledged the dimensions chosen to fold into this example cybersecurity effectiveness index are not necessarily the same dimensions an enterprise may use.
- There is no one way to measure cybersecurity effectiveness, but there are fundamental principles whose application can increase the likelihood that enterprise cybersecurity programs will be successful.

Fundamental Principles *(4 of 4)*

- As described in the rest of this appendix, OM quantifies almost any object (such as enterprise cybersecurity functional area or capability) in terms of value scales that help tie measurement to familiar enterprise language.
- The graphic notionally depicts OM combining multiple *value scale* measurements into an overall OM*Index* score (in other words, an overall index).

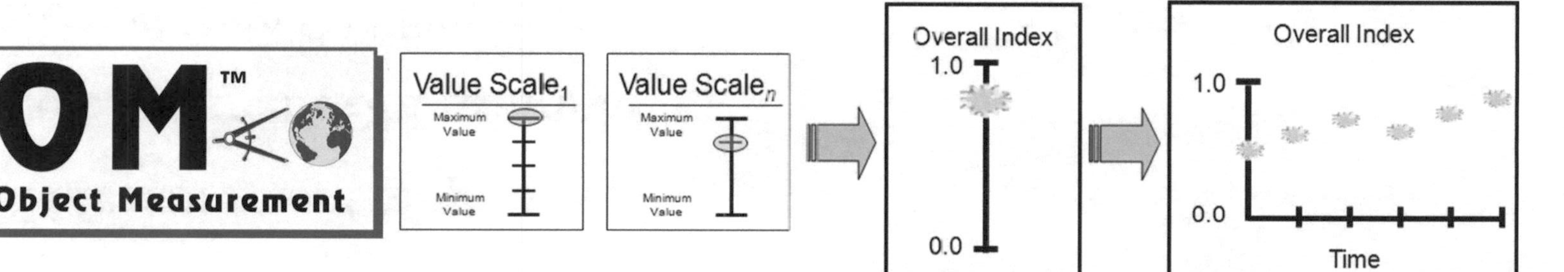

- Although the OM*Index*, like the Consumer Price Index, folds a number of individual measurements into a single quantity, the index can be "unfolded" to gain insight into the underlying measurements.
- Even though OM can measure almost anything, OM is not a measurement silver bullet.

Topics

- OM*Index* Equation
- OM Steps
- OM Value Scales
- OM Measurement Map
- Expert Judgment OM Example
- Observed Data OM Example
- Other Cybersecurity-Related Measurements

OM*Index* Equation *(1 of 2)*

General Equation

- The graphic depicts the general OM*Index* Equation, where vector dimensions are expressed in terms of object attributes.
- Each attribute can be weighted, and there are no mathematical limits to the number of attributes.
- However, keep in mind that enterprise measurement programs will fail if they are too onerous.
- Note that the denominator is set up to normalize the OM*Index*.
  - In other words, restrict the OM*Index* range from zero to one.
- Removing the denominator eliminates this normalization.

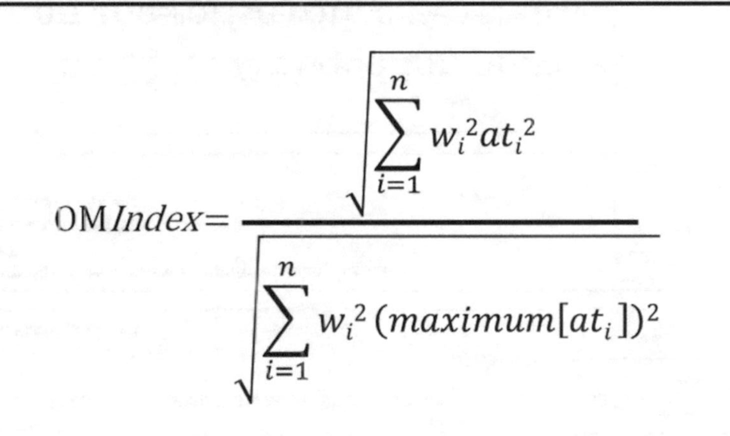

$$\mathrm{OM}\mathit{Index} = \frac{\sqrt{\sum_{i=1}^{n} w_i^2 at_i^2}}{\sqrt{\sum_{i=1}^{n} w_i^2 (maximum[at_i])^2}}$$

where at_i = object attribute measurement
n = number of object attribute measurements
w_i = weighting factor for object attribute at_i
maximum $[at_i]$ = maximum value of at_i

OM*Index* Equation (2 of 2)

Example Equations

- The graphic depicts three examples of how the OM*Index* equation can be used.
- ***Example 1*** represents the case in which an object is characterized by five attributes.
- ***Example 2*** represents the case in which the first attribute is considered twice as important as the other attributes.
- ***Example 3*** represents the case in which the second and third attributes are suppressed.

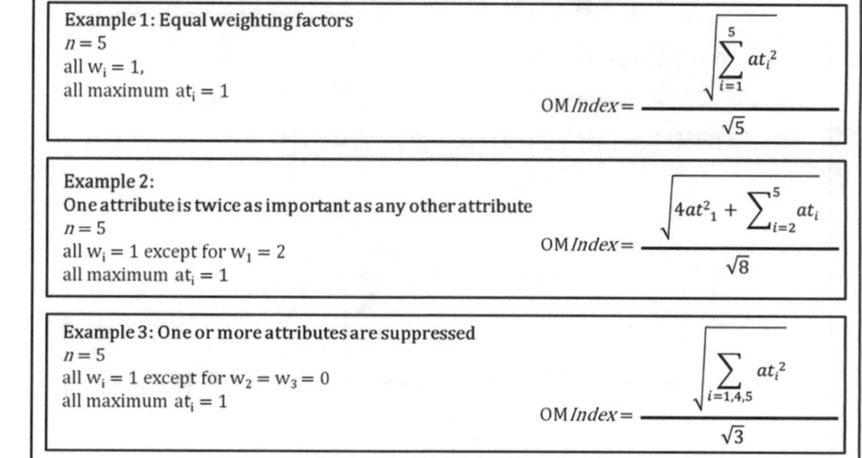

Example 1: Equal weighting factors
$n = 5$
all $w_i = 1$,
all maximum $at_i = 1$
$\text{OM}\mathit{Index} = \dfrac{\sqrt{\sum_{i=1}^{5} at_i^2}}{\sqrt{5}}$
Example 2:
One attribute is twice as important as any other attribute
$n = 5$
all $w_i = 1$ except for $w_1 = 2$
all maximum $at_i = 1$
$\text{OM}\mathit{Index} = \dfrac{\sqrt{4at^2_1 + \sum_{i=2}^{5} at_i}}{\sqrt{8}}$
Example 3: One or more attributes are suppressed
$n = 5$
all $w_i = 1$ except for $w_2 = w_3 = 0$
all maximum $at_i = 1$
$\text{OM}\mathit{Index} = \dfrac{\sqrt{\sum_{i=1,4,5} at_i^2}}{\sqrt{3}}$

- The OM*Index* Equation provides an enterprise with a generalized measurement methodology that can be tailored to specific enterprise measurement requirements.

OM Steps

- OM includes the following steps:
  - ***Step 1***: Define the questions the enterprise wants to answer.
  - ***Step 2***: Select appropriate object(s) to measure for collecting relevant data to answer the defined enterprise questions.
  - ***Step 3***: For each object, define the object characteristics to measure.
  - ***Step 4***: For each characteristic, create a value scale with tick marks and corresponding tick-mark descriptions in plain, unambiguous language.
  - ***Step 5***: Measure each characteristic by (a) using expert judgment to form an opinion and matching the opinion with the appropriate value scale(s) and tick-mark value(s), or (b) matching the observed data with the appropriate value scale(s) and tick-mark value(s).
  - ***Step 6***: Substitute the selected tick-mark numeric values into an appropriate OM equation to calculate the overall index.

OM Value Scales *(1 of 5)*

Fundamental Principles (1 of 2)

- Value scales help associate an enterprise vocabulary (that is, language) with measurement.
- The challenge is to establish value scales to make meaningful measurements.
- For this study guide, ***meaningful*** means "the enterprise uses the measurements to determine whether and where cybersecurity needs to be improved."
- OM value scale types include the following:
  - Discrete
  - Binary
  - Sliding
- Value scales have minimum and maximum numeric values, along with plain language description on the tick-mark labels.

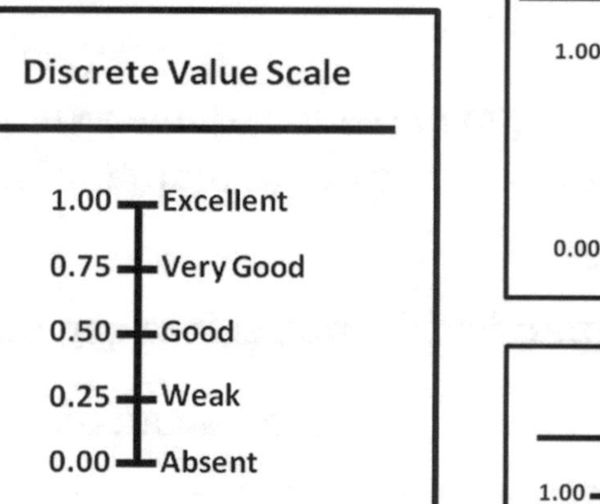

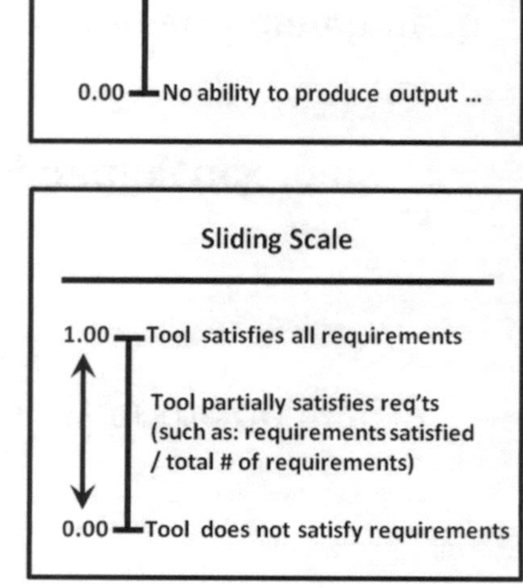

- The numeric range of values is not restricted to zero (0.00) to one (1.00) and can accommodate any numeric range.

OM Value Scales *(2 of 5)*

Fundamental Principles (2 of 2)

- The enterprise decides what terms define its value scales.
- ***Discrete value scales*** allow for *distinct interim* numeric values and corresponding tick-mark labels (for example, 0.00 = Absent; 0.25 = Weak, and so on).
- ***Binary value scales*** are often used to measure *on/off* or *yes/no* or *desired behavior/lack of desired behavior*.
- ***Sliding value scales*** measure a *minimum* numeric value, a *partial* numeric value based on a ratio, and a *maximum* numeric value.
- Value scale ***tick-mark labels*** need to be defined in everyday enterprise language to aid in communicating measurement results.

Discrete Value Scale

1.00 Excellent
0.75 Very Good
0.50 Good
0.25 Weak
0.00 Absent

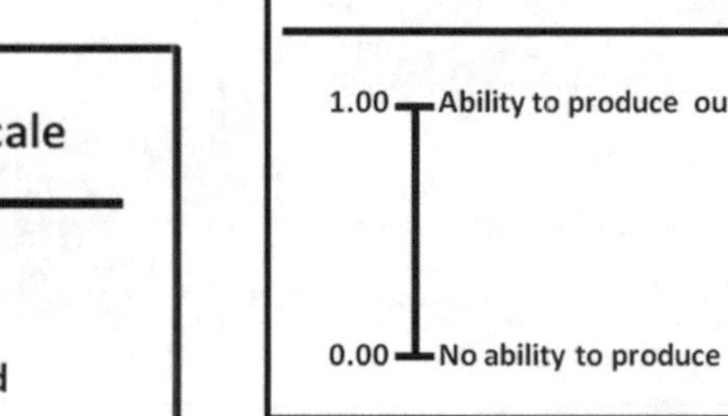

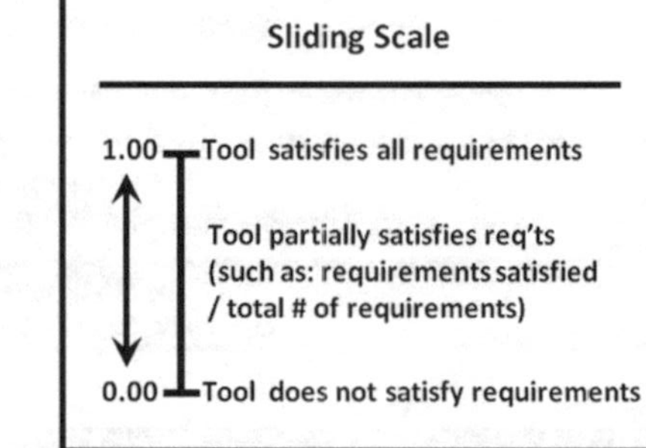

- There is ***no one set of terms*** (that is, numeric values and tick-mark labels) that define value scales.

OM Value Scales *(3 of 5)*

Example Expert Judgment Value Scales (1 of 2)

- Experts have their own experience-based language to describe their area of expertise to non-experts.
- Such language often embodies their educated guesses or intuitive judgment.
- The graphic depicts a value scale defined in expert judgment language for any ***cybersecurity functional area***.
- Expert judgment language may be somewhat "squishy," but it enables the expert to designate a particular value scale tick mark and its corresponding value as appropriate for the situation.
- For example:
  – If an expert thinks a functional area is ***poorly*** supported and has a ***very low level*** of maturity, then the expert would designate ***0.25*** as the appropriate value for the situation.

Any ESCA Functional Area (FA)
(Expert Judgment Value Scale)

- 1.00 – Excellent: FA has most of the capabilities that would be effective against anticipated threats, and those capabilities are very mature and operating properly.
- 0.75 – Very Good: FA has numerous capabilities, and those capabilities have relatively few major issues.
- 0.50 – Good: FA is supported, with important capabilities present, but also with issues that hinder the effectiveness of those capabilities.
- 0.25 – Poor: FA is poorly supported, and has a very low level of maturity.
- 0.00 – Absent: FA has no or very few capabilities present and is ineffective at providing enterprise protection.

Enterprise Cybersecurity Architecture
(Cybersecurity Functional Areas)

- Systems Administration
- Network Security
- Application Security
- Endpoint, Server, and Device Security
- Identity, Authentication, and Access Management
- Data Protection and Cryptography
- Monitoring, Vulnerability, and Patch Management
- High Availability, Disaster Recovery, and Physical Protection
- Incident Response
- Asset Management and Supply Chain
- Policy, Audit, E-Discovery, and Training

OM Value Scales *(4 of 5)*

Example Expert Judgment Value Scales (2 of 2)

- Similarly, the graphic depicts an example of an expert measuring any ***cybersecurity functional area capability***.
- For example:
  - If an expert thinks a functional area capability is ***present***, but with only ***limited utilization*** or ***major issues*** with its design or operation that ***sharply limit*** its effectiveness, then the expert would designate ***0.50*** as the appropriate value for the situation.
- The expert judgment scales described here are not set in stone and may be somewhat ***squishy***.
- Example expert value scales are provided as starting points for consideration.
- Each enterprise needs to create its own ***meaningful*** value scales.

Any ECSA Capability
(Expert Judgment Value Scale)

Value	Description
1.00	Excellent: Capability is present, well-implemented, and being utilized as designed to protect the enterprise.
0.75	Very Good: Capability is present and implemented, but not being fully utilized or the capability is fully-utilized, but has issues with its design or operation.
0.50	Good: Capability is present, but with only limited utilization or major issues with its design or operation that sharply limit its effectiveness.
0.25	Poor: Capability is in a pilot or partially-operational state with very limited functionality or effectiveness.
0.00	Absent: Capability is not present.

Functional Area	Capabilities	
Systems Administration (SA)	• Bastion hosts • Out-of-Band (OOB) management • Network isolation • Integrated Lights-Out (ILO), Keyboard Video Mouse (KVM), and power controls • Virtualization and Storage Area Network (SAN) management	• Separation of administration from services • Multi-factor authentication for Systems Administrators (SAs) • Administrator audit trail(s) • Command logging and analytics
Network Security (NS)	• Switches and routers • Software Defined Networking (SDN) • Domain Name System (DNS) and Dynamic Host Configuration Protocol (DHCP) • Network Time Protocol (NTP) • Network service management • Firewall and virtual machine firewall • Network Intrusion Detection / Network Intrusion Prevention System (IDS / IPS)	• Wireless networking (Wi-Fi) • Packet intercept and capture • Secure Sockets Layer (SSL) intercept • Network Access Control (NAC) • Virtual Private Networking (VPN) and Internet Protocol Security (IPSec) • Network Traffic Analysis (NTA) • Network Data Analytics (NDA)
Application Security (AS)	• E-mail security • Webshell detection • Application firewalls • Database firewalls • Forward proxy and web filters	• Reverse proxy • Data Leakage Protection (DLP) • Secure application and database software development • Software code vulnerability analysis
Endpoint, Server, and Device Security (ESDS)	• Local administrator privilege restrictions • Computer security and logging policies • Endpoint and media encryption • Computer access controls • Forensic imaging support for investigations • Virtual desktop / thin clients • Mobile Device Management (MDM) • Anti-virus / anti-malware	• Application whitelisting • In-memory malware detection • Host firewall and intrusion detection • "Gold code" software images • Security Technical Implementation Guides (STIGs) • Always-on Virtual Private Networking (VPN) • File integrity and change monitoring

OM Value Scales *(5 of 5)*

Example Observed Data Value Scales

- Observed data value scales are similar in structure to expert judgment value scales.
  - Minimum value
  - Maximum value
  - Tick mark labels
- ***However,*** the tick-mark labels represent ***observable events***, also known as "measurement triggers."
- Each tick-mark label can be ***observed*** as opposed to the ***expert judgment*** value scale tick-mark labels.
- The graphic depicts an observed data value scale for a specific capability, ***Virtualization and Storage Area Network Management***.
- As with expert judgment value scales, there is ***no one set of terms*** that defines observed data value scales.

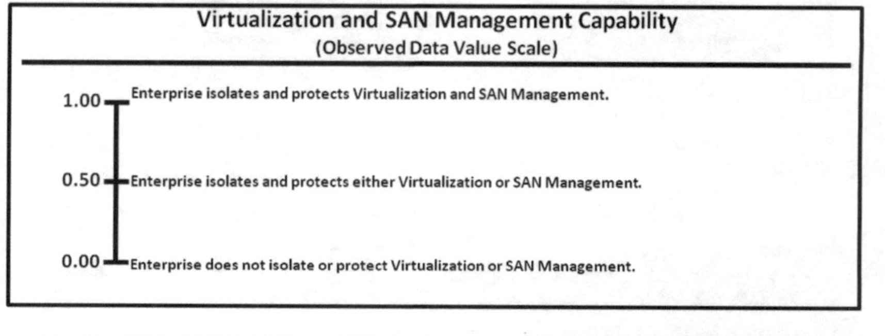
Virtualization and SAN Management Capability
(Observed Data Value Scale)
1.00
Enterprise isolates and protects Virtualization and SAN Management.
0.50
Enterprise isolates and protects either Virtualization or SAN Management.
0.00
Enterprise does not isolate or protect Virtualization or SAN Management.

Functional Area	Capabilities	
Systems Administration (SA)	• Bastion hosts • Out-of-Band (OOB) management • Network isolation • Integrated Lights-Out (ILO), Keyboard Video Mouse (KVM), and power controls • Virtualization and Storage Area Network (SAN) management	• Separation of administration from services • Multi-factor authentication for Systems Administrators (SAs) • Administrator audit trail(s) • Command logging and analytics
Network Security (NS)	• Switches and routers • Software Defined Networking (SDN) • Domain Name System (DNS) and Dynamic Host Configuration Protocol (DHCP) • Network Time Protocol (NTP) • Network service management • Firewall and virtual machine firewall • Network Intrusion Detection / Network Intrusion Prevention System (IDS / IPS)	• Wireless networking (Wi-Fi) • Packet intercept and capture • Secure Sockets Layer (SSL) intercept • Network Access Control (NAC) • Virtual Private Networking (VPN) and Internet Protocol Security (IPSec) • Network Traffic Analysis (NTA) • Network Data Analytics (NDA)
Application Security (AS)	• E-mail security • Webshell detection • Application firewalls • Database firewalls • Forward proxy and web filters	• Reverse proxy • Data Leakage Protection (DLP) • Secure application and database software development • Software code vulnerability analysis
Endpoint, Server, and Device Security (ESDS)	• Local administrator privilege restrictions • Computer security and logging policies • Endpoint and media encryption • Computer access controls • Forensic imaging support for investigations • Virtual desktop / thin clients • Mobile Device Management (MDM) • Anti-virus / anti-malware	• Application whitelisting • In-memory malware detection • Host firewall and intrusion detection • "Gold code" software images • Security Technical Implementation Guides (STIGs) • Always-on Virtual Private Networking (VPN) • File integrity and change monitoring

OM Measurement Map *(1 of 2)*

Basic Structure

- To help define and organize value scales for an object to be measured, it is convenient to create an OM measurement map.
- The graphic depicts two generic measurement maps that can be used in concert with the OM Six-Step Methodology.
  - The upper half of the graphic depicts Object A in terms of a number of characteristics and value scales.
  - The lower half of the graphic depicts Object B in terms of a number of characteristics, sub-characteristics, and value scales.
- Measurement maps define value scales at the lowest level (far right-hand side of map).

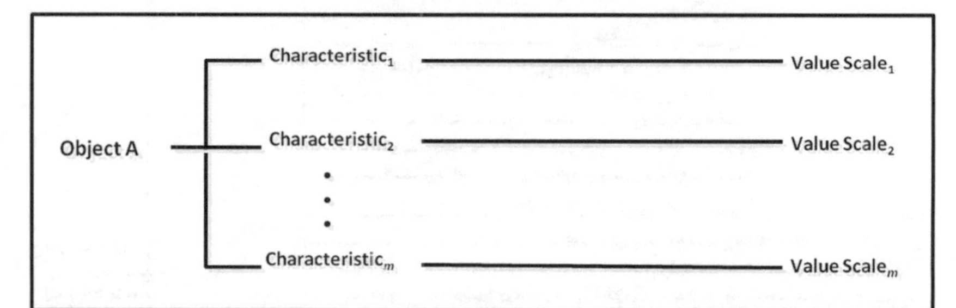

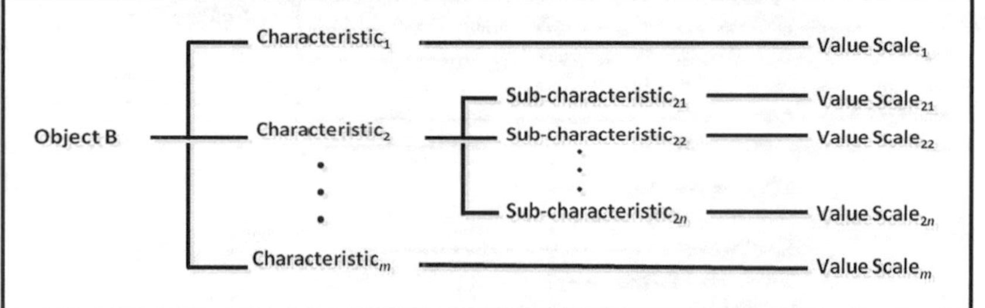

- A measurement map helps define objects in unambiguous terms and represents, in part, the scope of what is to be measured.
- The defined objects, via value scales, provide a consistent measurement vocabulary.

OM Measurement Map *(2 of 2)*

Example Enterprise Cybersecurity Program Assessment Measurement Map

- The graphic depicts an example measurement map established for conducting an enterprise cybersecurity program assessment.
- Assessment is structured and scoped, in part, by the following components:
  - ***Risk mitigations*** associated with a cyberattack sequence
  - ***Functional areas*** defined in terms of enterprise cybersecurity capabilities
  - ***Security operations*** associated with enterprise day-to-day security activities

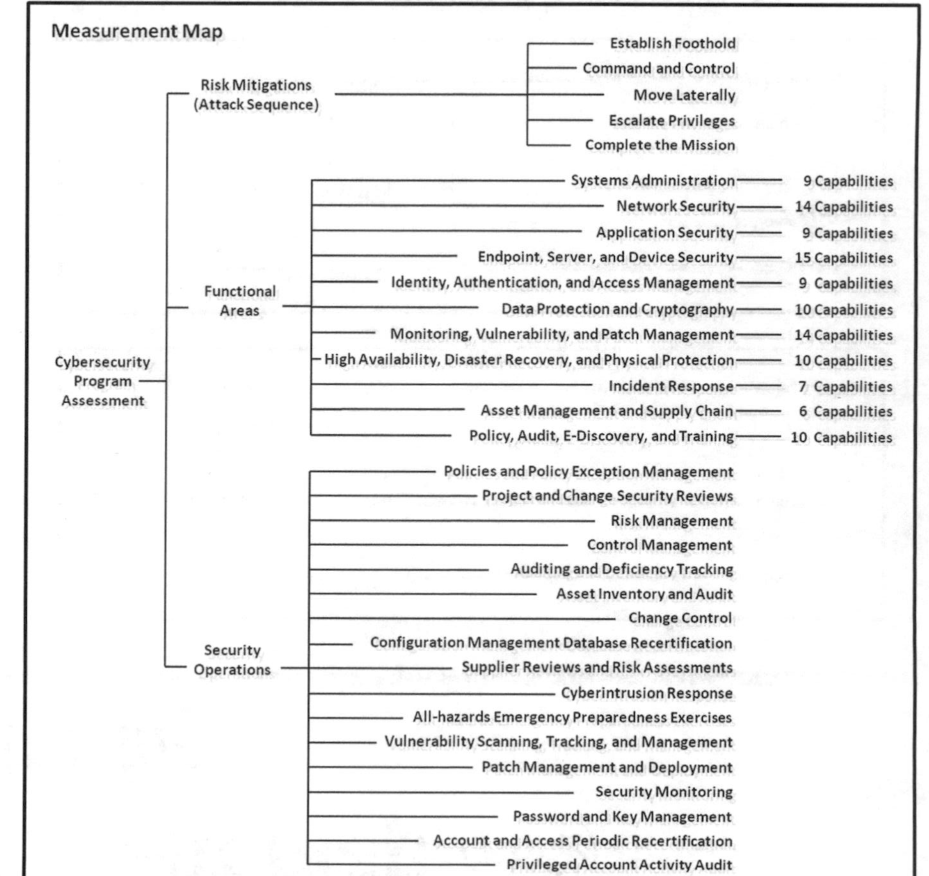

Expert Judgment OM Example *(1 of 8)*

OM Six-Step Methodology

- ***Step 1***: Define the questions the enterprise wants to answer.
  - *How effective is the current enterprise security posture?*
- ***Step 2***: Select appropriate object(s) to measure for collecting relevant data to answer the defined enterprise questions.
  - *Enterprise Cybersecurity Effectiveness depends on the selection of appropriate objects to defend the enterprise against cyberattacks.*
- ***Step 3***: For each object, define the object characteristics to measure.
  - *Enterprise cybersecurity effectiveness has the following 11 functional areas that will be the characteristics for measurement.*

Cybersecurity Functional Areas
• Systems Administration
• Network Security
• Application Security
• Endpoint, Server, and Device Security
• Identity, Authentication, and Access Management
• Data Protection and Cryptography
• Monitoring, Vulnerability, and Patch Management
• High Availability, Disaster Recovery, and Physical Protection
• Incident Response
• Asset Management and Supply Chain
• Policy, Audit, E-Discovery, and Training

Expert Judgment OM Example *(2 of 8)*

OM Six-Step Methodology

- ***Step 4***: For each characteristic, create a value scale with tick marks and corresponding tick-mark descriptions in plain, unambiguous language.
  - *Use the cybersecurity functional area value scale below to define expert judgment value scales for the 11 cybersecurity functional areas.*

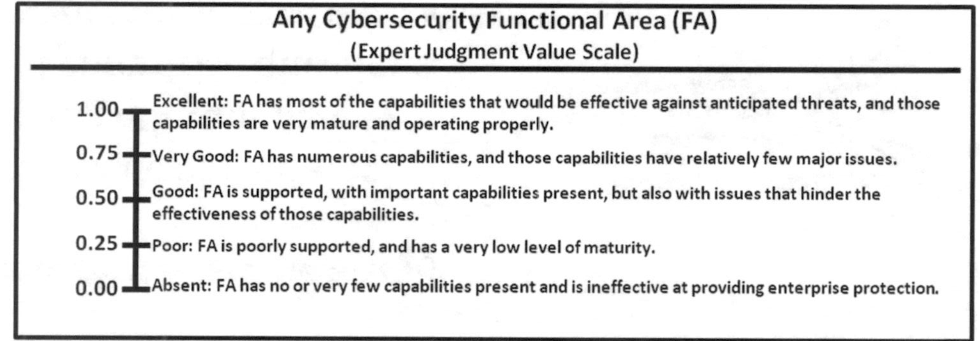
Any Cybersecurity Functional Area (FA)
(Expert Judgment Value Scale)
1.00
Excellent: FA has most of the capabilities that would be effective against anticipated threats, and those capabilities are very mature and operating properly.
0.75
Very Good: FA has numerous capabilities, and those capabilities have relatively few major issues.
0.50
Good: FA is supported, with important capabilities present, but also with issues that hinder the effectiveness of those capabilities.
0.25
Poor: FA is poorly supported, and has a very low level of maturity.
0.00
Absent: FA has no or very few capabilities present and is ineffective at providing enterprise protection.

Expert Judgment OM Example *(3 of 8)*

OM Six-Step Methodology

- ***Step 4 (continued)***
  - *The graphic shows expert judgment value scales.*

  Excellent: FA[1] has most of the capabilities that would be effective against anticipated threats, and those capabilities are very mature and operating properly.

  Very Good: FA has numerous capabilities, and those capabilities have relatively few major issues.

  Good: FA is supported, with important capabilities present, but also with issues that hinder the effectiveness of those capabilities.

  Poor: FA is poorly supported, and has a very low level of maturity.

  Absent: FA has no or very few capabilities present and is ineffective at providing enterprise protection.

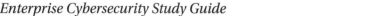

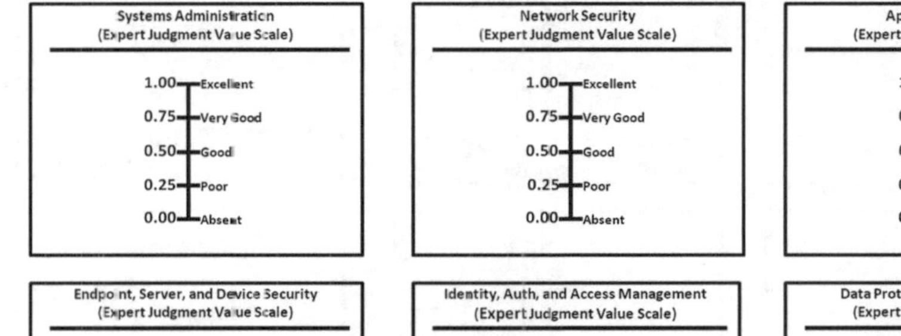
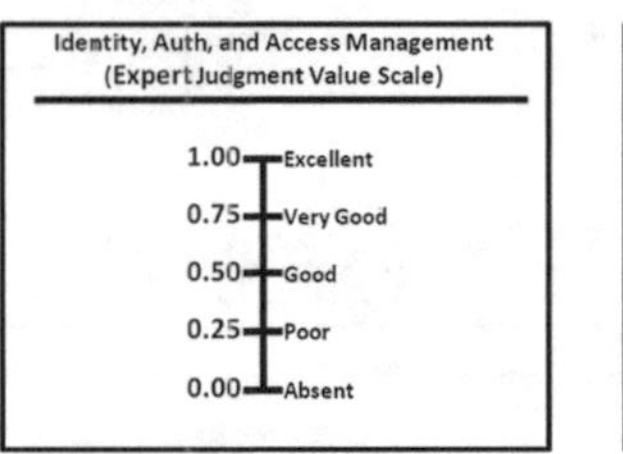
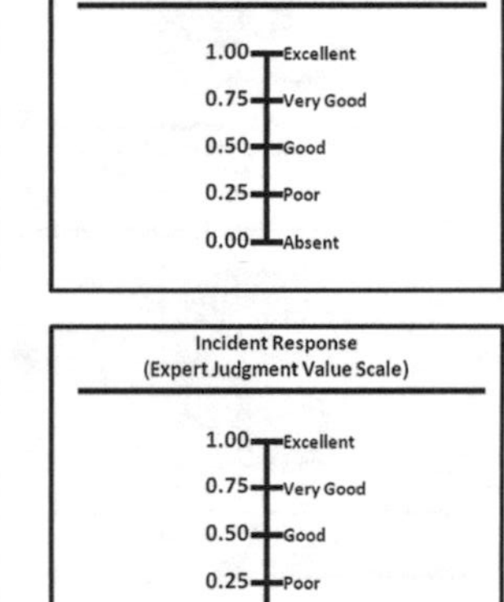
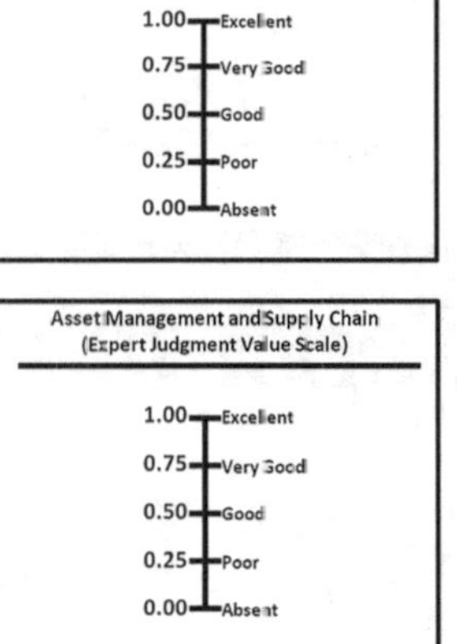
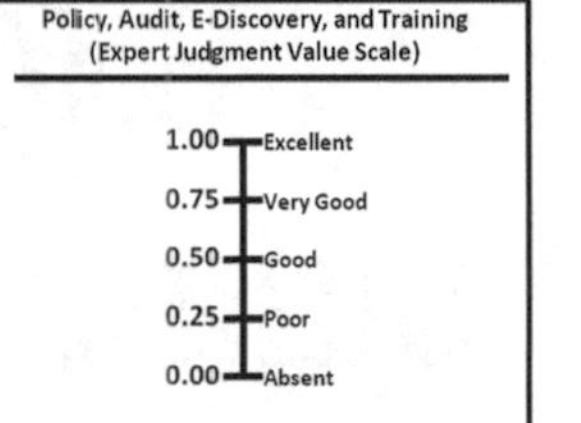

[1]**FA** = Functional area

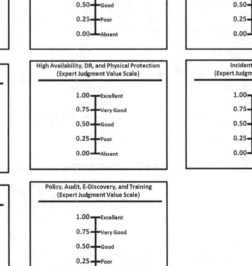

Expert Judgment OM Example *(4 of 8)*

OM Six-Step Methodology

- ***Step 5***: Measure each characteristic (in other words, 11 enterprise cybersecurity functional areas) by using expert judgment to form an opinion and matching the opinion with the appropriate value scale and tick-mark values.
  - *The graphic shows value scales with example expert judgment measurements indicated by circled values.*

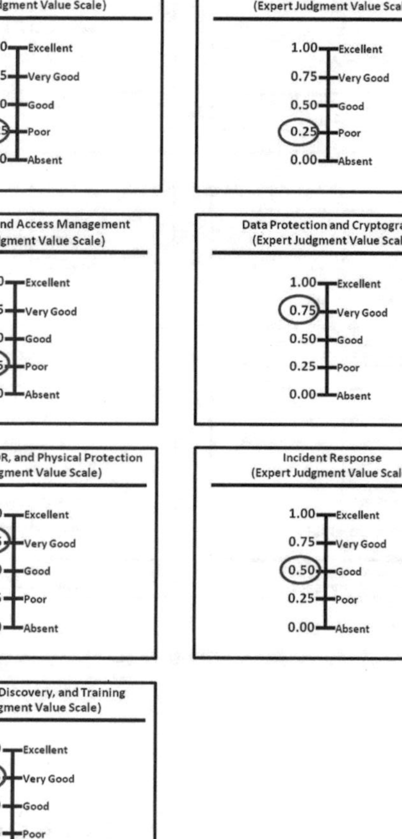
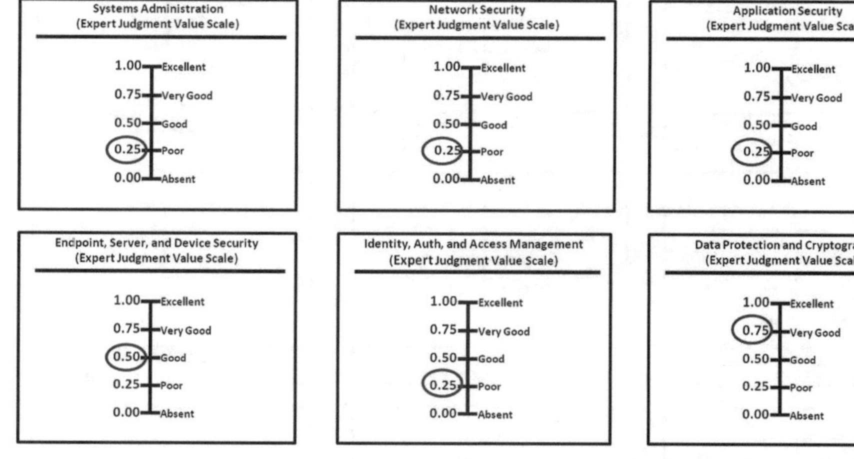
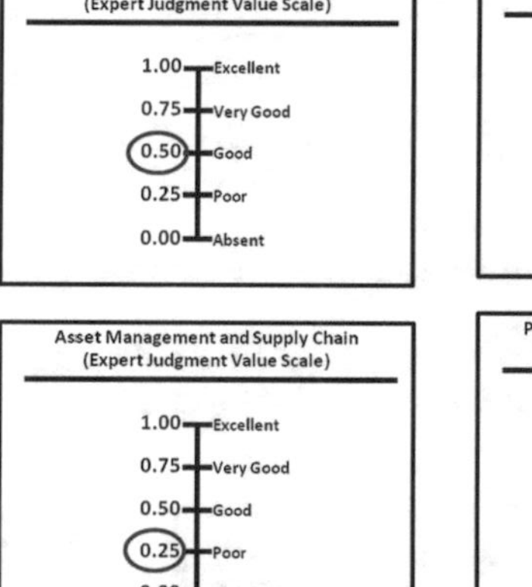

Expert Judgment OM Example *(5 of 8)*

OM Six-Step Methodology

- ***Step 6***: Substitute the selected tick-mark numeric values into an appropriate OM equation to calculate an overall index.
  - *Once the functional areas have been scored, the measurements can be aggregated together into an Object Measurement Index.*
  - *For this example, the upper graphic shows the expert judgment Cybersecurity Effectiveness Index,* CSE*Index.*
  - *The resulting* CSE*Index = 0.52,*[2] *which is greater than "good" and less than "very good."*
  - *The lower graphic illustrates one way to visualize* CSE*Index = 0.52.*

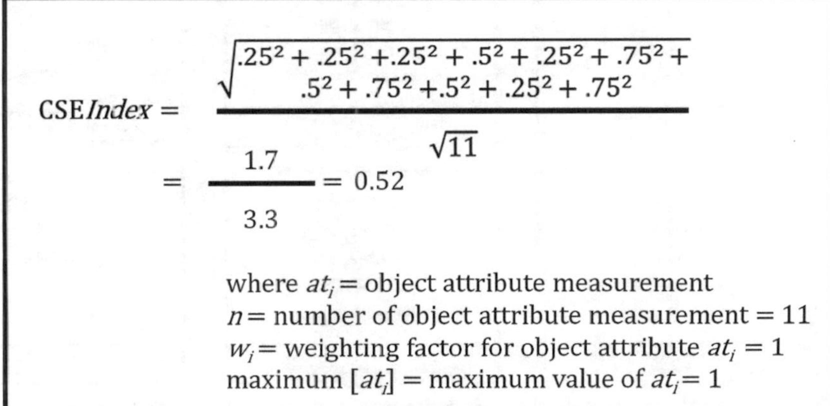

$$\text{CSE}\mathit{Index} = \frac{\sqrt{.25^2 + .25^2 + .25^2 + .5^2 + .25^2 + .75^2 + .5^2 + .75^2 + .5^2 + .25^2 + .75^2}}{\sqrt{11}}$$

$$= \frac{1.7}{3.3} = 0.52$$

where at_i = object attribute measurement
n = number of object attribute measurement = 11
w_i = weighting factor for object attribute $at_i = 1$
maximum $[at_i]$ = maximum value of $at_i = 1$

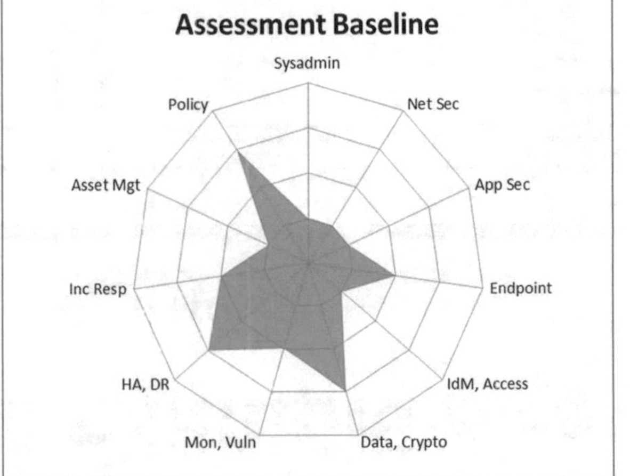

[2]Due to a rounding error in the companion *Enterprise Cybersecurity* book, this CSE*Index* value of 0.52 is different than the CSE*Index* value of 0.48 found on page 394 (***Figure F-11***) and page 396 (***Figure F-14***).

Expert Judgment OM Example *(6 of 8)*

OM Six-Step Methodology

- Value Scales can be used to visualize changes in cybersecurity functional area effectiveness over time.
- Since measurement is used, in part, to increase cybersecurity effectiveness, assume
  - the enterprise implemented an improvement program based on the measurement results; and
  - some time has elapsed after the original measurements were taken.
- *New expert judgment measurements (green ellipses and dashed arrows) were recorded after the cybersecurity improvements were implemented for 9 of 11 functional areas.*

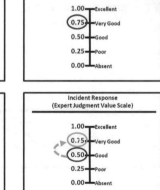

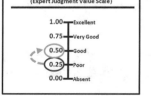

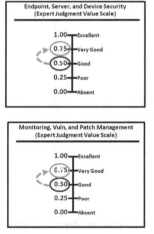

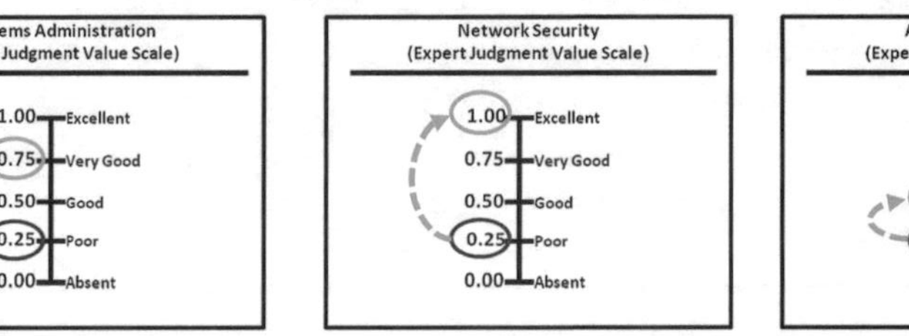
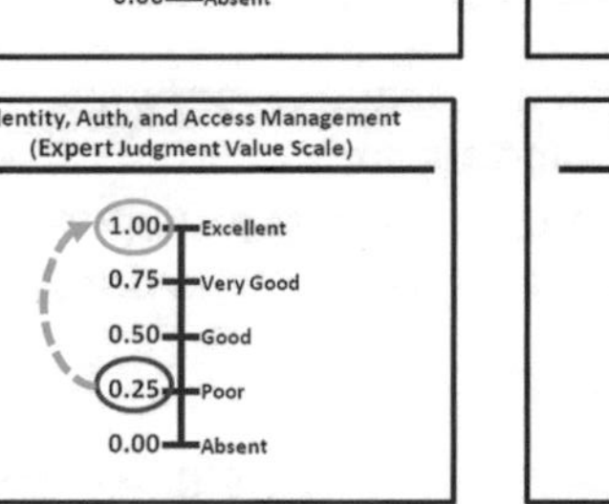
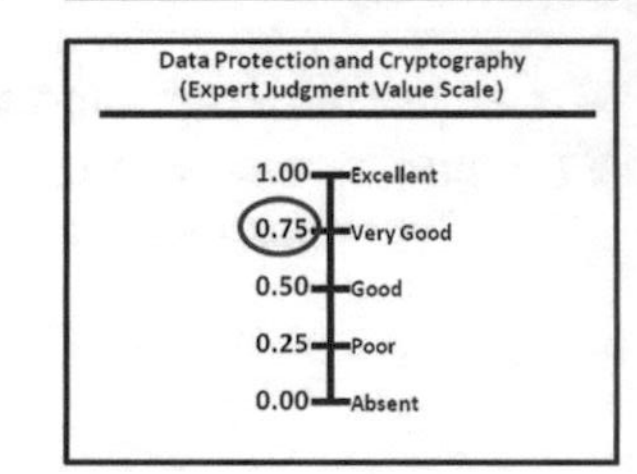
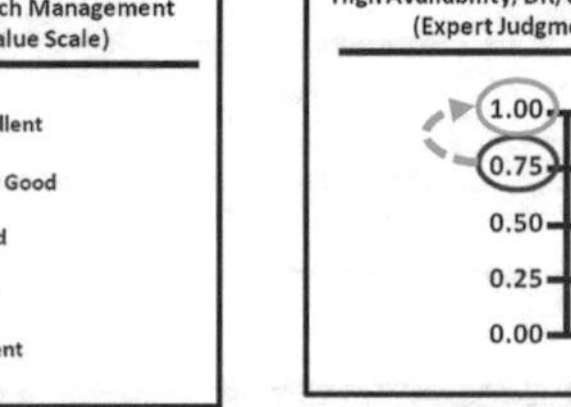
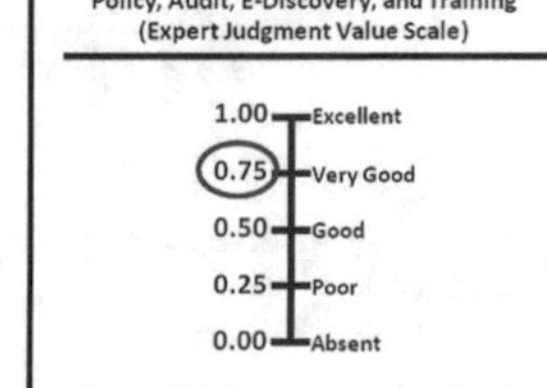
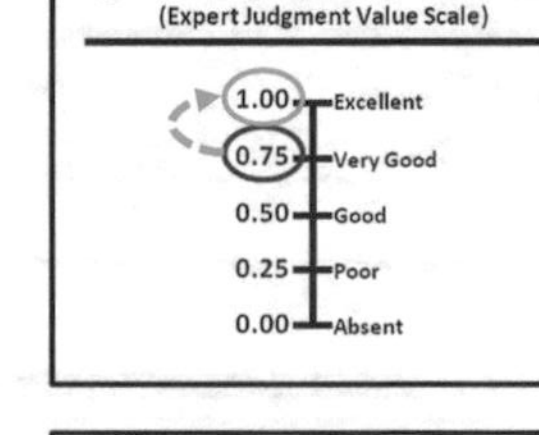
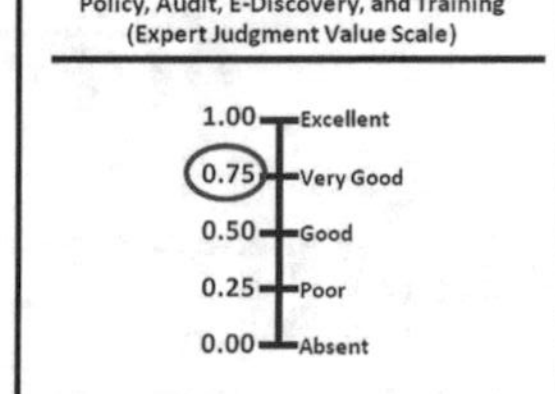
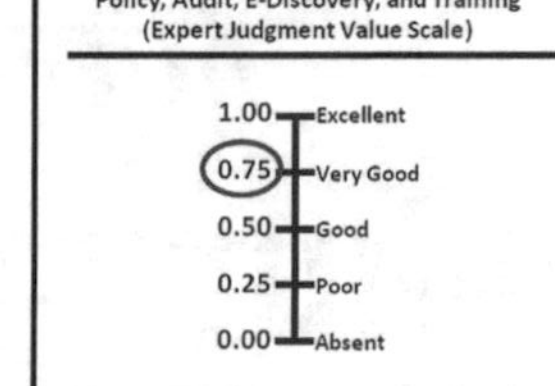

Expert Judgment OM Example *(7 of 8)*

OM Six-Step Methodology

- The OM equation can then be used to calculate an updated overall index to reflect changes in cybersecurity functional area effectiveness over time.
- ***Repeat Step 6***: Substitute the updated selected tick-mark numeric values into an appropriate OM equation to calculate an overall index.
  - *For this example, the upper graphic shows the expert judgment Cybersecurity Effectiveness Index, CSEIndex.*
  - *The resulting* CSE*Index = 0.79, which is greater than "very good" and less than "excellent."*
  - *The lower graphic illustrates one way to visualize* CSE*Index = 0.79.*

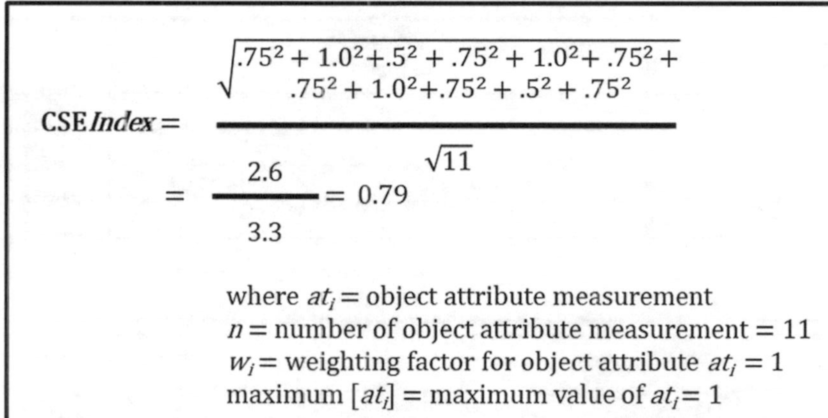

$$\text{CSE}\mathit{Index} = \frac{\sqrt{.75^2 + 1.0^2 + .5^2 + .75^2 + 1.0^2 + .75^2 + .75^2 + 1.0^2 + .75^2 + .5^2 + .75^2}}{\sqrt{11}}$$

$$= \frac{2.6}{3.3} = 0.79$$

where at_i = object attribute measurement
n = number of object attribute measurement = 11
w_i = weighting factor for object attribute $at_i = 1$
maximum $[at_i]$ = maximum value of $at_i = 1$

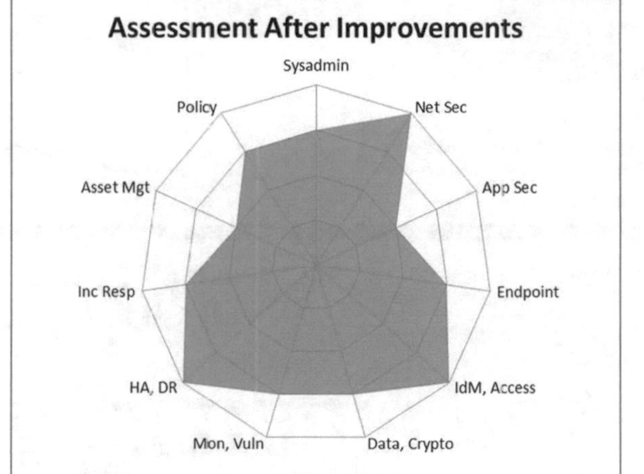

Expert Judgment OM Example *(8 of 8)*

OM Six-Step Methodology

- The top graphic depicts the expert judgment measurement results.
  - Original (or baseline) measurements, where CSE*Index* = 0.52
  - Updated measurements after improvements, where CSE*Index* = 0.79
- The bottom graphic depicts cybersecurity assessment results tracked over time and helps to communicate results of specific infrastructure investments.

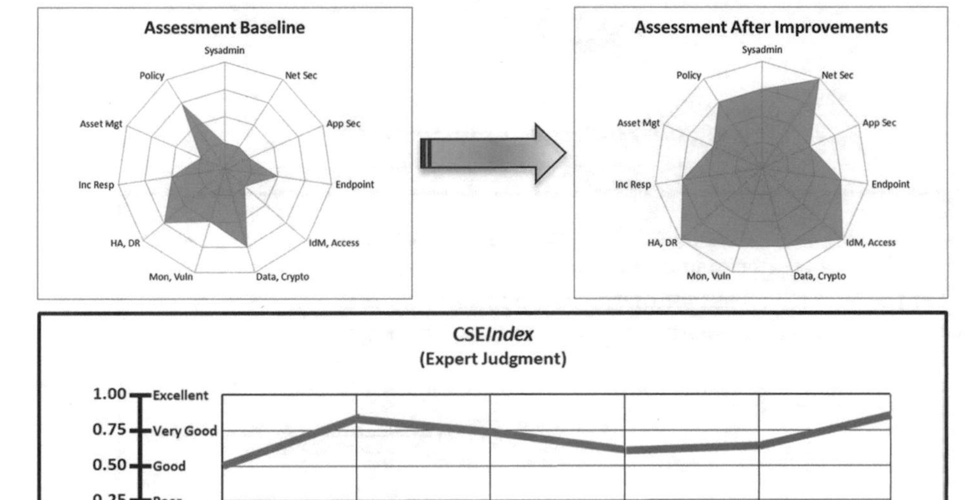

- The OM*Index* Equation provides direct linkage between the defined functional area value scales and an expert's judgment.
- This expressed linkage is tied to enterprise cybersecurity improvement activities.
- By tracking CSE*Index* over time, the enterprise has a means for using expert judgment to guide its ongoing cyberdefense improvement activities.

Observed Data OM Example *(1 of 8)*

OM Six-Step Methodology

- The next set of pages describe an observed data example, examining a single functional area and its capabilities
- ***Step 1***: Define the questions the enterprise wants to answer.
  - *How effective is the current systems administration functional area?*
- ***Step 2***: Select appropriate object(s) to measure for collecting relevant data to answer the defined enterprise questions.
  - *Systems Administration effectiveness in defending the enterprise against cyberattacks.*
- ***Step 3***: For each object, define the object's characteristics.

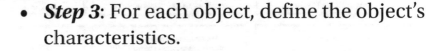

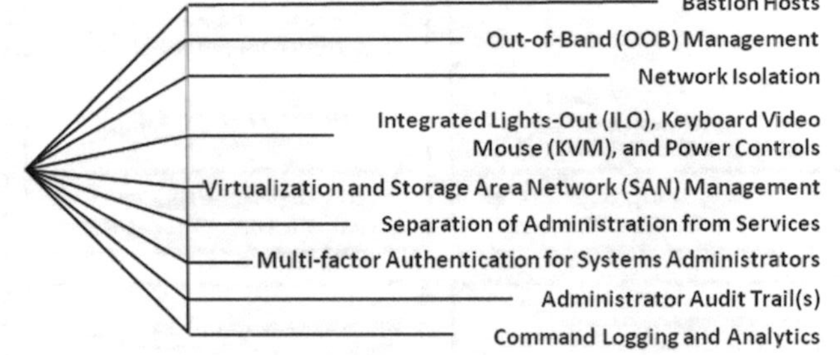

  - *This step is different from the expert judgment measurement example as nine individual Systems Administration capabilities are to be measured vs. the eleven enterprise cybersecurity functional areas.*

Observed Data OM Example *(2 of 8)*

OM Six-Step Methodology

- ***Step 4***: For each characteristic, create a value scale with tick marks and corresponding tick-mark descriptions in plain, unambiguous language.
  - *The graphic shows observed data cybersecurity capability value scales for Systems Administration.*

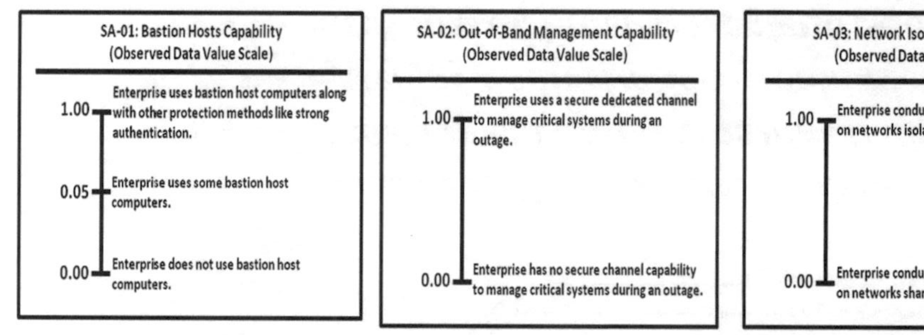
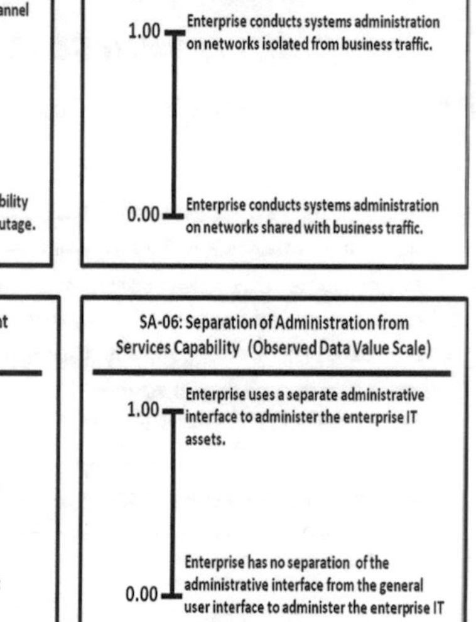
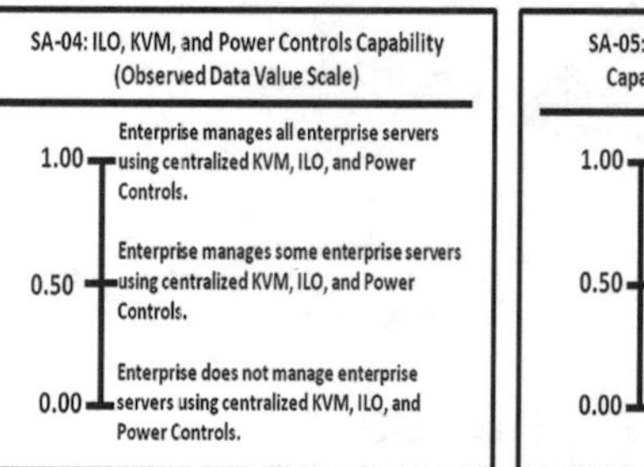
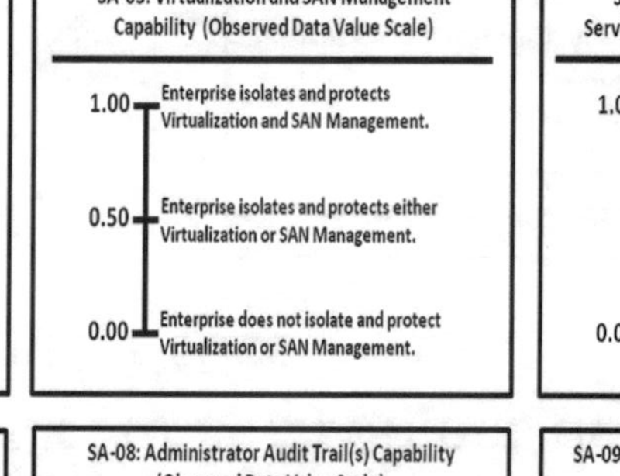
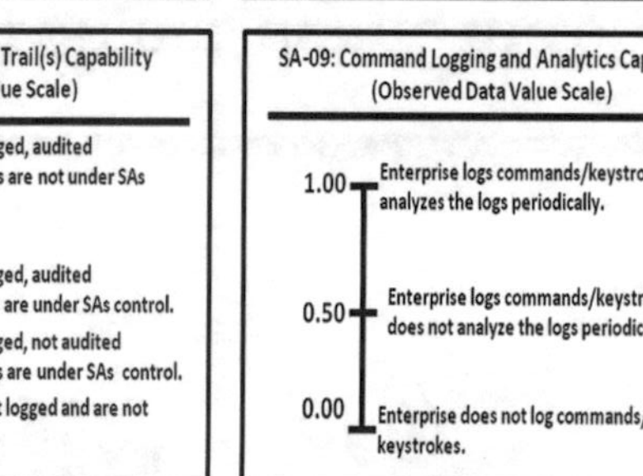
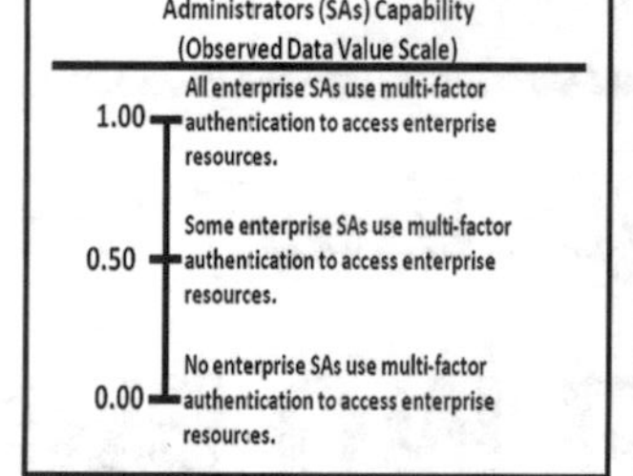
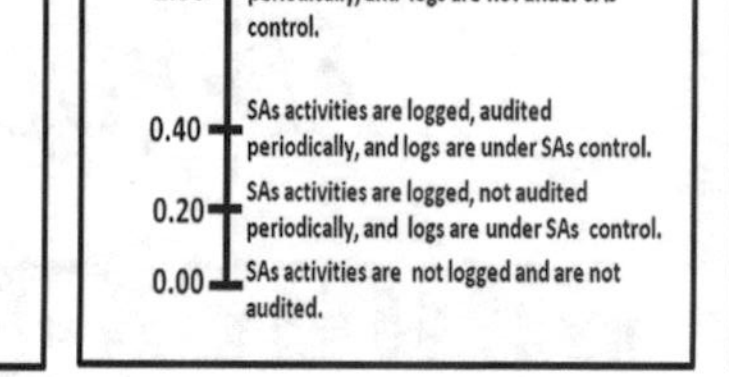

SA-01: Bastion Hosts Capability (Observed Data Value Scale)
1.00 Enterprise uses bastion host computers along with other protection methods like strong authentication.
0.05 Enterprise uses some bastion host computers.
0.00 Enterprise does not use bastion host computers.
SA-02: Out-of-Band Management Capability (Observed Data Value Scale)
1.00 Enterprise uses a secure dedicated channel to manage critical systems during an outage.
0.00 Enterprise has no secure channel capability to manage critical systems during an outage.
SA-03: Network Isolation Capability (Observed Data Value Scale)
1.00 Enterprise conducts systems administration on networks isolated from business traffic.
0.00 Enterprise conducts systems administration on networks shared with business traffic.
SA-04: ILO, KVM, and Power Controls Capability (Observed Data Value Scale)
1.00 Enterprise manages all enterprise servers using centralized KVM, ILO, and Power Controls.
0.50 Enterprise manages some enterprise servers using centralized KVM, ILO, and Power Controls.
0.00 Enterprise does not manage enterprise servers using centralized KVM, ILO, and Power Controls.
SA-05: Virtualization and SAN Management Capability (Observed Data Value Scale)
1.00 Enterprise isolates and protects Virtualization and SAN Management.
0.50 Enterprise isolates and protects either Virtualization or SAN Management.
0.00 Enterprise does not isolate and protect Virtualization or SAN Management.
SA-06: Separation of Administration from Services Capability (Observed Data Value Scale)
1.00 Enterprise uses a separate administrative interface to administer the enterprise IT assets.
0.00 Enterprise has no separation of the administrative interface from the general user interface to administer the enterprise IT assets.
SA-07: Multi-factor Authentication for Systems Administrators (SAs) Capability (Observed Data Value Scale)
1.00 All enterprise SAs use multi-factor authentication to access enterprise resources.
0.50 Some enterprise SAs use multi-factor authentication to access enterprise resources.
0.00 No enterprise SAs use multi-factor authentication to access enterprise resources.
SA-08: Administrator Audit Trail(s) Capability (Observed Data Value Scale)
1.00 SAs activities are logged, audited periodically, and logs are not under SAs control.
0.40 SAs activities are logged, audited periodically, and logs are under SAs control.
0.20 SAs activities are logged, not audited periodically, and logs are under SAs control.
0.00 SAs activities are not logged and are not audited.
SA-09: Command Logging and Analytics Capability (Observed Data Value Scale)
1.00 Enterprise logs commands/keystrokes and analyzes the logs periodically.
0.50 Enterprise logs commands/keystrokes but does not analyze the logs periodically.
0.00 Enterprise does not log commands/ keystrokes.

Observed Data OM Example *(3 of 8)*

OM Six-Step Methodology

- ***Step 5***: Measure each characteristic (in other words, nine Systems Administration capabilities) by matching the observed data with the appropriate systems administration capability value scales and tick-mark values.
  - *The graphic shows value scales with example observed data measurements indicated by circled values.*

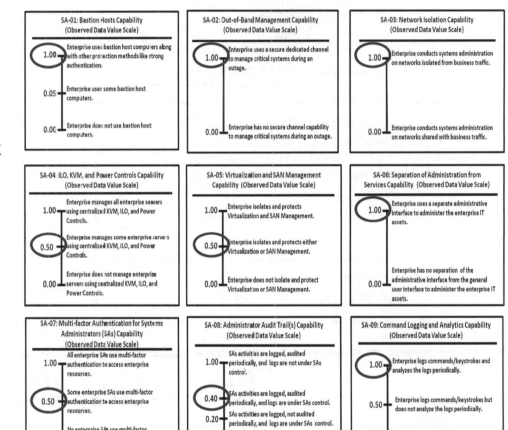

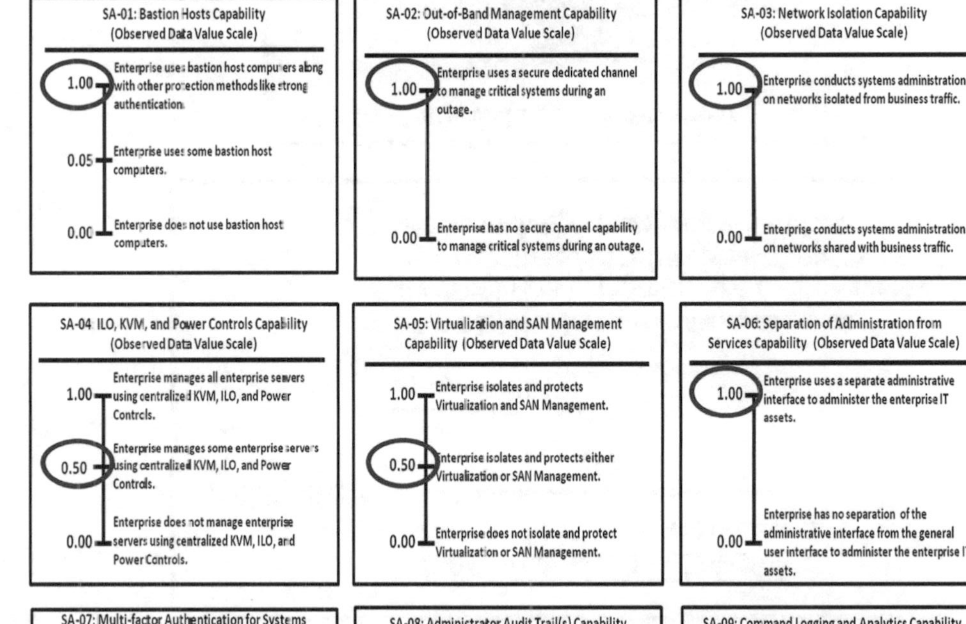

Observed Data OM Example *(4 of 8)*

OM Six-Step Methodology

- ***Step 6***: Substitute the selected tick-mark numeric values into an appropriate OM equation to calculate an overall index.
  - *Once the Systems Administration capabilities have been scored, the measurements can be aggregated together into an Object Measurement Index.*
  - *For this example, the upper graphic shows the observed data Systems Administration Effectiveness Index, SACSEIndex.*
  - *The resulting* SACSE*Index = 0.81.*
  - *The lower graphic illustrates one way to visualize* SACSE*Index = 0.81.*

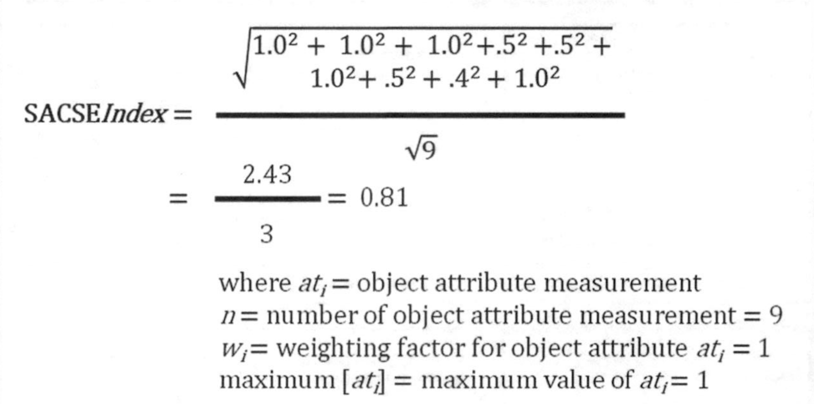

$$\text{SACSE}\mathit{Index} = \frac{\sqrt{1.0^2 + 1.0^2 + 1.0^2 + .5^2 + .5^2 + 1.0^2 + .5^2 + .4^2 + 1.0^2}}{\sqrt{9}}$$
$$= \frac{2.43}{3} = 0.81$$
where at_i = object attribute measurement
n = number of object attribute measurement = 9
w_i = weighting factor for object attribute $at_i = 1$
maximum $[at_i]$ = maximum value of $at_i = 1$

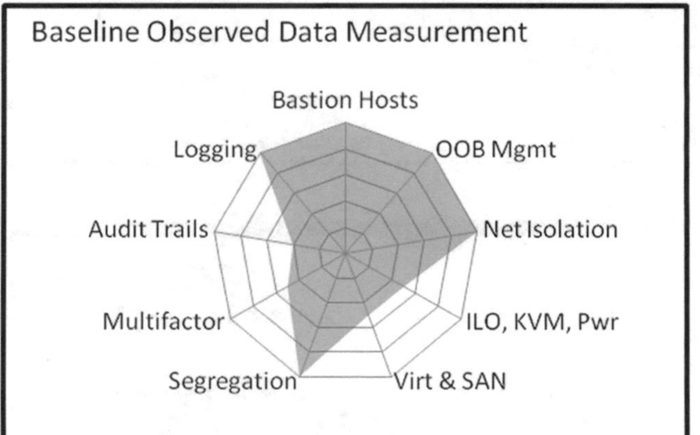

Observed Data OM Example *(5 of 8)*

OM Six-Step Methodology

- What does 0.81 mean?
  Systems Administration Cybersecurity Effectiveness is exactly what was observed (in other words, the observed data) as follows:
  - *Enterprise uses Bastion Host computers along with other protection methods such as strong authentication.*
  - *Enterprise uses a secure, dedicated channel to manage critical systems during an outage.*
  - *Enterprise conducts systems administration on networks isolated from business traffic.*
  - *Enterprise manages some enterprise servers using centralized KVM, ILO, and Power Controls.*
  - *Enterprise isolates and protects either Virtualization or SAN Management.*

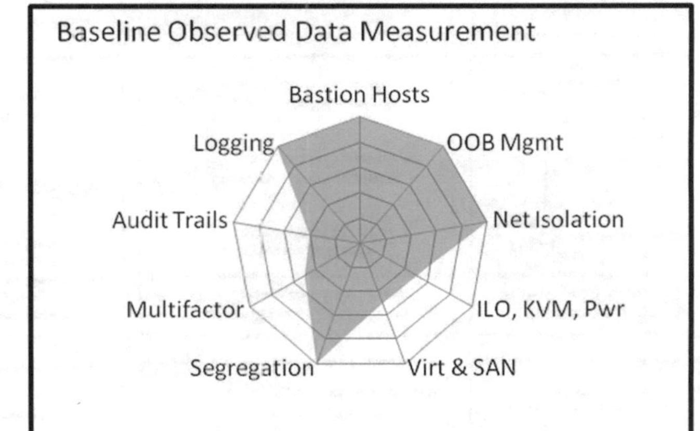

  - *Enterprise uses a separate administrative interface to administer the enterprise IT assets.*
  - *Some enterprise Systems Administrators (SAs) use multifactor authentication to access enterprise resources.*
  - *SAs activities are logged and audited periodically, and logs are under SA control.*
  - *Enterprise logs commands/keystrokes and analyzes the logs periodically.*

Observed Data OM Example *(6 of 8)*

OM Six-Step Methodology

- Value Scales can be used to visualize changes in cybersecurity capability effectiveness over time.
- Since measurement is used, in part, to increase cybersecurity effectiveness, assume
  - the enterprise implemented an improvement program based on the measurement results; and
  - some time has elapsed after the original measurements were taken.
- *New observed data measurements (green ellipses and dashed arrows) were recorded after the cybersecurity improvements were implemented for 2 of 9 capabilities.*

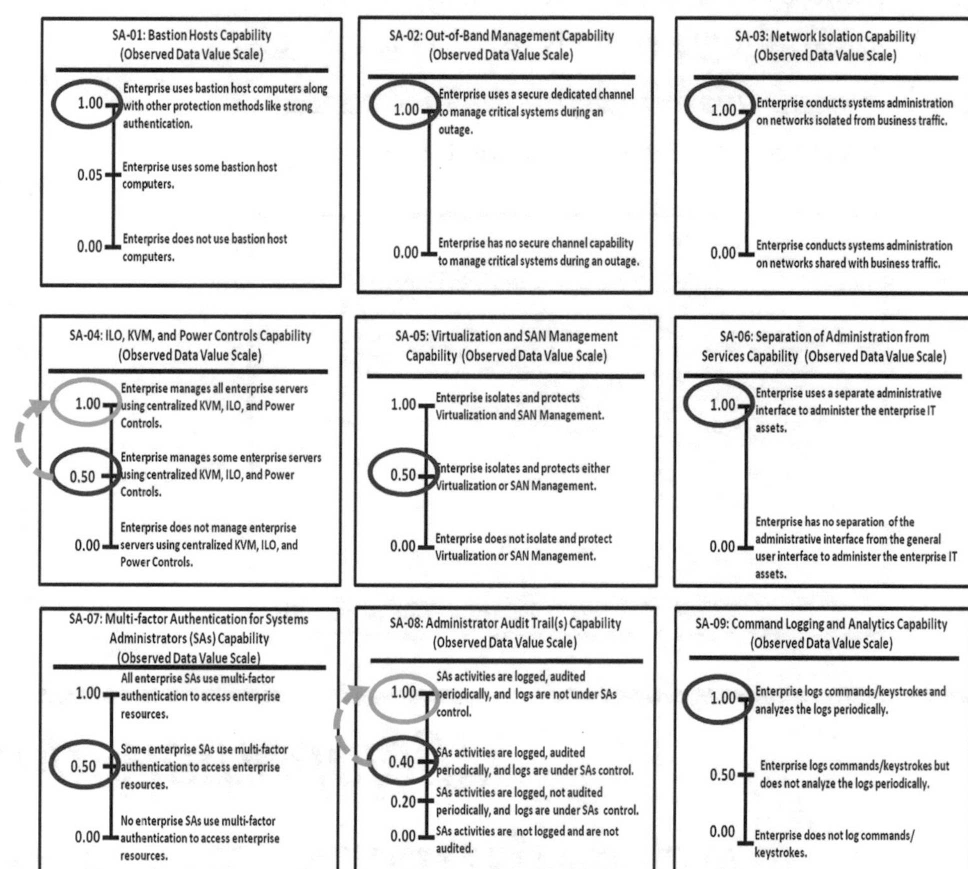

SA-01: Bastion Hosts Capability (Observed Data Value Scale)
1.00 Enterprise uses bastion host computers along with other protection methods like strong authentication.
0.05 Enterprise uses some bastion host computers.
0.00 Enterprise does not use bastion host computers.
SA-02: Out-of-Band Management Capability (Observed Data Value Scale)
1.00 Enterprise uses a secure dedicated channel to manage critical systems during an outage.
0.00 Enterprise has no secure channel capability to manage critical systems during an outage.
SA-03: Network Isolation Capability (Observed Data Value Scale)
1.00 Enterprise conducts systems administration on networks isolated from business traffic.
0.00 Enterprise conducts systems administration on networks shared with business traffic.
SA-04: ILO, KVM, and Power Controls Capability (Observed Data Value Scale)
1.00 Enterprise manages all enterprise servers using centralized KVM, ILO, and Power Controls.
0.50 Enterprise manages some enterprise servers using centralized KVM, ILO, and Power Controls.
0.00 Enterprise does not manage enterprise servers using centralized KVM, ILO, and Power Controls.
SA-05: Virtualization and SAN Management Capability (Observed Data Value Scale)
1.00 Enterprise isolates and protects Virtualization and SAN Management.
0.50 Enterprise isolates and protects either Virtualization or SAN Management.
0.00 Enterprise does not isolate and protect Virtualization or SAN Management.
SA-06: Separation of Administration from Services Capability (Observed Data Value Scale)
1.00 Enterprise uses a separate administrative interface to administer the enterprise IT assets.
0.00 Enterprise has no separation of the administrative interface from the general user interface to administer the enterprise IT assets.
SA-07: Multi-factor Authentication for Systems Administrators (SAs) Capability (Observed Data Value Scale)
1.00 All enterprise SAs use multi-factor authentication to access enterprise resources.
0.50 Some enterprise SAs use multi-factor authentication to access enterprise resources.
0.00 No enterprise SAs use multi-factor authentication to access enterprise resources.
SA-08: Administrator Audit Trail(s) Capability (Observed Data Value Scale)
1.00 SAs activities are logged, audited periodically, and logs are not under SAs control.
0.40 SAs activities are logged, audited periodically, and logs are under SAs control.
0.20 SAs activities are logged, not audited periodically, and logs are under SAs control.
0.00 SAs activities are not logged and are not audited.
SA-09: Command Logging and Analytics Capability (Observed Data Value Scale)
1.00 Enterprise logs commands/keystrokes and analyzes the logs periodically.
0.50 Enterprise logs commands/keystrokes but does not analyze the logs periodically.
0.00 Enterprise does not log commands/keystrokes.

Observed Data OM Example *(7 of 8)*

OM Six-Step Methodology

- The OM equation can then be used to calculate an updated overall Systems Administration index to reflect changes in capability effectiveness over time.
- ***Repeat Step 6***: Substitute the updated selected tick-mark numeric values into an appropriate OM equation to calculate an overall index.
  - *For this example, the upper graphic shows the observed data Systems Administration Cybersecurity Effectiveness Index, SACSEIndex.*
  - *The resulting* SACSE*Index = 0.91.*
  - *The lower Graphic illustrates one way to visualize* SACSE*Index = 0.91.*

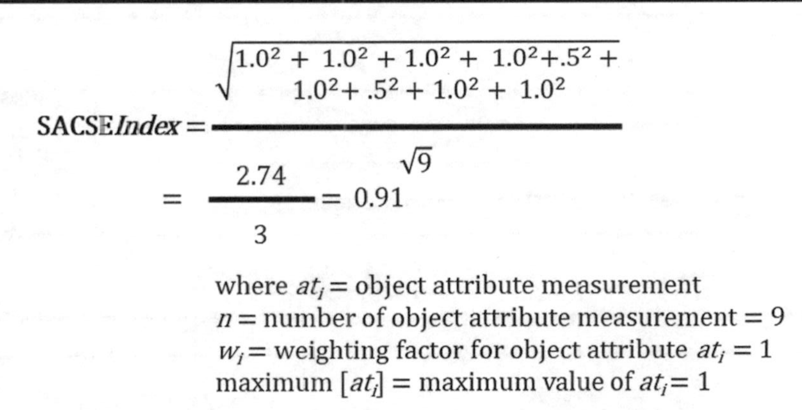

$$\text{SACSE}\textbf{\textit{Index}} = \frac{\sqrt{1.0^2 + 1.0^2 + 1.0^2 + 1.0^2 + .5^2 + 1.0^2 + .5^2 + 1.0^2 + 1.0^2}}{\sqrt{9}}$$

$$= \frac{2.74}{3} = 0.91$$

where at_i = object attribute measurement
n = number of object attribute measurement = 9
w_i = weighting factor for object attribute $at_i = 1$
maximum $[at_i]$ = maximum value of $at_i = 1$

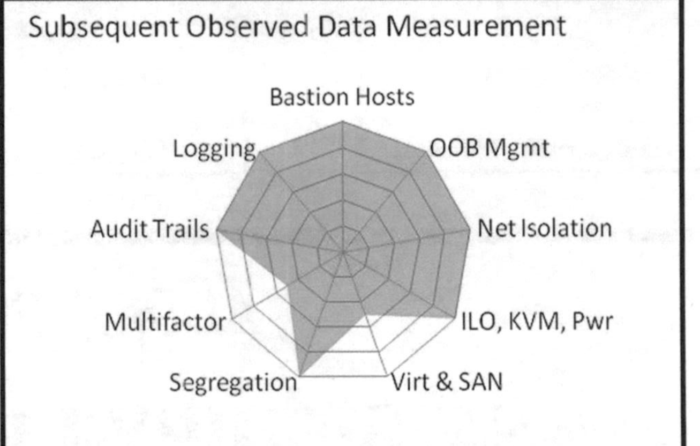

Observed Data OM Example *(8 of 8)*

OM Six-Step Methodology

- The top graphic depicts the observed data measurement results.
  - Original (or baseline) measurements, where SACSE*Index* = 0.81
  - Updated measurements after improvements, where SACSEIndex = 0.91
- The bottom graphic depicts cybersecurity assessment results tracked over time and helps to communicate results of specific infrastructure investments.

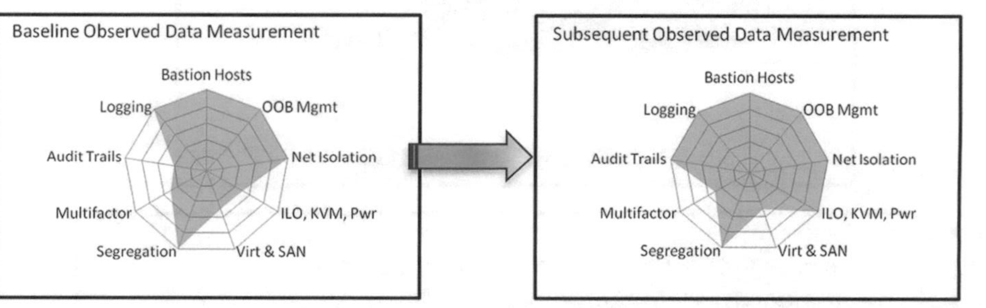

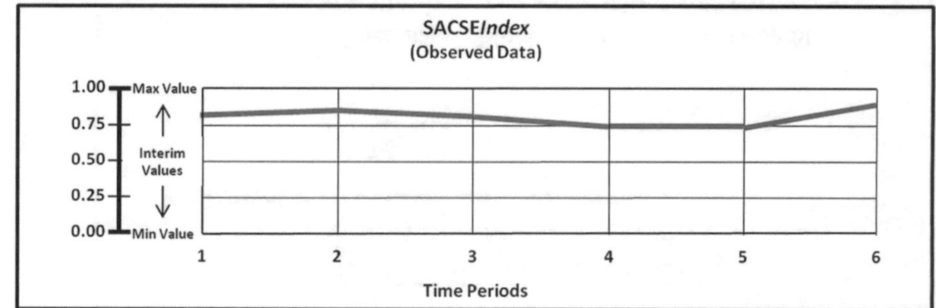

- The OM*Index* Equation provides direct linkage between the defined cybersecurity capability value scales and observed data.
- This expressed linkage is tied to enterprise cybersecurity improvement activities.
- By tracking SACSE*Index* over time, the enterprise has a means for using observed data to guide its ongoing cyberdefense improvement activities.

Other Cybersecurity-Related Measurements *(1 of 6)*

Two-Step Measurement Approach (1 of 2)

- In addition to OM-based cybersecurity measurement,
  - it may be useful for an enterprise to establish other cybersecurity program measurements.
  - *What attributes of the cybersecurity program are of interest to measure?*
  - *Which activities contribute to successfully securing the enterprise from cyberattacks?*
- An effective enterprise cybersecurity program protects the enterprise in a cost-effective manner that balances
  - technology, process, people, budgets, and external compliance requirements, while supporting the business mission as much as possible.
- This section presents a high-level, two-step measurement approach that can be used to effect cyberdefense improvement.
  - ***Step 1***: The application of metrics to cyberdefense activities to provide insight into the extent to which these activities are, or are not, contributing to effective cyberdefense.
  - ***Step 2***: Those activities that are not contributing to effective cyberdefense will be modified (or eliminated) until they do. These modification are what *cyberdefense improvement* means.
- Improvements are measured individually and then averaged to provide insight into what cyberdefense areas have improved or not improved.

Other Cybersecurity-Related Measurements *(2 of 6)*

Two-Step Measurement Approach (2 of 2)

- Measurement, in part, involves collecting data and putting it into a meaningful form for cyberdefense improvement purposes.
- Such activities should not be onerous because they will get in the way of the cyberdefense program.
  - Metrics need to be simple to collect and analyze.
  - However, simplicity can cause the metrics to be limited regarding the insight they provide into cyberdefense workings.
  - For the near term, the enterprise should collect some simple metrics to see if they help highlight activities that should be changed to effect cyberdefense improvement.
  - More sophisticated cybersecurity measurements can be added if needed.
- This section presents example cybersecurity measurements for the first three security operational processes in the graphic below.

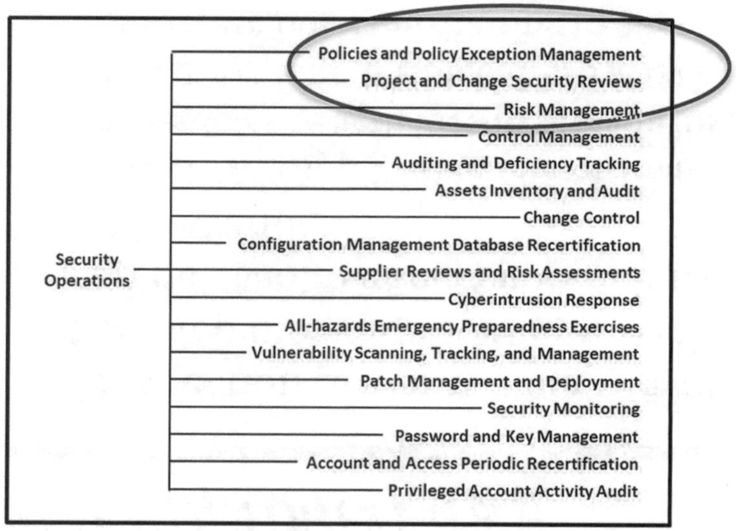

Security Operations
- Policies and Policy Exception Management
- Project and Change Security Reviews
- Risk Management
- Control Management
- Auditing and Deficiency Tracking
- Assets Inventory and Audit
- Change Control
- Configuration Management Database Recertification
- Supplier Reviews and Risk Assessments
- Cyberintrusion Response
- All-hazards Emergency Preparedness Exercises
- Vulnerability Scanning, Tracking, and Management
- Patch Management and Deployment
- Security Monitoring
- Password and Key Management
- Account and Access Periodic Recertification
- Privileged Account Activity Audit

Other Cybersecurity-Related Measurements *(3 of 6)*

Policies and Policy Exception Management

- The top graphic depicts the Policies and Policy Exception Management process that maintains enterprise policies, as well as exceptions to those policies.
  - Enterprises may be good at establishing cybersecurity policies and maintaining them, but managing exceptions tends to be more problematic.
  - Policy exceptions need to be formally approved and then re-certified on a regular basis.
- Security needs to observe policy exceptions to watch out for cases where the "exception becomes the rule."
- The bottom graphic depicts two example metrics that provide a quantitative means for assessing the extent to which enterprise cybersecurity policies are integrated into the enterprise business culture.

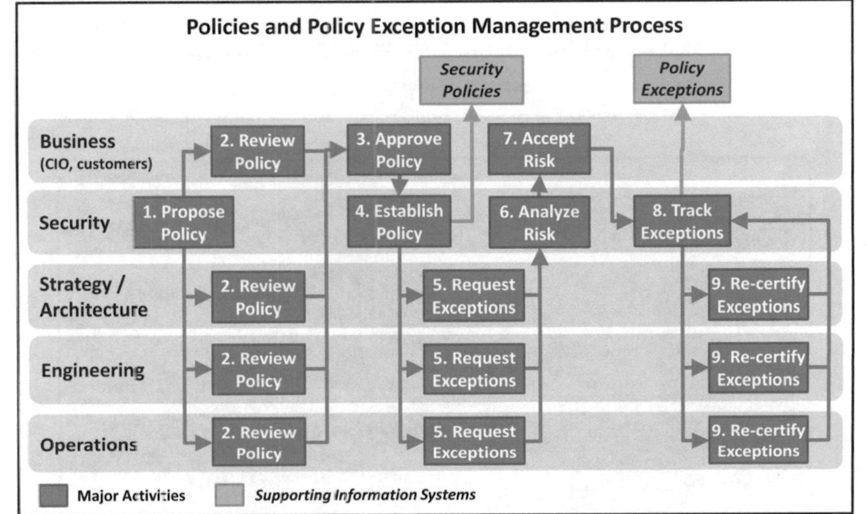

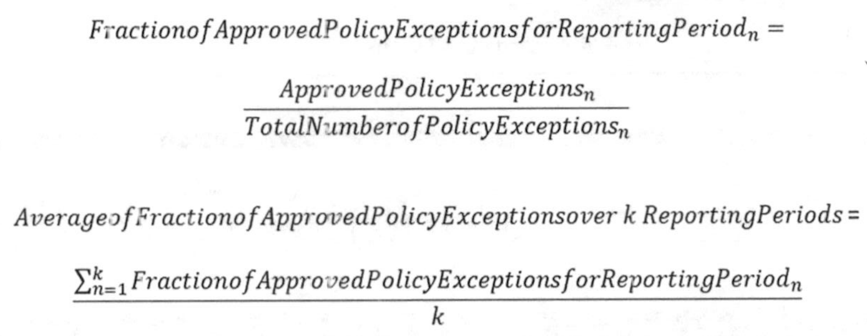

$$FractionofApprovedPolicyExceptionsforReportingPeriod_n = \frac{ApprovedPolicyExceptions_n}{TotalNumberofPolicyExceptions_n}$$

$$AverageofFractionofApprovedPolicyExceptionsover\ k\ ReportingPeriods = \frac{\sum_{n=1}^{k} FractionofApprovedPolicyExceptionsforReportingPeriod_n}{k}$$

Other Cybersecurity-Related Measurements *(4 of 6)*

Project and Change Security Reviews

- The top graphic depicts the Project and Change Security Reviews process that ensures, in part, that IT systems are designed and deployed with cybersecurity capabilities "baked in" and practical.
  - Should be integrated into the larger systems development life cycle
  - Can also be integrated into the management gates of the enterprise IT project and change process
- Cybersecurity needs to be considered on major IT initiatives as well as associated initiative risks and mitigations.
- The bottom graphic depicts two example metrics that provide a quantitative means for assessing the extent to which cybersecurity is designed and deployed with "baked-in" cybersecurity capabilities.

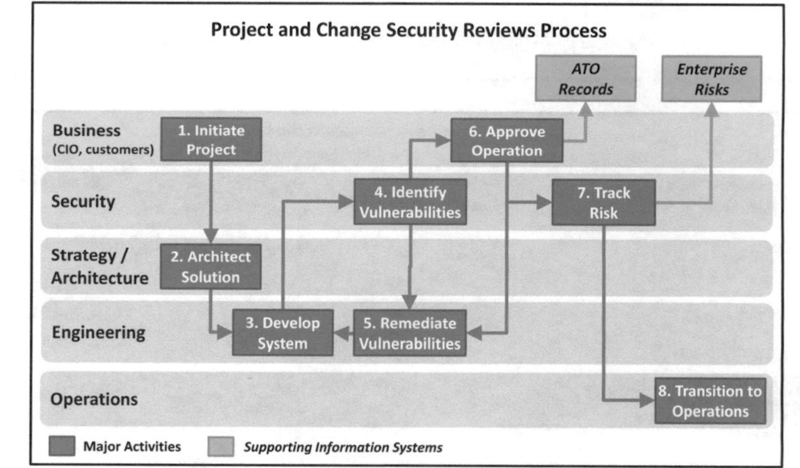

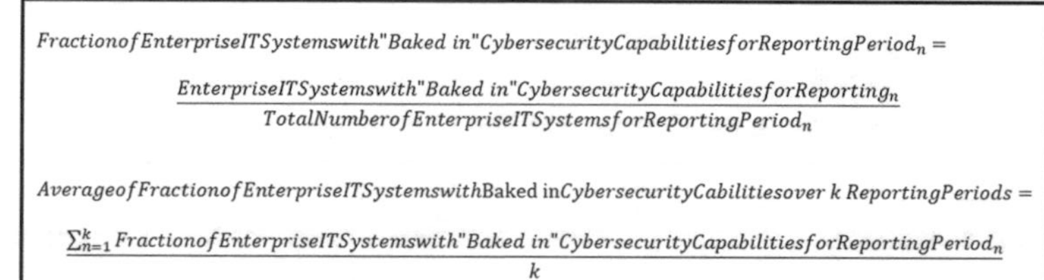

- These measurements provide a visible "yardstick" for portraying the enterprise's security posture with respect to project and change security reviews.

Other Cybersecurity-Related Measurements *(5 of 6)*

Risk Management (1 of 2)

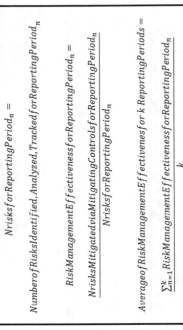

- The top graphic depicts the Risk Management process that helps the CISO track risks in terms of the risks' business impact, not their technological impact.
  - Risks should be technology-agnostic.
  - Technology factors into the risk process as vulnerabilities are identified and exploited by attackers.
  - Consequently, associated business risks can increase and possibly require additional mitigations.
- The bottom graphic depicts three example metrics that provide a quantitative means for assessing the extent to which identified, analyzed, and tracked risks are mitigated over time.

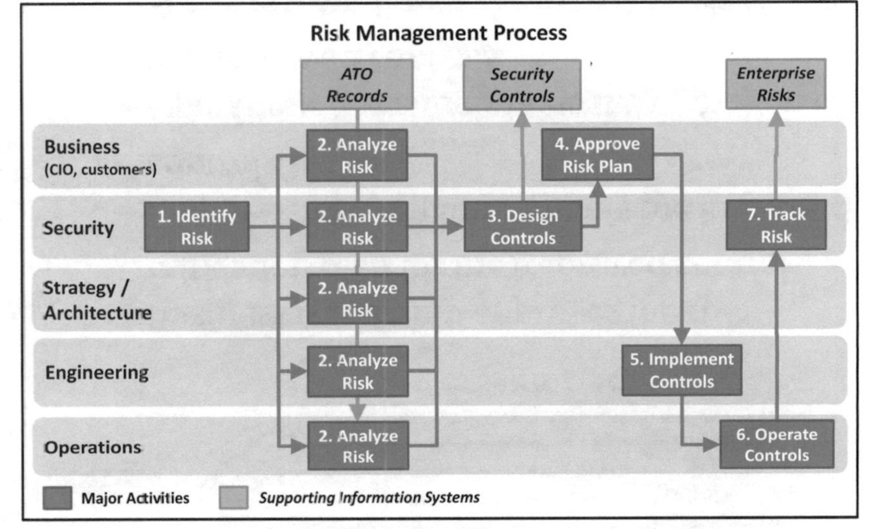

$$NrisksforReportingPeriod_n =$$

$$NumberofRisksIdentified, Analyzed, TrackedforReportingPeriod_n$$

$$RiskManagementEffectivenessforReportingPeriod_n =$$

$$\frac{NrisksMitigatedviaMitigatingControlsforReportingPeriod_n}{NrisksforReportingPeriod_n}$$

$$AverageofRiskManagementEffectivenesfor\ k\ ReportingPeriods =$$

$$\frac{\sum_{n=1}^{k} RiskManagementEffectivenessforReportingPeriod_n}{k}$$

Other Cybersecurity-Related Measurements *(6 of 6)*

Risk Management *(2 of 2)*

- These Risk Management measurements offer the enterprise a means for improving cybersecurity functional areas that may be falling short in dealing effectively with risks.
  - Enterprise may find for a given reporting period there have been successful cyberattack incidents linked to the e-mails of one or more enterprise users.
  - Possible starting point for mitigating the risk of e-mail security breaches may point to a shortfall in the ***E-mail Security Capability*** of the ***Application Security Functional Area***.
- The mitigation process may trigger an upgrade to the enterprise risk management process for the ***E-mail Security Capability***.
  - Security team designs better controls for the E-mail Security Capability.

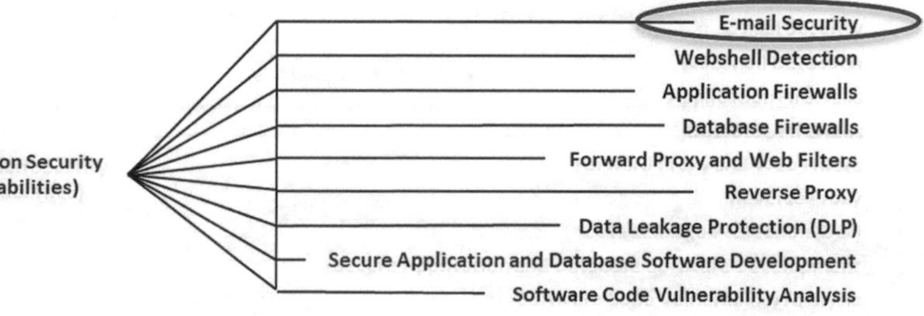

  - Business leadership approves the risk mitigation plan for the improved controls.
  - Engineering team implements the improved controls.
  - Operations team maintains the operation of the improved controls.
  - Security team tracks the extent to which the E-mail Security breaches may have been mitigated.
  - This tracking would show up in the updates to the risk management metrics in subsequent reporting periods.

APPENDIX D

Cybersecurity Sample Assessment

S. E. Donaldson et al., *Enterprise Cybersecurity Study Guide*, https://doi.org/10.1007/978-1-4842-3258-3_19

Overview *(1 of 2)*

- The purpose of this appendix is to bring together a previously introduced hierarchy of cybersecurity concepts into three worked-out numerical examples and address the following questions:
  - *What is the enterprise quantitative effectiveness in defending itself against cyberattacks?*
  - *How does the enterprise quantitatively improve this effectiveness?*
- A cybersecurity program lends itself well to performing top-down security assessments at progressively increasing levels of detail.
  - Each assessment level can be performed independently.
  - Assessments can be done in progressive passes to get increasing detail focusing on the areas of greatest interest.
  - Multiple passes help to gain a greater understanding of the enterprise security posture and areas for improvement.

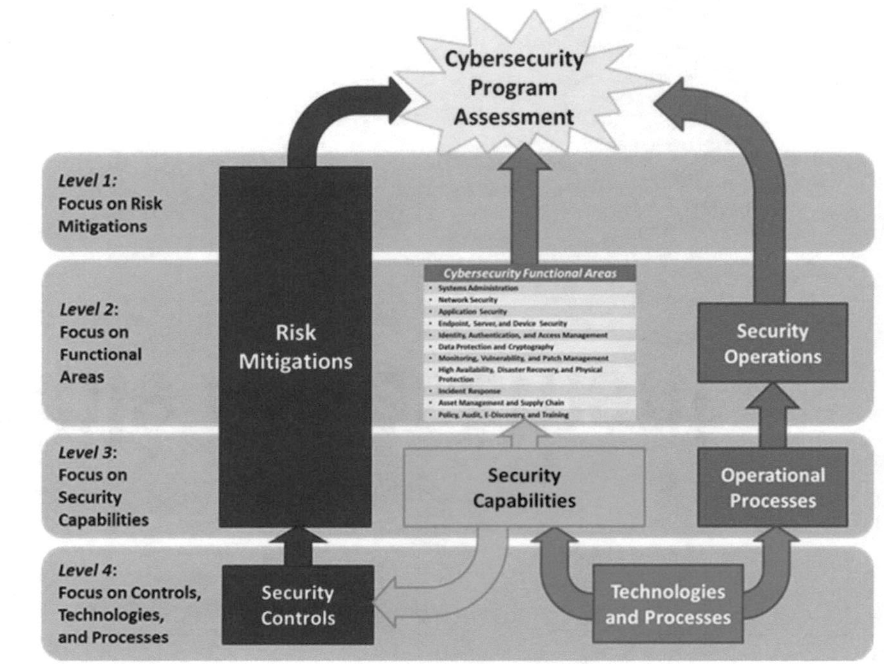

- The graphic depicts a top-down ***Cybersecurity Program Assessment*** framework with four levels of focus and detail.

Overview *(2 of 2)*

- *A Cybersecurity Program Assessment* can consist of one or more assessments.
  - ***Level 1 Assessment***
    - Very high-level assessment that focuses on risk mitigations using expert judgment
  - ***Level 2 Assessment***
    - High-level assessment that focuses on functional areas using expert judgment
    - Extends Level 1 results to consider functional areas and security operations
  - ***Level 3 Assessment***
    - Detailed assessment that focuses on capabilities using observed data
    - Extends Level 1 results to consider functional areas at the capabilities level and security operations considering individual operational processes using expert judgment
  - ***Level 4 Assessment***
    - More detailed assessment that considers controls, technologies, and/or processes using expert judgment or observed data

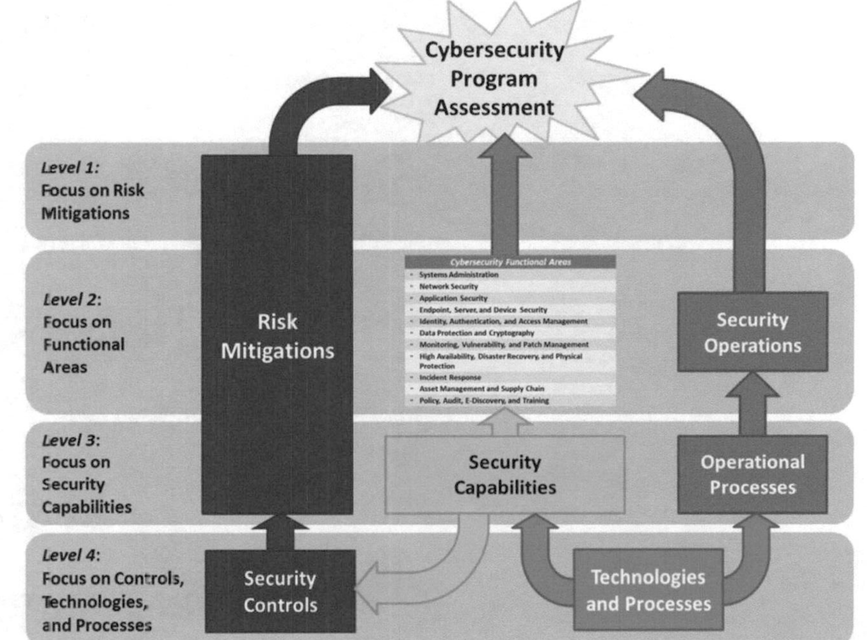

Note: Level 4 Assessment is not addressed in this appendix.

- Worked-out example numerical assessments illustrate how an enterprise can obtain answers to questions posed about its cybersecurity effectiveness and its evolution.

Topics

- Sample Assessment Scope and Methodology
- *Level 1 Assessment*: Focus on Risk Mitigations
- *Level 2 Assessment*: Focus on Functional Areas
- *Level 3 Assessment*: Focus on Capabilities

Sample Assessment Scope and Methodology

Overview

- This appendix presents three sample assessments for a hypothetical enterprise.
  - ***Level 1 Assessment*** focuses on risk mitigations against all steps of the attack sequence.
  - ***Level 2 Assessment*** focuses on functional areas.
  - ***Level 3 Assessment*** focuses on security capabilities.
- These three sample assessments
  - analyze a ***single security scope*** consisting of the enterprise's general-purpose IT environment
  - use the Object Measurement Methodology to identify the attributes for evaluation and score those attributes
  - combine the scores into a single ***Cybersecurity Program Assessment Index*** that represents the enterprise's security posture

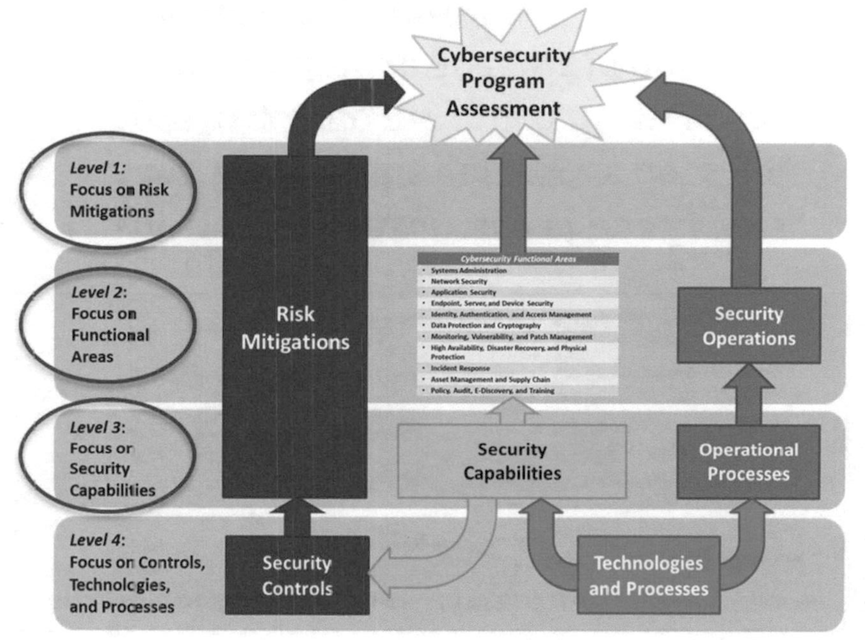

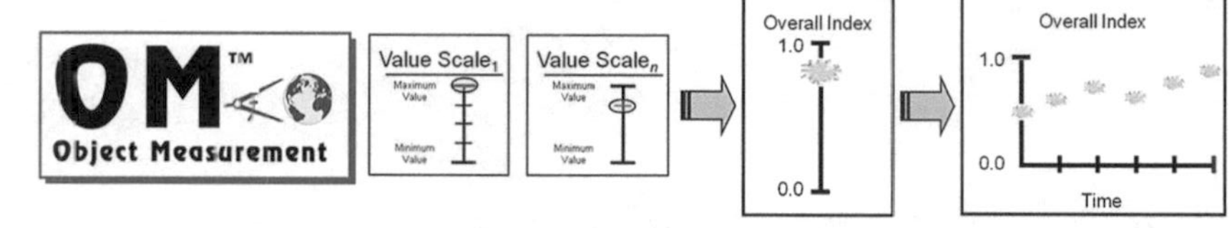

Level 1 Assessment: Focus on Risk Mitigations *(1 of 10)*

Context

- Level 1 assessment involves analyzing the *enterprise cybersecurity attack sequence.*
- Assessment security scope
  - is enterprise's general-purpose IT environment; and
  - considers how well the cybersecurity controls are ***reducing*** the ***probability*** and the ***impact*** of attacks making it through each step of the attack sequence.
- This assessment is an exploratory assessment providing a high-level evaluation of enterprise's overall cybersecurity posture.
  - Results used to help direct further cybersecurity assessments.
  - Since assessment is only looking at risk mitigations, it does not account for other cybersecurity details that could be critically important.

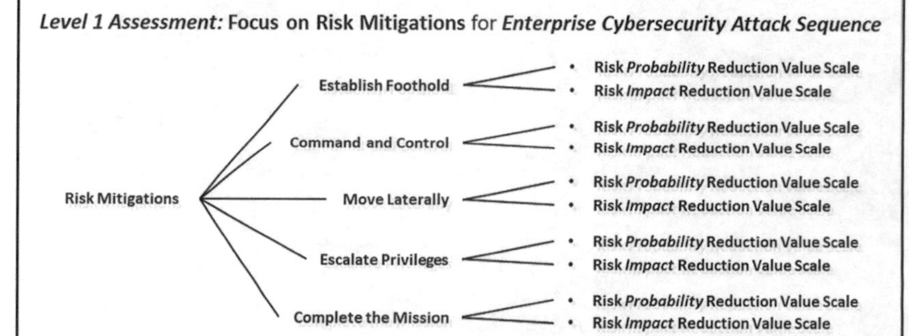

- The primary advantage of this ***Level 1 Assessment*** is the enterprise does not have to go into too much detail or spend too much time in analysis to obtain executive-level results.

Level 1 Assessment: Focus on Risk Mitigations *(2 of 10)*

Object Measurement Steps (1 of 8)

- ***OM Step 1***
  - *What is the strength of the enterprise's cybersecurity when **only considering risk mitigations** to reduce the probability or impact of targeted cyberattacks?*
- ***OM Step 2***
  - ***Risk mitigations*** against attack sequence steps
    1. Establish foothold
    2. Command and control
    3. Move laterally
    4. Escalate privileges
    5. Complete the mission
- ***OM Step 3***
  - For each attack sequence step, the object characteristics will be measured using expert judgment as follows:
    - ***Risk probability reduction*** that represents the amount that attacks are less likely to succeed at the specific step of the attack sequence due to the presence of controls that disrupt, detect, delay, or defeat the attack
    - ***Risk impact reduction*** that represents the amount that the impact of an attack is reduced at the specific step of the attack sequence due to the presence of controls that disrupt, detect, delay, or defeat the attack
  - A cybersecurity expert will use the above two characteristics and use ***expert judgment*** to define corresponding value scales and then evaluate the enterprise's cybersecurity controls' effectiveness.

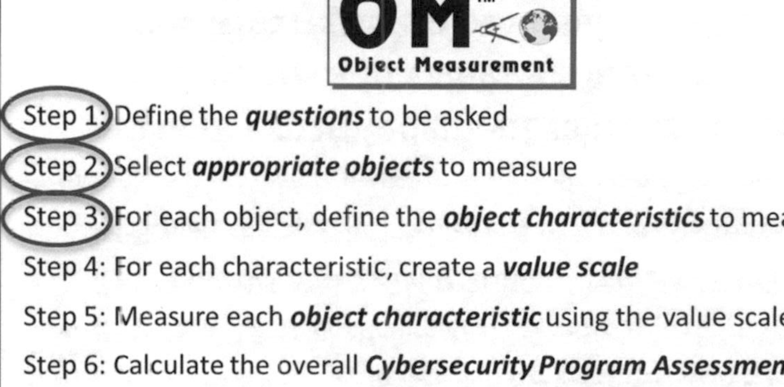

OM™
Object Measurement
Step 1: Define the questions to be asked
Step 2: Select appropriate objects to measure
Step 3: For each object, define the object characteristics to measure
Step 4: For each characteristic, create a value scale
Step 5: Measure each object characteristic using the value scale
Step 6: Calculate the overall Cybersecurity Program Assessment Index

Level 1 Assessment: Focus on Risk Mitigations *(3 of 10)*

Object Measurement Steps (2 of 8)

- ***OM Step 4***
  - The expert defines the value scales for (1) risk probability reduction and (2) risk impact reduction, as shown below.

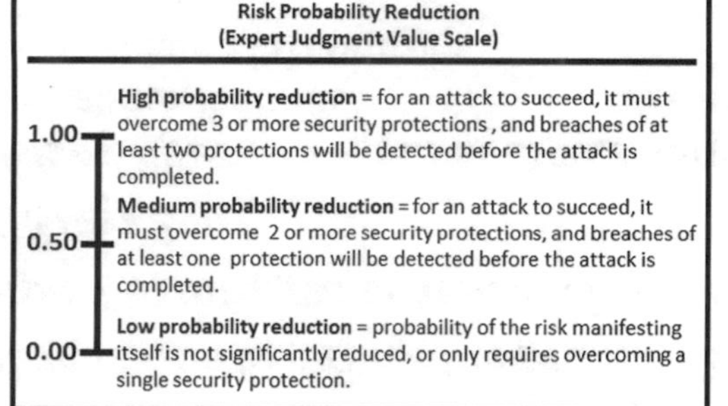

Risk Probability Reduction
(Expert Judgment Value Scale)
1.00
High probability reduction = for an attack to succeed, it must overcome 3 or more security protections, and breaches of at least two protections will be detected before the attack is completed.
0.50
Medium probability reduction = for an attack to succeed, it must overcome 2 or more security protections, and breaches of at least one protection will be detected before the attack is completed.
0.00
Low probability reduction = probability of the risk manifesting itself is not significantly reduced, or only requires overcoming a single security protection.

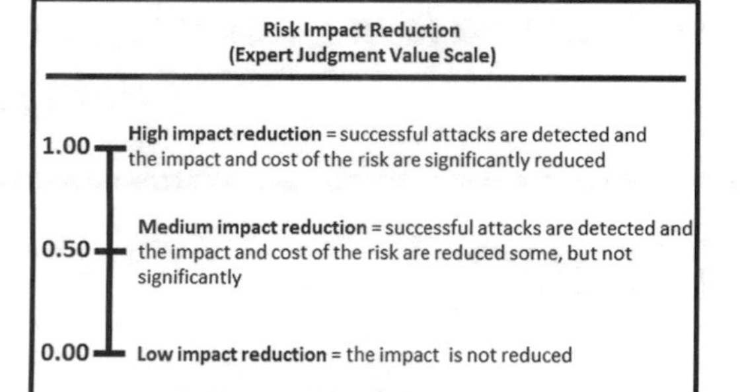

Risk Impact Reduction
(Expert Judgment Value Scale)
1.00
High impact reduction = successful attacks are detected and the impact and cost of the risk are significantly reduced
0.50
Medium impact reduction = successful attacks are detected and the impact and cost of the risk are reduced some, but not significantly
0.00
Low impact reduction = the impact is not reduced

OM™
Object Measurement

Step 1: Define the ***questions*** to be asked

Step 2: Select ***appropriate objects*** to measure

Step 3: For each object, define the ***object characteristics*** to measure

Step 4: For each characteristic, create a ***value scale***

Step 5: Measure each ***object characteristic*** using the value scale

Step 6: Calculate the overall ***Cybersecurity Program Assessment Index***

  - These expert judgment value scales provide definitions and values for ***high***, ***medium***, and ***low*** with regard to probability reduction and impact reduction
- It is possible for the risk mitigations of a step of the attack sequence to
  - reduce the probability of attack but not the impact; and
  - reduce the impact but not the probability of attack.

Level 1 Assessment: Focus on Risk Mitigations *(4 of 10)*

Object Measurement Steps *(3 of 8)*

- ***OM Step 4:*** For each characteristic, create a ***value scale (continued):***
  - Once the expert judgment value scales are defined, their values can be combined using an appropriate OM equation.
  - However, the graphic shows an alternative way to combine their values via an ***OM Scoring Matrix***.
  - The matrix combines the value scales in a way that is simpler than using the full OM equation, but produces similar results.

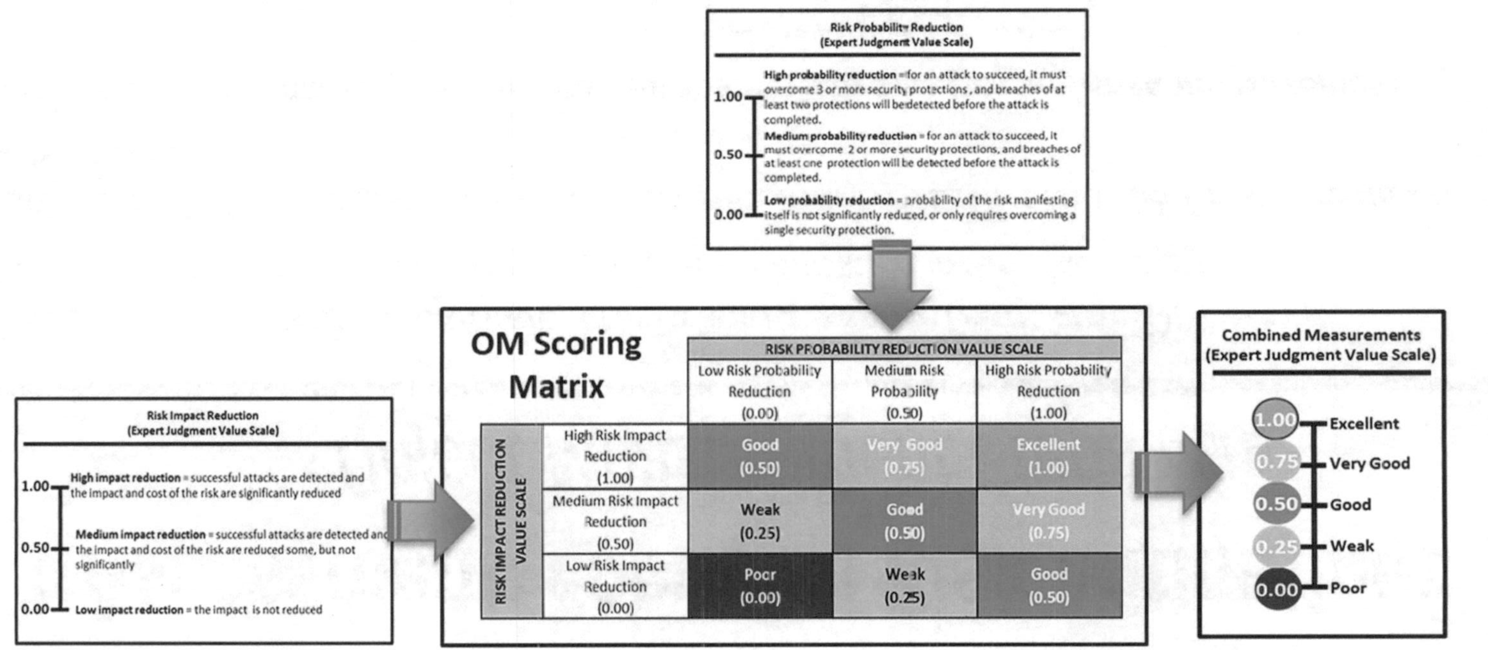

	Low Risk Probability Reduction (0.00)	Medium Risk Probability (0.50)	High Risk Probability Reduction (1.00)
High Risk Impact Reduction (1.00)	Good (0.50)	Very Good (0.75)	Excellent (1.00)
Medium Risk Impact Reduction (0.50)	Weak (0.25)	Good (0.50)	Very Good (0.75)
Low Risk Impact Reduction (0.00)	Poor (0.00)	Weak (0.25)	Good (0.50)

Level 1 Assessment: Focus on Risk Mitigations *(5 of 10)*

Object Measurement Steps *(4 of 8)*

- ***OM Step 4:*** For each characteristic, create a ***value scale (continued):***
  - The matrix defines a ***combined*** expert judgment value scale for an assessment.
  - Inputs to the OM Scoring Matrix are the ***risk probability reduction*** and ***risk impact reduction*** expert measurements.
  - Matrix converts the expert judgment measurements into a ***single combined measurement***.

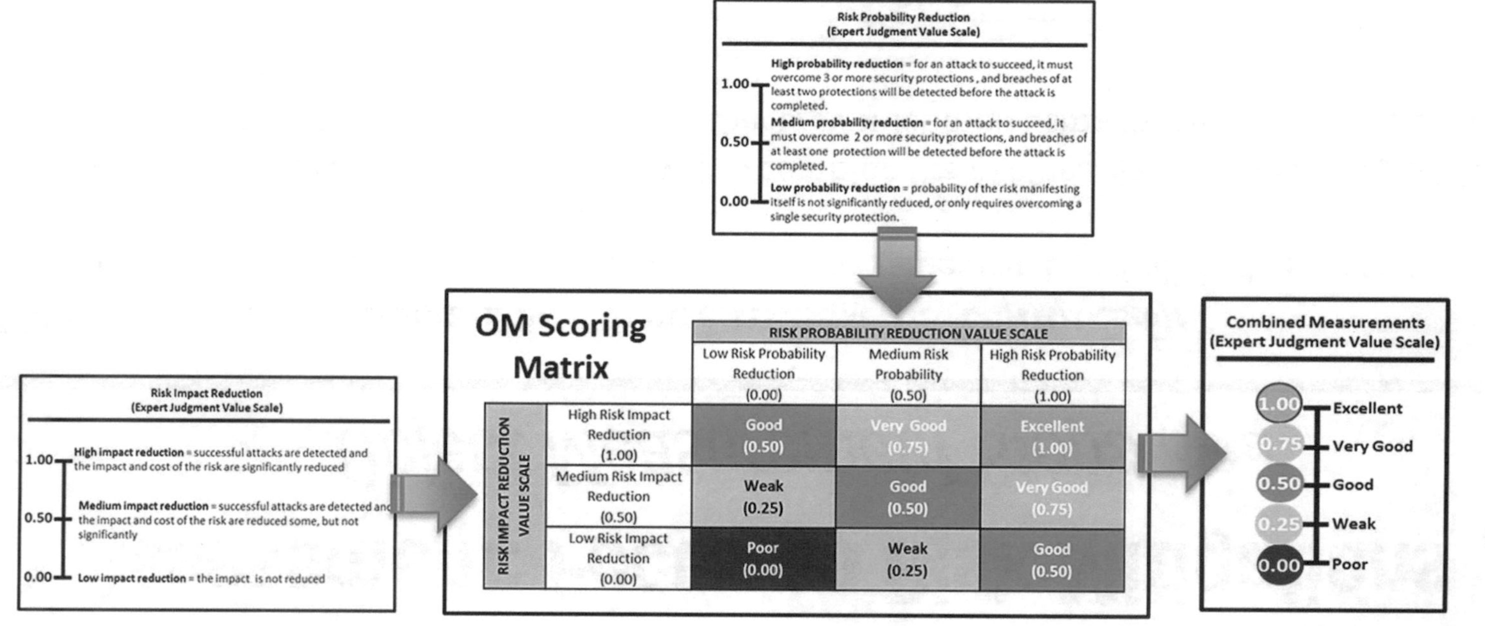

	Low Risk Probability Reduction (0.00)	Medium Risk Probability (0.50)	High Risk Probability Reduction (1.00)
High Risk Impact Reduction (1.00)	Good (0.50)	Very Good (0.75)	Excellent (1.00)
Medium Risk Impact Reduction (0.50)	Weak (0.25)	Good (0.50)	Very Good (0.75)
Low Risk Impact Reduction (0.00)	Poor (0.00)	Weak (0.25)	Good (0.50)

Level 1 Assessment: Focus on Risk Mitigations *(6 of 10)*

Object Measurement Steps *(5 of 8)*

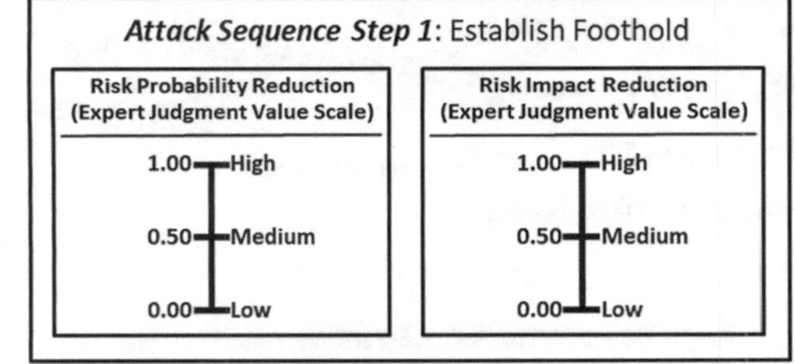

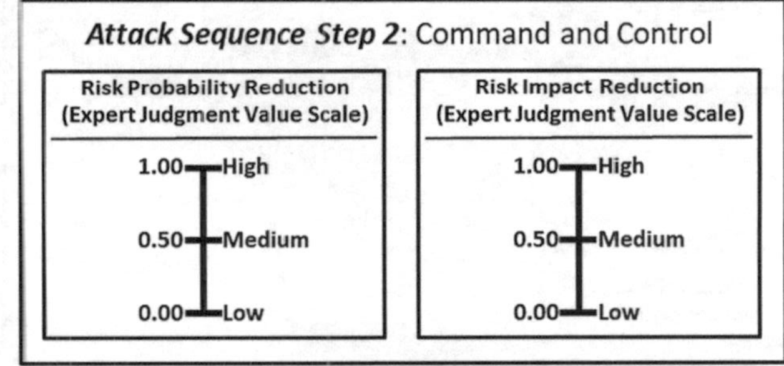

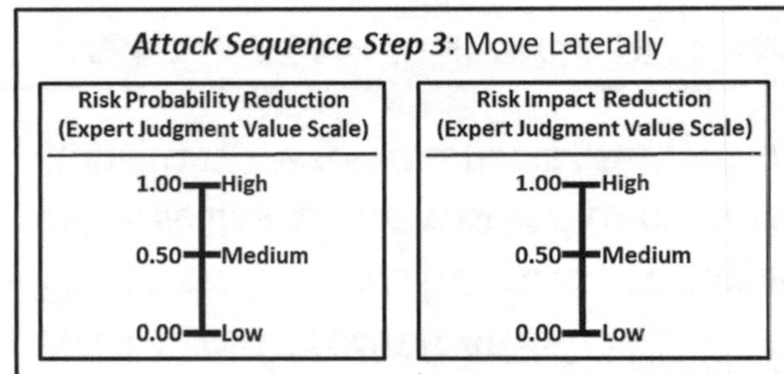

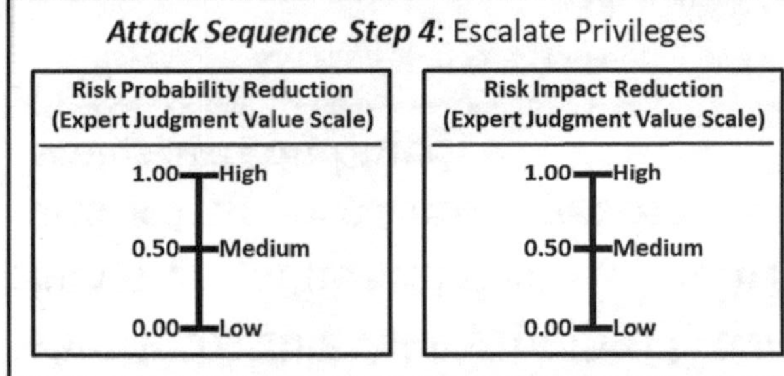

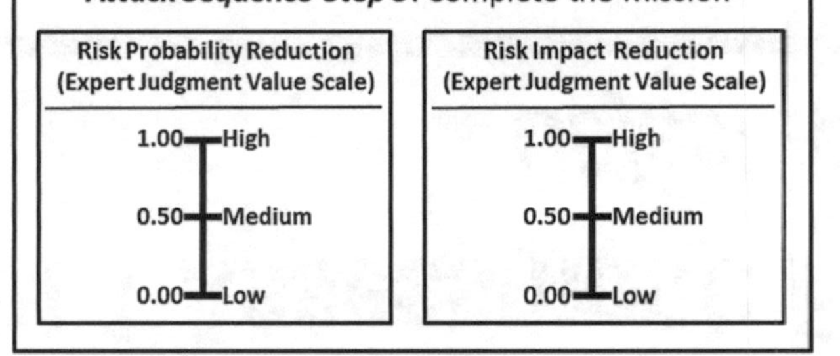

- ***OM Step 4:*** For each characteristic, create a ***value scale (continued):***
  - An ***OM Measurement Pane*** can be created to help record assessment measurements.
  - Level 1 expert judgment value scales are simplified here for display purposes only.

Level 1 Assessment: Focus on Risk Mitigations *(7 of 10)*

Object Measurement Steps *(6 of 8)*

- ***OM Step 4:*** For each characteristic, create a ***value scale (continued):***
  - The graphic shows how the two expert judgment value scales are networked to the attack sequence steps that are related to risk mitigations.

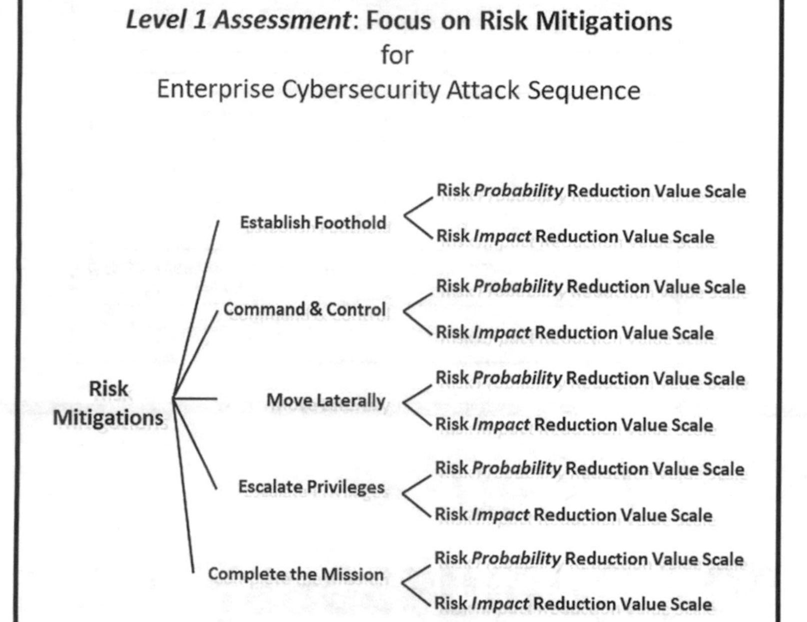

  - Using the OM Scoring Matrix, the graphic shows possible values for the (1) two expert judgment value scales and (2) individual attack sequence steps when the two value scales are combined.

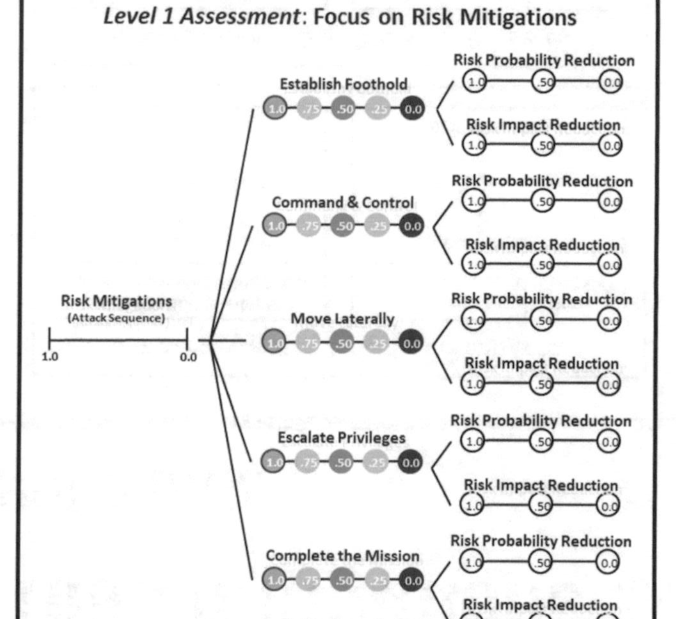

Level 1 Assessment: Focus on Risk Mitigations *(8 of 10)*

Object Measurement Steps (7 of 8)

- ***OM Step 5***: Measure each ***object characteristic*** using a value scale.

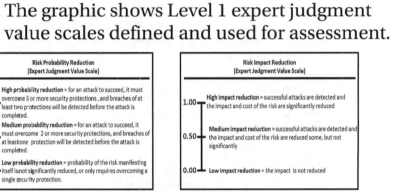

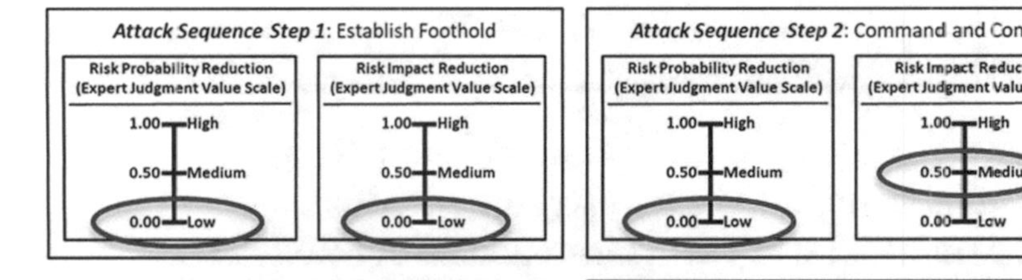

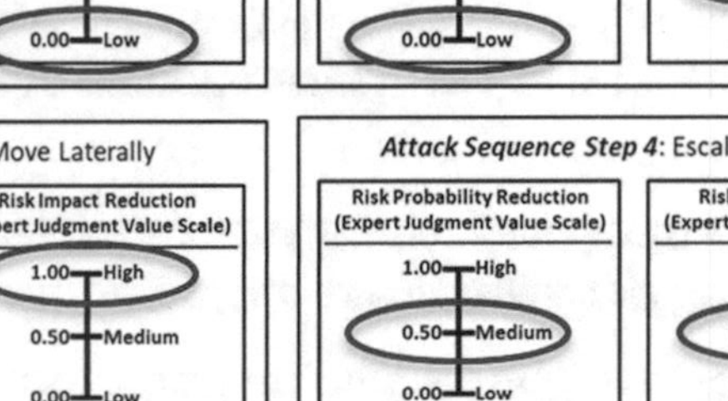

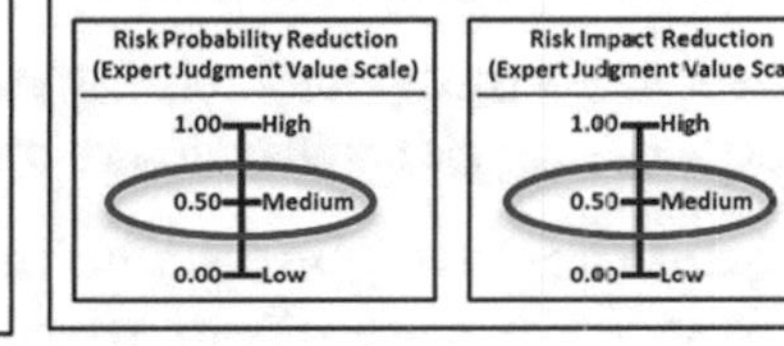

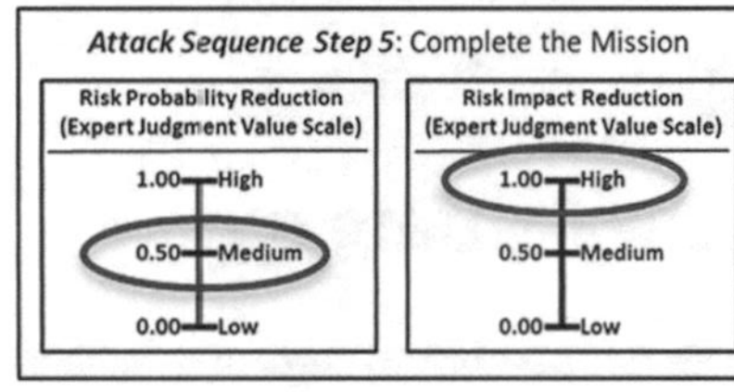

  - Each attack sequence step value is tied to a definition expressed in enterprise cybersecurity language that helps explain the underlying meaning of the numbers and preserves, in part, the context of this assessment.

- The graphic shows Level 1 expert judgment value scales defined and used for assessment.

Risk Probability Reduction (Expert Judgment Value Scale)

- 1.00 — **High probability reduction** = for an attack to succeed, it must overcome 3 or more security protections, and breaches of at least two protections will be detected before the attack is completed.
- 0.50 — **Medium probability reduction** = for an attack to succeed, it must overcome 2 or more security protections, and breaches of at least one protection will be detected before the attack is completed.
- 0.00 — **Low probability reduction** = probability of the risk manifesting itself is not significantly reduced, or only requires overcoming a single security protection.

Risk Impact Reduction (Expert Judgment Value Scale)

- 1.00 — **High impact reduction** = successful attacks are detected and the impact and cost of the risk are significantly reduced
- 0.50 — **Medium impact reduction** = successful attacks are detected and the impact and cost of the risk are reduced some, but not significantly
- 0.00 — **Low impact reduction** = the impact is not reduced

- Expert judgment risk mitigation values for each of the five attack sequence steps and their combined measurement based on **OM Scoring Matrix** are shown in the graphic below.

Level 1 Assessment Focusing on Risk Mitigations (Attack Sequence Steps)	Risk Probability Reduction	Risk Impact Reduction	Combined Measurements
1. Establish Foothold	Low = 0.00	Low = 0.00	0.00
2. Command and Control	Low = 0.00	Medium = 0.50	0.25
3. Move Laterally	Low = 0.00	High = 1.00	0.50
4. Escalate Privileges	Medium = 0.50	Medium = 0.50	0.50
5. Complete the Mission	Medium = 0.50	High = 1.00	0.75

Level 1 Assessment: Focus on Risk Mitigations *(9 of 10)*

Object Measurement Steps *(8 of 8)*

- ***OM Step 6***: Calculate the overall ***Cybersecurity Program Assessment Index.***
  - The graphic to the right shows
    - recorded ***expert value judgments*** in terms of risk probability and impact reductions (see ellipses);
    - the resulting ***attack sequence step metrics*** based on the OM Scoring Matrix (see solid circles with numbers); and
    - how the overall **Level1_*Index*** is calculated with an appropriate OM index equation as shown in the graphic below.

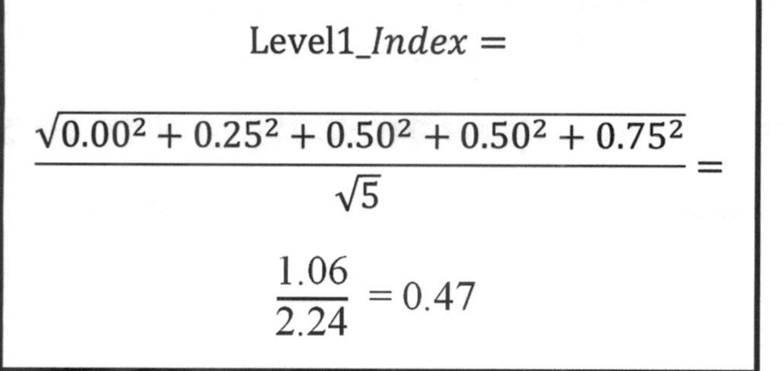

$$\text{Level1\_}Index = \frac{\sqrt{0.00^2 + 0.25^2 + 0.50^2 + 0.50^2 + 0.75^2}}{\sqrt{5}} = \frac{1.06}{2.24} = 0.47$$

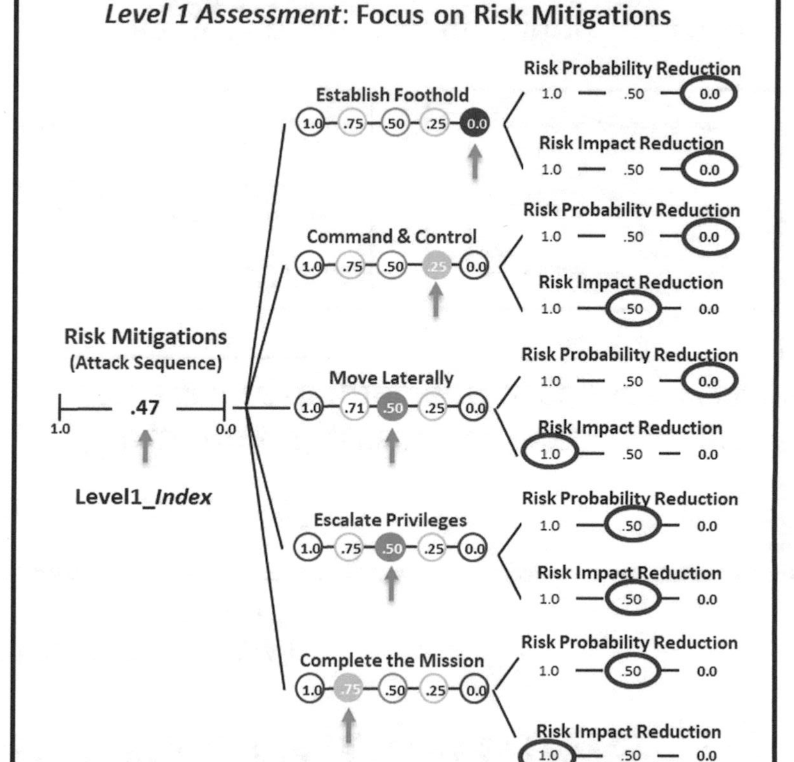

Level 1 Assessment: Focus on Risk Mitigations *(10 of 10)*

What does a Level1_*Index = 0.47 or 47% really mean?*

- The result represents the enterprise's cybersecurity effectiveness as determined from the expert judgment terms used to define the expert judgment value scales.
- By navigating the measurement map from left to right, the Level1_*Index* score can be unfolded and traced back to the expert judgment value scales.
- For example, ***Escalate Privileges* = 0.50** means
  - ***Risk Probability Reduction* = 0.50**
    - ***Medium probability reduction*** = For an attack to succeed, it must overcome two or more security protections, and breaches of at least one protection will be detected before the attack is complete.
  - ***Risk Impact Reduction* = 0.50**
    - ***Medium impact reduction*** = Successful attacks are detected and the impact and cost of the risk are reduced some, but not significantly.

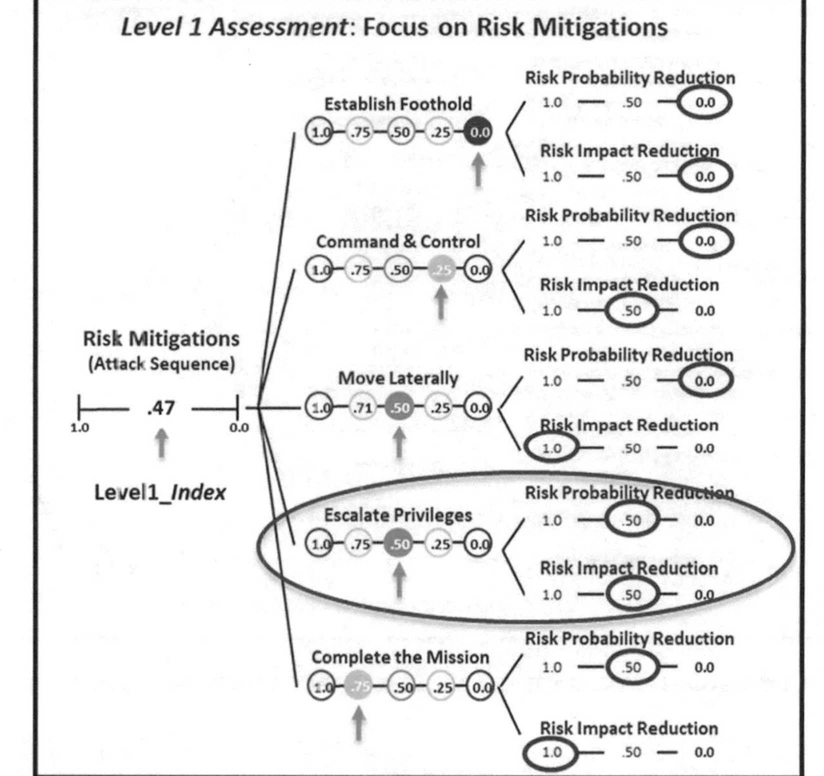

Level 2 Assessment: Focus on Functional Areas *(1 of 14)*

Context (1 of 2)

- Level 2 assessment involves analyzing
  - Risk Mitigations,
  - Cybersecurity Functional Areas, and
  - Security Operations.
- Assessment security scope
  - Consists of enterprise's general-purpose IT environment
- Assessment considers
  - how well cybersecurity controls are ***reducing*** the ***probability*** and ***impact*** of cybersecurity attacks;
  - how ***effectively*** the functional areas are ***reducing*** potential ***security gaps*** and ***security issues***; and
  - how ***comprehensively*** the security operations are ***utilized***.

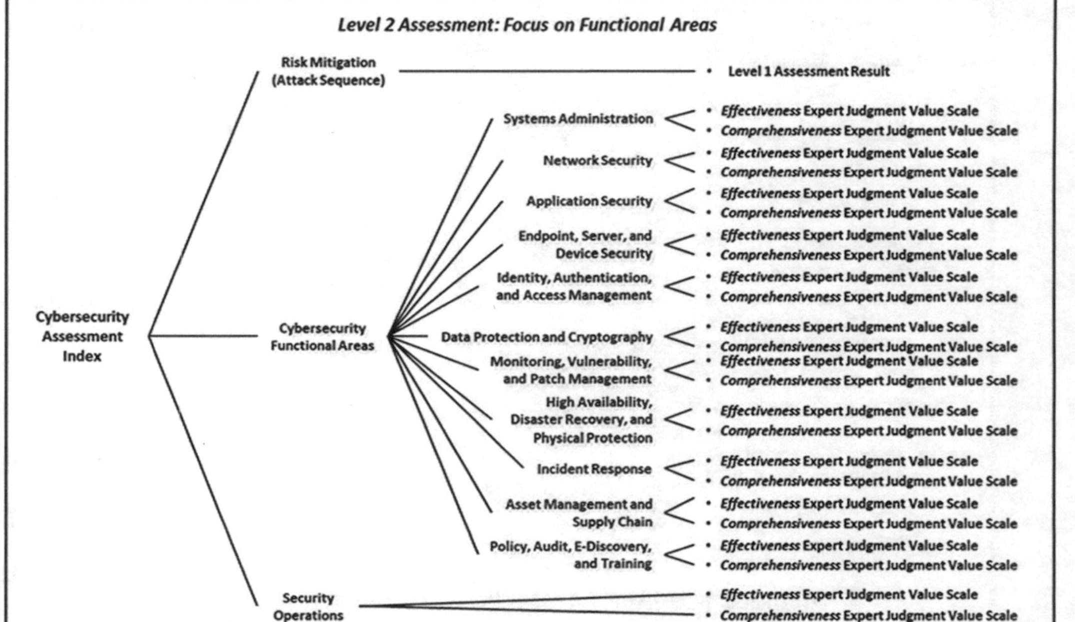

Level 2 Assessment: Focus on Functional Areas (2 of 14)

Context (2 of 2)

- Assessment
  - reflects expert judgment evaluating each functional area in its entirety;
  - does not account for other cybersecurity details that could be critically important:
    - cybersecurity capabilities,
    - processes, and
    - technologies;
  - Might be performed via a telephone interview or at a leadership whiteboard session; and
  - has the purpose of getting quickly to a high-level impression of the enterprise's cybersecurity posture.
- Results can be used to support or validate strategic decisions about which cybersecurity areas need focus and which areas do not.

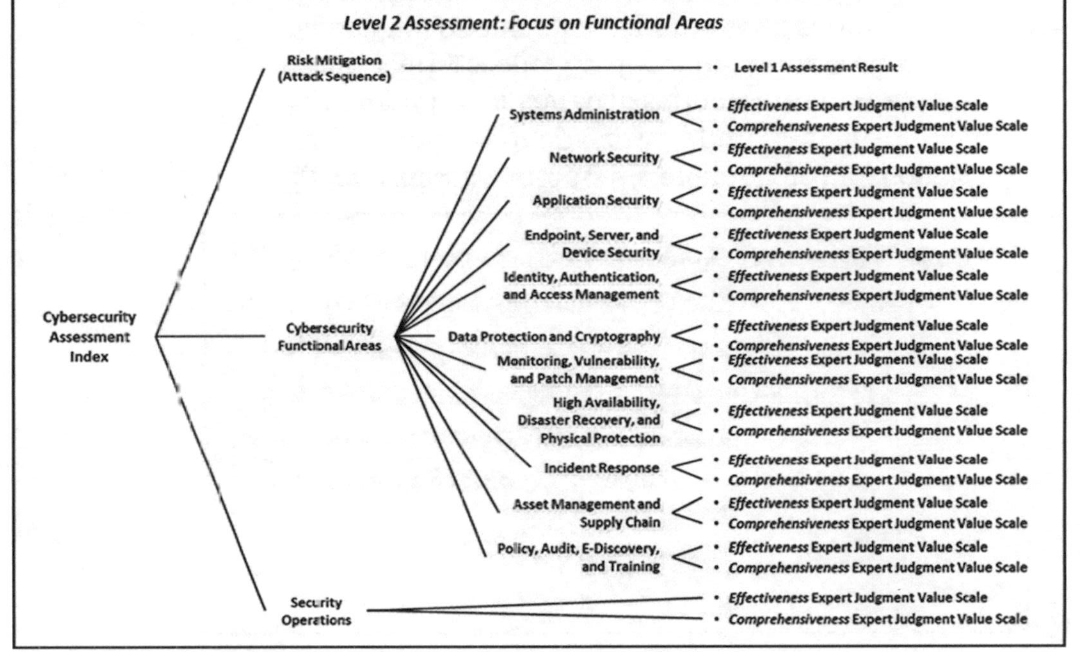

Level 2 Assessment: Focus on Functional Areas *(3 of 14)*

Object Measurement Steps (1 of 9)

- ***OM Step 1***
  - *What is the strength of the enterprise's cybersecurity when considering a high-level evaluation of risk mitigations, cybersecurity functional areas, and a high-level assessment of security operations?*
- ***OM Step 2***
  - Select the appropriate objects to measure.
    1. ***Risk mitigations*** against attack sequence steps with regard the Level 1 Assessment
    2. ***Cybersecurity functional areas***
    3. ***Security operations***
- ***OM Step 3***
  - For risk mitigations, the Level1_*Index* is to be simply carried over from the previous example assessment.
  - Cybersecurity functional areas and security operations will be measured using expert judgment as follows:

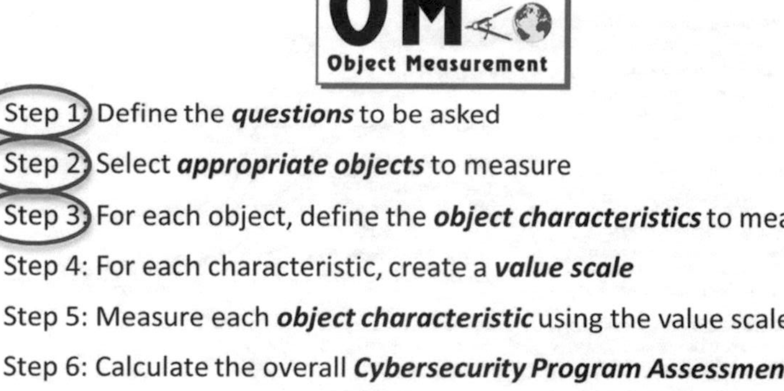

- ***Effectiveness*** represents the amount the functional area capabilities or operational processes are present and properly configured to support the applicable cybersecurity scope. The functional area is effective if the capabilities or operational processes it contains are mature and working properly, even if there are only a few of them.
- ***Comprehensiveness*** represents the amount the functional area capabilities or operational processes are being actively used to support the applicable cybersecurity scope. The functional area is comprehensive if it contains many of the capabilities and operational processes, even if they are not mature or working properly.

Level 2 Assessment: Focus on Functional Areas *(4 of 14)*

Object Measurement Steps *(2 of 9)*

- ***OM Step 4***
  - The expert defines the value scales for (1) effectiveness and (2) comprehensiveness, as shown below.

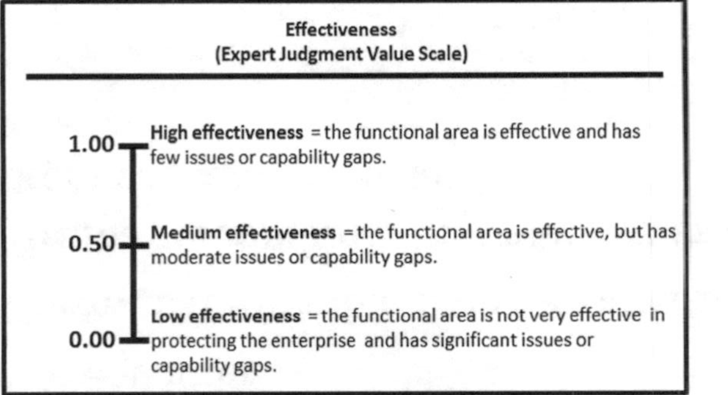

Effectiveness
(Expert Judgment Value Scale)
1.00
High effectiveness = the functional area is effective and has few issues or capability gaps.
0.50
Medium effectiveness = the functional area is effective, but has moderate issues or capability gaps.
0.00
Low effectiveness = the functional area is not very effective in protecting the enterprise and has significant issues or capability gaps.

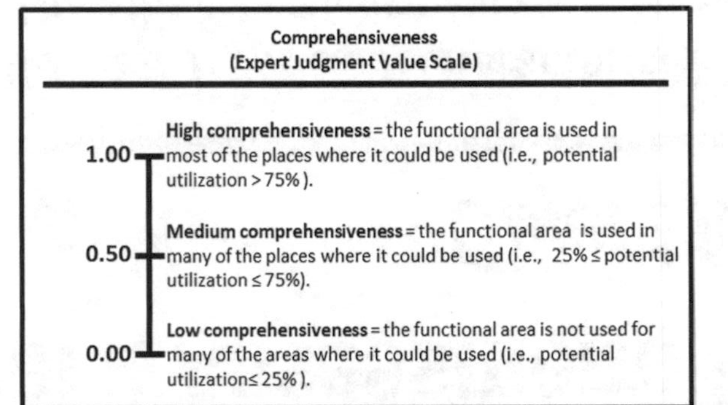

Comprehensiveness
(Expert Judgment Value Scale)
1.00
High comprehensiveness = the functional area is used in most of the places where it could be used (i.e., potential utilization > 75%).
0.50
Medium comprehensiveness = the functional area is used in many of the places where it could be used (i.e., 25% ≤ potential utilization ≤ 75%).
0.00
Low comprehensiveness = the functional area is not used for many of the areas where it could be used (i.e., potential utilization≤ 25%).

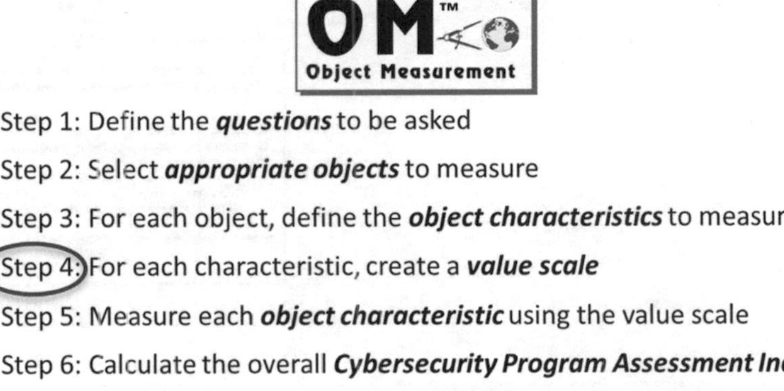

OM™
Object Measurement
Step 1: Define the questions to be asked
Step 2: Select appropriate objects to measure
Step 3: For each object, define the object characteristics to measure
Step 4: For each characteristic, create a value scale
Step 5: Measure each object characteristic using the value scale
Step 6: Calculate the overall Cybersecurity Program Assessment Index

  - These expert judgment value scales provide definitions and values for ***high***, ***medium***, and ***low*** with regard to effectiveness and comprehensiveness.

- It is possible for a functional area to be
  - effective but not comprehensive; and
  - comprehensive but not effective.

Level 2 Assessment: Focus on Functional Areas *(5 of 14)*

Object Measurement Steps (3 of 9)

- ***OM Step 4:*** For each characteristic, create a ***value scale (continued):***
  - Once the expert judgment value scales are defined, their values can be combined using an appropriate OM equation.
  - However, the graphic shows an alternative way to combine their values via an ***OM Scoring Matrix***.
  - The matrix combines the value scales in a way that is simpler than using the full OM equation, but produces similar results.

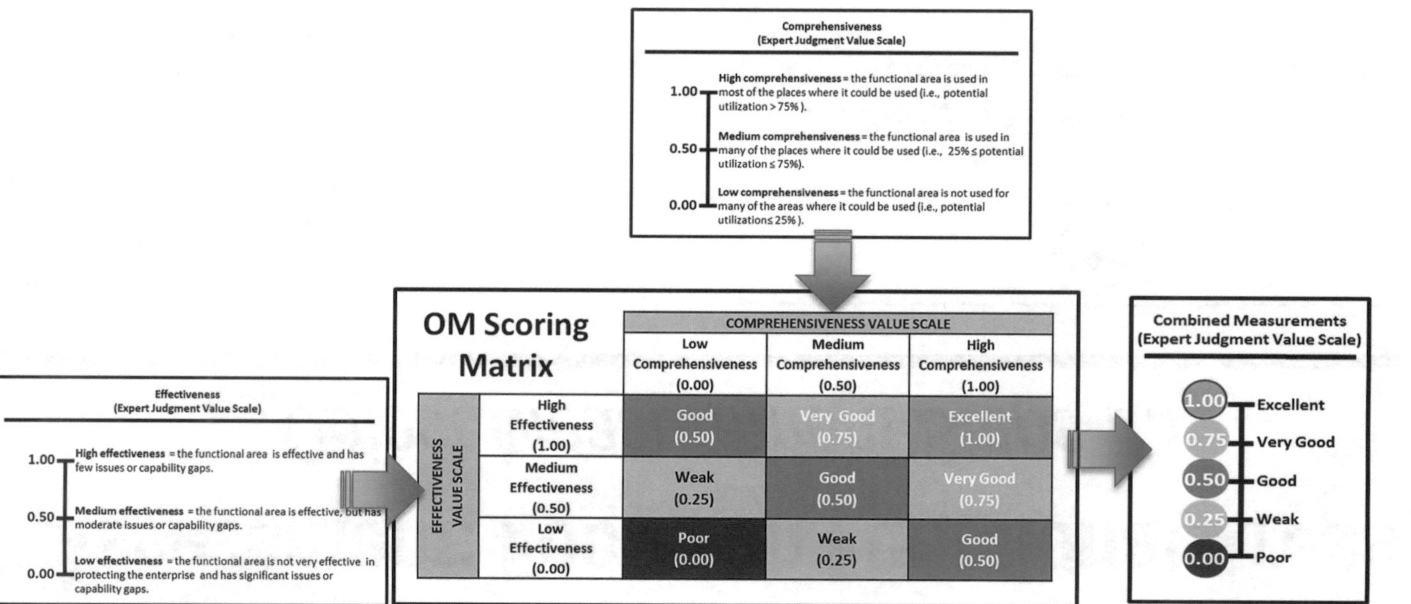

Level 2 Assessment: Focus on Functional Areas *(6 of 14)*

Object Measurement Steps *(4 of 9)*

- ***OM Step 4:*** For each characteristic, create a ***value scale (continued):***
  - The matrix defines a ***combined*** expert judgment value scale for an assessment.
  - Inputs to the OM Scoring Matrix are the ***comprehensiveness*** and ***effectiveness*** expert measurements.
  - The matrix converts the expert judgment measurements into a ***single combined measurement***.

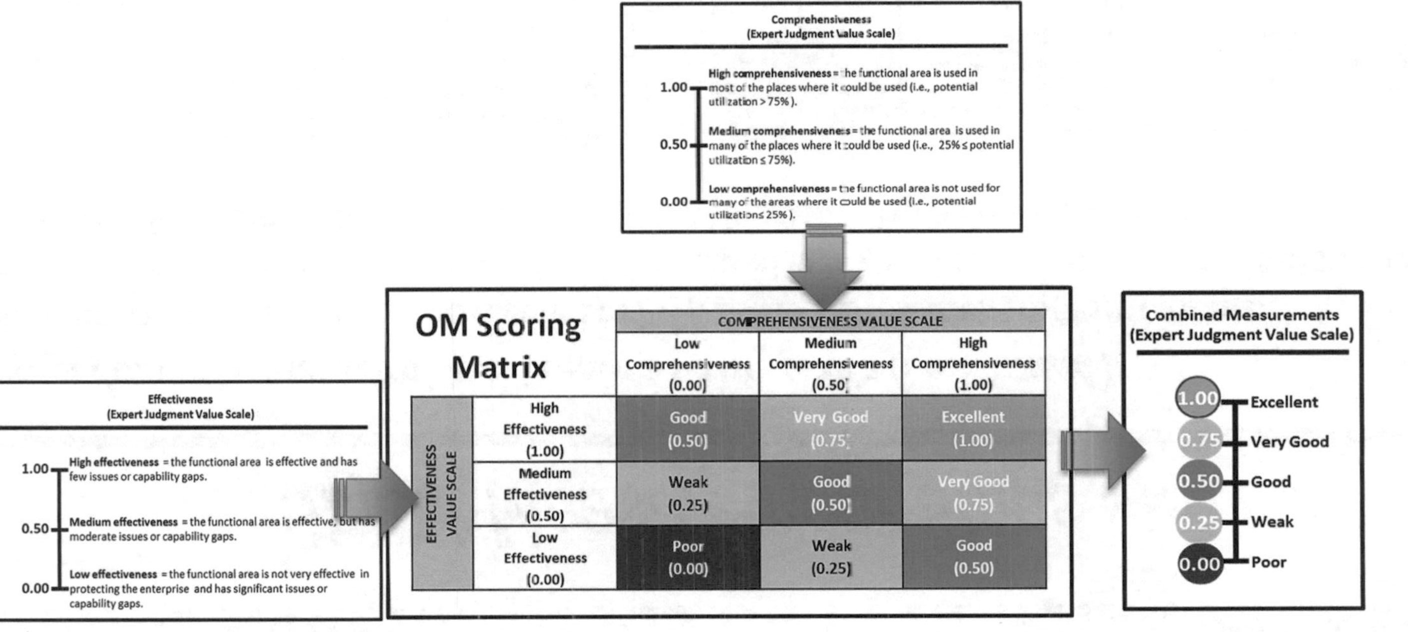

Level 2 Assessment: Focus on Functional Areas *(7 of 14)*

Object Measurement Steps *(5 of 9)*

- ***OM Step 4:*** For each characteristic, create a ***value scale (continued):***
  - An ***OM Measurement Pane*** can be created to help record assessment measurements.
  - The graphic shows measurement panes for 11 functional areas, and one for security operations (lower-right).
  - Level 2 expert judgment value scales are simplified here for display purposes only.

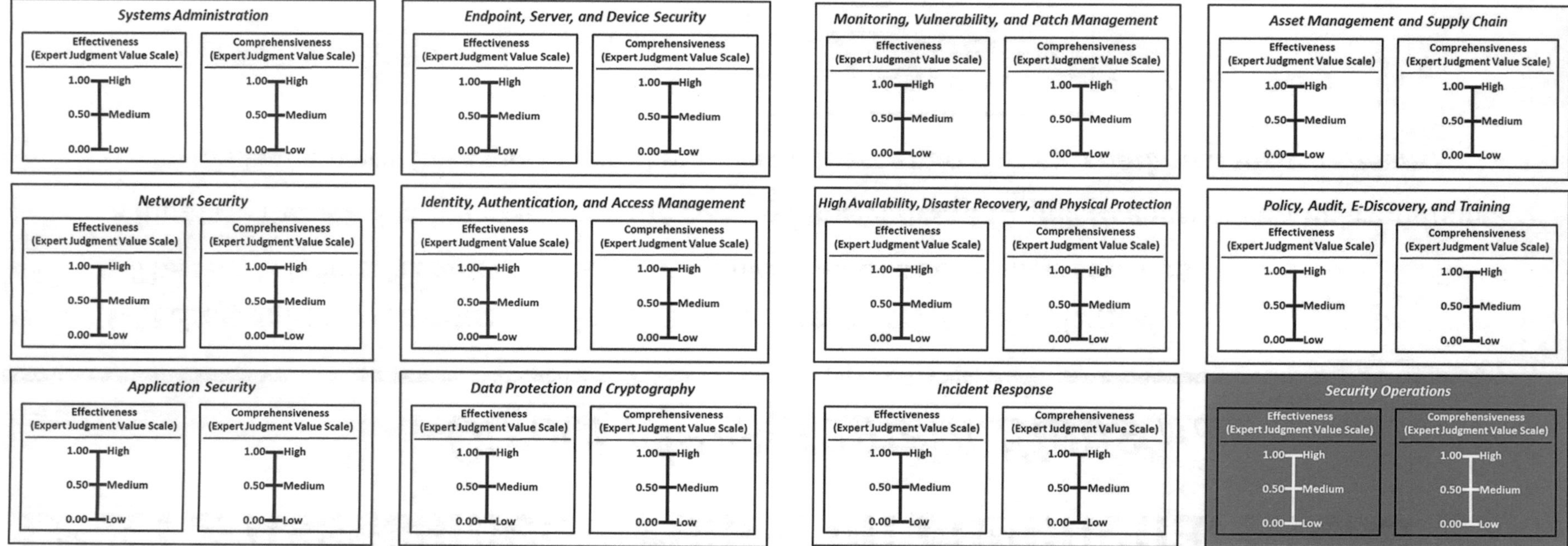

Level 2 Assessment: Focus on Functional Areas *(8 of 14)*

Object Measurement Steps *(6 of 9)*

- ***OM Step 4:*** For each characteristic, create a ***value scale (continued):***
  - The graphic shows how the two expert judgment value scales are networked to individual cybersecurity functional areas and overall security operations.

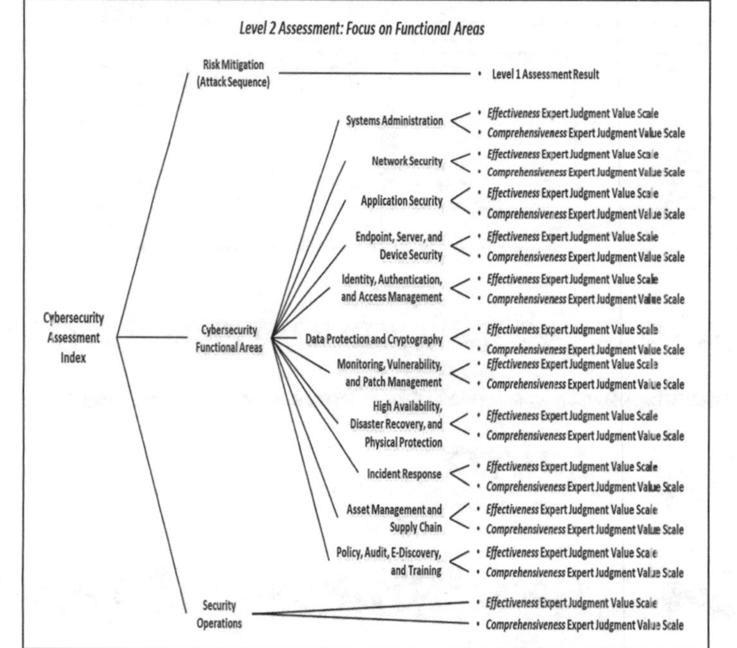

- Using the OM Scoring Matrix, the graphic shows possible values for the two expert judgment value scales. Also shown are possible ***combined*** values for (1) individual cybersecurity functional areas and (2) overall security operations.

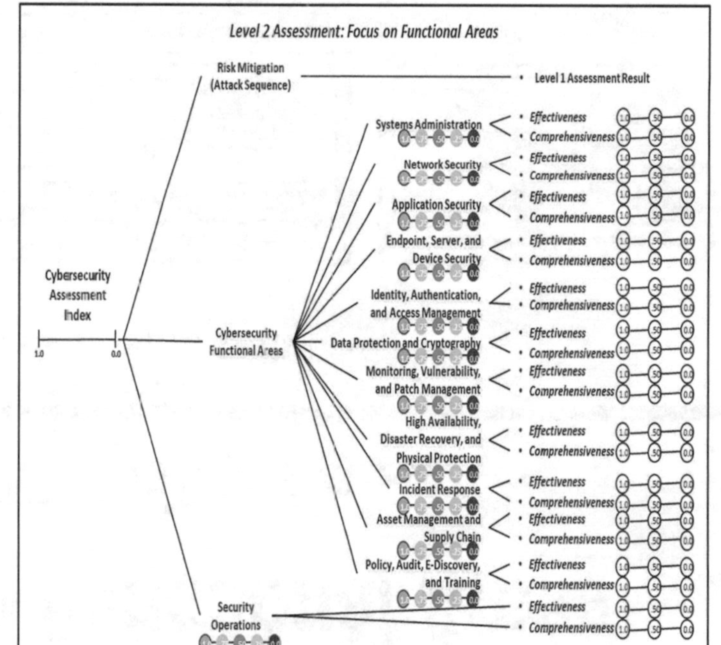

Level 2 Assessment: Focus on Functional Areas *(9 of 14)*

Object Measurement Steps *(7 of 9)*

- ***OM Step 5***: Measure each ***object characteristic*** using a value scale.

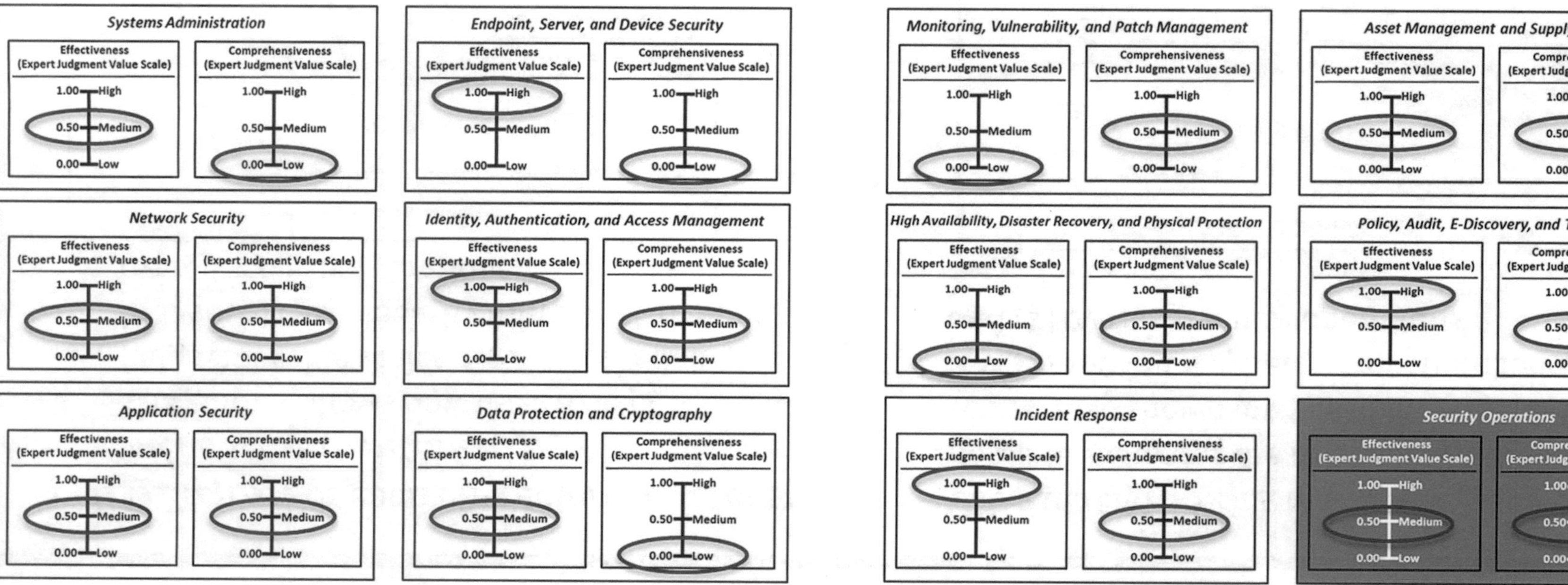

- Each value is tied to a definition expressed in enterprise cybersecurity language that helps explain the underlying meaning of the numbers and preserves, in part, the context of the assessment.

Level 2 Assessment: Focus on Functional Areas *(10 of 14)*

Object Measurement Steps (8 of 9)

- ***OM Step 5:** Measure each **object characteristic** using a value scale **(continued)***
  - The top graphic shows Level 2 expert judgment value scales defined and used for this assessment.
  - The bottom graphic shows expert judgment values for risk mitigations, functional areas, and overall security operations.
    - The Risk Mitigations value is carried over from Level 1 Assessment.
    - Functional Area Values are expressed in terms of effectiveness, comprehensiveness, and combined measurements.
    - Security Operations value is expressed in terms of effectiveness, comprehensiveness, and combined measurements.

Effectiveness
(Expert Judgment Value Scale)

- 1.00 — **High effectiveness** = the functional area or is effective and has few issues or capability gaps.
- 0.50 — **Medium effectiveness** = the functional area is effective, but has moderate issues or capability gaps.
- 0.00 — **Low effectiveness** = the functional area is not very effective in protecting the enterprise and has significant issues or capability gaps.

Comprehensiveness
(Expert Judgment Value Scale)

- 1.00 — **High comprehensiveness** = the functional area is used in most of the places where it could be used (i.e., potential utilization > 75%).
- 0.50 — **Medium comprehensiveness** = the functional area is used in many of the places where it could be used (i.e., 25% ≤ potential utilization ≤ 75%).
- 0.00 — **Low comprehensiveness** = the functional area is not used for many of the areas where it could be used (i.e., potential utilization≤ 25%).

Level 2 Assessment Focusing on Functional Areas (Risk Mitigations, Functional Areas, and Security Operations)	Effectiveness	Comprehensiveness	Combined Measurements
Risk Mitigations (carried over from Level 1 Assessment)	N/A	N/A	0.47
Systems Administration	Medium = 0.50	Low = 0.00	0.25
Network Security	Medium = 0.50	Medium = 0.50	0.50
Application Security	Medium = 0.50	Medium = 0.50	0.50
Endpoint, Server, and Device Security	High = 1.00	Low = 0.00	0.50
Identity, Authentication, and Access Management	High = 1.00	Medium = 0.50	0.75
Data Protection and Cryptography	Medium = 0.50	Low = 0.00	0.25
Monitoring, Vulnerability, and Patch Management	Low = 0.00	Medium = 0.50	0.25
High Availability, Disaster Recovery, and Physical Protection	Medium = 0.50	Medium = 0.50	0.50
Incident Response	High = 1.00	Medium = 0.50	0.75
Asset Management and Supply Chain	Medium = 0.50	Medium = 0.50	0.50
Policy, Audit, E-Discovery, and Training	High = 1.00	Medium = 0.50	0.75
Security Operations	Medium = 0.50	Medium = 0.50	0.50

Level 2 Assessment: Focus on Functional Areas *(11 of 14)*

Object Measurement Steps *(9 of 9)*

- ***OM Step 6***: Calculate the overall ***Cybersecurity Program Assessment Index***.
  - The graphic shows
    - recorded ***expert value judgments*** in terms of effectiveness and comprehensiveness (see ellipses);
    - resulting ***functional area metrics*** and overall ***security operations metric*** based on the OM Scoring Matrix (see solid circles with numbers); and
    - how the overall **Level2_*Index*** is calculated with an appropriate OM*Index* equation, as shown below.

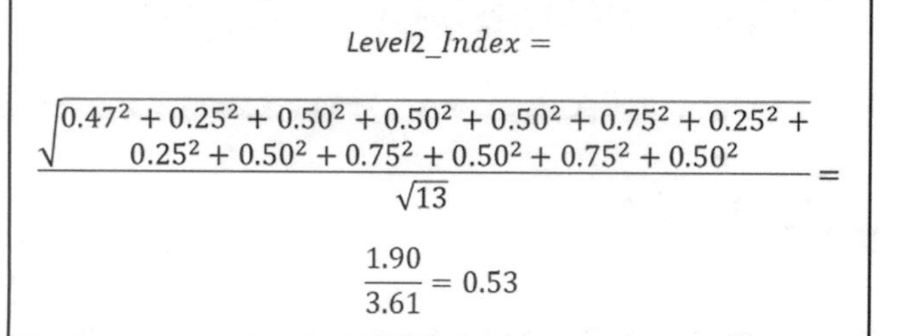

$$Level2\_Index = \frac{\sqrt{0.47^2 + 0.25^2 + 0.50^2 + 0.50^2 + 0.50^2 + 0.75^2 + 0.25^2 + 0.25^2 + 0.50^2 + 0.75^2 + 0.50^2 + 0.75^2 + 0.50^2}}{\sqrt{13}} =$$

$$\frac{1.90}{3.61} = 0.53$$

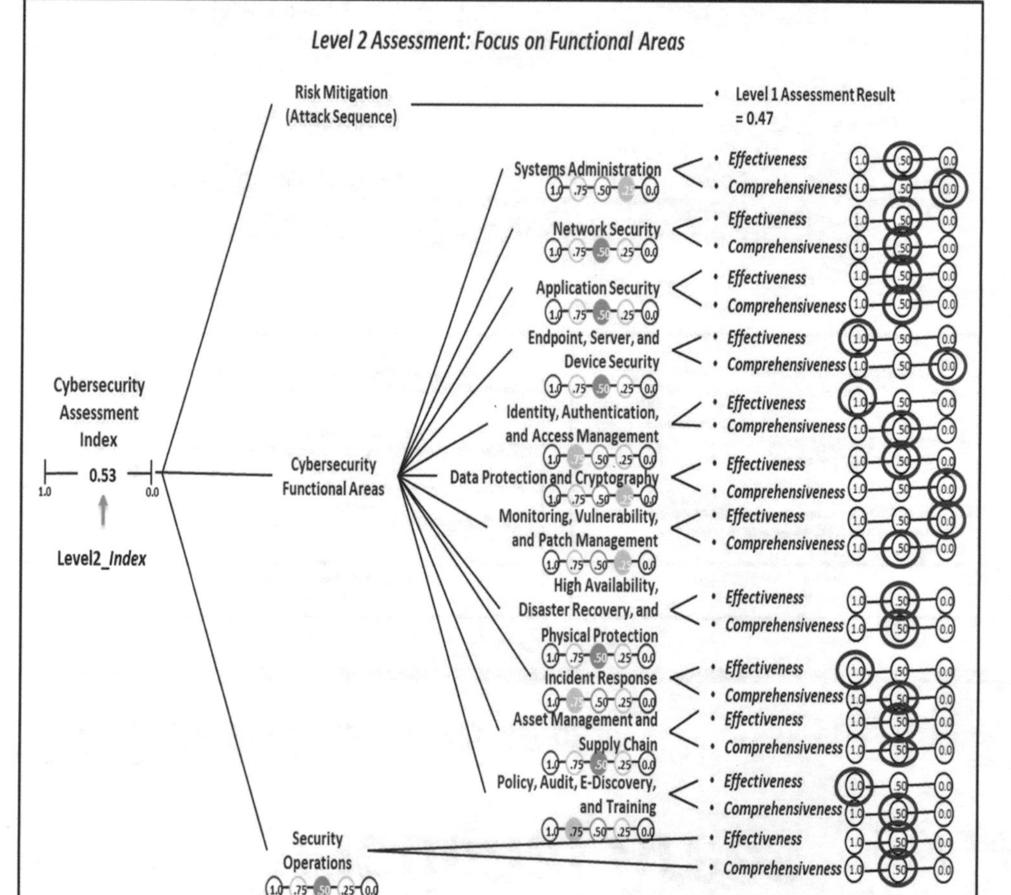

Level 2 Assessment: Focus on Functional Areas *(12 of 14)*

What does a Level2_*Index = 0.53 or 53% really mean?*

- The result represents the enterprise's cybersecurity effectiveness as determined from the expert judgment terms used to define the expert judgment value scales.
- By navigating the measurement map from left to right, the Level2_*Index* score can be unfolded and traced back to the expert judgment value scales.
- For example, ***Incident Response* = *0.75*** means the following:
  - ***Effectiveness* = *1.0***
    - High Effectiveness = The functional area is effective and has few capability gaps.
  - ***Comprehensiveness* = *0.50***
    - Medium Effectiveness = The functional area is used in many of the places where it could be used (in other words, 25% ≤ potential utilization ≤ 75%).

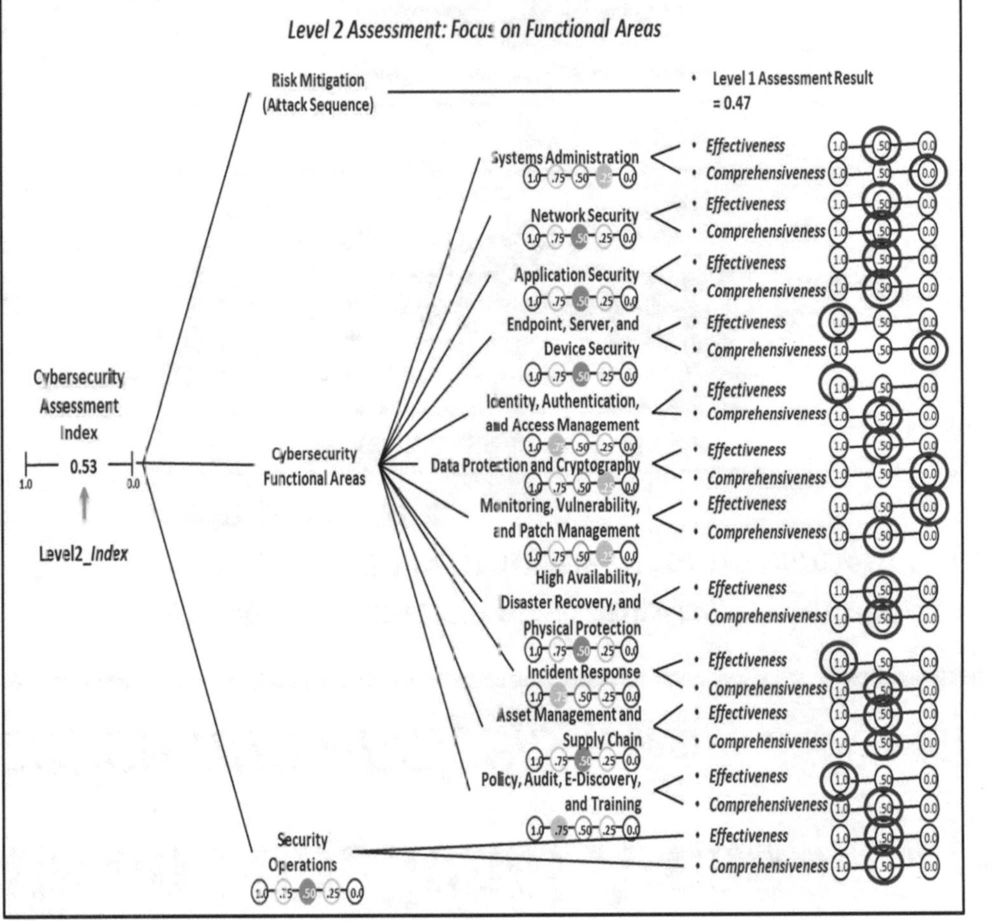

Level 2 Assessment: Focus on Functional Areas *(13 of 14)*

Results Visualization and Analysis (1 of 2)

- The upper graphic visualizes assessment results using a vertical bar (column) chart.
  - Functional areas can be quickly compared to one another.
  - Weak functional areas can be identified for subsequent improvement.
  - Values are shown on a scale from 0% to 100% while previous values were shown on a scale from 0 to 1.0; values are the same.
- The bottom graphic visualizes the results using a spider chart (also known as a radar chart).
  - Useful for emphasizing that all the functional areas should be of approximately equal effectiveness (that is, the target value) for overall enterprise cybersecurity to be effective
- Three functional areas scoring the lowest stand out compared to the rest.
  - Systems Administration
  - Data Protection and Cryptography
  - Monitoring, Vulnerability, and Patch Management

- Weak functional areas may be exploitable and should be prioritized for investment and improvement.

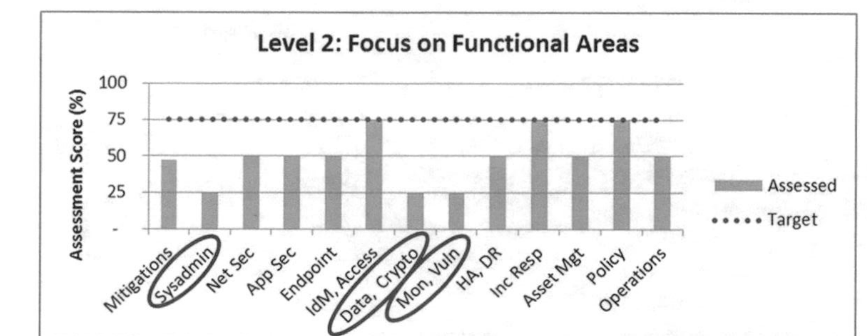

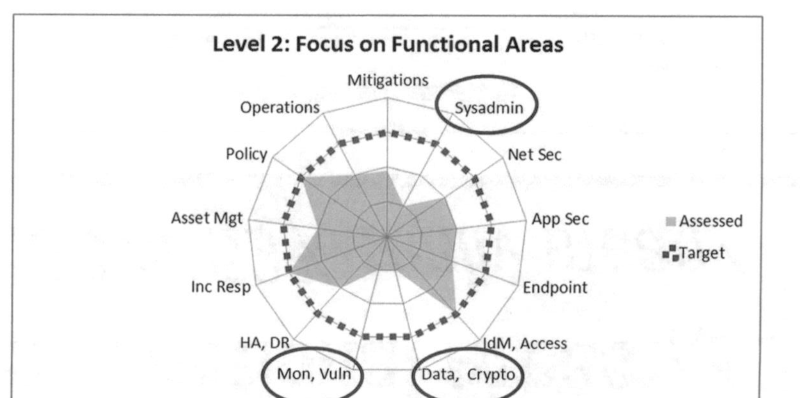

Level 2 Assessment: Focus on Functional Areas *(14 of 14)*

Results Visualization and Analysis *(2 of 2)*

- Both graphics show a ***target*** value at 75% (0.75).
  - Represent the enterprise's cybersecurity goal for the example security scope
  - Make it easy to see at a glance where deficiencies lie
  - Help leadership to understand the magnitude of the gap between what is present and what is desired
- Target value does not necessarily need to be 100% (1.0).
  - Business leadership sets the target bar to an acceptable level to balance
    - competing interests of business expediency and cybersecurity protection; and
    - controlling security costs and the impacts security can have on productivity.

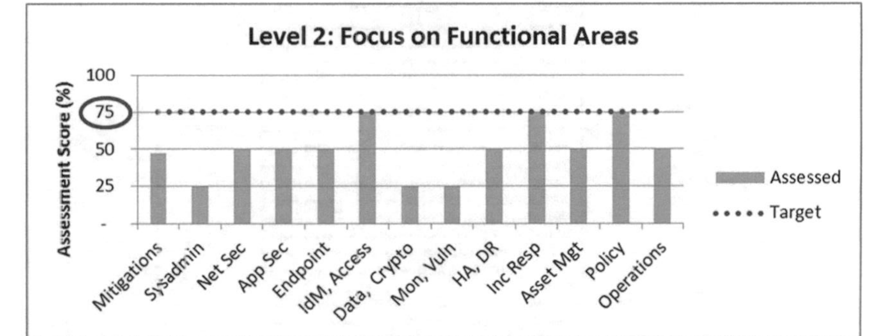

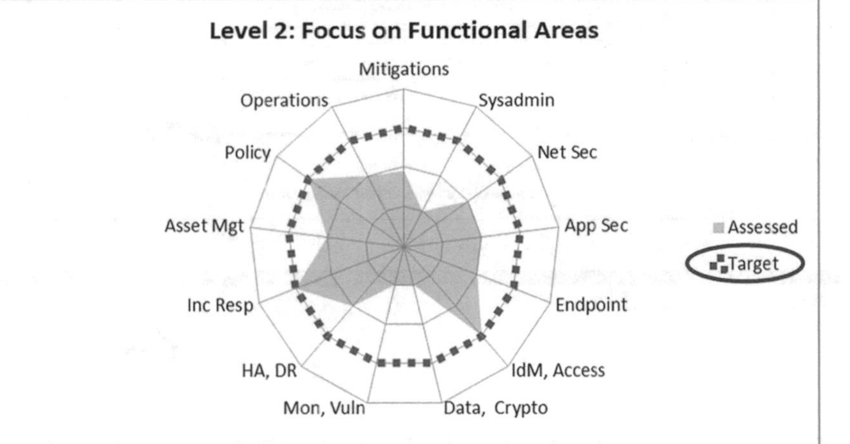

Level 3 Assessment: Focus on Capabilities *(1 of 30)*

Context *(1 of 2)*

- Level 3 assessment involves analyzing
  - risk mitigations,
  - functional areas, and
  - security operations.
- Assessment security scope
  - consists of enterprise's general-purpose IT environment.
- Assessment
  - incorporates the ***expert judgment*** results of the Level 1 Risk Mitigations Assessment of the five-step enterprise attack sequence;
  - uses ***observed data*** to assess the 113 enterprise cybersecurity functional area capabilities;
  - uses ***expert judgment*** to evaluate the 17 operational processes; and
  - uses ***object measurement equation*** to calculate aggregate scores for each functional area and security operations.

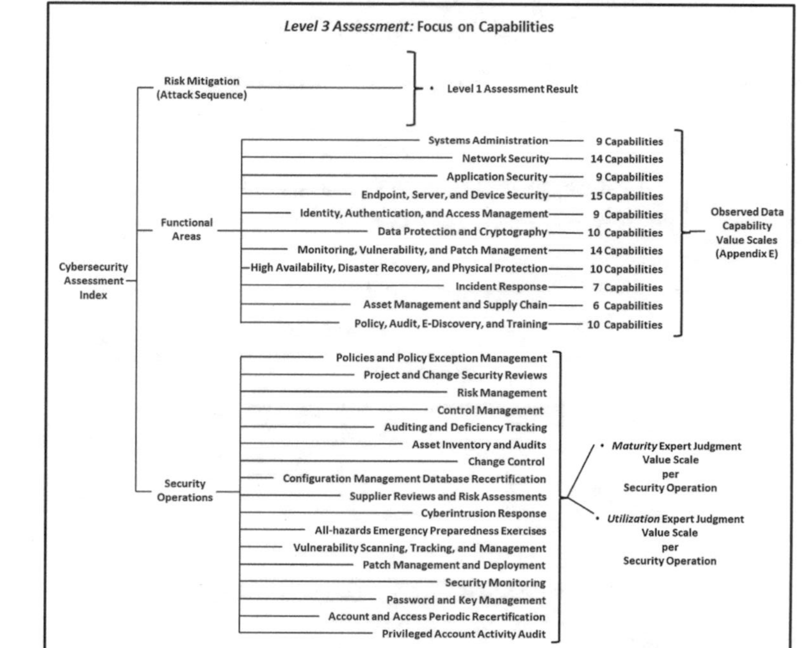

- The scores for Risk Mitigation, Functional Areas, and Security Operations are combined together to get a single Level3_*Index* value for the entire enterprise security scope.

Level 3 Assessment: Focus on Capabilities *(2 of 30)*

Context *(2 of 2)*

- Assessment (continued)
  - includes a detailed analysis of the enterprise's cybersecurity capabilities and operational processes;
  - uses observed data rather than expert data for most of its data gathering;
  - is significantly more detailed than Level 1 and Level 2 Assessments; and
  - requires a commensurately greater level of effort to perform.
- When performed by an external assessor, it generally requires onsite visits and interviews with IT leadership involved with each of the functional areas and their capabilities.
- Once completed, it delivers a detailed view of the enterprise's cybersecurity posture that can then be used to support detailed strategic, programmatic, and tactical decision-making.

Functional Area	Capabilities	
Systems Administration (SA)	• Bastion hosts • Out-of-Band (OOB) management • Network isolation • Integrated Lights-Out (ILO), Keyboard Video Mouse (KVM), and power controls • Virtualization and Storage Area Network (SAN) management	• Separation of administration from services • Multi-factor authentication for Systems Administrators (SAs) • Administrator audit trail(s) • Command logging and analytics
Network Security (NS)	• Switches and routers • Software Defined Networking (SDN) • Domain Name System (DNS) and Dynamic Host Configuration Protocol (DHCP) • Network Time Protocol (NTP) • Network service management • Firewall and virtual machine firewall • Network Intrusion Detection / Network Intrusion Prevention System (IDS / IPS)	• Wireless networking (Wi-Fi) • Packet intercept and capture • Secure Sockets Layer (SSL) intercept • Network Access Control (NAC) • Virtual Private Networking (VPN) and Internet Protocol Security (IPSec) • Network Traffic Analysis (NTA) • Network Data Analytics (NDA)
Application Security (AS)	• E-mail security • Webshell detection • Application firewalls • Database firewalls • Forward proxy and web filters	• Reverse proxy • Data Leakage Protection (DLP) • Secure application and database software development • Software code vulnerability analysis
Endpoint, Server, and Device Security (ESDS)	• Local administrator privilege restrictions • Computer security and logging policies • Endpoint and media encryption • Computer access controls • Forensic imaging support for investigations • Virtual desktop / thin clients • Mobile Device Management (MDM) • Anti-virus / anti-malware	• Application whitelisting • In-memory malware detection • Host firewall and intrusion detection • "Gold code" software images • Security Technical Implementation Guides (STIGs) • Always-on Virtual Private Networking (VPN) • File integrity and change monitoring
Identity, Authentication, and Access Management (IAAM)	• Identity life cycle management • Enterprise directory • Multi-factor authentication • Privilege management and access control • Identity and access audit trail and reporting	• Lightweight Directory Access Protocol (LDAP) • Kerberos, RADIUS, 802.1x • Federated authentication • Security Assertion Markup Language (SAML)
Data Protection and Cryptography (DPC)	• Secure Sockets Layer (SSL) and Transport Layer Security (TLS) • Digital certificates (Public Key Infrastructure [PKI]) • Key hardware protection (Smart cards, Trusted Platform Modules [TPMs], and Hardware Security Modules [HSMs])	• One-Time Password (OTP) and Out-of-Band (OOB) authentication • Key life cycle management • Digital signatures • Complex passwords • Data encryption and tokenization • Brute force attack detection • Digital Rights Management (DRM)
Monitoring, Vulnerability, and Patch Management (MVPM)	• Operational performance monitoring • System and network monitoring • System configuration change detection • Privilege and access change detection • Log aggregation • Data analytics • Security Information and Event Management (SIEM)	• Network and computer vulnerability scanning • Penetration testing • Patch management and deployment • Rogue network device detection • Rogue wireless access point detection • Honeypots / honeynets / honeytokens • Security Operations Center (SOC)
High Availability, Disaster Recovery, and Physical Protection (HADRPP)	• Clustering • Load balancing, Global Server Load Balancing (GSLB) • Network failover, subnet spanning • Virtual machine snapshots and cloning • Data mirroring and replication	• Backups and backup management • Off-site storage • Facilities protection • Physical access controls • Physical security monitoring
Incident Response (IR)	• Threat information • Incident tracking • Forensic tools • Computer imaging	• Indicators of Compromise (IOCs) • Black hole server • Regulatory / legal coordination
Asset Management and Supply Chain (AMSC)	• Asset management databases • Configuration Management Databases (CMDB) • Change management databases	• Software inventory and license management • Supplier certification processes • Secure disposal, recycling, and data destruction
Policy, Audit, E-Discovery, and Training (PAET)	• Governance, Risk, and Compliance (GRC), with reporting • Compliance and control frameworks (SOX, PCI, others) • Audit frameworks • Customer Certification and Accreditation (C&A)	• Policy and policy exception management • Risk and threat management • Privacy compliance • E-Discovery tools • Personnel security and background checks • Security awareness and training

Level 3 Assessment: Focus on Capabilities *(3 of 30)*

Object Measurement Steps *(1 of 22)*

- ***OM Step 1***
  - *What is the strength of the enterprise's cybersecurity when considering a detailed evaluation of risk mitigations, 113 functional area cybersecurity capabilities, and 17 security operational processes?*
- ***OM Step 2***
  - Select the appropriate objects to measure.
    - ***Risk mitigations***: 5 attack sequence steps
    - ***Functional area capabilities***: 113 capabilities in the 11 functional areas
    - ***Operational processes***: 17 processes and supporting information systems
- ***OM Step 3***
  - Risk mitigations will be evaluated using ***expert judgment*** based on their effectiveness in reducing the probability and the impact of the attack sequence.
  - The 113 functional area capabilities will be objectively evaluated using ***observed data***.

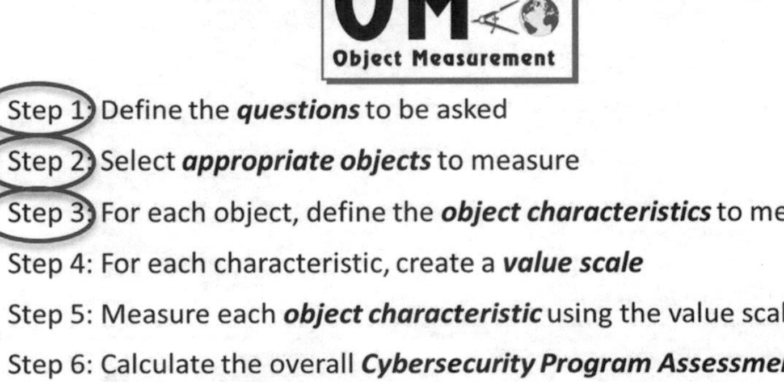

  - The 17 operational processes will be evaluated using ***expert judgment*** as follows:
    - ***Maturity*** represents how mature the operational process is in terms of how consistently it is performed, the quality of the data it maintains, and its ability to handle exceptions and special cases. A mature operational process is robust and reliable, uses appropriate supporting tools and technologies, and is consistently performed using documented procedures.

Level 3 Assessment: Focus on Capabilities *(4 of 30)*

Object Measurement Steps *(2 of 22)*

- ***OM Step 3:*** For each object, define the ***object characteristics*** to measure ***(continued):***
  - ***Utilization*** represents how comprehensively the enterprise utilizes the operational process across the assessed scope. A well-utilized process is used everywhere it should be used with safeguards in place to ensure it cannot be bypassed, ignored, or arbitrarily exempted.
  - It is possible for an operational process to be mature but not utilized, or well utilized but immature.
- ***OM Step 4***: For each characteristic, create a ***value scale***.
  - ***Risk mitigations*** values will be carried over from the Level 1 Assessment along with their associated *expert judgment* value scales.
  - ***The 113 capabilities*** of the 11 functional areas will be assessed using the *observed data* value scales that are defined in Appendix E of this study guide.
  - ***The 17 operational processes*** will be evaluated using *expert judgment* maturity and utilization value scales.

- The expert defines the value scales for (1) maturity and (2) utilization in terms of high, medium, and low values, as shown below.

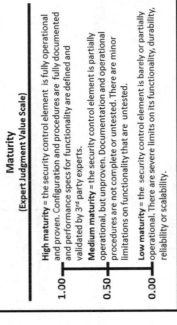

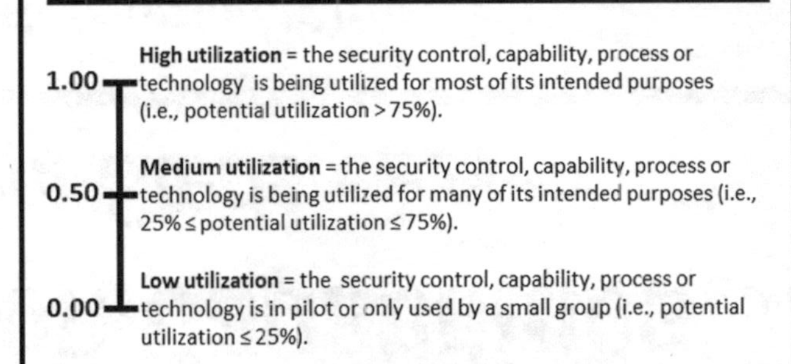

Utilization
(Expert Judgment Value Scale)

- 1.00 — **High utilization** = the security control, capability, process or technology is being utilized for most of its intended purposes (i.e., potential utilization > 75%).
- 0.50 — **Medium utilization** = the security control, capability, process or technology is being utilized for many of its intended purposes (i.e., 25% ≤ potential utilization ≤ 75%).
- 0.00 — **Low utilization** = the security control, capability, process or technology is in pilot or only used by a small group (i.e., potential utilization ≤ 25%).

Level 3 Assessment: Focus on Capabilities *(5 of 30)*

Object Measurement Steps (3 of 22)

- ***OM Step 4:*** For each characteristic, create a ***value scale (continued):***
  - Once the expert judgment value scales are defined, their values can be combined using an appropriate OM equation.
  - However, the graphic shows an alternative way to combine ***expert measurement*** values via an ***OM Scoring Matrix.***
  - The matrix combines the value scales in a way that is simpler than using the full OM equation, but produces similar results.

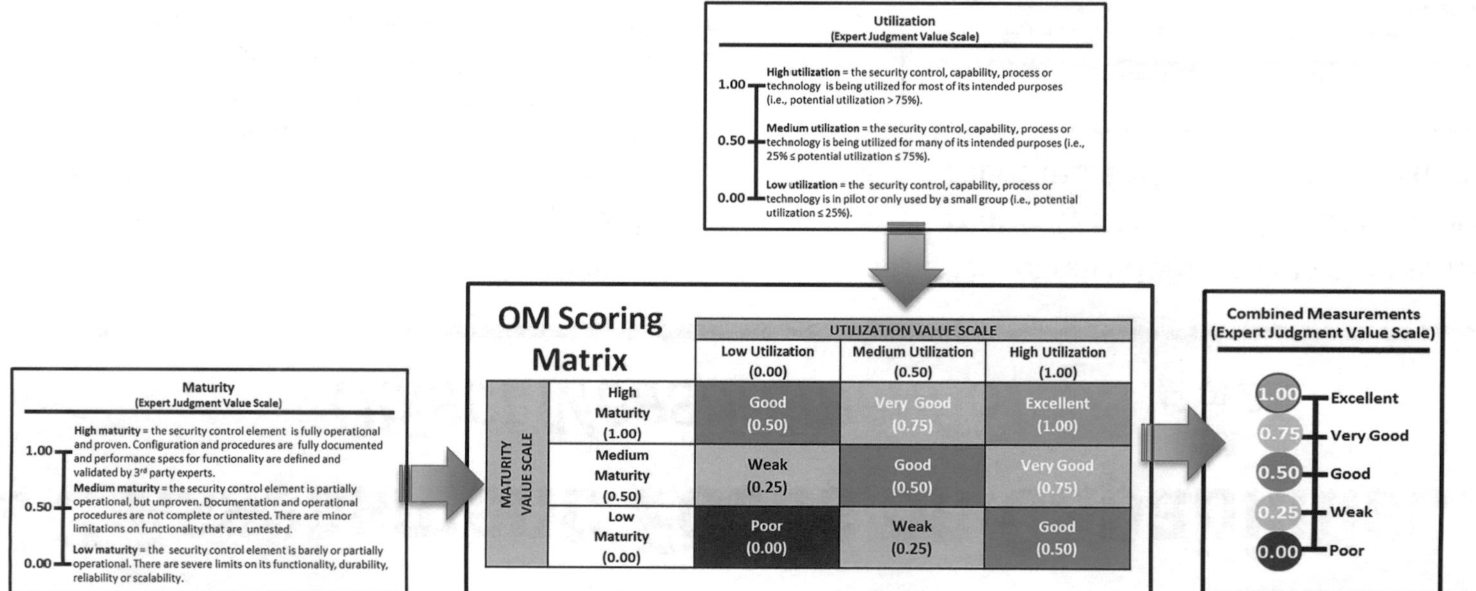

Utilization
(Expert Judgment Value Scale)
1.00
High utilization = the security control, capability, process or technology is being utilized for most of its intended purposes (i.e., potential utilization > 75%).
0.50
Medium utilization = the security control, capability, process or technology is being utilized for many of its intended purposes (i.e., 25% ≤ potential utilization ≤ 75%).
0.00
Low utilization = the security control, capability, process or technology is in pilot or only used by a small group (i.e., potential utilization ≤ 25%).
Maturity
(Expert Judgment Value Scale)
1.00
High maturity = the security control element is fully operational and proven. Configuration and procedures are fully documented and performance specs for functionality are defined and validated by 3rd party experts.
0.50
Medium maturity = the security control element is partially operational, but unproven. Documentation and operational procedures are not complete or untested. There are minor limitations on functionality that are untested.
0.00
Low maturity = the security control element is barely or partially operational. There are severe limits on its functionality, durability, reliability or scalability.
OM Scoring Matrix
UTILIZATION VALUE SCALE
MATURITY VALUE SCALE
Low Utilization (0.00)
Medium Utilization (0.50)
High Utilization (1.00)
High Maturity (1.00)
Good (0.50)
Very Good (0.75)
Excellent (1.00)
Medium Maturity (0.50)
Weak (0.25)
Good (0.50)
Very Good (0.75)
Low Maturity (0.00)
Poor (0.00)
Weak (0.25)
Good (0.50)
Combined Measurements
(Expert Judgment Value Scale)
1.00 Excellent
0.75 Very Good
0.50 Good
0.25 Weak
0.00 Poor

Level 3 Assessment: Focus on Capabilities *(6 of 30)*

Object Measurement Steps *(4 of 22)*

- ***OM Step 4:*** For each characteristic, create a ***value scale (continued):***
  - The matrix defines a ***combined*** expert judgment value scale for an assessment.
  - Inputs to the OM Scoring Matrix are the ***utilization*** and ***maturity*** expert measurements.
  - The matrix converts the expert judgment measurements into a ***single combined measurement***.

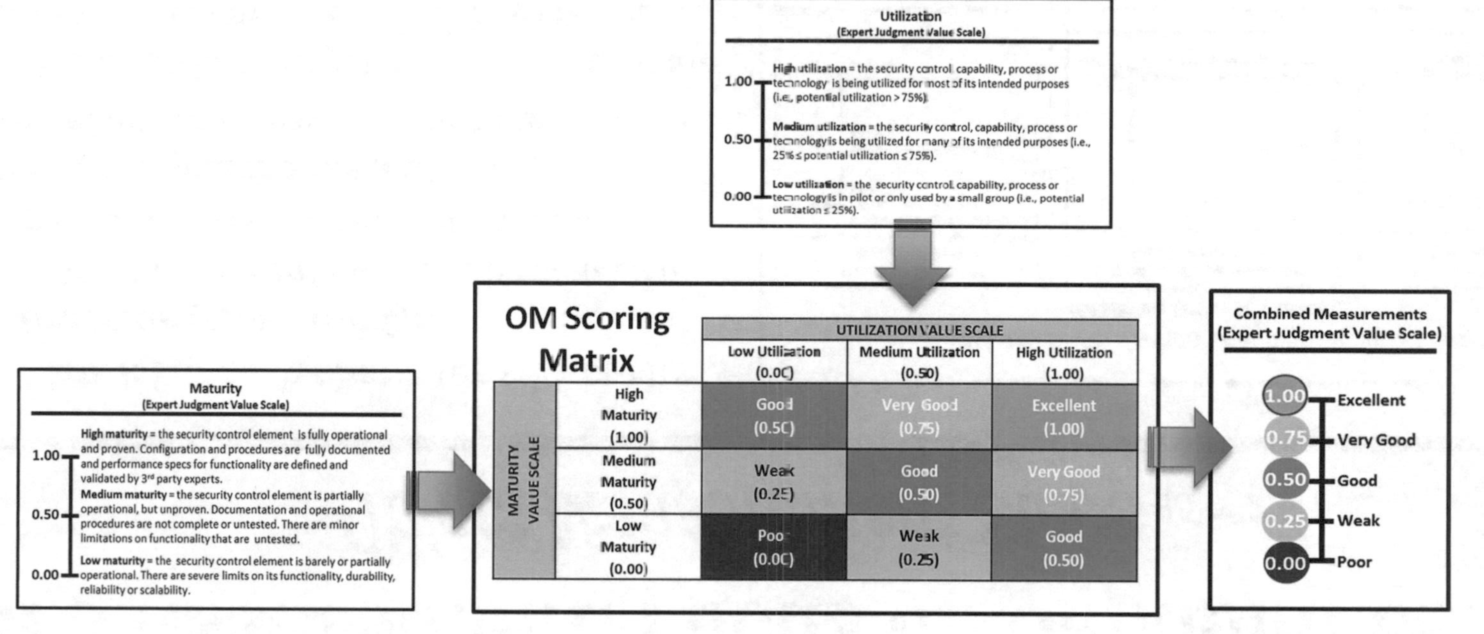

Level 3 Assessment: Focus on Capabilities *(7 of 30)*

Object Measurement Steps *(5 of 22)*

- ***OM Step 4:*** For each characteristic, create a ***value scale (continued):***
  - An ***OM Measurement Pane*** can be created to help record assessment measurements.
  - The graphic presents the ***Systems Administration*** measurement pane.
  - Similar measurement panes can be created for the other functional areas, but they are not shown here.
- As assessment complexity increases, it is helpful to have measurement panes.
  - Help explain the underlying meaning of the assessment because each "tick mark" is defined by enterprise language
  - Help organize possible measurements
  - Help with recording measurement
  - Help preserve, in part, the context of the assessment

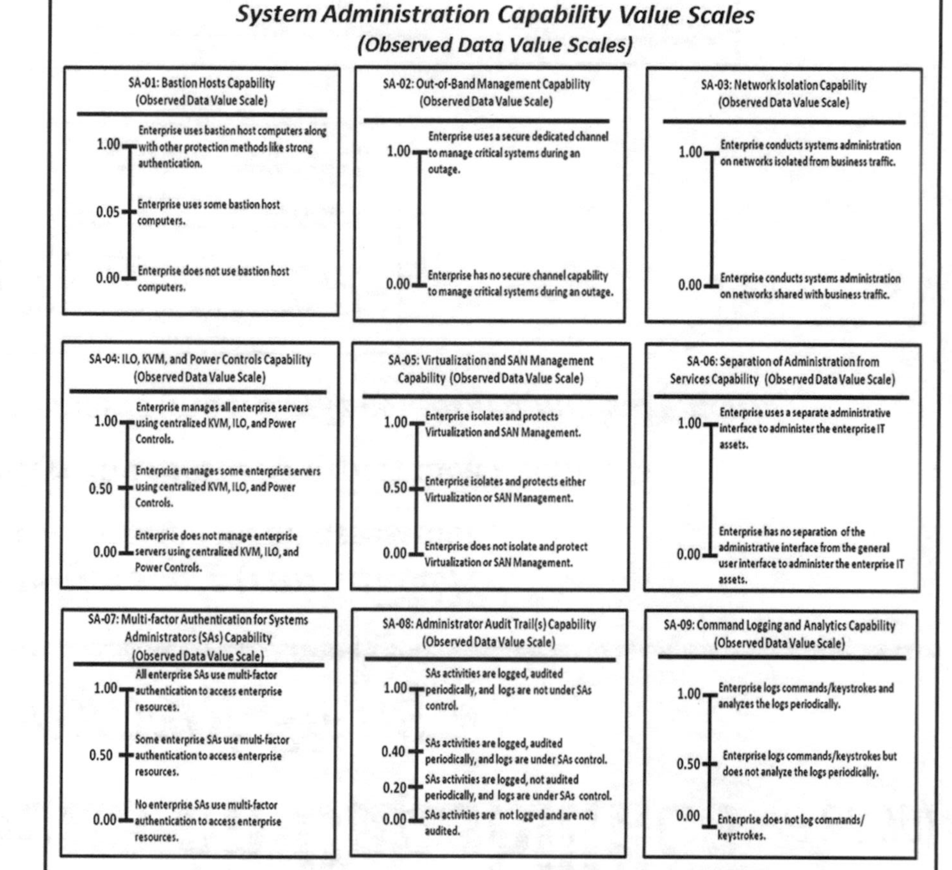

Level 3 Assessment: Focus on Capabilities *(8 of 30)*

Object Measurement Steps *(6 of 22)*

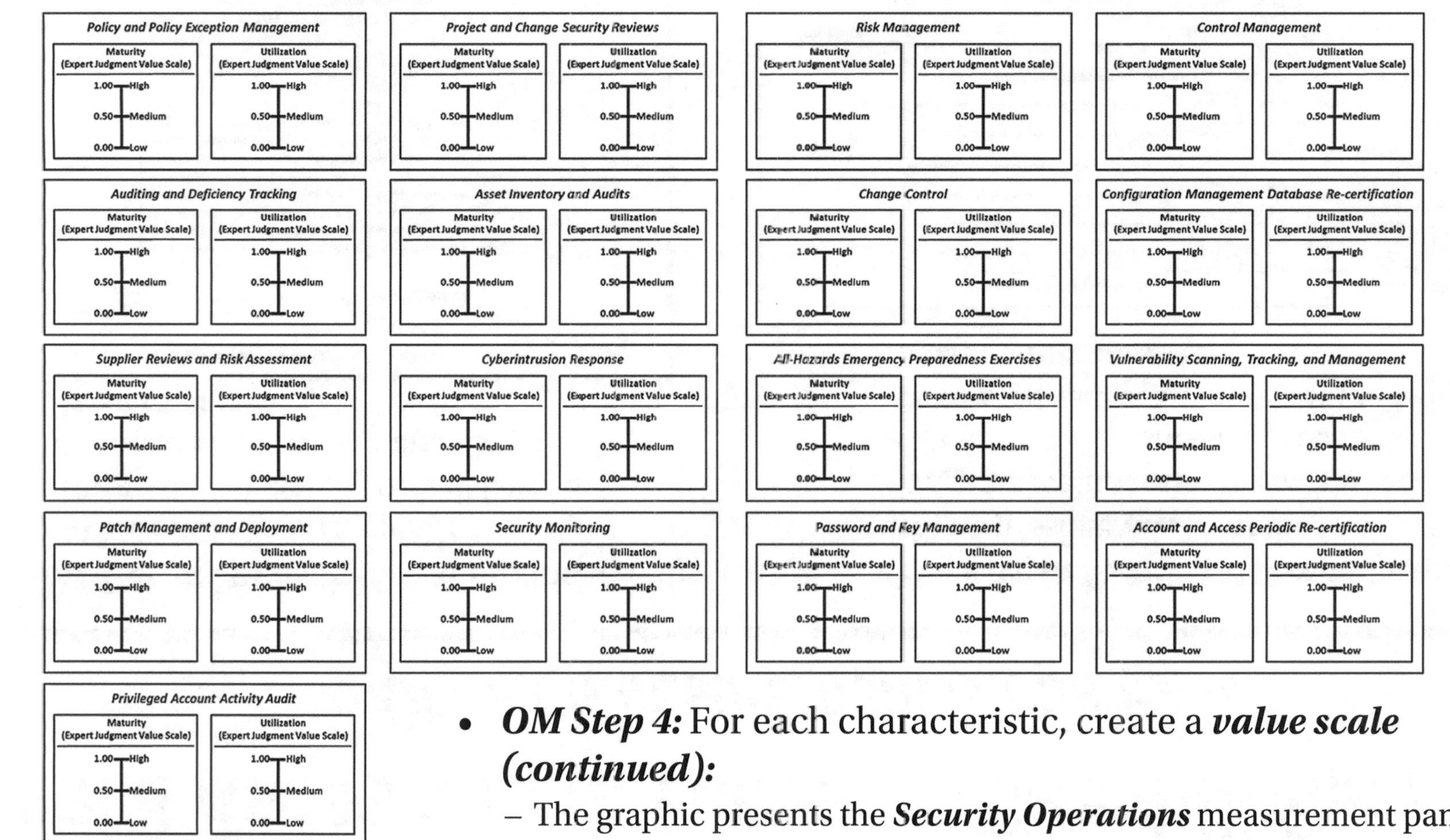

- ***OM Step 4:*** For each characteristic, create a ***value scale (continued):***
  - The graphic presents the ***Security Operations*** measurement pane.

Level 3 Assessment: Focus on Capabilities *(9 of 30)*

Object Measurement Steps *(7 of 22)*

- ***OM Step 4:*** For each characteristic, create a ***value scale (continued):***
  - The graphic shows the overall Level 3 Assessment: Focus on Capabilities ***Measurement Map***.

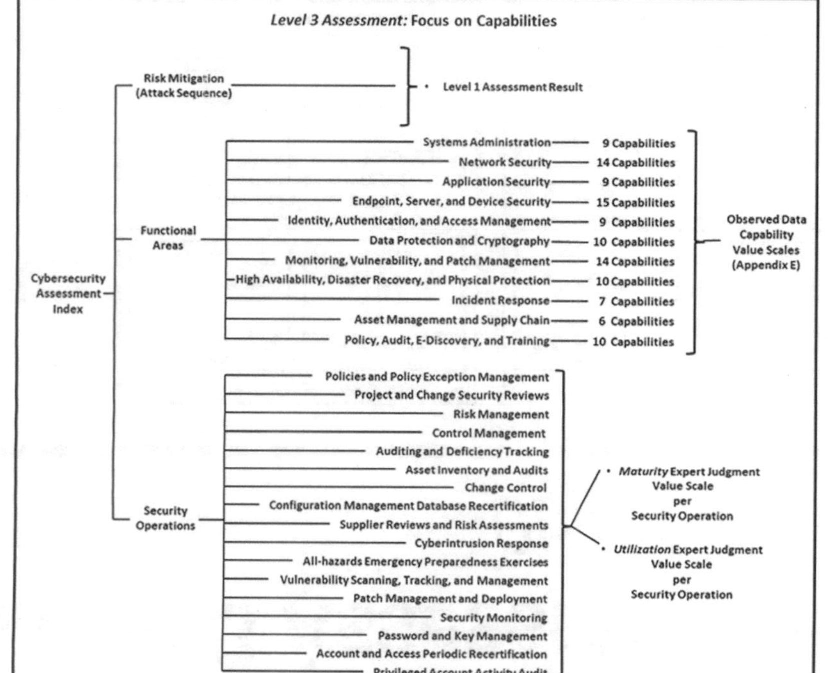

- Using the OM Scoring Matrix, the graphic shows possible values for the two expert judgment value scales regarding Security Operations. Also shown are possible ***combined*** values for individual security operations processes.

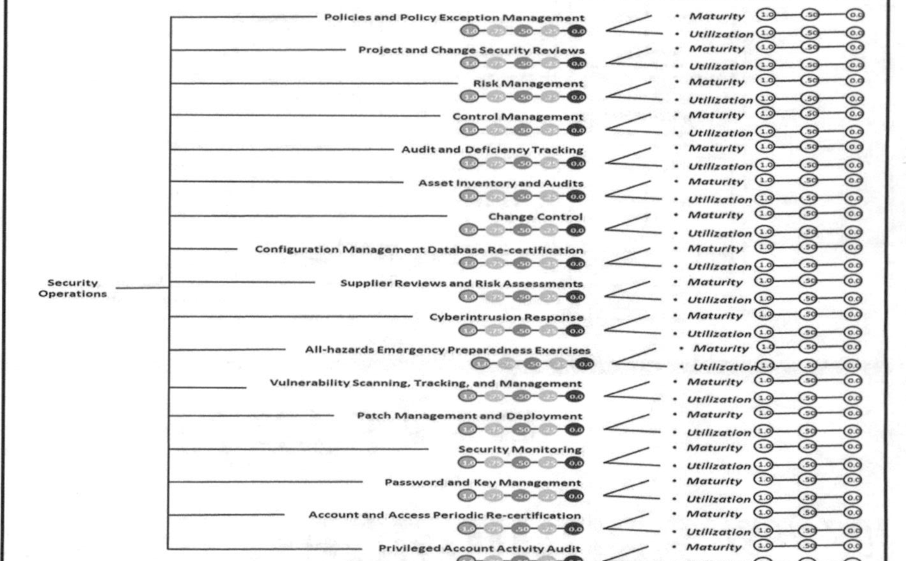

Level 3 Assessment: Focus on Capabilities *(10 of 30)*

Object Measurement Steps *(8 of 22)*

- ***OM Step 5***: Measure each ***object characteristic*** using a value scale.
  - Involves assessing the 113 capabilities by functional area, along with the 17 operational processes
    - Data collection for the capabilities uses ***observed data*** based on the ***value scales in Appendix E*** of this study guide.
    - Data collection for the security operational processes uses ***expert judgment*** based on the ***utilization*** and ***maturity*** values scales.
  - The graphic shows the systems administration measurement pane with recorded ***observed data measurement*** indicated by circled values.
    - Similar measurement panes can be used to record observed data measurements for the other functional areas and capabilities, but such measurement panes will not be shown here.
    - However, the following slides present the ***observed data*** values for the ***113 capabilities*** of the 11 functional areas in a tabular form.

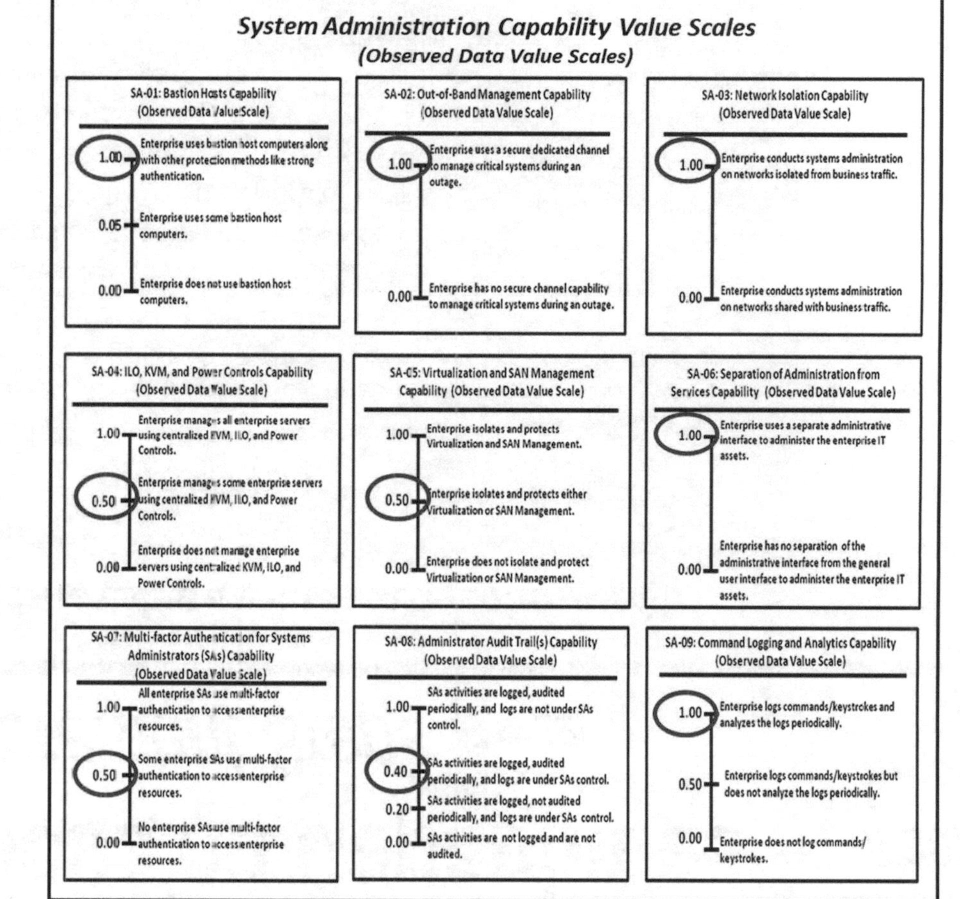

Level 3 Assessment: Focus on Capabilities *(11 of 30)*

Object Measurement Steps *(9 of 22)*

- ***OM Step 5***: Measure each ***object characteristic*** using a value scale ***(continued):***

Systems Administration (SA): 9 Capabilities	Observation (From Appendix G)	Observed Data
SA-01: Bastion hosts	Enterprise uses some bastion host computers.	0.50
SA-02: Out-of-Band (OOB) management	Enterprise has no secure channel capability to manage critical systems during an outage.	0.00
SA-03: Network isolation	Enterprise conducts systems administration on networks shared with business traffic.	0.00
SA-04: Integrated Lights-Out (ILO), Keyboard Video Mouse (KVM), and power controls	Enterprise manages some enterprise servers using centralized KVM, ILO, and power controls.	0.50
SA-05: Virtualization and Storage Area Network (SAN) management	Enterprise isolates and protects either virtualization or SAN management.	0.50
SA-06: Separation of administration from services	Enterprise has no separation of the administrative interface from the general user interface to administer the enterprise IT assets.	0.00
SA-07: Multi-factor authentication for Systems Administrators (SAs)	Some enterprise systems administrators use multi-factor authentication to access enterprise resources.	0.50
SA-08: Administrator audit trail(s)	SAs activities are logged, but not audited periodically, and logs are under SAs control.	0.20
SA-09: Command logging and analytics	Enterprise logs commands/keystrokes but does not analyze the logs periodically.	0.50
	Systems Administration Index:	**0.38**

Level 3 Assessment: Focus on Capabilities *(12 of 30)*

Object Measurement Steps *(10 of 22)*

- ***OM Step 5***: Measure each ***object characteristic*** using a value scale ***(continued):***

Network Security (NS): 14 Capabilities	Observation (From Appendix G)	Observed Data
NS-01: Switches and routers	Management and operation of some switches and routers are conducted through a secure centralized console. Logical and physical access to some of these devices is restricted to a small group with "need-to-access" basis.	0.50
NS-02: Software Defined Networking (SDN)	Enterprise utilizes SDN to deploy, manage, upgrade and retire some networking devices.	0.50
NS-03: Domain Name System (DNS) and Dynamic Host Configuration Protocol (DHCP)	Enterprise installs Standard DNS.	0.00
NS-04: Network Time Protocol (NTP)	Enterprise uses some capability other than NTP (for example, Chrony, OpenNTPD) to synchronize some system clocks to a master clock for accurate time stamping of logged events.	0.30
NS-05: Network service management	Enterprise uses only some of the security/protection mechanisms listed.	0.50
NS-06: Firewall and virtual machine firewall	Firewalled network zones are set up to separate some high-risk systems servers from low-risk internal systems. Network architecture is designed to manage logically the flow of data traffic and also get visibility.	0.50
NS-07: Network Intrusion Detection / Network Intrusion Prevention System (IDS / IPS)	Only IDS is implemented and IPS is in learning mode.	0.50
NS-08: Wireless networking (Wi-Fi)	Enterprise uses standard vendor-provided default configuration (including default administrator password).	0.00
NS-09: Packet intercept and capture	Packet intercept and capture tools are deployed to collect network traffic, and observe the throughput of the tool and network performance.	0.50
NS-10: Secure Sockets Layer (SSL) intercept	All SSL encrypted inbound traffic and some SSL outbound network traffic are examined.	0.40
NS-11: Network Access Control (NAC)	Network access control is deployed in learning mode.	0.50
NS-12: Virtual Private Networking (VPN) and Internet Protocol Security (IPSec)	VPN is deployed with two-factor authentication solution for some external or remote users.	0.50
NS-13: Network Traffic Analysis (NTA)	Enterprise uses network traffic analysis to analyze the volume of some network traffic.	0.50
NS-14: Network Data Analytics (NDA)	Enterprise has network data analytics but does not use it.	0.40
	Network Security Index:	**0.44**

Level 3 Assessment: Focus on Capabilities *(13 of 30)*

Object Measurement Steps *(11 of 22)*

- ***OM Step 5***: Measure each ***object characteristic*** using a value scale ***(continued):***

Application Security (AS): 9 Capabilities	Observation (From Appendix G)	Observed Data
AS-01: E-mail security	Enterprise deploys some e-mail protections.	0.50
AS-02: Webshell detection	Enterprise deploys webshell detection tools for some applications.	0.50
AS-03: Application firewalls	Enterprise deploys application firewalls in detection and learning mode for some applications.	0.50
AS-04: Database firewalls	Enterprise deploys firewalls in detection and learning mode for some databases.	0.50
AS-05: Forward proxy and web filters	Enterprise deploys forward proxy and web filters in enforcement mode for some outgoing requests from internal servers to the Internet.	0.50
AS-06: Reverse proxy	Enterprise deploys reverse proxy to mask the internal network from some Internet users.	0.50
AS-07: Data Leakage Protection (DLP)	Enterprise does not deploy DLP tools.	0.00
AS-08: Secure application and database software development	Secure application and database software development standards are partially utilized.	0.50
AS-09: Software code vulnerability analysis	Enterprise does not deploy software code vulnerability analysis tools.	0.00
	Application Security Index:	**0.44**

Level 3 Assessment: Focus on Capabilities *(14 of 30)*

Object Measurement Steps *(12 of 22)*

- ***OM Step 5***: Measure each ***object characteristic*** using a value scale **(*continued*):**

Endpoint, Server, and Device Security (ESDS): 15 Capabilities	Observation (From Appendix G)	Observed Data
ESDS-01: Local administrator privilege restrictions	Some users have local administrative privileges on their end-point computing devices.	0.50
ESDS-02: Computer security and logging policies	Enterprise implements ESDS computer security logging and log monitoring on an ad hoc basis.	0.10
ESDS-03: Endpoint and media encryption	Enterprise deploys some endpoint and media encryption.	0.50
ESDS-04: Computer access controls	Enterprise uses some computer access controls.	0.50
ESDS-05: Forensic imaging support for investigations	Enterprise does not deploy forensic imaging policies, procedures or tools to support criminal investigations.	0.00
ESDS-06: Virtual desktop / thin clients	Enterprise converts some of privately-owned resources to virtual desktops that are kept current with latest security patches and updates.	0.50
ESDS-07: Mobile Device Management (MDM)	Enterprise deploys MDM solution to allow some personally-owned mobile devices to connect to the enterprise network.	0.50
ESDS-08: Anti-virus / anti-malware	Enterprise deploys anti-virus/anti-malware software to protect some enterprise end-point devices.	0.50
ESDS-09: Application whitelisting	Enterprise does not use application whitelisting.	0.00
ESDS-10: In-memory malware detection	Enterprise does not have in-memory malware detection.	0.00
ESDS-11: Host firewall and intrusion detection	Enterprise deploys host firewall, and intrusion detection systems are in learning mode.	0.50
ESDS-12: "Gold code" software images	Enterprise develops and uses "Gold Code" software images, but there is no protection mechanism to secure the images.	0.50
ESDS-13: Security Technical Implementation Guides (STIGs)	Enterprise uses only default installation to install systems.	0.00
ESDS-14: Always-on Virtual Private Networking (VPN)	Enterprise uses "always-on" VPN to encrypt some network traffic, but monitoring capability does not exist.	0.50
ESDS-15: File integrity and change monitoring	Enterprise monitors file system changes of critical network systems.	0.50
	Endpoint, Server, and Device Security Index:	**0.41**

Level 3 Assessment: Focus on Capabilities *(15 of 30)*

Object Measurement Steps *(13 of 22)*

- ***OM Step 5***: Measure each ***object characteristic*** using a value scale ***(continued):***

Identity, Authentication, and Access Management (IAAM): 9 Capabilities	Observation (From Appendix G)	Observed Data
IAAM-01: Identity life cycle management	Enterprise manages some enterprise user identities.	0.50
IAAM-02: Enterprise directory	Enterprise uses enterprise directory to manage some users' identities, authorizations and digital/networking resources.	0.50
IAAM-03: Multi-factor authentication	Enterprise deploys multi-factor authentication for some enterprise resources.	0.50
IAAM-04: Privilege management and access control	Enterprise does not deploy privilege management and access control tools.	0.00
IAAM-05: Identity and access audit trail and reporting	Enterprise deploys an audit trail capability to support regulatory compliance and investigations for some user actions.	0.50
IAAM-06: Lightweight Directory Access Protocol (LDAP)	Enterprise deploys LDAP capability without security option implemented.	0.50
IAAM-07: Kerberos, RADIUS, 802.1x	Enterprise does not deploy Kerberos, RADIUS, 802.1x authentication protocols.	0.00
IAAM-08: Federated authentication	Enterprise deploys federated authentication services for identity sharing and trust with third-party suppliers.	1.00
IAAM-09: Security Assertion Markup Language (SAML)	Enterprise implements SAML to enable federated authentication and enhances single sign-on user experience.	1.00
	Identity, Authentication, and Access Management Index:	**0.60**

Level 3 Assessment: Focus on Capabilities *(16 of 30)*

Object Measurement Steps *(14 of 22)*

- ***OM Step 5***: Measure each ***object characteristic*** using a value scale ***(continued):***

Data Protection and Cryptography (DPC): 10 Capabilities	Observation (From Appendix G)	Observed Data
DPC-01: Secure Sockets Layer (SSL) and Transport Layer Security (TLS)	Enterprise uses SSL or TLS technology for some user and server interactive sessions.	0.50
DPC-02: Digital certificates (Public Key Infrastructure [PKI])	Enterprise does not deploy PKI components.	0.00
DPC-03: Key hardware protection	Enterprise deploys some key hardware protections.	0.50
DPC-04: One-Time Password (OTP) and Out-of-Band (OOB) authentication	Enterprise does not deploy OTP and OOB authentication services.	0.00
DPC-05: Key life cycle management	Enterprise does not deploy key life cycle management.	0.00
DPC-06: Digital signatures	Enterprise uses electronic signatures to identify some third-party users, and relevant processes.	0.50
DPC-07: Complex passwords	Enterprise has password complexity policies.	1.00
DPC-08: Data encryption and tokenization	Enterprise does not use data encryption or tokenization.	0.00
DPC-09: Brute force attack detection	Enterprise deploys either preventive controls or detection controls.	0.50
DPC-10: Digital Rights Management (DRM)	Enterprise does not deploy DRM.	0.00
	Data Protection and Cryptography Index:	**0.45**

Level 3 Assessment: Focus on Capabilities *(17 of 30)*

Object Measurement Steps *(15 of 22)*

- ***OM Step 5***: Measure each ***object characteristic*** using a value scale ***(continued):***

Monitoring, Vulnerability, and Patch Management (MVPM): 14 Capabilities	Observation (From Appendix G)	Observed Data
MVPM-01: Operational performance monitoring	Enterprise deploys operational performance monitoring for some critical systems.	0.50
MVPM-02: System and network monitoring	Enterprise deploys system and network monitoring for some critical systems.	0.50
MVPM-03: System configuration change detection	Enterprise does not deploy system configuration change detection.	0.00
MVPM-04: Privilege and access change detection	Enterprise does not deploy privilege and access change detection.	0.00
MVPM-05: Log aggregation	Enterprise does not deploy log aggregation.	0.00
MVPM-06: Data analytics	Enterprise does not deploy data analytics.	0.00
MVPM-07: Security Information and Event Management (SIEM)	Enterprise does not deploy SIEM.	0.00
MVPM-08: Network and computer vulnerability scanning	Enterprise deploys network and computer vulnerability scanning across some systems.	0.50
MVPM-09: Penetration testing	Penetration testing is not performed.	0.00
MVPM-10: Patch management and deployment	Enterprise does not deploy centralized patch management and deployment capability.	0.00
MVPM-11: Rogue network device detection	Enterprise deploys rogue network device detection capability to a portion of the enterprise.	0.50
MVPM-12: Rogue wireless access point detection	Enterprise uses "war-driving" method to detect rogue wireless access points.	0.50
MVPM-13: Honeypots / honeynets / honeytokens	Enterprise does not deploy honeypots, honeynets, or honeytokens.	0.00
MVPM-14: Security Operations Center (SOC)	SOC is not available.	0.00
	Monitoring, Vulnerability, and Patch Management Index:	**0.30**

Level 3 Assessment: Focus on Capabilities *(18 of 30)*

Object Measurement Steps *(16 of 22)*

- ***OM Step 5***: Measure each ***object characteristic*** using a value scale **(*continued*):**

High Availability, Disaster Recovery, and Physical Protection (HADRPP): 10 Capabilities	Observation (From Appendix G)	Observed Data
HADRPP-01: Clustering	Enterprise deploys clustering for some critical systems.	0.50
HADRPP-02: Load balancing, Global Server Load Balancing (GSLB)	Enterprise deploys load balancing and GSLB for some critical applications and systems.	0.50
HADRPP-03: Network failover, subnet spanning	Enterprise does not deploy network failover or subnet spanning.	0.00
HADRPP-04: Virtual machine snapshots and cloning	Enterprise implements virtual machine snapshots and cloning for some critical servers.	0.50
HADRPP-05: Data mirroring and replication	Enterprise deploys data mirroring and replication for some critical servers.	0.50
HADRPP-06: Backups and backup management	Enterprise manages backups on per system basis, but does not have a centralized backup status view.	0.50
HADRPP-07: Off-site storage	Off-site backup storage is within the same building or facility.	0.00
HADRPP-08: Facilities protection	Enterprise develops a draft facilities protection plan.	0.50
HADRPP-09: Physical access controls	Enterprise partially deploys physical access controls within the enterprise.	0.50
HADRPP-10: Physical security monitoring	Enterprise collects physical security logs, but regular physical security monitoring is not deployed.	0.50
High Availability, Disaster Recovery, and Physical Protection Index:		**0.45**

Level 3 Assessment: Focus on Capabilities *(19 of 30)*

Object Measurement Steps *(17 of 22)*

- ***OM Step 5***: Measure each ***object characteristic*** using a value scale ***(continued):***

Incident Response (IR): 7 Capabilities	Observation (From Appendix G)	Observed Data
IR-01: Threat information	Enterprise collects threat information from various authoritative sources and disseminates it to analysts.	1.00
IR-02: Incident tracking	Enterprise deploys incident tracking tools capability to a portion of the enterprise.	0.50
IR-03: Forensic tools	Enterprise deploys forensic tools, but data handling methodology does not exist.	0.50
IR-04: Computer imaging	Enterprise deploys computer imaging tools capability to a portion of the enterprise.	0.50
IR-05: Indicators of Compromise (IOCs)	Enterprise collects IOCs and makes then available for investigations.	1.00
IR-06: Black hole server	Enterprise deploys black hole server capability to a portion of the enterprise.	0.50
IR-07: Regulatory / legal coordination	Enterprise follows some chain of custody procedures.	0.50
	Incident Response Index:	**0.68**

Level 3 Assessment: Focus on Capabilities *(20 of 30)*

Object Measurement Steps *(18 of 22)*

- ***OM Step 5***: Measure each ***object characteristic*** using a value scale ***(continued):***

Asset Management and Supply Chain (AMSC): 6 Capabilities	Observation (From Appendix G)	Observed Data
AMSC-01: Asset management databases	Enterprise deploys an asset management database with some assets in the database.	0.50
AMSC-02: Configuration Management Databases (CMDB)	Enterprise deploys a CMDB with some configuration items managed.	0.50
AMSC-03: Change management databases	Enterprise deploys change management databases with some change requests processed by it.	0.50
AMSC-04: Software inventory and license management	Enterprise deploys a software inventory and license management capability, but a centralized software inventory does not exist.	0.50
AMSC-05: Supplier certification processes	Enterprise conducts supplier certification security checks on some suppliers before contract award.	0.50
AMSC-06: Secure disposal, recycling, and data destruction	Enterprise deploys secure disposal, recycling and data destruction capabilities for some enterprise IT assets.	0.50
	Asset Management and Supply Chain Index:	**0.50**

Level 3 Assessment: Focus on Capabilities *(21 of 30)*

Object Measurement Steps *(19 of 22)*

- ***OM Step 5***: Measure each ***object characteristic*** using a value scale ***(continued):***

Policy, Audit, E-Discovery, and Training (PAET): 10 Capabilities	Observation (From Appendix G)	Observed Data
PAET-01: Governance, Risk, and Compliance (GRC), with reporting	Enterprise deploys a GRC program limited to IT risks and does not account for regulatory compliance requirements.	0.50
PAET-02: Compliance and control frameworks	Enterprise deploys individual compliance and control frameworks to meet individual legal, regulatory and customer-driven requirements.	0.50
PAET-03: Audit frameworks	Audit scope is limited to legal, regulatory and customer-driven requirements.	0.50
PAET-04: Customer Certification and Accreditation (C&A)	Enterprise deploys a formal C&A process for some assets and services.	0.50
PAET-05: Policy and policy exception management	Enterprise deploys a policy and policy exception management capability without a follow-up/re-approval process on expired exceptions.	0.50
PAET-06: Risk and threat management	Enterprise deploys a risk and threat management capability to some enterprise IT processes and services.	0.50
PAET-07: Privacy compliance	Enterprise deploys a privacy compliance capability to some enterprise IT processes and services.	0.50
PAET-08: E-Discovery tools	Enterprise conducts e-discovery manually.	0.50
PAET-09: Personnel security and background checks	Human Resources performs pre-employment security and background checks on all potential employees.	1.00
PAET-10: Security awareness and training	Enterprise deploys security awareness program and annual training.	1.00
	Policy, Audit, E-Discovery, and Training Index:	**0.63**

Object Measurement Steps *(20 of 22)*

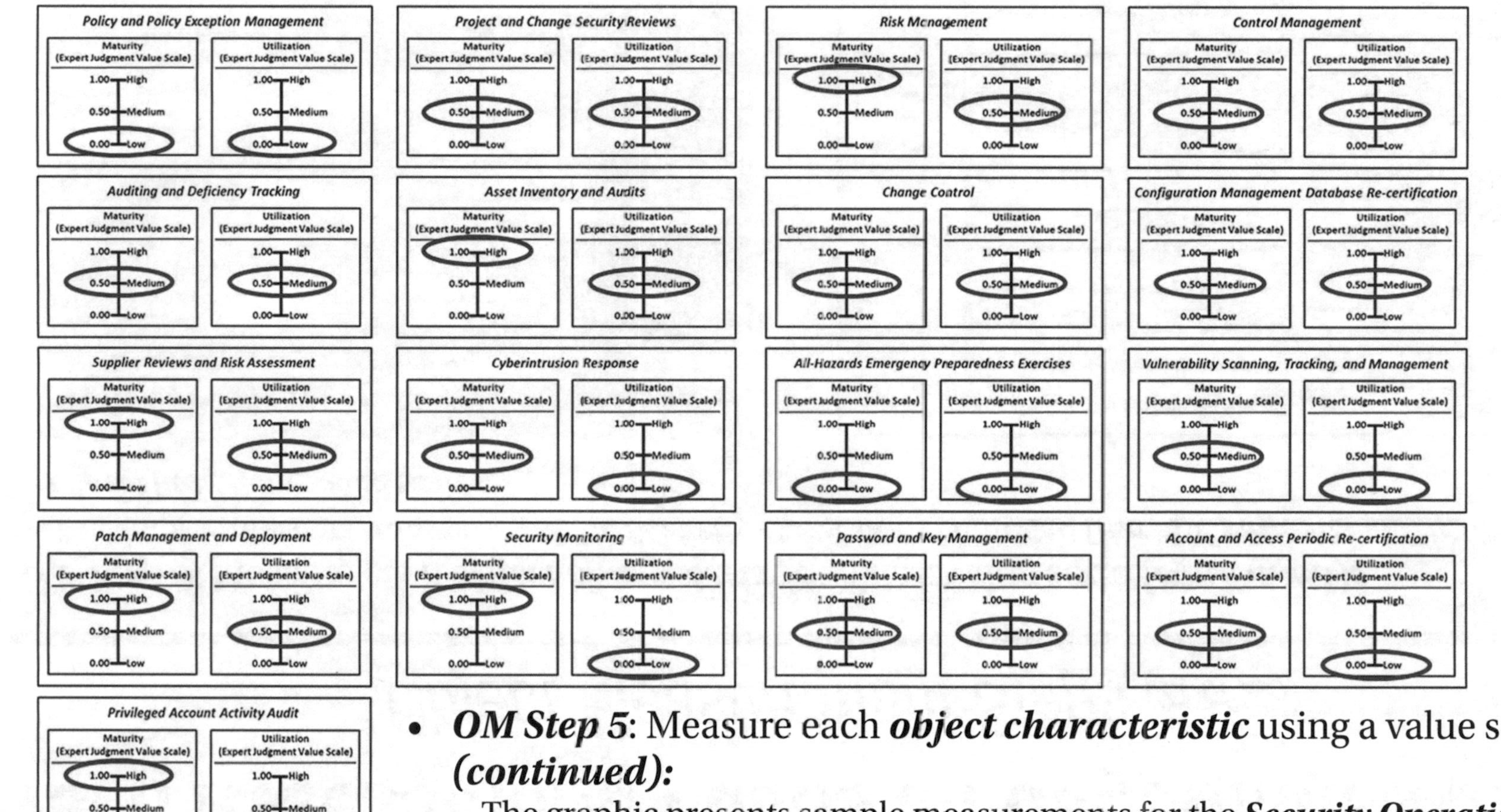

- ***OM Step 5***: Measure each ***object characteristic*** using a value scale ***(continued)***:
  - The graphic presents sample measurements for the ***Security Operations*** 17 operational processes using ***expert judgment*** value scales.

Level 3 Assessment: Focus on Capabilities *(23 of 30)*

Object Measurement Steps (21 of 22)

- ***OM Step 5:*** Measure each ***object characteristic*** using a value scale ***(continued):***
  - The graphic presents summaries of the ***Security Operations*** compiled from the ***maturity*** and ***utilization expert judgment*** value scales.

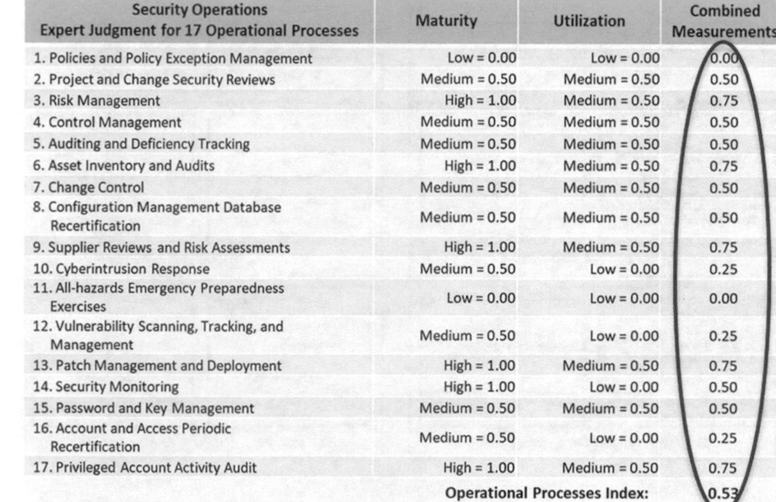

Security Operations Expert Judgment for 17 Operational Processes	Maturity	Utilization	Combined Measurements
1. Policies and Policy Exception Management	Low = 0.00	Low = 0.00	0.00
2. Project and Change Security Reviews	Medium = 0.50	Medium = 0.50	0.50
3. Risk Management	High = 1.00	Medium = 0.50	0.75
4. Control Management	Medium = 0.50	Medium = 0.50	0.50
5. Auditing and Deficiency Tracking	Medium = 0.50	Medium = 0.50	0.50
6. Asset Inventory and Audits	High = 1.00	Medium = 0.50	0.75
7. Change Control	Medium = 0.50	Medium = 0.50	0.50
8. Configuration Management Database Recertification	Medium = 0.50	Medium = 0.50	0.50
9. Supplier Reviews and Risk Assessments	High = 1.00	Medium = 0.50	0.75
10. Cyberintrusion Response	Medium = 0.50	Low = 0.00	0.25
11. All-hazards Emergency Preparedness Exercises	Low = 0.00	Low = 0.00	0.00
12. Vulnerability Scanning, Tracking, and Management	Medium = 0.50	Low = 0.00	0.25
13. Patch Management and Deployment	High = 1.00	Medium = 0.50	0.75
14. Security Monitoring	High = 1.00	Low = 0.00	0.50
15. Password and Key Management	Medium = 0.50	Medium = 0.50	0.50
16. Account and Access Periodic Recertification	Medium = 0.50	Low = 0.00	0.25
17. Privileged Account Activity Audit	High = 1.00	Medium = 0.50	0.75
		Operational Processes Index:	0.53

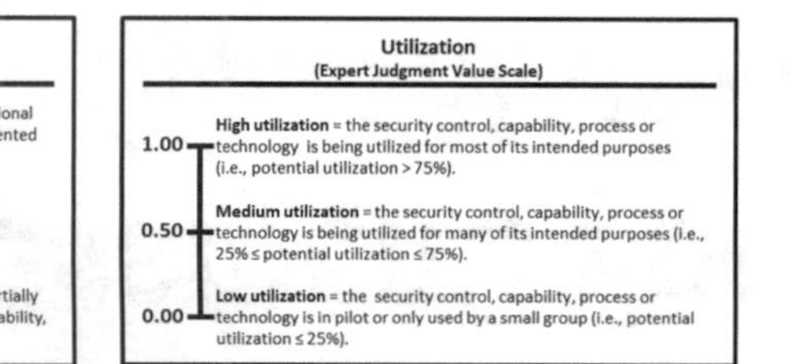

Maturity
(Expert Judgment Value Scale)

1.00 — **High maturity** = the security control element is fully operational and proven. Configuration and procedures are fully documented and performance specs for functionality are defined and validated by 3rd party experts.

0.50 — **Medium maturity** = the security control element is partially operational, but unproven. Documentation and operational procedures are not complete or untested. There are minor limitations on functionality that are untested.

0.00 — **Low maturity** = the security control element is barely or partially operational. There are severe limits on its functionality, durability, reliability or scalability.

Utilization
(Expert Judgment Value Scale)

1.00 — **High utilization** = the security control, capability, process or technology is being utilized for most of its intended purposes (i.e., potential utilization > 75%).

0.50 — **Medium utilization** = the security control, capability, process or technology is being utilized for many of its intended purposes (i.e., 25% ≤ potential utilization ≤ 75%).

0.00 — **Low utilization** = the security control, capability, process or technology is in pilot or only used by a small group (i.e., potential utilization ≤ 25%).

Security Operations
Policies and Policy Exception Management
Project and Change Security Reviews
Risk Management
Control Management
Audit and Deficiency Tracking
Asset Inventory and Audits
Change Control
Configuration Management Database Re-certification
Supplier Reviews and Risk Assessments
Cyberintrusion Response
All-hazards Emergency Preparedness Exercises
Vulnerability Scanning, Tracking, and Management
Patch Management and Deployment
Security Monitoring
Password and Key Management
Account and Access Periodic Re-certification
Privileged Account Activity Audit

Level 3 Assessment: Focus on Capabilities *(24 of 30)*

Object Measurement Steps *(22 of 22)*

- ***OM Step 6***: Calculate the overall cybersecurity ***Program Assessment Index.***
  - The graphic presents summaries of the program assessment measurements for ***Risk Mitigations***, 11 ***Functional Areas***, and ***Security Operations***.

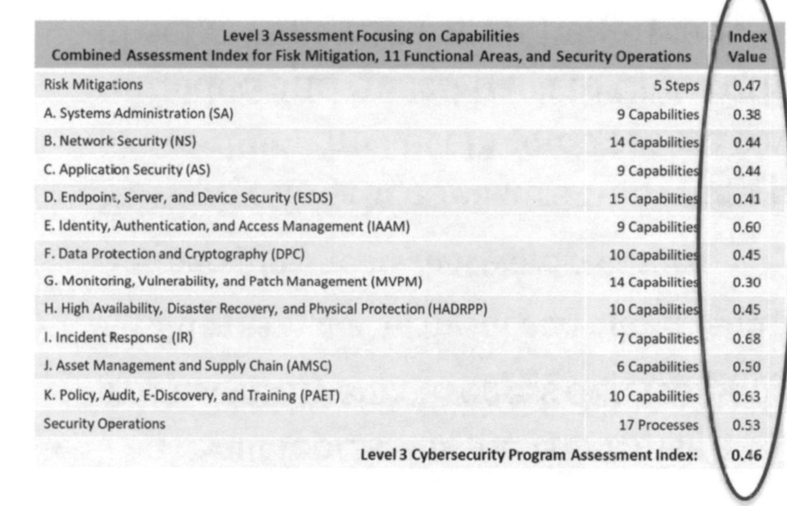

Level 3 Assessment Focusing on Capabilities Combined Assessment Index for Fisk Mitigation, 11 Functional Areas, and Security Operations		Index Value
Risk Mitigations	5 Steps	0.47
A. Systems Administration (SA)	9 Capabilities	0.38
B. Network Security (NS)	14 Capabilities	0.44
C. Application Security (AS)	9 Capabilities	0.44
D. Endpoint, Server, and Device Security (ESDS)	15 Capabilities	0.41
E. Identity, Authentication, and Access Management (IAAM)	9 Capabilities	0.60
F. Data Protection and Cryptography (DPC)	10 Capabilities	0.45
G. Monitoring, Vulnerability, and Patch Management (MVPM)	14 Capabilities	0.30
H. High Availability, Disaster Recovery, and Physical Protection (HADRPP)	10 Capabilities	0.45
I. Incident Response (IR)	7 Capabilities	0.68
J. Asset Management and Supply Chain (AMSC)	6 Capabilities	0.50
K. Policy, Audit, E-Discovery, and Training (PAET)	10 Capabilities	0.63
Security Operations	17 Processes	0.53
Level 3 Cybersecurity Program Assessment Index:		**0.46**

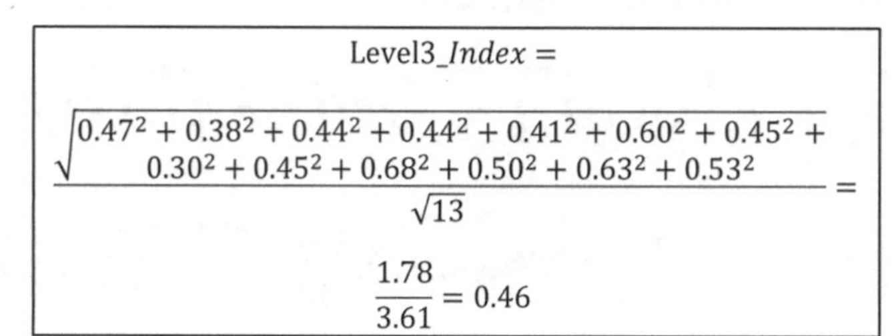

$$\text{Level3\_}Index =$$

$$\frac{\sqrt{\begin{array}{c}0.47^2 + 0.38^2 + 0.44^2 + 0.44^2 + 0.41^2 + 0.60^2 + 0.45^2 + \\ 0.30^2 + 0.45^2 + 0.68^2 + 0.50^2 + 0.63^2 + 0.53^2\end{array}}}{\sqrt{13}} =$$

$$\frac{1.78}{3.61} = 0.46$$

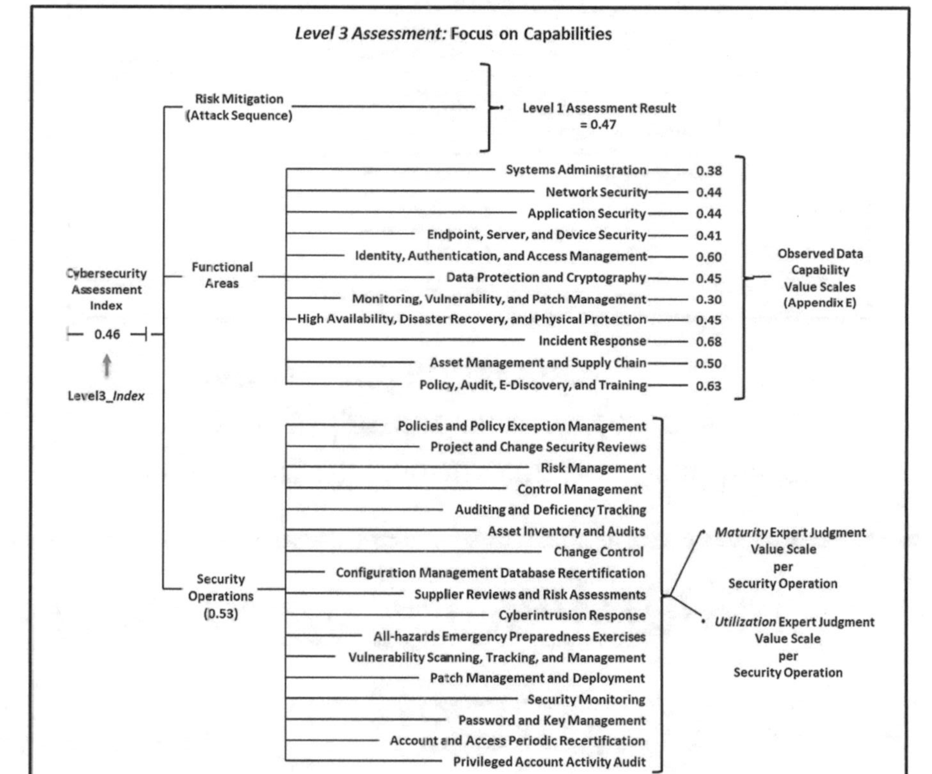

Level 3 Assessment: Focus on Capabilities *(25 of 30)*

What does a Level3_*Index = 0.46 or 46% really mean?*

- The result represents the enterprise's cybersecurity effectiveness determined from
  - values assigned to the observations; and
  - expert judgments that were recorded.
- By navigating the measurement map from left to right, the Level3_*Index* score can be unfolded and traced back to those original observations and expert judgments.
  - Risk mitigations can be traced back to the Level 1 Assessment expert judgment value scales regarding ***risk probability reduction*** and ***risk impact reduction***.
  - Functional areas can be traced back to the cybersecurity capability observed data value scales (for example, Systems Administration: ***Bastion hosts, Out-of-Band (OOB) management, Network isolation***, and so on).
  - Security operations can be traced back to expert judgment value scales regarding ***maturity*** and ***utilization***.

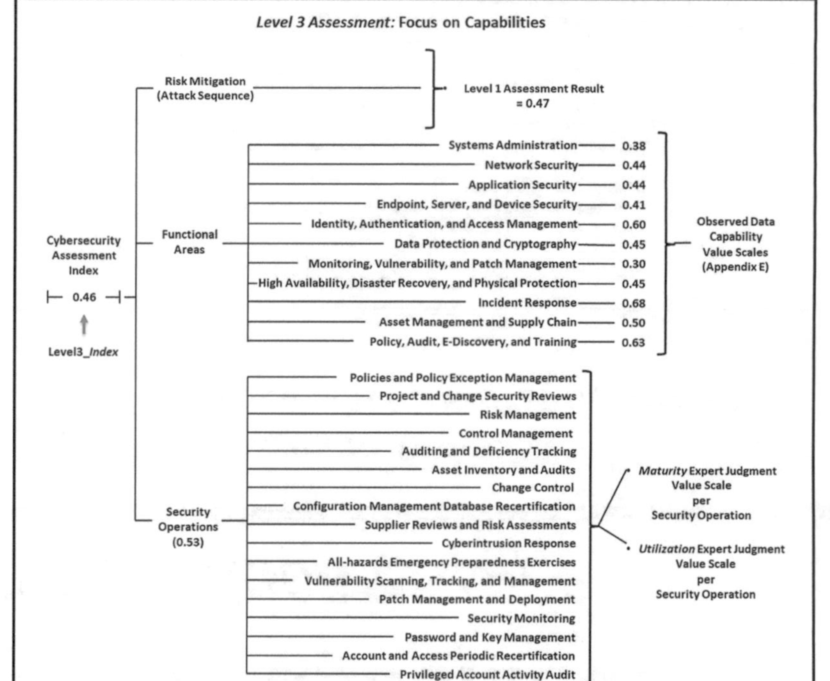

Level 3 Assessment: Focus on Capabilities *(26 of 30)*

Results Visualization and Analysis

- The upper graphic visualizes assessment results using a vertical bar (column) chart from 0% to 100%.
  - Functional areas can be quickly compared to one another.
  - Weak functional areas can be identified for subsequent improvement.
- The bottom graphic visualizes the results using a spider chart (also known as a radar chart).
  - Useful for emphasizing that all the functional areas should be of approximately equal effectiveness (that is, the target value) for overall enterprise cybersecurity to be effective
- Level 3 graphics
  - Capture security scope's overall cybersecurity effectiveness to a higher level of precision than Level 2 Assessment due to more detailed underlying observations
- Level 3 Assessment
  - Captures the status of the functional areas in greater granularity
  - Provides clarity on which functional areas are the weakest when compared to the others, or to the scope's cybersecurity target value

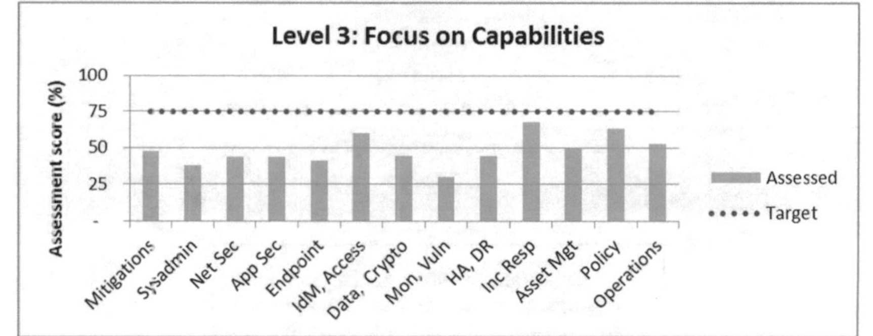

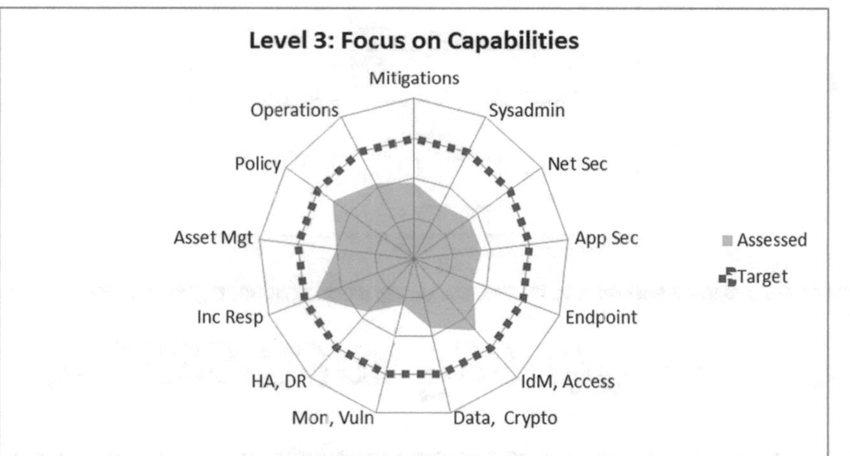

Level 3 Assessment: Focus on Capabilities *(27 of 30)*

Comparing Cybersecurity Assessment Results

- OM*Index* is a powerful tool.
  - Assesses and measures an enterprise's cybersecurity posture
  - Models potential effects of cybersecurity projects or improvements
- Different assessment levels.
  - use different values scales to rate the characteristics of the enterprise's cybersecurity;
  - apply those scales using the level of granularity appropriate to the assessment; and
  - produce results that are not entirely analogous, but use a common rating scale.
- The lower graphic shows the OM*Indices* calculated from the three sample assessments.
  - Scores are similar but not identical.
  - All scores represent the evaluated scope's overall security posture based on different sets of source data.

$$\text{OM}Index = \frac{\sqrt{\sum_{i=1}^{n} w_i^2 at_i^2}}{\sqrt{\sum_{i=1}^{n} w_i^2 (maximum[at_i])^2}}$$

where at_i = object attribute measurement
n = number of object attribute measurements
w_i = weighting factor for object attribute at_i
maximum $[at_i]$ = maximum value of at_i

Cybersecurity Program Assessment	Assessment Index
Level 1 Assessment: Focus on Risk Mitigations	0.47
Level 2 Assessment: Focus on Functional Areas	0.53
Level 3 Assessment: Focus on Capabilities	0.49

- Assessments that are to be compared to one another should be performed at the same level of assessment so the evaluated criteria and value scales are all the same.

Level 3 Assessment: Focus on Capabilities *(28 of 30)*

Using Cybersecurity Assessment Results *(1 of 3)*

- Enterprise value scale language
  - helps explain the underlying meaning of the OM numbers; and
  - preserves, in part, the context of each assessment.
- Future assessments may not involve the same cybersecurity expert(s).
  - New experts can use the same value scales for their assessments.
  - This helps ensure past and future results can be objectively compared to one another.
  - It allows an enterprise to continuously track its cybersecurity posture over time.
- Simply stated, the **OM*Index is much more than a number*** … it quantitatively represents the entire assessment and its objective.

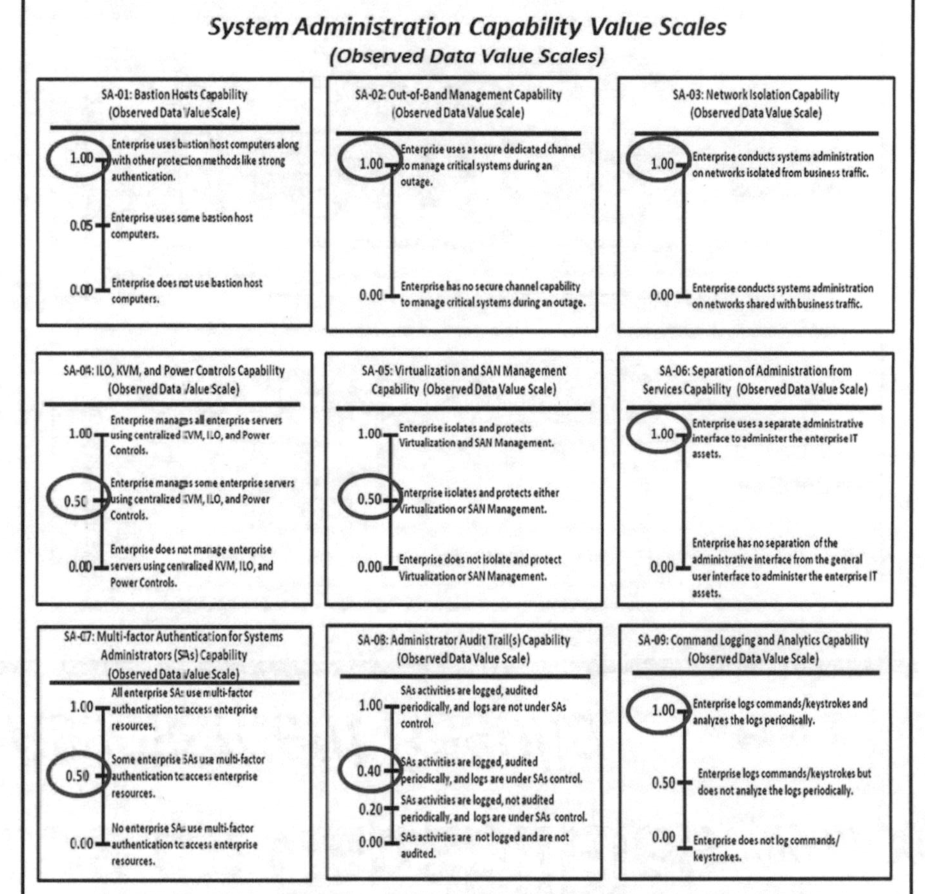

Level 3 Assessment: Focus on Capabilities *(29 of 30)*

Using Cybersecurity Assessment Results *(2 of 3)*

- Once the enterprise has an assessed security scope,
  - cybersecurity improvements can be modeled; and
  - ***what-if*** analyses and comparisons can be performed.
- Modeling involves
  - calculating the OM*Index* for the baseline security scope;
  - adjusting the input values to reflect desired changes to the risk mitigation measures, cybersecurity capabilities, or operational processes; and
  - the OM*Index* then being recalculated as if the improvements are already completed and the effect on the index being observed.

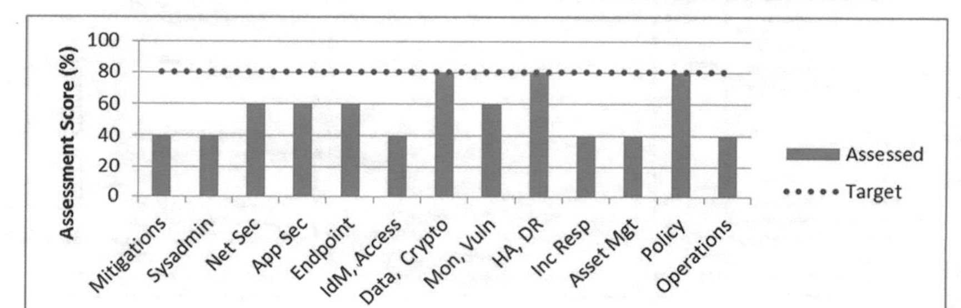

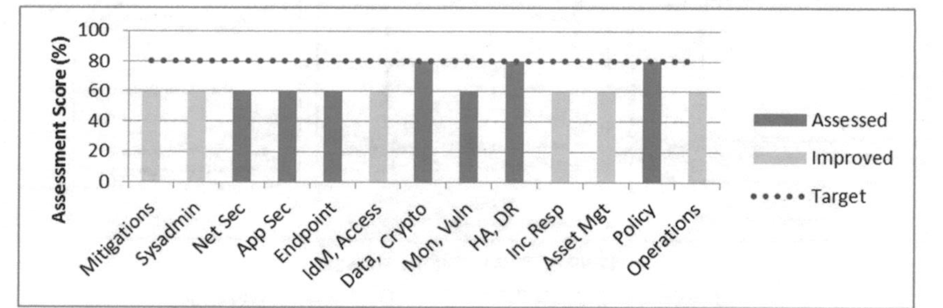

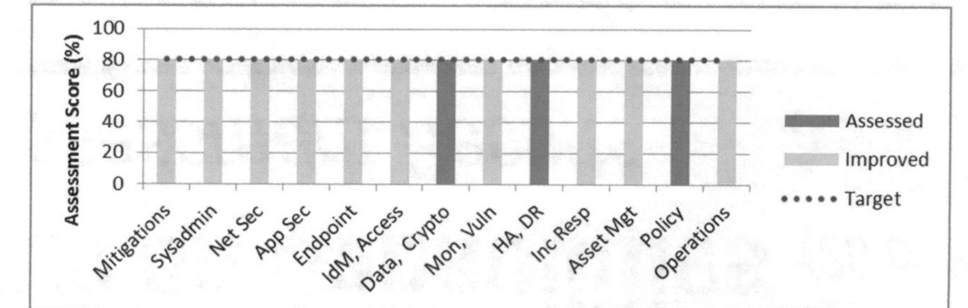

Level 3 Assessment: Focus on Capabilities *(30 of 30)*

Using Cybersecurity Assessment Results *(3 of 3)*

- ***Bang for the Buck*** modeling
  - estimates the project's value vs. its cost;
  - calculates the OM*Index* before a cybersecurity improvement project is begun and after it is completed; and
  - reflects quantitively the amount the enterprise's cybersecurity is expected to improve when the project is completed vs. the project's cost or effort.
- By modeling this calculation for different proposed projects, the enterprise can get an idea of which projects might be the most effective or cost-effective at improving the cybersecurity posture.
- This, in turn, helps business leaders
  - focus on those project that deliver the greatest potential results at the lowest costs; and
  - make well-informed decisions regarding cybersecurity improvements compared with other business priorities.

Starting Security Level
Initial Assessment: 55%

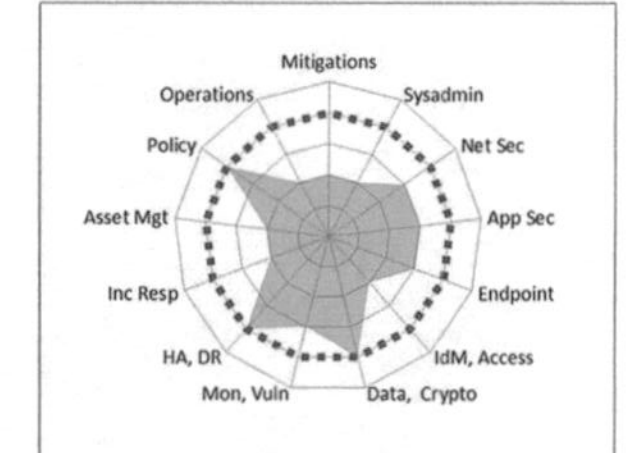

Deficient Areas Remediated
Updated Assessment: 65%

Target Security Level
Achieved: 80%

APPENDIX E

Cybersecurity Capability Value Scales

S. E. Donaldson et al., *Enterprise Cybersecurity Study Guide*, https://doi.org/10.1007/978-1-4842-3258-3_20

Overview

- This appendix provides example Object Measurement (OM) ***observed data*** value scale definitions for 113 cybersecurity capabilities.
  - Grouped by 11 functional areas
  - Minimum and maximum numeric values from 0.00 to 1.00, but scales can accommodate any numeric range
  - Tick marks with plain language descriptions to help associate an enterprise's vocabulary with measurement activities
  - ***No one set of terms*** (that is, numeric value and tick-mark labels) that defines value scales

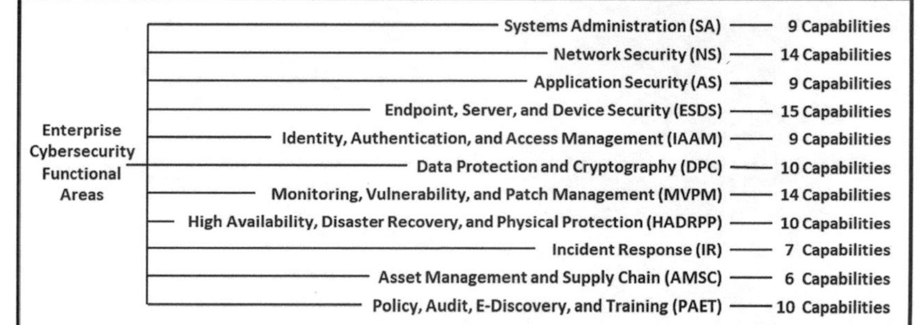

- In the end, an enterprise needs meaningful measurements.
- ***Meaningful*** here means "the enterprise uses the measurements, in part, to determine whether and where cybersecurity needs to be improved."

Topics

- This appendix contains value scales for each of 113 cybersecurity capabilities, grouped into 11 functional areas:
  - Systems Administration
  - Network Security
  - Applications Security
  - Endpoint, Server, and Device Security
  - Identity, Authentication, and Access Management
  - Data Protection and Cryptography
  - Monitoring, Vulnerability, and Patch Management
  - High Availability, Disaster Recovery, and Physical Protection
  - Incident Response
  - Asset Management and Supply Chain
  - Policy, Audit, E-Discovery, and Training

Functional Area	Capabilities	
Systems Administration (SA)	• Bastion hosts • Out-of-Band (OOB) management • Network isolation • Integrated Lights-Out (ILO), Keyboard Video Mouse (KVM), and power controls • Virtualization and Storage Area Network (SAN) management	• Separation of administration from services • Multi-factor authentication for Systems Administrators (SAs) • Administrator audit trail(s) • Command logging and analytics
Network Security (NS)	• Switches and routers • Software Defined Networking (SDN) • Domain Name System (DNS) and Dynamic Host Configuration Protocol (DHCP) • Network Time Protocol (NTP) • Network service management • Firewall and virtual machine firewall • Network Intrusion Detection / Network Intrusion Prevention System (IDS / IPS)	• Wireless networking (Wi-Fi) • Packet intercept and capture • Secure Sockets Layer (SSL) intercept • Network Access Control (NAC) • Virtual Private Networking (VPN) and Internet Protocol Security (IPSec) • Network Traffic Analysis (NTA) • Network Data Analytics (NDA)
Application Security (AS)	• E-mail security • Webshell detection • Application firewalls • Database firewalls • Forward proxy and web filters	• Reverse proxy • Data Leakage Protection (DLP) • Secure application and database software development • Software code vulnerability analysis
Endpoint, Server, and Device Security (ESDS)	• Local administrator privilege restrictions • Computer security and logging policies • Endpoint and media encryption • Computer access controls • Forensic imaging support for investigations • Virtual desktop / thin clients • Mobile Device Management (MDM) • Anti-virus / anti-malware	• Application whitelisting • In-memory malware detection • Host firewall and intrusion detection • "Gold code" software images • Security Technical Implementation Guides (STIGs) • Always-on Virtual Private Networking (VPN) • File integrity and change monitoring
Identity, Authentication, and Access Management (IAAM)	• Identity life cycle management • Enterprise directory • Multi-factor authentication • Privilege management and access control • Identity and access audit trail and reporting	• Lightweight Directory Access Protocol (LDAP) • Kerberos, RADIUS, 802.1x • Federated authentication • Security Assertion Markup Language (SAML)
Data Protection and Cryptography (DPC)	• Secure Sockets Layer (SSL) and Transport Layer Security (TLS) • Digital certificates (Public Key Infrastructure [PKI]) • Key hardware protection (Smart cards, Trusted Platform Modules [TPMs], and Hardware Security Modules [HSMs])	• One-Time Password (OTP) and Out-of-Band (OOB) authentication • Key life cycle management • Digital signatures • Complex passwords • Data encryption and tokenization • Brute force attack detection • Digital Rights Management (DRM)
Monitoring, Vulnerability, and Patch Management (MVPM)	• Operational performance monitoring • System and network monitoring • System configuration change detection • Privilege and access change detection • Log aggregation • Data analytics • Security Information and Event Management (SIEM)	• Network and computer vulnerability scanning • Penetration testing • Patch management and deployment • Rogue network device detection • Rogue wireless access point detection • Honeypots / honeynets / honeytokens • Security Operations Center (SOC)
High Availability, Disaster Recovery, and Physical Protection (HADRPP)	• Clustering • Load balancing, Global Server Load Balancing (GSLB) • Network failover, subnet spanning • Virtual machine snapshots and cloning • Data mirroring and replication	• Backups and backup management • Off-site storage • Facilities protection • Physical access controls • Physical security monitoring
Incident Response (IR)	• Threat information • Incident tracking • Forensic tools • Computer imaging	• Indicators of Compromise (IOCs) • Black hole server • Regulatory / legal coordination
Asset Management and Supply Chain (AMSC)	• Asset management databases • Configuration Management Databases (CMDB) • Change management databases	• Software inventory and license management • Supplier certification processes • Secure disposal, recycling, and data destruction
Policy, Audit, E-Discovery, and Training (PAET)	• Governance, Risk, and Compliance (GRC), with reporting • Compliance and control frameworks (SOX, PCI, others) • Audit frameworks • Customer Certification and Accreditation (C&A)	• Policy and policy exception management • Risk and threat management • Privacy compliance • E-Discovery tools • Personnel security and background checks • Security awareness and training

Systems Administration *(1 of 3)*

Functional Area	Capabilities
Systems Administration (SA)	• Bastion hosts • Out-of-Band (OOB) management • Network isolation • Integrated Lights-Out (ILO), Keyboard Video Mouse (KVM), and power controls • Virtualization and Storage Area Network (SAN) management • Separation of administration from services • Multi-factor authentication for Systems Administrators (SAs) • Administrator audit trail(s) • Command logging and analytics

Systems Administration (9 Capabilities)

- Bastion Hosts
- Out-of-Band (OOB) Management
- Network Isolation
- Integrated Lights-Out (ILO), Keyboard Video Mouse (KVM), and Power Controls
- Virtualization and Storage Area Network (SAN) Management
- Separation of Administration from Services
- Multi-factor Authentication for Systems Administrators
- Administrator Audit Trail(s)
- Command Logging and Analytics

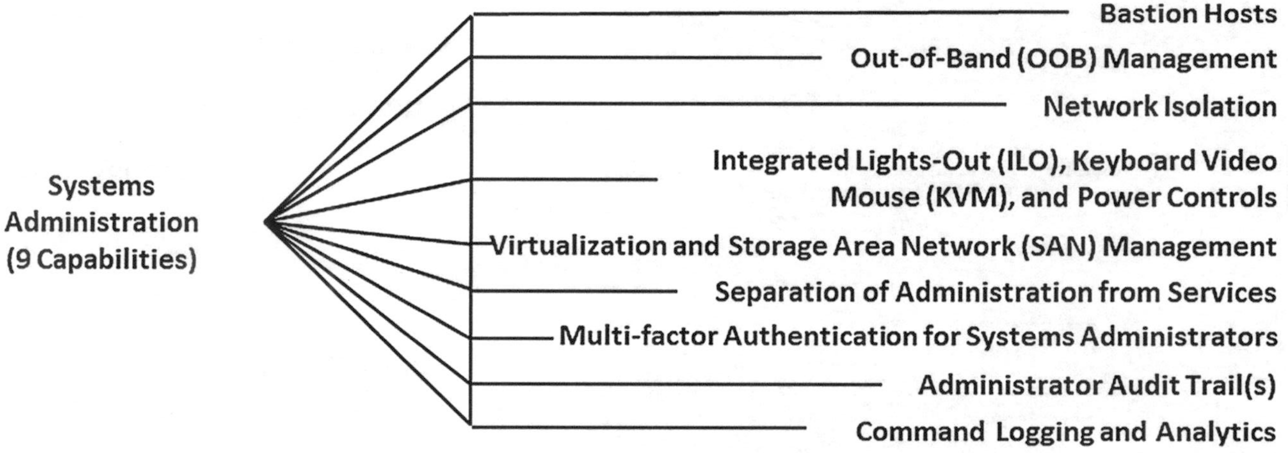

Systems Administration *(2 of 3)*

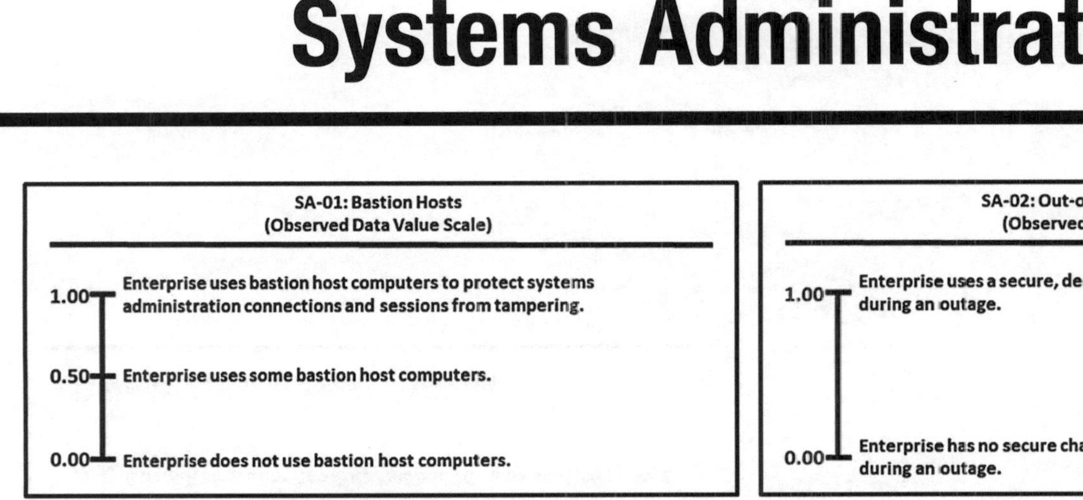

SA-01: Bastion Hosts
(Observed Data Value Scale)

- 1.00 — Enterprise uses bastion host computers to protect systems administration connections and sessions from tampering.
- 0.50 — Enterprise uses some bastion host computers.
- 0.00 — Enterprise does not use bastion host computers.

SA-03: Network Isolation
(Observed Data Value Scale)

- 1.00 — Enterprise conducts systems administration on networks isolated from business traffic.
- 0.00 — Enterprise conducts systems administration on networks shared with business traffic.

SA-05: Virtualization and SAN Management
(Observed Data Value Scale)

- 1.00 — Enterprise isolates and protects Virtualization and SAN Management.
- 0.50 — Enterprise isolates and protects either Virtualization or SAN Management.
- 0.00 — Enterprise does not isolate and protect Virtualization or SAN Management.

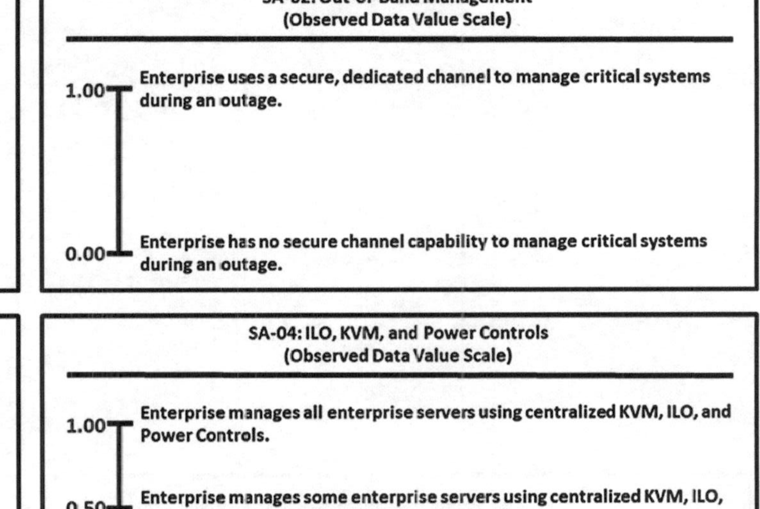

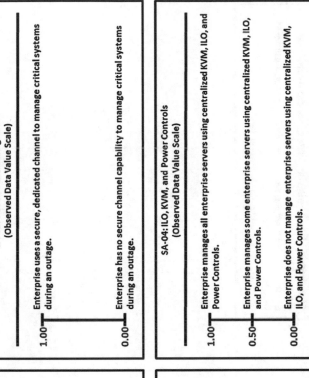

SA-02: Out-of-Band Management
(Observed Data Value Scale)

- 1.00 — Enterprise uses a secure, dedicated channel to manage critical systems during an outage.
- 0.00 — Enterprise has no secure channel capability to manage critical systems during an outage.

SA-04: ILO, KVM, and Power Controls
(Observed Data Value Scale)

- 1.00 — Enterprise manages all enterprise servers using centralized KVM, ILO, and Power Controls.
- 0.50 — Enterprise manages some enterprise servers using centralized KVM, ILO, and Power Controls.
- 0.00 — Enterprise does not manage enterprise servers using centralized KVM, ILO, and Power Controls.

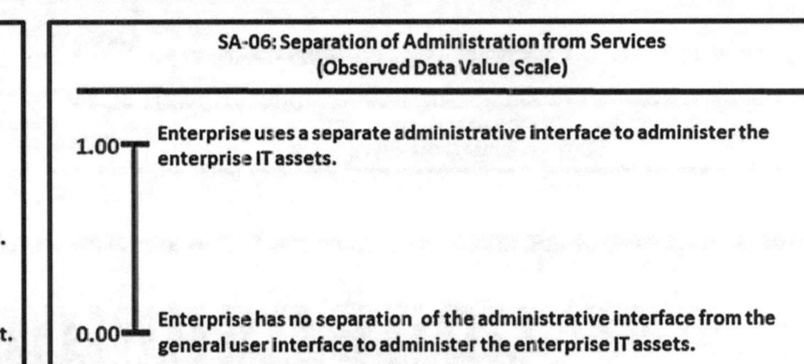

SA-06: Separation of Administration from Services
(Observed Data Value Scale)

- 1.00 — Enterprise uses a separate administrative interface to administer the enterprise IT assets.
- 0.00 — Enterprise has no separation of the administrative interface from the general user interface to administer the enterprise IT assets.

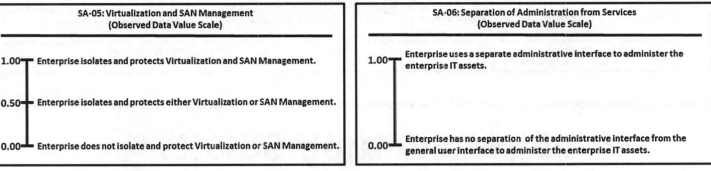

Systems Administration *(3 of 3)*

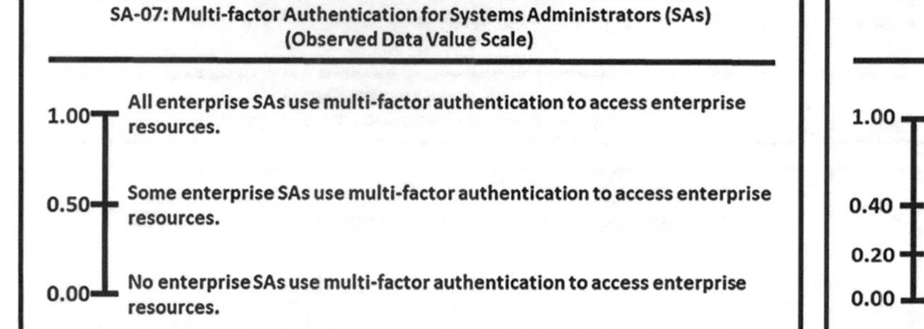

SA-07: Multi-factor Authentication for Systems Administrators (SAs)
(Observed Data Value Scale)
1.00
All enterprise SAs use multi-factor authentication to access enterprise resources.
0.50
Some enterprise SAs use multi-factor authentication to access enterprise resources.
0.00
No enterprise SAs use multi-factor authentication to access enterprise resources.

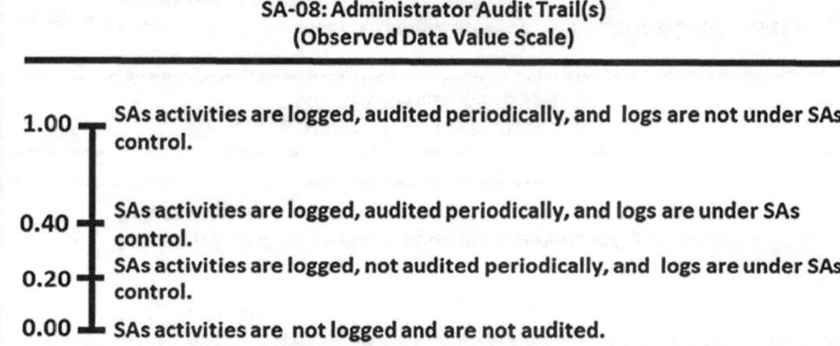

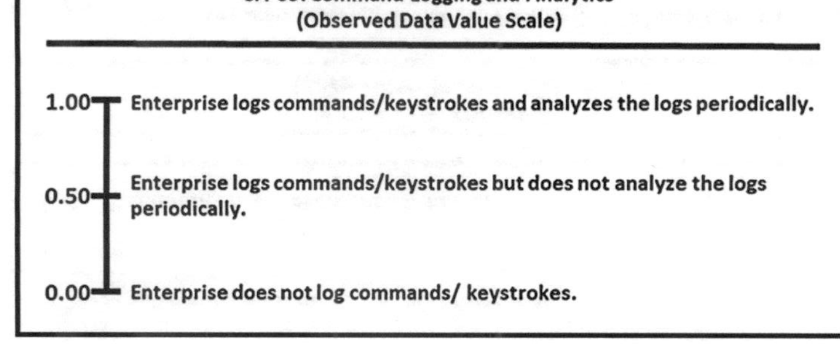

SA-09: Command Logging and Analytics
(Observed Data Value Scale)
1.00
Enterprise logs commands/keystrokes and analyzes the logs periodically.
0.50
Enterprise logs commands/keystrokes but does not analyze the logs periodically.
0.00
Enterprise does not log commands/ keystrokes.

Network Security *(1 of 4)*

Functional Area	Capabilities	
Network Security (NS)	• Switches and routers • Software Defined Networking (SDN) • Domain Name System (DNS) and Dynamic Host Configuration Protocol (DHCP) • Network Time Protocol (NTP) • Network service management • Firewall and virtual machine firewall • Network Intrusion Detection / Network Intrusion Prevention System (IDS / IPS)	• Wireless networking (Wi-Fi) • Packet intercept and capture • Secure Sockets Layer (SSL) intercept • Network Access Control (NAC) • Virtual Private Networking (VPN) and Internet Protocol Security (IPSec) • Network Traffic Analysis (NTA) • Network Data Analytics (NDA)

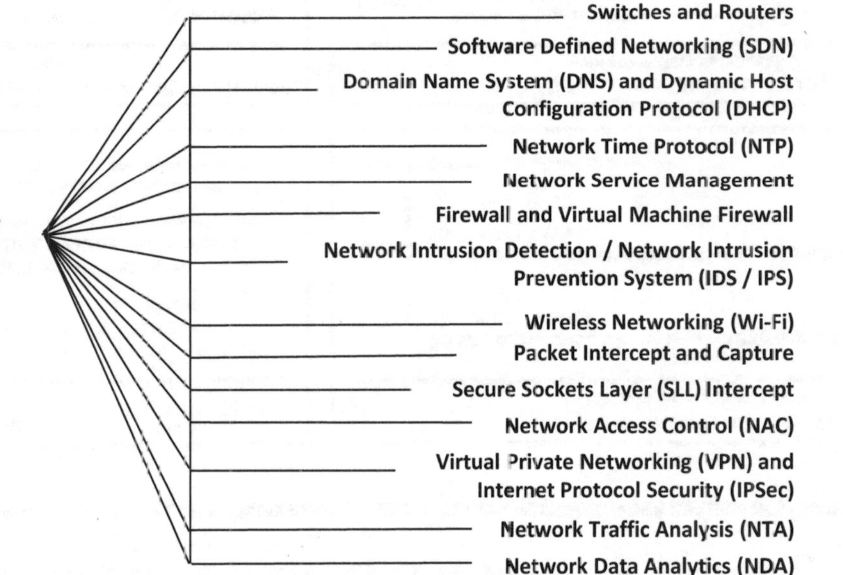

Network Security *(2 of 4)*

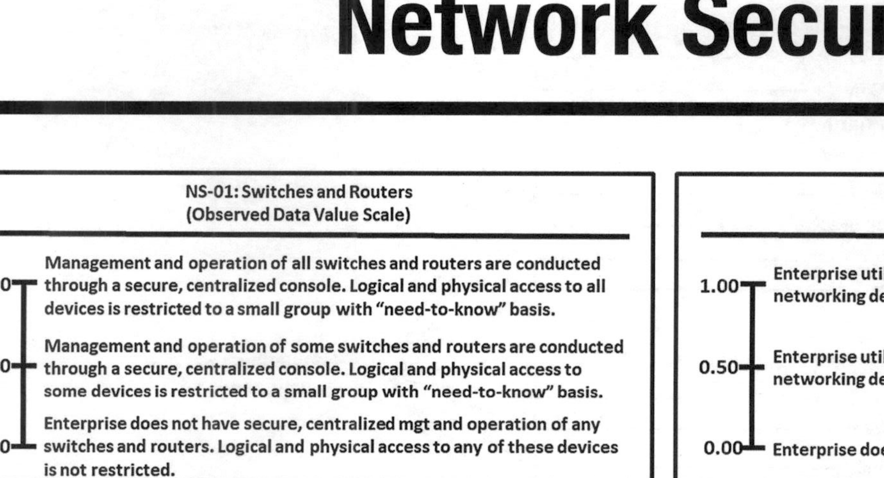

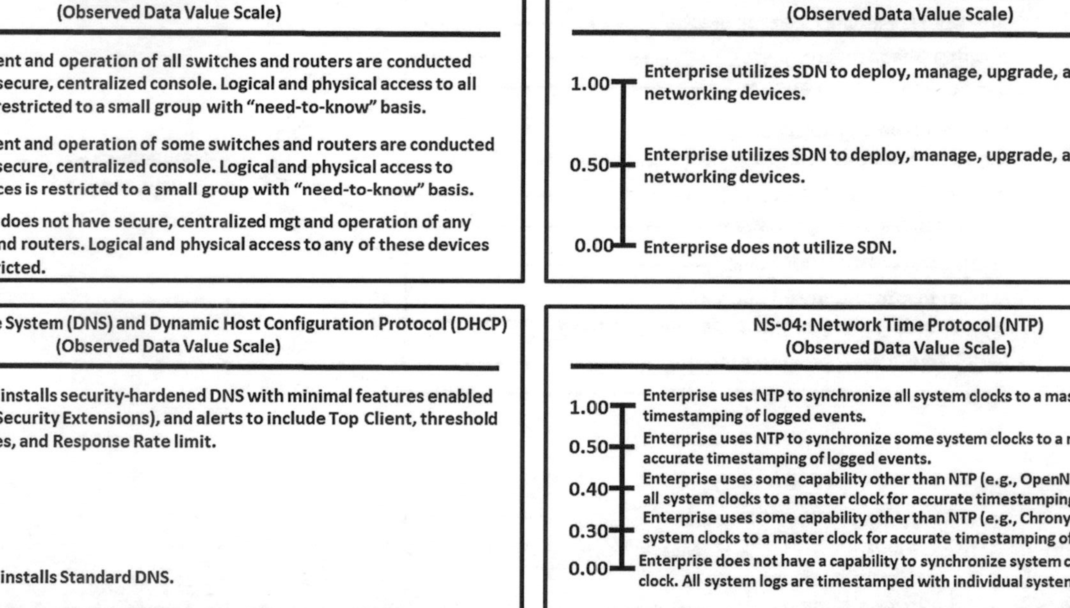

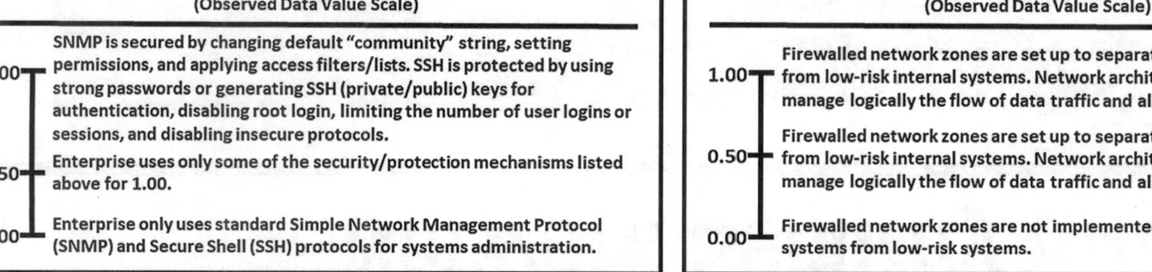

NS-01: Switches and Routers
(Observed Data Value Scale)

- 1.00 — Management and operation of all switches and routers are conducted through a secure, centralized console. Logical and physical access to all devices is restricted to a small group with "need-to-know" basis.
- 0.50 — Management and operation of some switches and routers are conducted through a secure, centralized console. Logical and physical access to some devices is restricted to a small group with "need-to-know" basis.
- 0.00 — Enterprise does not have secure, centralized mgt and operation of any switches and routers. Logical and physical access to any of these devices is not restricted.

NS-02: Software Defined Networks
(Observed Data Value Scale)

- 1.00 — Enterprise utilizes SDN to deploy, manage, upgrade, and retire all networking devices.
- 0.50 — Enterprise utilizes SDN to deploy, manage, upgrade, and retire some networking devices.
- 0.00 — Enterprise does not utilize SDN.

NS-03: Domain Name System (DNS) and Dynamic Host Configuration Protocol (DHCP)
(Observed Data Value Scale)

- 1.00 — Enterprise installs security-hardened DNS with minimal features enabled (e.g., DNS Security Extensions), and alerts to include Top Client, threshold DNS queries, and Response Rate limit.
- 0.00 — Enterprise installs Standard DNS.

NS-04: Network Time Protocol (NTP)
(Observed Data Value Scale)

- 1.00 — Enterprise uses NTP to synchronize all system clocks to a master clock for accurate timestamping of logged events.
- 0.50 — Enterprise uses NTP to synchronize some system clocks to a master clock for accurate timestamping of logged events.
- 0.40 — Enterprise uses some capability other than NTP (e.g., OpenNTPD) to synchronize all system clocks to a master clock for accurate timestamping of logged events.
- 0.30 — Enterprise uses some capability other than NTP (e.g., Chrony) to synchronize some system clocks to a master clock for accurate timestamping of logged events.
- 0.00 — Enterprise does not have a capability to synchronize system clocks to a master clock. All system logs are timestamped with individual system clocks.

NS-05: Network Service Management
(Observed Data Value Scale)

- 1.00 — SNMP is secured by changing default "community" string, setting permissions, and applying access filters/lists. SSH is protected by using strong passwords or generating SSH (private/public) keys for authentication, disabling root login, limiting the number of user logins or sessions, and disabling insecure protocols.
- 0.50 — Enterprise uses only some of the security/protection mechanisms listed above for 1.00.
- 0.00 — Enterprise only uses standard Simple Network Management Protocol (SNMP) and Secure Shell (SSH) protocols for systems administration.

NS-06: Firewall and Virtual Machine Firewall
(Observed Data Value Scale)

- 1.00 — Firewalled network zones are set up to separate all high-risk systems from low-risk internal systems. Network architecture is designed to manage logically the flow of data traffic and also provide visibility.
- 0.50 — Firewalled network zones are set up to separate some high-risk systems from low-risk internal systems. Network architecture is designed to manage logically the flow of data traffic and also provide visibility.
- 0.00 — Firewalled network zones are not implemented to separate high-risk systems from low-risk systems.

Network Security *(3 of 4)*

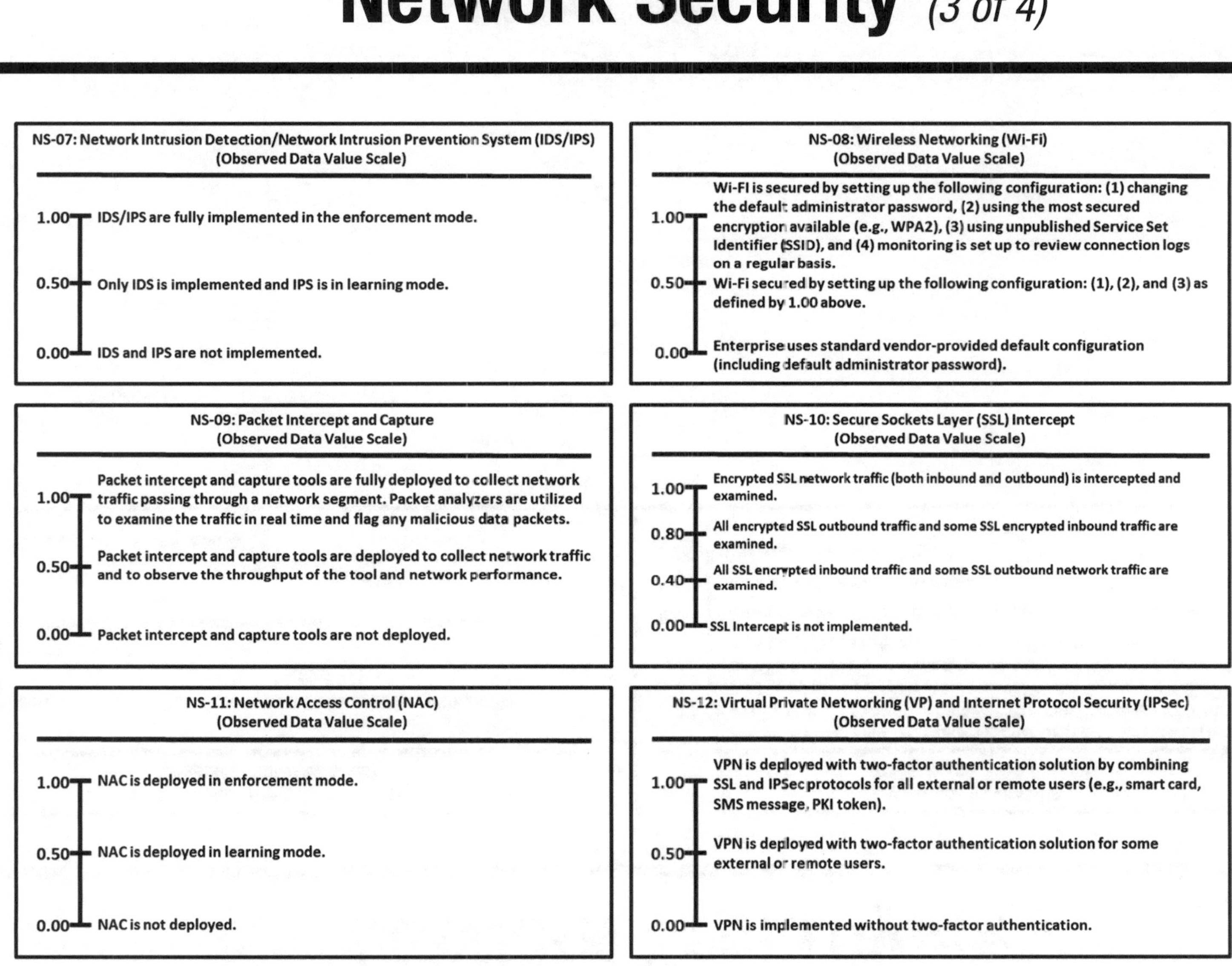

NS-07: Network Intrusion Detection/Network Intrusion Prevention System (IDS/IPS)
(Observed Data Value Scale)
1.00
IDS/IPS are fully implemented in the enforcement mode.
0.50
Only IDS is implemented and IPS is in learning mode.
0.00
IDS and IPS are not implemented.
NS-08: Wireless Networking (Wi-Fi)
(Observed Data Value Scale)
1.00
Wi-FI is secured by setting up the following configuration: (1) changing the default administrator password, (2) using the most secured encryption available (e.g., WPA2), (3) using unpublished Service Set Identifier (SSID), and (4) monitoring is set up to review connection logs on a regular basis.
0.50
Wi-Fi secured by setting up the following configuration: (1), (2), and (3) as defined by 1.00 above.
0.00
Enterprise uses standard vendor-provided default configuration (including default administrator password).
NS-09: Packet Intercept and Capture
(Observed Data Value Scale)
1.00
Packet intercept and capture tools are fully deployed to collect network traffic passing through a network segment. Packet analyzers are utilized to examine the traffic in real time and flag any malicious data packets.
0.50
Packet intercept and capture tools are deployed to collect network traffic and to observe the throughput of the tool and network performance.
0.00
Packet intercept and capture tools are not deployed.
NS-10: Secure Sockets Layer (SSL) Intercept
(Observed Data Value Scale)
1.00
Encrypted SSL network traffic (both inbound and outbound) is intercepted and examined.
0.80
All encrypted SSL outbound traffic and some SSL encrypted inbound traffic are examined.
0.40
All SSL encrypted inbound traffic and some SSL outbound network traffic are examined.
0.00
SSL Intercept is not implemented.
NS-11: Network Access Control (NAC)
(Observed Data Value Scale)
1.00
NAC is deployed in enforcement mode.
0.50
NAC is deployed in learning mode.
0.00
NAC is not deployed.
NS-12: Virtual Private Networking (VP) and Internet Protocol Security (IPSec)
(Observed Data Value Scale)
1.00
VPN is deployed with two-factor authentication solution by combining SSL and IPSec protocols for all external or remote users (e.g., smart card, SMS message, PKI token).
0.50
VPN is deployed with two-factor authentication solution for some external or remote users.
0.00
VPN is implemented without two-factor authentication.

Network Security *(4 of 4)*

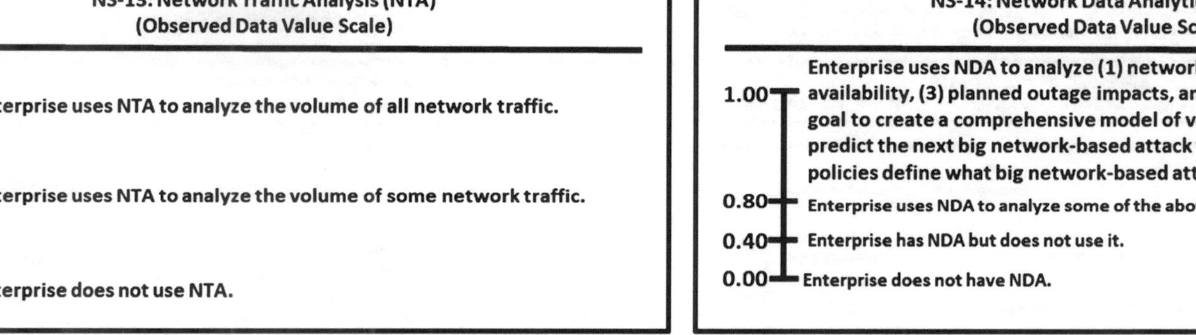

NS-13: Network Traffic Analysis (NTA)
(Observed Data Value Scale)

- 1.00 — Enterprise uses NTA to analyze the volume of all network traffic.
- 0.50 — Enterprise uses NTA to analyze the volume of some network traffic.
- 0.00 — Enterprise does not use NTA.

NS-14: Network Data Analytics (NDA)
(Observed Data Value Scale)

- 1.00 — Enterprise uses NDA to analyze (1) network traffic trends, (2) network availability, (3) planned outage impacts, and (4) network traffic with a goal to create a comprehensive model of various network threats to predict the next big network-based attack where network security policies define what big network-based attack means.
- 0.80 — Enterprise uses NDA to analyze some of the above items to achieve the goal.
- 0.40 — Enterprise has NDA but does not use it.
- 0.00 — Enterprise does not have NDA.

Application Security *(1 of 3)*

Functional Area	Capabilities	
Application Security (AS)	• E-mail security • Webshell detection • Application firewalls • Database firewalls • Forward proxy and web filters	• Reverse proxy • Data Leakage Protection (DLP) • Secure application and database software development • Software code vulnerability analysis

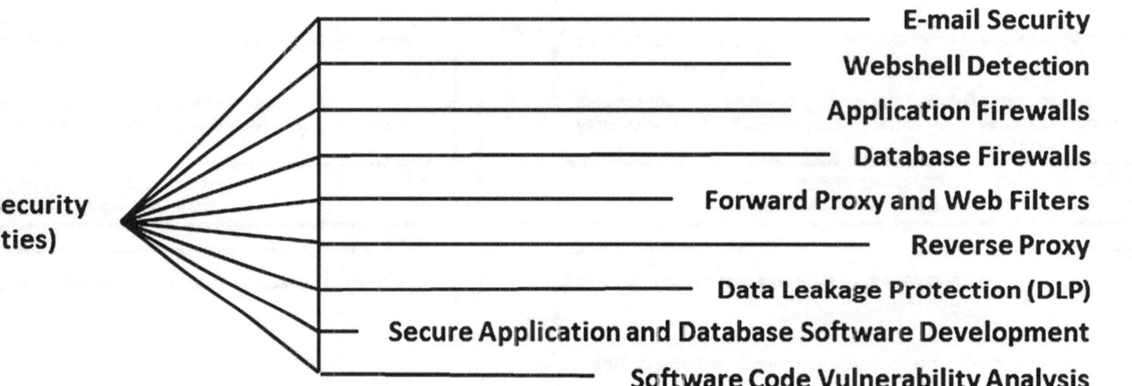

Application Security *(2 of 3)*

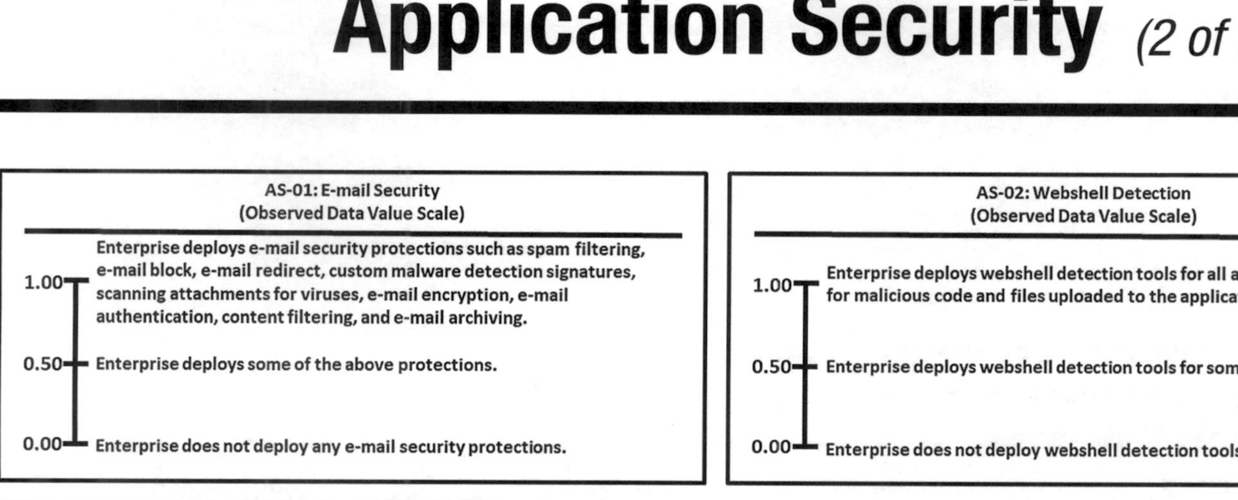

AS-01: E-mail Security
(Observed Data Value Scale)

- 1.00 — Enterprise deploys e-mail security protections such as spam filtering, e-mail block, e-mail redirect, custom malware detection signatures, scanning attachments for viruses, e-mail encryption, e-mail authentication, content filtering, and e-mail archiving.
- 0.50 — Enterprise deploys some of the above protections.
- 0.00 — Enterprise does not deploy any e-mail security protections.

AS-02: Webshell Detection
(Observed Data Value Scale)

- 1.00 — Enterprise deploys webshell detection tools for all applications to scan for malicious code and files uploaded to the applications.
- 0.50 — Enterprise deploys webshell detection tools for some applications.
- 0.00 — Enterprise does not deploy webshell detection tools.

AS-03: Application Firewalls
(Observed Data Value Scale)

- 1.00 — Enterprise deploys application firewalls in detection and enforcement mode to stop malicious data packets reaching all applications.
- 0.50 — Enterprise deploys application firewalls in detection and learning mode for some applications.
- 0.00 — Enterprise does not deploy application firewalls.

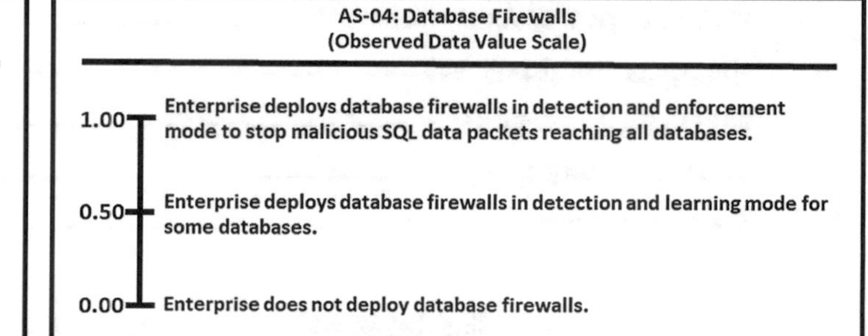

AS-04: Database Firewalls
(Observed Data Value Scale)

- 1.00 — Enterprise deploys database firewalls in detection and enforcement mode to stop malicious SQL data packets reaching all databases.
- 0.50 — Enterprise deploys database firewalls in detection and learning mode for some databases.
- 0.00 — Enterprise does not deploy database firewalls.

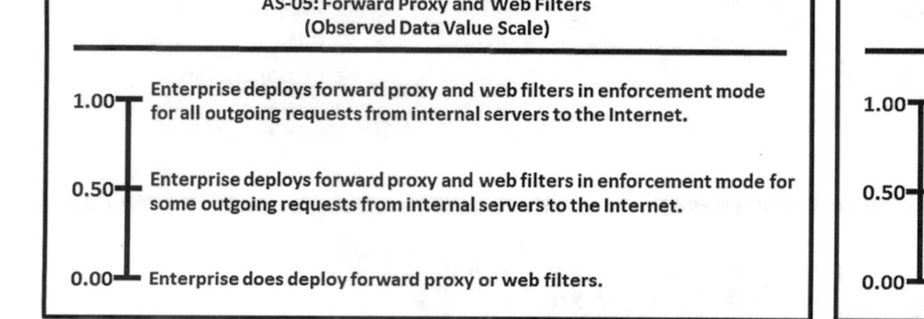

AS-05: Forward Proxy and Web Filters
(Observed Data Value Scale)

- 1.00 — Enterprise deploys forward proxy and web filters in enforcement mode for all outgoing requests from internal servers to the Internet.
- 0.50 — Enterprise deploys forward proxy and web filters in enforcement mode for some outgoing requests from internal servers to the Internet.
- 0.00 — Enterprise does deploy forward proxy or web filters.

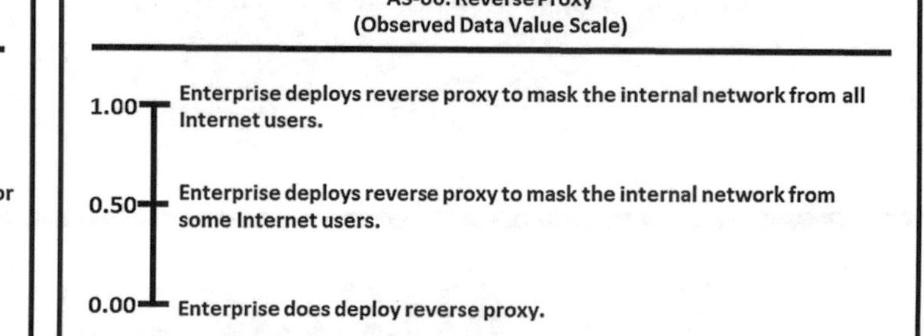

AS-06: Reverse Proxy
(Observed Data Value Scale)

- 1.00 — Enterprise deploys reverse proxy to mask the internal network from all Internet users.
- 0.50 — Enterprise deploys reverse proxy to mask the internal network from some Internet users.
- 0.00 — Enterprise does deploy reverse proxy.

Application Security *(3 of 3)*

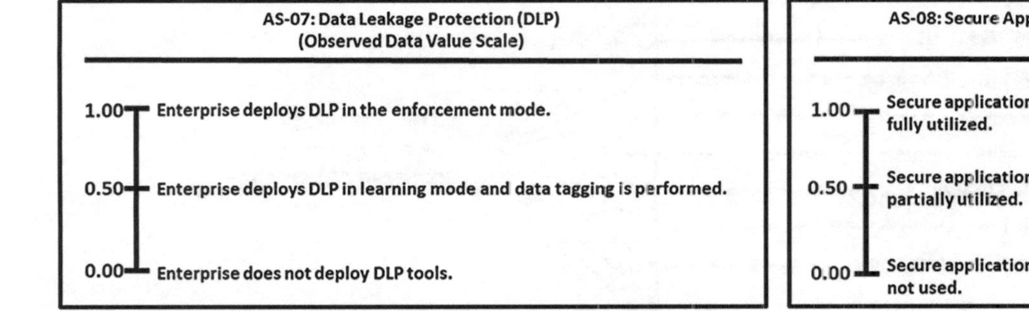

AS-07: Data Leakage Protection (DLP)
(Observed Data Value Scale)
1.00 Enterprise deploys DLP in the enforcement mode.
0.50 Enterprise deploys DLP in learning mode and data tagging is performed.
0.00 Enterprise does not deploy DLP tools.

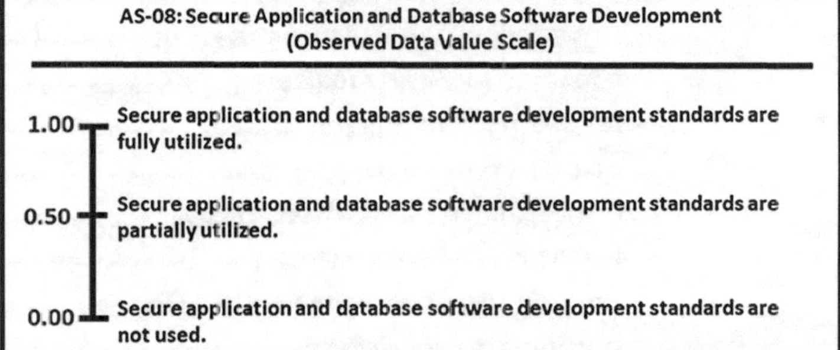

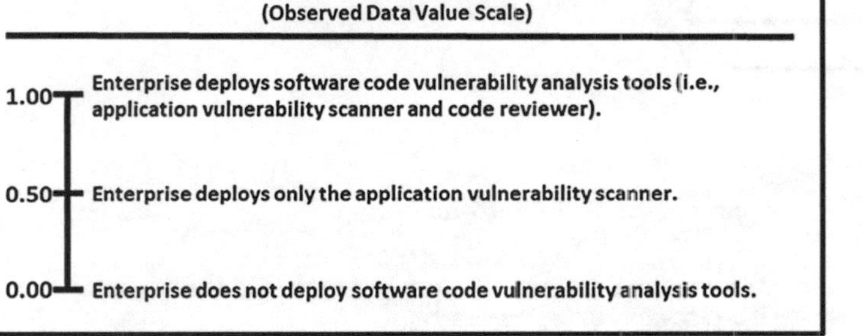

AS-09: Software Code Vulnerability Analysis
(Observed Data Value Scale)
1.00 Enterprise deploys software code vulnerability analysis tools (i.e., application vulnerability scanner and code reviewer).
0.50 Enterprise deploys only the application vulnerability scanner.
0.00 Enterprise does not deploy software code vulnerability analysis tools.

Endpoint, Server, and Device Security *(1 of 4)*

Functional Area	Capabilities	
Endpoint, Server, and Device Security (ESDS)	• Local administrator privilege restrictions • Computer security and logging policies • Endpoint and media encryption • Computer access controls • Forensic imaging support for investigations • Virtual desktop / thin clients • Mobile Device Management (MDM) • Anti-virus / anti-malware	• Application whitelisting • In-memory malware detection • Host firewall and intrusion detection • "Gold code" software images • Security Technical Implementation Guides (STIGs) • Always-on Virtual Private Networking (VPN) • File integrity and change monitoring

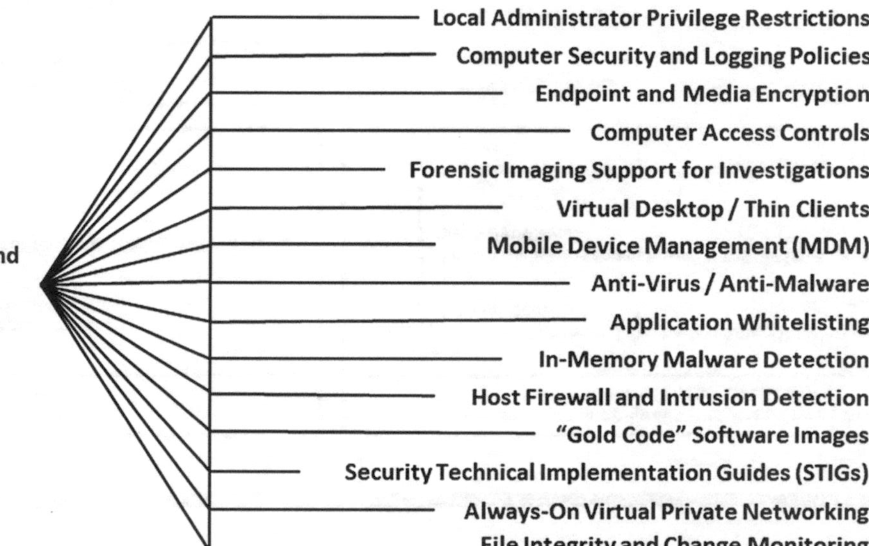

Endpoint, Server, and Device Security *(2 of 4)*

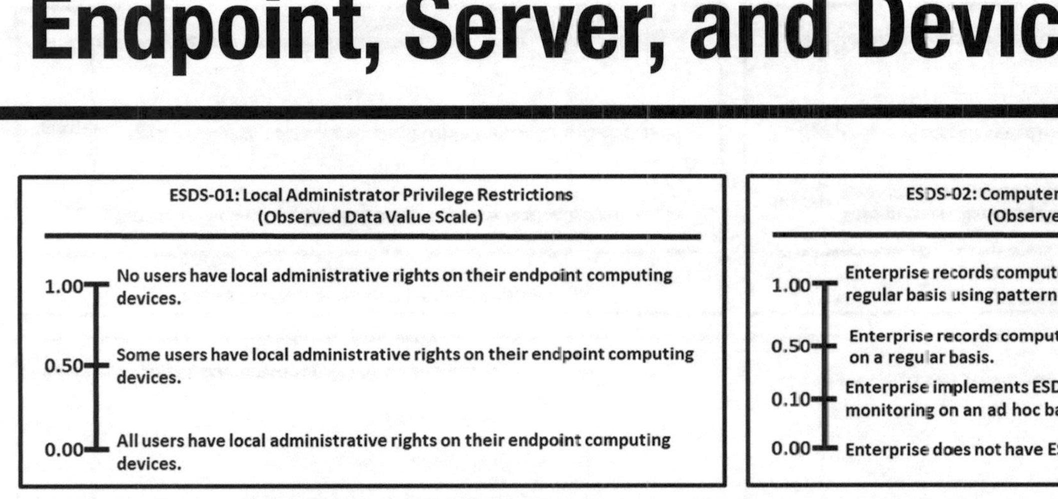

ESDS-01: Local Administrator Privilege Restrictions
(Observed Data Value Scale)

- 1.00 — No users have local administrative rights on their endpoint computing devices.
- 0.50 — Some users have local administrative rights on their endpoint computing devices.
- 0.00 — All users have local administrative rights on their endpoint computing devices.

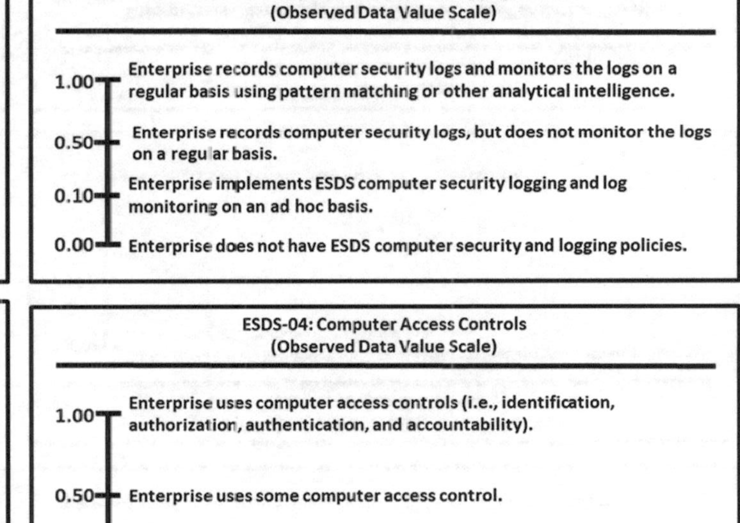

ESDS-02: Computer Security and Logging Policies
(Observed Data Value Scale)

- 1.00 — Enterprise records computer security logs and monitors the logs on a regular basis using pattern matching or other analytical intelligence.
- 0.50 — Enterprise records computer security logs, but does not monitor the logs on a regular basis.
- 0.10 — Enterprise implements ESDS computer security logging and log monitoring on an ad hoc basis.
- 0.00 — Enterprise does not have ESDS computer security and logging policies.

ESDS-03: Endpoint and Media Encryption
(Observed Data Value Scale)

- 1.00 — Enterprise deploys endpoint and media encryption protection.
- 0.50 — Enterprise deploys some endpoint and media encryption.
- 0.00 — Enterprise does not deploy endpoint and media encryption.

ESDS-04: Computer Access Controls
(Observed Data Value Scale)

- 1.00 — Enterprise uses computer access controls (i.e., identification, authorization, authentication, and accountability).
- 0.50 — Enterprise uses some computer access control.
- 0.00 — Enterprise does not use computer access control.

ESDS-05: Forensic Imaging Support for Investigations
(Observed Data Value Scale)

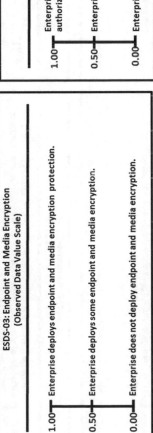

- 1.00 — Enterprise deploys forensic imaging policies, procedures, and tools governing what electronic data (at rest or in transmission) is recovered and analyzed to support criminal investigations.
- 0.00 — Enterprise does not deploy forensic imaging policies, procedures, or tools to support criminal investigations.

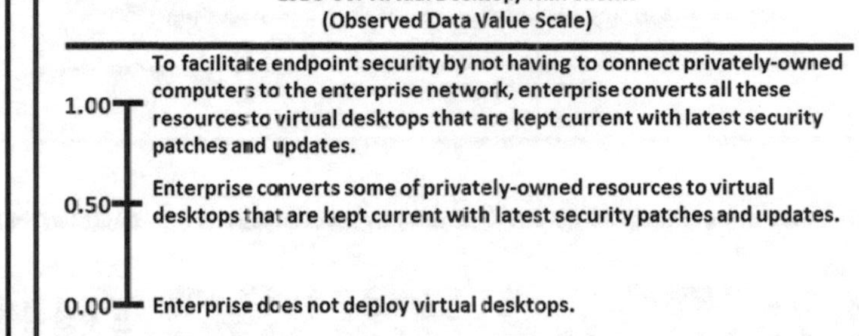

ESDS-06: Virtual Desktop/Thin Clients
(Observed Data Value Scale)

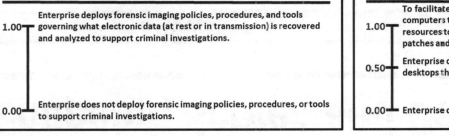

- 1.00 — To facilitate endpoint security by not having to connect privately-owned computers to the enterprise network, enterprise converts all these resources to virtual desktops that are kept current with latest security patches and updates.
- 0.50 — Enterprise converts some of privately-owned resources to virtual desktops that are kept current with latest security patches and updates.
- 0.00 — Enterprise does not deploy virtual desktops.

Endpoint, Server, and Device Security *(3 of 4)*

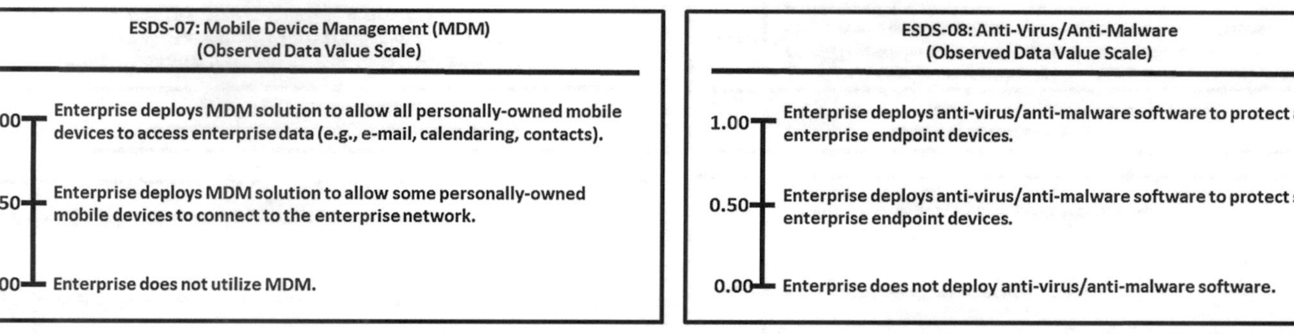

ESDS-07: Mobile Device Management (MDM)
(Observed Data Value Scale)
1.00
Enterprise deploys MDM solution to allow all personally-owned mobile devices to access enterprise data (e.g., e-mail, calendaring, contacts).
0.50
Enterprise deploys MDM solution to allow some personally-owned mobile devices to connect to the enterprise network.
0.00
Enterprise does not utilize MDM.
ESDS-08: Anti-Virus/Anti-Malware
(Observed Data Value Scale)
1.00
Enterprise deploys anti-virus/anti-malware software to protect all enterprise endpoint devices.
0.50
Enterprise deploys anti-virus/anti-malware software to protect some enterprise endpoint devices.
0.00
Enterprise does not deploy anti-virus/anti-malware software.

ESDS-09: Application Whitelisting
(Observed Data Value Scale)

- 1.00 — Enterprise creates an approved list of applications allowed to execute within the enterprise; if a non-whitelist application tries to execute, it is blocked for subsequent analysis.
- 0.00 — Enterprise does not use application whitelisting.

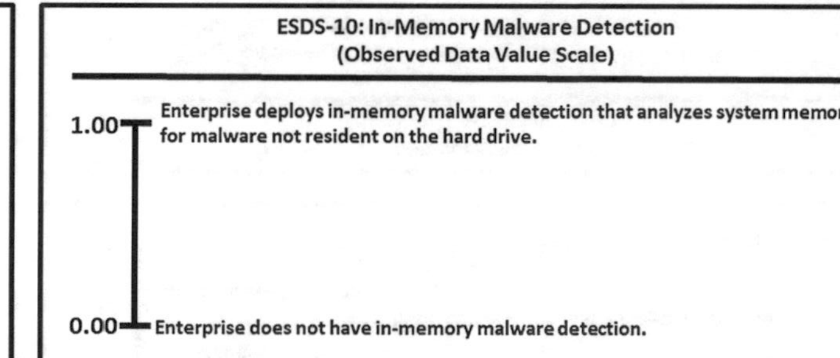

ESDS-10: In-Memory Malware Detection
(Observed Data Value Scale)
1.00
Enterprise deploys in-memory malware detection that analyzes system memory for malware not resident on the hard drive.
0.00
Enterprise does not have in-memory malware detection.

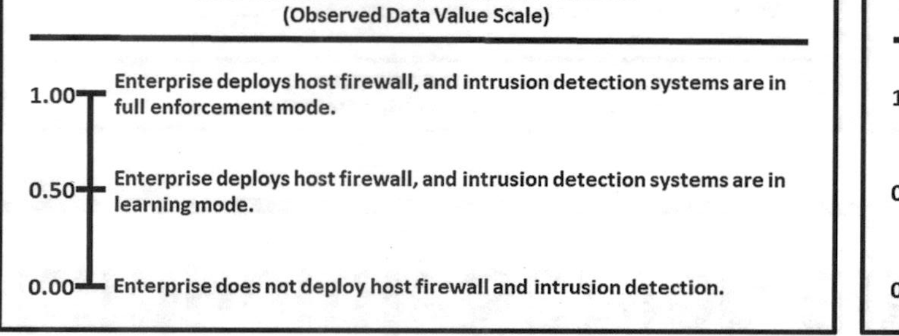

ESDS-11: Host Firewall and Intrusion Detection
(Observed Data Value Scale)
1.00
Enterprise deploys host firewall, and intrusion detection systems are in full enforcement mode.
0.50
Enterprise deploys host firewall, and intrusion detection systems are in learning mode.
0.00
Enterprise does not deploy host firewall and intrusion detection.

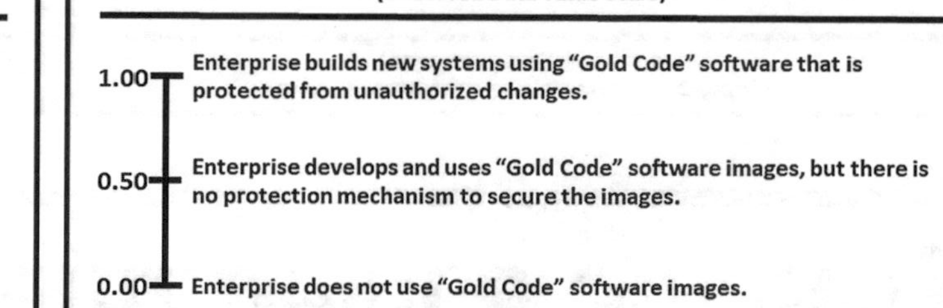

ESDS-12: "Gold Code" Software Images
(Observed Data Value Scale)
1.00
Enterprise builds new systems using "Gold Code" software that is protected from unauthorized changes.
0.50
Enterprise develops and uses "Gold Code" software images, but there is no protection mechanism to secure the images.
0.00
Enterprise does not use "Gold Code" software images.

Endpoint, Server, and Device Security *(4 of 4)*

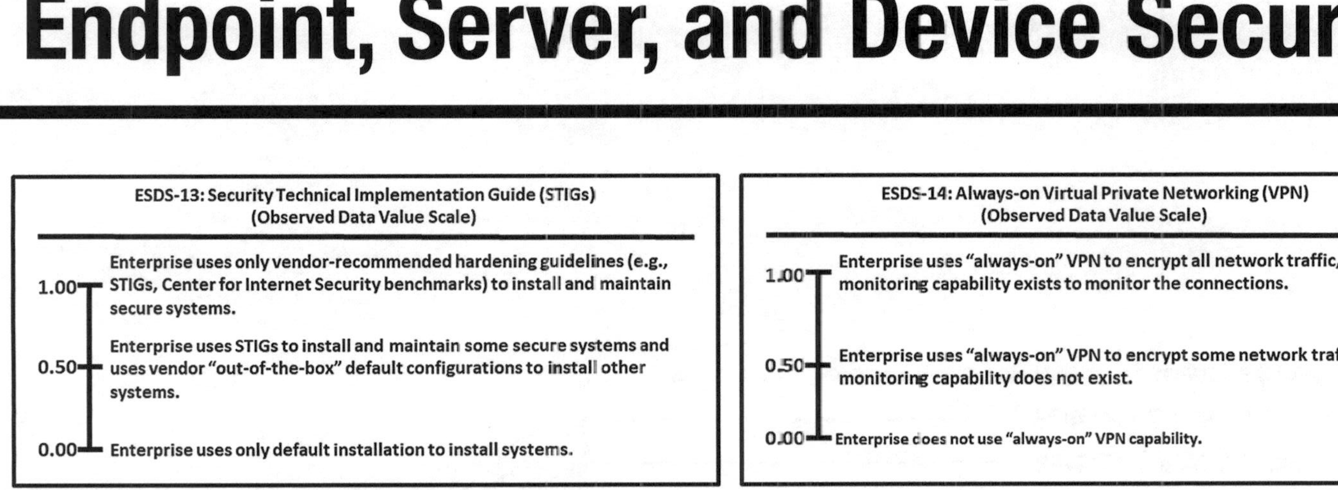

ESDS-13: Security Technical Implementation Guide (STIGs)
(Observed Data Value Scale)
1.00
Enterprise uses only vendor-recommended hardening guidelines (e.g., STIGs, Center for Internet Security benchmarks) to install and maintain secure systems.
0.50
Enterprise uses STIGs to install and maintain some secure systems and uses vendor "out-of-the-box" default configurations to install other systems.
0.00
Enterprise uses only default installation to install systems.
ESDS-15: File Integrity and Change Monitoring
(Observed Data Value Scale)
1.00
Enterprise monitors file system changes of all networked systems to uncover, for example, malicious software, viruses, and malicious file changes.
0.50
Enterprise monitors file system changes of critical systems.
0.00
Enterprise does not deploy file integrity and change monitoring.

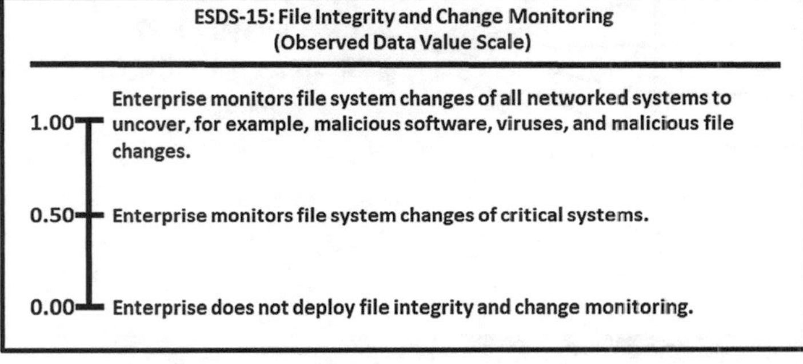

ESDS-14: Always-on Virtual Private Networking (VPN)
(Observed Data Value Scale)
1.00
Enterprise uses "always-on" VPN to encrypt all network traffic, and monitoring capability exists to monitor the connections.
0.50
Enterprise uses "always-on" VPN to encrypt some network traffic, but monitoring capability does not exist.
0.00
Enterprise does not use "always-on" VPN capability.

Identity, Authentication, and Access Management *(1 of 3)*

Functional Area	Capabilities	
Identity, Authentication, and Access Management (IAAM)	• Identity life cycle management • Enterprise directory • Multi-factor authentication • Privilege management and access control • Identity and access audit trail and reporting	• Lightweight Directory Access Protocol (LDAP) • Kerberos, RADIUS, 802.1x • Federated authentication • Security Assertion Markup Language (SAML)

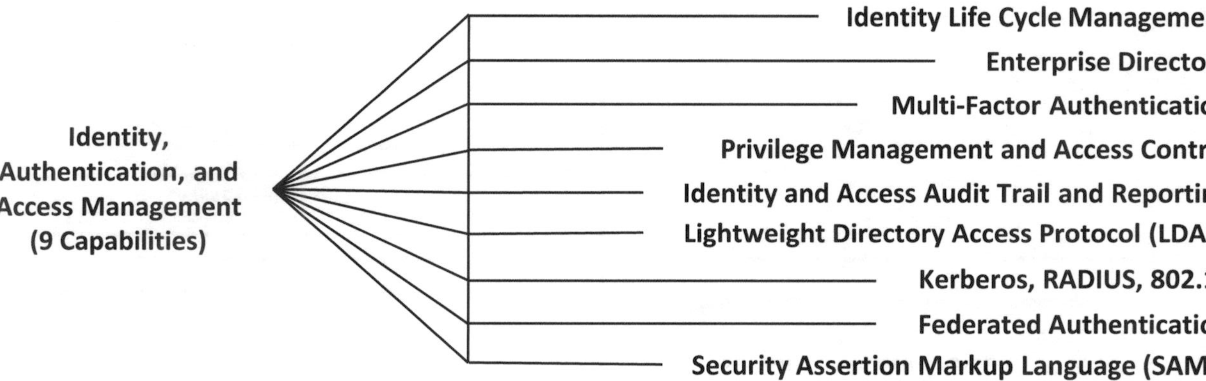

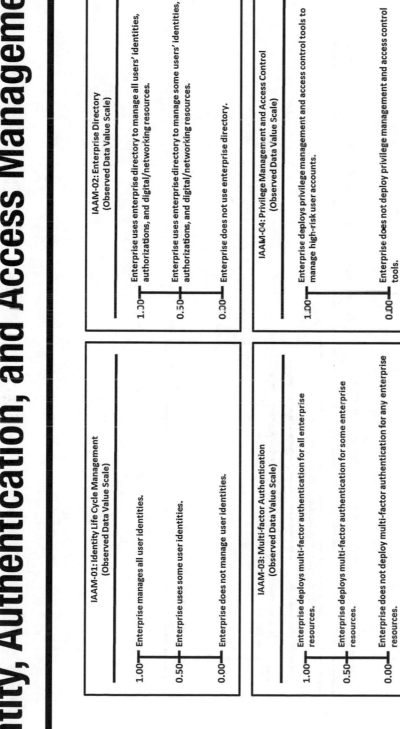

Identity, Authentication, and Access Management *(2 of 3)*

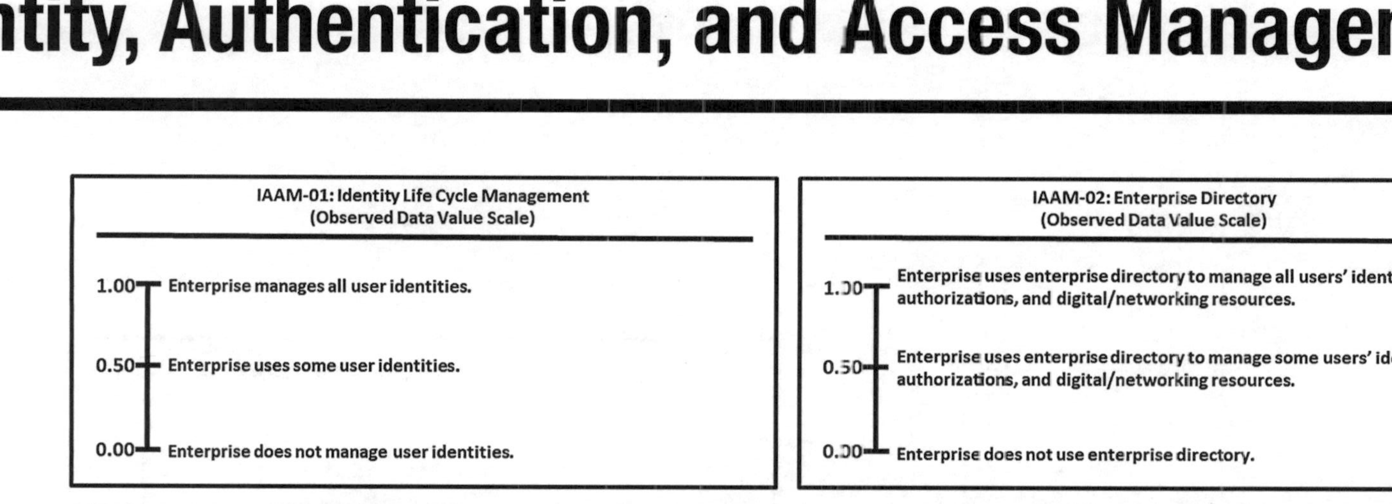

IAAM-01: Identity Life Cycle Management
(Observed Data Value Scale)
1.00 Enterprise manages all user identities.
0.50 Enterprise uses some user identities.
0.00 Enterprise does not manage user identities.
IAAM-02: Enterprise Directory
(Observed Data Value Scale)
1.00 Enterprise uses enterprise directory to manage all users' identities, authorizations, and digital/networking resources.
0.50 Enterprise uses enterprise directory to manage some users' identities, authorizations, and digital/networking resources.
0.00 Enterprise does not use enterprise directory.
IAAM-03: Multi-factor Authentication
(Observed Data Value Scale)
1.00 Enterprise deploys multi-factor authentication for all enterprise resources.
0.50 Enterprise deploys multi-factor authentication for some enterprise resources.
0.00 Enterprise does not deploy multi-factor authentication for any enterprise resources.
IAAM-05: Identity and Access Audit Trail and Reporting
(Observed Data Value Scale)
1.00 Enterprise deploys an audit trail capability to support regulatory compliance and investigations for all user actions.
0.50 Enterprise deploys an audit trail capability to support regulatory compliance and investigations for some user actions.
0.00 Enterprise does not deploy an audit trail capability.

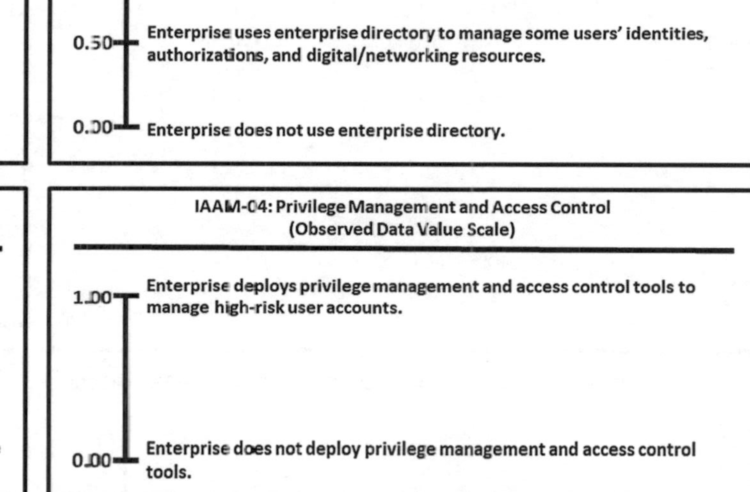

IAAM-04: Privilege Management and Access Control
(Observed Data Value Scale)
1.00 Enterprise deploys privilege management and access control tools to manage high-risk user accounts.
0.00 Enterprise does not deploy privilege management and access control tools.

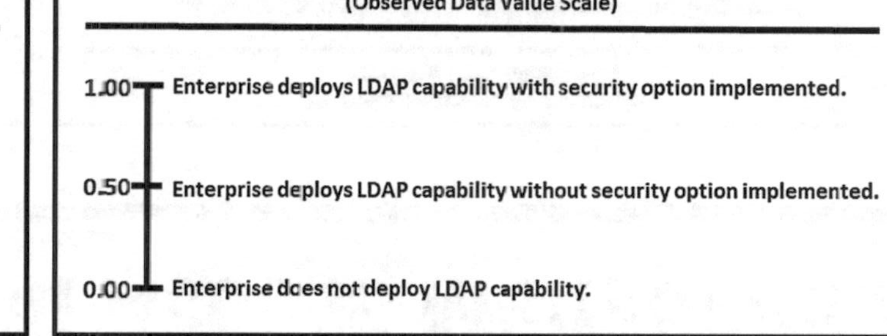

IAAM-06: Lightweight Directory Access Protocol (LDAP)
(Observed Data Value Scale)
1.00 Enterprise deploys LDAP capability with security option implemented.
0.50 Enterprise deploys LDAP capability without security option implemented.
0.00 Enterprise does not deploy LDAP capability.

Identity, Authentication, and Access Management *(3 of 3)*

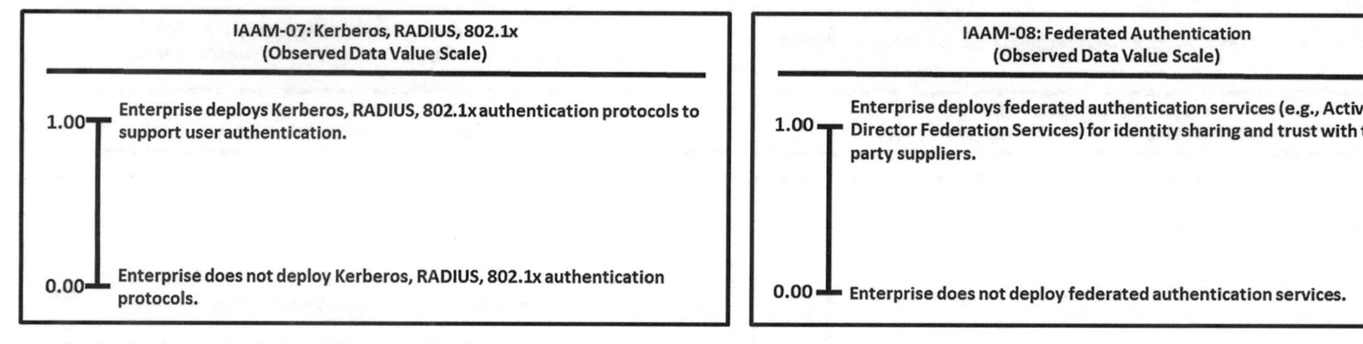

IAAM-07: Kerberos, RADIUS, 802.1x
(Observed Data Value Scale)
1.00
Enterprise deploys Kerberos, RADIUS, 802.1x authentication protocols to support user authentication.
0.00
Enterprise does not deploy Kerberos, RADIUS, 802.1x authentication protocols.
IAAM-08: Federated Authentication
(Observed Data Value Scale)
1.00
Enterprise deploys federated authentication services (e.g., Active Director Federation Services) for identity sharing and trust with third-party suppliers.
0.00
Enterprise does not deploy federated authentication services.

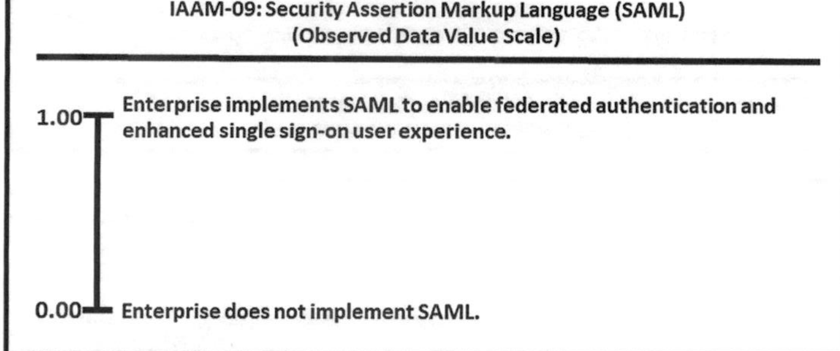

IAAM-09: Security Assertion Markup Language (SAML)
(Observed Data Value Scale)
1.00
Enterprise implements SAML to enable federated authentication and enhanced single sign-on user experience.
0.00
Enterprise does not implement SAML.

Data Protection and Cryptography *(1 of 3)*

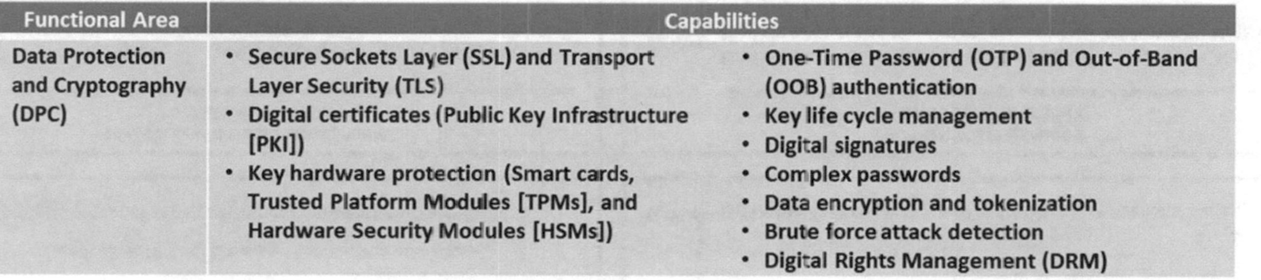

Functional Area	Capabilities	
Data Protection and Cryptography (DPC)	• Secure Sockets Layer (SSL) and Transport Layer Security (TLS) • Digital certificates (Public Key Infrastructure [PKI]) • Key hardware protection (Smart cards, Trusted Platform Modules [TPMs], and Hardware Security Modules [HSMs])	• One-Time Password (OTP) and Out-of-Band (OOB) authentication • Key life cycle management • Digital signatures • Complex passwords • Data encryption and tokenization • Brute force attack detection • Digital Rights Management (DRM)

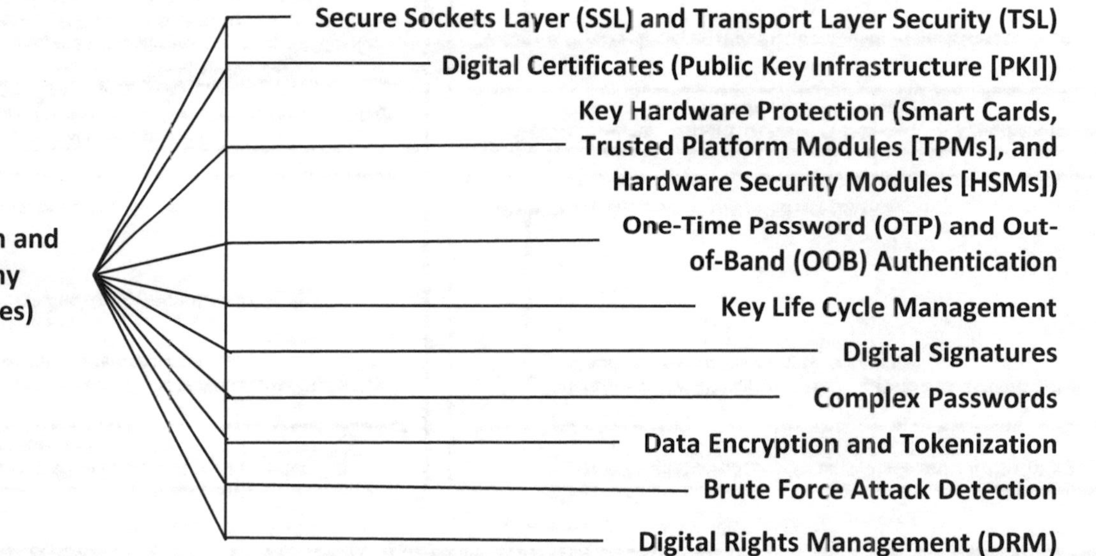

Data Protection and Cryptography *(2 of 3)*

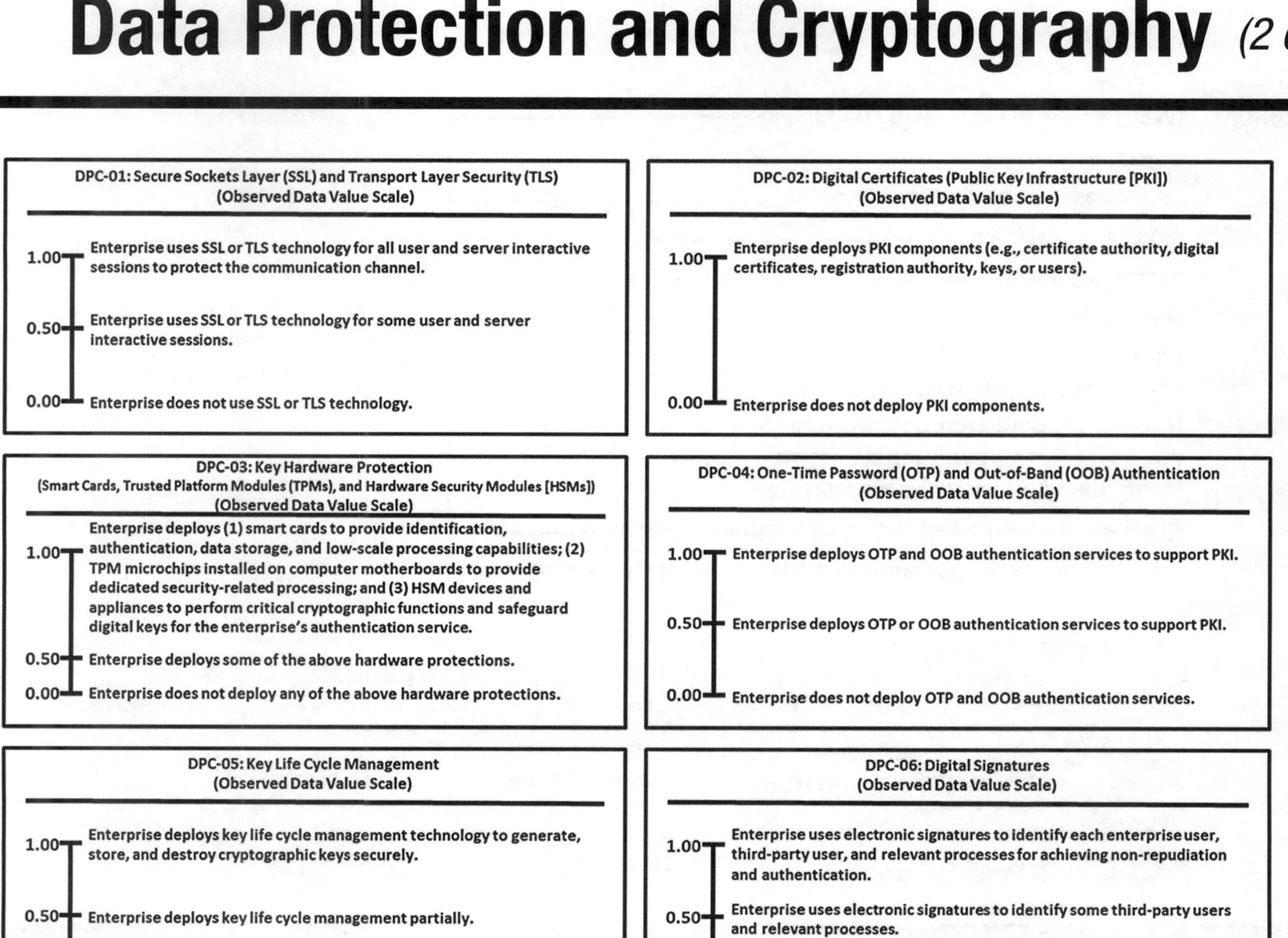

DPC-01: Secure Sockets Layer (SSL) and Transport Layer Security (TLS)
(Observed Data Value Scale)
1.00
Enterprise uses SSL or TLS technology for all user and server interactive sessions to protect the communication channel.
0.50
Enterprise uses SSL or TLS technology for some user and server interactive sessions.
0.00
Enterprise does not use SSL or TLS technology.
DPC-02: Digital Certificates (Public Key Infrastructure [PKI])
(Observed Data Value Scale)
1.00
Enterprise deploys PKI components (e.g., certificate authority, digital certificates, registration authority, keys, or users).
0.00
Enterprise does not deploy PKI components.
DPC-03: Key Hardware Protection
(Smart Cards, Trusted Platform Modules (TPMs), and Hardware Security Modules [HSMs])
(Observed Data Value Scale)
1.00
Enterprise deploys (1) smart cards to provide identification, authentication, data storage, and low-scale processing capabilities; (2) TPM microchips installed on computer motherboards to provide dedicated security-related processing; and (3) HSM devices and appliances to perform critical cryptographic functions and safeguard digital keys for the enterprise's authentication service.
0.50
Enterprise deploys some of the above hardware protections.
0.00
Enterprise does not deploy any of the above hardware protections.
DPC-04: One-Time Password (OTP) and Out-of-Band (OOB) Authentication
(Observed Data Value Scale)
1.00
Enterprise deploys OTP and OOB authentication services to support PKI.
0.50
Enterprise deploys OTP or OOB authentication services to support PKI.
0.00
Enterprise does not deploy OTP and OOB authentication services.
DPC-05: Key Life Cycle Management
(Observed Data Value Scale)
1.00
Enterprise deploys key life cycle management technology to generate, store, and destroy cryptographic keys securely.
0.50
Enterprise deploys key life cycle management partially.
0.00
Enterprise does not deploy key life cycle management.
DPC-06: Digital Signatures
(Observed Data Value Scale)
1.00
Enterprise uses electronic signatures to identify each enterprise user, third-party user, and relevant processes for achieving non-repudiation and authentication.
0.50
Enterprise uses electronic signatures to identify some third-party users and relevant processes.
0.00
Enterprise does not use electronic signatures.

Data Protection and Cryptography *(3 of 3)*

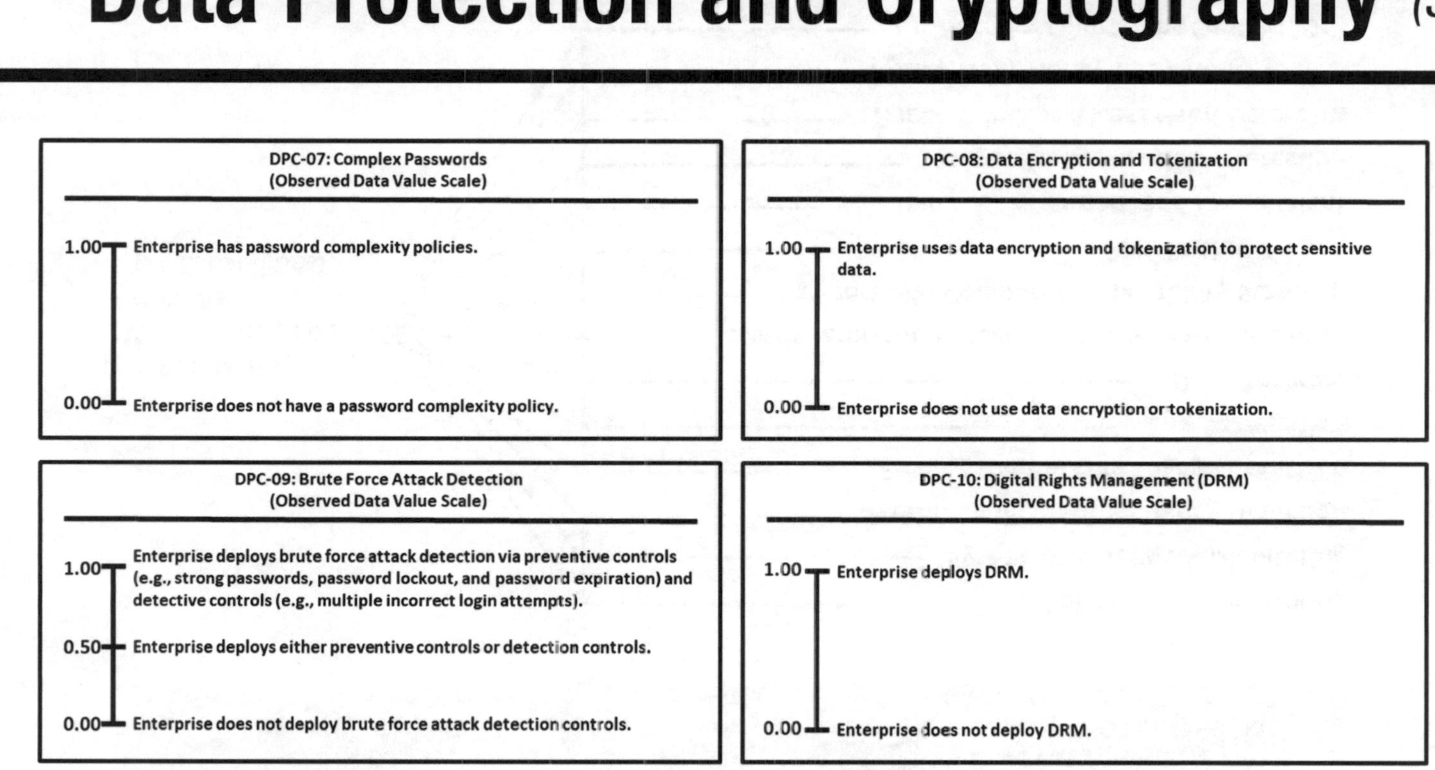

DPC-07: Complex Passwords
(Observed Data Value Scale)
1.00
Enterprise has password complexity policies.
0.00
Enterprise does not have a password complexity policy.
DPC-08: Data Encryption and Tokenization
(Observed Data Value Scale)
1.00
Enterprise uses data encryption and tokenization to protect sensitive data.
0.00
Enterprise does not use data encryption or tokenization.
DPC-09: Brute Force Attack Detection
(Observed Data Value Scale)
1.00
Enterprise deploys brute force attack detection via preventive controls (e.g., strong passwords, password lockout, and password expiration) and detective controls (e.g., multiple incorrect login attempts).
0.50
Enterprise deploys either preventive controls or detection controls.
0.00
Enterprise does not deploy brute force attack detection controls.
DPC-10: Digital Rights Management (DRM)
(Observed Data Value Scale)
1.00
Enterprise deploys DRM.
0.00
Enterprise does not deploy DRM.

Monitoring, Vulnerability, and Patch Management *(1 of 4)*

Functional Area	Capabilities	
Monitoring, Vulnerability, and Patch Management (MVPM)	• Operational performance monitoring • System and network monitoring • System configuration change detection • Privilege and access change detection • Log aggregation • Data analytics • Security Information and Event Management (SIEM)	• Network and computer vulnerability scanning • Penetration testing • Patch management and deployment • Rogue network device detection • Rogue wireless access point detection • Honeypots / honeynets / honeytokens • Security Operations Center (SOC)

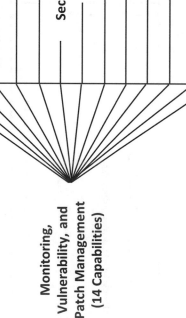

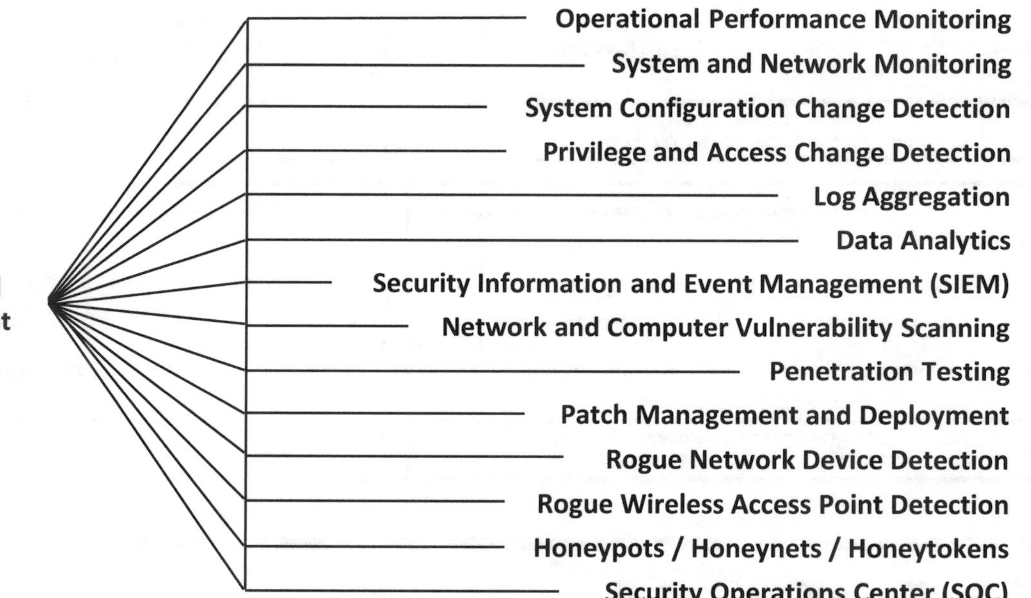

Monitoring, Vulnerability, and Patch Management *(2 of 4)*

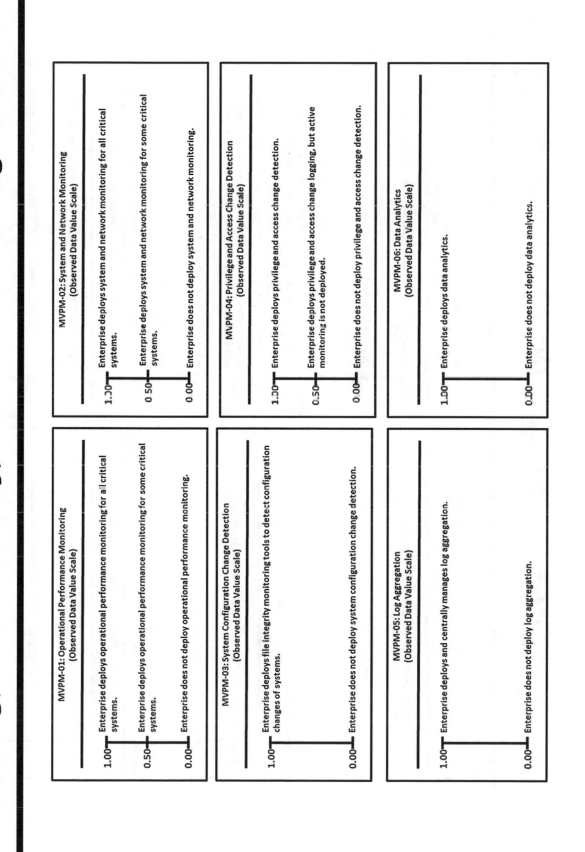

MVPM-01: Operational Performance Monitoring (Observed Data Value Scale)

Value	Description
1.00	Enterprise deploys operational performance monitoring for all critical systems.
0.50	Enterprise deploys operational performance monitoring for some critical systems.
0.00	Enterprise does not deploy operational performance monitoring.

MVPM-02: System and Network Monitoring (Observed Data Value Scale)

Value	Description
1.00	Enterprise deploys system and network monitoring for all critical systems.
0.50	Enterprise deploys system and network monitoring for some critical systems.
0.00	Enterprise does not deploy system and network monitoring.

MVPM-03: System Configuration Change Detection (Observed Data Value Scale)

Value	Description
1.00	Enterprise deploys file integrity monitoring tools to detect configuration changes of systems.
0.00	Enterprise does not deploy system configuration change detection.

MVPM-04: Privilege and Access Change Detection (Observed Data Value Scale)

Value	Description
1.00	Enterprise deploys privilege and access change detection.
0.50	Enterprise deploys privilege and access change logging, but active monitoring is not deployed.
0.00	Enterprise does not deploy privilege and access change detection.

MVPM-05: Log Aggregation (Observed Data Value Scale)

Value	Description
1.00	Enterprise deploys and centrally manages log aggregation.
0.00	Enterprise does not deploy log aggregation.

MVPM-06: Data Analytics (Observed Data Value Scale)

Value	Description
1.00	Enterprise deploys data analytics.
0.00	Enterprise does not deploy data analytics.

Monitoring, Vulnerability, and Patch Management *(3 of 4)*

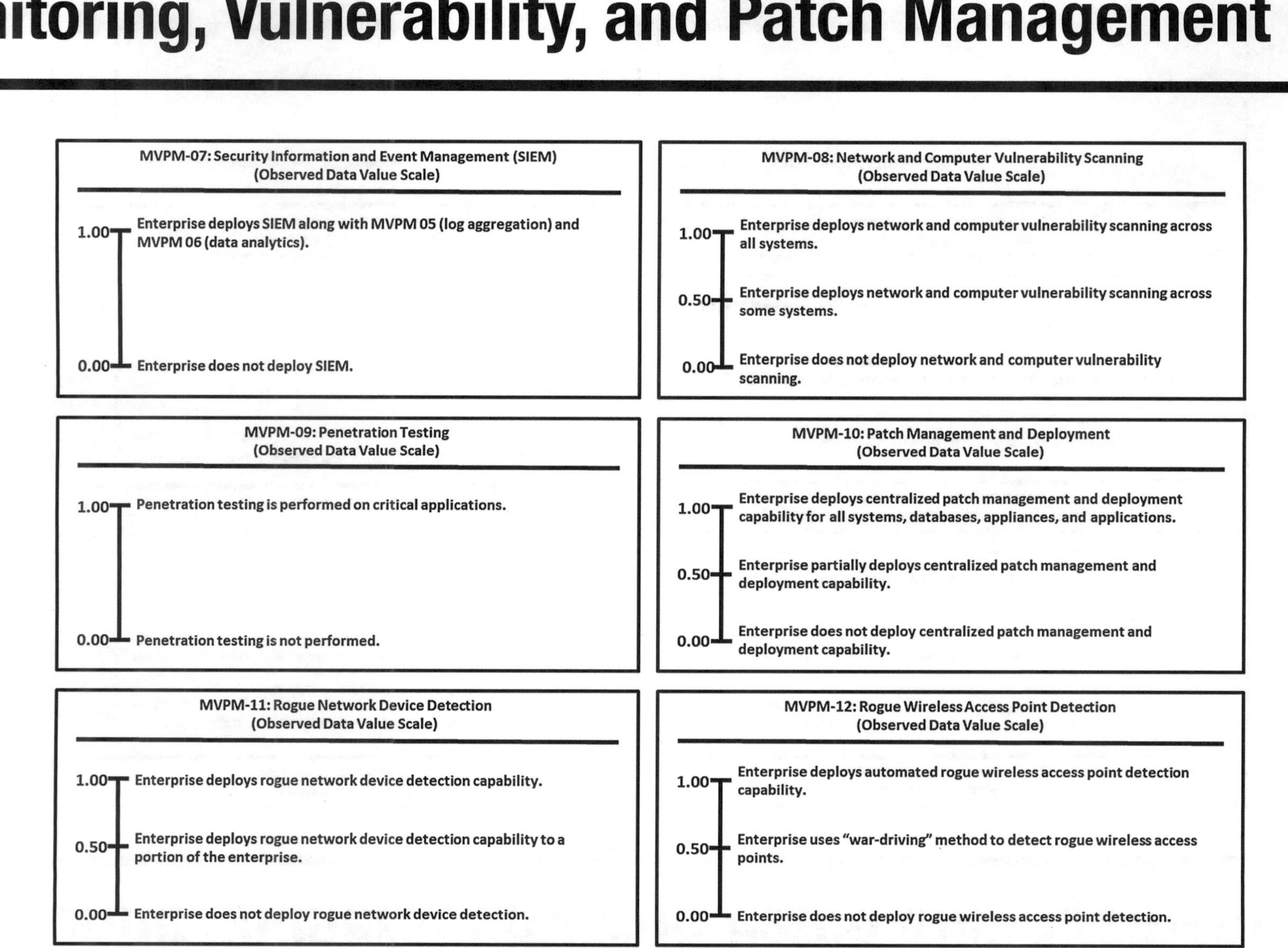

MVPM-07: Security Information and Event Management (SIEM)
(Observed Data Value Scale)
1.00
Enterprise deploys SIEM along with MVPM 05 (log aggregation) and MVPM 06 (data analytics).
0.00
Enterprise does not deploy SIEM.
MVPM-08: Network and Computer Vulnerability Scanning
(Observed Data Value Scale)
1.00
Enterprise deploys network and computer vulnerability scanning across all systems.
0.50
Enterprise deploys network and computer vulnerability scanning across some systems.
0.00
Enterprise does not deploy network and computer vulnerability scanning.
MVPM-09: Penetration Testing
(Observed Data Value Scale)
1.00
Penetration testing is performed on critical applications.
0.00
Penetration testing is not performed.
MVPM-10: Patch Management and Deployment
(Observed Data Value Scale)
1.00
Enterprise deploys centralized patch management and deployment capability for all systems, databases, appliances, and applications.
0.50
Enterprise partially deploys centralized patch management and deployment capability.
0.00
Enterprise does not deploy centralized patch management and deployment capability.
MVPM-11: Rogue Network Device Detection
(Observed Data Value Scale)
1.00
Enterprise deploys rogue network device detection capability.
0.50
Enterprise deploys rogue network device detection capability to a portion of the enterprise.
0.00
Enterprise does not deploy rogue network device detection.
MVPM-12: Rogue Wireless Access Point Detection
(Observed Data Value Scale)
1.00
Enterprise deploys automated rogue wireless access point detection capability.
0.50
Enterprise uses "war-driving" method to detect rogue wireless access points.
0.00
Enterprise does not deploy rogue wireless access point detection.

Monitoring, Vulnerability, and Patch Management *(4 of 4)*

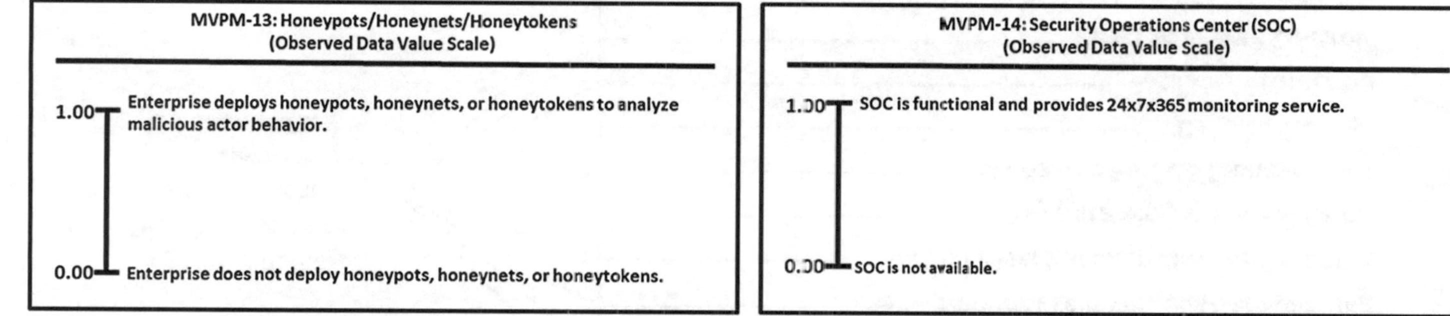

MVPM-13: Honeypots/Honeynets/Honeytokens
(Observed Data Value Scale)
1.00
Enterprise deploys honeypots, honeynets, or honeytokens to analyze malicious actor behavior.
0.00
Enterprise does not deploy honeypots, honeynets, or honeytokens.
MVPM-14: Security Operations Center (SOC)
(Observed Data Value Scale)
1.00
SOC is functional and provides 24x7x365 monitoring service.
0.00
SOC is not available.

High Availability, Disaster Recovery, and Physical Protection *(1 of 3)*

Functional Area	Capabilities	
High Availability, Disaster Recovery, and Physical Protection (HADRPP)	• Clustering • Load balancing, Global Server Load Balancing (GSLB) • Network failover, subnet spanning • Virtual machine snapshots and cloning • Data mirroring and replication	• Backups and backup management • Off-site storage • Facilities protection • Physical access controls • Physical security monitoring

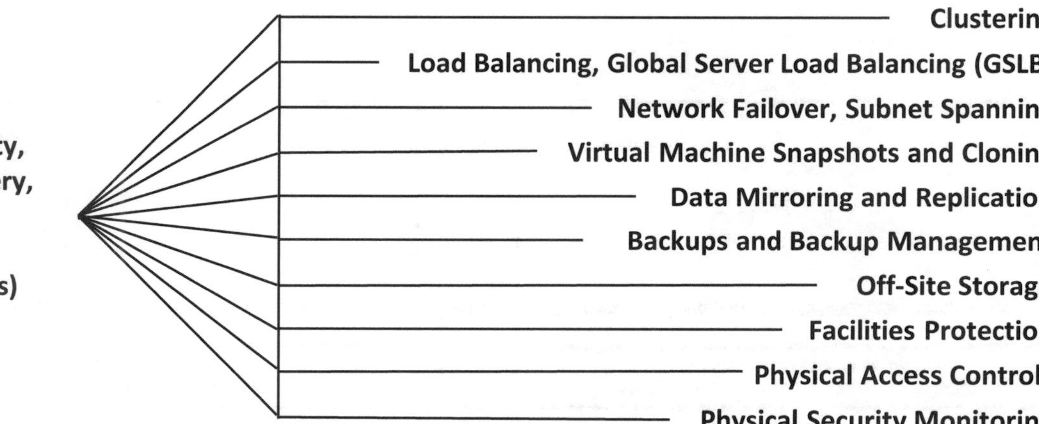

High Availability, Disaster Recovery, and Physical Protection *(2 of 3)*

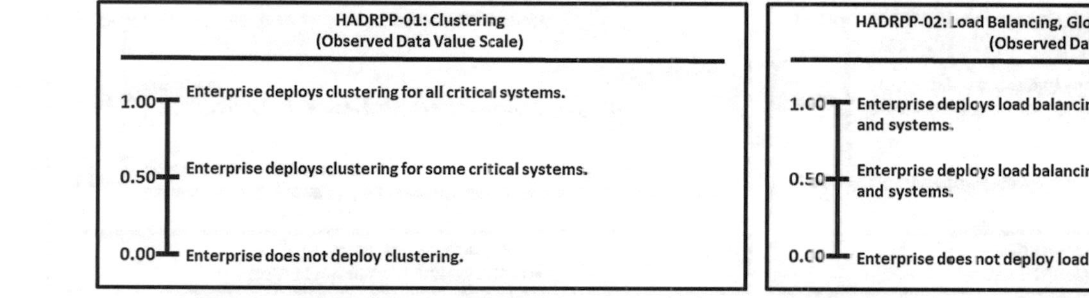

HADRPP-01: Clustering
(Observed Data Value Scale)
1.00 Enterprise deploys clustering for all critical systems.
0.50 Enterprise deploys clustering for some critical systems.
0.00 Enterprise does not deploy clustering.

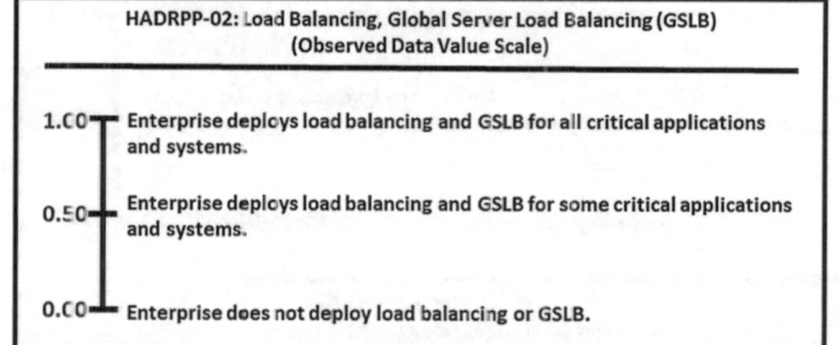

HADRPP-02: Load Balancing, Global Server Load Balancing (GSLB)
(Observed Data Value Scale)
1.00 Enterprise deploys load balancing and GSLB for all critical applications and systems.
0.50 Enterprise deploys load balancing and GSLB for some critical applications and systems.
0.00 Enterprise does not deploy load balancing or GSLB.

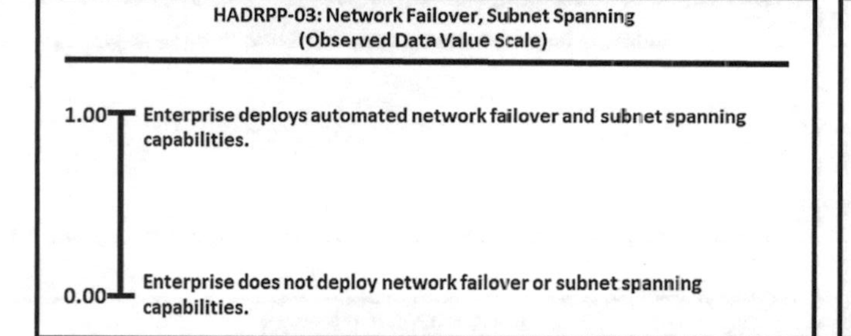

HADRPP-03: Network Failover, Subnet Spanning
(Observed Data Value Scale)
1.00 Enterprise deploys automated network failover and subnet spanning capabilities.
0.00 Enterprise does not deploy network failover or subnet spanning capabilities.

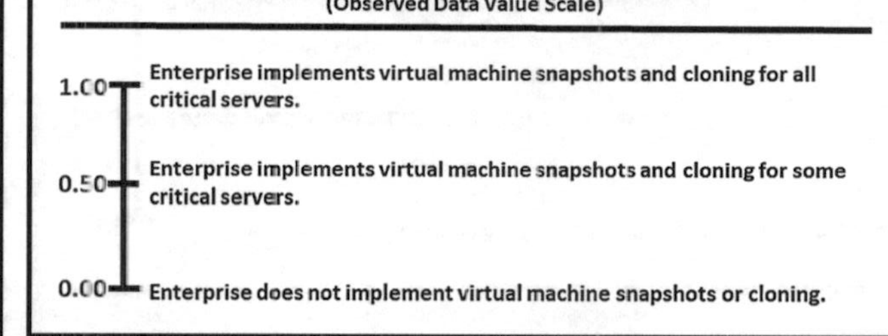

HADRPP-04: Virtual Machine Snapshots and Cloning
(Observed Data Value Scale)
1.00 Enterprise implements virtual machine snapshots and cloning for all critical servers.
0.50 Enterprise implements virtual machine snapshots and cloning for some critical servers.
0.00 Enterprise does not implement virtual machine snapshots or cloning.

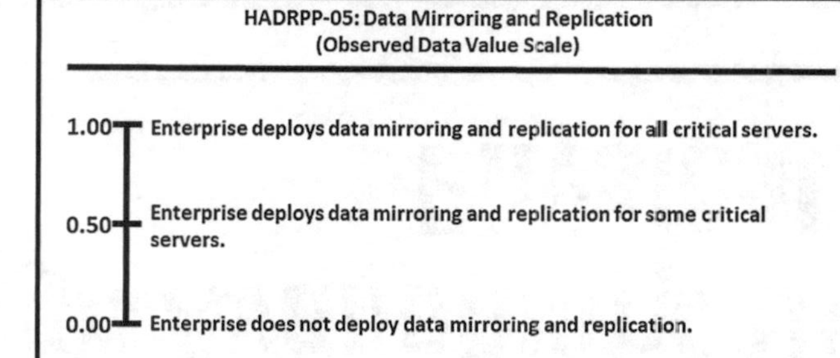

HADRPP-05: Data Mirroring and Replication
(Observed Data Value Scale)
1.00 Enterprise deploys data mirroring and replication for all critical servers.
0.50 Enterprise deploys data mirroring and replication for some critical servers.
0.00 Enterprise does not deploy data mirroring and replication.

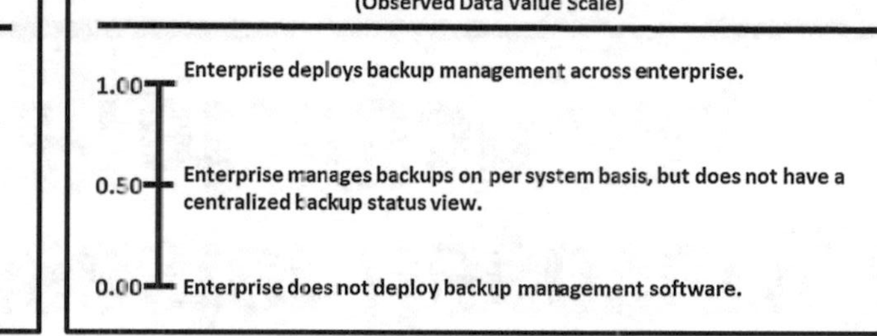

HADRPP-06: Backups and Backup Management
(Observed Data Value Scale)
1.00 Enterprise deploys backup management across enterprise.
0.50 Enterprise manages backups on per system basis, but does not have a centralized backup status view.
0.00 Enterprise does not deploy backup management software.

High Availability, Disaster Recovery, and Physical Protection *(3 of 3)*

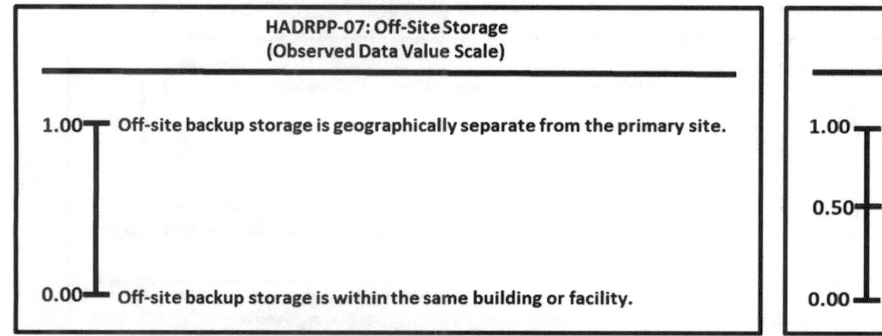

HADRPP-07: Off-Site Storage
(Observed Data Value Scale)
1.00
Off-site backup storage is geographically separate from the primary site.
0.00
Off-site backup storage is within the same building or facility.

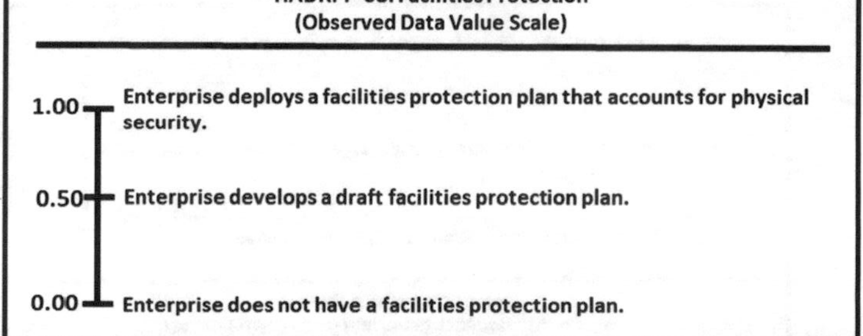

HADRPP-08: Facilities Protection
(Observed Data Value Scale)
1.00
Enterprise deploys a facilities protection plan that accounts for physical security.
0.50
Enterprise develops a draft facilities protection plan.
0.00
Enterprise does not have a facilities protection plan.

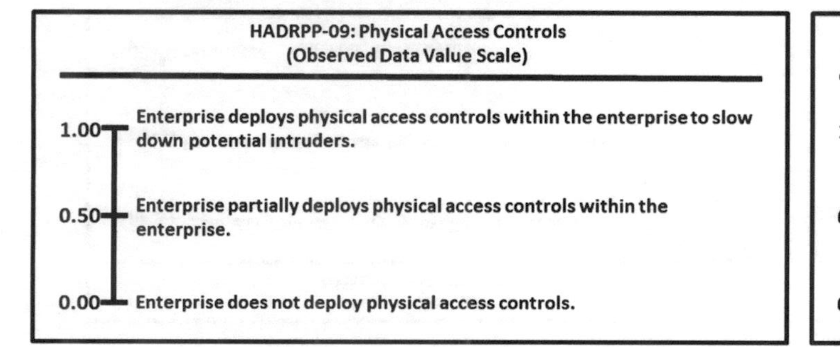

HADRPP-09: Physical Access Controls
(Observed Data Value Scale)
1.00
Enterprise deploys physical access controls within the enterprise to slow down potential intruders.
0.50
Enterprise partially deploys physical access controls within the enterprise.
0.00
Enterprise does not deploy physical access controls.

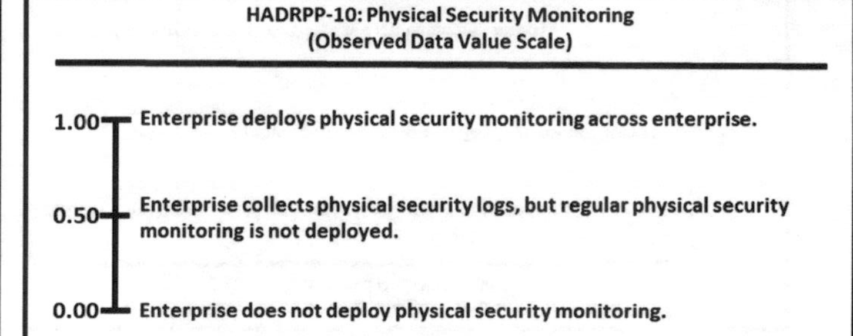

HADRPP-10: Physical Security Monitoring
(Observed Data Value Scale)
1.00
Enterprise deploys physical security monitoring across enterprise.
0.50
Enterprise collects physical security logs, but regular physical security monitoring is not deployed.
0.00
Enterprise does not deploy physical security monitoring.

Incident Response *(1 of 3)*

Functional Area	Capabilities	
Incident Response (IR)	• Threat information • Incident tracking • Forensic tools • Computer imaging	• Indicators of Compromise (IOCs) • Black hole server • Regulatory / legal coordination

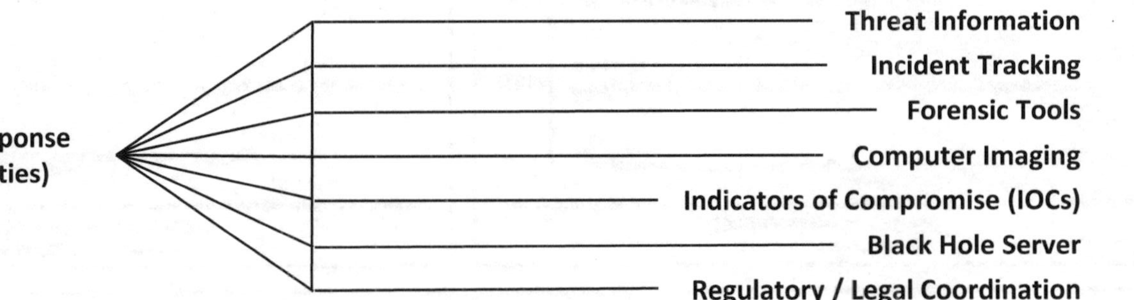

Incident Response *(2 of 3)*

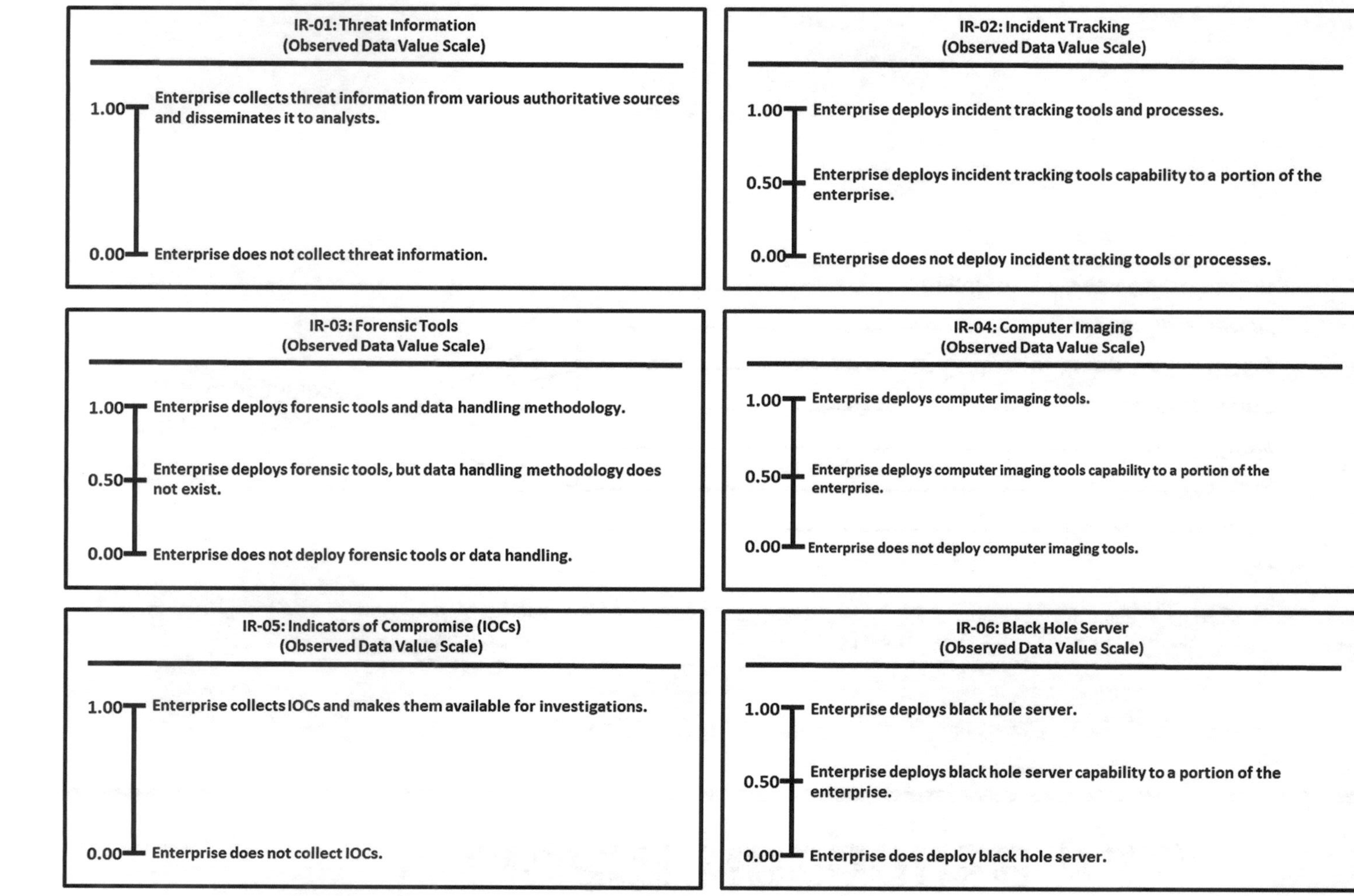

IR-01: Threat Information
(Observed Data Value Scale)
1.00 Enterprise collects threat information from various authoritative sources and disseminates it to analysts.
0.00 Enterprise does not collect threat information.
IR-02: Incident Tracking
(Observed Data Value Scale)
1.00 Enterprise deploys incident tracking tools and processes.
0.50 Enterprise deploys incident tracking tools capability to a portion of the enterprise.
0.00 Enterprise does not deploy incident tracking tools or processes.
IR-03: Forensic Tools
(Observed Data Value Scale)
1.00 Enterprise deploys forensic tools and data handling methodology.
0.50 Enterprise deploys forensic tools, but data handling methodology does not exist.
0.00 Enterprise does not deploy forensic tools or data handling.
IR-04: Computer Imaging
(Observed Data Value Scale)
1.00 Enterprise deploys computer imaging tools.
0.50 Enterprise deploys computer imaging tools capability to a portion of the enterprise.
0.00 Enterprise does not deploy computer imaging tools.
IR-05: Indicators of Compromise (IOCs)
(Observed Data Value Scale)
1.00 Enterprise collects IOCs and makes them available for investigations.
0.00 Enterprise does not collect IOCs.
IR-06: Black Hole Server
(Observed Data Value Scale)
1.00 Enterprise deploys black hole server.
0.50 Enterprise deploys black hole server capability to a portion of the enterprise.
0.00 Enterprise does deploy black hole server.

Incident Response *(3 of 3)*

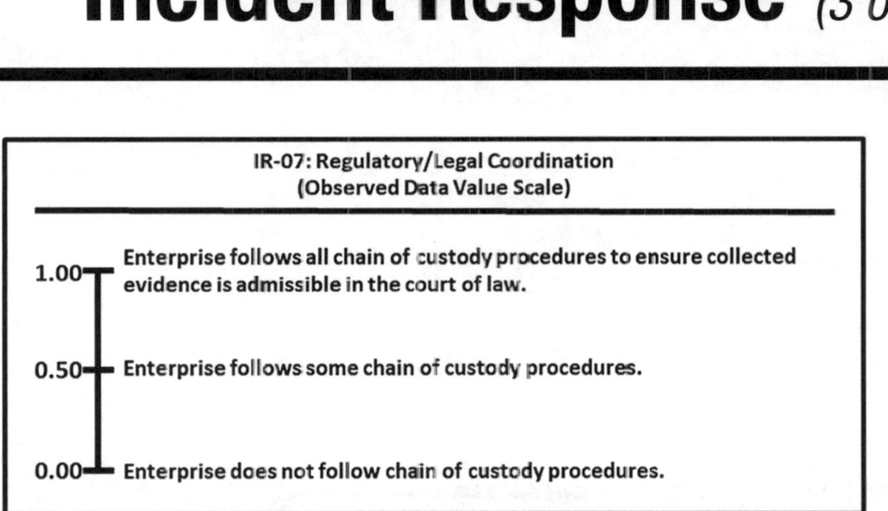

IR-07: Regulatory/Legal Coordination
(Observed Data Value Scale)
1.00
Enterprise follows all chain of custody procedures to ensure collected evidence is admissible in the court of law.
0.50
Enterprise follows some chain of custody procedures.
0.00
Enterprise does not follow chain of custody procedures.

Asset Management and Supply Chain *(1 of 2)*

Functional Area	Capabilities	
Asset Management and Supply Chain (AMSC)	• Asset management databases • Configuration Management Databases (CMDB) • Change management databases	• Software inventory and license management • Supplier certification processes • Secure disposal, recycling, and data destruction

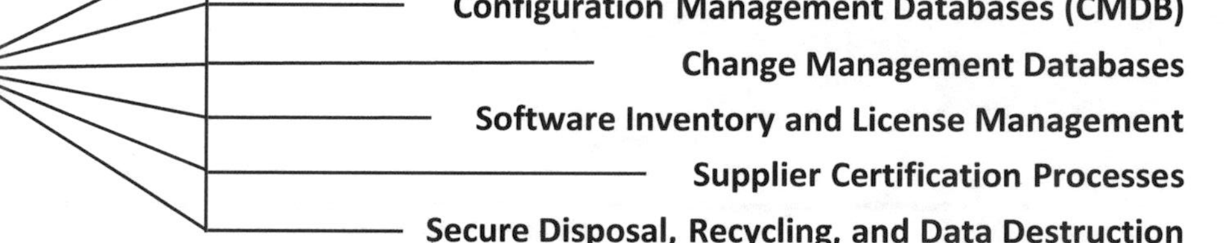

Asset Management and Supply Chain *(2 of 2)*

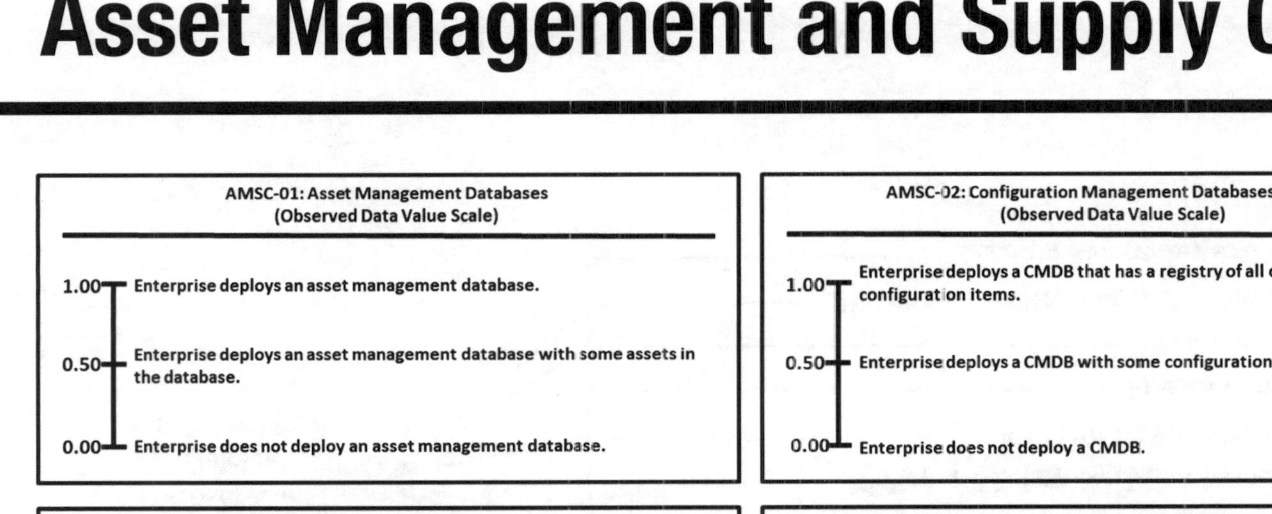

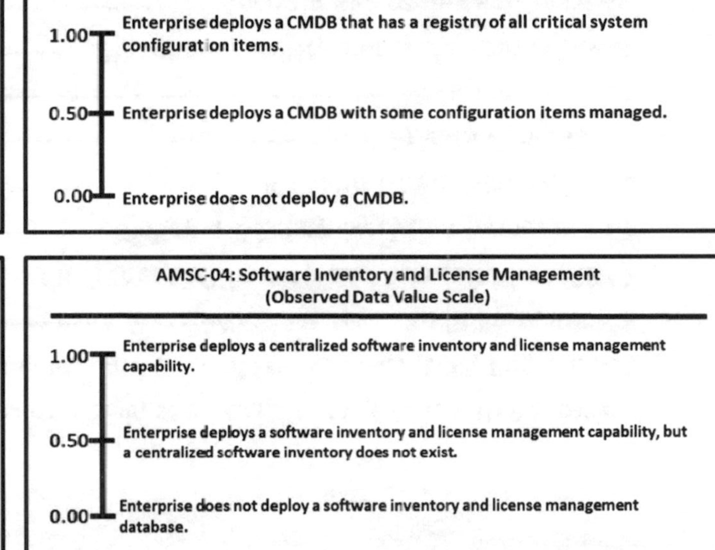

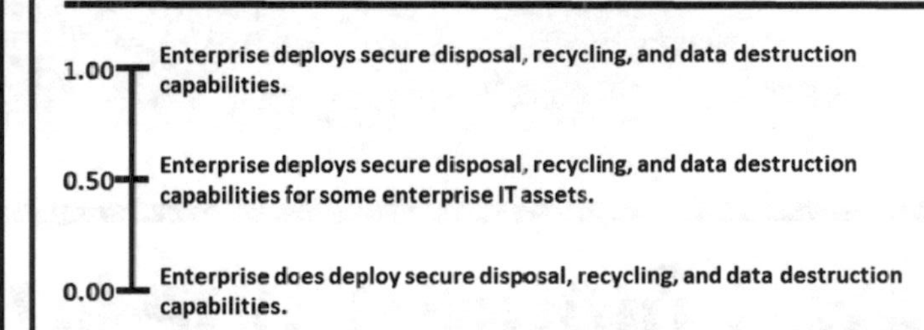

AMSC-01: Asset Management Databases
(Observed Data Value Scale)
1.00 Enterprise deploys an asset management database.
0.50 Enterprise deploys an asset management database with some assets in the database.
0.00 Enterprise does not deploy an asset management database.
AMSC-02: Configuration Management Databases (CMDB)
(Observed Data Value Scale)
1.00 Enterprise deploys a CMDB that has a registry of all critical system configuration items.
0.50 Enterprise deploys a CMDB with some configuration items managed.
0.00 Enterprise does not deploy a CMDB.
AMSC-03: Change Management Databases
(Observed Data Value Scale)
1.00 Enterprise deploys change management databases to process change requests for all baselined systems.
0.50 Enterprise deploys change management databases with some change requests processed by it.
0.00 Enterprise does not deploy a change management database.
AMSC-04: Software Inventory and License Management
(Observed Data Value Scale)
1.00 Enterprise deploys a centralized software inventory and license management capability.
0.50 Enterprise deploys a software inventory and license management capability, but a centralized software inventory does not exist.
0.00 Enterprise does not deploy a software inventory and license management database.
AMSC-05: Supplier Certification Processes
(Observed Data Value Scale)
1.00 Enterprise conducts supplier certification security checks on all suppliers before contract award.
0.50 Enterprise conducts supplier certification security checks on some suppliers before contract award.
0.00 Enterprise does not perform supplier certification security checks before contract award.
AMSC-06: Secure Disposal, Recycling, and Data Destruction
(Observed Data Value Scale)
1.00 Enterprise deploys secure disposal, recycling, and data destruction capabilities.
0.50 Enterprise deploys secure disposal, recycling, and data destruction capabilities for some enterprise IT assets.
0.00 Enterprise does deploy secure disposal, recycling, and data destruction capabilities.

Policy, Audit, E-Discovery, and Training (PAET) *(1 of 3)*

Functional Area	Capabilities	
Policy, Audit, E-Discovery, and Training (PAET)	• Governance, Risk, and Compliance (GRC), with reporting • Compliance and control frameworks (SOX, PCI, others) • Audit frameworks • Customer Certification and Accreditation (C&A)	• Policy and policy exception management • Risk and threat management • Privacy compliance • E-Discovery tools • Personnel security and background checks • Security awareness and training

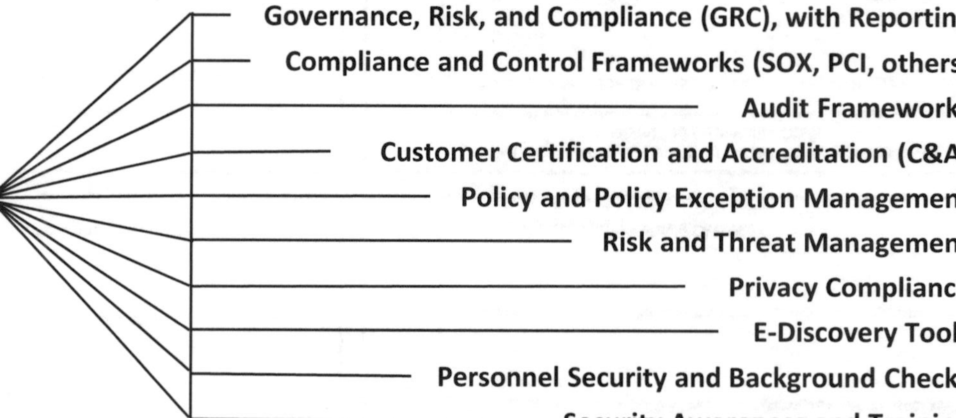

Policy, Audit, E-Discovery, and Training (PAET) *(2 of 3)*

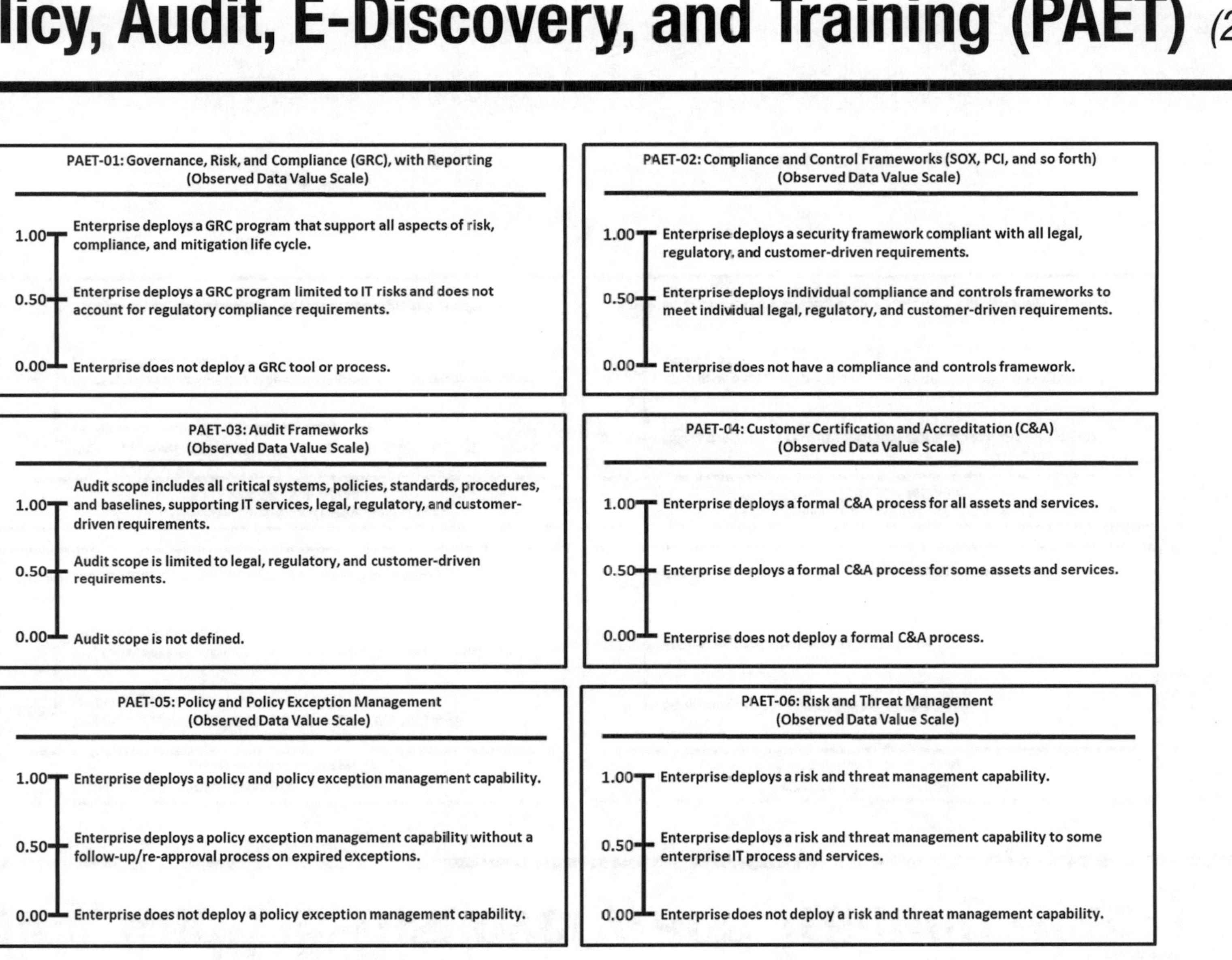

PAET-01: Governance, Risk, and Compliance (GRC), with Reporting
(Observed Data Value Scale)
1.00 Enterprise deploys a GRC program that support all aspects of risk, compliance, and mitigation life cycle.
0.50 Enterprise deploys a GRC program limited to IT risks and does not account for regulatory compliance requirements.
0.00 Enterprise does not deploy a GRC tool or process.
PAET-02: Compliance and Control Frameworks (SOX, PCI, and so forth)
(Observed Data Value Scale)
1.00 Enterprise deploys a security framework compliant with all legal, regulatory, and customer-driven requirements.
0.50 Enterprise deploys individual compliance and controls frameworks to meet individual legal, regulatory, and customer-driven requirements.
0.00 Enterprise does not have a compliance and controls framework.
PAET-03: Audit Frameworks
(Observed Data Value Scale)
1.00 Audit scope includes all critical systems, policies, standards, procedures, and baselines, supporting IT services, legal, regulatory, and customer-driven requirements.
0.50 Audit scope is limited to legal, regulatory, and customer-driven requirements.
0.00 Audit scope is not defined.
PAET-04: Customer Certification and Accreditation (C&A)
(Observed Data Value Scale)
1.00 Enterprise deploys a formal C&A process for all assets and services.
0.50 Enterprise deploys a formal C&A process for some assets and services.
0.00 Enterprise does not deploy a formal C&A process.
PAET-05: Policy and Policy Exception Management
(Observed Data Value Scale)
1.00 Enterprise deploys a policy and policy exception management capability.
0.50 Enterprise deploys a policy exception management capability without a follow-up/re-approval process on expired exceptions.
0.00 Enterprise does not deploy a policy exception management capability.
PAET-06: Risk and Threat Management
(Observed Data Value Scale)
1.00 Enterprise deploys a risk and threat management capability.
0.50 Enterprise deploys a risk and threat management capability to some enterprise IT process and services.
0.00 Enterprise does not deploy a risk and threat management capability.

Policy, Audit, E-Discovery, and Training (PAET) *(3 of 3)*

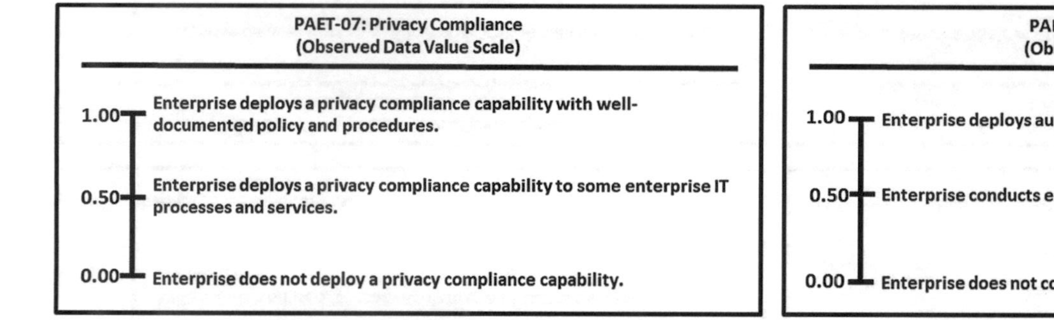

PAET-07: Privacy Compliance
(Observed Data Value Scale)
1.00
Enterprise deploys a privacy compliance capability with well-documented policy and procedures.
0.50
Enterprise deploys a privacy compliance capability to some enterprise IT processes and services.
0.00
Enterprise does not deploy a privacy compliance capability.

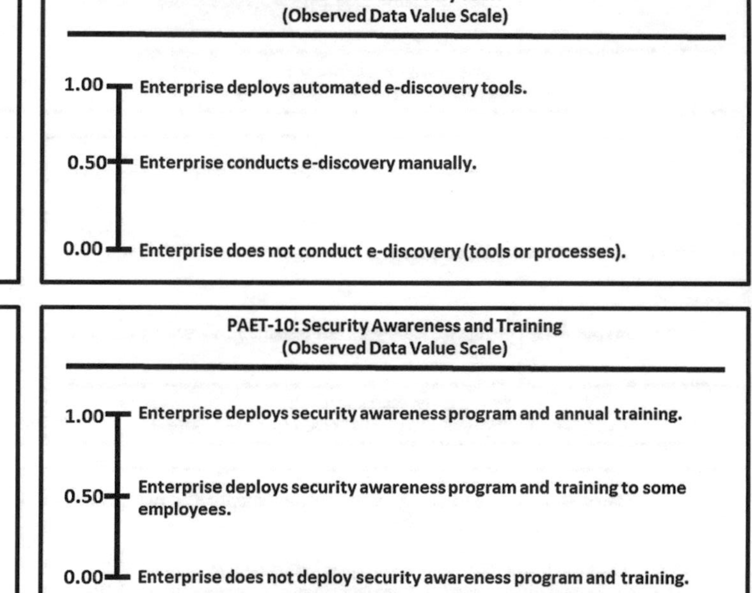

PAET-08: E-Discovery Tools
(Observed Data Value Scale)
1.00
Enterprise deploys automated e-discovery tools.
0.50
Enterprise conducts e-discovery manually.
0.00
Enterprise does not conduct e-discovery (tools or processes).
PAET-10: Security Awareness and Training
(Observed Data Value Scale)
1.00
Enterprise deploys security awareness program and annual training.
0.50
Enterprise deploys security awareness program and training to some employees.
0.00
Enterprise does not deploy security awareness program and training.

PAET-09: Personnel Security and Background Checks
(Observed Data Value Scale)

- 1.00 — Human Resources (HR) performs pre-employment security and background checks on all potential employees.
- 0.50 — HR performs pre-employment security and background checks on some potential employees.
- 0.00 — HR does not perform personnel security and background checks.

Index

S. E. Donaldson et al., *Enterprise Cybersecurity Study Guide*, https://doi.org/10.1007/978-1-4842-3258-3

D

E

F

G

H

I, J, K

L

M

N

O

P, Q

R

S

T, U

V, W, X, Y, Z

Printed in the United States
By Bookmasters